MICROECONOMICS

First Canadian Edition

DAVID C. COLANDER
Middlebury College

PETER S. SEPHTON
University of New Brunswick

Represented in Canada by:

Times Mirror
Professional Publishing Ltd.

IRWIN

Toronto • Chicago • Bogotá • Boston • Buenos Aires
Caracas • London • Madrid • Mexico City • Sydney

Dedicated to the memory of Frank Knight and Thorstein Veblen, both of whose economics have significantly influenced the contents of this book.

Part opener photos

Part 1: Reuters/Bettmann
Part 2: Michael Polselli

Irwin Book Team

Publisher: *Roderick T. Banister*
Developmental editor: *Sabira Hussain*
Marketing manager: Murray Moman
Production supervisor: *Bob Lange*
Assistant manager, graphics: *Charlene R. Perez*
Coordinator, graphics and desktop services: *Keri Johnson*
Photo resercher: *Michelle Oberhoffer*
Project editor: *Lynne Basler*
Senior designer: *Heidi J. Baughman*
Compositor: *Better Graphics, Inc.*
Typeface: *10/12 Times Roman*
Printer: *Webcrafters, Inc.*

Times Mirror
Higher Education Group

ISBN: 0-256-17575-6
Library of Congress Catalog Number: 95-78247

Printed in the United States of America
1 2 3 4 5 6 7 8 9 0 WEB 2 1 0 9 8 7 6 5

Preface

One of the first lessons of writing is: Know for whom you are writing. This book is written for students; this preface, however, is written for professors. Why? The answer is simple—the students for whom this book was written don't read prefaces; they don't read anything in a textbook unless it is assigned (and sometimes they don't even read that). Their interests lie in the real world, not texts. The style and structure of the body of this text is made to turn on such students, as much as they can be turned on, to economic ideas. Alas, we recognize that we will fail with many, but we sincerely believe that our success rate of actually getting students to read this textbook will likely be higher than will be the success rate for other economic textbooks written in standard professorial style.

We also recognize that students will never get a chance to read this text unless the professor chooses the book, which is why we write this preface for professors—they read prefaces. (If you're one of those rare students who read textbook prefaces, read on; it will give you a sense of what will be coming in the course.)

The Canadian edition keeps most of the distinctive components and style of the American editions, so we begin this preface with the key elements of those earlier prefaces.

Why Write another Book?

Why write a new introductory economics textbook? Since we are economists, the answer must be that the expected benefits outweighed the expected costs. But that doesn't mean we had our bank balances in mind when we decided to write this book. Quite honestly, there are easier ways of earning money. There had to be some other benefits out there. For us, those other benefits had to do with a belief about how economics should be taught—what was important and what was not.

Before we started writing this book we had done quite a bit of research on economic education. As part of that research, graduate students in a number of top graduate programs were surveyed and interviewed. Two of the most disturbing things we discovered were that economic institutions and economic literature were being given short shrift in graduate economics education. For example, in response to the question, "How important is a knowledge of economic literature to being successful as an economist?" only 10 percent of the students responded that it was very important, while 43 percent said it was unimportant. In response to the question, "How important to achieving success as an economist is having a thorough knowledge of the economy?" only 3 percent said it was very important, while 68 percent said it was unimportant.

We believe that the majority of the profession is concerned with these results. Certainly the students we interviewed were concerned. They said they believed that institutions and literature were very important. Their survey responses simply indicated their perception of how people succeed in the profession, but the current situation was not the way it should be. Almost all economists we know believe that students need to know economic literature and have a thorough knowledge of the institutions. Without the appropriate background knowledge of institutions and literature, all the technical skills in the world aren't going to provide one with the economic sensibility necessary to understand what's going on in the economy or to decide whether or not a model is relevant.

As we thought about these results and considered our own teaching, we realized that the problem was not only in graduate schools; it had filtered down to undergraduate texts. As we looked through the texts, we saw excellent discussions of technical issues and of models, but little discussion of economic sensibility. These books didn't even try to provide the intellectual context within which those models developed or the institutional context to which those models were to be applied. The standard texts had settled into teaching technique for the sake of technique and had shifted away from teaching economic sensibility.

We decided that if we were serious about playing a role in reinstituting economic sensibility and a knowledge of institutions and literature in economic education, we would have to write an introductory textbook that did that. We took it as a challenge. Meeting that challenge was what drove us to write this book.

Teaching Economic Sensibility

The question we faced was: How do you incorporate economic sensibility into a textbook? Economic sensibility is more than a knowledge of modelling techniques; it is a mindset in which one's lens of the world is a latticework of ascending cost/benefit frameworks in which one is deciding on the optimal degree of rationality. Economic sensibility is an enforced reasonableness that provides insight into complicated issues; it is a perspective, not a technique. The argument we heard in favour of teaching technique was that economic sensibility could not be taught. We reject that argument. Economic sensibility may be hard to teach because it does not come naturally for most people, but it can and must be taught. The question is: How do you teach it? The answer we came to: Enthusiastically.

Economics with Passion

We are first and foremost economics teachers; we are excited by economics. We find economic ideas relevant, challenging, and exciting. In our lectures, we try to convey that excitement, and if the lecture is going right, we can feel the excitement in our students. Then off they go to read the text. All too often when they return to class, the fire in their eyes is gone; the textbook has lulled them into complacency. Those who know us know that we can put up with many things (not quietly, but nonetheless put up with), but one of those things isn't complacency. We want students to think, to argue, to challenge, to get passionate about the ideas. We encourage this reaction from students not just because economists' ideas deserve to be treated passionately, but also because, through a combination of passion and reason, eventually students achieve economic sensibility. We decided what was missing from most textbooks was the passion. We promised ourselves our book would retain the passion.

Now there's no way we're going to get passionate about Slutsky equations, phase diagrams, indifference curves, or an AS/AD model. Mathematicians may get passionate about such things, we don't. We do get passionate about the insight economics gives one into the problems, we, as individuals and as society, must face: the budget deficit, TANSTAAFL, the environment, and agricultural subsidies. If the techniques help in understanding the ideas, fine, but if they don't, goodbye to the techniques.

Passion without Bias

While not all textbooks are written by passionless people, the conventional wisdom is that authors should hide their passion to make their books more marketable. In some ways this makes sense—often passion and ideological bias go together. Many economists' passions are ideologically linked, and if you remove the ideology, you remove the passion. Good economic sensibility cannot be—and cannot even appear to be—biased; if passion is purged in maintaining neutrality, it is purged for a good cause.

But passion and ideological bias need not go together. We believe it is possible for a passionate textbook to be reasonably objective and unbiased. And we set out to write a book that would be as unbiased as possible (but not more so) and to do so without masking our passion for economic ideas. Various techniques allow us to do this. For example, to keep the students interested in the ideas rather than focusing on technique, we present some ideas in a debate format with two passionate believers on both sides arguing the points. The debate format makes the arguments come alive; they are no longer technical issues that must be memorized, they are passionate ideas.

A Conversational Tone

To transmit that sense of passion to the students, we needed a writing style that allowed it to come through. Quite honestly, textbookese douses passion faster than a cold shower. So this book is not written in textbookese. It's written in conversational English—we're talking to the students.

The conversational tone is not a monotone; it ebbs and flows depending on the nature of the material. Sometimes, in the analytic parts, the style approaches textbookese; the important technical aspects of economics require technical writing. When we hit those parts, we tell the students and encourage them to stick with us. But, even here we try to provide intuitive explanations that students can relate to.

The use of conversational style has two effects. First, it eliminates the sense some students have that textbooks provide the "truth." When the textbook authors are real people with peccadilloes and warts, the students won't accept what he or she says unless it makes sense to them. Approaching a textbook with a "show me" attitude stimulates true learning. Second, the conversational style keeps the students awake. If students' heads are nodding as they read a chapter, they're not learning. Now we know this book is not *Catcher in the Rye;* it's a textbook conveying sometimes complex ideas. But the excitement about economic ideas and the real world comes through.

The approach we take allows us to deal simply with complicated ideas. For example, in the book we discuss modern interpretations of Keynesian and Classical economics, real business cycles, strategic pricing, the theory of the second best, rent-seeking, Pareto optimality, and challenges to Pareto optimality. The conversational style conveys the essence of these complex topics to students in a nontechnical fashion without tying the student's brains up in technical tourniquets.

Models in Historical and Institutional Context

Discussing only the minimum of techniques necessary for the students to understand the ideas allows us more leeway to get into, and discuss, institutional and historical issues as they relate to current policy. Models without context are meaningless, and you'll find more historical and institutional issues in this book than in other principles books. The book has numerous maps; the discussion conveys the sense that geography, history, and psychology are important, even though it touches on them only tangentially.

One of the ways in which this historical and institutional approach shows up is in the complete coverage of the changing nature of economic systems. Socialism is undergoing enormous changes, and students are interested in what is happening and why it is happening. Their questions cannot be answered with technical models, but they can be discussed informally in a historical context. And that's what this book does.

The Invisible Forces

We've incorporated in the book a pedagogical device we've found useful where we want to include the social and political forces that affect reality. That device is to convey to students a picture of reality being controlled not only by the invisible hand, but also by the invisible foot (politics) and the invisible handshake (social and cultural forces). This *invisible forces* imagery lets us relate economists' abstract models to the real world; it allows us to discuss the real-world interface between economics, politics, and social forces. What makes this device effective is that students can picture these three invisible forces fighting each other to direct real world events; that image allows them to put economic models into perspective.

Some Short Prefatory Comments on the Canadian Edition

A question the reader might have, and one that we asked ourselves long and hard, is: "If the American editions were so good, why not just use the U.S. book in Canada? Why write a Canadian edition?" The most important reason is that Canadian economic history and Canadian institutions differ significantly from those in the United States. To turn on Canadian students to economics—to teach economic sensibility in Canada—we've got to take advantage of Canada's unique institutional and cultural heritage.

In our view, the existing Canadian textbooks just didn't foster the economic sensibility we wanted of our students. We knew we could provide a passionate alternative that would nurture Canadian students—particularly those whose background in quantitative methods was limited and who believed that economics was a course in technique. And, yes, while we do tell our students that "math is fun, math is our friend"—we also tell them that math is just a tool; it's not the essence of economics. We really do believe that models without context are meaningless and that students *need* to understand how Canadian social and political forces affect real world events.

Our Colloquial Writing Style

It's pretty clear that our writing style (and our style in general) isn't professorial. We agree; it isn't. But in our view, students would learn a lot more if professors were a lot less professorial. If students see us as people, they will be encouraged to think through what we have to say, and to challenge us when they think we're wrong. That's the purpose of education—to get students to think. True, it would be nice if students had a love of learning and were thirsting for knowledge. Unfortunately, the reality is that 99% of them don't. It's our job as teachers to make learning fun and exciting for students who don't want to learn, and either get them to learn, or to flunk them out. Being less professional makes us more real to students and makes learning more fun.

We see the course and the book as an entry point to an enormous store of information, not as the ultimate source. We want to motivate students to learn on their own, to read on their own, to think on their own. These desires have to be taught, and they can only be taught in a language that students can relate to. We believe in going in steps with students, not in leaps. The traditional textbookese is too much a leap for most students to make. It's not a step from the stuff they normally read; it's a leap that most of them aren't willing to make—the same type of leap it is for most of us teachers of economics to read the *Journal of Economic Theory.* There may be some relevant information in those articles, but most of us teachers aren't going to find out because the language the ideas are presented in is incomprehensible to us. So too with a text; it has to talk to students, otherwise they won't read it.

People to Thank

A book this size is not the work of two people, despite the fact that only two are listed as authors. So many people have contributed so much to this book that it is hard to know where to begin thanking them. But we must begin somewhere, so let us begin by thanking the innumerable referees who went through the various versions of the text and kept us on track:

Gary Berman
Humber College

Aurelia Best
Centennial College

Samuel Boutilier
University College of Cape Breton

Chris Clark
British Columbia Institute of Technology

Campion Dormuth
Palliser Institute SIAST

Sam Fefferman
The Northern Alberta Institute of Technology

Peter Fortura
Algonquin College

Donald Garrie
Georgian College

Michael Hare
University of Toronto

Matlub Hussain
Dawson College

Ernie Jacobson
The Northern Alberta Institute of Technology

Cheryl Jenkins
John Abbott College

Susan Kamp
University of Alberta

Gregg Levis
Georgian College

Sonja Novkovic
Saint Mary's University

Don Reddick
Kwantlen College

Michael Rushton
University of Regina

Balbir Sahni
Concordia University

Marlyce Searcy
Palliser Institute SIAST

Annie Spears
University of Prince Edward Island

We cannot thank these reviewers enough. They corrected many of our mistakes, they explained to us how a text can contribute to good teaching, and they kept us focused on combining teaching economic sensibility with economic models. They provided us with page upon page of detailed comments and suggestions for improvement. The book strongly reflects their input and is much more usable because of that input.

There were many faculty and students who have informally pointed out aspects of the book that they liked, or did not like. There are so many that we can't remember them all, but those who especially deserve thanks include John Brander, Beverly Cook, Vaughan Dickson, Stephen Law, Heather Lebrecque, Maurice Tugwell, Linda Williams, and Weiqui Yu. We especially want to thank Maurice Tugwell of Acadia University for providing us with problems and exercises for inclusion in the textbook.

Massaging the Manuscript into a Book

In this edition we had immense help from Brad Mullin, Jim MacGee, and Helen Reiff. They all did great jobs, and we thank them.

In this entire process many people at Times Mirror Professional Publishing (TMPP) are extremely important and helpful. One is Milt Vacon, a sales rep at TMPP, who convinced us that we should work on this project. Another is Rod Banister, the publisher at TMPP. He believed in the project early on, and has seen to it that the book has gone forward and prospered. Then there's Sabira Hussain, our development editor. To understand Sabira's role, you have to understand a bit about us. We're difficult to work with. We're outlandish perfectionists, sticklers about deadlines, and rather blunt in our assessments. We don't like excuses or bureaucracy. We want things done perfectly, yesterday. Given these characteristics, the fact that we coexist with publish houses is unexplainable—except for the existence of people like Sabira within the publishing houses. Sabira is superb. She almost always gets things done perfectly, yesterday, and when she doesn't, she offers no excuses—she simply gets them done today. She operates in a bureaucracy without losing sight of her main duty—to get the job done competently and professionally. She's a gem, and we thank her.

The actual production process of a four-color introductory book is complicated. It requires enormous efforts. Luckily, we had Lynne Basler, project editor, directing the manuscript through the process. She did a superb job, as did all the players in the production process: Tom Serb, the copy editor; Heidi Baughman, the designer who made the book look good; Bob Lange, the production manager, who worked with Better Graphics, Inc., the typesetter, and Webcrafters, Inc., the printer.

Of course, as they did their superb job, they created more work for us, reading the galley proofs, the page proofs, and doing all the final checking that must be done in an effort to eliminate those pesky errors that occur out of nowhere. Helen Reiff went over the manuscript with her fine-tooth comb and discerning eyes, and we went over it with our rake and 20/400 vision, and together we caught things overlooked until then. We thank her enormously for doing what we cannot do, and apologize to her for complaining that she is so picky.

Then, there are the sales reps who are the core of a textbook publishing company. As we traveled around the country giving lectures, we met with many of the TMPP sales reps, discussing the book and learning to see it through their eyes. There are a number we remember very well; they sent us books, comments, and talked with us for hours about publishing and TMPP. We thank them sincerely. TMPP has one great set of sales representatives out there, and we thank them for getting behind the book.

Creating the Package

These days an introductory economics book is much more than a single book; it is an entire package, and numerous people have worked on the package. The supplements and their authors include:

Instructor's Manual prepared by Peter Sephton and Paul Estenson (includes *Experiments in Teaching and in Understanding Economics* by David Colander and Andreas Ortman).

Study Guide for use with Microeconomics prepared by Susan Kamp, Douglas W. Copeland, Richard Trieff, and Benjamin Shlaes.

Testbank to Accompany Microeconomics prepared by Susan Kamp and Susan Dadres.

Micro-interactive Software prepared by Peter Sephton and Paul Estenson.

Classic Readings in Economics, edited by David Colander and Harry Landreth.

Economics: An Honors Companion, by Sunder Ramaswamy, Kailash Khandke, Jenifer Gamber and David Colander.

Case Studies in Microeconomics, selections from *The Wall Street Journal*, edited by David Colander and Jenifer Gamber.

We want to say thank you to all the supplements authors for making a high-quality and innovative supplements package to the text.

Then there's our wives, Pat and Sue, and our children, who gave us the time we needed to work on this edition. Only after it was finished did we realize how absolutely necessary their sacrifices were to getting this book out.

As you can see, although our names are on the book, many people besides us deserve the credit. We thank them all.

Data Acknowledgements

All Statistics Canada sources are reproduced by authority of the Minister of Industry, 1995, and are adopted from the following sources:

Canadian Economic Observer, Catalogue 11–010
Canada Year Book 1994, Catalogue 11–402E
Historical Statistics of Canada, 2nd Edition, Catalogue 11–516E
The Labour Force, Catalogue 71–001
Consumer Prices and Price Index, Catalogue 62–010
National Income and Expenditure Accounts, Catalogue 13–001
National Balance Sheet Accounts, Catalogue 13–214
Unemployment Insurance Statistics, Catalogue 73–001
Selected Income Statistics, Catalogue 93–331
Employment Income by Occupation, Catalogue 93–332
Income Distributions by Size in Canada, Catalogue 13–207
Income After Tax Distributions by Size in Canada, Catalogue 13–210
Annual Report of the Minister of Industry, Science, and Technology under The Corporations and Labours Unions Act, Part 1, Corporations, Catalogue 61–210

Readers wishing additional information on data provided through the cooperation of Statistics Canada may obtain copies of related publications by mail from:

Publications Sales, Statistics Canada, Ottawa, Ontario, K1A0T6, by calling (613) 951–7277, or toll-free 800–267–6677. Readers may also facsimile their order by dialing (613) 951–1584.

Brief Contents

PART 1
Introduction

PART 2
Microeconomics

Contents

PART 2

Microeconomics

I

Microeconomic Theory: The Basics

III

Factor Markets

IV

Microeconomic Policy Debates

About the Authors

David Colander is the Christian A. Johnson Distinguished Professor of Economics at Middlebury College. He has authored, coauthored, or edited 30 books and over 90 articles on a wide range of economic topics.

He earned his B.A. at Columbia College and his M.Phil and Ph.D. at Columbia University. He also studied at the University of Birmingham in England and at Wilhelmsburg Gymnasium in Germany. Professor Colander has taught at Columbia College, Vassar College, and the University of Miami, as well as having been a consultant to Time-Life Films, a consultant to Congress, a Brookings Policy Fellow, and Visiting Scholar at Nuffield College, Oxford. Recently, he spent two months in Bulgaria, where he worked with former professors of political economy on how to teach Western economics.

He belongs to a variety of professional associations and has served on the Board of Directors and as vice president of the History of Economic Thought Society, the Eastern Economics Association, and is on the Board of Advisors of the *Journal of Economic Perspectives*. He is also on the Editorial Board of *The Journal of Economic Methodology* and *The Eastern Economics Journal*. He is currently the president of the Eastern Economic Association.

Peter Sephton is a Professor of Economics at the University of New Brunswick in Fredericton. He has authored and coauthored over 30 journal articles on a wide variety of topics.

He earned his B.A. at McMaster University, and both his M.A. and Ph.D. at Queen's University. Professor Sephton has taught at Queen's University, the University of Regina, the University of New Brunswick, and Saint Thomas University. He has also been a consultant to the International Monetary Fund, to Provincial governments, to environmental engineering firms, and in legal cases. He has also held positions at the Bank of Canada, the Ontario Ministry of Treasury and Economics, and the Federal Business Development Bank.

Professor Sephton has written a large number of instructional materials. Most recently, he wrote materials for use in the open access distance learning course in International Finance at Athabasca University.

He is married to Sue, and together they have two children: Bill, 10, and Jenny, 8. In his spare time, he coaches both of their soccer teams.

TASMAN SEA
NEW ZEALAND
North Cape
Auckland
Wellington
Christchurch
Dunedin
South I.
Stewart I.
Bounty Is.
Antipodes Is.
Campbell I.
Auckland Is.
(N.Z.)

PART 1

Introduction

PART

Section I is an introduction, and an introduction to an introduction sounds a little funny. But other sections have introductions, so it seemed a bit funny not to have an introduction to Section I and besides, as you will see, we're a little funny ourselves (which, in turn, has two interpretations; you will, we're sure, decide which of the two is appropriate). It will, however, be a very brief introduction, consisting of questions you probably have and some answers to those questions.

SOME QUESTIONS AND ANSWERS

Why study economics?
Because it's neat and interesting and helps provide insight into events that are constantly going on around you.

Why is this book so big?
Because there's lots of important information in it and because the book is designed so your teacher can pick and choose. You'll likely not be required to read all of it, but once you start, you'll probably read it all anyhow (Would you believe?)

Why does this book cost so much?
To answer this question you'll have to read the book.

Will this book make me rich?
No.

Will this book make me happy?
It depends.

This book doesn't seem to be written in normal textbook style. Is this book really written by two professors?
Yes, but they are really different, as you'll soon see.

Will the entire book be like this?
No, the introduction is just trying to rope you in. Much of the book will be hard going. Learning happens to be a difficult process: no pain, no gain. But the authors aren't sadists; they try to make learning as pleasantly painful as possible.

What do the authors' students think of them?
Weird—definitely weird—and hard. But fair, interesting, and sincerely interested in getting us to learn. (Answer written by our students.)

So there you have it. Answers to the questions that you might never have thought of if they hadn't been put in front of you. We hope they give you a sense of us and the approach we'll use in the book. There are some neat ideas in it. Let's now briefly consider what's in the first five chapters.

A SURVEY OF THE FIRST FIVE CHAPTERS

This first section is really an introduction to the rest of the book. It gives you the background necessary to have the latter chapters make sense. Chapter 1 gives you an overview of the entire field of economics as well as an introduction to our style. Chapter 2 introduces you to supply and demand, and shows you not only the power of those two concepts, but also the limitations.

Chapter 3 tries to put supply and demand in context. It discusses evolving economic systems and how economic forces interact with political and social forces. In it you'll see how the power of supply and demand analysis is strengthened when it's interpreted with a knowledge of economic institutions. Chapters 4 and 5 then introduce you to some of those economic institutions. Chapter 4 concentrates on domestic institutions; Chapter 5 concentrates on international institutions. Now let's get on with the show.

CHAPTER 1

Economics and Economic Reasoning

In my vacations, I visited the poorest quarters of several cities and walked through one street after another, looking at the faces of the poorest people. Next I resolved to make as thorough a study as I could of Political Economy.

~ Alfred Marshall

After reading this chapter, you should be able to:

1. State five important things to learn in economics.
2. Explain how to make decisions by comparing marginal costs and marginal benefits.
3. Define opportunity cost, and explain its relationship to economic reasoning.
4. Demonstrate opportunity cost with a production possibility curve.
5. State the principle of increasing opportunity cost.
6. Explain real-world events in terms of three "invisible forces."
7. Differentiate between microeconomics and macroeconomics.
8. Distinguish among positive economics, normative economics, and the art of economics.

When an artist looks at the world, he sees colour. When a musician looks at the world, she hears music. When an economist looks at the world, she sees a symphony of costs and benefits.[1] The economist's world might not be as colourful or as melodic as the others' worlds, but it's more practical. If you want to understand what's going on in the world that's really out there, you need to know economics.

We hardly have to convince you of this fact if you keep up with the news. Unemployment is up; inflation is down; the dollar is down; interest rates are up; businesses are going bankrupt. . . . The list is endless. So let's say you grant us that economics is important. That still doesn't mean that it's worth studying. The real question then is: How much will you learn? Most of what you learn depends on you, but part depends on the teacher and another part depends on the textbook. On both these counts, you're in luck; since your teacher chose this book for your course, you must have a super teacher.[2]

WHAT ECONOMICS IS ABOUT

1 Five important things to learn in economics are:
1. Economic reasoning
2. Economic terminology
3. Economic insights
4. Economic institutions
5. Economic policy options.

Five important things to learn in economics are:

1. Economic reasoning.
2. Economic terminology.
3. Insights economists have about economic issues, and theories that lead to those insights.
4. Information about economic institutions.
5. Information about the economic policy options facing society today.

By no coincidence, this book discusses economic reasoning, economic terminology, economic insights, economic institutions, and economic policy options.

Let's consider each in turn.

Economic Reasoning

Economic reasoning Making decisions on the basis of costs and benefits.

The most important thing you'll learn is **economic reasoning**—how to think like an economist. People trained in economics think in a certain way. They analyze everything critically; they compare the costs and the benefits of every issue and make decisions based, in part, on those costs and benefits. As we'll see later in this chapter, economists are human beings, and when they *make* choices, their decisions are coloured by their own views of how to deal with scarcity. As we'll see, part of good decision making is being able first to explain observed choices without taking sides on any issue: economists are trained to *explain* observed choices. For example, say you're trying to decide whether protecting baby seals is a good policy or not. Economists are trained to put their emotions aside and ask: What are the costs of protecting baby seals, and what are the benefits? Thus, they are open to the argument that the benefits of allowing baby seals to be killed might exceed the costs. To think like an economist is to address almost all issues using a cost/benefit approach.

Economic reasoning, once learned, is infectious. If you're susceptible, being exposed to it will change your life. It will influence your analysis of everything, including issues normally considered outside the scope of economics. For example,

---

[1]Authors are presented with a problem today. Our language has certain ambiguous words that can be interpreted as affording unequal treatment to women. For example, we use the term *man* both to describe all human beings and to describe a specific group of human beings. Similarly, we use the pronoun *he* when we mean all people. One can avoid such usage by writing *he and she* and *men and women* or *human beings,* and in much of this book these terms will be used, although every so often either the masculine or feminine term will appear. This is to see if you notice and to encourage you to think of possible sexist aspects in your own usage.

If you are wondering whether you are sexist, consider the following riddle: A father and son are in a car accident. The father is killed and the boy is injured. When the boy is brought to the hospital, the doctor on emergency room duty says, "I can't operate on him—he's my son." How can this be? If it doesn't seem like a riddle, good; if it does, whenever you see an occupation that is not gender-specific, think *man or woman* until the riddle is no longer a riddle.

[2]This book is written by two people, not a machine. That means that we have our quirks, our odd senses of humour, and our biases. All textbook writers do. Most textbooks have the quirks and eccentricities edited out so that all the books read and sound alike—professional, but dull. We choose to sound like ourselves—sometimes professional, sometimes playful, and sometimes stubborn. In our view, that makes the book more human and less dull. So forgive us our quirks—don't always take us too seriously—and we'll try to keep you awake when you're reading this book at 3 a.m., on the morning of the exam. If you think it's a killer to read a book this long, you ought to try writing one.

you will likely use economic reasoning to decide the possibility of getting a date for Saturday night, and who will pay for dinner. You will likely use it to decide whether to read this book, whether to attend class, whom to marry, and what kind of work to go into after you graduate. This is not to say that economic reasoning will provide all the answers. As you will see throughout this book, real-world questions are inevitably complicated, and economic reasoning simply provides a framework within which to approach a question.

Economic Terminology

Second, there's economic terminology, which is tossed around by the general public with increasing frequency. *GDP, corporations,* and *money supply* are just a few of the terms whose meaning any educated person in modern society needs to know. If you go to a party, don't know these terms, and want to seem intelligent, you'll have to nod knowingly. It's much better to actually *know* when you nod knowingly.

Two terms we want to introduce to you immediately are the *economy* and *economics.* The **economy** is the institutional structure through which individuals in a society coordinate their diverse wants or desires. **Economics** is the study of the economy. That is, economics is the study of how human beings in a society *coordinate* their wants and desires.

Economy The institutional structure through which individuals in a society coordinate their diverse wants or desires.

Economics The study of how human beings coordinate their wants.

One of society's largest problems is that individuals want more than is available, given the work they're willing to do. If individuals can be encouraged to work more and consume less, that problem can be reduced. Coordination often involves coercion; it involves limiting people's wants and increasing the amount of work individuals are willing to do to fulfill those wants.

Many of society's coordination problems involve scarcity. Therefore, economics is sometimes defined as the study of the allocation of scarce resources to satisfy individuals' wants or desires. We focus the definition on coordination rather than on scarcity to emphasize that the quantity of goods and services available depends on human action: individuals' imaginations, innovativeness, and willingness to do what needs to be done.

The reality of our society is that many people would rather play than help solve society's problems. So the basic economic problem involves inspiring people to do things that other people want them to do, and not to do things that other people don't want them to do. Thus, economics is the study of how to get people to do things they're not wild about doing (such as studying) and not to do things they *are* wild about doing (such as eating all the lobster they like), so that the things some people want to do are consistent with the things other people want them to do.

Economic Insights

Third, you'll learn about some general insights economists have gained into how the economy functions—how an economy seems to proceed or progress without any overall plan or coordinating agency. It's almost as if an invisible hand were directing economic traffic. These insights are often based on **economic theory**—generalizations about the workings of an abstract economy. Theory ties together economists' terminology and knowledge about economic institutions and leads to economic insights.

Economic theory Generalizations about the working of an abstract economy.

We're so used to the economy's functioning that we may not realize how amazing it is that the economy works as well as it does. Imagine for a moment that you're a visitor from Mars. You see the Canadian economy functioning relatively well. Stores are filled with goods. Most people have jobs. So you ask, "Who's in charge of organizing and coordinating the economic activities of the 30 million people in Canada?" The answer you get is mind boggling: "No one. The invisible hand of the market does it all." Economic theory helps explain such mind-boggling phenomena.

Economic Institutions

Fourth, you'll learn about economic institutions: how they work, and why they sometimes don't work. An **economic institution** is a physical or mental structure that significantly influences economic decisions. Corporations, governments, and cultural norms are all economic institutions. Many economic institutions have social, political, and religious dimensions. For example, your job often influences your social standing. In addition, many social institutions, such as the family, have economic functions. If

Economic institution Physical or mental stuctures that significantly influence economic decisions.

A REMINDER 

FIVE IMPORTANT THINGS TO LEARN IN ECONOMICS

To understand the economy, you need to learn:

1. Economic reasoning.
2. Economic terminology.
3. Economic insights economists have gained in thinking about economics.
4. Information about economic institutions.
5. Information about economic policy options facing society today.

any institution significantly affects economic decisions, we include it as an economic institution because you must understand that institution if you are to understand how the economy functions.

Cultural norms Standards people use when they determine whether a particular activity or behaviour is acceptable.

Since **cultural norms** may be an unfamiliar concept to you, let's consider how such norms affect economies. A cultural norm is a standard people use when they determine whether a particular activity or behaviour is acceptable. For example, religious rules once held that Catholics shouldn't eat meat on Friday, so Friday became a day to eat fish. The prohibition ended in the 1960s, but the tendency to eat fish on Friday has endured. In North America today, more fish is consumed on Fridays than on any other day of the week. This fact can be understood only if you understand the cultural norm that lies behind it. Similarly, in Canada more hams are bought in April and more turkeys are bought in October and December than in other months; more pork is consumed per capita in Sweden than in Israel. Can you explain why?

Economic institutions differ significantly among countries. For example, in Germany banks are allowed to own companies; in the United States they cannot. This causes a difference in the flow of resources into investment. Or alternatively, in Japan, antitrust laws (laws under which companies can combine or coordinate their activities) are loose; in Canada they are restrictive. This causes differences in the nature of competition in the two countries.

Besides helping you understand the economy, knowledge of economic institutions also directly benefits you. How do firms decide whom to hire? How do banks work? How does unemployment insurance work? What determines how much a Japanese car will cost you? How much does the government require your boss to deduct from your paycheque? Knowing the answers to these real-world questions will make your life easier.

Economic Policy Options

Economic policy An action (or inaction) taken, usually by government, to influence economic events.

Fifth, you'll learn about economic policy options facing our country. An **economic policy** is an action (or inaction) taken, usually by government, to influence economic events. Examples of economic policy questions are: How should the government deal with the next recession? (Alas, we can be sure that there will be a next recession.) What should the government do about the budget deficit? Will lowering interest rates stimulate the economy? Should government allow two large companies to merge? You won't get specific answers to these questions; instead, you'll simply learn what some of the policy options are, and what advantages and disadvantages each option offers.

A GUIDE TO ECONOMIC REASONING

2 If the benefits of doing something exceed the costs, do it. If the costs of doing something exceed the benefits, don't do it.

Let's now look at each of these five issues more carefully. We'll start with economic reasoning. In the economic way of thinking, every choice has costs and benefits, and decisions are made by comparing the two. The rules are simple:

If the benefits of doing something exceed the costs, do it.
If the costs of doing something exceed the benefits, don't do it.

Marginal Costs and Marginal Benefits

Economists have found that, when one is considering a choice among a variety of alternatives, often it's unnecessary to look at total benefits and total costs. All one need look at are marginal costs and marginal benefits. These are key concepts in economics, and it pays to learn them early on.

ECONOMIC KNOWLEDGE IN ONE SENTENCE: TANSTAAFL

A REMINDER 

Once upon a time, Tanstaafl was made king of all the lands. His first act was to call his economic advisors and tell them to write up all the economic knowledge the society possessed. After years of work, they presented their monumental effort: 25 volumes, each about 400 pages long. But in the interim, King Tanstaafl had become a very busy man, what with running a kingdom of all the lands and everything. Looking at the lengthy volumes, he told his advisors to summarize their findings in one volume.

Despondently, the economists returned to their desks, wondering how they could summarize what they'd been so careful to spell out. After many more years of rewriting, they were finally satisfied with their one-volume effort, and tried to make an appointment to see the king. Unfortunately, affairs of state had become even more pressing than before, and the king couldn't take the time to see them. Instead he sent word to them that he couldn't be bothered with a whole volume, and ordered them, under threat of death (for he had become a tyrant), to reduce the work to one sentence.

The economists returned to their desks, shivering in their sandals and pondering their impossible task. Thinking about their fate if they were not successful, they decided to send out for one last meal. Unfortunately, when they were collecting money to pay for the meal, they discovered they were broke. The disgusted delivery man took the last meal back to the cook, and the economists started down the path to the beheading station. On the way, the delivery man's parting words echoed in their ears. They looked at each other and suddenly they realized the truth. "We're saved!" they screamed. "That's it! That's economic knowledge in one sentence!" They wrote the sentence down and presented it to the king, who thereafter fully understood all economic problems. (He also gave them a good meal.) The sentence?

There Ain't No Such Thing As A Free Lunch—TANSTAAFL.

Marginal means additional or incremental. So a **marginal cost** is the additional cost to you over and above the costs you have already incurred. Consider, for example, attending class. You've already paid your tuition, so the marginal (or additional) cost of going to class does not include tuition.

Marginal cost The change in cost associated with a change in quantity.

Similarly, with marginal benefit. The **marginal benefit** of reading this chapter is the *additional* knowledge you get from reading it. If you already knew everything in this chapter before you picked up the book, the marginal benefit of reading it now is zero, except that you now know you are prepared for class, whereas before you might only have suspected you were prepared.

Marginal benefit Additional benefit above what you've already derived.

Comparing marginal (additional) costs with marginal (additional) benefits will often tell you how you should adjust your activities to be as well off as possible. If the marginal benefit of engaging in an activity exceeds the marginal cost of doing so, you should do it. But if the marginal benefit is less than the marginal cost, you should do something else.

As an example, let's consider a discussion we might have with a student who tells us that she is too busy to attend class. We respond, "Think about the tuition you've spent for this class—it works out to about $10 a lecture." She answers that the book she reads for class is a book that we wrote, and that we wrote it so clearly she fully understands everything. She goes on:

> I've already paid the tuition and, whether I go to class or not, I can't get any of the tuition back, so the tuition doesn't enter into my marginal cost decision. The marginal cost to me isn't the tuition; it's what I could be doing with the hour instead of spending it in class. Because I value my time at $75 an hour [people who understand everything value their time highly], and even though I've heard that your lectures are super, I estimate that the marginal benefit of your class is only $50. The marginal cost, $75, exceeds the marginal benefit, $50, so I don't attend class.

We would congratulate her on her diplomacy and her economic reasoning, but tell her that we give a quiz every week, that students who miss a quiz fail the quiz, that those who fail all the quizzes fail the course, and that those who fail the course do not graduate. In short, she is underestimating the marginal benefits of attending the course. Correctly estimated, the marginal benefits of attending class exceed the marginal costs of cutting class. So she should attend class.

There's much more to be said about economic reasoning, but that will come later. For now, all you need remember is that, in economic thinking, *all things have a cost—*

Economic decision rule If benefits exceed costs, do it. If costs exceed benefits, don't do it.

and a benefit. Decisions are made on the basis of the **economic decision rule:** If benefits exceed costs, do it. If costs exceed benefits, don't do it.

Economics and Passion

Recognizing that everything has a cost is reasonable, but it's a reasonableness that many people don't like. It takes some of the passion out of life. It leads you to consider possibilities such as these:

- Saving some peoples' lives with liver transplants might not be worth the cost. The money might be better spent on nutritional programs that would save 20 lives for every 2 lives you might save with transplants.
- Maybe we shouldn't try to eliminate all pollution, because the cost of doing so may be too high. To eliminate all pollution would be to forgo too much of some other good activity.
- Buying a stock that went up 20 percent wasn't necessarily the greatest investment if in doing so you had to forgo some other investment that would have paid you a 30 percent return.
- It might make sense for the automobile industry to save $12 per car by not installing a safety device, even though without the safety device some people will be killed.

You get the idea. This kind of reasonableness is often criticized for being cold-blooded. But, not surprisingly, economists first reason economically; the social and moral implications of their conclusions are integrated later.

Economists' reasonableness isn't universally appreciated. Businesses love the result; others aren't so sure, as one of us discovered some years back when a girlfriend said she was leaving. "Why?" I asked. "Because," she responded, "you're so, so . . . reasonable." It took me many years after she left to learn what she already knew: There are many types of reasonableness, and not everyone thinks an economist's reasonableness is a virtue. We'll discuss such issues later; for now, let us simply warn you that, for better or worse, studying economics will lead you to view questions in a cost/benefit framework.

Opportunity Cost

Opportunity cost The benefit forgone, or the cost, of the best alternative to the activity you've chosen. In economic reasoning, the cost is less than the benefit

3 Opportunity cost is the basis of cost-benefit economic reasoning: it is the benefit forgone, or the cost of the best alternative to the activity you've chosen. In economic reasoning, that cost is less than the benefit of what you've chosen.

Putting economists' cost/benefit rules into practice isn't easy. To do so, you have to be able to choose and measure the costs and benefits correctly. Economists have devised the concept of opportunity cost to help you do that. The **opportunity cost** of undertaking an activity is the benefit forgone by undertaking that activity. The benefit forgone is the benefit that you might have gained from choosing the next-best alternative. To obtain the benefit of something, you must give up (forgo) something else—namely, the next-best alternative. All activities that have a next-best alternative have an opportunity cost.

Let's consider some examples. The opportunity cost of going out once with Natalia (or Nathaniel), the most beautiful woman (attractive man) in the world, might well be losing your solid steady, Margo (Mike). The opportunity cost of cleaning up the environment might be a reduction in the money available to assist low-income individuals. The opportunity cost of having a child might be two boats, three cars, and a two-week vacation each year for five years.

Examples are endless, but let's consider two that are particularly relevant to you: your choice of courses and your decision about how much to study. Let's say you're a full-time student and at the beginning of the term you had to choose four or five courses to take. Taking one precluded taking some other, and the opportunity cost of taking an economics course may well have been not taking a course on theatre. Similarly with studying: you have a limited amount of time to spend studying economics, studying some other subject, sleeping, or partying. The more time you spend on one activity, the less time you have for another. That's opportunity cost.

Notice how neatly the opportunity cost concept takes into account costs and benefits of all other options, and converts these alternative benefits into costs of the decision you're now making. This conversion helps you to compare costs and benefits and to select the activity with the largest difference between benefits and costs.

Opportunity costs have always made choice difficult, as we see in the early 19th-century engraving, "One or the Other." *Bleichroeder Print Collection, Baker Library, Harvard Business School.*

The relevance of opportunity cost isn't limited to your individual decisions. Opportunity costs are also relevant to government's decisions, which affect everyone in society. A common example is the guns-versus-butter debate. The resources that a society has are limited; therefore, its decision to use those resources to have more guns (more weapons) means that it must have less butter (fewer consumer goods). Thus, when society decides to spend $10 billion more on improved military hardware, the opportunity cost of that decision is $10 billion not spent on helping the homeless, paying off some of the national debt, or spending $10 billion on health care.

The opportunity cost concept has endless implications. It can even be turned upon itself. For instance, it takes time to think about alternatives; that means that there's a cost to being reasonable, so it's only reasonable to be somewhat unreasonable. If you followed that argument, you've caught the economic bug. If you didn't, don't worry. Just remember the opportunity cost concept for now. We'll infect you with economic thinking in the rest of the book.

The Production Possibility Table

We've just gone over opportunity cost. We're now going to review the same concept—only this time numerically and graphically. Opportunity cost can be seen numerically with a **production possibility table,** which lists a choice's opportunity cost by summarizing what alternative outputs you can achieve with your inputs. An **output** is simply a result of an activity—your grade in a course is an output. An **input** is what you put in to achieve that output. In this example, study time is an input.

Production possibility table Table that lists a choice's opportunity costs.

Output The result of an activity.

Input What you put in to achieve output.

Let's present the study time/grades example numerically. To do so we must be more precise. Say you have exactly 20 hours a week to devote to two courses: economics and history. (So, maybe we're a bit optimistic.) Grades are given numerically and you know that the following relationships exist: if you study 20 hours in economics, you'll get a grade of 100, 18 hours—94, and so forth.[3]

Let's say that the best you can do in history is a 98 with 20 hours of study a week; 19 hours of study guarantee you a 96, and so on. The production possibility table in Exhibit 1 (a) shows the highest combination of grades you can get with various allocations of the 20 hours available for studying the two subjects. One possibility is getting 100 in economics and 58 in history. Another is getting 70 in economics and 78 in history.

Notice that the opportunity cost of studying one subject rather than the other is embodied in the production possibility table. The information in the table comes from experience; we are assuming that you've discovered that if you transfer an hour of

[3]Throughout the book we'll be presenting numerical examples to help you understand the concepts. The numbers we choose are often arbitrary. After all, we have to choose something. As an exercise, you might choose different numbers that apply to your own life and work out the argument using those numbers. For those who don't want to make up their own numbers, the study guide has examples with different numbers.

ADDED DIMENSION

DEALING WITH MATH ANXIETY

Knowing our students, we can see the red flags rising, the legs tensing up, the fear flooding over many of you. Here it comes—the math and the graphs.

We wish we could change things by saying to you, "Don't worry—mathematics and graphical analysis are easy." But we can't. That doesn't mean math and graphical analysis aren't easy. They are. They're wonderful tools that convey ideas neatly and efficiently. But we've had enough teaching experience to know that somewhere back in elementary school some teacher blew it and put about 40 percent of you off mathematics for life. A tool that scares you to death is not useful; it can be a hindrance, not a help, to learning. We also know that nothing your current teacher or we now can say, write, or do is going to change that for most of those 40 percent. On the other hand, we've had a little bit of luck with about 10 percent of the 40 percent (which makes 4 percent—4 out of 100 students) with the following "conspiracy explanation." So we'll try it on you. Here's what we tell them.

Economics is really simple. Economists know that it is, and they also know that if word got around about how simple economics is, few students would take economics. But economists are smart. They make economics seem more difficult than it is by couching simple economic ideas in graphs. The graphs convince many students that economics is really hard, allowing economics professors to teach simple ideas that the students think are hard.

About 4 percent of our students become so mad at the thought of being duped that they overcome their math anxiety. The rest just wonder whether these teachers are for real.

If avoiding being duped means something to you, believe the preceding story; if it doesn't, don't. But whatever you do, try to follow the numerical and graphical examples carefully, because they not only cement the knowledge into your minds, they also present the ideas we're discussing in a rigorous manner.

The ideas conveyed in the numerical and graphical examples will be explained in words, and the graphical analysis (the type of mathematical explanation most used in introductory economics) generally will simply be a more precise presentation of the accompanying discussion in words. In some economics courses, understanding the words may be enough, but in most, the exams pose the questions in graphical terms, so there's no getting around the need to understand the ideas graphically. And it is simple. (Appendix B discusses the basics of graphical analysis.)

study from economics to history, you'll lose 3 points on your grade in economics and gain 2 points in history. Thus, the opportunity cost of a 2-point rise in your history grade is a 3-point decrease in your economics grade.

The Production Possibility Curve

Production possibility curve A curve measuring the maximum combination of outputs that can be obtained from a given number of inputs.

The information in the production possibility table can also be presented graphically in a diagram. This graphical presentation of the opportunity cost concept is called the **production possibility curve.** This curve indicates the maximum combination of outputs you can obtain from a given number of inputs.

A production possibility curve is created from a production possibility table by mapping the table in a two-dimensional graph. We've taken the information from the table in Exhibit 1 (a) and mapped it into Exhibit 1 (b). The history grade is mapped, or plotted, on the horizontal axis; the economics grade is on the vertical axis.

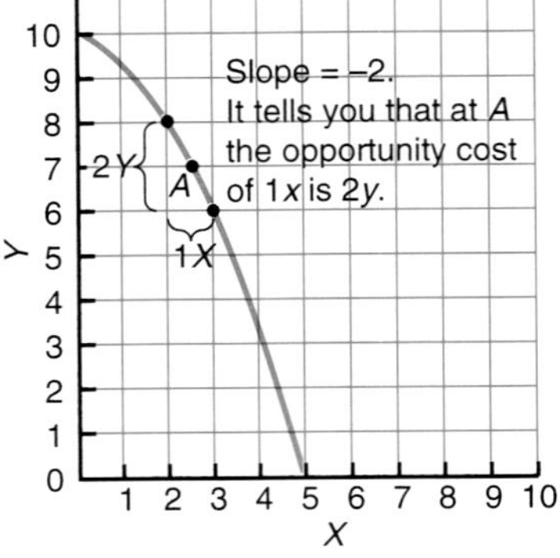

4 Remember this graph: The slope tells you the opportunity cost of good *X* in terms of good *Y*. You have to give up 2*Y* to get 1*X* when you're around point *A*.

As you can see from the bottom row of Exhibit 1 (a), if you study economics for all 20 hours and study history for 0 hours, you'll get grades of 100 in economics and 58 in history. Point *A* in Exhibit 1 (b) represents that choice. If you study history for all 20 hours and study economics for 0 hours, you'll get a 98 in history and a 40 in economics. Point *E* represents that choice. Points *B, C,* and *D* represent three possible choices between these two extremes.

Notice that the production possibility curve slopes downward from left to right. That means that there is an inverse relationship (a trade-off) between grades in economics and grades in history. The better the grade in economics, the worse the grade in history, and vice versa. That downward slope represents the opportunity cost concept—you get more of one benefit only if you get less of another benefit.

The production possibility curve not only represents the opportunity cost concept; it also measures the opportunity cost. For example, in Exhibit 1 (b), say you want to raise your grade in history from a 94 to a 98 (move from point *D* to point *E*). The opportunity cost of that 4-point increase would be a 6-point decrease in your economics grade, from 46 to 40.

Hours of study in history	Grade in history	Hours of study in economics	Grade in economics
20	98	0	40
19	96	1	43
18	94	2	46
17	92	3	49
16	90	4	52
15	88	5	55
14	86	6	58
13	84	7	61
12	82	8	64
11	80	9	67
10	78	10	70
9	76	11	73
8	74	12	76
7	72	13	79
6	70	14	82
5	68	15	85
4	66	16	88
3	64	17	91
2	62	18	94
1	60	19	97
0	58	20	100

(a) Production possibility table

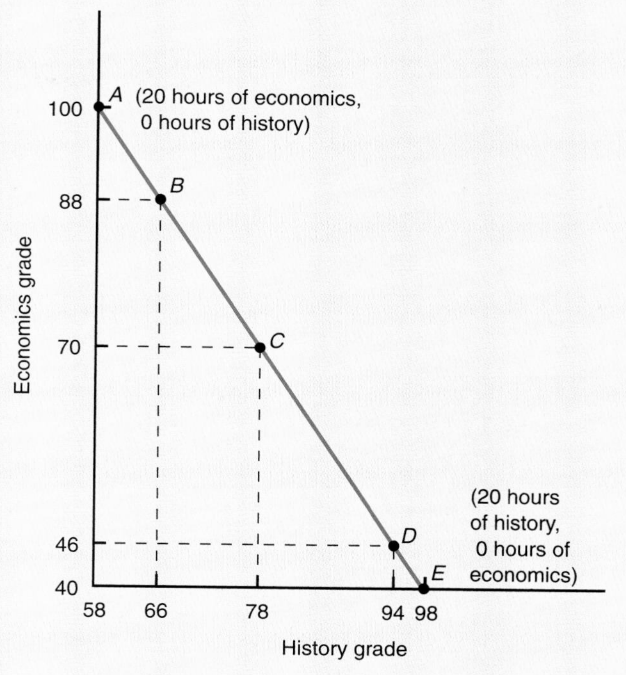

(b) Production possibility curve

EXHIBIT 1 A Production Possibility Table and Curve for Grades in Economics and History

The production possibility table (**a**) shows the highest combination of grades you can get with only 20 hours available for studying economics and history.

The information in the production possibility table in (**a**) can be plotted on a graph, as is done in (**b**). The grade received in economics is on the vertical axis, and the grade received in history is on the horizontal axis.

To summarize, the production possibility curve demonstrates that:

1. There is a limit to what you can achieve, given the existing institutions, resources, and technology.
2. Every choice you make has an opportunity cost. You can get more of something only by giving up something else.

Increasing Marginal Opportunity Cost We chose an unchanging trade-off in the study time/grade example because it made the initial presentation of the production possibility curve easier. Since, by assumption, you could always trade two points on your history grade for three points on your economics grade, the production possibility curve was a straight line. But is that the way we'd expect reality to be? Probably not. The production possibility curve is generally bowed outward, as in Exhibit 2 (b).

Why? To make the answer more concrete, let's talk specifically about society's choice between eating (cheeseburgers) and spending on entertainment (CDs). The information in Exhibit 2 (b) is derived from the table in Exhibit 2 (a).

Let's see what the shape of the curve means in terms of numbers. Let's start with society producing only CDs (point *A*). Giving up a CD initially gains us a lot of cheeseburgers (4), moving us to point *B*. The next two CDs we give up gains us slightly fewer cheeseburgers (point *C*). If we continue to trade cheeseburgers for CDs, we find that at point *D* we gain almost no cheeseburgers from giving up a CD. The opportunity cost of choosing cheeseburgers over CDs increases as we increase the production of cheeseburgers.

The reason the opportunity cost of cheeseburgers increases as we consume more cheeseburgers is that some resources are relatively better suited to producing cheese-

EXHIBIT 2 A Production Possibility Table and Curve

The table in (**a**) contains information on the trade-off between the production of cheeseburgers and CDs. This information has been plotted on the graph in (**b**). Notice in (**b**) that as we move along the production possibility curve from *A* to *F*, trading CDs for cheeseburgers, we get fewer and fewer cheeseburgers for each CD given up. That is, the opportunity cost of choosing cheeseburgers over CDs increases as we increase the production of cheeseburgers. This concept is called the principle of increasing marginal opportunity cost. The phenomenon occurs because some resources are better suited for the production of CDs than for the production of cheeseburgers, and we use the better ones first.

% resources devoted to production of cheeseburgers	Number of cheeseburgers	% resources devoted to production of CDs	CDs	Row
0	0	100	15	*A*
20	4	80	14	*B*
40	7	60	12	*C*
60	9	40	9	*D*
80	11	20	5	*E*
100	12	0	0	*F*

(a) Production possibility table

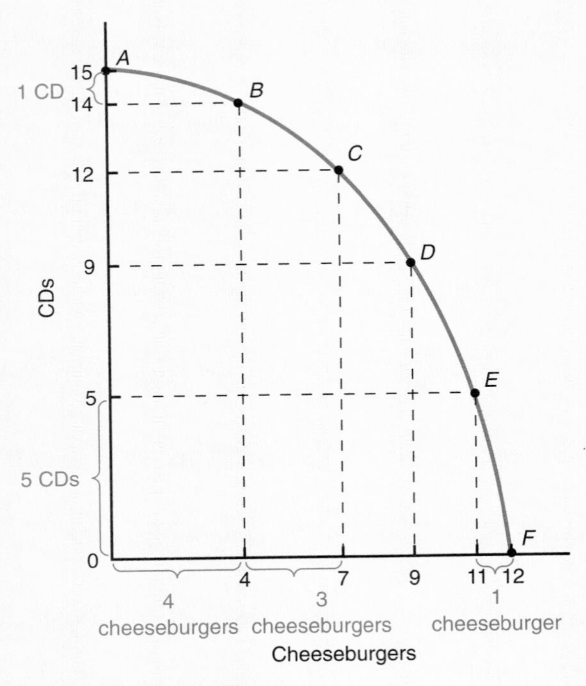

(b) Production possibility curve

Comparative advantage The ability to produce a good at a lower opportunity cost (forgone production of another good) than another country or resource can.

burgers, while others are relatively better suited to producing CDs. Put in economists' terminology, some resources have a comparative advantage over other resources in the production of CDs, while other resources have a comparative advantage in the production of cheeseburgers. A resource has a **comparative advantage** in the production of a good when, compared to other resources, it's relatively better suited to producing that good than to producing another good.

When making small amounts of cheeseburgers and large amounts of CDs, in the production of those cheeseburgers we use the resources whose comparative advantage is in the production of cheeseburgers. All other resources are devoted to producing CDs. Because the resources used in producing cheeseburgers aren't good at producing CDs, we're not giving up many CDs to get those cheeseburgers. As we produce more and more of a good, we must use resources whose comparative advantage is in the production of the other good—in this case, more suitable for producing CDs than for producing cheeseburgers. As we remove resources from the production of CDs to get the same additional amount of cheeseburgers, we must give up increasing numbers of CDs. An alternative way of saying this is that the opportunity cost of producing cheeseburgers becomes greater as the production of CDs increases. As we continue to increase the production of cheeseburgers, the opportunity cost of more cheeseburgers becomes very high because we're using resources to produce cheeseburgers that have a strong comparative advantage for producing CDs.

Let's consider two more specific examples. Say Canada suddenly decides it needs more wheat. To get additional wheat, we must devote additional land to growing it. This land is less fertile than the land we're already using, so our additional output of wheat per acre of land devoted to wheat will be less. Alternatively, consider the use of relief pitchers in a baseball game. If only one relief pitcher is needed, the manager sends in the best; if he must send in a second one, then a third, and even a fourth, the likelihood of winning the game decreases.

For many of the choices society must make, opportunity costs tend to increase as we choose more and more of an item. The reason is that resources are not easily adapt-

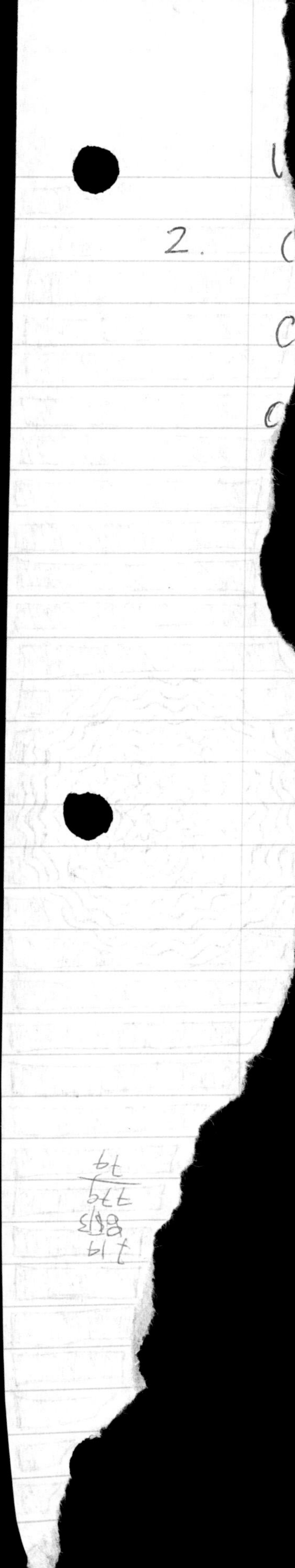

2.

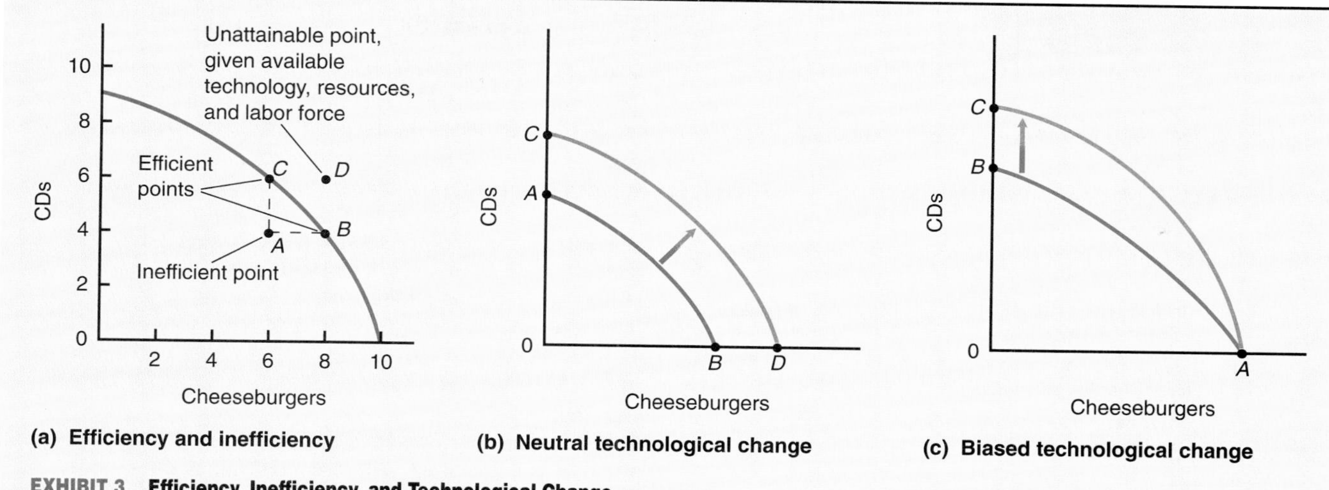

EXHIBIT 3 Efficiency, Inefficiency, and Technological Change

The production possibility curve helps us see what is meant by efficiency. At point *A*, in (**a**), all inputs are used to make 6 cheeseburgers and 4 CDs. This is inefficient since there is a way to obtain more of one without giving up any of the other; that is, to obtain 6 cheeseburgers and 6 CDs (point *C*) or 4 CDs and 8 cheeseburgers (point *B*). All points inside the production possibility curve are inefficient. With fixed inputs and given technology, we cannot go beyond the production possibility curve. For example, point *D* is unattainable.

A technological change that improves production techniques will shift the production possibility curve outward, as shown in both (**b**) and (**c**). How the curve shifts outward depends on how technology improves. For example, if we become more efficient in the production of both CDs and cheeseburgers, the curve will shift out as in (**b**). If we become more efficient in producing CDs, but not in producing cheeseburgers, then the curve will shift as in (**c**).

able from the production of one good to the production of another. Such a phenomenon about choice is so common, in fact, that it has acquired a name: the **principle of increasing marginal opportunity cost.** That principle states:

Principle of increasing marginal opportunity cost In order to get more of something, one must give up ever-increasing quantities of something else.

> *In order to get more of something, one must give up ever-increasing quantities of something else.*

In other words, initially the opportunity costs of an activity are low, but they increase the more we concentrate on that activity. Sometimes this law is called the flowerpot law because, if it didn't hold, all the world's food could be grown in a flowerpot. But it can't be. As we add more seeds to a fixed amount of soil, there won't be enough nutrients or room for the roots, so output per seed decreases.

5 The principle of increasing marginal opportunity cost states that opportunity costs increase the more you concentrate on the activity. In order to get more of something, one must give up ever-increasing quantities of something else.

Efficiency We like, if possible, to get as much output as possible from a given amount of inputs or resources. That's how **productive efficiency** is defined: achieving as much output as possible from a given amount of inputs or resources. We would like to be efficient. The production possibility curve helps us see what is meant by productive efficiency. Consider point *A* in Exhibit 3 (a), which is inside the production possibility curve. If we are producing at point *A*, we are using all our resources to produce 6 cheeseburgers and 4 CDs. Point *A* represents **inefficiency,** since with the same inputs we could be getting either 8 cheeseburgers and 4 CDs (point *B*) or 6 CDs and 6 cheeseburgers (point *C*). Both points *B* and *C* represent efficiency, as long as we prefer more to less. We always want to move our production out to a point on the production possibility curve.

Productive efficiency Getting as much output for as few inputs as possible.

Inefficiency Getting less output from inputs which, if devoted to some other activity, would produce more output.

Why not move out farther, say to point *D*? If we could, we would, but by definition the production possibility curve represents the most output we can get from a certain combination of inputs. So point *D* is unattainable, given our resources and technology.

When technology improves, when more resources are discovered, or when the economic institutions get better at fulfilling our wants, we can get more output with the same inputs. What this means is that when technology or an economic institution

ADDED DIMENSION 

RESOURCES, INPUTS, TECHNOLOGY, AND OUTPUT

Production involves transforming inputs into outputs. For example, seeds, soil, and labour (inputs) combine to produce wheat (output). Many introductory economics texts call inputs *resources* and divide those inputs into three resources: land, labour, and capital. Economists in the 1800s, often called *Classical economists,* discussed production as a means of transforming land, labour, and capital into outputs. Classical economists divided all inputs into those three categories because they were interested in answering the question: How is income divided among landowners, workers, and capitalists? The three divisions helped them focus on that question: landowners' income was rent, workers' income was wages, and capitalists' income was profit.

Modern advanced analysis of production doesn't follow this threefold division. Instead, the modern analysis is more abstract and tells how inputs in general are transformed into outputs in general. Modern economic theory has moved away from the traditional division because the division of income among these three groups isn't central to the questions economists are now asking.

But that leaves open the problem: What division of resources makes the most sense? The answer depends on what question you're asking. For example, in the grade example in this chapter, your time was the input, while in the CDs-and-cheeseburgers example the inputs were machines, natural resources, and labour. In the most abstract categorization, the ultimate resources are space (represented by land), time (represented by labour), and matter (represented by capital). Thus, in one way of looking at it, the traditional distinction is still relevant. But in another way, it isn't. It directs our focus of analysis away from some important inputs. For example, one of the inputs that economists now focus on is *entrepreneurship,* the ability to organize and get something done. Entrepreneurship is an important input that's distinct from labour. Most listings of general resources today include entrepreneurship.

Here's another important point about resources. The term *resource* is often used with the qualifier *natural,* as in the phrase *natural resources.* Coal, oil, and iron are all *called natural resources.* Be careful about that qualifier *natural.* Whether something is or isn't a natural resource depends on the available technology. And technology is unnatural. For example, at one time a certain black gooey stuff was not a resource—it was something that made land unusable. When people learned that the black gooey stuff could be burned as a fuel, oil became a resource. What's considered a resource depends on technology. If solar technology is ever perfected, oil will go back to being black gooey stuff.

improves, the entire production possibility curve shifts outward from *AB* to *CD* in Exhibit 3 (b). How the production possibility curve shifts outward depends on how the technology improves. For example, say we become more efficient in producing CDs, but not more efficient in producing cheeseburgers. Then the production possibility curve shifts outward to *AC* in Exhibit 3 (c).

Policies that costlessly shift the production possibility curve outward are the most desirable policies because they don't require us to decrease our consumption of one good to get more of another. Alas, they are the most infrequent. Improving technology and institutions and discovering more resources are not costless; generally there's an opportunity cost of doing so that must be taken into account.

Economics, Institutions, and the Production Possibility Curve One of the important lessons one learns in economics is that *decisions are made in context:* What makes sense in one context may not make sense in another. For example, say you're answering the question: Would society be better off if students were taught literature or if they were taught agriculture? The answer depends on the institutional context. In a developing country whose goal is large increases in material output, teaching agriculture may make sense. In a developed country, where growth in material output is less important, literature may make sense.

Recognizing the contextual nature of decisions is important in interpreting the production possibility curve. Because decisions are contextual, what the production possibility curve looks like depends on the existing institutions, and the analysis can only be applied in institutional context. The production possibility curve is not a purely technical phenomenon. The curve is an *engine of analysis* to make contextual choices, not a definitive tool to decide what one should do in all cases.

Distribution and Productive Efficiency In discussing the production possibility curve, we avoided questions of distribution: Who gets what? But such questions cannot be ignored in real-world situations. Specifically, if the method of production is tied to a particular

In the 1990s, oil has remained an important natural resource. *Bettman Newsphotos.*

income distribution and choosing one method will help some people but hurt others, we can't say that one method of production is efficient and the other inefficient, even if one method produces more total output than the other. The term **efficiency** involves achieving a goal as cheaply as possible. The term has meaning only in regard to a specified goal. Say, for example, that we have a society of ascetics who believe that consumption above some minimum is immoral. For such a society, producing more for less (productive efficiency) would not be efficient since consumption is not its goal. Or say that we have a society that cares that what is produced is fairly distributed. An increase in output that goes to only one person and not to anyone else would not necessarily be efficient.

Efficiency Achieving a goal as cheaply as possible. (16)

In our society, however, most people prefer more to less, and many policies have relatively small distributional consequences. On the basis of the assumption that more is better than less, economists use their own kind of shorthand for such policies and talk about efficiency as identical to productive efficiency—increasing total output. But it's important to remember the assumption under which that shorthand is used: that the distributional effects that accompany the policy aren't undesirable and that we, as a society, prefer more output.

The Production Possibility Curve and Tough Choices

The production possibility curve represents the tough choices society must make. Not everyone recognizes these choices. For example, politicians often talk as if the production possibility curve were nonexistent. They promise voters the world, telling them, "If you elect me, you can have more of everything." When they say that, they obscure the hard choices and increase their probability of getting elected.

Economists do the opposite. They promise little except that life is tough, and they continually point out that seemingly free lunches often involve significant hidden costs. Alas, political candidates who exhibit such reasonableness seldom get elected. Economists' reasonableness has earned economics the nickname, *the dismal science.*

Economics and the Invisible Forces

The opportunity cost concept applies to all aspects of life. It embodies *economic forces.* **Economic forces** are the forces of scarcity; when there isn't enough to go around, goods must be rationed. **Rationing** is a structural mechanism for determining who gets what. For example, dormitory rooms are often rationed by lottery, and permission to register in popular classes is often rationed by a first-come, first-registered

Economic forces The forces of scarcity (when there isn't enough to go around, goods must be rationed).

Rationing Structural mechanism for determining who gets what.

Market force Economic force to which society has given relatively free rein so that it has been able to work through the market.

Invisible hand Economic forces, that is, the price mechanism; the rise and fall of prices that guides our actions in a market.

6 Economic reality is controlled by three invisible forces:

1. The invisible hand (economic forces);
2. The invisible handshake (social and historical forces); and
3. The invisible foot (political and legal forces).

Invisible handshake Social and historical forces that play a role in deciding whether to let market forces operate.

Invisible foot Political and legal forces that play a role in deciding whether to let market forces operate.

rule. The same with food: If food weren't rationed, there wouldn't be enough to go around, so it must be rationed—by charging a price for it. All scarce goods or rights must be rationed in some fashion.

Rationing reflects scarcity and economic forces. One of the important choices that a society must make is whether to allow these economic forces to operate freely and openly or to try to rein them in. When society gives an economic force relatively free rein so that an economic force works through the market, it's called a **market force.**

Market forces ration by changing prices. When there's a shortage, the price goes up. When there's a surplus, the price goes down. Much of this book will be devoted to analyzing how the market works like an invisible hand, guiding economic forces to coordinate individual actions and allocate scarce resources. The **invisible hand** is the price mechanism, the rise and fall of prices that guides our actions in a market.

Societies can't choose whether or not to allow economic forces to operate—economic forces are always operating. However, societies may choose whether to allow market forces to predominate. Other forces play a major role in deciding whether to let market forces operate. We'll call these other forces the **invisible handshake** (social and historical forces) and the **invisible foot** (political and legal forces). Economic reality is determined by a contest among these three invisible forces.

Let's consider an example in which the invisible handshake prevents an economic force from becoming a market force: the problem of getting a date for Saturday night. If a school (or a society) has significantly more people of one sex than the other (let's say more men than women), some men may well find themselves without a date—that is, men will be in excess supply—and will have to find something else to do, say study or go to a movie by themselves. An "excess supply" person could solve the problem by paying someone to go out with him or her, but that would probably change the nature of the date in unacceptable ways. It would be revolting to the person who offered payment and to the person who was offered payment. That unacceptability is an example of the invisible handshake in action—the complex of social and cultural norms that guides and limits our activities. People don't try to buy dates because the invisible handshake prevents them from doing so. The invisible handshake makes the market solution for dating inappropriate.

Now let's consider another example in which it's the invisible foot—political and legal influences—that stops economic forces from becoming market forces. Say you decide that you can make some money by producing and selling your own brand of beer from your basement apartment. You try to establish a small business, but suddenly you experience the invisible foot in action. Alcoholic beverages can only be sold by government license, so you'll be prohibited from selling your beer. Economic forces—the desire to make money—led you to want to enter the business, but in this case the invisible foot squashes the invisible hand.

Often the invisible foot and invisible handshake work together against the invisible hand. For example, in Canada there aren't enough babies to satisfy all the couples who desire them. Babies born to particular sets of parents are rationed—by luck. Consider a group of parents, all of whom want babies. Those who can, have a baby; those who can't have one, but want one, try to adopt. Adoption agencies ration the available babies. Who gets a baby depends on whom people know at the adoption agency and on the desires of the birth mother, who can often specify the socioeconomic background (and many other characteristics) of the family in which she wants her baby to grow up. That's the economic force in action; it gives more power to the supplier of something that's in short supply.

If our society allowed individuals to buy and sell babies, that economic force would be translated into a market force. The invisible hand would see to it that the quantity of babies supplied would equal the quantity of babies demanded at some price. The market, not the adoption agencies, would do the rationing.[4]

[4]Even though it's against the law, some babies are nonetheless "sold" on a semilegal, or what is called a gray, market. In the United States in the early 1990s, "market price" for a healthy baby was about U.S. $30,000. If it were legal to sell babies (and if people didn't find having babies in order to sell them morally repugnant), the price would be much lower, since there would be a larger supply of babies.

THE INVISIBLE FORCES

ADDED DIMENSION

Ideas are encapsulated in metaphors, and Adam Smith's "invisible hand" metaphor has been a central one in economics since 1776. It's a neat metaphor, but it sometimes makes economic forces seem to be the only forces guiding the direction of society. And that just ain't so.

In the 1970s and 1980s, a number of modern-day economists attempted to broaden the dimensions of economic analysis. To explain what they were doing, they introduced metaphors for two other invisible forces. The term *invisible handshake* was coined by Arthur Okun, an American economist working at an economic "think tank". Okun argued that social and historical forces—the invisible handshake—often prevented the invisible hand from working.

The term *invisible foot* was coined by Stephen Magee. Magee summarized the argument of a large number of economists that individuals often use politics to get what they want, expressing this phenomenon with the invisible foot metaphor. Government action to benefit particular pressure groups is the invisible foot. By the late 1980s, these two additional terms were commonly used by the group of economists who were struggling to integrate economic insights with social and political insights.

Most people, including us, find the idea of selling babies repugnant. But why? It's the strength of the invisible handshake backed up and strengthened by the invisible foot.

What is and isn't allowable differs from one society to another. For example, in Russia, until recently, private businesses were against the law, so not many people started their own businesses. In the United States, until the 1970s, it was against the law to hold gold except in jewelry, so most people refrained from holding gold. Ultimately a country's laws and social norms determine whether the invisible hand will be allowed to work.

The invisible foot and invisible handshake are active in all parts of your life. The invisible foot influences many of your everyday actions. You don't practice medicine without a license; you don't sell body parts or certain addictive drugs. These actions are all against the law. But many people do sell alcohol; that's not against the law if you have a permit. The invisible handshake also influences us. You don't make profitable loans to your friends (you don't charge your friends interest); you don't charge your children for their food (parents are supposed to feed their children); many sports and media stars don't sell their autographs (some do, but many consider the practice tacky); you don't lower the wage you'll accept in order to get a job away from someone else. The list is long. You cannot understand economics without understanding the limitations that political and social forces—the invisible foot and the invisible handshake—place on economic actions.

In summary, what happens in a society can be seen as the reaction and interaction of these three forces: the invisible hand (economic forces), the invisible foot (political and legal forces), and the invisible handshake (social and historical forces). Economics has a role to play in sociology, history, and politics, just as sociology, history, and politics have roles to play in economics. While different branches of economics attempt to offer an explanation for political forces (public choice theory), legal forces (law and economics), and social forces (institutional economics), it is important to remember that good economic theory must take into account how these forces interact with decision making.

Economics is about the real world. Throughout this book we'll use the invisible forces analogy to talk about real-world events and the interrelationships of economics, history, sociology, and politics.

ECONOMIC TERMINOLOGY

Economic terminology needs little discussion. It simply needs learning. As terms come up in discussion, you'll begin to recognize them. Soon you'll begin to understand them, and finally you'll begin to feel comfortable using them. In this book we're trying to describe how economics works in the real world, so we introduce you to many of the terms that occur in business and in discussions of the economy. Learning economic vocabulary, like learning German or French vocabulary, isn't fun. It's not

A REMINDER  WINSTON CHURCHILL AND LADY ASTOR

There are many stories about Nancy Astor, the first woman elected to Britain's Parliament. A vivacious, fearless American woman, she married into the English aristocracy and, during the 1930s and 1940s, became a bright light on the English social and political scenes, which were already quite bright.

One story told about Lady Astor is that she and Winston Churchill, the unorthodox genius who had a long and distinguished political career and who was Britain's prime minister during World War II, were sitting in a pub having a theoretical discussion about morality. Churchill suggested that as a thought experiment Lady Astor ponder the question: If a man were to promise her a huge amount of money—say £1 million—for the privilege, would she sleep with him? Lady Astor did ponder the question for a while and finally answered, yes, she would, if the money were guaranteed. Churchill then asked her if she would sleep with him for £5. Her response was sharp: "Of course not. What do you think I am—a prostitute?" This time Churchill won the battle of wits by answering, "We have already established that fact; we are now simply negotiating about price."

One moral that economists might draw from this story is that economic incentives, if high enough, can have a powerful influence on behaviour. An equally important moral of the story is that noneconomic incentives can also be very strong. Why do most people feel it's wrong to sell sex for money, even if they would be willing to do so if the price were high enough? Keeping this second moral in mind will significantly increase your economic understanding of real-world events.

something that's easily taught in classes. It's something that's learned by study and repetition outside the class. Learning vocabulary takes repetition and memorization, but no one ever said all learning is fun.

Whenever possible we'll integrate the introduction of new terminology into the discussion so that learning it will seem painless. In fact we've already introduced you to a number of economic terms: *opportunity cost, the invisible hand, market forces,* and *economic forces,* just to name a few. By the end of the book we'll have introduced you to hundreds more.

ECONOMIC INSIGHTS

Economists have thought about the economy for a long time, so it's not surprising that they've developed some insights into the way it works.

General insights are often embodied in a *particular economic theory*—a formulation of highly abstract, deductive relationships that capture inherent empirically-observed tendencies of economies. Theories are inevitably too abstract to apply in specific cases and, thus, these theories are often embodied, in turn, in economic models and economic principles that place the generalized insights of the theory in a more specific contextual setting. Then these theories, models, and principles are empirically tested (as best one can) to ensure that they correspond to reality. While these models and principles are less general than theories, they are still usually too general to apply in specific cases. Theories, models, and principles must be combined with a knowledge of real-world economic institutions to arrive at specific policy recommendations.

You've already been introduced to one economic principle, the principle of increasing marginal opportunity cost, which is an insight about the relationship among outputs: In order to get more of one output, you must give up ever-increasing quantities of another output. That principle can be applied to a wide variety of examples, so you need to learn only the principle, not each specific example.

To see the importance of principles, think back to grade school when you learned to add. You didn't memorize the sum of 147 and 138; instead you learned a principle of addition. The principle says that when adding 147 and 138, you first add 7 + 8, which you memorized was 15. You write down the 5 and carry the 1, which you add to 4 + 3 to get 8. Then add 1 + 1 = 2. So the answer is 285. When you know that one principle, you know how to add millions of combinations of numbers.

The Invisible Hand Theory

In the same way, knowing a theory gives you insight into a wide variety of economic phenomena, even though you don't know the particulars of each phenomenon. For example, much of economic theory deals with the *pricing mechanism* and how the market operates to coordinate *individuals' decisions.* Economists have come to the following insights:

> *When the quantity supplied is greater than the quantity demanded, price has a tendency to fall.*
> *When the quantity demanded is greater than the quantity supplied, price has a tendency to rise.*

Using these generalized insights, economists have developed a theory of markets that leads to the further insight that, under certain conditions, the market will coordinate individuals' decisions, allocating scarce resources *efficiently* so society moves out to its production possibility curve, not inside it. An efficient economy is one that reaps the maximum amount of outputs from the available inputs. Economists call the insight that a market economy will allocate resources efficiently the **invisible hand theory.**

Invisible hand theory The insight that a market economy will allocate resources efficiently.

Theories and the models used to represent them are enormously efficient methods of conveying information, but they're also necessarily abstract. They rely upon simplifying assumptions, and *if you don't know the assumptions, you don't know the theory.* The result of forgetting assumptions could be similar to what happens if you forget that you're supposed to add numbers in columns. Forgetting that, yet remembering all the steps, can lead to a wildly incorrect answer. For example,

$$\begin{array}{r} 471 \\ +\ 327 \\ \hline 5037 \end{array} \text{ is wrong.}$$

Knowing the assumptions of theories and models allows you to progress beyond gut reaction and better understand the strengths and weaknesses of various economic systems. Let's consider a central economic assumption: The assumption that individuals behave rationally—that what they choose reflects what makes them happiest, given the constraints. If that assumption doesn't hold, the invisible hand theory doesn't hold.

Presenting the invisible hand theory in its full beauty is an important part of any economics course. Presenting the assumptions upon which it is based and the limitations of the invisible hand is likewise an important part of the course. We'll do both throughout the book.

Economic Theory and Stories

Economic theory, and the models in which that theory is presented, often developed as a shorthand way of telling a story. These stories are important; they make the theory come alive and convey the insights that give economic theory its power. In this book we present plenty of theories and models, but they're accompanied by stories that provide the context that makes them relevant.

At times, because there's much new terminology, discussing models and theories takes up much of the presentation time and becomes a bit oppressive. That's the nature of the beast. As Albert Einstein said, "Theories should be as simple as possible, but not more so." When a theory or a model becomes oppressive, pause and think about the underlying story that the theory is meant to convey. That story should make sense and be concrete. If you can't translate the theory into a story, you don't understand the theory.

Microeconomics and Macroeconomics

Economic theory is divided into two parts: microeconomic theory and macroeconomic theory. Microeconomic theory considers economic reasoning from the viewpoint of individuals and firms and builds up from there to an analysis of the whole economy. We'll define **microeconomics** as *the study of individual choice, and how that choice is influenced by economic forces.* Microeconomics studies such things as the pricing policies of firms, households' decisions on what to buy, and how markets allocate resources among alternative ends. Our discussions of opportunity cost and the production possibility curve were based on microeconomic theory. It is from microeconomics that the invisible hand theory comes.

Microeconomics The study of individual choice, and how that choice is influenced by economic forces.

As one builds up from microeconomic analysis to an analysis of the entire society,

7 Microeconomic theory considers economic reasoning from the viewpoint of individuals and builds up; macroeconomics considers economic reasoning from the aggregate and builds down.

everything gets rather complicated. Many economists try to simplify matters by taking a different approach—a macroeconomic approach—first looking at the aggregate, or whole, and then breaking it down into components. A micro approach would analyze a person by looking first at each individual cell and then building up. A macro approach would start with the person and then go on to his or her components—arms, legs, fingernails, feelings, and so on. Put simply, microeconomics analyzes from the parts to the whole; macroeconomics analyzes from the whole to the parts.

In recent years the analysis of macroeconomic issues—inflation, unemployment, business cycles, and growth—has used more and more microeconomic analysis to supplement it. Thus, many economists now define macroeconomics as the study of inflation, unemployment, business cycles, and growth. We'll compromise and define **macroeconomics** as *the study of inflation, unemployment, business cycles, and growth primarily from the whole to the parts—focusing on aggregate relationships and supplementing that analysis with microeconomic insights.*

Macroeconomics The study of inflation, unemployment, business cycles, and growth primarily from the whole to the parts, focusing on aggregate relationships and supplementing its analysis with microeconomic insights.

To demonstrate the relationship between micro and macro analysis, let's consider again the production possibility curve, which is based on microeconomic principles. If unemployment is high, the economy is operating inside the production possibility curve and hence may be operating inefficiently. In that case, reducing unemployment can be costless. But it might also be that current institutions require such a high level of unemployment in order to prevent other problems like inflation. In that case, reducing unemployment is not costless; it involves significant, and probably costly, institutional changes. Similarly, macroeconomic growth shifts the production possibility curve outward, but that growth may be best explained by changes in microeconomic factors, such as technological change and resource endowments. Thus, even though the production possibility curve is derived from microeconomic principles, it can be used to discuss macroeconomic issues.

Neither macro nor micro is prior to the other. Clearly, macro results follow from micro decisions, but micro decisions are formed with a macro context, and can only be understood within that context. We need to be able to simultaneously develop a microfoundation of macro, and a macrofoundation of micro. The macro foundation of micro provides the institutional context within which micro decisions are made, and the micro foundation of macro provides the contextual relationship between individual decisions and aggregate outcomes.

ECONOMIC INSTITUTIONS

To know whether you can apply economic theory to reality, you must know about economic institutions. Economic institutions are complicated combinations of historical circumstance and economic, cultural, social, and political pressures. Economic institutions are all around you and affect your everyday life. For example, let's consider three economic institutions: schools, corporations, and cultural norms. Where you go to school determines the kind of job you'll get. Corporations determine what products are available to buy. Cultural norms determine what you identify as legitimate business activities. Understanding economic institutions requires the wisdom of experience, tempered with common sense—all combined with a desire to understand rather than to accept without question.

Economic institutions sometimes seem to operate in quite different manners than economic theory says they do. For example, economic theory says that prices are determined by supply and demand. However, a knowledge of economic institutions says that prices are set by rules of thumb—often by what are called cost-plus-markup rules. (That is, you determine what your costs are, multiply by 1.4 or 1.5, and the result is the price you set.) Economic theory says that supply and demand determine who's hired; a knowledge of economic institutions says that hiring is often done on the basis of whom you know, not by economic forces.

These apparent contradictions have two complementary explanations. First, economic theory abstracts from many issues. These issues may account for the differences. Second, there's no contradiction; economic principles often affect decisions from behind the scenes. For instance, supply and demand pressures determine what the price markup over cost will be. In this case, the invisible handshake is guided by the invisible hand. In all cases, however, to apply economic theory to reality—to gain the full value of economic insights—you've got to have a sense of economic institutions.

ECONOMIC POLICY OPTIONS

The final goal of the course is to present the economic policy options facing our society today. For example, should the government restrict mergers between firms? Should it run a budget deficit? Should it do something about the international trade deficit? Should it decrease taxes?

We saved our discussion of this goal for last because there's no sense talking about policy options unless you know some economic terminology, some economic theory, and something about economic institutions. Once you know something about those, you're in a position to consider the policy options available for dealing with the economic problems our society faces.

The first thing to note about policies is that they have many dimensions. Some policies operate within existing institutions without affecting them. Others indirectly change institutions. Still others are designed to change institutions directly. Policies that affect institutions are much more difficult to analyze (because their effects on institutions are generally indirect and nebulous) and to implement (since existing institutions often create benefits for specific individuals who don't want them changed) than are policies that don't affect institutions. For example, consider establishing a government program to promote research. Seems like a good thing—right? But such a policy might undermine the role of existing institutions already promoting research, and the net result of the program might be less, not more, research. When analyzing such policies, we need to take this effect on institutions into account.

On the other hand, policies that directly change institutions, while much more difficult to implement than policies that don't, also offer the largest potential for gain. They shift the production possibilities curve, whereas policies that operate within existing institutions simply move society closer to the frontier.

Let's consider an example. In the 1990s, a number of countries decided to abandon socialist institutions and put market economies in place. The result: output in those countries fell enormously as the old institutions fell. Eventually, these countries hope, once the new market institutions are predominant, output will bounce back and further gains will be made. But the temporary hardships these countries are experiencing show the enormous difficulty of implementing policies involving major institutional changes.

We have found it helpful in thinking about institutions to make an analogy to the computer, which has an operating system, software which works within that operating system, and what might be called nested software—software that only works within other software. What's efficient within one software package or operating system may be totally inefficient within another. To use a computer effectively, you must understand the interaction of the different levels of the software. To carry out economic policy effectively, one must understand the interaction and the various levels of institutions.

Let's consider an example: unemployment insurance and seasonal workers. In 1956 the Canadian Unemployment Assistance Act was introduced to protect workers during short periods of unemployment. The program has evolved to the point where it now provides benefits for workers leaving the labour force temporarily because of illness, pregnancy, work-sharing, and job-training programs. A recent study suggests that as many as 80 percent of the 1,800,000 claimants in 1989 were people who had previously received benefits. Critics argue that workers in seasonal industries abuse the unemployment insurance program since it is being used, year after year, to stabilize income. Critics argue that seasonal workers should search for jobs that offer employment year-round. This is not to say that we should not have programs to protect seasonal workers against unemployment; it is only to say that we must build into our policies their effect on institutions.

Objective Policy Analysis

Objective Term applied to "analysis," meaning that the analysis keeps your subjective views—your value judgements—separate.

Subjective Term applied to "analysis," meaning that the analysis reflects the analyst's views of how things should be.

Positive economics The study of what is, and how the economy works.

Normative economics The study of what the goals of the economy should be.

8 *Positive economics* is the study of what is, and how the economy works.
Normative economics is the study of what the goals of the economy should be.
The *art of economics* is the application of the knowledge learned in positive economics to the achievement of the goals determined in normative economics.

In thinking about policy, we must keep a number of points in mind. The most important is that good economic policy analysis is **objective.** Objective analysis does not say, "This is the way things should be," reflecting a goal established by the analyst. That would be **subjective** analysis. Instead it says, "This is the way the economy works, and if society (or the individual or firm for whom you're doing the analysis) wants to achieve a particular goal, this is how it might go about doing so." Objective analysis keeps your subjective views—your value judgements—separate.

To make clear the distinction between objective and subjective analysis, economists have divided economics into three categories: *positive economics, normative economics,* and the *art of economics.* **Positive economics** is the study of what is, and how the economy works. It asks such questions as: How does the market for hog bellies work? How do price restrictions affect market forces? These questions fall under the heading of economic theory. **Normative economics** is the study of what the goals of the economy should be. In discussing such questions, economists must carefully delineate whose goals they are discussing. One cannot simply assume that one's own goals for society are society's goals. Normative economics asks such questions as: What should the distribution of income be? What should tax policy be designed to achieve?

The **art of economics** relates positive economics to normative economics; it is the application of the knowledge learned in positive economics to the achievement of the goals one has determined in normative economics. It looks at such questions as: To achieve a certain distribution of income, how would you go about it, given the way the economy works?[5] Most policy discussions fall under the art of economics.

In each of these three branches of economics, economists separate their own value judgements from their objective analysis as much as possible. The qualifier "as much as possible" is important, since some value judgements inevitably sneak in. We are products of our environment, and the questions we ask, the framework we use, and the way we interpret empirical evidence all embody value judgements and reflect our background.

Maintaining objectivity is easiest in positive economics, where one is simply trying to understand how the economy works. In positive economics, one is working with abstract models. Maintaining objectivity is harder in normative economics. It's easy to jump from the way you think the world should be to believing that society agrees with you, and hence not to be objective about whose normative values you are using.

It's hardest to maintain objectivity in the art of economics because it embodies all the problems of both positive and normative economics. It's about how to achieve certain normative ends given the way the economy works, but it also adds more problems. Because noneconomic forces affect policy, to practice the art of economics one must make judgements about how these noneconomic forces work. These judgements are likely to embody one's own value judgements. So one must be exceedingly careful to be as objective as possible in practicing the art of economics.

One of the best ways to find out about feasible economic policy options is to consider how other countries do something and compare their approach to ours. For example, health care is supplied quite differently in various countries. To decide how to improve health care policy in Canada, policy makers study how the United States and Britain do it, and make judgements about whether the approaches those countries take will fit existing Canadian institutions. Comparative institutional analysis is an important part of the art of economics.

Policy and the Invisible Forces

When you think about the policy options facing society, you'll quickly discover that the choice of policy options depends on much more than economic theory. One must take into account historical precedent plus social, cultural, and political forces. In an

[5]This three-part distinction was made back in 1896 by a famous economist, John Neville Keynes, father of John Maynard Keynes, the economist who developed macroeconomics. This distinction was instilled into modern economics by Milton Friedman, among others, in the 1950s. They, however, downplayed the art of economics, which J. N. Keynes had seen as central to understanding the economists' role in policy.

economics course, we don't have time to analyze these forces in as much depth as we'd like. That's one reason there are separate history, political science, sociology, and anthropology courses.

But we don't want to pretend that these forces don't play an important role in policy decisions. They do. That's why we use the invisible force terminology when we cover these other issues. It allows us to integrate the other forces without explaining in depth how they work. We'll use this terminology when discussing policy and applying economic insights to policy questions. In economics, we focus the analysis on the invisible hand, and much of economic theory is devoted to how the economy would operate if the invisible hand were the only force operating. But as soon as we apply theory to reality and policy, we must take into account the other invisible forces.

Students will find that *Canadian Business Economics* contains useful articles on topical economic issues.

An example will make our point more concrete. Most economists agree that holding down or eliminating tariffs (taxes on imports) and quotas (numerical limitations on imports) makes good economic sense. They strongly advise governments to follow a policy of free trade. Do governments follow free trade policies? Almost invariably they do not. The invisible foot—politics—leads society in a different direction. If you're advising a policy maker, you need to point out that these other forces must be taken into account, and how other forces should (if they should) and can (if they can) be integrated with your recommendations.

Here's another example. Economic analysis devoid of institutional content would say that the world would be more efficient if we allowed Canadian citizenship to be bought and sold. But to advise policies that would legally allow a market for buying and selling Canadian citizenship would be to recommend a kind of efficiency that goes against historical, cultural, and social norms. The invisible handshake and the invisible foot would prevent the policies from being introduced, and any economist who proposed them would probably be banished to an ivory or other type of tower.

CONCLUSION

There's tons more that could be said by way of introducing you to economics, but an introduction must remain an introduction. As it is, this chapter should have:

1. Introduced you to economic reasoning.
2. Surveyed what we're going to cover in this book.
3. Given you an idea of our writing style and approach.

We'll be spending long hours together over the coming term, and before entering into such a commitment it's best to know your partner. While we won't know you, by the end of this book you'll know us. Maybe you won't love us as our mothers do, but you'll know us.

This introduction was our opening line. We hope it also conveyed the importance and relevance that belong to economics. If it did, it has served its intended purpose. Economics is tough, but tough can be fun.

CHAPTER SUMMARY

- Learning economics consists of learning: economic reasoning, economic terminology, economic insights, economic institutions, and economic policy options.
- Economic reasoning structures all questions in a cost/benefit frame: If the benefits of doing something exceed the costs, do it. If the costs exceed the benefits, don't.
- Often economic decisions can be made by comparing marginal costs and marginal benefits.
- "There ain't no such thing as a free lunch" (TANSTAAFL) embodies the opportunity cost concept.
- The production possibility curve embodies the opportunity cost concept.
- Economic reality is controlled and directed by three invisible forces: the invisible hand, the invisible foot, and the invisible handshake.
- Economics can be divided into microeconomics and macroeconomics.
- Economics also can be subdivided into positive economics, normative economics, and the art of economics.

KEY TERMS

art of economics *(24)*
comparative advantage *(14)*
cultural norm *(8)*
economic decision rule *(10)*
economic forces *(17)*
economic institution *(7)*
economic policy *(8)*
economic reasoning *(6)*
economic theory *(7)*
economics *(7)*
economy *(7)*
efficiency *(17)*
inefficiency *(15)*
input *(11)*
invisible foot *(18)*
invisible hand *(18)*
invisible hand theory *(21)*
invisible handshake *(18)*
macroeconomics *(22)*
marginal benefit *(9)*
marginal cost *(9)*
market force *(18)*
microeconomics *(21)*
normative economics *(24)*
objective *(24)*
opportunity cost *(10)*
output *(11)*
positive economics *(24)*
principle of increasing marginal opportunity cost *(15)*
production possibility curve *(12)*
production possibility table *(11)*
productive efficiency *(15)*
rationing *(17)*
subjective *(24)*

QUESTIONS FOR THOUGHT AND REVIEW

The number after each question represents the estimated degree of critical thinking required. (1 = almost none; 10 = deep thought.)

1. Design a grade production possibility table and curve that embody the principle of increasing marginal opportunity cost. *(4)*
2. What would the production possibility curve look like if there were decreasing marginal opportunity costs? Explain. Think of an example of decreasing marginal opportunity costs. *(8)*
3. Show how a production possibility curve would shift if a society became more productive in its output of widgets but less productive in its output of wadgets. *(5)*
4. List two microeconomic and two macroeconomic problems. *(2)*
5. Does economic theory prove that the free market system is best? Why? *(4)*
6. Calculate, using the best estimates you can make:
   a. Your opportunity cost of attending your next class.
   b. Your opportunity cost of taking this course.
   c. Your opportunity cost of attending yesterday's lecture in this course. *(6)*
7. List two recent choices you made and explain why you made those choices in terms of marginal benefits and marginal costs. *(5)*
8. Individuals have two kidneys but most of us need only one. People who have lost both kidneys through accident or disease must be hooked up to a dialysis machine, which cleanses waste from their bodies. Say a person who has two good kidneys offers to sell one of them to someone whose kidney function has been totally destroyed. The seller asks $30,000 for the kidney, and the person who has lost both kidneys accepts the offer. Who benefits from the deal? Who is hurt? Should a society allow such market transactions? Why? *(9)*
9. Is a good economist always objective? Why? *(4)*
10. When all people use economic reasoning, inefficiency is impossible, because if the cost of reducing that inefficiency were greater than the benefits, the efficiency would be eliminated. Thus, if people use economic reasoning, it's impossible to be on the interior of a production possibility curve. Is this statement true or false? Why? *(8)*

PROBLEMS AND EXERCISES

1. A country has the following production possibility table:

Resources devoted to clothing	Output of clothing	Resources devoted to food	Output of food
100%	20	0	0
80	16	20	5
60	12	40	9
40	8	60	12
20	4	80	14
0	0	100	15

   a. Draw the country's production possibility curve.
   b. What's happening to marginal opportunity costs as output of food increases?
   c. Say the country gets better at the production of food. What will happen to the production possibility curve?
   d. Say the country gets equally better at producing food and producing clothing. What will happen to the production possibility curve?
2. Go to two stores: a supermarket and a convenience store.

   a. Write down the cost of a litre of milk in each.
   b. The prices are most likely different. Using the terminology used in this chapter, explain why that is the case and why anyone would buy milk in the store with the higher price.
   c. Do the same exercise with shirts or dresses in Wal-Mart (or its equivalent) and Eaton's (or its equivalent).
3. Suppose we learn that lawns occupy more land in Canada than any single crop, such as corn. This means that Canada is operating inefficiently and hence is at a point inside the production possibility frontier. Right? If not, what does it mean?
4. Groucho Marx is reported to have said that "The secret of success is honest and fair dealing. If you can fake those, you've got it made." What would likely happen to society's production possibility curve if everyone could fake honesty? Why? (Hint: Remember that society's production possibility curve reflects more than just technical relationships.)
5. Adam Smith, who wrote *The Wealth of Nations* and is seen as the father of modern economics, also wrote *The Theory of Moral Sentiments* in which he argued that society would be better off if people weren't so selfish and were more considerate of others. How does this view fit with the discussion of economic reasoning presented in the chapter?
6. Trade agreements like the North American Free Trade Agreement (NAFTA) attempt to eliminate trade barriers and encourage economic growth. Using production possibility curves for Canada, Mexico, and the United States, show how you think the trade agreement will affect each economy. Is there any reason for you to expect that one country will benefit more than the others? How could you illustrate that on your figures?
7. In 1995, Newfoundland fishermen wanted to hunt seals for meat. Suppose you were hired by the fishermen to lobby the government. What would you argue? If you were hired by an animal rights group to oppose the hunt, what arguments would you use?
8. In 1995, Canada and the European Union had a fight about overfishing in the waters surrounding Canada. Canada argued that excessive fishing with new technologies would decrease the future catch. In terms of the production possibility curve for fish, what were they arguing? How would your answer differ if it were the production possibility curve for fish and beef?

APPENDIX A

Economics in Perspective

All too often, students study economics out of context. They're presented with sterile analysis and boring facts to memorize, and are never shown how economics fits into the large scheme of things. That's bad; it makes economics seem boring—but economics is not boring. Every so often throughout this book, sometimes in the appendixes and sometimes in boxes, we'll step back and put the analysis in perspective, giving you an idea from whence the analysis sprang and its historical context. In educational jargon, this is called *enrichment.*

We begin here with economics itself.

First, its history: In the 1500s there were few universities. Those that existed taught religion, Latin, Greek, philosophy, history, and mathematics. No economics. Then came the *Enlightenment* (about 1700) in which reasoning replaced God as the explanation of why things were the way they were. Pre-Enlightenment thinkers would answer the question, "Why am I poor?" with, "Because God wills it." Enlightenment scholars looked for a different explanation. "Because of the nature of land ownership" is one answer they found.

Such reasoned explanations required more knowledge of the way things were, and the amount of information expanded so rapidly that it had to be divided or categorized for an individual to have hope of knowing a subject. Soon philosophy was subdivided into science and philosophy. In the 1700s, the sciences were split into natural sciences and social sciences. The amount of knowledge kept increasing, and in the late 1800s and early 1900s social science itself split into subdivisions: economics, political science, history, geography, sociology, anthropology, and psychology. Many of the insights about how the economic system worked were codified in Adam Smith's *The Wealth of Nations,* written in 1776. Notice that this is before economics as a subdiscipline developed, and Adam Smith could also be classified as an anthropologist, a sociologist, a political scientist, and a social philosopher.

Throughout the 18th and 19th centuries, economists such as Adam Smith, Thomas Malthus, John Stuart Mill, David Ricardo, and Karl Marx were more than economists; they were social philosophers who covered all aspects of social science. These writers were subsequently called *Classical economists.* Alfred Marshall continued in that classical tradition, and his book, *Principles of Economics,* published in the late 1800s, was written with the other social sciences much in evidence. But Marshall also changed the questions economists ask; he focused on those questions that could be asked in a graphical supply/demand framework. In doing so he began what is called *neoclassical economics.* Marshall's analysis forms the basis of much of what's currently taught in undergraduate microeconomics courses.

In the 1930s, as economists formalized Marshall's insights, many other social science insights were removed. By the 1950s, these social sciences were cemented into college curricula and organized into college departments. Economists learned economics; sociologists learned sociology.

For a while economics got lost in itself, and economists learned little else. Marshall's analysis was downplayed, and the work of more formal economists of the 1800s (such as Leon Walras, Francis Edgeworth, and Antoine Cournot) was seen as the basis of the science of economics. Economic analysis that focuses only on formal interrelationships is called *Walrasian economics.*

Thus, in the 1990s, there are two branches of neoclassical economics: Marshallian and Walrasian. The Marshallian branch sees economics as a way of thinking and integrates insights from other disciplines. The Walrasian branch sees economics as a logical science and excludes other social sciences. This book falls solidly in the Marshallian tradition. It sees economics as a way of thinking—as an engine of analysis used to understand real-world phenomena, not as a logical exercise in deductive reasoning. Our strong belief is that in undergraduate school one should learn Marshallian economics; in graduate school one can learn Walrasian economics.

Marshallian economics is both an art and a science. It sees institutions as well as political and social dimensions of reality as important, and it shows you how economics ties into those dimensions.

Graphish
The Language of Graphs

A picture is worth 1,000 words. Economists, being efficient, like to present ideas in graphs, which are a type of picture. But a graph is worth 1,000 words only if the person looking at the graph knows the graphical language—Graphish, we'll call it. (It's a bit like English.) Graphish is usually written on graph paper. If the person doesn't know *Graphish*, the picture isn't worth any words and Graphish can be babble.

We have enormous sympathy for students who don't understand Graphish. A number of our students get thrown for a loop by graphs. They understand the idea, but Graphish confuses them. This appendix is for them, and for those of you like them. It's a primer in Graphish.

Two Ways to Use Graphs

In this book we use graphs in two ways:

1. To present an economic model or theory visually; to show how two variables interrelate.
2. To present real-world data visually. To do this, we use primarily bar charts, line charts, and pie charts.

Actually, these two ways of using graphs are related. They are both ways of presenting visually the *relationship* between two things.

Graphs are built around a number line, or axis, like the one in Exhibit B1 (a). The numbers are generally placed in order, equal distances from one another. That number line allows us to represent a number at an appropriate point on the line. For example, point *A* represents the number 4.

The number line in Exhibit B1 (a) is drawn horizontally, but it doesn't have to be; it can also be drawn vertically, as in Exhibit B1 (b).

How we divide our axes, or number lines, into intervals, is up to us. In Exhibit B1 (a), we called each interval 1; in Exhibit B1 (b), we called each interval 10. Point *A* appears after 4 intervals of 1 (starting at 0 and reading from left to right), so it represents 4. In Exhibit B1 (b), where each interval represents 10, to represent 5, we place point *B* halfway in the interval between 0 and 10.

So far, so good. Graphish developed when a vertical and a horizontal number line were combined, as in Exhibit B1 (c). When the number lines are put together they're called *axes.* (Each line is an axis. *Axes* is the plural of *axis.*) We now have a two-dimensional space in which *one point can represent two numbers.* (This two-dimensional space is called a *coordinate space.*) For example, point *A* in Exhibit B1 (c) represents the numbers (4, 5)—4 on the horizontal number line and 5 on

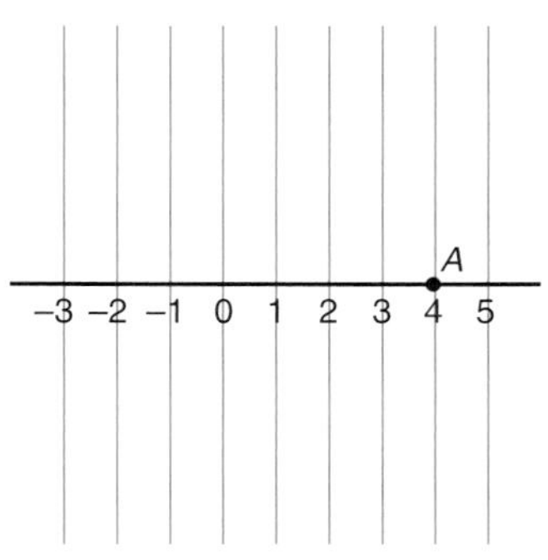

(a) Horizontal number line

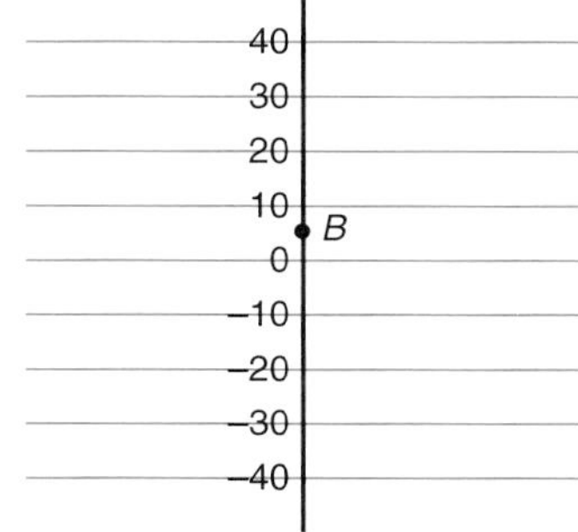

(b) Vertical number line

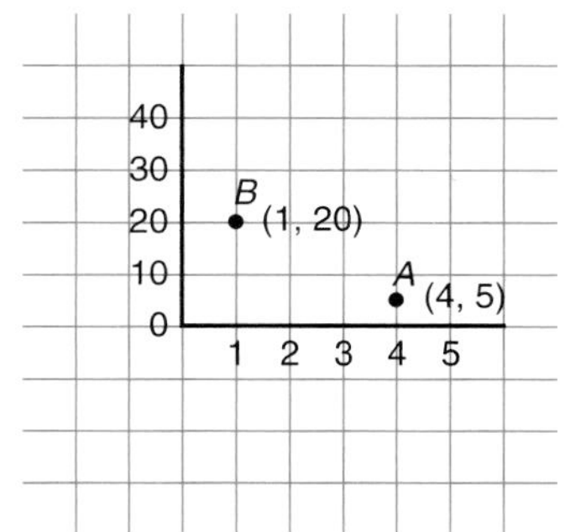

(c) Coordinate system

EXHIBIT B1 **Horizontal and Vertical Number Lines and a Coordinate System**

the vertical number line. Point *B* represents the numbers (1, 20). (By convention, the horizontal numbers are written first.)

Being able to represent two numbers with one point is neat because it allows the relationships between two numbers to be presented visually instead of having to be expressed verbally, which is often cumbersome. For example, say the cost of producing 6 units of something is $4 per unit and the cost of producing 10 units is $3 per unit. By putting both these points on a graph, we can visually see that producing 10 costs less per unit than does producing 6.

Another way to use graphs to present real-world data visually is to use the horizontal line to represent time. Say that we let each horizontal interval equal a year, and each vertical interval equal $100 in income. By graphing your income each year, you can obtain a visual representation of how your income has changed over time.

Graphs can be used to show any relationship between two variables. (*Variables* are what economists call the units that are measured on the horizontal and vertical axes.) As long as you remember that graphs are simply a way of presenting a relationship visually, you can keep graphs in perspective.

Using Graphs in Economic Modelling We use graphs throughout the book as we present economic models, or simplifications of reality. A few terms are often used in describing these graphs, and we'll now go over them. Consider Exhibit B2 (a), which lists the number of pens bought per day (column 2) at various prices (column 1).

We can present the table's information in a graph by combining the pairs of numbers in the two columns of the table and representing, or plotting, them on two axes. We do that in Exhibit B2 (b).

By convention, when graphing a relationship between price and quantity, economists place price on the vertical axis and quantity on the horizontal axis.

EXHIBIT B2 A Table and Graphs Showing the Relationships between Price and Quantity

Price of pens (in dollars)	Quantity of pens bought per day	Row
3.00	4	*A*
2.50	5	*B*
2.00	6	*C*
1.50	7	*D*
1.00	8	*E*

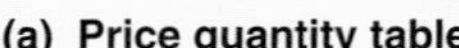

(a) Price quantity table

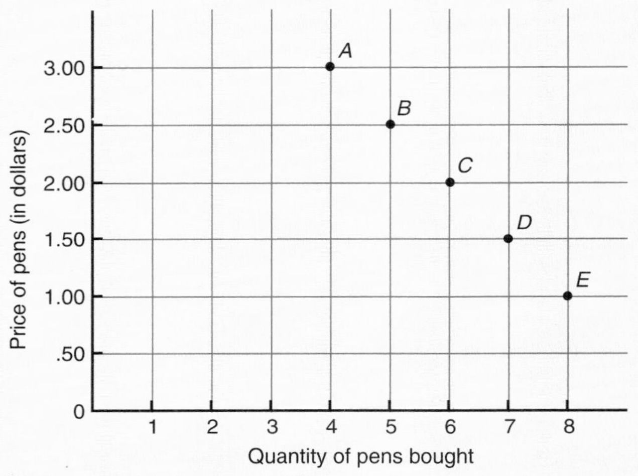

(b) From a table to a graph (1)

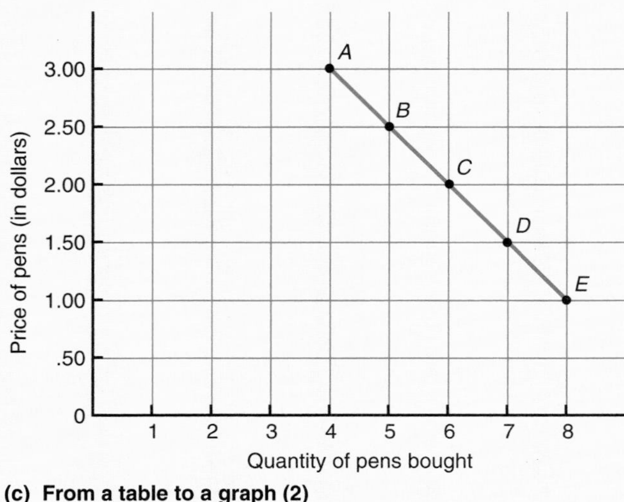

(c) From a table to a graph (2)

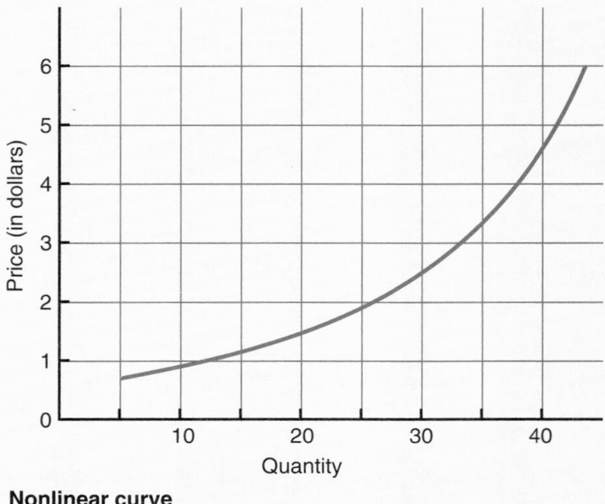

(d) Nonlinear curve

We can now connect the points, producing a line like the one in Exhibit B2 (c). With this line, we interpolate the numbers between the points. That is, we make the reasonable assumption (which makes for a nice visual presentation) that the relationship between the variables is the same *between* the points as it is at the points. This assumption is called the *interpolation assumption.* It allows us to think of a line as a collection of points and therefore to connect the points into a line.

Even though the line in Exhibit B2 (c) is straight, economists call any such line drawn on a graph a *curve.* Because it's straight, the curve in Exhibit B2 (c) is called a *linear curve.* Notice that this curve starts high on the left-hand side and goes down to the right. Economists say any curve that looks like that is downward-sloping. They also say that a *downward-sloping* curve represents an *inverse* relationship between the two variables: When one goes up, the other goes down. In this example, the line demonstrates an inverse relationship between price and quantity—that is, when the price of pens goes up, the quantity bought goes down.

Exhibit B2 (d) presents a curve that really is curved. It starts low on the left-hand side and goes up to the right. Such curves are called *nonlinear curves.* Economists say any curve that goes up to the right is upward-sloping. An *upward-sloping* curve represents a direct relationship between the two variables (what's measured on the horizontal and vertical lines). In a direct relationship, when one variable goes up, the other goes up too. *Downward-sloping* and *upward-sloping* are terms you need to memorize if you want to read, write, and speak Graphish, keeping graphically in your mind the image of the relationships they represent.

Slope One can, of course, be far more explicit about how much the curve is sloping upward or downward. To be more explicit, mathematicians define the term slope as the change in the value on the vertical axis divided by the change in the value on the horizontal axis. Sometimes it's presented as "rise over run":

$$\text{Slope} = \frac{\text{Rise}}{\text{Run}} = \frac{\text{Change in value on vertical axis}}{\text{Change in value on horizontal axis}}$$

Slopes of Linear Curves In Exhibit B3, we present five linear curves and measure their slopes. Let's go through an example to show how we can measure slope. To do so, we must pick two points. Let's use points *A* (6, 8) and *B* (7, 4) on curve *a*. Looking at these points, we see that as we move from 6 to 7 on the horizontal axis, we move from 8 to 4 on the vertical axis. So when the number on the vertical axis falls by 4, the number on the horizontal axis increases by 1. That means the slope is −4 divided by 1, or −4.

Notice that the inverse relationships represented by the two downward-sloping curves, *a* and *b,* have negative slopes, and that the direct relationships represented by the two upward-sloping curves, *c* and *d*, have positive slopes. Notice also that the flatter the curve, the smaller the numerical value of the slope; and the more vertical, or steeper, the curve, the larger the numerical value of the slope. There are two extreme cases:

1. When the curve is horizontal (flat), the slope is zero.
2. When the curve is vertical (straight up and down), the slope is infinite (larger than large).

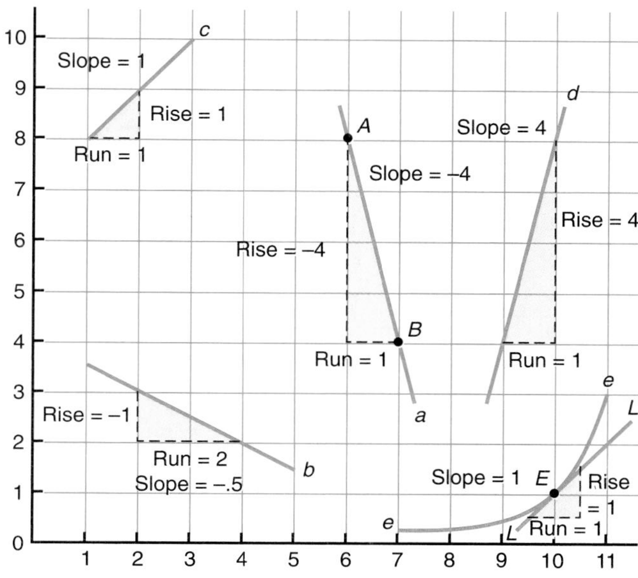

EXHIBIT B3 Slopes of Curves

Knowing the term *slope* and how it's measured lets us describe verbally the pictures we see visually. For example, if we say a curve has a slope of zero, you should picture in your mind a flat line; if we say "a curve with a slope of minus one," you should picture a falling line that makes a 45-degree angle with the horizontal and vertical axes. (It's the hypotenuse of an equilateral triangle with the axes as the other two sides.)

Slopes of Nonlinear Curves The preceding examples were of linear (straight) curves. With nonlinear curves—the ones that really do curve—the slope of the curve is constantly changing. As a result, we must talk about the slope of the curve at a particular point, rather than the slope of the whole curve. How can a point have a slope? Well, it can't really, but it can almost, and if that's good enough for mathematicians, it's good enough for us.

Defining the slope of a nonlinear curve is a bit more difficult. The slope at a given point on a nonlinear curve is determined by the slope of a linear (or straight) line that's tangent to that curve. (A line that's tangent to a curve is a line that just touches the curve, and touches it only at one point in the immediate vicinity of the given point.) In Exhibit B3, the line *LL* is tangent to the curve *ee* **at** point *E*. The slope of that line, and hence the slope

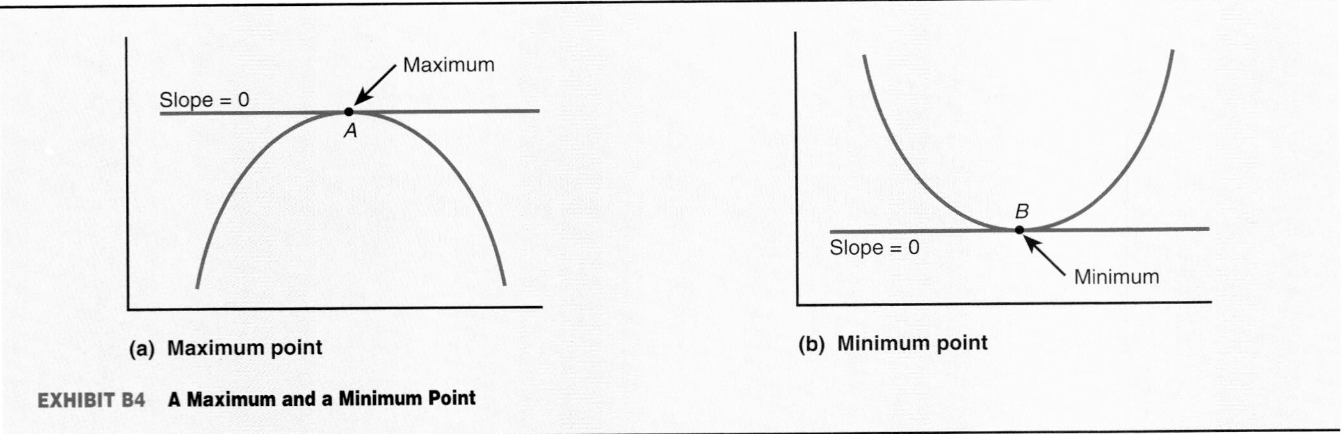

(a) Maximum point
(b) Minimum point

EXHIBIT B4 A Maximum and a Minimum Point

of the curve at the one point where the line touches the curve, is +1.

Maximum and Minimum Points Two points on a nonlinear curve deserve special mention. These points are the ones for which the slope of the curve is zero. We demonstrate those in Exhibit B4 (a) and (b). (At point *A*, we're at the top of the curve so it's at a maximum point; at point *B*, we're at the bottom of the curve so it's at a minimum point.) These maximum and minimum points are often referred to by economists, and it's important to realize that the value of the slope of the curve at each of these points is zero.

There are, of course, many other types of curves, and much more can be said about the curves we've talked about. We won't do so because, for purposes of this course, we won't need to get into those refinements. We've presented as much Graphish as you need to know for this book.

Presenting Real-World Data in Graphs

The previous discussion treated the Graphish terms that economists use in presenting models which focus on hypothetical relationships. Economists also use graphs in presenting actual economic data. Say, for example, that you want to show how exports have changed over time. Then you would place years on the horizontal axis (by convention) and exports on the vertical axis, as in Exhibit B5 (a) and (b). Having done so, you can either connect the data, as in (a), or fill in the areas under the points for that year, as in (b). The first is called a *line graph;* the second is called a *bar graph.*

Another type of graph is a *pie chart,* such as the one presented in Exhibit B5 (c). A pie chart is useful in visu-

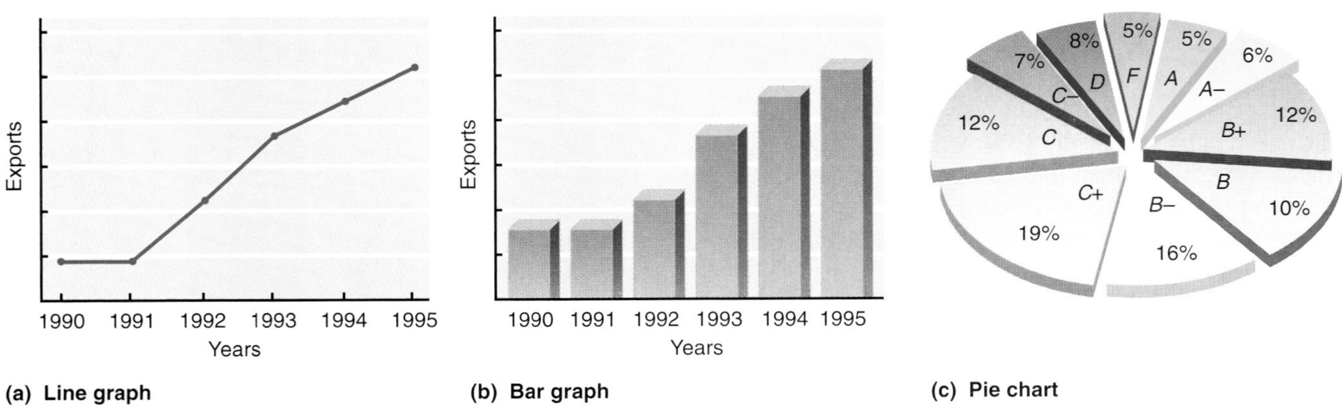

(a) Line graph
(b) Bar graph
(c) Pie chart

EXHIBIT B5 Presenting Information Visually

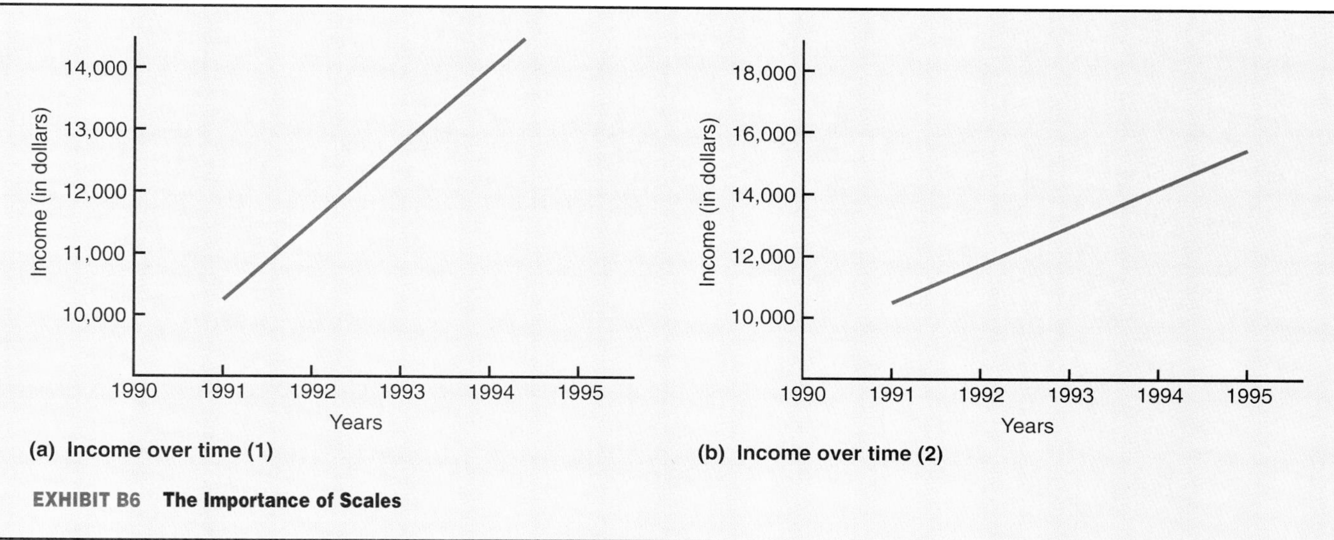

(a) Income over time (1)

(b) Income over time (2)

EXHIBIT B6 The Importance of Scales

ally presenting how a total amount is divided. The uncut pie is the total amount, and the pie pieces reflect the percentage of the whole pie that the various components make up. Exhibit B5 (c) shows the division of grades on a test we gave. Notice that 5 percent of the students got As.

There are other types of graphs, but they're all variations on line and bar graphs and pie charts. Once you understand these three basic types of graphs, you shouldn't have any trouble understanding the other types.

Interpreting Graphs about the Real World Understanding Graphish is important, because if you don't, you can easily misinterpret the meanings of graphs. For example, consider the two graphs in Exhibit B6 (a) and (b). Which graph demonstrates the larger rise in income? If you said (a), you're wrong. The intervals in the vertical axes differ, and if you look carefully you'll see that the curves in both graphs represent the same combination of points. So when considering graphs, always make sure you understand the markings on the axes. Only then can you interpret the graph.

Let's now review what we've covered.

- A graph is a picture of points on a coordinate system in which the points denote relationships between numbers.
- A downward-sloping line represents an inverse relationship or a negative slope.
- An upward-sloping line represents a direct relationship or a positive slope.
- Slope is measured by rise over run, or a change of y (the number measured on the vertical axis) over a change in x (the number measured on the horizontal axis).
- The slope of a point on a nonlinear curve is measured by the rise over run of a line tangent to that point.
- At the maximum and minimum points of a nonlinear curve, the value of the slope is zero.
- In reading graphs, one must be careful to understand what's being measured on the vertical and horizontal axes.

CHAPTER 2

Supply and Demand

Teach a parrot the terms supply and demand and you've got an economist.

~Thomas Carlyle

After reading this chapter, you should be able to:

1. State the law of demand.
2. Explain the importance of opportunity cost and substitution to the laws of supply and demand.
3. Draw a demand curve from a demand table.
4. Distinguish a shift in demand from a movement along the demand curve.
5. State the law of supply.
6. Draw a supply curve from a supply table.
7. Distinguish a shift in supply from a movement along the supply curve.
8. State the three dynamic laws of supply and demand.
9. Demonstrate the effect of a price ceiling and a price floor on a market.

Supply and demand. Supply and demand. Roll the phrase around your mouth, savour it like a good wine. *Supply* and *demand* are the most-used words in economics. And for good reason. They provide a good off-the-cuff answer for any economic question. Try it.

Why are bacon and oranges so expensive this winter? *Supply and demand.*

Why are interest rates falling? *Supply and demand.*

Why can't I find decent wool socks any more? *Supply and demand.*

The importance of the interplay of supply and demand makes it only natural that, early in any economics course, you must learn about supply and demand. Let's start with demand.

DEMAND

Poets and songwriters use literary license. Take the classic song by the Rolling Stones entitled "You Can't Always Get What You Want." Whether the statement is or isn't true depends on how you define *want.* If you define *want* as "being sufficiently desirous of something so that you do what's necessary to buy the good," then in a market in which prices are flexible, you *can* always get what you want. The reason: what you want depends on what the price is. If, however, you define *want* as simply "being desirous of something," then there are many unfulfilled "wants," such as our wanting expensive sports cars. We want to own Maseratis. But, we must admit, we're not willing to do what's necessary to own one. If we really wanted to own one, we'd mortgage everything we own, increase our income by doubling the number of hours we work, not buy anything else, and get that car. But we don't do any of those things, so there's a question of whether we really want the car. Sure, we'd want one if it cost $10,000, but from our actions it's clear that, at $290,000, we don't really want it. If *want* is defined as "being sufficiently desirous of something that you will do what's necessary to buy the good," you can always get what you want, because your willingness to pay the going price for something is the only way to tell whether you really want it. What you want at a low price differs from what you want at a high price. The quantity you demand varies inversely—in the opposite direction—with the price.

Prices are the tool by which the invisible hand—the market—coordinates individuals' desires and limits how much people are willing to buy—how much they really want. When goods are scarce, the market reduces people's desires for those scarce goods; as their prices go up, people buy fewer of them. As goods become abundant, their prices go down, and people want more of them. The invisible hand sees to it that what people want (do what's necessary to get) matches what's available. In doing so, the invisible hand coordinates individuals' wants. While you can't always get what you want at a low price, you can get it at some price—maybe a super-high price. It isn't surprising that the Stones chose the other definition of *want;* it's unlikely that their song would have become a hit had they put in the appropriate qualifier. You can't dance to "You Can't Always Get What You Want at the Price You Want."

The Law of Demand

1 The law of demand states that the quantity of a good demanded is inversely related to the good's price. When price goes up, quantity demanded goes down.

What makes the qualifier appropriate is the **law of demand:**

More of a good will be demanded the lower its price, other things constant.

Or alternatively:

Less of a good will be demanded the higher its price, other things constant.

This law is fundamental to the invisible hand's ability to coordinate individuals' desires: as prices change, people change how much of a particular good they're willing to buy.

Demand Schedule of quantities of a good that will be bought per unit of time at various prices.

Quantity demanded A specific amount that will be demanded per unit of time at a specific price. Refers to a point on a demand curve.

To be clear about the meaning of the law of demand, economists differentiate the concepts *demand* and *quantity demanded.* **Demand** refers to a schedule of quantities of a good that will be bought per unit of time at various prices. **Quantity demanded** refers to a specific amount that will be demanded per unit of time at a specific price.

In graphical terms, *demand* refers to the entire **demand curve** which tells how much of a good will be bought at various prices. *Quantity demanded* refers to a point

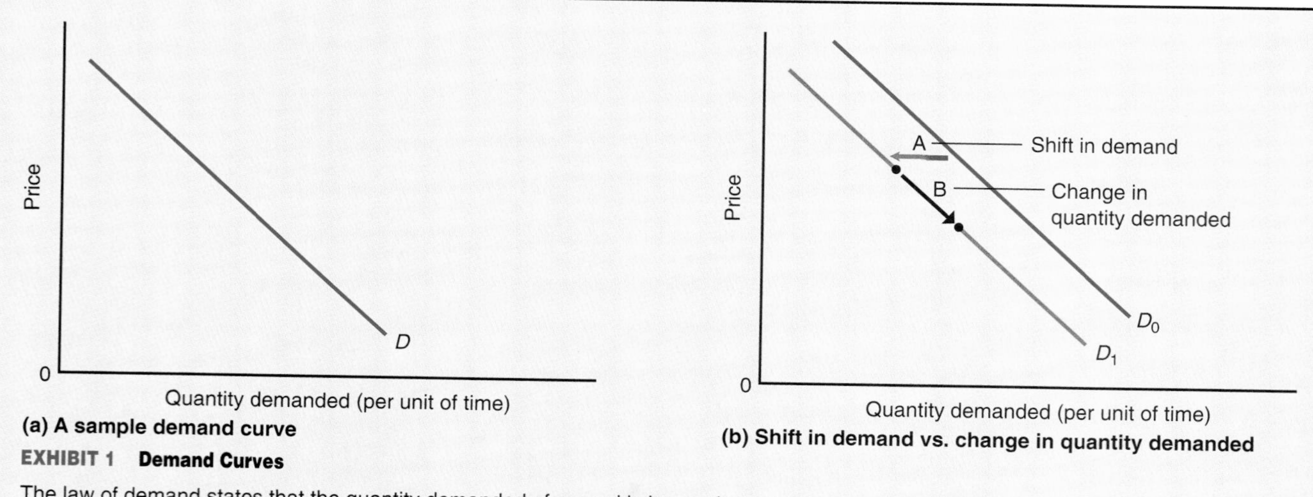

(a) A sample demand curve

(b) Shift in demand vs. change in quantity demanded

EXHIBIT 1 Demand Curves

The law of demand states that the quantity demanded of a good is inversely related to the price of that good. As the price of a good goes up, the quantity demanded goes down so the demand curve is downward sloping as in Exhibit 1(a). Exhibit 1(b) shows the distinction between a shift in demand (arrow A) brought about by a shift in a nonprice factor, and a change in quantity demanded—a movement along a demand curve—brought about by a change in price (arrow B).

on a demand curve, so when economists talk about movements along a demand curve, they mean changes in quantity demanded.

Demand curve Curve that tells how much of a good will be bought at various prices.

Exhibit 1 (a) shows a demand curve. In graphical terms, the law of demand states that the quantity demanded of a good is inversely related to that good's price, other things constant. As the price goes up, the quantity demanded goes down. As you can see in Exhibit 1 (a), price and quantity are inversely related, so the demand curve slopes downward to the right. Exhibit 1 (b) distinguishes between a shift in demand—a shift of the entire demand curve as shown by Arrow A—and a change in quantity demanded—a movement along a demand curve as shown by Arrow B.

Just think of something you'd really like but can't afford. If the price is cut in half, you—and other consumers—become more likely to buy it. Quantity demanded goes up as price goes down.

Just to be sure you've got it, let's consider a real-world example: scalpers and the demand for hockey tickets. Standing outside a sold-out game between Montreal and Pittsburgh in Montreal, we saw tickets that normally cost $15 sell for $75. There were few takers—that is, there was little demand at that price. We figured that as soon as the game started, prices would drop and the quantity demanded (at a lower price) would rise, but this didn't happen until well after the start of the game. As the price dropped to $60, then $50, quantity demanded increased; when the price dropped to $35, the quantity demanded soared. That's the law of demand in action.

Other Things Constant To understand the law of demand, you must understand the terminology used to discuss that law and the assumptions upon which that law is based. Let's first consider the phrase, "Other things constant."

Other things constant An assumption that places a limitation on the implications that can be drawn from any supply/demand analysis. The elements of the particular analysis are considered under the assumption that all other elements that could affect the analysis remain constant (whether they actually remain constant or not).

Notice that in stating the law of demand, we put in a qualification: **other things constant.**[1] That's three extra words, and unless they were important we wouldn't have put them in. But what does "other things constant" mean? Say that over a period of two years, the price of cars rises as the number of cars sold likewise rises. That seems to violate the law of demand, since the number of cars sold should have fallen in response to the rise in price. Looking at the data more closely, however, we see that a third factor has also changed: individuals' income has increased overall. As income increases, people buy more cars, increasing the demand for cars.

[1]*Other things constant* is a translation of the Latin phrase *ceteris paribus.* Sometimes economists just use *ceteris paribus* without translating it.

The increase in price works as the law of demand states—it decreases the number of cars bought. But in this case, income doesn't remain constant; it increases. That rise in income increases the demand for cars. That increase in demand outweighs the decrease in quantity demanded that results from a rise in price, so ultimately more cars are sold. If you want to study the effect of price alone—which is what the law of demand refers to—you must make adjustments to hold income constant when you make your study. That's why the qualifying phrase *other things constant* is an important part of the law of demand.

This qualifying phrase, "other things constant," places a limitation on the implications that can be drawn from any analysis based on the law of demand. Alfred Marshall, one of the originators of this law, emphasized these limitations, arguing that it is as much of a mistake to apply supply/demand analysis to areas where these assumptions do not hold as it is not to apply it to those areas where it does apply. To emphasize this point he argued that the law of demand is directly applicable to *partial equilibrium* issues—issues in which other things can reasonably be assumed to remain constant—and that supply/demand analysis should be called **partial equilibrium analysis** (we'll explain just what we mean by *equilibrium* in a moment). He admonished his students to remember that partial equilibrium analysis is incomplete because it assumes other things equal. That it is incomplete does not mean that it cannot be used for other issues, but when applied to issues where other things do not remain constant, it must be used with an educated common sense and one must keep in the back of one's mind what does not remain constant.

Partial equilibrium analysis Analysis of a part of a whole; it initially assumes all other things remain equal.

How much somebody wants to buy a good depends on many other things besides its price. These include individuals' tastes, prices of other goods, and even the weather. Those other factors must remain constant if you're to make a valid study of the effect of an increase in the price of a good on the quantity demanded of it. In practice it's impossible to keep all other things constant, so you have to be careful when you say that when price goes up, quantity demanded goes down. It's likely to go down, but it's always possible that something besides price has changed.

Economists recognize that many things besides price affect demand. They call them **shift factors of demand.** A shift factor of demand is something, other than the good's price, that affects how much of the good is demanded. Important shift factors of demand include:

Shift factors of demand Something, other than the good's price, that affects how much of the good is demanded.

1. Society's income.
2. The prices of other goods.
3. Tastes.
4. Expectations.

These aren't the only shift factors. In fact anything—except the good's price changes—that affects demand (and many things do) is a shift factor. This includes changes in the income of our trading partners, changes in exchange rates, and changes in population, just to name a few. While economists agree these shift factors are important, they believe that no shift factor influences how much is demanded as consistently as the price of the specific item does. That's what makes economists focus first on price as they try to understand the world. That's why economists make the law of demand central to their analysis.

Relative Price A second qualification is that the law of demand refers to a good's **relative price.** The relative price of a good is the price of that good compared to the price of another good or combination of goods. For example, if the price of a compact disc is \$11 and the price of an apple is 50 cents, the relative price of CDs compared to the price of apples is \$11/ \$0.50 = 22. In other words, you can buy 22 apples with one CD or one CD with 22 apples.

Relative price The price of a good relative to the price level.

The actual price you pay for the goods you buy is called *the money price.* You don't say that a CD has a price of 22 apples; you say that a CD has a price of \$11. But don't let that fool you. While the \$11 may not look like a relative price, it is. It is the price of the CD compared to a composite price for all other goods. That composite price for all other goods is the price of money. What's the price of money? It's simply how much you'll pay for money. Most people will pay $1 for $1, so the price of $1 is $1. The money price of $11 means that you can trade one CD for 11 "loonies."

Money is not desired for its own sake. You want dollar coins only because you can trade them for something else. You have in the back of your mind a good sense of what else you could do with that $11—what the opportunity cost of spending it on a CD is. You could buy, say, three Big Macs, a double order of fries, and a vanilla shake for $11. The opportunity cost of buying the CD is that big tray of fast food. Thus the money price of an item represents the price of that item relative to the prices of all other goods.

As long as your sense of what that opportunity cost is doesn't change, money price is a good representation of relative price. Over short periods the opportunity cost of $1 doesn't change. Over longer periods, though, because of inflation, money prices are not a good representation of relative prices. Say, for instance, that money prices (including your wage) on average go up 10 percent. (When this happens, economists say the price level has gone up by 10 percent.) Also say the money price of a CD goes up by 2 percent. Has the relative price of CDs gone up or down? Since the *average* money price has gone up 10 percent and the money price of a CD has risen by 2 percent, the relative price of a CD has fallen by 8 percent. The law of demand would say that the quantity of CDs demanded would increase because the relative price has gone down, even though the money price has gone up.

The use of money prices makes life easier for members of society, but it makes life harder for economics students, who must remember that, even though they see the money price of an item as an absolute number, it is actually a relative price.

2 The law of demand is based upon individuals' ability to substitute.

We emphasize that the law of demand refers to relative price because the explanation for it involves demanders' ability to *substitute* some other good for that good. If a good's relative price goes up, some people will substitute some other good for it because that substitute's relative price goes down. For example, if the money price of compact discs rises and the money price of music tapes doesn't rise, individuals will substitute music tapes for CDs.

The Demand Table

As we emphasized in Chapter 1, introductory economics depends heavily on graphs and graphical analysis—translating ideas into graphs and back again into words. So let's graph the demand curve.

Exhibit 2 (a) describes Alice's demand for renting videocassettes. In this example, the demand is for the temporary use of a videocassette. For example, at a price of $2, Alice will buy the use of six cassettes per week.

There are a number of points about the relationship between the number of videos Alice rents and the price of renting them that are worth mentioning. First, the relationship follows the law of demand: as the rental price rises, quantity demanded decreases. Second, quantity demanded has a specific *time dimension* to it. In this example it is the number of cassette rentals per week that is referred to, not the number of cassettes rented per day, hour, or year. Without the time dimension, the table wouldn't provide us with any useful information. Nine cassette rentals per year is quite a different concept from nine cassette rentals per week. Third, the cassette rentals that Alice buys are interchangeable—the ninth cassette rental doesn't significantly differ from the first, third, or any other cassette rental.

The concept of interchangeable goods causes economists significant problems in discussing real-world demand schedules because the quality of goods often differs in the real world. A pink Volkswagen is quite different from a gray Aston Martin, yet they're both cars. Luckily, in textbooks interchangeable goods cause few problems because we can pick and choose among examples. Textbook authors simply avoid examples that raise significant quality problems. However, it's only fair to point out that in the real world economists spend a great deal of time adjusting their analyses for differences in quality among goods.

EXHIBIT 2 From a Demand Table to a Demand Curve

The demand table in (**a**) is translated into a demand curve in (**b**). Each point on the table corresponds to a point on the curve. For example, point *A* on the graph represents row *A* in the table: Alice demands 9 videocassette rentals at a price of 50 cents. A demand curve is constructed by plotting all points from the demand table and connecting the points by a line.

	Price (in dollars)	Cassette rentals demanded per week
A	0.50	9
B	1.00	8
C	2.00	6
D	3.00	4
E	4.00	2

(a) A demand table

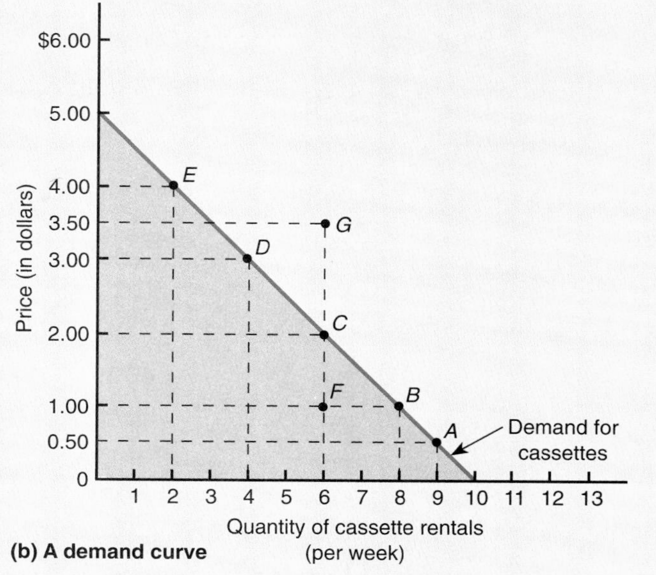

(b) A demand curve

Two final points are already familiar to you. They are, fourth, the price the table refers to is a relative price even though it is expressed as a money price, and fifth, the schedule assumes that everything else is held constant.

From a Demand Table to a Demand Curve

Exhibit 2 (b) translates Exhibit 2 (a)'s information into a graph. Point *A* (quantity = 9, price = \$.50) is graphed first at the (9, \$.50) coordinates. Next we plot points *B, C, D,* and *E* in the same manner and connect the resulting dots with a solid line. The result is the demand curve, which graphically conveys the same information that's in the demand table. Notice that the demand curve is downward sloping (from left to right), indicating that the law of demand holds in the example. When a curve slopes downward to the right, we say that there is an inverse relationship between the price and the quantity demanded.

Demand table

Q	*P*
2	5
4	3

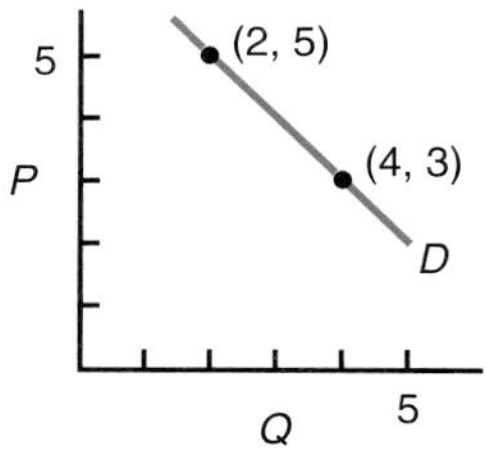

The demand curve represents the *maximum price* that an individual will pay for various quantities of a good; the individual will happily pay less. For example, say someone offers Alice six cassette rentals at a price of \$1 each (point *F* of Exhibit 2 (b)). Will she accept? Sure; she'll pay any price within the shaded area to the left of the demand curve. But if someone offers her six rentals at \$3.50 each (point *G*), she won't accept. At a rental price of \$3.50, she's willing to buy only three cassette rentals.

Individual and Market Demand Curves

Market demand curve
The horizontal sum of all individual demand curves.

Normally, economists talk about market demand curves rather than individual demand curves. A **market demand curve** is the horizontal sum of all individual demand curves. Market demand curves are what most firms are interested in. Firms don't care whether individual A or individual B buys their good; they care that *someone* buys their good.

It's a good graphical exercise to add the individual demand curves together to create a market demand curve. We do that in Exhibit 3. In it we assume that the market consists of three buyers, Alice, Pierre, and Jonas, whose demand tables are given in Exhibit 3 (a). Alice and Pierre have demand tables similar to the demand tables discussed previously. At a price of \$3, Alice rents four cassettes; at a price of \$2, she rents six. Jonas is an all-or-nothing individual. He rents one cassette as long as the price is equal to or below \$1; otherwise he rents nothing. If you plot Jonas's demand curve, it's a vertical line. However, the law of demand still holds: as price increases, quantity demanded decreases.

EXHIBIT 3 From Individual Demands to a Market Demand Curve

The table (**a**) shows the demand schedules for Alice, Pierre, and Jonas. Together they make up the market for videocassette rentals. Their total quantity demanded (market demand) for videocassette rentals at each price is given in column 5. As you can see in (**b**), Alice's, Pierre's, and Jonas' demand curves can be added together to get the total market demand curve. For example, at a price of $2, Jonas demands 0, Pierre demands 3, and Alice demands 6, for a market demand of 9 (point *D*).

	(1)	(2)	(3)	(4)	(5)
	Price (in dollars)	Alice	Pierre	Jonas	Market demand
A	0.50	9	6	1	16
B	1.00	8	5	1	14
C	1.50	7	4	0	11
D	2.00	6	3	0	9
E	2.50	5	2	0	7
F	3.00	4	1	0	5
G	3.50	3	0	0	3
H	4.00	2	0	0	2

(a) A demand table

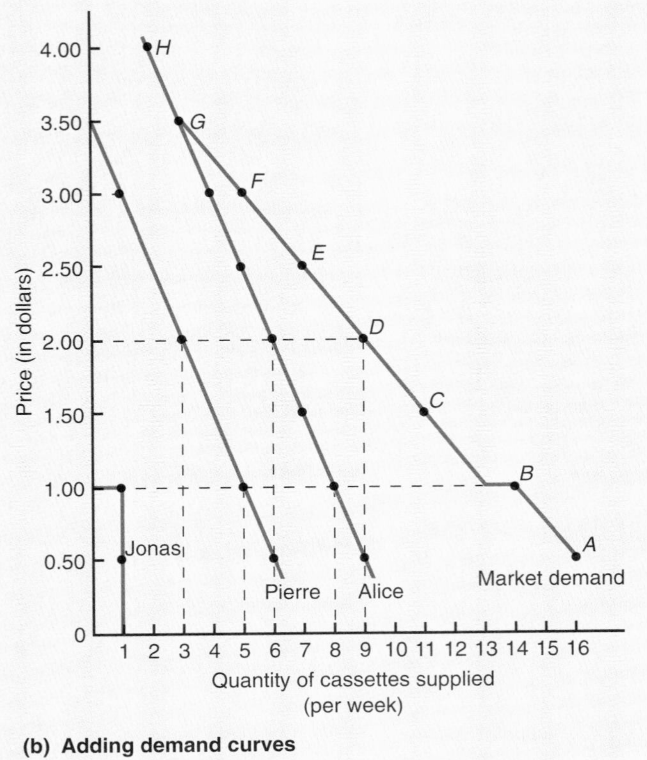

(b) Adding demand curves

3 To derive a demand curve from a demand table, you plot each point on the demand table on a graph and connect the points. For example:

The quantity demanded by each demander is listed in columns 2, 3, and 4 of Exhibit 3 (a). Column 5 gives total market demand; each entry is the sum of the entries in columns 2, 3, and 4. For example, at a price of $3 (row *F*), Alice demands four cassette rentals, Pierre demands one, and Jonas demands zero, for a total market demand of five cassette rentals.

Exhibit 3 (b) shows three demand curves: one each for Alice, Pierre, and Jonas. The market, or total, demand curve is the horizontal sum of the individual demand curves. To see that this is the case, notice that if we take the quantity demanded at $1 by Alice (8), Pierre (5), and Jonas (1) (row *B*, columns 2, 3, and 4), they sum to 14, which is point *B* (14, $1) on the market demand curve. We can do that for each level of price. Alternatively, we can simply add the individual quantities demanded prior to graphing (which we do in column 5 of Exhibit 3 (a)) and graph that total in relation to price. Not surprisingly, we get the same total market demand curve.

In practice, of course, firms don't measure individual demand curves, so they don't sum them up in this fashion. Instead, they estimate total demand. Still, summing up individual demand curves is a useful exercise because it shows you how the market demand curve is made up of the sum (the horizontal sum, graphically speaking) of the individual demand curves, and it gives you a good sense of where market demand curves come from. It also shows you that, even if individuals don't respond to small changes in price, the market demand curve can still be smooth and downward sloping. That's because for the market, the law of demand is based on two phenomena:

1. At lower prices, existing demanders buy more.
2. At lower prices, new demanders (some all-or-nothing demanders like Jonas) enter the market.

Shifts in Demand versus Movement along a Given Demand Curve

As we have emphasized already, the demand curves we draw assume other things are held constant. That is, we assume the price of the good, not shift factors, is causing the demand curve to be downward sloping. To distinguish between the effects of price and

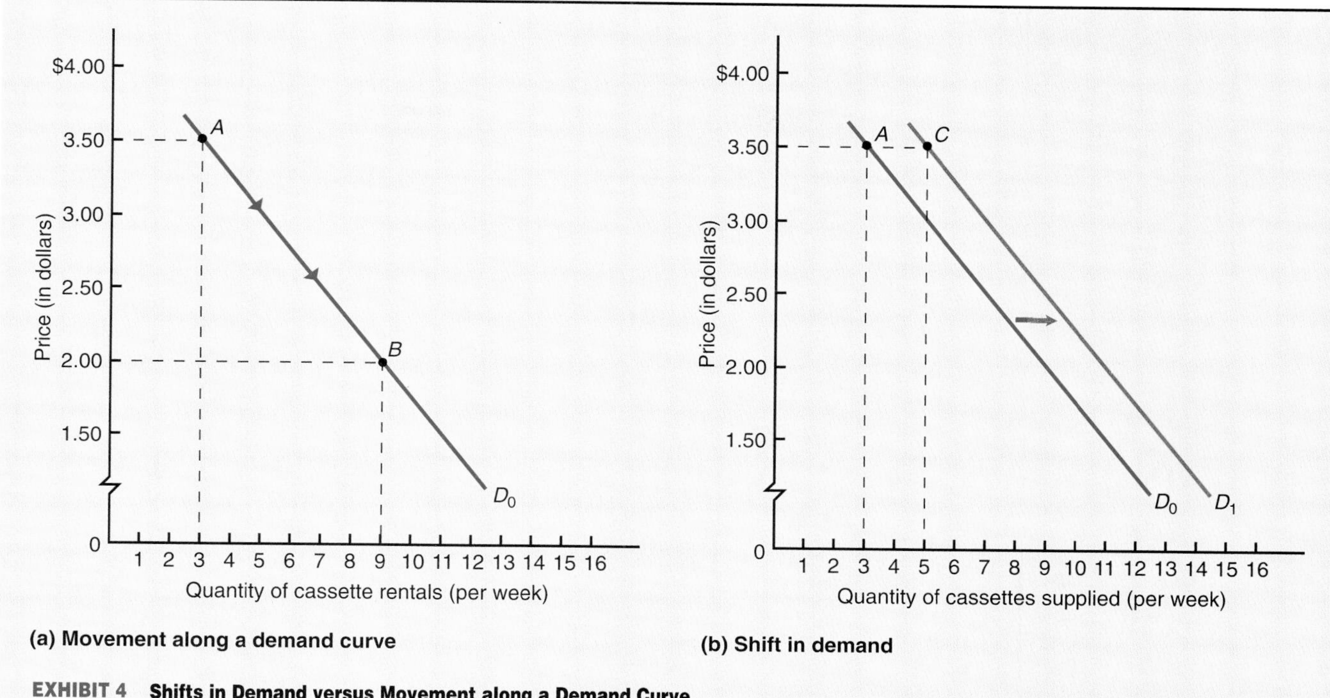

EXHIBIT 4 Shifts in Demand versus Movement along a Demand Curve

A change in price causes a movement along the demand curve. For example, in (**a**), if the price of videocassette rentals is $3.50, 3 rentals will be demanded (point *A*). If the price falls to $2, the quantity of rentals demanded will be 9 (point *B*). Thus, the fall in price brings about a movement along the demand curve, from point *A* to point *B*.

A shift factor change causes a shift in demand. For example, in (**b**), at the price of $3.50, 3 cassette rentals will be demanded (point *A*), but if income rises while price remains the same, people are willing to buy 5 cassette rentals for $3.50 (point *C*) instead of only 3. An increase in income causes the entire demand curve to shift outward from D_0 to D_1.

the effects of shift factors on how much of a good is demanded, we need some terminology.

As we stated above, if how much is demanded is affected by price, we call that effect a change in the quantity demanded. Since a demand curve tells us how much is demanded at different prices, a change in the quantity demanded is represented graphically by a **movement along the demand curve.** If how much is demanded is affected by a shift factor, there is said to be a **shift in demand.** Since a change in a shift factor changes how much would be bought at each different price, a change in demand means that the entire demand curve shifts, to either the right or the left. Thus, a change in a shift factor causes a *shift* in demand; a change in price causes a *movement* along the demand curve. Differentiating between a shift in demand and movement along the demand curve is important but difficult, so it's useful to differentiate the two types of change graphically. We do so for this example in Exhibit 4.

Movement along a demand curve Method of representing a change in the quantity demanded. Graphically, a change in quantity demanded will cause a movement along the demand curve.

Shift in demand If how much of a good is demanded is affected by a shift factor, there is said to be a shift in demand. Graphically, a shift in demand will cause the entire demand curve to shift.

Exhibit 4 (a) shows the effect of a change in the price of cassettes from $3.50 to $2. Point *A* (quantity demanded 3, price $3.50) represents the starting point. Now the price falls to $2 and the quantity demanded rises from 3 to 9, so we move along the demand curve to point *B*. Notice the demand curve (D_0) has already been drawn to demonstrate the effect that price has on quantity.

Now let's say that the price of $3.50 doesn't change but income rises and, as it does, quantity demanded rises to 5. Thus, at a price of $3.50, 5 cassette rentals are demanded rather than only 3. That point is represented by point *C* in Exhibit 4 (b). But if income causes a rise in quantity demanded at a price of $3.50, it will also likely cause an increase in the quantity demanded at all other prices. The demand curve will not remain where it was, but will shift to D_1 to the right of D_0. Because of the change in income, the entire demand curve has shifted. Thus, we say a change in this shift factor has caused a shift in demand.

4 Changes in quantity demanded are shown by movements along a demand curve. Shifts in demand are shown by a shift of the entire demand curve.

A REMINDER 

SIX THINGS TO REMEMBER WHEN CONSIDERING A DEMAND CURVE

- A demand curve had better follow the law of demand: when price rises, quantity demanded falls; and vice versa.
- The horizontal axis—quantity—has a time dimension.
- The quantities are of the same quality.
- The vertical axis—price—is a relative price.
- The curve assumes everything else is held constant.
- Effects of price changes are shown by movements along the demand curve. Effects of anything else on demand (shift factors) are shown by shifts of the entire demand curve.

To see if you understand, say the local theatre decides to let everyone in for free. What will happen to demand for videocassettes? If your answer is there will be a shift in demand—the entire demand curve will shift leftward—you've got it. Just to be sure, let's try one last example. Say tastes change: couch potatoes are out, hard bodies are in. What will happen to the demand for cassettes? The entire demand curve shifts left some more.

The difference between shifts in demand and movements along the demand curve deserves emphasis:

- A change in a shift factor causes a shift in demand (a shift of the entire demand curve).
- A change in price of a good causes a change in the quantity demanded (a movement along an existing demand curve).

SUPPLY

Factors of production Resources, or inputs, necessary to produce goods.

In one sense, supply is the mirror image of demand. Individuals control the inputs, or resources, necessary to produce goods. Such resources are often called **factors of production.** Individuals' supply of these factors to the market mirrors other individuals' demand for those factors. For example, say you decide you want to rest rather than weed your garden. You hire someone to do the weeding; you demand labour. Someone else decides she would prefer more income instead of more rest; she supplies labour to you. You trade money for labour; she trades labour for money. Here supply is the mirror image of demand.

Firm Economic institution that transforms factors of production into consumer goods.

For a large number of goods, however, the supply process is more complicated than demand. As Exhibit 5 shows, for a large number of goods, there's an intermediate step in supply. Individuals supply factors of production to firms. **Firms** are organizations of individuals that transform factors of production into consumable goods.

Let's consider a simple example. Say you're a taco technician. You supply your labour to the factor market. The taco company demands your labour (hires you). The taco company combines your labour with other inputs like meat, cheese, beans, and tables, and produces many tacos (production) which it supplies to customers in the goods market. For produced goods, supply depends not only on individuals' decisions to supply factors of production; it also depends on firms' ability to produce—to transform those factors of production into consumable goods.

The supply process of produced goods can be much more complicated. Often there are many layers of firms—production firms, wholesale firms, distribution firms, and retailing firms—each of which passes on in-process goods to the next-layer firm. Real-world production and supply of produced goods is a multistage process.

The supply of nonproduced goods is more direct. Individuals supply their labour in the form of services directly to the goods market. For example, an independent contractor may repair your washing machine. That contractor supplies his labour directly to you.

Thus, the analysis of the supply of produced goods has two parts: an analysis of the supply of factors of production to households and to firms, and an analysis of why firms transform those factors of production into consumable goods and services.

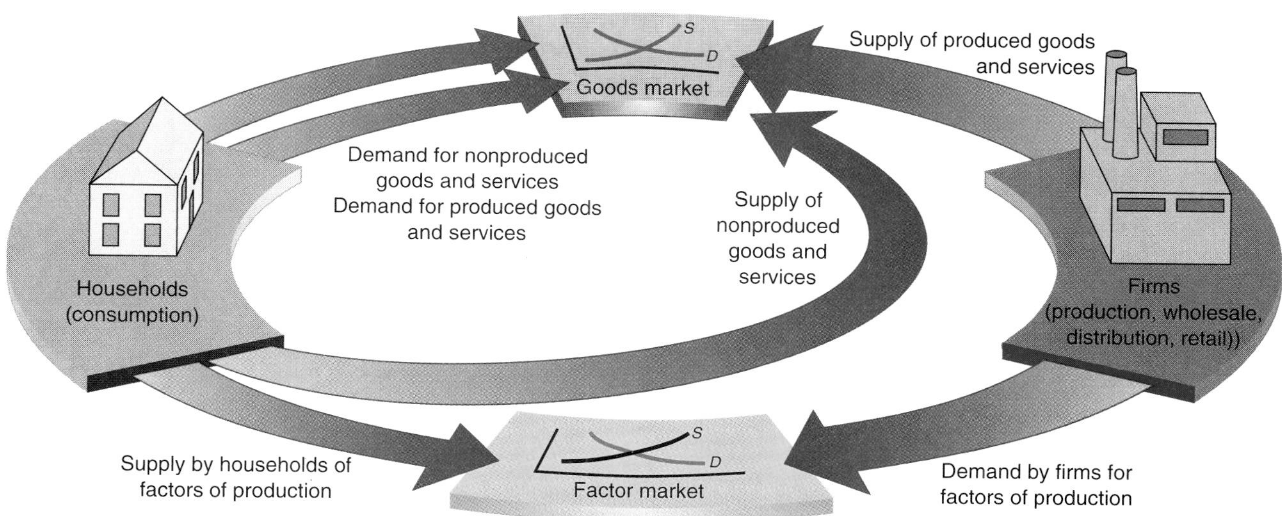

EXHIBIT 5 Transformation of Factors of Production into Consumable Goods and Services

Supply refers to the quantities that will be bought at various prices. When goods are simply traded, supply and demand both come from households. One household supplies the good; another household demands the good. When you mow a neighbour's yard for a fee, you are supplying a nonproduced good.

With produced goods and services, such as a television and insurance, the supply process is more complicated. Households supply factors; firms demand factors and use those factors to produce goods and services. These produced goods are then supplied to households.

In talking about supply, the same convention exists that we used for demand. **Supply** refers to the various quantities offered for sale at various prices. **Quantity supplied** refers to a specific quantity offered for sale at a specific price.

There's also a law of supply that corresponds to the law of demand. The **law of supply** states that the quantity supplied of a good is positively related to that good's price, other things constant. Specifically:

Law of supply: More of a good will be supplied the higher its price, other things constant.

Or:

Law of supply: Less of a good will be supplied the lower its price, other things constant.

Price regulates quantity supplied just as it regulates quantity demanded. Like the law of demand, the law of supply is fundamental to the invisible hand's (the market's) ability to coordinate individuals' actions. Notice how the supply curve in Exhibit 6 (a) slopes upward to the right. That upward slope captures the law of supply. It tells us that the quantity supplied varies directly—in the same direction—with the price.

The same graphical distinction holds for the terms *supply* and *quantity supplied* as for the terms *demand* and *quantity demanded.* In graphical terms, supply refers to the entire supply curve because a supply curve tells us how much will be offered for sale at various prices. *Quantity supplied* refers to a point on a supply curve, so if you refer to movements along a supply curve, you're talking about changes in the quantity supplied. The distinction between a shift in supply and a change in quantity supplied is shown in Exhibit 6 (b). A shift in supply—a shift of the entire supply curve—is shown by Arrow A. A change in the quantity supplied—a movement along the entire supply curve—is shown by Arrow B.

What accounts for the law of supply? When the price of a good rises, individuals and firms can rearrange their activities in order to supply more of that good to the market, substituting production of that good for production of other goods. Thus, the same psychological tendency of individuals that underlies the law of demand—their

The Law of Supply

Supply A schedule of quantities of goods that will be offered to the market at various prices.

Quantity supplied A specific quantity of a good offered for sale at a specific price. Refers to a point on a supply curve.

Law of supply More of a good will be supplied the higher its price, other things constant. Also can be stated as: Less of a good will be supplied the lower its price, other things constant.

5 The law of supply states that the quantity supplied of a good is directly related to the good's price. When prices go up, quantity supplied goes up.

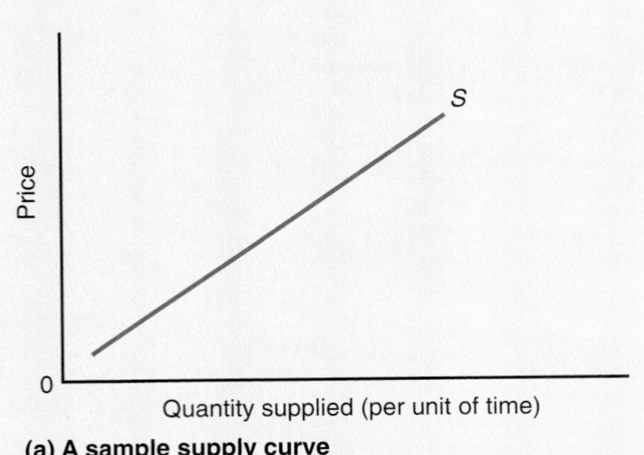

(a) A sample supply curve

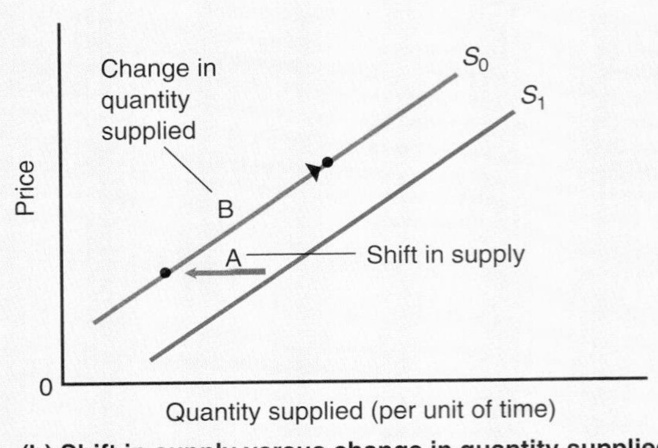

(b) Shift in supply versus change in quantity supplied

EXHIBIT 6 The Supply Curve

The supply curve in (**a**) demonstrates graphically the law of supply, which states that the quantity supplied of a good is directly related to that good's price, other things held constant. The supply curve is upward sloping. Exhibit (**b**) distinguishes between a shift in supply—a shift of the entire supply curve as shown by arrow *A*—and a change in the quantity supplied—a movement along a supply curve as shown by arrow *B*.

determination to want more for less—underlies the law of supply. Individuals and firms want the highest price they can get for the smallest possible quantity they can supply.

With firms, there's a second explanation of the law of supply. Assuming firms' costs are constant, a higher price means higher profits (the difference between a firm's revenues and its costs). The expectation of those higher profits leads it to increase output as price rises, which is what the law of supply states.

Other Things Constant As with the law of demand, the first qualification of the law of supply is that it assumes other things are held constant. Thus, if the price of wheat rises and quantity supplied falls, you'll look for something else that changed—for example, a drought might have caused the drop in quantity supplied. Your expectations would go as follows: Had there been no drought, the quantity supplied would have increased in response to the rise in price, but because there was a drought, the supply decreased, which caused prices to rise.

As with the law of demand, the law of supply represents economists' off-the-cuff response to the question: What happens to quantity supplied if price rises? If the law seems to be violated, economists search for some other variable that has changed. As was the case with demand, these other variables that might change are called *shift factors*.

This "other things constant" assumption is as important to the law of supply as it is to the law of demand. It limits the direct application of supply/demand analysis to microeconomics. To see why, consider a macroeconomic example (one which affects the entire economy). Say that all firms in an economy cut output—decrease supply—by 10 percent. Is it reasonable to assume that other things remain constant? In answering this question, think about the demand for a firm's product. As all firms cut production, peoples' income will fall and their demand for goods will fall (income is a shift factor). So when considering the aggregate economy, when considering macro issues, changes in aggregate supply and changes in the quantity of aggregate supply will likely be interrelated with changes in aggregate demand. This interaction is one of the primary reasons economists separate the micro analysis presented in this chapter from macro analysis.

Relative Price A second qualification is that the law of supply refers to *relative price*. The reason is that, like the law of demand, the law of supply is based on individuals' and firms' ability to substitute production of this good for another, or vice versa. If the

EXHIBIT 7 From a Supply Table to a Supply Curve

As with market demand, market supply is determined by adding all individual supplies at a given price. Three suppliers—Ann, Barry, and Charlie—make up the market of videocassette suppliers. The total market supply is the sum of their individual supplies at each price (shown in column 5 of (**a**).

Each of the individual supply curves and the market supply curve have been plotted in (**b**). Notice how the market supply curve is the horizontal sum of the individual supply curves.

	(1)	(2)	(3)	(4)	(5)
Row	Price (in dollars)	Ann's supply	Barry's supply	Charlie's supply	Market supply
A	0.00	0	0	0	0
B	0.50	1	0	0	1
C	1.00	2	1	0	3
D	1.50	3	2	0	5
E	2.00	4	3	0	7
F	2.50	5	4	0	9
G	3.00	6	5	0	11
H	3.50	7	5	2	14
I	4.00	8	5	2	15

(a) A supply table

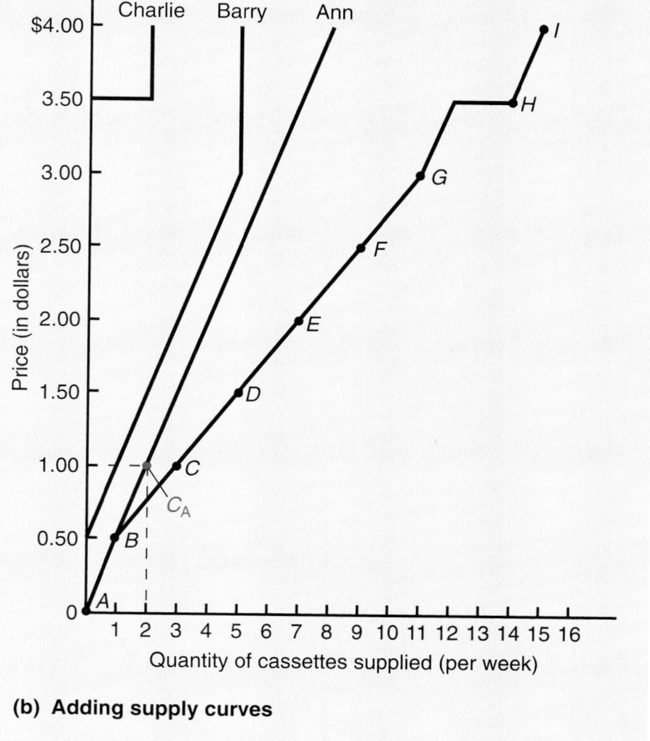

(b) Adding supply curves

price of corn rises relative to the price of wheat, farmers will grow less wheat and more corn. If both prices rise by equal percentages, the relative price won't change and it won't be worthwhile to substitute one good for another.

The Supply Table

Remember Exhibit 3 (a)'s demand table for cassette rentals. In Exhibit 7 (a), columns 2 (Ann), 3 (Barry), and 4 (Charlie), we follow the same reasoning to construct a supply table for three hypothetical cassette suppliers. Each supplier follows the law of supply: when price rises, they supply more, or at least as much as they did at a lower price.

From a Supply Table to a Supply Curve

Exhibit 7 (b) takes the information in Exhibit 7 (a)'s supply table and translates it into a graph of Ann's supply curve. For instance, point C_A on Ann's supply curve corresponds to the information in column 2, row *C*. Point C_A is at a price of $1 and a quantity of 2. Notice that Ann's supply curve is upward sloping, meaning that price is positively related to quantity. Charlie's and Barry's supply curves are similarly derived.

6 To derive a supply curve from a supply table, you plot each point on the supply table on a graph and connect the points.

The supply curve represents the set of *minimum prices* an individual seller will accept for various quantities of a good. The market's invisible hand stops suppliers from charging more than the market price. If suppliers could escape the market's invisible hand and charge a higher price, they would gladly do so. Unfortunately for them, and fortunately for consumers, a higher price encourages other suppliers to begin selling cassettes. Competing suppliers' entry into the market places a limit on the price any supplier can charge.

Individual and Market Supply Curves

The market supply curve is derived from individual supply curves in precisely the same way that the demand curve was. To emphasize the symmetry in reasoning, we've made the three suppliers quite similar to the three demanders. Ann (column 2) will supply 2 at $1; if price goes up to $2 she increases her supply to 4. Barry (column 3) begins supplying at $1, and at $3 supplies 5, the most he'll supply, regardless of how

ADDED DIMENSIONS  SUPPLY, PRODUCTION, AND PROFIT

Many goods must be produced—that is, inputs must be physically transformed before they become desirable goods. Production is complicated and requires a separate analysis before it can be integrated into our analysis.

In what's called *Walrasian economics* (named after famous Swiss economist Leon Walras), the problem of production is assumed away; his is an analysis of a trading economy. This is important to recognize since it's Walrasian economics that provides the logical underpinnings for supply/demand analysis. In Walrasian economics, individuals have certain goods they trade; at some prices they sell, at some (lower) prices they buy. It is in this sense that supply is simply the mirror image of demand.

An easy way to see that supply is a mirror image of demand is to think about your supply of hours of work. When we talk of work, we say you're supplying hours of work at $6 per hour. But that same supply of work can be thought of as demand for leisure time. If, at $6 an hour, you choose to work 8 hours a day, you're simultaneously choosing to keep 16 hours for yourself (24 hours a day minus the 8 hours spent working). If we talk in terms of leisure, we speak of demand for leisure; if we talk of work, we speak of supply of labour. One is simply the mirror image of the other.

Another approach to economics is *Marshallian economics* (named after Alfred Marshall, a famous English economist). Marshallian economics does include an analysis of production. It relates costs of production with what firms are willing to sell. The reason production is difficult to integrate with an analysis of supply is that, with many production processes, per-unit costs fall as production increases. For example, in the 1920s Henry Ford produced a lot more model T cars than he had produced before; he even produced more of his cars than any of his competitors produced of their cars. As he produced more, costs per unit fell and the price of cars fell. Even today many businesses will tell you that if they can increase demand for their good, their per-unit costs and their price will go down. Such examples don't violate the law of supply. Costs per unit fall because of the nature of production. As the nature of production changes, the upward-sloping supply curve shifts outward.

There's another point we should mention about supply. Sometimes students get the impression from textbooks that supply and demand simply exist—that firms can go out, find demand curves, and start supplying. That's not a realistic picture of how the economy works. Demand curves aren't there for students or firms to see. Producing goods and supplying them inevitably involves risk and uncertainty. A company like General Motors may spend $1 billion designing a certain type of car, only to find that consumers don't like its style, or that another company has produced a car consumers like better. In that case, GM suffers a large loss.

To compensate for the potential for losses, suppliers also have the potential to make a profit on goods they sell. When the price of a good is high compared to costs of the resources used in production, expected profits are high, so more producers are encouraged to take the risk. When the price of a good is low compared to the costs, fewer firms take the risk because expected profits are low. Thus, profit is a motivating force of supply in a market economy.

high price rises. Charlie (column 4) has only two units to supply. At a price of $3.50 he'll supply that quantity, but higher prices won't get him to supply any more.

We sum horizontally the individual supply curves to get the market supply curve. In Exhibit 7 (a) (column 5), we add together Ann's, Barry's, and Charlie's supply to arrive at the market supply curve, which is graphed in Exhibit 7 (b). Notice each point on it corresponds to the information in columns 1 and 5 for a particular row. For example, point *H* corresponds to a price of $3.50 and a quantity of 14.

The market supply curve's upward slope is determined by two different sources: by existing suppliers supplying more and by new suppliers entering the market. Sometimes existing suppliers may not be willing to increase their quantity supplied in response to an increase in prices, but a rise in price often brings brand new suppliers into the market. For example, a rise in teachers' salaries will have little effect on the amount of teaching current teachers do, but it will increase the number of people choosing to be teachers.

Shifts in Supply versus Movement along a Given Supply Curve

Just as there can be shifts in the demand curve resulting from shift factors, so too can there be shifts in the supply curve caused by shift factors. Important shift factors of supply include:

1. Changes in the prices of inputs used in the production of a good.
2. Changes in technology.
3. Changes in suppliers' expectations.
4. Changes in taxes and subsidies.

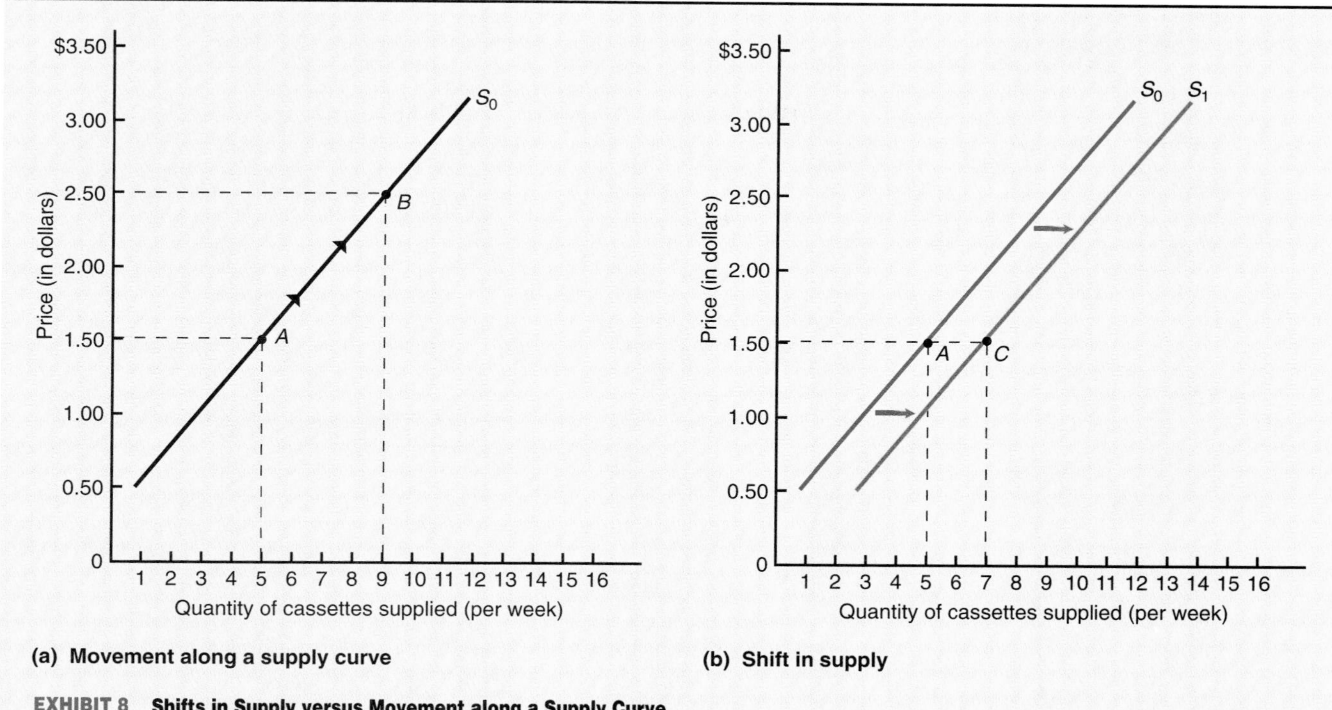

EXHIBIT 8 Shifts in Supply versus Movement along a Supply Curve
A change in the price of a good results in a movement along the supply curve. For example, in **(a)** if the price of videocassette rentals is \$1.50, 5 cassettes would be supplied (point *A*). But if the price of cassette rentals increases for some reason, say to \$2.50, suppliers would increase supply to 9 (point *B*). The change in price results in a movement along the supply curve from point *A* to point *B*.

Shift factors cause a shift in the supply curve. For example, in **(b)**, at the price of \$1.50, 5 cassettes would be supplied (point *A*). If some new technology were introduced, lowering the cost of producing the cassette, then suppliers would supply 7 cassettes at the price of \$1.50 (point *C*). An improvement in technology results in a shift in the supply curve from S_0 to S_1.

These aren't all the shift factors; as was the case with demand, anything that affects supply other than the good's own price is a shift factor. Each of these shift factors will cause a **shift in supply,** whereas a change in the price causes a **movement along the supply curve.**

Shift in supply If how much of a good is supplied is affected by a shift factor, there is said to be a shift in supply. Graphically, a shift in supply will cause the entire supply curve to shift.

Movement along the supply curve Method of representing a change in the quantity supplied. Graphically, a change in quantity demanded will cause a movement along the supply curve.

As with demand, it's useful to graph an example of a shift in supply and to differentiate that from a movement along the supply curve. Exhibit 8 does this for our example. Exhibit 8 (a) shows the effect of a change in the price of cassettes from \$1.50 to \$2.50. Point *A* (5, \$1.50) represents the starting point. Now, for some reason, price rises to \$2.50 and the quantity supplied rises to 9 (point *B*). Because of the price increase, there's a movement along the supply curve.

Now, however, let's say that there's an improvement in technology: a new type of cassette that's cheaper to make than the existing cassette. Such an advance in technology shifts the supply curve outward to the right. Why? Because it lowers costs for each unit sold, enabling suppliers to offer more for sale at each price. An improvement in technology is shown in Exhibit 8 (b). Notice that the entire supply curve shifts from S_0 to S_1, showing that for each price, the quantity supplied will be greater. For example, at price \$1.50, 5 cassettes are supplied; but after the technological improvement, at price \$1.50, 7 cassettes are supplied. The same reasoning holds for any price.

7 Just as with demand, it is important to distinguish between a shift in supply (a shift of the entire supply curve) and a movement along a supply curve (a change in the quantity supplied due to a change in price).

Do we see such shifts in the supply curve often? Yes. A good example is computers. For the past 30 years, technological changes have continually shifted computers' supply curve to the right.

This should give you an idea of factors that shift supply, and should cement for you the difference between a shift in supply and a movement along a supply curve. But in case it didn't, here it is one more time:

A REMINDER 

SIX THINGS TO REMEMBER WHEN CONSIDERING A SUPPLY CURVE

- A supply curve follows the law of supply. When price rises, quantity supplied increases; and vice versa.
- The horizontal axis—quantity—has a time dimension.
- The quantities are of the same quality.
- The vertical axis—price—is a relative price.
- The curve assumes everything else is constant.
- Effects of price changes are shown by movements along the supply curve. Effects of nonprice determinants of supply are shown by shifts of the entire supply curve.

Shift in supply: A change in a nonprice factor—a shift of the entire supply curve.

Movement along a supply curve: A change in the quantity supplied due to a change in price—a movement along a supply curve.

THE MARRIAGE OF SUPPLY AND DEMAND

Thomas Carlyle, the English historian who dubbed economics "the dismal science," also wrote this chapter's introductory tidbit, "Teach a parrot the words *supply* and *demand* and you've got an economist." In Chapter 1, we hope we convinced you that economics is not dismal. In the rest of this chapter, we hope to convince you that while supply and demand are important to economics, parrots don't make good economists. If students think that when they've learned the terms *supply* and *demand* they've learned economics, they're mistaken. Those terms are just labels for the ideas behind supply and demand, and it's the ideas that are important. What's relevant about supply and demand isn't the labels but how the concepts interact. For instance, what happens if quantity supplied doesn't equal quantity demanded? It's in understanding the interaction of supply and demand that economics becomes interesting *and relevant.*

The First Dynamic Law of Supply and Demand

Excess supply Quantity supplied is greater than quantity demanded.

Excess demand Quantity demanded is greater than quantity supplied.

8 The three dynamic laws of supply and demand are:
1. If Qd > Qs, P increases; if Qs > Qd, P decreases.
2. The larger Qs − Qd, the faster P falls; the larger Qd − Qs, the faster P rises.
3. If Qd = Qs, P does not change.

First dynamic law of supply and demand When quantity demanded is greater than quantity supplied, prices tend to rise; when quantity supplied is greater than quantity demanded, prices tend to fall.

When you have a market in which neither suppliers nor demanders can organize and in which prices are free to adjust, economists have a good answer for the question: What happens if quantity supplied doesn't equal quantity demanded? If quantity supplied is greater than quantity demanded (that is, if there is **excess supply,** a surplus), some suppliers won't be able to sell all their goods. Each supplier will think: "Gee, if I offer to sell it for a bit less, I'll be the lucky one who sells my good; someone else will be stuck with not selling their good." But because all suppliers with excess goods will be thinking the same thing, the price in the market will fall. As that happens, demanders will increase their quantity demanded. So the movement toward equilibrium caused by excess supply is on both the supply and demand sides.

The reverse is also true. Say that instead of excess supply, there's **excess demand** (a shortage): quantity demanded is greater than quantity supplied. There are more demanders who want the good than there are suppliers selling the good. Let's consider what's likely to go through demanders' minds. They'll likely call long-lost friends who just happen to be sellers of that good and tell them it's good to talk to them and, by the way, don't they want to sell that . . .? Suppliers will be rather pleased that so many of their old friends have remembered them, but they'll also likely see the connection between excess demand and their friends' thoughtfulness. To stop their phones from ringing all the time, they'll likely raise their price. The reverse is true for excess supply. It's amazing how friendly suppliers become to potential demanders when there's excess supply.

This tendency for prices to rise when demand exceeds supply and for prices to fall when supply exceeds demand is a phenomenon economists call the **first dynamic law of supply and demand:**

When quantity demanded is greater than quantity supplied, prices tend to rise; when quantity supplied is greater than quantity demanded, prices tend to fall.

Exhibit 9 shows the first dynamic law of supply and demand by the arrows

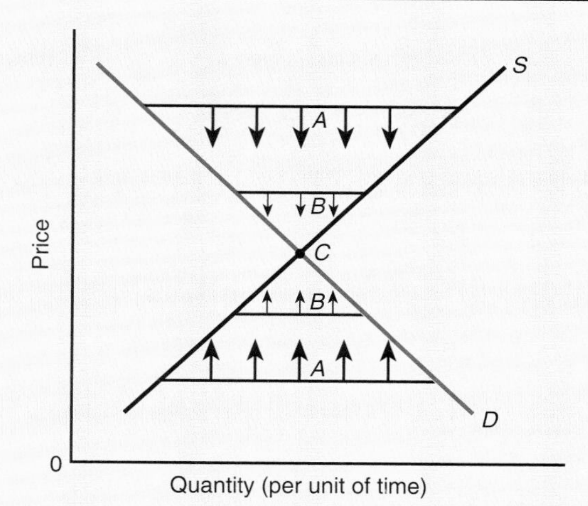

EXHIBIT 9 The Dynamic Laws of Supply and Demand

The dynamic laws of supply and demand tell us what forces will be set in motion when the quantity supplied does not equal the quantity demanded.

In this example, supply (line *S*) and demand (line *D*) are in balance at point *C*. When supply is greater than demand, there is downward pressure on price; when demand is greater than supply, there is upward pressure on price. The greater the difference between supply and demand, the greater the pressure on price, as indicated by the larger arrows at *A* and smaller arrows at *B*.

labelled *A*. With excess supply the arrows push price down; with excess demand the arrows push price up. It's called a *dynamic law* because *dynamic* refers to change and this law refers to how prices change, not to what prices will be.

The Second Dynamic Law of Supply and Demand

How much pressure will there be for prices to rise or fall? That too will likely depend on differences between quantity supplied and quantity demanded. The greater the difference, the more pressure there is on individuals to raise or lower prices. If you're a seller (supplier) and all your old friends are calling you (there's major excess demand), you'll simply put a message on your answering machine saying, "The price has gone up 200 percent or 300 percent. If you're still interested in talking about old times, stay on the line. Otherwise, it was nice knowing you." If, however, only a couple of old friends call you (there's only minor excess demand), you'll probably raise your price only slightly. Or if you're a buyer (demander) and there's major excess supply, you'll leave the following message: "If you're trying to sell me anything, I'm broke and can only pay less than what you ask."

Thus, the **second dynamic law of supply and demand is:**

In a market, the larger the difference between quantity supplied and quantity demanded, the greater the pressure on prices to rise (if there is excess demand) or fall (if there is excess supply).

Second dynamic law of supply and demand In a market, the larger the difference between quantity supplied and quantity demanded, the greater the pressure on prices to rise (if there is excess demand) or fall (if there is excess supply).

The second dynamic law of supply and demand is demonstrated by the smaller *B* arrows in Exhibit 9. Because the difference between quantity supplied and quantity demanded is less than before, the upward and downward pressures aren't as strong.

The Third Dynamic Law of Supply and Demand

People's tendencies to change prices exist as long as there's some difference between quantity supplied and quantity demanded. But the change in price brings the laws of supply and demand into play. As price falls, quantity supplied decreases as some suppliers leave the business (the law of supply); and as some people who originally weren't really interested in buying the good think, "Well, at this low price, maybe I do want to buy," quantity demanded increases (the law of demand). Similarly, when price rises, quantity supplied will increase (the law of supply) and quantity demanded will decrease (the law of demand).

Whenever quantity supplied and quantity demanded are unequal, price tends to change. If, however, quantity supplied and quantity demanded are equal, price will stay the same because no one will have an incentive to change it. This observation leads to the **third dynamic law of supply and demand:**

When quantity supplied equals quantity demanded, prices have no tendency to change.

Third dynamic law of supply and demand When quantity supplied equals quantity demanded, prices have no tendency to change.

A REMINDER  THE DYNAMIC LAWS OF SUPPLY AND DEMAND

1. When quantity demanded is greater than quantity supplied, prices tend to rise; when quantity supplied is greater than quantity demanded, prices tend to fall.
2. The larger the difference between quantity supplied and quantity demanded, the faster prices will rise (if there is excess demand) or fall (if there is excess supply).
3. When quantity supplied equals quantity demanded, prices have no tendency to change.

The third dynamic law of supply and demand is represented by point *C* in Exhibit 9. At point *C* there's no upward or downward pressure on price.

The Graphical Marriage of Demand and Supply

Exhibit 10 shows supply and demand curves for cassettes and demonstrates the operation of the dynamic laws of supply and demand. Let's consider what will happen to the price of cassettes in four cases:

1. When the price is $3;
2. When the price is $2.50;
3. When the price is $1.50; and
4. When the price is $2.25.

1. When price is $3, quantity supplied is 11 and quantity demanded is only 5. Excess supply is 6. At a price of $3, individual demanders can get all they want, but most suppliers can't sell all they wish; they'll be stuck with cassettes that they'd like to sell. Suppliers will tend to offer their goods at a lower price and demanders, who see plenty of suppliers out there, will bargain harder for an even lower price. Both these forces will push the price down as indicated by the *A* arrows in Exhibit 10.
2. When price falls from $3 to $2.50, the pressures are the same kind as in (1), only they're weaker, because excess supply is smaller. There aren't as many dissatisfied suppliers searching for ways to sell their cassettes. Generally, the rate at which prices fall depends on the size of the gap between quantity supplied and quantity demanded. This smaller pressure is shown by the *B* arrows in Exhibit 10.

Now let's start from the other side.

3. Say price is $1.50. The situation is now reversed. Quantity supplied is 5 and quantity demanded is 11. Excess demand is 6. Now it's demanders who can't get what they want and suppliers who are in the strong bargaining position. The pressures will be on price to rise in the direction of the *C* arrows in Exhibit 10.
4. At $2.25, price is at its equilibrium: quantity supplied equals quantity demanded. Suppliers offer to sell 8 and demanders want to buy 8, so there's no pressure on price to rise or fall. Price will tend to remain where it is (point *E* in Exhibit 10).

Equilibrium

Equilibrium A concept in which the dynamic forces cancel each other out.

Equilibrium price The price toward which the invisible hand (economic forces) drives the market.

The concept of equilibrium appears often throughout this text. You need to understand what equilibrium is and what it isn't. The concept itself comes from physics—classical mechanics. To say something is in **equilibrium** is to say that the dynamic forces pushing on it cancel each other out. For example, a book on a desk is in equilibrium because the upward force exerted on the book by the desk equals the downward pressure exerted on the book by gravity. In supply and demand analysis, equilibrium means that the upward pressure on price is exactly offset by the downward pressure on price. **Equilibrium price** is the price toward which the invisible hand drives the market.

So much for what equilibrium is. Now let's consider what it isn't.

First, equilibrium isn't inherently good or bad. It's simply a state in which dynamic pressures offset each other. Some equilibria are awful. Say two countries are

EXHIBIT 10 The Marriage of Supply and Demand

Combining supply and demand lets us see the dynamic laws of supply and demand. These laws tell us the pressures on price when there is excess demand (there is upward pressure on price) or excess supply (there is downward pressure on price). Understanding these pressures is essential to understanding how to apply economics to reality.

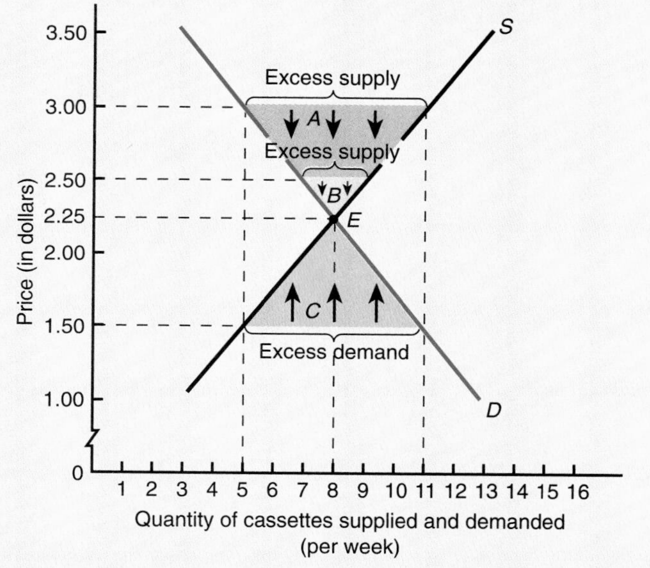

engaged in a poison gas war against each other and both sides are snuffed out. An equilibrium will have been reached, but there's nothing good about it.

Second, equilibrium isn't a state of the world. It's a characteristic of the framework you use to look at the world. A framework for looking at the world is called a **model.** The same situation could be seen as an equilibrium in one framework and as a disequilibrium in another. Say you're describing a car that's speeding along at 100 kilometres an hour. That car is changing position relative to objects on the ground. Its movement could be, and generally is, described as if it were in disequilibrium. However, if you consider this car relative to another car going 100 kilometres an hour, the cars could be modeled as being in equilibrium because their positions relative to each other aren't changing.

Model Framework for looking at the world.

Understanding that equilibrium is a characteristic of the framework of analysis, not of the real world, is important in applying economic models to reality. For example, in the preceding description we said equilibrium occurs where supply equals demand. In a model where the invisible hand is the only force operating, that's true. In the real world, however, other forces—political and social forces—are operating. These will likely push price away from that supply/demand equilibrium. Were we to consider a model that included all these forces—political, social, and economic—equilibrium would be likely to exist where supply isn't equal to demand. In the real world, the invisible hand, foot, and handshake often work in different directions and vary in strength. For example:

- In agricultural markets, farmers use political pressure (the invisible foot) to obtain higher-than-supply/demand-equilibrium prices. Generally they succeed, so agricultural prices rise above the supply/demand-equilibrium price. The laws of supply and demand assume no political pressures on prices.
- In labour markets, social pressures often offset economic pressures and prevent unemployed individuals from accepting work at lower wages than currently employed workers (the invisible handshake). Similarly, when there's a strike, social pressures prevent people who don't have jobs from taking jobs strikers have left. People who do take those jobs are called names like *scab* or *strike-breaker,* and they don't like those names. A pure supply and demand model, though, assumes everyone who wants a job will try to become a scab.

ADDED DIMENSION

PUBLIC CHOICE AND RENT-SEEKING ECONOMIC MODELS

Economics is a developing discipline, so the models used in one time period aren't necessarily the models used in another. In their research, economists debate which models are best and how to integrate more insights into their existing models.

Two groups of economists who've recently pushed back the frontiers of economics are the *public choice economists* and the *neoclassical political economists.* Public choice economists, led by Gordon Tullock and James Buchanan, argue that the political dimension must be part of economists' models. To integrate the political dimension, they apply economic analysis to politics and consider how economic forces affect the laws that are enacted and how, in turn, those laws affect economics. Their work was instrumental in leading to the invisible foot metaphor discussed in Chapter 1, and won James Buchanan a Nobel prize in 1986.

Neoclassical political economists share with public choice economists the view that the political dimension must be part of economists' models, and have developed a variety of formal models that significantly modify earlier models' predictions. Many of their models focus on rent seeking (how suppliers can restrict supply and thereby create rents for themselves). *Rent* is defined as an income earned when supply is restricted. For example, say a carpenter's union limits the number of people who can do carpentry. The supply of carpenters will decrease and existing carpenters will earn a higher wage that includes a rent component. Rents can be created either by using politics (the invisible foot) or by special agreements (the invisible handshake). Hence, neoclassical political economists are at the forefront of the movement to broaden economic analysis.

Although the formal analyses of both these groups haven't been adopted by the majority of economists, other economists often use their informal results and insights. Throughout this book we'll discuss these and other groups' views, but we'll focus on the mainstream model that the majority of economists use.

- In product markets, suppliers conspire to limit entry by other suppliers. They work hard to get Parliament to establish tariffs and make restrictive regulations (the invisible foot). They also devise pricing strategies that scare off other suppliers and allow them to hold their prices higher than a supply/demand equilibrium. A pure supply and demand model assumes no conspiring at all.
- In the housing rental markets, consumers often organize politically and get local government to enact rent controls (ceilings on rents that can be charged for apartments). Here's an example of government (the invisible foot) putting downward pressure on price.

If social and political forces were included in the analysis, they'd provide a counterpressure to the dynamic forces of supply and demand. The result would be an equilibrium with continual excess supply or excess demand. The invisible hand pushing toward a supply/demand equilibrium would be thwarted by other invisible forces pushing in the other direction.

A formal political/social/economic model that included all these forces simultaneously would be complicated, and economists are still working on perfecting one. Meanwhile economists, in their formal analysis, focus on a pure supply and demand model in which only the invisible hand is operating. That model lets you see clearly the economic forces at work. When economists apply the pure supply/demand model to reality, however, they discuss the effects of these other forces.

In this book we'll introduce you to both the formal model (in which only market forces are operating) and the informal model (in which all forces are operating).

Changes in Supply and Demand

To ensure that you understand the supply and demand graphs throughout the book and can apply them, let's go through three examples. Exhibit 11 (a) deals with an increase in demand; Exhibit 11 (b) deals with a decrease in supply.

Let's consider again the supply and demand for cassette rentals. In Exhibit 11 (a), the supply is S_0 and initial demand is D_0. They meet at an equilibrium price of \$2.25 and a quantity demanded of 8 (point A). Now say demand for cassette rentals increases from D_0 to D_1. At a price of \$2.25, the quantity of cassette rentals supplied will be 8 and the quantity demanded will be 10; excess demand of 2 exists.

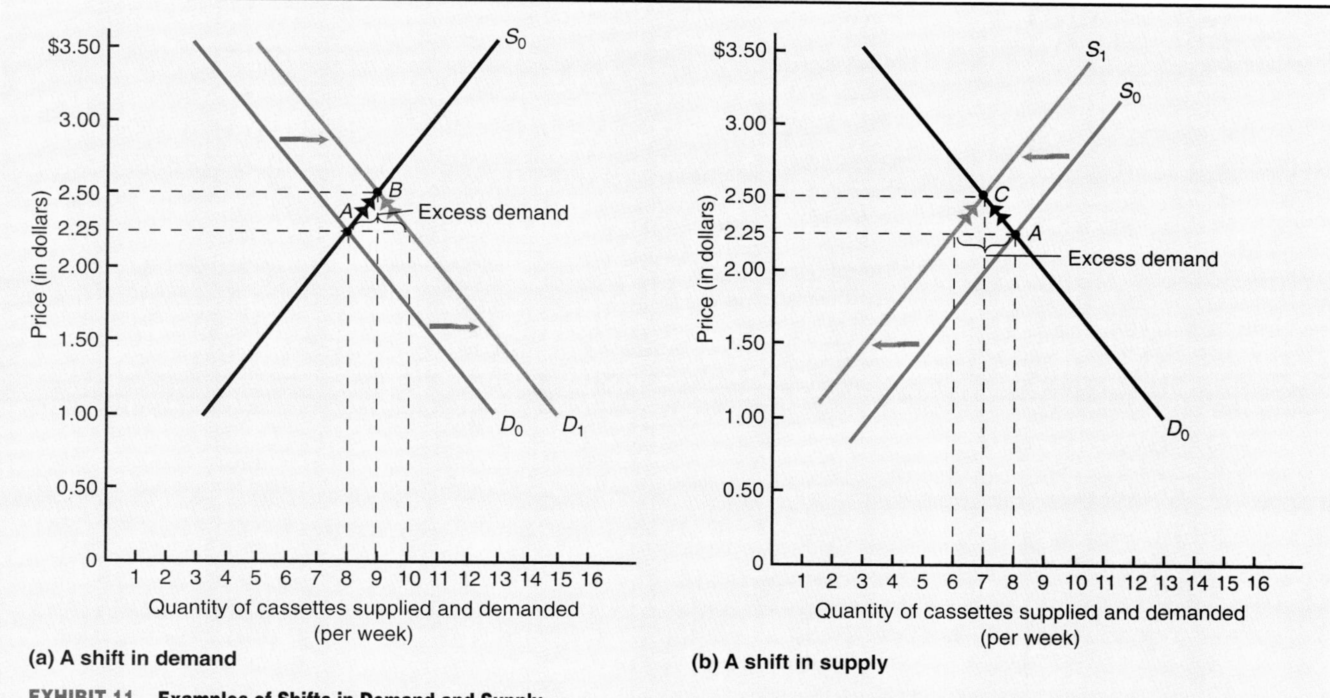

EXHIBIT 11 Examples of Shifts in Demand and Supply

When there is an increase in demand (the demand curve shifts outward), there is upward pressure on the price, as shown in (**a**). If there is an increase in demand from D_0 to D_1, the quantity of cassette rentals that was demanded at a price of $2.25, 8, increases to 10, but the quantity supplied remains at 8. This excess demand tends to cause prices to rise. Eventually, a new equilibrium is reached at the price of $2.50, where the quantity supplied and the quantity demanded is 9.

If supply of cassettes decreases, then the entire supply curve shifts inward to the left, as shown in (**b**), from S_0 to S_1. At the price of $2.25, the quantity supplied has now decreased to 6 cassettes, but the quantity demanded has remained at 8 cassettes. The excess demand tends to force the price upward. Eventually, an equilibrium is reached at the price of $2.50 and quantity 7 (point *C*).

As the first dynamic law of supply and demand dictates, the excess demand pushes prices upward in the direction of the small arrows, decreasing the quantity demanded. As it does so, movement takes place along both the supply curve and the demand curve. The first dynamic law of supply and demand tells us that price will be pushed up.

The upward push on price decreases the gap between the quantity supplied and the quantity demanded. As the gap is decreased, the upward pressure decreases, as the second dynamic law requires. But as long as that gap exists at all, price will be pushed upward until the new equilibrium price ($2.50) and new quantity (9) are reached (point *B*). At point *B* the third dynamic law of supply and demand takes hold: quantity supplied equals quantity demanded. So the market is in equilibrium. Notice that the adjustment is twofold: The higher price brings about equilibrium by both increasing the quantity supplied (from 8 to 9) and decreasing the quantity demanded (from 10 to 9).

Exhibit 11 (b) begins with the same situation that we started with in Exhibit 11 (a); the initial equilibrium quantity and price are 8 and $2.25 (point *A*). In this example, however, instead of demand increasing, let's assume supply decreases—say because some suppliers change what they like to do, and decide they will no longer supply this good. That means that the entire supply curve shifts inward to the left (from S_0 to S_1). At the initial equilibrium price of $2.25, the quantity demanded is greater than the quantity supplied. Two more cassettes are demanded than are supplied. (Excess demand = 2.)

ADDED DIMENSION 

HISTORICAL TIME, HISTORESES, AND "TENDENCY TOWARD EQUILIBRIUM" ANALYSIS

A model can be interpreted many different ways, and knowing the various interpretations is as central to understanding the lesson of the model as is knowing the technical aspects of the model. For example, most models we use in economics are equilibrium models; they have a definite equilibrium toward which they move. To use such an equilibrium model to analyze a problem is not to believe that the equilibrium of the model is the one that will be reached in the real world. Other forces may, and often do, prevent that equilibrium from being reached. Moreover, the process of moving toward an equilibrium may change the equilibrium one is aiming at. A model only captures certain aspects of reality. To interpret that model, other aspects must be added in.

When the movement toward equilibrium can affect the equilibrium, there is what is called *histores*es or *path dependency* present. When path dependency exists, as it often does, the supply/demand model is incomplete and the equilibrium of the supply/demand model isn't the equilibrium that one would expect. For example, say the price of a pair of Nike sneakers is $200. These $200 sneakers have lots of snob appeal. Now, say, demand declines, and Nike lowers prices. The falling price causes people to think that Nikes are no longer "in," and *because of the fall in price,* tastes change and the demand falls further. In our supply/demand model, such effects are ruled out by our "other things constant" assumption. The real world need not, and generally does not, follow this assumption.

In the analysis of large changes in the economy or small changes in the aggregate economy, the "other things constant" assumption is inevitably broken because movements along a supply curve cause income to change which causes shifts of the demand curve. To capture these interactive effects we need a different analysis, which is where *macroeconomics* comes in. Macroeconomics goes beyond microeconomic supply and demand and tries to include an analysis of interactive effects. (We write "tries to" because macro hasn't done a great job in understanding these interactive effects.)

Another way in which the "other things constant" assumption is violated is demonstrated in the irreversibility of many actions. For example, say you decide to paint your bike pink in a fit of pink-passion. The cost: $2.98 for the spray can. Now you see the newly-painted bike and decide pink isn't your colour—you want it back to the original colour. You *might* be able to remove the paint at a cost of $75—but probably you can't get the pink paint off. After you've painted the bike, "other things are no longer constant"; you cannot turn back time by pressing a rewind button. Or say you sawed a 10-foot 2x4 to 8′4″. Then, you discover that you really wanted an 8′5″ 2x4. You don't simply run the saw backwards and try again.

The point of these examples is that reality happens in historical time where many actions are irreversible, or are reversible at a much higher cost than was the cost of getting to the situation you'd like to reverse. Supply/demand analysis doesn't capture that dimension of reality, so that dimension must be added back to the analysis in the interpretation.

Economists recognize these problems, but nonetheless they use supply/demand analysis which assumes these problems away to keep the analysis simple. But they keep these limitations in the back of their minds, and add them back, where appropriate, when applying the model to a real-world problem.

As the dynamic laws of supply and demand require, this excess demand exerts upward pressure on price. Price is pushed in the direction of the small arrows. As the price rises, the upward pressure on price is reduced (in accord with the second dynamic law of supply and demand) but will still exist until the new equilibrium price, $2.50, and new quantity, 7, are reached. At $2.50, the quantity supplied equals the quantity demanded. The adjustment has involved a movement along the demand curve and the new supply curve. As price rises, quantity supplied is adjusted upward and quantity demanded is adjusted downward until quantity supplied equals quantity demanded where the new supply curve intersects the demand curve at point *C,* an equilibrium of 7 and $2.50.

We leave a final example as an exercise for you. Demonstrate graphically how the price of computers could have fallen dramatically in the past 10 years, even as demand increased. (Hint: Supply has shifted even more, so even at lower prices, far more computers have been supplied than were being supplied 10 years ago.)

SUPPLY AND DEMAND IN ACTION: OIL PRICE FLUCTUATIONS

Now that we've discussed the basic analysis and its limitations, we can apply the supply/demand model to a real-world situation.

Exhibit 12 (a) shows the changes in the U.S. dollar price of oil from 1973 to 1993. Exhibit 12 (b) demonstrates the supply/demand forces associated with those changes in the period 1973–81, during which the price of oil went up substantially. Prior to the

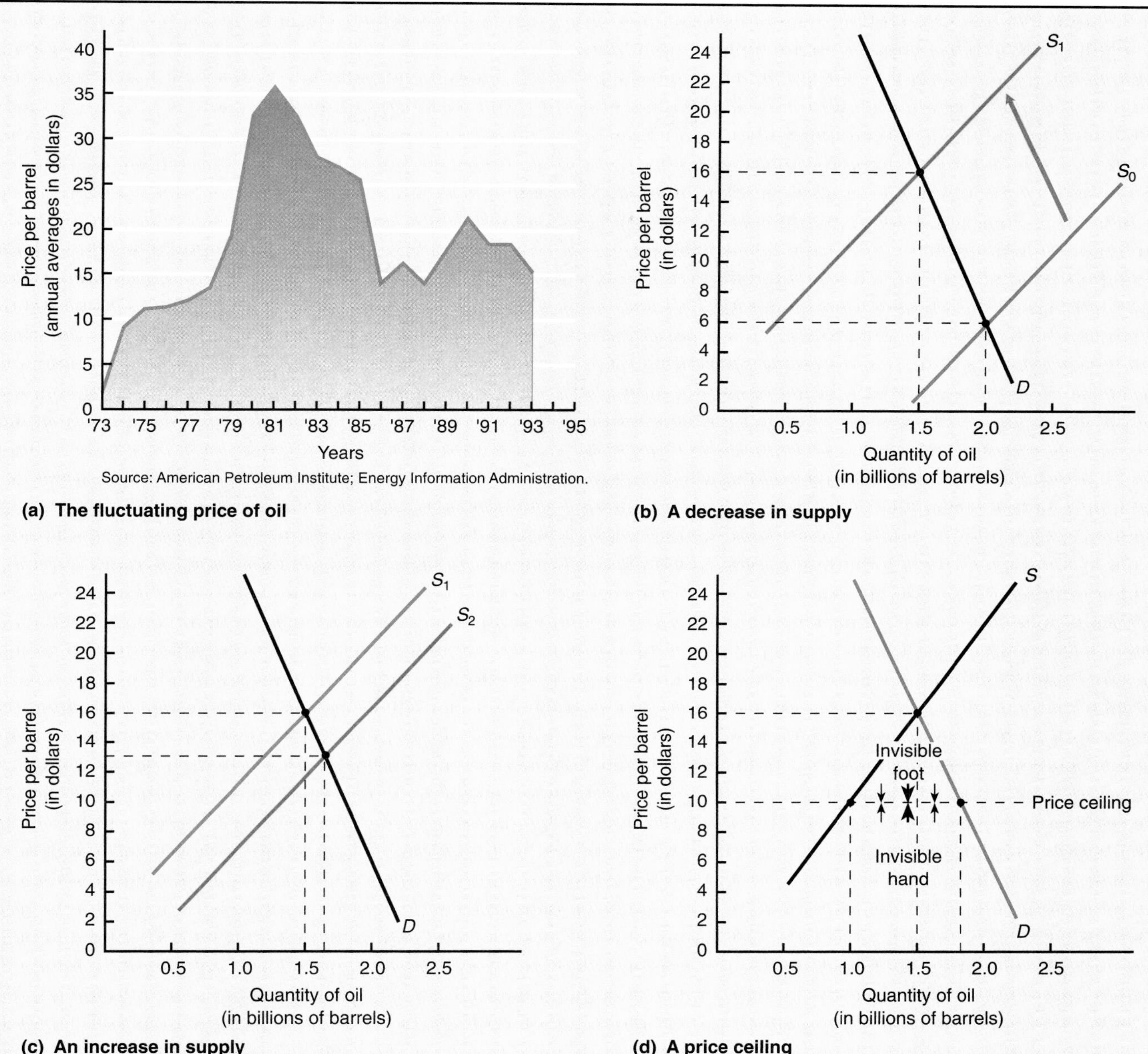

EXHIBIT 12 Supply, Demand, and Changing Oil Prices

More money for less oil: (**a**) Shows the price of oil in the 1970s through 1993. In (**b**), (**c**), and (**d**), we see what happened in supply and demand terms in the period from 1973 to 1988. In the early 1970s, OPEC members decided to limit their supply of oil to 1.5 billion barrels, represented by a shift in curve S_1 in (**b**). Initially, supplying 2 billion barrels of oil at $6 per barrel gave them a revenue of $12 billion, but with restricted supply, the price of oil per barrel rose to $16, giving OPEC members a revenue of $24 billion ($1.5 billion x $16). New exploration shifted the supply curve out, lowering price to $13, as in (**c**).

Graph (**d**) shows the response of a market to a price ceiling such as the one imposed in the 1970s in the United States. In (**d**) the invisible hand is not allowed to operate; quantity demanded exceeds quantity supplied; and the result is shortage. In the 1970s, people lined up to buy limited supplies of gas for their cars.

1970s, its price had been relatively stable. In the early 1970s, at a series of meetings of countries who were members of OPEC (the Organization of Petroleum Exporting Countries), some delegates who had studied economics pointed out how OPEC could get more for less. They argued that if they could somehow all decide to limit oil production (to decrease supply), then even though each of them produced less, actually each would make more money. Exhibit 12 (b) shows why.

The long lines and shortages of the 1974 gas crisis are typical results of a price ceiling.© *George Gardner/The Image Works.*

Initially the quantity supplied was 2 billion barrels and the U.S. dollar price per barrel was \$6. Total OPEC revenue was U.S. \$12 billion (U.S. \$6 × 2 billion). Now say OPEC shifts supply back from S_0 to S_1. The quantity of oil supplied falls to 1.5 billion barrels and the price of oil rises to U.S. \$16 per barrel. Now members' revenue is U.S. \$24 billion (U.S. \$16 × 1.5 billion). In cutting production by 25 percent they double their revenues! Even though each producer is selling less oil, each is earning more income. And that's what OPEC did. The member countries restricted supply, and the price of oil started rising drastically worldwide.

The high price provoked a reaction among a large number of non-OPEC oil suppliers (and from OPEC members who could hide their oil sales from other members). They increased their quantity of oil supplied significantly, causing an upward movement along the original supply curve. At the same time oil exploration boomed, shifting the oil supply curve out to S_2 in Exhibit 12 (c). These new discoveries of oil shifted oil's total supply curve rightward, even as most OPEC countries held their oil back. As supply was responding to higher prices and shortages, so too was quantity demanded. As the price rose, the quantity demanded fell. As people switched to fuel-efficient cars and set the thermostats in their homes lower, there was a resulting movement along the demand curve. By the late 1980s, the invisible hand had effectively broken OPEC's limitation on supply, and price fell to between U.S. \$12 and \$15 a barrel, as shown in Exhibit 12 (c), approximately where it would have been (after adjustment for inflation) had OPEC never organized to limit supply. (Why not use Canadian dollar figures? Many commodities, including oil, are typically priced in world markets in terms of U.S. dollars.)

Price ceiling A government-imposed limit on how high a price can be charged.

Before these adjustments occurred, the sudden jump in oil price caused political reactions both at home and abroad. The invisible foot put downward pressure on the price of oil in North America. It led to **price ceilings** (government-imposed limits on how high a price can be charged). This political pressure prevented the price of oil from rising to the full new supply/demand equilibrium. The result was an oil short-

THE SUPPLY AND DEMAND FOR CHILDREN

A REMINDER

In Chapter 1, we distinguished between an economic force and a market force. Economic forces are operative in all aspects of our lives; market forces are economic forces that are allowed to be expressed through a market. Our examples in this chapter are of market forces—of goods sold in a market—but supply and demand can also be used to analyze situations in which economic, but not market, forces operate. An economist who is adept at this is Gary Becker of the University of Chicago. He has applied supply and demand analysis to a wide range of issues, even the supply of and demand for children.

Becker doesn't argue that children should be bought and sold. But he does argue that economic considerations play a large role in people's decisions on how many children to have. In farming communities, children can be productive early in life; by age six or seven, they can work on a farm. In an advanced industrial community, children provide pleasure, but generally don't contribute productively to family income. Even getting them to help around the house can be difficult.

Becker argues that since the price of having children is lower for a farming society than for an industrial society, farming societies will have more children per family. Quantity of children demanded will be larger. And that's what we find. Developing countries that rely primarily on farming often have three, four, or more children per family. Industrial societies average fewer than two children per family.

age—the quantity of oil demanded was greater than the quantity of oil supplied. There were dire predictions that North Americans would freeze to death or wouldn't be allowed to use energy-intensive products. While there were shortages, Canada was better off than the United States, since by the mid-1960s we were able to supply more than half of our domestic needs—a much higher proportion than the United States was able to supply. In fact, in the United States some people were killed at the gas pumps by frustrated motorists vying for position.

Exhibit 12 (d) shows how such a price ceiling will cause such shortages. The price ceiling is U.S. $10, even though the supply/demand equilibrium price is U.S. $16. Quantity supplied is 1 billion barrels, while quantity demanded is 1.8 billion barrels. The difference between quantity supplied and quantity demanded reflects the number of people going without oil. When the invisible foot or invisible handshake prevents price from rising to the equilibrium price, the invisible hand doesn't disappear. It places upward pressure on price while the invisible foot places downward pressure on price. In this case the invisible hand won out, and the price ceilings were eliminated, allowing the price of oil to rise substantially. The rise in price eliminated the shortages.

9 An effective price ceiling will cause Qd > Qs.

It isn't only price ceilings that have predictable effects. **Price floors** (government-imposed limits on how low a price can be charged) also do. A price floor such as the minimum wage or a government-imposed mandatory price for milk creates a situation of excess supply. The quantity supplied exceeds the quantity demanded, and some way must be found to ration the available quantity demanded among the suppliers. We'll deal with these issues in detail later.

Price floor A government-imposed limit on how low a price may be.

CONCLUSION

Throughout the book, we'll be presenting examples of supply and demand. So we'll end this chapter here because its intended purposes have been served. What were those intended purposes? First, the discussion and examples should have exposed you to enough economic terminology and economic thinking to allow you to proceed to our more complicated examples. Second, the discussion should also have set your mind to work putting the events around you into a supply/demand framework. Doing that will give you new insights into the events that shape all our lives. Finally, this chapter should have made you wary of applying supply/demand analysis to the real world without considering the other invisible forces out there battling the invisible hand.

CHAPTER SUMMARY

- The law of demand (supply): More (less) of a good will be demanded (supplied) the lower its price, other things constant. The demand curve is negatively sloped while the supply curve is positively sloped.
- A market demand (supply) curve is the sum of all individual demand (supply) curves.
- A shift in quantity demanded (supplied) is a movement along the demand (supply) curve. A shift in demand (supply) is a shift of the entire demand (supply) curve.
- The laws of supply and demand refer to relative prices; they hold true because individuals can substitute other goods for the one we're examining.
- When quantity demanded is greater than quantity supplied, there is excess demand and prices tend to rise. When quantity supplied is greater than quantity demanded, there is excess supply and prices tend to fall.
- When quantity supplied equals quantity demanded, prices have no tendency to change. At that price, producers want to sell the same number of units that consumers want to buy.
- When demand shifts right, the equilibrium price rises. When supply shifts right, the equilibrium price falls.

KEY TERMS

demand *(35)*
demand curve *(35)*
equilibrium *(50)*
equilibrium price *(50)*
excess demand *(48)*
excess supply *(48)*
factors of production *(42)*
firms *(42)*
first dynamic law of supply and demand *(48)*
law of demand *(35)*
law of supply *(43)*
market demand curve *(39)*
model *(51)*
movement along the demand curve *(41)*
movement along the supply curve *(47)*
other things constant *(36)*
partial equilibrium analysis *(37)*
price ceiling *(56)*
price floor *(57)*
quantity demanded *(35)*
quantity supplied *(43)*
relative price *(37)*
second dynamic law of supply and demand *(49)*
shift factors of demand *(37)*
shift in demand *(41)*
shift in supply *(47)*
supply *(43)*
third dynamic law of supply and demand *(49)*

QUESTIONS FOR THOUGHT AND REVIEW

The number after each question represents the estimated degree of critical thinking required. (1 = almost none; 10 = deep thought.)

1. Draw a demand curve from the following demand table. *(1)*

Price	Quantity
37	20
47	15
57	10
67	5

2. Draw a market demand curve from the following demand table. *(1)*

P	D_1	D_2	D_3	Market Demand
37	20	4	8	32
47	15	2	7	24
57	10	0	6	16
67	5	0	5	10

3. It has just been reported that eating meat is bad for your health. Using supply and demand curves, demonstrate the report's likely effect on the price and quantity of steak sold in the market. *(3)*
4. Toronto has had residential rent control for many years. Using supply/demand analysis, explain what effect eliminating those controls would probably have. *(4)*
5. Draw a market supply curve from the following supply table. *(1)*

P	S_1	S_2	S_3	Market Supply
37	0	4	14	18
47	0	8	16	24
57	10	12	18	40
67	10	16	20	46

6. Show, using supply and demand curves, the likely effect of a minimum wage law. If you were a worker, would you support or oppose minimum wage laws? Why? *(6)*

7. Distinguish the effect of a shift factor of demand from the effect of a change in price on the demand curve. *(3)*
8. Say Canada were to legalize the sale of certain currently illegal drugs. Using supply/demand analysis, show what effect legalization would have on the price of those drugs and on the quantity bought. *(7)*
9. Mary has just stated that normally, as price rises, supply will increase. Her teacher grimaces. Why? *(5)*
10. Supply/demand analysis states that equilibrium occurs where quantity supplied equals quantity demanded, but in Canadian agricultural markets quantity supplied almost always exceeds quantity demanded. How can this be? *(5)*

PROBLEMS AND EXERCISES

1. You're given the following individual demand tables for comic books.

Price	John	Liz	Alex
$ 2	4	36	24
4	4	32	20
6	0	28	16
8	0	24	12
10	0	20	8
12	0	16	4
14	0	12	0
16	0	8	0

   a. Determine the market demand table.
   b. Graph the individual and market demand curves.
   c. If the current market price is $4, what's total market demand? What happens to total market demand if price rises to $8?
   d. Say that an advertising campaign increases demand by 50 percent. Illustrate graphically what will happen to the individual and market demand curves.
2. Draw hypothetical supply and demand curves for tea. Show how the equilibrium price and quantity will be affected by each of the following occurrences:
   a. Bad weather wreaks havoc with the tea crop.
   b. A medical report implying tea is bad for your health is published.
   c. A technological innovation lowers the cost of producing tea.
   d. Consumers' income falls.
   e. The government imposes a $5 per kilo price ceiling on tea.
   f. The government imposes a $15 per kilo price ceiling on tea.
   g. The government imposes a $15 per kilo price floor on tea.
3. "Scalping" is the name given to the buying of tickets at a low price and reselling them at a high price. Consider the following information: At the beginning of the season:
   a. Tickets sell for $27 and are sold out in pre-season.
   b. Halfway through the season, rival teams have maintained unbeaten records. Resale price of tickets rises to $200.
   c. One week before playing each other, rival teams have remained unbeaten and are ranked 1-2. Ticket price rises to $600.
   d. Three days before the game, price falls to $400.

   Demonstrate, using supply/demand analysis and words, what might have happened to cause these fluctuations in price.
4. In some areas, "scalping" is against the law, although enforcement of these laws is spotty (difficult).
   a. Using supply/demand analysis and words, demonstrate what a weakly enforced anti-scalping law would likely do to the price of tickets in 3*b,* 3*c,* and 3*d.*
   b. Using supply/demand analysis and words, demonstrate what a strongly enforced anti-scalping law would likely do to the price of tickets in 3*b,* 3*c,* and 3*d.*
5. This is a question concerning what economists call "the identification problem." Say you go out and find figures on the quantity bought of various products. You will find something like the following:

Product	Year	Quantity	Average Price
VCRs	1990	100,000	$210
	1991	110,000	220
	1992	125,000	225
	1993	140,000	215
	1994	135,000	215
	1995	160,000	220

   Plot these figures on a graph.
   a. Have you plotted a supply curve, a demand curve, or what?
   b. If we assume that the market for VCRs is competitive, what information would you have to know to determine whether these are points on a supply curve or on a demand curve?
   c. Say you know that the market is one in which suppliers set the price and allow the quantity to vary. Could you then say anything more about the curve you have plotted?
   d. What information about shift factors would you expect to find to make these points reflect the law of demand?
6. Apartments in Vancouver are often hard to find. You believe one of the reasons is that there are rent controls.
   a. Demonstrate graphically how rent controls could make apartments hard to find.
   b. Often one can get an apartment if one makes a side payment to the current tenant. Can you explain why?
   c. What would be the likely effect of eliminating rent controls?

d. What is the political appeal of rent controls?

7. You're a commodity trader and you've just heard a report that the winter wheat harvest will be 2.09 billion bushels, a 44 percent jump, rather than an expected 35 percent jump to 1.96 billion bushels.
   a. What would you expect would happen to wheat prices?
   b. Demonstrate graphically the effect you suggested in *a.*
8. Mushrooms grow best in carbon-rich soil. The years immediately following a forest fire provide ideal growing conditions for mushrooms. Nowadays wild mushrooms are in demand, which has led to the development of the mushroom-picking profession (individuals travel around to various woods and forests to pick mushrooms).
   Mushroom-pickers often complain that they face a catch-22. Whenever the picking is easy, the prices are low, and whenever the pickings are slim, the prices are high. Can you explain, using supply and demand analysis, why they face this catch-22 situation?
9. Consider the example of ticket scalpers in Montreal presented in the text. Explain why the scalpers didn't lower price until well into the third period (and then what's the point of going to the game?). Use the concept of historical time and path-dependency in your answer.
10. In Canada, gasoline costs much less than it does in Italy. What effect is the price differential likely to have on:
    a. The size of cars in Canada and in Italy?
    b. The use of public transportation in Canada and in Italy?
    c. The fuel efficiency of cars in Canada and in Italy?

CHAPTER 3

The Economic Organization of Society

In capitalism man exploits man;
in socialism it's the other way 'round.
~Abba Lerner

After reading this chapter, you should be able to:

1. List three central questions that every economy must answer.
2. Define capitalism and socialism.
3. Explain how capitalist and socialist economies answer the three central economic questions.
4. Give a brief overview of the history of economic systems: how feudalism begat mercantilism which begat capitalism, and how capitalism and socialism continue to evolve.
5. Explain how markets coordinate economic decisions.
6. Explain what is meant by the phrase "Socialism is the longest path from capitalism to capitalism."

The scene is the People's Court in Bucharest, Romania, December 25, 1989. The newly deposed dictator of Romania, Nicolae Ceausescu, and his wife, Elena, are on trial for crimes against the state.

Judge: *What have you done for society?*

Nicolae Ceausescu: *I built hospitals.*

Judge: *What about the food shortage?*

Nicolae Ceausescu: *The people have 440 pounds of corn a year.*

Judge: *You destroyed the Romanian people and their economy.*

Elena Ceausescu: *I gave my entire life for our people.*

Judge: *We condemn the two of you to death.*

On that same day, Elena and Nicolae Ceausescu were executed by a firing squad for economic crimes against the Romanian people.

The political and economic turmoil in the formerly socialist countries have been much in the news in the early 1990s. And with good reason. The Soviet Union is no more; most republics of the former Soviet Union have forsaken socialism and are struggling to introduce a market economy. These events involve some of the most far-reaching changes in the nature of economic systems that the world has seen since the 1930s—changes so major that some social scientists have called the developments "the end of history." Such a sweeping statement is more than a tad too strong, but the developments are certainly important. What's more, they provide us with a good vehicle to introduce some broader issues involving economic systems and the workings of markets.

ECONOMIC SYSTEMS: CAPITALISM AND SOCIALISM

Economic system The set of economic institutions that determine a country's important economic decisions.

In Chapter 1, we discussed how an **economic system** (the set of economic institutions that determine a country's important economic decisions) works via the interaction of three invisible forces: the invisible hand (economic forces), invisible foot (political forces), and invisible handshake (social forces).

An economic system is closely tied to a political system through which people decide what their society desires. In a democracy, voting procedures determine society's will. In an autocracy, a ruling individual or group of individuals decides what society's desires are. Besides determining what a society wants, an economic system must see that individuals' decisions about what they do are coordinated with what society wants, and with what other individuals do. Coordination is necessary so that the commodities that the market wants match the commodities that are available.

1 Three central questions that economy must answer:
1. *What* to produce.
2. *How* to produce it.
3. *For whom* to produce it.

Before we discuss how the invisible forces operate, we need to consider what people can reasonably expect from an economic system. They can expect it to produce the goods that people want in a reasonably efficient way and to distribute those goods reasonably fairly. Put another way, people can reasonably expect that an economic system will decide:

1. *What* to produce.
2. *How* to produce it.
3. *For whom* to produce it.

These three decisions that an economic system must make are necessarily vague because what people expect is vague. But when people feel that an economic system hasn't given them what they want, the result isn't always so vague—as the Ceausescus found out.

Planning, Politics, and Markets

In making their three decisions, societies have a problem. Usually what individuals, on their own, want to do isn't consistent with what "society" wants them to do. Society would often like people to consider what's good for society, and to fit what's good for themselves into what society wants them to do. For example, say society has garbage, and society determines that your neighbourhood is the best place to set up a garbage dump. Even if you agree a garbage dump is needed, you probably won't want it in your neighbourhood. This **NIMBY** (**N**ot **I**n **M**y **B**ack **Y**ard) attitude has become familiar in the 1990s.

NIMBY A short way to express "Not In My Back Yard" when a community objects to a proposed development in its neighbourhood.

Another area in which individual goals and social goals come into conflict is in producing and consuming goods. Individuals generally like to consume much more than they like to produce, so society has the problem of scarcity. It must provide incentives for people to produce more and consume less. It's a sure sign that an economic system isn't working when there are important things that need to be done, but many people are sitting around doing nothing because the system doesn't provide individuals with the incentive to do that work.

How hard is it to make the three decisions we've listed? Imagine for a moment the problem of living in a family: the fights, arguments, and questions that come up. "Do I have to do the dishes?" "Why can't I have piano lessons?" "Bobby got a new jacket. How come I didn't?" "Mom likes you best." Now multiply the size of the family by millions. The same fights, the same arguments, the same questions—only for society the problems are millions of times more complicated than for one family.

How do you solve these complicated coordination problems? Do you create an organization to tell people what to do and when to do it? Or do you let people do what they want, subject to a set of rules? The two main economic systems the world has used in the past 50 years—capitalism and socialism—answer these questions differently.

Capitalism

Capitalism is an economic system based upon private property and the market in which, in principle, individuals decide how, what, and for whom to produce. Under capitalism, individuals are encouraged to follow their own self-interest, while market forces of supply and demand are relied upon to coordinate economic activity. Distribution is to each individual according to his or her ability, effort, and inherited property.

2A Capitalism is an economic system based on private property and the market. It gives private property rights to individuals, and relies on market forces to coordinate economic activity.

Reliance upon market forces doesn't mean that political, social, and historical forces play no role in coordinating economic decisions, because the other forces influence how the market works. For a market to exist, **private property rights** (in which control over an asset or a right is given to a private individual or firm) must be allocated and defended by government. The concept of private ownership must exist and must be accepted by individuals in society. When you say, "This car is mine," it means that it is unlawful for someone else to take it. If someone takes it without your permission, he or she is subject to punishment through the legal system. Private property rights include intellectual property too—when you come up with the design for the proverbial "new and improved mousetrap," that's your intellectual property. When a television entertainer switches networks, that may be a result of a willingness to pay more for her talent—her intellectual property.

Private property rights Control of an asset or a right given to an individual or a firm.

Markets work through a system of rewards and payments. If you do something, you get paid for doing that something; if you get something, you pay for that something. How much you get is determined by how much you give. This relationship seems fair to most people. But there are instances when it doesn't seem fair. Say someone is unable to work. Should that person not get anything? How about Joe down the street who was given $10 million by his parents? Is it fair that he gets lots of toys like Corvettes and skiing trips to Whistler, and doesn't have to work, while the rest of us have to work 40 hours a week and maybe go to school at night?

We'll consider those questions about fairness in a later chapter. For now, all we want to present is the underlying concept of fairness that capitalism embodies: "Them that works, gets; them that don't, starve."[1] In capitalism, individuals are encouraged to follow their own self-interest.

[1]How come the professors get to use rotten grammar but scream when they see rotten grammar in your papers? Well, that's fairness for you. Actually, we should say a bit more about writing style. All writers are expected to know correct grammar; if they don't, they don't deserve to be called writers. Once one knows grammar, one can individualize his or her writing style, breaking the rules of grammar where the metre and flow of the writing require it. Right now you're still proving that you know grammar so, in papers handed in to your teacher, you shouldn't break the rules of grammar until you've proven to the teacher that you know them. We've written a large number of books and journal articles, so our editors give us a bit more leeway than your teachers will give you.

In capitalist economies, individuals are free to do whatever they want as long as it's legal. The market is relied upon to see that what people want to get, and want to do, is consistent with what's available. If there's not enough of something to go around (if there's excess demand), its price goes up; if more of something needs to get done, the price given to individuals willing to do it goes up. If something isn't wanted or doesn't need to be done (if there's excess supply), its price goes down. Under capitalism, fluctuations in prices coordinate individuals' wants.

Chapters 1 and 2 told how the market works. By almost all accounts, capitalism has been an extraordinarily successful economic system. Since much of this book will be devoted to explaining capitalist economies' success, and since capitalism is probably somewhat familiar to you already (to take the course you had to pay a price determined by your institution—your tuition—giving you direct experience with capitalism), let's discuss socialism first.

Socialism in Theory

2B Socialism is an economic system that tries to organize society in the same way as do most families—all people should contribute what they can, and get what they need.

In theory, socialism is an economic system based upon individuals' good will toward others, not their own self-interests.

You can best understand the idea behind theoretical socialism by thinking about how decisions are made in a family. In most families, decisions about who gets what are determined by usually benevolent parents. When Sabin gets a new coat and his sister Sally doesn't, it's because Sabin needs a coat while Sally already has two coats that fit her and are in good condition. Victor may be slow as molasses, but from his family he still gets as much as his superefficient brother Jerry. In fact, Victor may get more than Jerry because he needs extra help.

Markets have little role in most families. In our families, when food is placed on the table we don't bid on what we want, with the highest bidder getting the food. In our families every person can eat all he or she wants, although if one child eats more than a fair share, that child gets a lecture on the importance of sharing—of seeing to it that everyone has already had a fair share before you take or even ask for seconds. "Be thoughtful; be considerate; and think of others first," are among the lessons that many families try to teach.

Socialism Economic system that tries to organize society in such a way that all people contribute what they can and get what they need, adjusting their own wants in accordance with what's available.

In theory, **socialism** is an economic system that tries to organize society in the same way as these families. Socialism tries to see that individuals get what they need. Socialism tries to get individuals to take other people's needs into account and to adjust their own wants in accordance with what's available. A capitalist economy expects people to be selfish; it relies on markets and competition to direct that selfishness to the general good. In socialist economies, individuals are urged to look out for the other person; if individuals' inherent goodness won't make them consider the general good, government will make them.[2]

Socialism in Practice

In practice, socialism became an economic system based on government ownership of the means of production, with economic activity governed by central planning. Because it is based on a system developed in the former Soviet Union, this is often called Soviet-style socialism.

In the 1980s, a number of countries had Soviet-style socialist economies. In the late 1980s and early 1990s, many of those countries were in turmoil. Total output in the economies had fallen significantly, and their economic and political systems were in chaos. Many of the countries undergoing major changes are shown in Exhibit 1. Why did these countries reject the economic system they had followed for almost 50 years (and almost 75 years in the former Soviet Union)? Some economists argue that Soviet-style socialism self-destructed because socialism did not offer acceptable answers to the questions an economic system must address. They claim socialism didn't provide individuals with incentives to produce enough. Soon, they say, the

[2]As you probably surmised, the above distinction is too sharp. Even in capitalist societies, one wants people to be selfless, but not too selfless. Children in capitalist societies are generally taught to be selfless, at least in dealing with friends and family. The difficulties parents and societies face is finding a midpoint between the two positions: selfless but not too selfless; selfish but not too selfish.

EXHIBIT 1 Socialist Countries in Transition

This map shows the most important formerly traditional socialist economies that are now going through major transitions. China and the former USSR were the largest socialist economies, although there were a number of socialist countries in Eastern Europe, Africa, and Asia.
Source: *CIA World Fact Book.*

world will have only one economic system: capitalism. Other economists argue that the Soviet-style socialism was not socialism at all—that, early on, Soviet-style socialism deviated from the socialistic path. True socialism was not rejected, these economists argue, because true socialism was never tried.

Defining Soviet-style socialism precisely is difficult because it embodies both political and economic features. We will concentrate on the economic features. Specifically, **Soviet-style socialism** uses administrative control or central planning to answer the questions *what, how,* and *for whom.* In a Soviet-style socialist economic system, government planning boards set society's goals and then give individuals directives as to how to achieve those goals.

Soviet-style socialism Economic system that uses central planning and government ownership of the means of production to answer the questions: what, how, and for whom.

Let's now discuss how a Soviet-style socialist country and a capitalist country might make different decisions about the what, how, and for whom questions. Let's consider two goods: designer jeans and whole-wheat bread. Compared to their cost in the formerly socialist countries, in most capitalist societies designer jeans are relatively inexpensive while whole-wheat bread is relatively expensive. Why? One reason is that central planners decide that designer jeans are frivolous luxury items, so they produce few or none and charge a high price for what they do produce. Similarly, they decide that whole-wheat bread is good for people, so they produce large quantities and price it exceptionally low. Planners, not supply and demand, determine what, how, and for whom to produce.

To accomplish planners' ends—getting people to do what planners think is best—requires stronger government control than exists in capitalist countries. To maintain

EXHIBIT 2 Capitalism's and Socialism's Answers to the Three Economic Questions

Central economic question	Capitalism's answer	Soviet-Style socialism's answer
What to produce?	What firms believe people want and will make the firm a profit.	What central planners believe is socially beneficial.
How to produce?	Businesspeople decide how to produce efficiently, guided by their desire to make a profit.	Central planners decide, guided by what they believe is good for the country (ideally).
For whom to produce?	Distribution according to ability and inherited wealth.	Distribution according to individuals' need (as determined by central planners).

3A Capitalism's answers to the central economic questions:

1. What to produce: what businesses believe people want, and is profitable.
2. How to produce: businesses decide how to produce efficiently, guided by their desire to make a profit.
3. For whom to produce: distribution according to individuals' ability and/or inherited wealth.

that control, government generally owns the means of production, such as factories and machines, and tells people where they will work and how much they will receive. In Soviet-style socialism, individuals' choices are limited and planners' choices, not individuals' choices, determine the answers to the central economic questions.

In summary, the three principal components of a Soviet-style socialist economy compared to a capitalist economy are:

3B Soviet-style socialism's answers to the three questions:

1. What to produce: what central planners believe is socially beneficial.
2. How to produce: central planners decide, based on what they think is good for the country.
3. For whom to produce: central planners distribute goods based on what they determine are individuals' needs.

1. Government ownership of the means of production, rather than private ownership as in capitalism. Central planners, rather than owners of businesses, decide what to produce.
2. Directed labour. A government planning board directs where workers will work and how much they will be paid, rather than workers making individual choices of employment based on wage levels in different jobs, as in capitalism.
3. Government-determined prices. Usually, high prices are charged for luxury goods and low prices for necessities, rather than market-determined prices as in capitalism.

There are, of course, markets in Soviet-style socialist economies. Just as in capitalist economies, individuals buy goods by going to the store. The difference between stores in the two kinds of economies is that, in a Soviet-style socialist economy, the government tells the storekeeper what goods will be offered, what price to charge, and how much of a good will be delivered to the store, while in a capitalist society, the storeowner can order as much of any good as he or she wants and can charge any price he or she wants—whatever the market will bear.

Differences between Soviet-Style Socialism and Capitalism

The difference between Soviet-style socialist economies and capitalist economies is not that Soviet-style socialist economies are planned economies and capitalist economies are unplanned. Both economies involve planning. **Planning** simply involves deciding—before the production takes place—what will be produced, how to produce it, and for whom it will be produced. The differences are in who does the planning, what they try to do in planning, and how the plans are coordinated.

Planning Deciding, before the production takes place, what will be produced, how to produce it, and for whom to produce it.

In capitalist countries, businesspeople do the planning. Businesspeople decide that they can sell designer jeans, Nintendo games, or economics textbooks. They target their likely customers and decide how much to produce and what price to charge. In Soviet-style socialist countries, government planners decide what people need and should have.

In an idealized capitalist society, businesses design their plans to maximize their profit; the market is relied upon to see that individual self-interest is consistent with society's interest. In an idealized socialist society, the government designs its plans to make society better.

In a capitalist economy, coordination of plans is left to the workings of the market. In a Soviet-style socialist economy, coordination is done by government planners.

Exhibit 2 summarizes how capitalism and Soviet-style socialism answer the three central economic questions: how, what, and for whom.

Soviet people happily tear down a statue of Lenin, which they saw as a symbol of Soviet-style socialism. Reuters/Bettmann.

Evolving Economic Systems

Capitalism and socialism have not existed forever. Capitalism came into existence in the mid-1700s; socialism came into existence in the early 1900s.

Both capitalism and socialism have changed over the years, and a look at their evolution will give us a good sense of the struggle among the invisible forces to dominate our lives. In the 1930s, during the Great Depression, capitalist countries integrated a number of what might be called *socialist institutions* with their existing institutions. Distribution was no longer, even in theory, only according to ability; need also played a role. Government's economic role in capitalist societies increased, and some of the how, what, and for whom decisions were transferred from the market to the government. For example, most capitalist nations established a welfare system and a social security system, providing an economic safety net for people whose incomes were inadequate for their needs.

The 1980s saw the reverse process take place, with socialism integrating some capitalist institutions with its existing institutions. Market sectors in socialist countries expanded, government's economic importance decreased, and some how, what, and for whom decisions were transferred from government to the market. Instead of being assigned jobs by the government, workers were often allowed to choose jobs themselves, and some firms were allowed to produce independently of planners' decisions. Even in cases where production decisions weren't transferred, socialist planning boards used market principles more and more in making their decisions.

The result has been a blending of economic systems and a blurring of the distinctions between capitalism and socialism. If the trend toward the use of market mechanisms in socialist countries continues, in the 21st century there may be only one general type of economic structure. It won't be pure socialism and it won't be pure capitalism. It will be a blend of the two.

For students of history, the recent changes in economic systems are not surprising. Economic systems are in a continual state of evolution. To understand recent movements in socialist countries and to put market institutions in perspective, in the next section we briefly consider the history and nature of economic systems.

THE HISTORY OF ECONOMIC SYSTEMS

4A Economic systems evolve because the institutions of the new system offer a better life for at least some—and usually a large majority—of the individuals in a society.

Remember the distinction between market and economic forces: Economic forces have always existed—they operate in all aspects of our lives; but market forces have not always existed. Markets are social creations societies use to coordinate individuals' actions. Markets developed, sometimes spontaneously, sometimes by design, because they offered a better life for at least some—and usually a large majority of—individuals in a society.

To understand why markets developed, it is helpful to look briefly at the history of the economic systems from which our own system descended.

Feudal Society: Rule of the Invisible Handshake

Let's go back in time to the year 1000, when Europe had no nation-states as we now know them. There was no coordinated central government, no unified system of law, no national patriotism, no national defense, although there was a strong religious institution simply called the Church that fulfilled some of these roles. There were few towns; most individuals lived in walled manors or "estates." These manors "belonged to" the "lord of the manor."[3] We say "belonged to" rather than "were owned by" because most of the empires or federations at that time were not formal nation-states that could organize, administer, and regulate ownership. There were no documents or deeds giving ownership of the land to an individual. Instead there was tradition, and in normal times nobody questioned the lord's right to the land. The land "belonged to" the lord because the land "belonged to" him—that's the way it was.

Because there was no central nation-state, the manor served many functions a nation-state would have served had it existed. The lord provided protection, often within a walled area surrounding the manor house or, if the manor was large enough, a castle. He provided administration and decided disputes. He also decided *what* would be done, *how* it would be done, and *who* would get what, but these decisions were limited. In the same way that the land belonged to the lord because that's the way it always had been, what people did and how they did it were determined by what they always had done. Tradition ruled the manor more than the lord did.

The Life of a Serf Individuals living on the land were called *serfs*. What serfs did was determined by what their fathers had done. If the father was a farmer, the son was a farmer. A woman followed her husband and helped him do what he did. That was the way it always had been and that's the way it was—tradition again.

Most serfs were farmers, and surrounding the manor were fields of about a half acre each. Serfs were tied by tradition to their assigned plots of land; according to tradition, they could not leave those plots and had to turn over a portion of their harvest to the lord every year. How much they had to turn over varied from manor to manor, but payments of half the total harvest were not unheard of. In return, the lord provided defense and organized the life of the manor—boring as it was. Thus, there was a type of trade between the serf and the lord, but it was nonnegotiable and did not take place through a market.

Feudalism Political system divided into small communities in which a few powerful people protect those who are loyal to them.

Problems of a Tradition-Based Society This system, known as **feudalism,** developed about the 8th and 9th centuries and lasted until about the 15th century, though in isolated countries such as Russia it continued well into the 19th century, and in all European countries its influence lingered for hundreds of years (as late as about 140 years ago in some parts of Germany). Such a long-lived system must have done some things right, and feudalism did: it answered the what, how, and for whom questions in an acceptable way.

But a tradition-based society has problems. In a traditional society, because someone's father was a baker, the son must also be a baker, and because a woman was a homemaker, she wouldn't be allowed to be anything but a homemaker. But what if Joe Blacksmith, Jr., the son of Joe Blacksmith, Sr., is a lousy blacksmith and longs to knead dough, while Joe Baker, Jr., would be a superb blacksmith but hates making pastry? Tough. Tradition dictated who did what. In fact, tradition probably arranged

[3]Occasionally the "lord" was a lady, but not often.

ADDED DIMENSION

MILESTONES IN ECONOMICS

6700 B.C.	First known coins (Iran).
3600 B.C.	First system of taxation (Mesopotamia).
2100 B.C.	First welfare system (Egypt).
2000 B.C.	Coins in general use.
2000 B.C.–500 A.D.	International trade flourishes.
100 B.C.	First corporation (Rome).
105 A.D.	Chinese invent paper (a cheap substance to replace parchment).
301 A.D.	First wage and price controls (Emperor Diocletian of Rome).
700–1400	Development of feudal estates.
1275	Development of tariffs in England.
1400–1800	End of feudal estates and development of private property and wage workers.
1600–1800	Mercantilism and state control of economic activity.
1700s	Development of paper money (France).
1750–1900	Industrial Revolution.
1760–1800	Enclosure movement in England, solidifying private property and market economy.
1776	Publication of Adam Smith's *Wealth of Nations.*
1860–1960	Development of social security and unemployment insurance (Germany).
1867	Publication of Karl Marx's *Das Kapital.*
1935–1970	Integration of socialist institutions into capitalism.
1988 onward	Socialist economies in upheaval adopt markets and capitalist institutions.

things so that we will never know whether Joe Blacksmith, Jr., would have made a superb baker.

As long as a society doesn't change too much, tradition operates reasonably well, although not especially efficiently, in holding the society together. However, when a society must undergo change, tradition does not work. Change means that the things that were done before no longer need to be done, while new things do need to get done. But if no one has traditionally done these new things, then they don't get done. If the change is important but a society can't figure out some way for the new things to get done, the society falls apart. That's what happened to feudal society. It didn't change when change was required.

Some individuals in feudal society just couldn't take life on the manor, and they set off on their own. Because there was no organized police force, they were unlikely to be caught and forced to return to the manor. Going hungry, being killed, or both, however, were frequent fates of an escaped serf. One place to which serfs could safely escape, though, was a town or city—the remains of what in Roman times had been thriving and active cities. These cities, which had been decimated by plagues, plundering bands, and starvation in the preceding centuries, nevertheless remained an escape hatch for runaway serfs because they relied far less on tradition than did manors. City dwellers had to live by their wits; many became merchants who lived predominantly by trading. They were middlemen; they would buy from one group and sell to another.

Trading in towns was an alternative to the traditional feudal order because trading allowed people to have an income independent of the traditional social structure. Markets broke down tradition. Initially merchants traded using barter (exchange of one kind of good for another): silk and spices from the Orient for wheat, flour, and artisan products in Europe. But soon a generalized purchasing power (money) developed as a medium of exchange. Money greatly expanded the possibilities of trading because its use meant that goods no longer needed to be bartered. They could be sold for money, which could then be spent to buy other goods.

4B Feudalism evolved into mercantilism because markets and the development of money allowed trade to expand, which undermined the traditional base of feudalism. Tradition that can be bought and sold is no longer tradition—it's just another commodity.

In the beginning, land was not one of the goods that could be traded, but soon the feudal lord who just had to have a silk robe but had no money was saying, "Why not?

I'll sell you a small piece of land so I can buy a shipment of silk." Once land became tradeable, the traditional base of the feudal society was undermined. Tradition that can be bought and sold is no longer tradition—it's just another commodity.

From Feudalism to Mercantilism

Toward the end of the Middle Ages, markets went from being a sideshow, a fair that spiced up peoples' lives, to being the main event. Over time, some traders and merchants started to amass fortunes that dwarfed those of the feudal lords. Rich traders settled down; existing towns and cities expanded and new towns were formed. As towns grew and as fortunes shifted from feudal lords to merchants, power in society shifted to the towns. And with that shift came a change in society's political and economic structure.

As these traders became stronger politically and economically, they threw their support behind a king (the strongest lord) in the hope that the king would expand their ability to trade. In doing so, they made the king even stronger. Eventually, the king became so powerful that his will prevailed over the will of the other lords and even over the will of the Church. As the king consolidated his power, nation-states as we know them today evolved. *The invisible foot—government—became an active influence on economic decision making.*

Mercantilism Economic system in which government doles out the rights to undertake economic activities.

As markets grew, feudalism evolved into **mercantilism** (an economic system in which the government determines the what, how, and for whom decisions by doling out the rights to undertake certain economic activities). Political rather than social forces came to control the central economic decisions.

The evolution of feudal systems into mercantilism occurred in somewhat this way: As cities and their markets grew in size and power relative to the feudal manors and the traditional economy, a whole new variety of possible economic activities developed. It was only natural that individuals began to look to a king to establish a new tradition that would determine who would do what. Individuals in particular occupations organized into groups called *guilds,* which were similar to strong labour unions today. These guilds, many of which had financed and supported the king, now expected the king and his government to protect their interests.

As new economic activities, such as trading companies, developed, individuals involved in these activities similarly depended on the king for the right to trade and for help in financing and organizing their activities. For example, in 1492, when Christopher Columbus had the wild idea that by sailing west he could get to the East Indies and trade for their riches, he went to Spain's Queen Isabella and King Ferdinand for financial support.

Since many traders had played and continued to play important roles in financing, establishing, and supporting the king, the king was usually happy to protect their interests. The government doled out the rights to undertake a variety of economic activities. By the late 1400s, Western Europe had evolved from a feudal to a mercantilist economy.

The mercantilist period was marked by the increased role of government, which could be classified in two ways: by the way it encouraged growth, and by the way it limited growth. Government legitimized and financed a variety of activities, thus encouraging growth. But government also limited economic activity in order to protect the monopolies of those it favoured, thus limiting growth. So mercantilism allowed the market to operate, but it kept the market under its control. The market was not allowed to respond freely to the laws of supply and demand.

From Mercantilism to Capitalism

The mercantilist period saw major growth in Western Europe, but mercantilism also unleashed new tensions within society. Like feudalism, mercantilism limited entry into economic activities. It used a different form of limitation—the invisible foot (politics) rather than the invisible handshake (social and cultural tradition)—but individuals who were excluded still felt unfairly treated.

Capitalists Businesspeople who have acquired large amounts of money and use it to invest in businesses.

The most significant source of tension was the different roles played by craft guilds and owners of new businesses, who were called **capitalists** or industrialists. Craft guild members were artists in their own crafts: pottery, shoemaking, and the like.

TRADITION AND TODAY'S ECONOMY

ADDED DIMENSION

In a tradition-based society, the invisible handshake (the social and cultural forces embodied in history) gives a society inertia (a tendency to resist change) which predominates over economic and political forces.

"Why did you do it that way?"
"Because that's the way we've always done it."

Tradition-based societies had markets, but those were peripheral, not central, to economic life. In feudal times what was produced, how it was produced, and for whom it was produced were primarily decided by tradition.

In today's economy, the market plays the central role in economic decisions. But that doesn't mean that tradition is dead. As we said in Chapter 1, tradition still plays a significant role in today's society, and, in many aspects of society, tradition still overwhelms the invisible hand. Consider the following:

1. The persistent view that women should be homemakers rather than factory workers, consumers rather than producers.
2. The raised eyebrows when a man is introduced as a nurse, secretary, homemaker, or member of any other profession conventionally identified as *women's work.*
3. Society's unwillingness to permit the sale of individuals or body organs.
4. Parents' willingness to care for their children without financial compensation.

Each of these tendencies reflects tradition's influence in Western society. Some are so deep-rooted that we see them as self-evident. Some of tradition's effects we like; others we don't—but we often take them for granted. Economic forces may work against these traditions, but the fact that they're still around indicates the continued strength of tradition in our market economy.

New business owners destroyed the art of production by devising machines to replace hand production. Machines produced goods cheaper and faster than craftsmen.[4] The result was an increase in supply and a downward pressure on the price, which was set by government. Craftsmen didn't want to be replaced by machines. They argued that machine-manufactured goods didn't have the same quality as hand-crafted goods, and that the new machines would disrupt the economic and social life of the community.

4C Mercantilism evolved into capitalism because the Industrial Revolution undermined the craft-guided mercantilist method of production. Machines produced goods cheaper and faster, making industrialists rich. They used their economic power to change the political support for mercantilism.

Industrialists were the outsiders with a vested interest in changing the existing system. They wanted the freedom to conduct business as they saw fit. Because of the enormous cost advantage of manufactured goods over crafted goods, a few industrialists overcame government opposition and succeeded within the mercantilist system. They earned their fortunes and became an independent political power.

Once again the economic power base shifted, and two groups competed with each other for power—this time, the guilds and the industrialists. The government had to decide whether to support the industrialists (who wanted government to loosen its power over the country's economic affairs) or the craftsmen and guilds (who argued for strong government limitations and for maintaining traditional values of workmanship). This struggle raged in the 1700s and 1800s. But during this time, governments themselves were changing. This was the Age of Revolutions, and the kings' powers were being limited by democratic reform movements—revolutions supported and financed in large part by the industrialists.

The Need for Coordination in an Economy One argument craftsmen put forward was that coordination of the economy was necessary, and the government had to be involved. If government wasn't going to coordinate economic activity, who would? To answer that question, a British moral philosopher named Adam Smith developed, in his famous book *The Wealth of Nations* (1776), the concept of the invisible hand, and used it to explain how markets could coordinate the economy without the active involvement of government. Smith wrote:

> Man has almost constant occasion for the help of his brethren, and it is in vain for him to expect it from their benevolence only. He will be more likely to prevail, if he can interest their self-love in his favour, and show them that it is for their own advantage to do for him what he requires of them. Whoever offers to another a bargain of any kind proposes

5 Markets coordinate economic activity by turning self-interest into social good. Competition directs individuals pursuing profit to do what society needs to have done.

[4]Throughout this section we use *men* to emphasize that these societies were strongly male-dominated. There were almost no businesswomen. In fact, a woman had to turn over her property to a man upon her marriage, and the marriage contract was written as if she were owned by her husband!

ADDED DIMENSION

THE RISE OF MARKETS IN PERSPECTIVE

Back in the Middle Ages, markets developed spontaneously. "You have something I want; I have something you want. Let's trade" is a basic human attitude we see in all aspects of life. Even children quickly get into trading: chocolate ice cream for vanilla, two action figures for a ride on a motor scooter. Markets institutionalize such trading by providing a place where people know they can go to trade. New markets are continually coming into existence. Today there are markets for baseball cards, pork bellies (which become bacon and pork chops), rare coins, and so on.

Throughout history, societies have tried to prevent some markets from operating because they feel those markets are ethically wrong or have undesirable side effects. Societies have the power to prevent markets. They make some kinds of markets illegal. In Canada, the addictive drug market, the baby market, and the sex market, to name a few, are illegal. In socialist countries, markets in a much wider range of goods (such as clothes, cars, and soft drinks) and activities (such as private business for individual profit) have been illegal.

But, even if a society prevents the market from operating, it cannot escape the dynamic laws of supply and demand. If there's excess supply, there will be downward pressure on prices; if there's excess demand, there will be upward pressure on prices. To maintain an equilibrium in which the quantity supplied does not equal the quantity demanded, a society needs a force to prevent the invisible hand from working. In the Middle Ages, that strong force was religion. The Church told people that if they got too far into the market mentality—if they followed their self-interest—they'd go to Hell.

Until recently in socialist society, the state has provided the preventive force. In their educational system, socialist countries would emphasize a more communal set of values. They taught students that a member of socialist society does not try to take advantage of other human beings but, rather, lives by the philosophy "From each according to his ability; to each according to his need."

For whatever reason—some say because true socialism wasn't really tried; others say because people's self-interest is too strong—the "from each according to his ability; to each according to his need" approach didn't work in socialist countries. They have switched (some say succumbed) to greater reliance on the market.

> to do this. Give me that which I want, and you shall have that which you want, is the meaning of every such offer; and it is in this manner that we obtain from one another the far greater part of those good offices which we stand in need of. It is not from the benevolence of the butcher, the brewer, or the baker, that we expect our dinner, but from their regard to their own interest. We address ourselves, not to their humanity but to their self-love, and never talk to them of our own necessities but of their advantages.

Smith argued that the market's invisible hand would guide suppliers' actions toward the general good. No government coordination was necessary.

Laissez-faire Economic policy of leaving coordination of individuals' wants to be controlled by the market.

With the help of economists such as Adam Smith, the industrialists' view won out. Government pulled back from its role in guiding the economy and adopted a **laissez-faire** policy, leaving coordination of the economy to the invisible hand. (*Laissez faire,* a French term, means "Let events take their course; leave things alone.")

Industrial Revolution Period (1750–1900) during which technology and machines rapidly modernized industrial production.

The Industrial Revolution The invisible hand worked; capitalism thrived. During the **Industrial Revolution,** which began about 1750 and continued through the late 1800s, machine production increased enormously, almost totally replacing hand production. The economy grew faster than ever before. Society was forever transformed. New inventions changed all aspects of life. James Watt's steam engine (1769) made manufacturing and travel easier. Eli Whitney's cotton gin (1793) changed the way cotton was processed. James Kay's flying shuttle (1733),[5] James Hargreaves's spinning jenny (1765), and Richard Arkwright's power loom (1769), combined with the steam engine, changed the way cloth was processed and the clothes people wore.

The need to mine vast amounts of coal to provide power to run the machines changed the economic and physical landscapes. The repeating rifle changed the nature of warfare. Modern economic institutions replaced guilds. Stock markets, insurance companies, and corporations all became important. Trading was no longer financed by

[5]The invention of the flying shuttle frustrated the textile industry because it enabled workers to weave so much cloth that the spinners of thread from which the cloth was woven couldn't keep up. This challenge to the textile industry was met by offering a prize to anyone who could invent something to increase the thread spinners' productivity. The prize was won when the spinning jenny was invented.

THE ROLE OF ECONOMISTS IN ECONOMIC TRANSITIONS

ADDED DIMENSION 

For economics to be relevant, it must have something to say about social policy. Good economists try to be objective and recommend policies that they believe would be good for society in general rather than for any particular group in society.

Deciding what is in society's interest isn't always easy. For economists, it requires interpreting what society wants and comparing different policies, using what economists believe is society's preference. That often means proposing policies that will help some people but hurt others.

Adam Smith's "invisible hand" argument for the free working of the market and against government intervention is a good example. Smith favoured a laissez-faire policy, meaning the government should not interfere with the operation of the economy. In this argument, Smith and other Classical economists found themselves aligned with the industrialists or manufacturers, who wanted the right to enter into markets as they saw fit, and against the guilds and independent artisans, who wanted government to control who did what.

These two groups each had different reasons for supporting laissez-faire policy, however. Industrialists supported the policy because they believed it benefited them. Sometimes they claimed policies that helped them actually benefited society, but they only made this argument because it helped make their case more persuasive. Economists supported the laissez-faire policy because they believed it benefited society.

It's not easy to decide which policies will benefit society when the policies you're looking at will help some people and hurt other people. It's hard to weigh a policy and decide whether the good that it will probably do outweighs the harm that it may cause.

Modern economists have spent a long time struggling with this problem. Some have avoided the problem. They have refused to advocate any policy that might hurt anyone, which pretty much eliminates advocating any policy at all. Good policy-oriented economists make working judgements of what they believe is in society's interest; these working judgements determine which policies they advocate.

In reality, economists' (or anyone's) arguments for the general good of society are unlikely to have much effect on the policies of any government unless their arguments coincide with the interests of one group or another. A policy of less government involvement favoured manufacturers over craftspeople. That the policy favoured manufacturers or industrialists isn't the reason economists favoured it (they argued that less government involvement would be good for society as a whole), but it is the reason industrialists supported laissez-faire, and the industrialists' support of laissez-faire was critical in getting the policy adopted in Britain in the late 1700s.

Once markets were established, the terms of the debate changed. Many economists stopped advocating laissez-faire policies. Good economists recognize the advantages of markets, but they also recognize the problems of markets.

government; it was privately financed (although government policies, such as colonial policies giving certain companies monopoly trading rights with a country's colonies, helped in that trading). The Industrial Revolution, democracy, and capitalism all arose in the middle and late 1700s. By the 1800s, they were part of the institutional landscape of Western society. Capitalism had arrived.

From Capitalism to ~~Socialism~~ *Welfare Capitalism*

Capitalism was marked by significant economic growth in the Western world. But it was also marked by human abuses—18-hour workdays, low wages, children as young as five years old slaving long hours in dirty, dangerous factories and mines—to produce enormous wealth for an elite few. Such conditions and inequalities led to criticism of the capitalist or market economic system.

Marx's Analysis The best-known critic of this system was Karl Marx, a German philosopher, economist, and sociologist who wrote in the 1800s and who developed an analysis of the dynamics of change in economic systems. Marx argued that economic systems are in a constant state of change, and that capitalism would not last. Workers would revolt, and capitalism would be replaced by a socialist economic system.

Marx saw an economy marked by tensions among economic classes. He saw capitalism as an economic system controlled by the capitalist class (businessmen). His class analysis was that capitalist society is divided into capitalist and worker classes. He said constant tension between these economic classes causes changes in the system. The capitalist class made large profits by exploiting the **proletariat** class (working class) and extracting what he called *surplus value* from workers who, according to Marx's labour theory of value, produced all the value inherent in goods. Surplus value was the profit that, according to Marx's normative views, capitalists

Proletariat The working class.

added to the price of goods. What economic analysis sees as recognizing a need that society has and fulfilling it, Marx saw as exploitation.

Marx argued that this exploitation would increase as production facilities became larger and larger and as competition among capitalists decreased. At some point, he believed, exploitation would lead to a revolt by the proletariat, who would overthrow their capitalist exploiters.

By the late 1800s, some of what Marx predicted had occurred, although not in the way that he thought it would. Production moved from small to large factories. Corporations developed, and classes became more distinct from one another. Workers were significantly differentiated from owners. Small firms merged and were organized into monopolies and trusts (large combinations of firms). The trusts developed ways to prevent competition among themselves and ways to limit entry of new competitors into the market. Marx was right in his predictions about these developments, but he was wrong in his prediction about society's response to them.

The Revolution that Did Not Occur Western society's response to the problems of capitalism was not a revolt by the workers. Whereas Marx said capitalism would fall because of the exploitation of workers by the owners of businesses or capitalists, what actually happened was that the market economy was modified by political forces. Governments stepped in to stop the worst abuses of capitalism. The hard edges of capitalism were softened.

Evolution, not revolution, was capitalism's destiny. The democratic state did not act, as Marx argued it would, as a mere representative of the capitalist class. Competing pressure groups developed; workers gained political power which offset the economic power of businesses.

In the late 1930s and the 1940s, workers dominated the political agenda. During this time, capitalist economies developed an economic safety net which included government-funded programs, such as public welfare and unemployment insurance, and established an extensive set of regulations affecting all aspects of the economy. Today, depressions are met with direct government policy. Anti-combines laws, regulatory agencies, and social programs of government softened the hard edges of capitalism. Laws were passed prohibiting child labour, mandating a certain minimum wage, and limiting the hours of work. Capitalism became what is sometimes called **welfare capitalism,** an economic system in which the market is allowed to operate, but in which government plays key roles in determining distribution and making the *what, how,* and *for whom* decisions.

Welfare capitalism Economic system in which the market operates but government regulates markets significantly.

Due to these developments, government spending now accounts for nearly half of all spending in Canada, and for more than half in some European countries. Were an economist from the late 1800s to return from the grave, he'd probably say socialism, not capitalism, exists in Western societies. Most modern-day economists wouldn't go that far, but they would agree that our economy today is better described as a welfare capitalist economy than as a capitalist, or even a market, economy. Because of these changes, Canada and Western European economies are a far cry from the competitive "capitalist" economy that Karl Marx criticized. Markets operate, but they are constrained by the government.

The concept *capitalism* developed to denote a market system controlled by one group in society, the capitalists. Looking at Western societies today, we see that domination by one group no longer characterizes Western economies. Although in theory capitalists control corporations through their ownership of shares of stock, in practice corporations are controlled in large part by managers. There remains an elite group who control business, but "capitalist" is not a good term to describe them. Managers, not capitalists, exercise primary control over business, and even their control is limited by laws or the fear of laws being passed by governments.

Governments in turn are controlled by a variety of pressure groups. Sometimes one group is in control; at other times, another. Government policies similarly fluctuate. Sometimes they are proworker, sometimes proindustrialist, sometimes progovernment, and sometimes prosociety.

From Feudalism to Socialism

You probably noticed that we crossed out "Socialism" in the previous section's heading and replaced it with "Welfare Capitalism." That's because capitalism did not evolve to socialism as Karl Marx predicted it would. Instead, Marx's socialist ideas took root in Russia, a society that the Industrial Revolution had in large part bypassed. Arriving at a different place and a different time than Marx predicted it would, socialism, you should not be surprised to read, arrived in a different way than Marx predicted. There was no revolution of the proletariat to establish socialism. Instead, there was World War I, which the Russians were losing, and there was Russia's feudal economy and government, which were crippled by the war effort. A small group of socialists overthrew the czar (Russia's king) and took over the government in 1917. They quickly pulled Russia out of the war, and then set out to organize a socialist society and economy.

Russian socialists tried to adhere to Marx's ideas, but they found that Marx had concentrated on how capitalist economies operate, not on how a socialist economy should be run. Thus, Russian socialists faced a huge task with little guidance. Their most immediate problem was how to increase production so that the economy could emerge from feudalism into the modern industrial world. In Marx's analysis, capitalism was a necessary stage in the evolution toward the ideal state for a very practical reason. The capitalists exploit the workers, but in doing so capitalists extract the necessary surplus—an amount of production in excess of what is consumed. That surplus had to be extracted in order to provide the factories and machinery upon which a socialist economic system would be built. But since there had been no capitalism in Russia, a true socialist state could not be established immediately. Instead, the socialists created an economic system that they called **state socialism.** The state would see to it that people worked for the common good until they could be relied on to do so on their own.

State socialism Economic system in which government sees to it that people work for the common good

Socialists saw state socialism as a transition stage to pure socialism. This transition stage still exploited the workers; when Joseph Stalin took power in Russia in the late 1920s, he took the peasants' and small farmers' land and turned it into collective farms. The government then paid farmers low prices for their produce. When farmers balked at the low prices, millions of them were killed.

Simultaneously, Stalin created central planning agencies which directed individuals on what to produce and how to produce it, and determined for whom things would be produced. During this period, *socialism* became synonymous with *central economic planning,* and Soviet-style socialism became the model of socialism in practice.

Also during this time, Russia took control of a number of neighbouring states and established the Union of Soviet Socialist Republics (USSR), the formal name of the Soviet Union. The Soviet Union also installed Soviet-dominated governments in a number of Eastern European countries. In 1949 most of China, under the rule of Mao Tse-tung, adopted Soviet-style socialist principles.

Since the late 1980s, the Soviet socialist economic and political structure has fallen apart. The Soviet Union as a political state broke up, and its former republics became autonomous. Eastern European countries were released from Soviet control. Now they faced a new problem: transition from socialism to a market economy. Why did the Soviet socialist economy fall apart? Because workers lacked incentives to work; production was inefficient; consumer goods were either unavailable or of poor quality; and high Soviet officials were exploiting their positions, keeping the best jobs for themselves and moving themselves up in the waiting lists for consumer goods. In short, the parents of the socialist family (the Communist party) were no longer acting benevolently; they were taking many of the benefits for themselves.

6 Socialism was an attempt to bring out people's social conscience, rather than their self-interest. Many of the countries that attempted to introduce socialism have recently reverted to capitalism.

Recent political and economic upheavals in Eastern Europe and the Soviet Union suggest that the kind of socialism these societies tried did not work. However, that

ADDED DIMENSION  SHAREHOLDERS AND STAKEHOLDERS

Corporations (businesses) are technically owned by the owners of capital (shareholders). In theory, at least, they control corporations by electing the officers (the people who make the *what, how,* and *for whom* production decisions). In practice, however, effective control of corporations is generally in the hands of a small group of managing officers.

In the debate about the possible future evolution of capitalism, the question of who controls business decisions is likely to take centre stage. Some reformers argue that the current system is wrong in both theory and practice. They argue that corporations should reflect the need of stakeholders (all the individuals who have a stake in a corporation's activities). Stakeholders include the corporation's shareholders and officers as well as workers, customers, and the community where the corporation operates. An economy in which all stakeholders, not just shareholders, elect the officers who make the *what, how,* and *for whom* decisions would still use the market. It would still be a market economy, but it would no longer be a capitalist economy.

failure does not mean that socialist goals are bad; nor does it mean that no type of socialism can ever work. To overthrow socialist-dominated governments it is not necessary to accept capitalism, and many citizens of these countries are looking for an alternative to both systems. Most, however, wanted to establish market economies.

From Socialism to ?

The upheavals in the former Soviet Union and Eastern Europe have left only China as a major power using a socialist economic system. But even in China there have been changes, and the Chinese economy is socialist in name only. Almost uncontrolled markets exist in numerous sectors of the economy. These changes have led some socialists to modify their view that state socialism is the path from capitalism to true socialism, and instead to joke: "Socialism is the longest path from capitalism to capitalism."

ECONOMIC SYSTEMS OF THE FUTURE

Our economic system will probably be different 30 years from now. If the debate between socialism and capitalism disappears, another debate will rise up to take its place. A new topic for debate may be: Who should be the decision makers in a market economy? In the Canadian economy in the late 1980s, a handful of financiers became celebrities by reaping billions of dollars in profits for themselves. Many people came to wonder whether an economic system that so glorified greed was really desirable, and in the 1990s some of those same financiers found themselves near bankruptcy, with the financial institutions they had controlled in ruins. Such widespread reactions may well lead to further evolution of the capitalist system.

Asian tigers Group of Asian countries that have achieved economic growth well above the level of other developing countries.

Also in the early and mid-1990s, the **Asian tigers**—a collection of Asian countries such as Singapore, South Korea, and Hong Kong—are the economic stars. As we will discuss in a later chapter, these countries' economies are similar to Japan's economy, which, in turn, has many similarities to mercantilism. In Japan, government and industrialists work closely together, and government plays a key role in the economy. Given the success of the Asian tigers, a push in North America toward a type of mercantilism similar to theirs exists. And so it's safe to predict that the 1990s will see further evolution of economic systems. With the advent of knowledge-based production, the lesson of history seems to be that change remains the one constant in economic systems.

CHAPTER SUMMARY

- Any economic system must answer three central questions:
  What to produce?
  How to produce it?
  For whom to produce it?
- In capitalism, the what, how, and for whom decisions are made by the market.
- In Soviet-style socialism, the what, how, and for whom decisions are made by government planning boards.
- Political, social, and economic forces are active in both capitalism and socialism.
- Economic systems are in a constant state of evolution.
- In feudalism, tradition rules; in mercantilism, the government rules; in capitalism, the market rules.
- In welfare capitalism, the market, the government, and tradition each rule components of the economy.
- Socialism is currently undergoing a major transition; Soviet-style socialism is almost dead, and the future structure of socialist society is unclear.

KEY TERMS

Asian tigers *(76)*
capitalism *(63)*
capitalists *(70)*
economic system *(62)*
feudalism *(68)*
Industrial Revolution *(72)*
laissez-faire *(72)*
mercantilism *(70)*
NIMBY *(63)*
planning *(66)*
private property rights *(63)*
proletariat *(73)*
socialism *(64)*
Soviet-style socialism *(65)*
state socialism *(75)*
welfare capitalism *(74)*

QUESTIONS FOR THOUGHT AND REVIEW

The number after each question represents the estimated degree of critical thinking required. (1 = almost none; 10 = deep thought.)

1. Is capitalism or socialism the better economic system? Why? *(9)*
2. What three questions must any economic system answer? *(2)*
3. How does Soviet-style socialism answer these three questions? *(3)*
4. How does capitalism answer these three questions? *(3)*
5. What arguments can you give for supporting a socialist organization of a family and a capitalist organization of the economy? *(6)*
6. Why did feudalism evolve into mercantilism? Could feudalism stage a return? Why? *(6)*
7. Why did mercantilism evolve into capitalism? Could mercantilism stage a return? Why? *(6)*
8. Some intellectuals have argued "history is ended" because of recent developments in socialist economies. Respond, basing your answer on Marx's analysis. *(7)*
9. A common joke in socialist countries in the early 1990s was that a person went into a free market store and asked how much a loaf of bread cost. "A dollar," said the clerk. "But that's outrageous. Down the street at the state-run store, it only costs a nickel." "So why don't you buy it there?" said the clerk. "Well," said the customer, "they don't have any." Using supply/demand analysis, show why this situation makes economic sense. *(4)*
10. The Heisenberg principle states that it's impossible to know the true nature of reality because in analyzing that reality, you change it. How might the Heisenberg principle apply to Marx's economic analysis? *(6)*

PROBLEMS AND EXERCISES

1. Suppose a Soviet-style socialist government decided to set all prices at the supply/demand equilibrium price.
   a. Show graphically what price they'd set.
   b. How would such an economy differ from a market economy?
   c. Do you think a socialist government could carry out that decision?
   d. Show graphically what would happen if it set the price too high and if it set the price too low.
   e. Which of the preceding two situations best describes what the actual situation was in socialist economies?
2. Poland, Bulgaria, and Hungary (all former socialist countries) were in the process of changing to a market economy in the early 1990s.
   a. Go to the library and find the latest information about their transitions.

   b. Explain what has happened in those countries, using the invisible hand, invisible handshake, and invisible foot metaphors.
3. Economists Edward Lazear and Robert Michael have calculated that the average family spends two-and-one-half times as much on each adult as they do on each child.
   a. Does this mean that children are deprived and that the distribution is unfair?
   b. Do you think these percentages change with family income? If so, how?
   c. Do you think that the allocation would be different in a family in a Soviet-style socialist country than in a capitalist country? Why?
4. One of the specific problems Soviet-style socialist economies had was keeping up with capitalist countries technologically.
   a. Can you think of any reason inherent to a centrally planned economy that would make innovation difficult?
   b. Can you think of any reason inherent in a capitalist country that would foster innovation?
   c. Joseph Schumpeter, a famous Harvard University economist of the 1930s, predicted that as firms in capitalist societies grew in size, they would innovate less. Can you suggest what his argument might have been?
   d. Schumpeter's prediction did not come true. Modern capitalist economies have had enormous innovations. Can you provide explanations why?
5. Canada's health care system is the envy of the Western world, but it is becoming increasingly expensive to maintain. Can you think of a reason why a capitalist economy like Canada would allow government-run health care? Why doesn't the United States adopt a similar system?
6. "Government restraint has affected the quality of medical care in Canada." Do you agree?

CHAPTER

4

Canadian Economic Institutions

The business of government is to keep the government out of business—that is, unless business needs government aid.

~Will Rogers

After reading this chapter, you should be able to:

1. Provide a bird's-eye view of the Canadian economy.
2. Explain the role of consumer sovereignty in the Canadian economy.
3. Go out and learn more about Canadian economic institutions on your own.
4. Summarize briefly the advantages and disadvantages of various types of business.
5. Explain why, even though households have the ultimate power, much of the economic decision making is done by business and government.
6. List two general roles of government and seven specific roles of government.

You saw in Chapter 2 that supply and demand are the driving forces behind the invisible hand. But the invisible hand doesn't operate in an invisible world; it operates in a very real world—a world of institutions that sometimes fight against, sometimes accept, and sometimes strengthen the invisible hand. Thus, to know how the invisible hand works in practice, we need to have some sense of economic institutions and data about the Canadian economy. Let's first look at some data.

A BIRD'S-EYE VIEW OF THE CANADIAN ECONOMY

The Canadian economic machine generates enormous economic activity and provides a high standard of living (compared to most other countries) for almost all its inhabitants. It also provides economic security for its citizens. Starvation is far from most people's minds. Exhibit 1 gives you an idea of what underlies the Canadian economy's strength. For example, in it you can see that Canada is a large country with a temperate climate across the south and taiga (forestland) and polar regions to the north, and a wide range of natural resources. It has excellent transportation facilities and a multicultural population, most of which speaks English and/or French. Its characteristics are, however, changing. Large-scale immigration is increasing the Asian population, especially on the west coast and in large cities such as Vancouver, Toronto, and Montreal.

The Importance of Geographic Economic Information

1 For a bird's-eye view of the Canadian economy see Exhibit 2.

Such geographic economic information is vitally important. To understand an economy you should know: Where are goods produced? Where are natural resources found? What natural resources does it lack? What are normal transportation routes? To keep their analyses simpler, economists often discuss economic problems without discussing geographic dimensions. But no discussion of an economy should forget that geographic dimensions of economic problems are significant. To determine whether to send our students off to the library to learn this information, we give them a quiz. We present them with two lists like those in the box on page 83. The list on the right gives 20 places in Canada. The list on the left gives a particular economic characteristic, such as an industry, product, activity, or natural condition that has been turned to economic advantage. Students are asked to match the numbers with important characteristics of each area.

If you can answer 15 or more of the 20 questions on this quiz correctly, we're impressed with your knowledge of economic geographic facts. If you answer fewer than 15, we strongly suggest learning more geographic facts. The study guide has a number of other projects, information, and examples. An encyclopedia has even more, and your library has a wealth of information. You could spend the entire semester acquiring facts. We're not suggesting that, but we *are* suggesting that you follow the economic news carefully and pay attention to where various *whats* are produced.

The positive attributes of the Canadian economy don't mean that Canada has no problems. Critics point out that crime is on the rise, drugs are omnipresent, economic resources such as oil and minerals are declining, the environment is deteriorating, the distribution of income is skewed toward the rich, and an enormous amount of economic effort goes into economic gamesmanship (real estate deals, stock market deals, deals about deals) which seems simply to reshuffle existing wealth, not to create new wealth. Internationally, the Canadian economy is the seventh largest among the western industrialized countries in terms of our total output of goods and services. While our output per capita is second only to that of the United States, Canada remains plagued by high levels of unemployment and an ever-increasing debt load. In short, the Canadian economy is great, but it's far from perfect.

Diagram of the Canadian Economy

Exhibit 2 diagrams the Canadian economy. Notice it's divided into three groups: business, households, and government. Households supply factors of production to business and are paid by business for doing so. The market where this interaction takes place is called a *factor market.* Business produces goods and services and sells them to households and government. The market where this interaction takes place is called the *goods market.*

EXHIBIT 1 CIA Information Survey on Canada: 1994

GEOGRAPHY

Total area: 9,976,140 km^2
Land area: 9,220,970 km^2
Comparative area: slightly larger than U.S.
Land boundaries: total 8,893 km, U.S. 8,893 km (includes 2,477 km with Alaska)
Coastline: 243,791 km
Maritime claims: *continental shelf* 200-m depth or to depth of exploitation; *exclusive fishing zone* 200 nm; *territorial sea* 12 nm; *International disputes* maritime boundary disputes with the US; Saint Pierre and Miquelon is focus of maritime boundary dispute between Canada and France
Climate: varies from temperate in south to subarctic and arctic in north
Terrain: mostly plains with mountains in west and lowlands in southeast
Natural resources: nickel, zinc, copper, gold, lead, molybdenum, potash, silver, fish, timber, wildlife, coal, petroleum, natural gas
Land use: arable land 5%; permanent crops 0%; meadows and pastures 3%; forest and woodland 35%; other 57%
Irrigated land: 8,400 km^2 (1989 est.)

PEOPLE

Population: 28,434,545 (July 1995 est.)
Population growth rate: 1.18% (1994 est.)
Birth rate: 13.74 births/1,000 population (1995 est.)
Death rate: 7.43 deaths/1,000 population (1995 est.)
Net migration rate: 4.55 migrant(s)/1,000 population (1995 est.)
Infant mortality rate: 6.9 deaths/1,000 live births (1994 est.)
Life expectancy at birth: total population 78.29 years; male 74.93 years; female 81.81 years (1995 est.)
Total fertility rate: 1.83 children born/woman (1995 est.)
Nationality: noun: Canadian(s); adjective: Canadian
Ethnic divisions: British Isles origin 40%, French origin 27%, other European 20%, indigenous Indian and Eskimo 1.5%
Religions: Roman Catholic 46%, United Church 16%, Anglican 10%, other 28%
Languages: English (official), French (official)
Literacy: (age 15 and over can read and write (1986)): total population 97%; male NA%; female NA%
Labor force: 13.38 million; *by occupation:* services 75%, manufacturing 14%, agriculture 4%, construction 3%, other 4% (1988)

ECONOMY

Overview: As an affluent, high-tech industrial society, Canada today closely resembles the U.S. in per capita output, market-oriented economic system, and pattern of production. Since World War II, the impressive growth of the manufacturing, mining, and service sectors has transformed the nation from a largely rural economy into one primarily industrial and urban. In the 1980s, Canada registered one of the highest rates of real growth among the OECD nations, averaging about 3.2%. With its great natural resources, skilled labor force, and modern capital plant, Canada has excellent economic prospects, although the country still faces high unemployment and a growing debt. Moreover, the continuing constitutional impasse between English- and French-speaking areas has observers discussing a possible split in the confederation; foreign investors have become edgy.
National product: GDP (purchasing power equivalent) $639.8 billion (1994)
National product real growth rate: 4.5% (1994)
National product per capita: $22,760 (1994)
Inflation rate (consumer prices): 0.2% (1994)
Unemployment rate: 9.6% (December 1994)
Budget: revenues $85 billion (Federal); expenditures $115.3 billion, including capital expenditures of $NA (FY93/94 est.)
Exports: $164.3 billion (f.o.b., 1994); *commodities:* newsprint, wood pulp, timber, crude petroleum, machinery, natural gas, aluminum, motor vehicles and parts, telecommunications equipment; *partners:* U.S., Japan, UK, Germany, South Korea, Netherlands, China
Imports: $151.5 billion (c.i.f., 1994); *commodities:* crude oil, chemicals, motor vehicles and parts, durable consumer goods, electronic computers; telecommunications equipment and parts; *partners:* U.S., Japan, UK, Germany, France, Mexico, Taiwan, South Korea
External debt: $243 billion (1993)
Industrial production: growth rate 4.8% (1993)
Electricity: capacity 108,090,000 kW; production 511 billion kWh consumption per capita 16,133 kWh (1993)
Industries: processed and unprocessed minerals, food products, wood and paper products, transportation equipment, chemicals, fish products, petroleum and natural gas
Agriculture: accounts for about 3% of GDP; one of the world's major producers and exporters of grain (wheat and barley); key source of U.S. agricultural imports; large forest resources cover 35% of total land area; commercial fisheries provide annual catch of 1.5 million metric tons, of which 75% is exported
Illicit drugs: illicit producer of cannabis for the domestic drug market; use of hydroponics technology permits growers to plant large quantities of high-quality marijuana indoors; growing role as a transit point for heroin and cocaine entering the U.S. market
Economic aid: donor; ODA and OOF commitments (1970–89), $7.2 billion
Currency: 1 Canadian dollar (Can$) = 100 cents
Exchange rates: Canadian dollars (Can$) per U.S.$1: 1.4129 (January 1995), 1.3636 (1994), 1.2901 (1993), 1.2087 (1992), 1.1457 (1991), 1.1668 (1990)
Fiscal year: 1 April – 31 March

COMMUNICATIONS

Railroads: 78,148 km total; two major transcontinental freight railway systems—Canadian National (government owned) and Canadian Pacific Railway; passenger service—VIA (government operated); 158 km is electrified
Highways: *total* 849,404 km; *paved* 253,692 km; *unpaved* gravel 595,712 km, earth 171,336 km
Inland waterways: 3,000 km, including Saint Lawrence Seaway
Pipelines: crude and refined oil 23,564 km; natural gas 74,980 km
Ports: Becancour, Churchill, Halifax, Montreal, New Westminister, Prince Rupert, Quebec, Saint John (New Brunswick), Saint John's (Newfoundland), Toronto, Vancouver
Merchant marine: 71 ships (1,000 GRT or over) totaling 617,010 878,819 DWT; bulk 17, cargo 10, chemical tanker 5, container 1, oil tanker 22, passenger 1, passenger-cargo 1, railcar carrier 2, roll-on/roll-off cargo 6, short-sea passenger 3, specialized tanker 2; *note:* does not include ships used exclusively in the Great Lakes
Airports: total 1,386 1,107; with permanent-surface runways 458; with runways over 3,659 m 4; with runways 2,440–3,659 m 29; with runways 1,220–2,439 m 326
Telecommunications: excellent service provided by modern media; 18.0 million telephones; broadcast stations—900 AM, 29 FM, 53 (1,400 repeaters) TV; 5 coaxial submarine cables; over 300 earth stations operating in INTELSAT (including 4 Atlantic Ocean and 1 Pacific Ocean) and domestic systems

Source: *CIA World Factbook*, 1994.

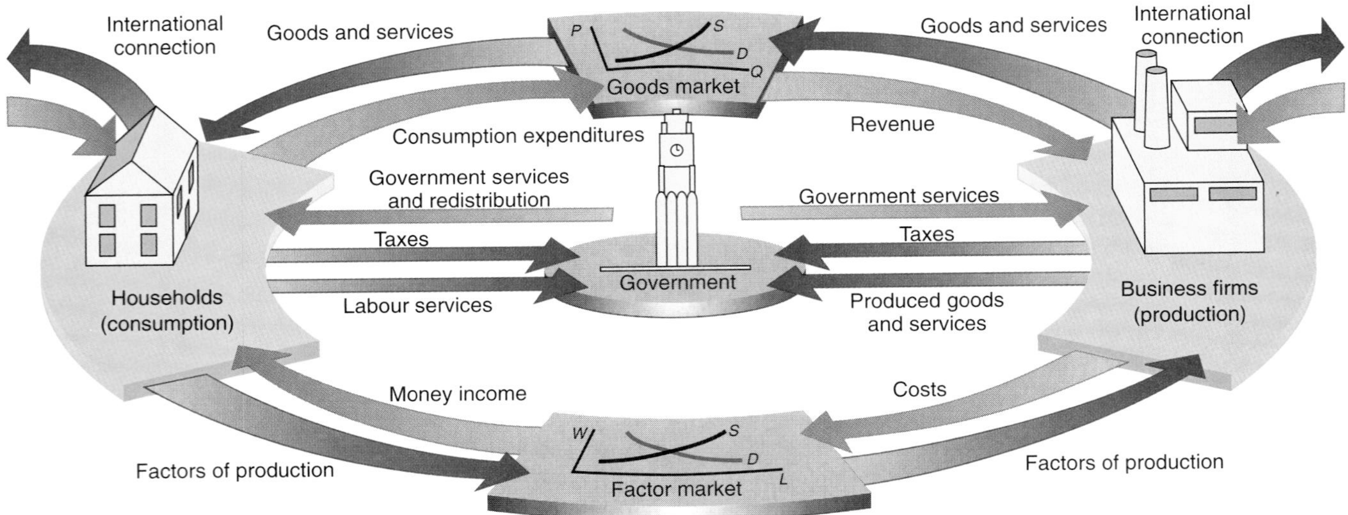

EXHIBIT 2 Diagrammatic Representation of the Canadian Economy

Notice also the arrows going out and coming in for both business and households. Those arrows represent the international connection, which we'll discuss in Chapter 5.

Finally, consider the arrows connecting government with households and business. Government taxes business and households. It buys goods and services from business and buys labour services from households. Then, with some of its tax revenue, it provides services to both business and households (roads, education) and gives some of its tax revenue directly back to individuals. In doing so, it redistributes income. But government also serves a second function. It oversees the interaction of business and households in the goods and factor markets. Government, of course, is not independent. Canada is a democracy, so households vote to determine who shall govern.

Exhibit 2 gave you an overview of the institutional organization of the Canadian economy. Let's now consider some specifics. First look at business, second at households, and finally at government.

BUSINESS

Business The private producing unit in our society.

Business is responsible for over 77 percent of Canadian production (government is responsible for the other 23 percent). In fact, any time a household decides to produce something, it becomes a business. **Business** is simply the name given to private producing units in our society.

Businesses in Canada decide *what* to produce, *how* much to produce, and *for whom* to produce it. They make these central economic decisions on the basis of their own feelings, which are influenced by market incentives. Anyone who wants to can start a business, provided he or she can come up with the required cash and meet the necessary regulatory requirements.

Entrepreneurship and Business

Entrepreneurship Labour services that involve high degrees of organizational skills, concern, and creativity.

Don't think of business as something other than people. Businesses are ultimately made up of a group of people organized together to accomplish some end. In terms of numbers, most businesses are one- or two-person operations. Home-based businesses, at least if they're part-time activities, are easy to start. All you have to do is say you're in business, and you are. If that business becomes complex enough and big enough to have employees (especially if it needs its own building), the difficulties begin. Before the business may expand its operations, a large number of licenses, permits, approvals, and forms must be obtained from various government agencies. That's why **entrepreneurship** (the ability to organize and get something done) is an important part of

ECONOMIC GEOGRAPHY OF CANADA

A REMINDER

The Quiz

In the first column, we list 20 economic characteristics. In the second and third columns, we list 20 provinces, cities, or areas of the country. Associate the locale with the proper characteristic by printing the letter on the line.

____ 1. Province hardest hit by fishing moratorium
____ 2. Over half of all manufacturing takes place here
____ 3. Island economy driven by tourism
____ 4. Maritime seaport serving U.S., Europe, and Africa
____ 5. Site of large GM plant
____ 6. Most of Canada's potash is produced here
____ 7. Grain is shipped through this system
____ 8. Majority of natural gas is produced here
____ 9. Hollywood producers like this western city
____ 10. Major commodity exchange is in this city
____ 11. Forestry is this province's largest manufacturing sector
____ 12. City where most of Canada's steel is produced
____ 13. Major stock exchange in this city
____ 14. Only officially bilingual province
____ 15. Nuclear energy produced in these provinces
____ 16. One of the largest freshwater bodies
____ 17. Geographically largest and most rural area
____ 18. You might move here to retire
____ 19. Major source of hydroelectric power
____ 20. World's largest producer of uranium

a. Niagara Falls
b. Saskatchewan
c. Winnipeg
d. Newfoundland
e. Hamilton
f. New Brunswick
g. Ont., Que., NB
h. Vancouver
i. Great Lakes
j. Oshawa
k. Alberta
l. St. Lawrence Seaway
m. Northwest Territories
n. Halifax
o. British Columbia
p. Toronto
q. Victoria
r. Canada
s. Ontario
t. Prince Edward Island

business. To give you a sense of what it's like to run a business, let's consider a real-world example.

Trials and Tribulations of Starting a Business

In 1982, Jane and Lee Corey wanted to start a business. Jane worked as a registered nurse and Lee worked as a biologist for the civil service. They decided that it would be fun to get into aquaculture, a new and growing industry in Atlantic Canada.

They found a site, bought it, and, after getting a building permit, began building. Because it was to be the home of a business, the building had to meet strict fire, electrical, and plumbing codes. They had to establish contacts with suppliers, get insurance, obtain permits from the city to comply with zoning, and satisfy all provincial and federal regulations surrounding their activities. They incorporated the new business as Corey Feed Mills Ltd., bought a machine, and started to produce aquaculture feeds and supplies.

All this costs a lot of money. Jane and Lee had to open a business chequing account with their bank. (They couldn't run all that expense through their personal chequing accounts because sound accounting practice requires people to keep their business cheques separate from their personal cheques.) They had to have some

Answers: 1–d, 2–s, 3–t, 4–n, 5–j, 6–b, 7–l, 8–k, 9–h, 10–c, 11–o, 12–e, 13–p, 14–f, 15–g, 16–i, 17–m, 18–q, 19–a, 20–r.

Corey Feed Mills Ltd. produces a wide range of pet and aquaculture products.

money to put in the business account. They used some of their savings, but they needed more funds. That meant they had to apply for a loan from the bank. The bank required them to present a formal business plan.

The company's first year of sales was less than $100,000—Lee took no salary for the first three years and Jane continued to work outside the business to provide an income to assure the bank that loan payments would be made. Over the next 10 years, all company profits were reinvested. New equipment and additional staff were needed to maintain increasing accounting, legal, and production demands. Employment grew to over 30 people in 1995.

Then, of course, there are taxes. Any business with employees must withhold taxes from their wages and send those taxes periodically to the various taxing authorities. This includes Canada Pension plan contributions, unemployment insurance contributions, federal income taxes, and provincial income taxes. There are also property taxes and sales taxes that the business, not the employees, must pay.

It took several years and hundreds of thousands of dollars to start the business. And this was a small business. Somebody without training and background in handling forms, taxes, and bureaucratic regulations usually doesn't do well in business. To such a person, entry into business isn't free; it isn't even possible. Still, many people try it, and many succeed. Their business was one of the successful ones. Today, Corey Feed products include an expanding line of pet and aquaculture foods which are sold across North America. The company is now turning to export markets worldwide.

Consumer Sovereignty and Business

2 Although businesses decide what to produce, they are guided by consumer sovereignty.

Consumer sovereignty The right of the individual to make choices about what is consumed and produced.

To say that businesses decide what to produce isn't to say that **consumer sovereignty** (the consumer's wishes) doesn't reign in Canada. Businesses decide what to produce based on what they believe will sell. A key question a person in Canada should ask about starting a business is: Can I make a profit from it? **Profit** is what's left over from total revenues after all the appropriate costs have been subtracted. Businesses that guess correctly what the consumer wants generally make a profit. Businesses that guess wrong generally operate at a loss.

People are free to start businesses for whatever purposes they want. No one asks them: "What's the social value of your term paper assistance business, your hair-replacement business, your fur coat business, or your textbook publishing business?" Yet the Canadian economic system is designed to channel individuals' desire to make a profit into the general good of society. That's the invisible hand at work. As long as the business doesn't violate a law and conforms to regulations, people in Canada are free to start whatever business they want, if they can get the money to finance it. That's a key difference between the Canadian market economy and a traditional Soviet-style economy where people weren't free to start a business even if they could get the financing.

Profit A return on entrepreneurial activity and risk taking.

Categories of Business

Exhibit 3 (a) shows a selection of various categories of Canadian businesses with their relative contributions to total output for each category. Output shares aren't necessarily the best indicator of the importance of various types of business to the economy. Exhibit 3 (b) ranks businesses by their relative employment.

Stages of Business

Stage of production Any of the various levels, such as manufacturing, wholesale, or retail, on which businesses are organized.

Businesses in Canada are organized on a variety of levels: manufacturing firms, wholesale firms, and retail firms. For most products, the manufacturer doesn't sell the product to you. Often products are sold five or six times before they reach the consumer. Each of these levels is called a **stage of production.** Thus, most firms *provide a service*—getting you the good when you want it—rather than producing the good. Firms are continually deciding whether to combine these stages of production under one firm, or whether to divide the stages up and allow many firms. Recently, for example, retailing firms such as Wal-Mart have been vertically integrating and combining various stages into their firms. Factory outlets are examples of manufacturing firms undertaking retailing functions.

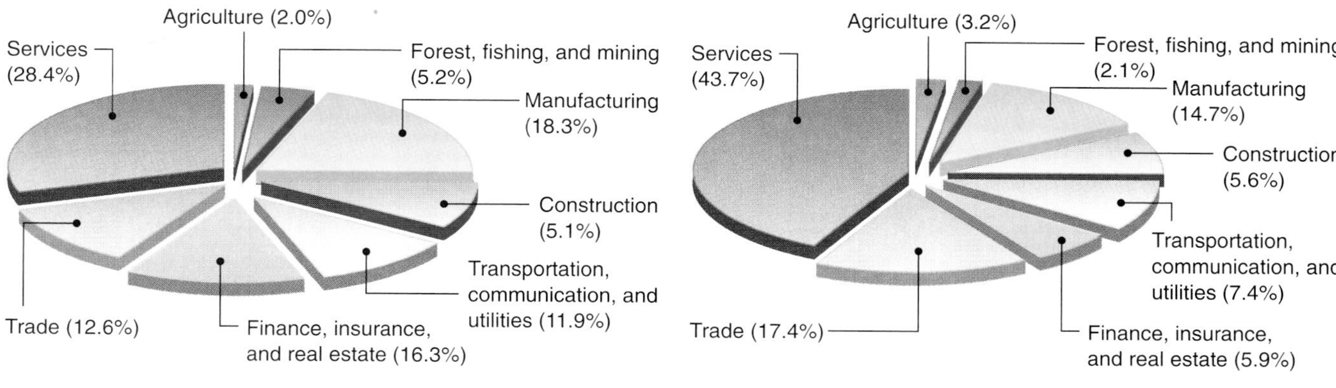

EXHIBIT 3 Importance and Size of Various Types of Business

The general types of business are listed here: (**a**) shows their relative share of output; (**b**) shows their relative importance by employment. Notice that less than half the population is involved in what most laypeople consider production—manufacturing, construction, mining, and agriculture.

Source: *Statistics Canada, CANSIM Database,* March 1995.

in the mid-1990s, it was only 18 percent. This is reflected in employment figures: manufacturing employment has fallen from about 27 percent in 1950 to about 15 percent in the mid-1990s. The reason is twofold: first, manufacturing has become more productive, so we get more output per worker; and second, we now import many more components of the products we produce. In the 1990s, parts of manufactured goods are produced around the world, and service jobs such as retailing have replaced manufacturing jobs.

3A The five largest industries in Canada are:

1. Services
2. Manufacturing
3. Finance, insurance, and real estate
4. Trade
5. Transportation, communication, and utilities.

The growing importance of the service sector to the economy has led some observers to say that we're in a postindustrial society. In their view, the Canadian economy today is primarily a service economy, not a production economy. So classifying the economy may or may not be helpful, but you should note how important the provision of services and the distribution of goods are to our economy.

From Manufacturer to You To give you a sense of the path of a good from manufacturer to ultimate buyer, let's consider a hypothetical example of a window. Clearview Window Limited bought the glass, wood, and machines needed to make the window from other companies, perhaps spending a total of $20 per window. Those purchases all fell within what is classified as wholesale trade. Clearview Window then assembled the components (cost of assembly: $60), making Clearview's total cost of the window $80.

One of us needed a window for his house, so he went down to Buildright, a local building supply store, which sells both wholesale to general contractors and retail to plain people who walk in off the street. Wholesale customers get a 20 percent discount from the retail price, which is deducted at the end of the month from the total bill they've run up. These wholesale customers charge their own customers the full retail price. We're plain people, so when one of us ordered a window, Buildright said the cost would be $200. However, it didn't have the right size in stock.

3B A useful way to learn about the economy is to trace the path of a product from raw material to final product.

Buildright stacked the order with orders from other customers and called up its Clearview distributor (who has a franchise from Clearview Window in the territory where we live) to place one big order for a number of windows, including the one we ordered. The Clearview distributor charged Buildright $140 for our window. The Clearview distributor keeps a pile of windows in stock which she replenishes from a shipment of newly made windows that come in once a month from the Clearview plant. For our window, she pays about $100 plus freight.

So it costs Clearview $80 to make our window; Clearview sells it to the distributor for $100 plus freight. The distributor needs to cover her costs for storage, handling,

ADDED DIMENSION

BALANCE SHEET AND INCOME STATEMENT

Accounting for revenues and expenditures is an important part of business. Elaborate methods of keeping track of those revenues and expenses have developed over the years. A firm's balance sheet (a statement of the firm's net worth at a point in time) is shown in (a) below.

Company Name
Balance Sheet
December 31, 1995

Assets*		Liabilities and Shareholders' Equity*	
Current assets	$13,859	Current liabilities	$12,675
Property, plant, and equipment	20,362	Long-term Liabilities	5,843
		Shareholders' equity	15,703
Total Assets	$34,221	Total liabilities and shareholders' equity	$34,221

*Dollars in millions

(a) Balance sheet

As you can see, the balance sheet is divided into assets on the left side and liabilities and shareholders' equity (also called net worth) on the right side. An *asset* is anything of value. An asset need not be a physical item. It might be a right to do something or use something. For example, landing rights are important assets of airline companies. A *liability* is an obligation. When a firm borrows money, it takes on a liability because it has an obligation to pay the money back to the lender. The totals of the two sides must be equal, since *shareholders' equity (net worth)* is defined as the difference between assets and liabilities. That is:

$$\text{Assets} = \text{Liabilities} + \text{Shareholders' equity}$$

or

$$\text{Assets} = \text{Liabilities} + (\text{Assets} - \text{Liabilities})$$
$$\text{Assets} = \text{Assets}.$$

The two sides of the equation are equal by definition. Both assets and liabilities are divided into various subcategories on a balance sheet, but at this stage, all you need to remember is the sheet's general structure.

Company Name
Statement of Income and Expenses*
For the Year Ending December 31, 1995

Sales	$8,710
Cost of goods sold	5,980
Gross profit	2,730
Operating expenses	1,509
Fixed interest payment	165
Income before federal income taxes	1,056
Federal income taxes	509
Net income	$ 547

*Dollars in millions

(b) Statement of income and expenditures

A firm's statement of income and expenses is shown in (b). Whereas a balance sheet measures a stock concept (a firm's position at a point in time), a statement of income and expenses measures a flow concept (the amount of income and expenses passing through a company during a particular period of time). A firm's sales, or total revenue, is given at the top. Then the cost of goods sold is subtracted from total revenue. The resulting number is called *gross profit,* although many income statements don't list gross profits. Next, operating costs and fixed interest payments are subtracted, giving earnings before taxes. Finally, income taxes are subtracted, giving the firm's net income.

ADDED DIMENSION

IS CANADA A POSTINDUSTRIAL SOCIETY?

Producing physical goods is only one of a society's economic tasks. Another task is to provide services (activities done for others). Services do not involve producing a physical good. When you get your hair cut, you buy a service, not a good. Much of the cost of the physical goods we buy actually is not a cost of producing the good, but is a cost of one of the most important services: distribution (getting the good to where the consumer is). After a good is produced, it has to get to the individuals who are going to consume it at the time they need it. If the distribution system gets botched up, it's as if the good had never been produced.

Let's consider a couple of examples. Take Christmas trees. Say you're sitting on 60,000 cut spruce trees in New Brunswick, but an ice storm prevents you from shipping them until December 26. Guess what? You're now stuck with 60,000 spruce trees and the problem of somehow getting rid of them. Or take hot dogs. How many of us have been irked that a hot dog that cost 25¢ to fix at home costs $2 at a football game? But a hot dog at home isn't the same as a hot dog at a game. Distribution of the good is as important as production; you're paying the extra $1.75 for distribution.

inventory, and billing, and of course she has to make a profit, so she sells the window to Buildright for $140. The owner of Buildright has to cover expenses and make a profit, so he sells us the window for $200 ($160—a 20 percent discount—if he thought we were wholesale customers).

Producing the good is only a small component of the cost. Distribution—getting the good where it is wanted when it is wanted—makes up 60 percent of the total cost of the window in this example. That large percentage is not unusual. The same story holds true for most goods you buy.

Given the importance of distribution, firms are always looking for new ways to make the distribution process more efficient. Recent approaches include just-in-time inventory systems in which computers track a firm's needs—the needed inputs are shipped to the firm just in time and its outputs are similarly shipped to customers just in time. Another new practice is for retail firms to keep instantaneous tabs on what is selling. That is why, when you buy something, the clerk has to type a whole load of numbers into the computerized cash register (or have the scanner read the bar code with a whole load of numbers). This practice lets the store know what's selling and what isn't so it knows what to order. This makes the distribution process more efficient, and thereby reduces the firm's costs, although it sometimes makes checkouts a pain.

Sizes of Business

Another way to classify businesses is by size. Contrary to popular belief, many sectors of Canada contain small (fewer than 100 employees), not large, firms. This is especially true in retail trade and construction industries. The notable exception is manufacturing, which has a group of large producers, such as auto manufacturers.

Exhibit 4 combines activity and size of firms, looking at the largest businesses in various types of activities.

A sector's relative size does not necessarily capture its importance to the economy. Take agriculture, for example. It's small in terms of both payroll and revenue, but if it stopped doing its job of providing our food, its importance would quickly become apparent. Similarly, the financial sector is relatively small, but modern industry couldn't function without a highly developed financial sector. Just as a missing bolt can bring a car to a sudden halt, so too can problems in one sector of the economy bring about a sudden halt to a much larger part of the economy.

Goals of Business

Another way to classify businesses is by their goals. They can be either for-profit businesses or nonprofit businesses. For-profit businesses keep their earnings after they pay expenses (if there are any to keep); **nonprofit businesses** try only to make enough money to cover their expenses with their revenues. If a nonprofit business winds up with a profit, that money goes into "reserves" where it's saved to use in case of later losses.

Nonprofit business Business that does not try to make a profit. It tries only to make enough money to cover its expenses with its revenues.

EXHIBIT 4 The Largest Canadian Businesses

The Top Five	Revenues (thousands)	Assets
General Motors of Canada Ltd.	$ 24,919,421	$ 8,050,837
BCE Inc.	21,670,000	38,092,000
Ford Motor Co. of Canada, Ltd.	20,100,600	5,029,000
Chrysler Canada Ltd.	15,722,000	4,317,800
George Weston Ltd.	13,002,000	4,744,000

Top Five Conglomerates	Revenues	Assets
Imasco Ltd.	$ 8,134,000	$53,482,000
Canadian Pacific Ltd.	7,053,000	16,912,300
Power Corp. of Canada	6,904,240	31,526,382
Noranda Inc.	6,633,000	11,836,000
Brascan Ltd.	6,149,000	4,244,800

Top Five Merchandisers	Revenues	Assets
George Weston Ltd.	$ 13,002,000	$ 4,744,000
Provigo Inc.	6,176,400	1,026,000
The Oshawa Group Ltd.	6,069,800	1,313,700
Hudson's Bay Co.	5,829,243	4,016,626
Canada Safeway Ltd.	4,628,300	1,153,900

Top Five Telecommunications Companies	Revenues	Assets
BCE Inc.	$ 21,670,000	$38,092,000
Anglo-Canadian Telephone Co.	2,550,000	4,965,000
TELUS Corp.	1,360,149	3,483,722
Rogers Cantel Mobile Communications Inc.	750,420	1,219,467
Teleglobe Inc.	643,000	1,934,400

Top Five Financial Institutions	Assets	Revenues
Royal Bank of Canada	$173,079,000	$13,434,000
Canadian Imperial Bank of Commerce	151,032,554	11,214,000
Bank of Montreal	138,175,000	9,108,000
Bank of Nova Scotia	132,928,000	9,376,000
Toronto-Dominion Bank	99,759,000	6,993,000

Source: *The Financial Post 500*, May 1995.

The goal of a nonprofit business is to serve the community or some segment of the community. Nonprofit businesses include all government-run businesses, some hospitals, pension funds, foundations, many fund-raising organizations such as the Canadian Cancer Society, most universities and colleges, and many museums. Working for a nonprofit organization doesn't mean working for free. Salaries are an expense of a business, and are paid by both for-profit and nonprofit firms. In fact, salaries paid to individuals managing nonprofit organizations can be higher than in for-profit organizations, and perks of the job can be fantastic.[1] But perks are classified as "expenses" and aren't included in "profits."

Why discuss the goals of business? Because the goals of business are central to economic theory and economists' insight into how economies function. In a pure capitalist country, all businesses are for-profit businesses. In a pure socialist country, all businesses are nonprofit. As we discussed in Chapter 3, Canada is far from a pure cap-

[1] *Perks* is short for *perquisites*. An example of a "fantastic" perk might be the business supplying you with a limousine and driver in Ottawa or Montreal, an unlimited expense account, trips to Europe and the Far East, and a condo in Victoria.

Advantages and Disadvantages of Various Forms of For-Profit Businesses

	Sole Proprietor	Partnership	Corporation
Advantages	1. Minimum bureaucratic hassle 2. Direct control by owner	1. Ability to share work and risks 2. Relatively easy to form	1. No personal liability 2. Increasing ability to get funds 3. Ability to shed personal income and gain added expenses
Disadvantages	1. Limited ability to get funds 2. Unlimited personal liability	1. Unlimited personal liability (even for partner's blunder) 2. Limited ability to get funds	1. Legal hassle to organize 2. Possible double taxation of income 3. Monitoring problems

italist country, and nonprofit businesses play significant roles in the Canadian economy.

Forms of Business

The three primary forms of business are sole proprietorships, partnerships, and corporations. Each of the different forms of business has certain advantages and disadvantages. These are summarized in the above table.

Sole proprietorships are the easiest to start and have the fewest bureaucratic hassles. **Partnerships**—businesses with two or more owners—create possibilities for sharing the burden, but they also create unlimited liability for each of the partners. **Corporations**—businesses that are treated as a person, and are legally owned by their stockholders who are not liable for the actions of the corporate "person"—are the largest form of business when measured in terms of receipts. Thus their income is taxed, which leads to charges of double taxation of income.

Sole proprietorship Business with only one owner.

Partnership Business with two or more owners.

Corporation Business that is treated like a person, legally owned by its stockholders. Its stockholders are not personally liable for the actions of the corporate "person."

When a corporation is formed, it issues **stock** (certificates of ownership in a company) which is sold or given to individuals. Proceeds of the sale of that stock make up what is called the *equity capital* of a company. Ownership of stock entitles you to vote in the election of a corporation's directors.

Corporations were developed as institutions to make it easier for company owners to be separated from company management. A corporation provides **limited liability** for the owners. Whereas with the other two forms of business, owners can lose everything they possess even if they have only a small amount invested in the company, in a corporation the owners can lose only what they have invested in that corporation. If you've invested $100, you can lose only $100. In the other kinds of business, even if you've invested only $100, you could lose everything; the business's losses must be covered by the individual owners.

4 The advantages and disadvantages of the three forms of business are shown in the table.

Limited liability The liability of a stockholder (owner) in a corporation; it is limited to the amount the stockholder has invested in the company.

Another advantage of corporations involves taxes. While it is true that corporate income is taxed, corporate expenses can be deducted and thus corporate "perks"—a hunting lodge in James Bay—which is actually a consumption good, can be rented tax free if one has a creative accountant.

A corporation's stocks can be distributed among as few as three persons or among millions of stockholders. Shares can be bought and sold either in an independent transaction between two people (an over-the-counter trade) or through a broker and a *stock exchange.* Appendix A provides a brief introduction to the stock market.

In corporations, there is a separation of ownership and control. Most shareholders have little input into the decisions a corporation makes. Instead, corporations are often controlled by their managers, who often run them for their own benefit as well as for the owners'. The reason is that owners' control of management is limited.

A large percentage of most corporations' shares are not even controlled by the owners; instead, they are controlled by financial institutions such as mutual funds (financial institutions that invest individuals' money for them) and by pension funds (financial institutions that hold people's money for them until it is to be paid out to them upon their retirement). Thus, ownership of corporations is another step removed from individuals.

Why is the question of who controls a firm important? Because economic theory assumes a business owners' goal is to maximize profits, which would be true of corporations if shareholders made the decisions. Managers don't have the same incentives to maximize profits that owners do. There's pressure on managers to maximize profits, but that pressure can often be weak or ineffective.

HOUSEHOLDS

Households Groups of individuals living together and making joint decisions.

The second classification we'll consider in this overview of Canadian economic institutions is households. **Households** (groups of individuals living together and making joint decisions) are the most powerful economic institution. They ultimately control government and business, the other two economic institutions. Households' votes in the political arena determine government policy; their decisions about supplying labour and capital determine what businesses will have available to work with; and their spending decisions or expenditures (the "votes" they cast with their dollars) determine what businesses will be able to sell.

While the ultimate power does in principle lie with the people and households, we, the people, have assigned much of that power to representatives. As we discussed above, corporations are only partially responsive to owners of their shares, and much of that ownership is once-removed from individuals. Ownership of 1,000 shares in a company with a total of 2 million shares isn't going to get you any influence over the corporation's activities. As a shareholder, you simply accept what the corporation does.

5 Although, in principle, ultimate power resides with the people and households (consumer sovereignty), in practice the representatives of the people—firms and government—are sometimes removed from the people and, in the short run, are only indirectly monitored by the people.

A major decision that corporations make independently of their shareholders concerns what to produce. True, ultimately we, the people, decide whether we will buy what business produces, but business spends a lot of money telling us what services we want, what products make us "with it," what books we want to read, and the like. Most economists believe that consumer sovereignty reigns—that we are not fooled or controlled by advertising. Still, it is an open question in some economists' minds whether we, the people, control business or the business representatives control people. There's similar debate in the political sphere of our lives. Members of Parliament feel only partially responsible to voters. (They feel slightly more responsible around election time.)

Because of this assignment of power to other institutions, in many spheres of the economy households are not active producers of output but merely passive recipients of income. That's why much of the discussion of the household sector focuses on the distribution of household income. Thus, our consideration of households will be short and will focus on their income and their role as suppliers of labour.

Household Types and Income

The Canadian population of about 30 million is composed of about 7 million households. Exhibit 6 looks at three ways income is divided up among households. Notice the relatively low incomes of female lone-parent households. Of similar interest is the regional distribution of income. With few exceptions, Ontario, Quebec, and British Columbia offer the highest median income. Because income determines how many goods and services a person will get, family structure and geographic location play a big role in the *for whom* department.

One political concern about income is whether it is fairly (equitably, as opposed to equally) distributed, and whether all households have sufficient income. That's a tough question to answer. For now, let us simply note that, unlike the United States, in Canada poverty is not defined by a "poverty line" based on a calculation of needs. Statistics Canada uses a **low-income cutoff** which defines low-income families as those who spend proportionately more (at least 20 percent more) than the average family on the necessities of life—food, clothing, and shelter. Using this measure, in

low-income cutoff The income level at which families spend at least 20 percent more than the average family on the necessities of life. Used by Statistics Canada to define low-income families.

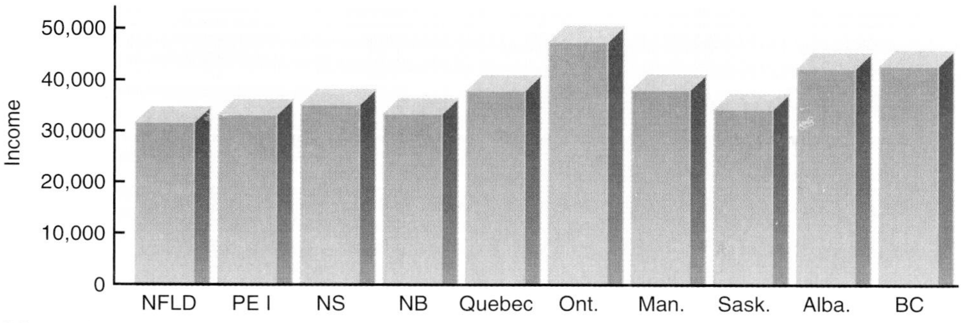

(a) Median income, all families

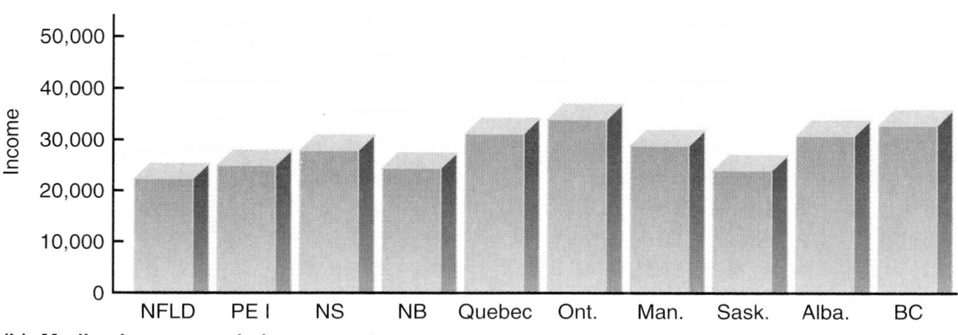

(b) Median income, male-lone parent

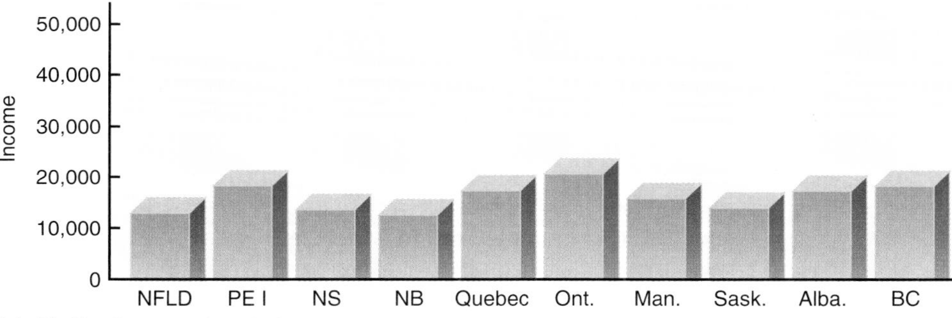

(c) Median income, female-lone parent

EXHIBIT 5 1990 Median Income by Family Structure and Province

These bar charts illustrate that median family income varied considerably by province and family structure in 1990.

Source: *Statistics Canada*, 93–331, 1993.

1993 there were almost 5 million Canadians living in low-income conditions—about one-sixth of the total population! As Exhibit 5 (c) suggests, the highest rate of incidence of low-income families were female lone-parent—almost 62 percent.

Households as Suppliers of Labour

The largest source of household income is wages and salaries (the income households get from labour). Households supply the labour with which businesses produce and government governs. In 1994, the total Canadian labour force was 14.8 million, about 10 percent (1.5 million) of whom were unemployed. The average Canadian work week in 1994 was about 42 hours.

Exhibit 6 divides Canadian employment by types of jobs and average salaries. Notice that many are service jobs, since Canada has become largely a service economy. Exhibit 7 shows that this greater emphasis on services rather than goods is continuing. Many of the fastest-growing jobs are in service industries; many of the fastest-declining are in manufacturing and agriculture.

Other divisions of jobs show even more differences. For example, physicians earn about $150,000 per year, lawyers often earn $100,000 per year, and CEOs of large cor-

EXHIBIT 6 Employment and Salaries for Various Types of Employment, 1991

Type of Job	Number of Full-Time Workers Female	Male	Average Earnings per Year Female	Male
Managerial, administrative and related occupations	462,000	882,000	$33,000	$51,000
Medicine and health	267,000	95,000	32,000	62,000
Service	338,000	405,000	17,000	31,000
Farming	47,000	166,000	13,000	21,000
Construction	9,000	349,000	26,000	35,000

Source: *Statistics Canada*, 93–332, 1993.

porations often make $1,000,000 per year or more. A beginning McDonald's employee generally makes less than $10,000.

One of the biggest changes in the labour market in the 1980s was unions' decline in importance. Labour unions are an economic institution closely associated with households. They were initially created to balance businesses' power. By organizing into unions, workers became an economic institution and gained a larger say in the production process. Unions pushed Canadian wages up relative to wages in other countries, and established in Canada some of the best working conditions in the world. But unions also had a negative effect; part of businesses' response to the high Canadian wages has been to move production facilities to countries where workers receive lower wages. That's one reason the Canadian manufacturing sector has declined relative to the service sector, and union membership and influence have fallen substantially. Service workers have far fewer unions, and their jobs are much more difficult to move to other countries.

People Power

An important way households influence government and business is in their cultural and ideological beliefs. Those beliefs determine what is allowable and what isn't. When those beliefs differ from the existing situation, "people power" has the potential to change the existing institutions significantly. For example, in Eastern Europe by the late 1980s, people's beliefs had become so inconsistent with the existing institutions that people demanded and brought about major economic and political reforms even though there was no formal mechanism, such as free elections, by which they could exert their power. People power goes beyond the power people exert in elections. People in an economy have a cultural sensibility, or outlook, which limits actions of both government and business.

Households can exert people power to keep government and business in line. Do people accept the existing situation, or do they feel business or government is wrong? To keep people power on their side, Canadian businesses spend a lot of money on public service and advertisements stating that they, the businesses, are good citizens.

Because of the importance of these cultural and social limitations to business (the invisible handshake), you need some sense of which way the invisible handshake will push. While summarizing the sensibility of a country's people is impossible, it is necessary to make the attempt because it is through those sensibilities—through informal, invisible channels—that households exert much of their power on the economy. Thus, in the next section, we will present our view of the sensibility of the Canadian people.

The Social, Cultural, and Ideological Sensibilities of Canadian People

Although, as we've pointed out, the actual Canadian economy is best described as welfare capitalism or a mixed economy due to a number of government programmes designed to blunt the sharp edge of the market's forces, the Canadian **ideology** (values held so deeply that they are not questioned) is, in word if not in deed, "let the market do it." Like maple syrup and motherhood, competition and freedom to undertake economic activities are seen as sacred. That is not to say that Canadians loathe government intervention. When markets fail to operate in a timely manner, Canadians are quick to call for government action.

EXHIBIT 7 Fastest-Growing Occupations in the 1990s

Software engineer	New Media packaging and marketing
Geriatric-care aide	English-as-a-second-language teacher
Human-resources facilitator	Derivatives trader
Financial counsellor	Wastemanagement
Genetic mapping	Information highway pothole repair

Source: The *Financial Post,* October 14, 1995, p.15.

Maple syrup and motherhood have changed over the years, and so has competition. In the Great Depression of the 1930s, the Canadian population's unbridled faith in the market was tested. Under Prime Minister R.B. Bennett, and later under Prime Minister Mackenzie King, numerous government programmes were developed to ease the market's harshness. Laws were passed establishing minimum prices at which goods could be sold. Labour was given the right to organize to achieve its ends; a new farm programme limited price fluctuations of agricultural goods; a welfare system, including social security programmes and unemployment insurance, was established. These laws and programmes are generally viewed as good.

With the advent of World War II (1939–45), defense spending zoomed and government spending as a percentage of total Canadian spending increased. After the war, the share of government spending on output declined, but the march of government programmes to regulate the market continued. In the decade following the war, the government sector's role increased further and the economy grew rapidly. The government took responsibility for maintaining high employment, and the safety net (a set of programmes that guaranteed individuals a minimum standard of living) was expanded.

During the postwar period, a number of special interest groups developed—we'll call them **interest groups.** They are involved in encouraging and protecting government spending in certain areas of the economy. For example, we could say there's a social-educational interest group which protects education interests, while a welfare interest group protects social benefits. These interest groups compete for government expenditures.

Interest groups Individuals and others who band together to encourage and protect government spending in certain areas of the economy.

These developments may seem to go against the cultural and ideological support the Canadian public gives the market. Support for the market and tolerance of vested interests seem contradictory, but people's ideological views need not be consistent, and they often aren't. A new and larger role for government in the market has been accepted by most people. They believe these programmes are proper, so now government programmes that restrict the market (for example, the social security system) are seen to be as fundamentally Canadian, as is the market.

Another important aspect of a people's sensibility is their view of morality. Compared to other countries, Canada has a relatively strict standard of economic morals—activities such as direct bribery and payoffs are illegal. (In some countries, these activities aren't illegal. In numerous others, they're illegal but openly tolerated.) The Canadian government bureaucracy, while considered by many to be inefficient, is generally thought to be honest and not corrupt; moreover, by international standards it's actually efficient. Around the fringes of standard morality there's still room for influence peddling, discreet payoffs, and trading favours, but by international standards of corruption they're small potatoes.

There's much more to be said about the cultural sensibilities of the Canadian people, but we'll stop here. Those of you unfamiliar with Canadian cultural and social norms can best find out about them by following the newspapers and by having discussions with friends. Our goal in presenting this material isn't to cover the Canadian people's social and cultural sensibilities completely—that would take a whole book by itself—but simply to remind you how important they are: How an economy functions, what types of policies can be instituted, and what people's perceptions of the economic problems are, are all shaped by its people's social, cultural, and ideological sensibilities. The invisible handshake is an important determinant of economic events.

GOVERNMENT

The third major Canadian economic institution we'll consider is government. Government plays two general roles in the economy. It's both a referee (setting the rules that determine relations between businesses and households) and an actor (collecting money in taxes and spending that money on its own projects, such as defence and education). Let's first consider government's role as an actor.

Government as an Actor

6A Two general roles of government are (1) as a referee and (2) as an actor.

Transfer payments Payments by government to individuals that are not in payment for goods or services.

Special purpose transfers Payments from the federal government to provincial and local governments for funding social spending on health care, welfare, and post-secondary education.

General purpose transfers Payments from the federal government to the provincial and local governments meant to reduce disparities between "have" and "have not" provinces.

Canada has a federal government system, which means we have various levels of government (federal, provincial, and municipal), each with its own powers. All levels of government combined consume about 48 percent of the country's total output and employ about 2.7 million individuals. The various levels of government also have a number of programmes that redistribute income through taxation or through a variety of social welfare and assistance programmes designed to help specific groups. Many of the programmes are based on a system of **transfer payments**—payments by governments to individuals that are not in payment for goods and services.

Provincial and Local Government Provincial and local governments employ over 1.9 million people and spend almost $230 billion a year. Provincial and local governments get much of their income from taxes: property taxes, consumption taxes, and provincial income taxes. They are also heavily reliant on general and special purpose transfers from the federal government. **Special purpose transfers** are primarily aimed at funding social spending on health care, welfare, and post-secondary education. **General purpose transfers** are equalization payments that are meant to reduce disparities between the "have" and the "have-not" provinces. They are supposed to provide for comparable levels of public service at comparable levels of taxation. They spend their tax revenues on social services, health care, administration, education (education through high school is available free in public schools), and roads. These activities fall within microeconomics, which we'll discuss when we study microeconomics.

Federal Government Probably the best way to get an initial feel for the federal government and its size is to look at the various categories of its tax revenues and expenditures in Exhibit 8. Notice that direct taxes from persons make up about 58 percent of the federal government's revenue, while direct taxes from businesses make up about 9 percent. That's more than 65 percent of the federal government's revenues, most of which shows up as a deduction from your paycheque. In Exhibit 9 (b), notice the federal government's two largest categories of spending are, first, transfers to persons, with expenditures on interest payments close behind.

Debt Accumulated deficits minus accumulated surpluses.

Interest payments are important because the Canadian government has a large debt. **Debt** is an amount of money that one owes to others. It is a stock concept, which corresponds to the liability portion of a company's balance sheet. The Canadian government has accumulated a large debt—over $500 billion in the mid-1990s, or over $20,000 per person. Interest must be paid on that debt, which explains why the budget's interest component is so high. The national debt has accumulated because the federal government has run almost continual budget deficits since the 1940s. A deficit is a flow concept that corresponds to the net income portion of a company's income statement. A **government budget deficit** occurs when government expenditures exceed government revenues—that is, when tax revenues fall short of budgeted expenditures and the government borrows to make up the difference. A **government budget surplus** occurs when revenues exceed expenditures.

Government budget deficit Situation when government expenditures exceed government revenues.

Government budget surplus Situation when government revenues exceed expectations.

Individuals like government programmes that assist them, and they pressure politicians to provide these programmes. However, people don't like the taxes they have to pay for those programmes, and they put pressure on politicians to lower taxes. These two pressures have resulted in the federal government's significant deficits since the 1970s.

Government as a Referee

Even if government spending made up only a small proportion of total expenditures, government would still be central to the study of economics. The reason is that, in a

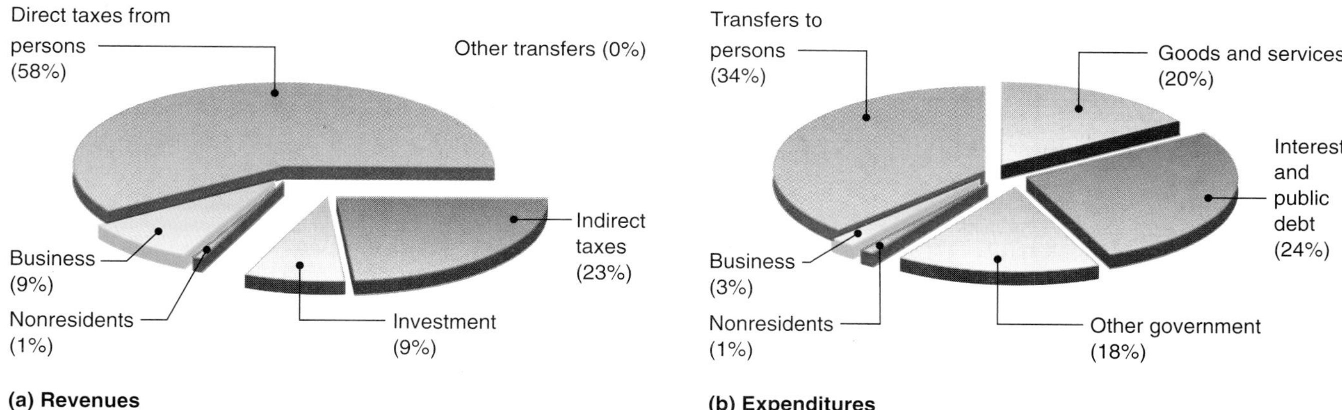

EXHIBIT 8 Federal Government Revenues and Expenditures: 1994

(a) Direct taxes from persons and indirect taxes are the largest sources of federal government revenues.

(b) Transfers to persons and interest on the public debt are the largest of federal government expenditures.
Source: *Statistics Canada,* CANSIM Database, March 1995.

market economy, government controls the interaction of business and households. Government sets the rules of interaction and acts as a referee, changing the rules when it sees fit. Government decides whether the invisible hand will be allowed to operate freely.

Government is involved in every interaction between households and business in the form of laws regulating that interaction. For example, in Canada today:

1. Businesses are not free to hire and fire whomever they want. They must comply with employment equity and labour laws. Even closing a plant requires a period of notice for many kinds of firms.
2. Many working conditions are subject to government regulation: safety rules, wage rules, overtime rules, hours-of-work rules, and the like.
3. Businesses cannot meet with other businesses to agree on prices they will charge.
4. Workers in a union cannot require all workers in a firm to join the union before they are hired. In some provinces, they cannot require workers to join the union at all.

Most of these laws evolved over time. Up until the 1930s, household members, in their roles as workers and consumers, had few rights. Businesses were free to hire and fire at will and, if they chose, to deceive and take advantage of consumers.

Over time, laws have changed. New laws to curb business abuses have been passed, and government agencies have been formed to enforce these laws. Now many people think the pendulum has swung too far the other way. They believe businesses are saddled with too many regulatory burdens.

One big question that we'll address throughout this book is: What referee role should the government play in an economy? For example, should government redistribute income from the rich to the poor through taxation? Should it allow a merger between two companies? Should it regulate air traffic? Should it regulate prices?

Since considering government's role will be a central element of the entire book, we'll present a few terms and roles now to establish a framework for the later chapters.

Economic Roles of Government We first consider the economic roles of government. These roles tend to be somewhat less controversial than its political roles.

Providing a Stable Institutional Framework A basic economic role of government is to provide a stable institutional framework (the set of rules determining what we can and

6B Seven specific roles of government are:
1. Providing a stable structure within which markets can operate.
2. Promoting workable, effective competition.
3. Correcting for external effects of individuals' decisions.
4. Providing public goods that the market doesn't adequately supply.
5. Ensuring economic stability and growth.
6. Providing acceptably fair distribution of society's production among its individuals.
7. Encouraging merit and discouraging demerit goods or activities.

can't do). Before people conduct business, they need to know the rules of the game and have a reasonable belief about what those rules will be in the future. The modern economy requires contractual arrangements to be made among individuals. These arrangements must be enforced if the economy is to operate effectively. Ultimately, only the government can create a stable environment and enforce contracts through its legal system. Where governments don't provide a stable environment, as often happens in developing countries, economic growth is difficult; usually such economies are stagnant. Liberia in the early 1990s is an example. As two groups there fought for political control, the Liberian economy stagnated.

Almost all economists believe that providing an institutional framework within which the market can operate is an important function of government. However, they differ significantly as to what the rules for such a system should be. Even if the rules are currently perceived as unfair, an argument can be made for keeping them. Individuals have already made decisions based on the existing rules, so it's unfair to them to change the rules in midstream. Stability of rules is a benefit to society.

Recent economic reforms in the former Soviet Union provide a good example of this point. First, the Soviets modified their rules to encourage profits and entrepreneurship. Within a year they changed the rules again, attacking entrepreneurs as profiteers and confiscating their earnings. Then they began to encourage entrepreneurship again, but the second time few entrepreneurs came forward because of fear that the rules would change once again. Then there was a conservative coup; then a reestablishment of the market. Finally the entire political structure fell apart, and the Soviet Union was no more.

When rules are perceived as unfair and changing them is also perceived as unfair, which often happens, the government finds itself in the difficult position of any referee, trying to strike a balance between the two degrees of unfairness.

Monopoly power Ability to prevent others from entering a business field, which enables a firm to raise its price.

Competition Ability of individuals to freely enter into business activities

Promoting Effective and Workable Competition One of the most difficult economic functions of government is its role in protecting and promoting competition. As we discussed above, Canadian ideology sees **monopoly power** as bad. Monopoly power is the ability of individuals or firms currently in business to prevent other individuals or firms from entering the same kind of business; thereby monopoly power can raise existing firms' prices. Similarly, Canadian ideology sees **competition** (individuals' or firms' ability to enter freely into business activities) as good. Government's job is to promote competition and prevent monopoly power from limiting competition.

What makes this a difficult function for government is that most individuals and firms believe that competition is far better for the other guy than it is for themselves, that their monopolies are necessary monopolies, and that competition facing them is unfair competition. For example, farmers support competition, but they also support government farm subsidies and import restrictions, which make it harder for foreign individuals to compete in Canada. Likewise, firms support competition, but they also support tariffs which protect them from foreign competition. Professionals, such as architects and engineers, support competition, but they also support professional licensing, which limits the number of competitors who can enter their field.

Externality A result of a decision that is not taken into account by the decision maker.

Correcting for Externalities When two people freely enter into a trade or agreement, they both believe that they will benefit from that trade. But unless they're required to do so, traders are unlikely to take into account the effect that that agreement or trade may have on others. (An effect of a trade or agreement on a third party that the people who made the trade did not take into account is called an *external effect* or **externality.**) An externality can be positive (in which case society as a whole benefits even more than the two traders) or negative (in which case society as a whole benefits less than the two parties). In either case, externalities provide a potential role for government. If one's goal is to benefit society as much as possible, trades with positive externalities should be encouraged, and trades with negative externalities should be restricted.

An example of a positive externality is education. When someone educates herself or himself, it is not only the person who is helped. All society benefits since better-educated people make better citizens and can often figure out new approaches to solving problems, solutions that benefit everyone.

An example of a negative externality is pollution. For example, when people use air conditioners, they'll probably let loose a small amount of chlorofluorocarbons, which go up into the earth's atmosphere and contribute to the destruction of the ozone layer. The ozone layer protects all living things by filtering some of the sun's ultraviolet light rays, which can contribute to cancer and other harmful or fatal conditions. Neither the firms that produce the air conditioners nor the consumers who buy them pay for the negative effect those chlorofluorocarbons have on society. This means that the destruction of the ozone layer is an externality—the result of an action that is not taken into account by traders.

When externalities exist, government has a potential role: to step in and change the rules so that the actors must take into account the effect of their actions on society as a whole. We emphasize that the role is a *potential* one, because government often has difficulty dealing with externalities in such a way that society gains. For example, even if the Canadian government totally banned chlorofluorocarbons, the problem wouldn't be solved because ozone layer destruction is an international, rather than a national, problem. We also emphasize *potential* because government isn't simply an institution trying to do good. It's an institution that reflects, and is often guided by, politics and vested interests. It's not clear that, given the political realities, government intervention to correct externalities would improve the situation. In later chapters we'll have a lot more to say about government's role in correcting for externalities.

Providing for Public Goods **Public goods** are goods whose consumption by one individual does not prevent their consumption by other individuals. This means that when a supplier supplies a public good to one person, he or she supplies the good to all. In contrast, a **private good** is one that, when consumed by one individual, cannot be consumed by other individuals. An example of a private good is an apple; once that apple is eaten, no one else can consume it.

Public goods Goods whose consumption by one individual does not prevent their consumption by other individuals.

Private good A good that, when consumed by one individual, cannot be consumed by other individuals.

An example of a public good is national defence. National defence must protect all individuals in the country; it cannot protect some people but leave others unprotected. Everyone agrees that national defence is needed. But will everyone, as individuals, supply it, or will everyone rely on someone else doing it? Self-interested people would like to enjoy the benefits of defence, while letting someone else pay for it. Because national defence is a public good, if someone else defends the country you're defended for free; you can be a **free rider.** Everyone has an incentive to be a free rider, but if everyone is a free rider, there won't be any defence. In such cases, government can step in to require that everyone pay part of the cost of national defence to make sure that no one is a free rider.

Free rider Person who participates in something for free because others have paid for it.

Ensuring Economic Stability and Growth In addition to providing general stability, government has the potential role of providing economic stability. If it's possible, most people would agree that government should prevent large fluctuations in the level of economic activity, maintain a relatively constant price level, and provide an economic environment conducive to economic growth. These aims are generally considered macroeconomic goals. They're justified as appropriate aims for government to pursue because they involve **macroeconomic externalities** (externalities that affect the levels of unemployment, inflation, or growth in the economy as a whole).

Macroeconomic externality Externality that affects the levels of unemployment, inflation, or growth in the economy as a whole.

Here's how a macroexternality could occur. When individuals decide how much to spend, they don't take into account the effects of their decisions on others; thus, there may be too much or too little spending. Too little spending often leads to unemployment. But in making their spending decisions, people don't take into account the fact that spending less might create unemployment. So their spending decisions can involve a macroexternality. Similarly, when people raise their price and don't consider its effect on inflation, they too might be creating a macroexternality.

Political Roles of Government The other group of possible roles for government, *political roles,* involves more controversial issues.

Providing for a Fair Distribution of Society's Income The first, and probably most controversial, of these roles concerns income distribution. Many believe the government should see that the economic system is fair, or at least is perceived as fair, by the majority of the people in the society.

Progressive tax Average tax rate increases with income.

Regressive tax Average tax rate decreases with income.

Proportional tax Average tax rate is constant with income.

But determining what's fair is a difficult philosophical question. Let's simply consider two of the many manifestations of the fairness problem. Should the government use a **progressive tax** (a tax whose rates increase as a person's income increases) to redistribute money from the rich to the poor? (A progressive income tax schedule might tax individuals at a rate of 15 percent for income up to $20,000; at 25 percent for income between $20,000 and $40,000; and at 35 percent for every dollar earned over $40,000.) Or should government impose a **regressive tax** (a tax whose rates decrease as income rises) to redistribute money from the poor to the rich? Or should government impose a flat or **proportional tax** (a tax whose rates are constant at all income levels, say 25 percent on every dollar of income, no matter what your total annual income is) and not redistribute money? Canada has chosen a somewhat progressive income tax.

Another tax question government faces is: Should there be *exemptions* (items of income that aren't taxed at all)? An exemption might be granted for $2,400 of income multiplied by the number of children the taxpayer has. A single mother with five children wouldn't be taxed at all on $12,000 ($2,400 × 5) of her annual income. Or is that a *tax loophole* (a legal but unfair exemption)? Many Canadian economists would argue that a more equitable approach is to give the mother a tax credit rather than an exemption. Economists can tell government the effects of various types of taxes and forms of taxation, but we can't tell government what's fair. That is for *the people,* through the government, to decide. Of course, interest groups place a great deal of pressure on the government, as we've already seen. Members of Parliament sometimes have a difficult time remembering just who *the people* really are.

Consider, for example, spending programmes targeted at historically depressed regions of the country. People in, for example, central Ontario or Alberta may have a hard time understanding why the federal government transfers millions of their tax dollars to firms in Atlantic Canada (through government agencies like the Atlantic Canada Opportunities Agency, known as ACOA) in an attempt to encourage regional economic development. Many might argue that regional development programmes are economically inefficient—and, while that might be true, we need to remember that economic institutions—such as the invisible handshake and the invisible foot—and political considerations colour every decision the government makes.

Determining Demerit and Merit Goods or Activities Another controversial role for government involves deciding what's best for people independently of their desires. The externality justification of government intervention assumes that individuals know what is best for themselves.

But what if people don't know what's best for themselves? What if they do know but don't act on that knowledge? For example, people might know that addictive drugs are bad for them but because of peer pressure, or because they just don't care, they may take addictive drugs anyway. Government action prohibiting such activities through law or high taxes may then be warranted. Goods or activities that are deemed bad for people even though they choose to use the goods or engage in the activities are known as **demerit goods or activities.** The addictive drug is a demerit good; using addictive drugs is a demerit activity.

Demerit goods or activities Things government believes are bad for you, although you may like them.

FINDING MORE INFORMATION ABOUT THE ECONOMY

ADDED DIMENSION 

No introductory book is able to provide you with all the information you should have about the economy. You should know about:

- Financial institutions, such as banks, insurance companies, and stock markets.
- The state of the economy: unemployment rates, inflation rates, and growth rates.
- The operations of business, such as advertising and assembly line production.

We'll provide general information on such topics, but you should get up-to-date specifics by following the economic news. Such current information is integral to any economics course. Where should you look? A good beginning is the following:

- Cursory: Business section of your local paper and network news on TV. A slim treatment of the economic issues, but at least it introduces you to the terms.
- One step up from cursory: Time, *Newsweek, MacLean's;* CBC, CTV, CNN on TV.
- Reasonably thorough: *Business Week, Forbes, Fortune, Canadian Business* magazines; "Question Period," "Venture," "Wall Street Week," and "The McNeil-Lehrer Report" on TV.
- Excellent: *The Economist, The Financial Post, The Financial Times, The Globe and Mail, The Wall Street Journal.*

Alternatively, there are some activities that government believes are good for people, even if people may not choose to engage in them. For example, government may believe that going to the opera or contributing to charity is a good activity. But in Canada only a small percentage of the population goes to the opera, and not everyone in Canada contributes to charity. Similarly, government may believe that whole-wheat bread is more nutritious than white bread. But many consumers prefer white bread. Activities and goods that government believes are good for you even though you may not choose to engage in the activities or consume the goods are known as **merit goods or activities,** and government support for them through subsidies or tax benefits may be warranted.

Merit goods or activities Things government believes are good for you, although you may not think so.

The Limits of Government Action

Economic theory doesn't say government should or shouldn't play any particular role in the economy. Those decisions depend on costs and benefits of government action. The public often perceives economic theory and economists as suggesting the best policy is a policy of laissez-faire, or government noninvolvement in the economy. Many economists do suggest a laissez-faire policy, but that suggestion is based on empirical observations of government's role in the past, not on economic theory.

Still, economists as a group generally favour less government involvement than does the general public. We suspect that the reason is that economists are taught to look below the surface at the long-run effect of government actions. They've discovered that the effects of government actions often aren't the intended effects, and that programmes frequently have long-run consequences that make the problems worse, not better. Economists, both liberal and conservative, speak in the voice of reason: "Look at all the costs; look at all the benefits. Then decide whether government should or should not intervene."

Political pressures often force government to act, regardless of what rational examination suggests. A good example is new air safety regulations after a plane crash. The public generally favours these overwhelmingly. Most economists we know say: "Wait. Don't act in haste. Consider the benefits and costs that would result." After careful consideration, advantages and disadvantages aren't always clear; some economists favour more regulation, some economists favour less regulation—but they all make their assessments on the basis of rational examination, not emotion.

CHAPTER SUMMARY

- The invisible hand doesn't operate in an invisible world. Knowing economics requires knowing real-world information.
- Views about government's appropriate role in the economy have changed over time.
- In Canada, businesses make the *what, how much,* and *for whom* decisions.
- Businesses, households, and government can be categorized in a variety of ways.
- Although businesses decide what to produce, they succeed or fail depending on their ability to meet consumers' desires. That's consumer sovereignty.
- The three main forms of business are corporations, sole proprietorships, and partnerships.
- Income is unequally divided among households. Whether that's bad, and whether anything should be done about it, are debatable.
- Governments play two general roles in the economy: (1) as a referee, and (2) as an actor.
- Government has seven possible economic roles in a capitalist society:
  1. Providing a stable institutional and legal structure within which markets can operate.
  2. Promoting workable and effective competition.
  3. Correcting for external effects of individuals' decisions.
  4. Providing public goods that the market doesn't adequately supply.
  5. Ensuring economic stability and growth.
  6. Providing an acceptably fair distribution of society's products among its individuals.
  7. Encouraging merit and discouraging demerit goods or activities.
- In deciding whether government has a role to play, economists look at the costs and benefits of a given role.

KEY TERMS

business *(82)*
competition *(96)*
consumer sovereignty *(84)*
corporation *(89)*
debt *(94)*
demerit goods or activities *(98)*
entrepreneurship *(82)*
externality *(96)*
free rider *(97)*
general purpose transfers *(94)*
government budget deficit *(94)*
government budget surplus *(94)*
households *(90)*
ideology *(92)*
interest groups *(93)*
limited liability *(89)*
low-income cutoff *(90)*
macroeconomic externality *(97)*
merit goods or activities *(99)*
monopoly power *(96)*
nonprofit business *(87)*
partnership *(89)*
private good *(97)*
profit *(84)*
progressive tax *(98)*
proportional tax *(98)*
public good *(97)*
regressive tax *(98)*
sole proprietorship *(89)*
special purpose transfers *(94)*
stage of production *(84)*
stock *(89)*
transfer payments *(94)*

QUESTIONS FOR THOUGHT AND REVIEW

The number after each question represents the estimated degree of critical thinking required. (1 = almost none; 10 = deep thought.)

1. A market system is often said to be based on consumer sovereignty—the consumer determines what's to be produced. Yet business decides what's to be produced. Can these two views be reconciled? How? If not, why? *(5)*
2. Should conservation be left to the free market to determine price and availability of resources, or is there a role for government intervention in the conservation debate? *(8)*
3. Canada is sometimes classified as a postindustrial society. What's meant by this? And, if it's an accurate classification, is it good or bad to be a postindustrial society? *(7)*
4. A nonprofit company will generally charge lower prices than a for-profit company in the same business because the nonprofit company doesn't factor a profit into its prices. True or false? Why? *(6)*
5. You're starting a software company in which you plan to sell software to your fellow students. What form of business organization would you choose? Why? *(5)*
6. The social security system is inconsistent with pure capitalism, but is almost an untouchable right of Canadians. How can this be? *(6)*
7. You've set up the rules for a game and started the game, but now realize that the rules are unfair. Should you change the rules? *(6)*
8. Say the government establishes rights to pollute so that without a pollution permit you aren't allowed to emit pollutants into the air, water, or soil. Firms are allowed to buy and sell these rights. In what way will this correct for an externality? *(9)*
9. What are two general roles of government and seven specific roles? *(3)*
10. According to polls, most economists classify themselves as liberal, but they generally favour less government involvement in the economy than does the general public. Why? *(7)*

PROBLEMS AND EXERCISES

1. Go to a store in your community.
   a. Ask what limitations the owners faced in starting their business.
   b. Were these limitations necessary?
   c. Should there have been more or fewer limitations?
   d. Under what heading of reasons for government intervention would you put each of the limitations?
   e. Ask what taxes the business pays and what benefits it believes it gets for those taxes.
   f. Is it satisfied with the existing situation? Why? What would it change?
2. You've been appointed to a provincial counterterrorist squad. Your assignment is to work up a set of plans to stop a group of 10 terrorists the government believes are going to disrupt the economy as much as possible with explosives.
   a. List their five most likely targets in your province, city, or town.
   b. What counterterrorist action would you take?
   c. How would you advise the economy to adjust to a successful attack on each of the targets?
3. The technology is now developing so that road use can be priced by computer. A computer in the surface of the road picks up a signal from your car and automatically charges you for the use of the road.
   a. How could this technological change contribute to ending bottlenecks and rush hour congestion?
   b. What are some of the problems that might develop with such a system?
   c. How would your transportation habits likely change if you had to pay to use roads?
4. Tom Rollins heads a new venture called Teaching Co. He has taped lectures at the top universities, packaged the lectures on audio- and videocassettes, and sells them for $90 and $150 per eight-hour series.
   a. Discuss whether such an idea could be expanded to include college courses that one could take at home.
   b. What are the technical, social, and economic issues involved?
   c. If it is technically possible and cost-effective, will the new venture be a success?
5. You've just been hired by a government department whose primary responsibility is to monitor the economic activities of foreign countries.
   a. What kind of information are you going to want to examine? Make a list of the ten most important topics. Now go to your library and try to find that information on any country of your choosing.
   b. How readily available was that information?
   c. If you wanted to disrupt that country's economy, on which sectors would you want to focus your energies?
   d. Now repeat this for Canada.
6. Boris Gaussware is a leading expert in the analysis of bankruptcy. He argues that government "red tape" is the primary cause of business failure in the nation. Do you agree? Ask someone who operates a business if they think red tape is what causes bankruptcies. What was their first reaction? Did they have any other explanation for why firms fail?
7. The government uses tax policy to redistribute income. The government also tries to set the rules of business so that firms know what they can and cannot do. Which of the seven roles of government would be applicable to these examples? Why?

Trading in Stocks

Small corporations' stock is usually traded *over-the-counter,* which doesn't mean you go in a store and walk up to the counter. *Over-the-counter* is an expression representing the stock exchange on which these stocks are bought and sold. An over-the-counter share has a *bid* price and a higher *ask* price. The bid price is the price someone has offered to pay for shares; the ask price is the price a shareholder has told her brokers she wants to get for her shares. Trades are usually made at some price between the bid and ask figures, with the broker collecting a commission for arranging a trade.

Exhibit A1 shows a typical stock exchange listing.

In order to buy or sell a Toronto Stock Exchange stock, you go to a stockbroker and say you want to buy or sell whatever stock you've decided on—say Ford Motor Company. The commission you're charged for having the broker sell you the stock (or sell it for you) varies. Any purchase of fewer than 100 shares of one corporation is called an *odd lot* and you'll be charged a higher commission than if you buy a 100-share lot or more.

There are a number of stock exchanges. The largest and most familiar is the Toronto Stock Exchange.

To judge how stocks as a whole are doing, a number of indexes have been developed. The one you're most likely to hear about in the news is the TSE 300. American indexes include Standard and Poor's (S&P 500), the Wilshire Index, and the Dow Jones Industrial Average.

When a share of a corporation's existing stock is sold on the stock exchange, corporations get no money from that sale. The sale is simply a transfer of ownership from one individual (or organization) to another. The only time a corporation gets money from the sale of stock is when it first issues the shares.

EXHIBIT A1 Stock Exchange Listings and Explanation

Source: The Globe and Mall, March 3, 1995, p. BB.

B8 Friday March 3, 1995 Globe and Mail Toronto

52-week high	52-week low	Stock	Sym	Div	High	Low	Close	Chg	Vol (100s)	Yield	P/E ratio
		A-B									
6 3/8	1.00	ABL Canada	ABL		1.05	1.00	1.05		1617		
20 1/2	14	AGF nv	AGF.PR.B	0.60	15	15	15		8	4.00	7.7
14 3/8	8	AIT Advanced	AIV		10 1/2	10 1/2	10 1/2		25		15.9
.145	0.10	AJ Perron	AJP		0.11	0.11	0.11	+0.01	350		
12 1/4	6 1/2	AT Plastics	ATP	0.18	11 1/8	11 1/8	11 1/8	−1/8	13	1.62	8.6
19 1/4	4.50	ATI Techs	ATY		7 1/2	7 1/2	7 1/2	+1/8	66		
12 1/8	6 5/8	ATS Automat	ATA		10	10	9 3/4	+1/8	37		15.0
14 5/8	3.95	Aberj	ABZ		8 1/8	8 1/4	8 1/2	−1/4	1570		
20 4/8	15 5/8	Abitibi-Price	A		17 3/8	17 1/4	17 1/2	−1/4	1368		
8 1/8	1.50	Accugraph j	ACU.A		7	6 1/2	6 3/8	+1/8	879		15.9
14 1/8	10 1/2	Acklands	ACK		12	11 3/8	11 5/8	−3/8	13		8.5
34 1/8	20 1/2	Acme Metal	AMK		21 1/2	20 3/4	21		22		6.2
0.48	0.15	Adex Mining	AMG		0.35	.325	.325	−0.15	4220		
5 1/4	2.70	Adrian Res	ADL		3.80	3.60	3.70	−0.15	573		
3.00	1.10	Advancd Grv j	AED		1.60	1.55	1.60	+0.05	186		
0.60	0.42	Advancd Ma	AMR		0.60	0.60	0.60		50		
7	4.50	Adventure El	AVN	0.14	5 1/2	5 1/2	5 1/2	+0.75	2	2.55	9.2
1.16	0.33	Advent	AVN.WT.A		0.45	0.35	0.35	−0.10	606		
19 3/8	11 1/4	Agnico Eagle	AGE	a0.10	13 1/8	13	13 1/4	+1/4	106	1.05	34.9
9 1/4	5 1/8	Agra nv	AGR.B	0.16	6 1/4	6 1/2	6 3/4	+1/4	58	2.37	
9 1/8	5 7/8	Agra Ind	AGR.A	0.14	7	7	7		51	2.00	
12 1/4	3.30	Aim Safety	AIM		9 7/8	9 1/2	9 3/4	−1/8	52		
18 1/8	10 1/4	Ainsworth Lu	ANS		11 1/8	11 1/4	11 1/4	−1/8	34		6.8
8 2/8	5 5/8	Air Canada	AC		7 5/8	7 3/8	7 3/8	−1/4	1385		6.8
3.15	1.75	Air Canad	AC.WT		2.00	1.80	1.80	−0.20	136		
5 1/4	2.30	Akita Dri nv	AKT.A		2.75	2.70	2.75	+0.05	9		4.6
22 1/4	16 1/8	Alberta Ener	AEC	0.40	18 3/4	18 1/2	18 5/8	−1/4	142	2.15	13.7
17 1/8	13 1/4	Alta Nat Gas	ANG	0.68	14 1/2	14 1/4	14 1/4	−1/4	275	4.77	11.5
38 3/8	27 1/8	Alcan	AL	a0.30	33 1/8	33 1/8	33 1/4	+1/8	3625	1.24	71.2
24 1/8	21 1/4	Alcan C	AL.PR.E	1.81	21 1/4	21 5/8	21 3/8		24	8.32	
2.25	0.50	Algo sv	AO.A		0.50	0.50	0.50	−0.09	10		
↑26	14	Algoma Cnti	ALC		26	24 3/4	26	+1	19		14.9
22 1/2	19 3/4	Algoma	AFC.PR.A	1.38	22	22	22	−1/2	497	6.25	
11 1/8	9	Algoma Steel	ALG		9 3/8	9 1/4	9 1/4	−1/8	15		
8 5/8	5 1/8	Allelix	AXB		5 5/8	5 5/8	5 5/8		10		
18 1/4	12 3/8	Alliance Com	AAC		14	13 1/4	14		44		11.0
25	16 1/4	Alliance Fore	ALP		23 1/2	22 1/4	22 3/4	−5/8	401		8.9
14 1/2	7	AlphaNet Tel	FAX		8 1/4	8 1/2	8 1/4	+1/4	32		
2.77	0.50	Altai Res	ATI		0.55	0.55	0.55		68		
6 1/2	2.35	Amer Eco	ECX		2.55	2.55	2.55		30		4.7
25 1/8	9 3/8	Amer Sensor	ASZ		12 1/4	12 3/4	12 1/8	+5/8	2543		

How to read the stock tables

1 2	3	4	5	6	7	8	9	10	11	12
↓↓ 52-week high low	↓ Stock	↓ Sym	↓ Div	↓ High	↓ Low	↓ Close	↓ Chg	↓ Vol (100s)	↓ Yield	↓ P/E ratio

1. Arrow up or down - new 52-week high or low in day's trading
2. 52-week high/low - highest and lowest inter-day price in past 52 weeks
3. Stock - abbreviated company name
4. Sym - Ticker symbol assigned to issue by exchange; .PR is preferred share, .WT is warrant, .UN is unit, .S means stacks are subject to regulation of the SEC Act, .W means when issued.
5. Div - Indicated annual dividend (excluding special dividends)
6. High - Highest inter-day trading price
7. Low - Lowest inter-day trading price
8. Close - Closing price
9. Chg - Change between closing price and previous closing board lot price
10. Vol - Number of shares traded in 100s; z preceding figure indicates sales are reported in full
11. Yield - expressed as percentage, calculated by dividing the dividend by current market price
12. P/E ratio - Price/earnings ratio; current stock price divided by the company's earnings per share from continuing operations for the latest 12 months

Footnotes

a - in U.S. dollars (on Canadian exchanges)
au - in Australian dollars
b - in British pounds or pence
c - in Canadian dollars (on U.S. exchanges)
cl - commercial/industrial stock (on the Vancouver Stock Exchange)
da - dividend in arrears
dc - dividends paid in Canadian dollars, but stock trades in U.S. funds
g - coming capital gains distribution will be paid to the current owner
in - inactive stock (on the VSE)
j - subject to special reporting rules
n - stock is new issue
nl - mutual fund with no front-end load or contingent deferred sales load
nv - non-voting
rc - in bankruptcy or receivership or being reorganized under the Bankruptcy Act, or securities assumed by such companies
rf - redemption fee or contingent deferred sales load may apply
rs - resource stock (VSE)
rv - shareholders' voting is restricted
s - indicates 52-week high-low range has been adjusted to reflect stock split or consolidation
sv - subordinate-voting
x - stock is trading ex-dividend
y - in Japanese yen.
Data supplied by Dow Jones Telerate Canada Inc.

CHAPTER 5

An Introduction to the World Economy

As for foreign exchange, it is almost as romantic as young love, and quite as resistant to formulae.

~H. L. Mencken

After reading this chapter, you should be able to:

1. Explain what is meant by *the industrial countries of the world* and *the developing countries of the world.*
2. State where in the world various resources are found and where goods are produced.
3. State two ways international trade differs from domestic trade.
4. Make sense of an exchange rate table in the newspaper.
5. Explain two important determinants of the trade balance.
6. List five important international economic institutions.
7. Give a brief economic history of the European Union and Japan since the 1940s.

International issues have always been at the centre of economic activity and economic policy in Canada. The Canadian economy is integrated with the world economy, and we cannot reasonably discuss Canadian economic issues without discussing the role that international considerations play in these issues. The aim of this chapter is to get you to start thinking about how the international marketplace affects the Canadian economy. Later in the course we'll examine the international dimensions of economic activity in much greater detail—by then you'll be well versed in Canada's dependence on the international economy.

Consider the clothes on your back. Most likely they were made abroad. Similarly with the cars you drive. It's likely that half of you drive a car that was made abroad. Of course, it's often difficult to tell. Just because a car has a Japanese or German name doesn't mean that it was produced abroad. Some Japanese and German companies now have manufacturing plants in Canada, and some Canadian firms have manufacturing plants abroad. When goods are produced by **global corporations** (corporations with substantial operations on both the production and sales sides in more than one country are called global, or multinational, corporations), corporate names don't always tell much about where a good is produced. As global corporations' importance

Global corporations Corporations with substantial operations on both the production and sales sides in more than one country. Another name for multinational corporations.

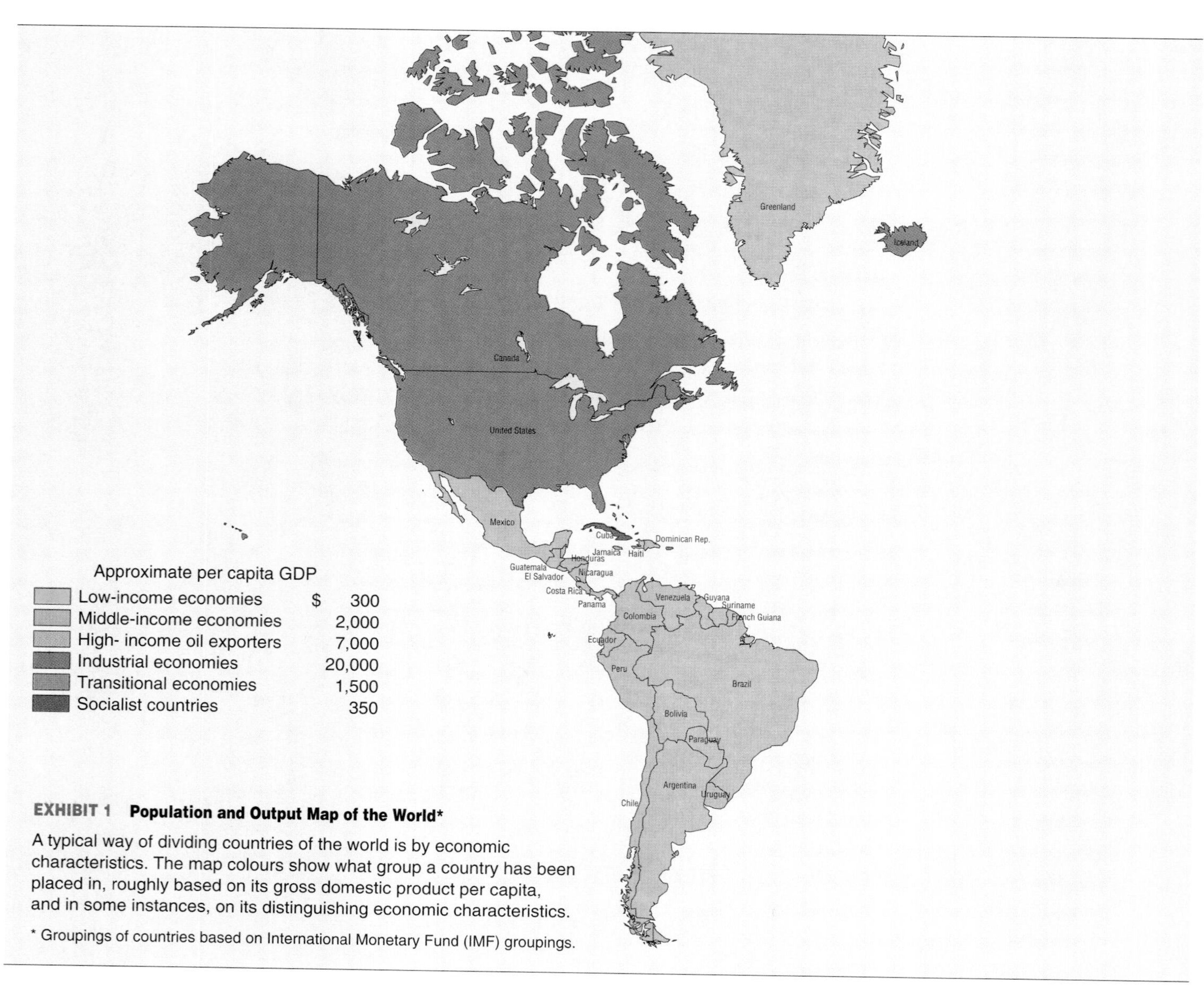

EXHIBIT 1 Population and Output Map of the World*

A typical way of dividing countries of the world is by economic characteristics. The map colours show what group a country has been placed in, roughly based on its gross domestic product per capita, and in some instances, on its distinguishing economic characteristics.

* Groupings of countries based on International Monetary Fund (IMF) groupings.

has grown, most manufacturing decisions are made in reference to the international market, not the domestic Canadian market.

The international connection means international economic problems and the policies of other countries—U.S. and European trade policies, developing countries' debt problems, questions of competitiveness, transfer of technology to China, Japanese microeconomic policy, Organization of Petroleum Exporting Countries (OPEC) pricing policies—all have moved to the centre of the economic stage. This chapter introduces you to such issues.

INTERNATIONAL ECONOMIC STATISTICS: AN OVERVIEW

Exhibit 1's map of the world is divided into categories based on per capita output (output per person, valued in U.S. dollars) and other relevant economic characteristics. *Industrial economies* (such as Canada, the United States, Germany, and Britain) have a large industrial production base. A second group of countries, such as Kuwait and Saudi Arabia, have high incomes, but don't have the industrial base. Since their high income is primarily based on oil exports, those countries are known as high-income *oil exporters*. The next two classifications, *middle-income economies* and *low-income economies* (or, as they are sometimes called, *developing economies*), make up

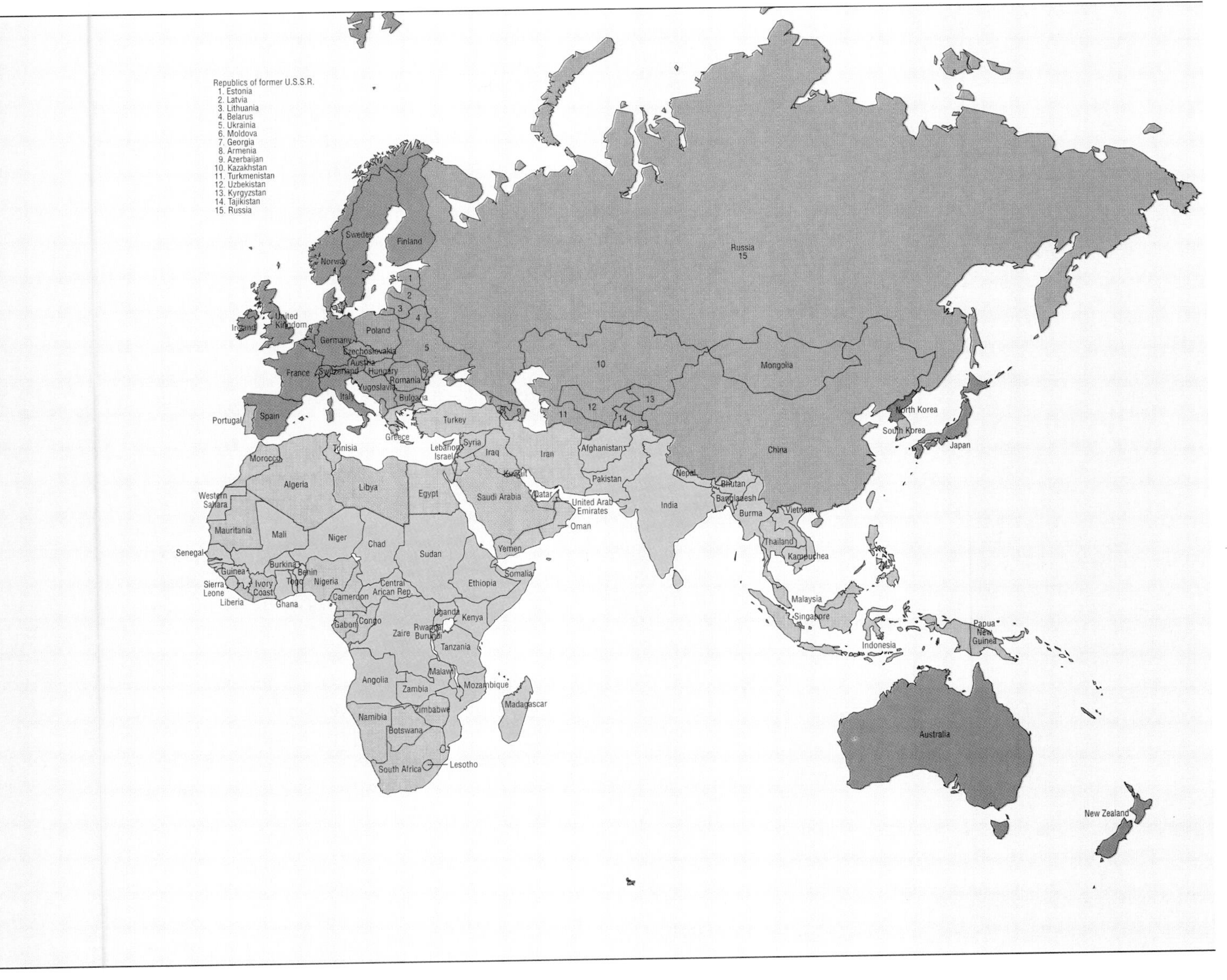

the majority of countries in the world. The *transitional economies* consist of the formerly socialist economies. These economies are in a period of flux and will probably be much in the news in the late 1990s. It is unclear what form of economic organization these transitional economies will take. The final category is *socialist economies;* only North Korea and Cuba still fit in this category.

1 The industrial countries of the world have a large industrial base and a per capita income of about $20,000 a year; the developing countries of the world include low- and medium-income economies that have a per capita income of between $300 and $2,000 a year.

This isn't the only method of classification. An alternative method is by region: Latin American, African, Middle Eastern, Asian, Western European, North American, and Eastern European countries. Since geographically grouped countries often share a cultural heritage, they also often face similar problems.

None of these classifications is airtight. Each country is different from every other, so no grouping works perfectly. Exhibit 1's classification system, based largely on output per person, is the most commonly used, and should give you a sense of what's meant by such classifications. The next time you hear "the industrial nations of the world" or "the developing countries of the world," you should be able to close your eyes and picture the relevant group of economies on a map or, at least, have a general idea of which countries are meant.

Economic Geography

Most classifications are based on a country's total output or production. Production statistics, however, don't necessarily capture a nation's importance or the strategic role it plays in the world economy. Consider Saudi Arabia. Its total output isn't particularly large, but since it's a major supplier of oil to the world, its strategic importance goes far beyond the relative size of its economy. Without its oil, many of the industrial countries of the world would come to a grinding halt. Similarly, Panama's production is minuscule, but its location on a narrow isthmus between the Atlantic and Pacific Oceans and the fact that the Panama Canal runs through its territory make Panama vital to the world economy.

These examples demonstrate why we need, besides a knowledge of countries' productive capacities, a knowledge of economic geography: Where do the world's natural resources lie? Which countries control them? What are the major trade routes? How are goods shipped from one place to another?

2 Some major producing areas for some important raw materials are:
Aluminum—Guinea, Australia
Cobalt—Zaire, Zambia, Russia
Copper—Chile, U.S., Poland
Iron—Russia, Brazil, Australia
Zinc—Canada, Australia, Russia

Exhibit 2 locates some of the world's major energy resources and trade routes. Note the major flow of energy resources from the Middle East: You can see why that region is so important to the world economy (oil and the Suez Canal). Other such resource maps would show why many countries treat South Africa with care (gold, many other alloying metals, and diamonds) and why Chile (with about 27 percent of all copper) is important to the world economy.

Differing Economic Problems

Imports Goods produced in foreign countries but sold in the home country.
Exports Goods produced in the home country but sold to foreign countries.

The economic problems countries face are determined by a variety of factors such as per capita income levels. High-income countries generally face quite different problems than low-income countries. Even two countries within the same group often face different problems. For example, the United States **imports** (buys goods produced in foreign countries) much more than it **exports** (sells U.S. goods to foreign countries), while the reverse is true for Japan. When trade disputes arise between Japan and the United States, as they did in 1993 and 1994, Canada gets caught in the crossfire. This is because the vast majority of our trade is with the United States. The result is that Canadian economic activity is highly sensitive to events originating abroad.

Although the identical economic insights apply to all countries, institutions differ substantially among countries. For example, many developing countries have few financial institutions, so when people there want to save, there's no way for them to do so. Similarly with transportation systems. If a firm wants to ship a good from Trois Rivières to Thunder Bay, it can use ships, trucks, trains, or planes. However, if an African firm wants to ship a good from one city to another in Zaire—say from Kinshasa to Lubumbashi—it must import trucks that can travel on unpaved or even nonexistent roads.

Comparative Advantage and Trade

One reason economies differ is that they produce different goods. Why? That's a question we'll explore in macroeconomics in a later chapter on international trade. For

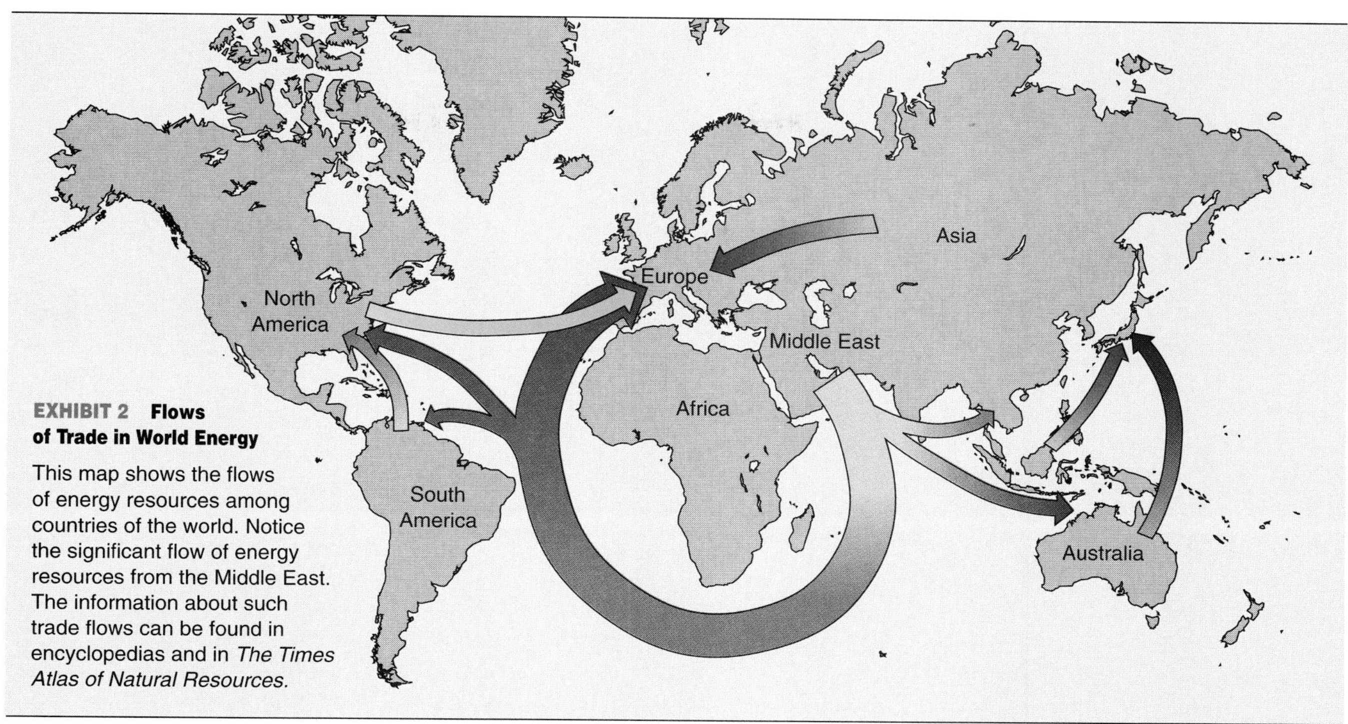

EXHIBIT 2 Flows of Trade in World Energy

This map shows the flows of energy resources among countries of the world. Notice the significant flow of energy resources from the Middle East. The information about such trade flows can be found in encyclopedias and in *The Times Atlas of Natural Resources.*

now, we'll simply introduce you to a key term in international trade which plays a major role in what different countries produce. That term is **comparative advantage.** A country has a comparative advantage in producing a good if it can produce that good at a lower opportunity cost (forgone production of another good) than another country can.

Comparative advantage The ability to produce a good at a lower opportunity cost (forgone production of another good) than another country can.

For example, say Canada can produce widgets at a cost of $4 apiece and wadgets at $4 apiece, while South Korea can produce widgets at a cost of 300 won apiece and wadgets at a cost of 100 won apiece. In Canada, the opportunity cost of one widget is one wadget. (Since each costs $4, Canada must reduce its production of wadgets by one to produce another widget.) In South Korea, the opportunity cost of a widget is three wadgets since it costs three times as much to produce a widget as it does to produce a wadget. Because Canada's opportunity cost of producing widgets is lower than South Korea's, Canada is said to have a comparative advantage in producing widgets. Similarly, South Korea is said to have a comparative advantage in producing wadgets because its opportunity cost of wadgets is one-third of a widget while Canada's opportunity cost of wadgets is one widget.

If one country has a comparative advantage in one good, the other country must necessarily have a comparative advantage in the other good. Notice how comparative advantage hinges on opportunity cost, not total cost. Even if one country can produce all goods cheaper than another country, trade between them is still possible since the opportunity costs of various goods differ.

There's much more to be said about comparative advantage and how changes in a nation's resource base force it to restructure its economy to take advantage of those changes. For now, we want you to remember that different countries produce different goods because opportunity costs vary considerably across countries.

Countries not only produce different goods, they also consume different goods. Exhibit 3 presents per capita consumption of some foods in selected countries. Notice the differences.

Other differences in consumption (and production) are explained by custom, history, and tradition. For example, Japanese traditionally eat rice with meals; Canadians eat bread and potatoes. Drinking alcoholic beverages in Russia is a time-honoured tradition; Muslim countries, such as Saudi Arabia, forbid consumption of

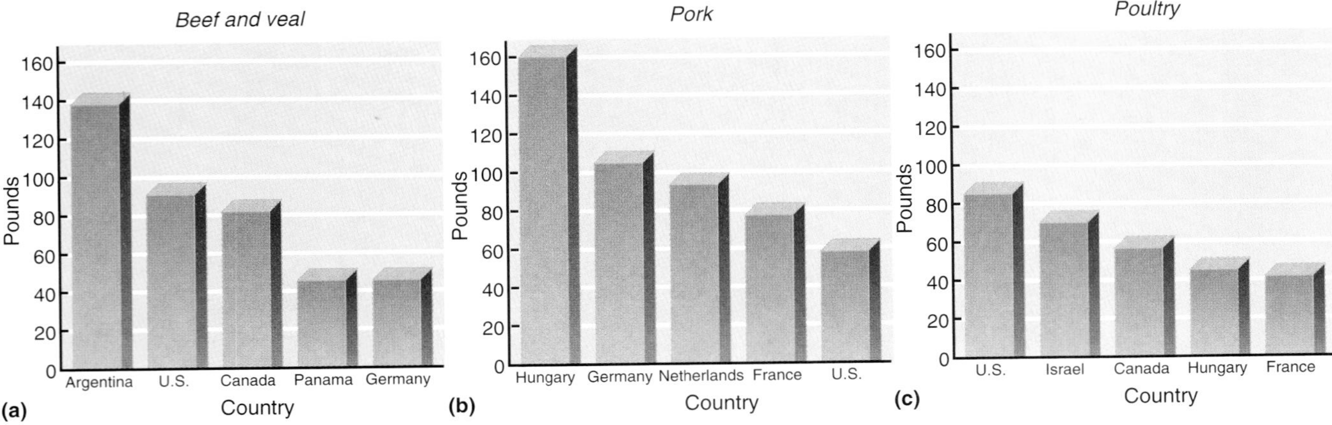

EXHIBIT 3 Per Capita Consumption of Different Commodities, 1990

In Exhibit 3 you can see the per capita consumption of selected goods in various countries. Notice that Canada consumes less beef and veal than does Argentina, and its consumption of poultry is small compared to the United States.

alcoholic beverages. Understanding international economic issues often requires an in-depth understanding of various countries' histories and cultures.

HOW INTERNATIONAL TRADE DIFFERS FROM DOMESTIC TRADE

3 Two ways in which *inter*national trade differs from *intra*national (domestic) trade are:
(1) International trade involves potential barriers to trade; and
(2) International trade involves multiple currencies.

Quotas Limitations on how much of a good can be shipped into a country.

Tariff tax A tax governments place on internationally traded goods—generally imports. Tariffs are also called *customs duties*.

Nontariff barriers Indirect regulatory restrictions on exports and imports.

Foreign exchange market Market in which one country's currency can be exchanged for another country's.

4 By looking at an exchange rate table, you can determine how much various goods will likely cost in different countries.

*Inter*national trade differs from *intra*national, or domestic trade in two ways. First, international trade involves potential barriers to the flow of inputs and outputs. Before they can be sold in Canada, international goods must be sent through Canada Customs; that is, when they enter Canada they are inspected by Canadian officials and usually charged fees, known as *customs*. A company in Vancouver can produce output to sell in any Canadian province without worrying that its right to sell will be limited; a producer outside the Canada boundary cannot. That is not to say that there aren't barriers to domestic trade: there are. These typically take the form of provincial regulations that attempt to protect local workers and firms from competition from outside the province. (In 1994, the provincial premiers announced their commitment to lessen interprovincial trade barriers and promised to introduce legislation to do so.) At any time, a foreign producer's right to sell in Canada can be limited by government-imposed **quotas** (limitations on how much of a good can be shipped into a country), **tariffs** (taxes on imports), and **nontariff barriers** (indirect regulatory restrictions on imports and exports).

The last category, indirect regulatory restrictions on imports and exports, may be unfamiliar to you, so let's consider an example. U.S. building codes require that plywood have fewer than, say, five flaws per sheet. Canadian building codes require that plywood have fewer than, say, two flaws per sheet. The different building codes are a nontariff barrier, making trade in building materials between the United States and Canada difficult.

The second way international trade differs from domestic trade is countries' use of different currencies. When people in one country sell something to people in another, they must find a way to exchange currencies as well as goods. **Foreign exchange markets** (markets where one currency can be exchanged for another) have developed to provide this service.

How many dollars will a Canadian have to pay to get a given amount of the currency of another country? That depends on the supply of and demand for that currency. To find what you'd have to pay, you look in the newspaper for the exchange rate set out in a foreign exchange table. Exhibit 4 shows such a table.

If you want shekels, you'll have to pay about 47 cents apiece. If you want Punt, one Punt will cost you $ 2.22. (If you're wondering what shekels and Punt are, look at Exhibit 4.)

A REMINDER

A WORLD ECONOMIC GEOGRAPHY QUIZ

Economic geography isn't much covered in most economics courses because it requires learning enormous numbers of facts. Universities and colleges are designed to teach you how to interpret and relate facts. Unfortunately, if you don't know facts, much of what you learn in university and college isn't going to do you much good. You'll be relating and interpreting air. The following quiz presents some facts about the world economy. On the left we list characteristics of countries or regions. On the right we list 20 countries or regions. Associate the characteristics with the country or region.

If you answer 15 or more correctly, you have a reasonably good sense of economic geography. If you don't, we strongly suggest learning more facts. The study guide has other projects, information, and examples. An encyclopedia has even more, and your library has a wealth of information. You could spend the entire term acquiring facts. We're not suggesting that; we are suggesting following the economic news carefully, paying attention to where various commodities are produced, and picturing in your mind a map whenever you hear about an economic event.

____ 1. Former British colony, now small independent island country famous for producing rum.
____ 2. Large sandy country contains world's largest known oil reserves.
____ 3. Very large country with few people produces 25 percent of the world's wool.
____ 4. Temperate country ideal for producing wheat, soybeans, fruits, vegetables, wine, and meat.
____ 5. Small tropical country produces abundant coffee and bananas.
____ 6. Has world's largest population and world's largest hydropower potential.
____ 7. Second-largest country in Europe; famous for wine and romance.
____ 8. Former Belgian colony has vast copper mines.
____ 9. European country; exports luxury clothing, footwear, and automobiles.
____ 10. Large country that has depleted many of its own resources but has enough coal to last its people for hundreds of years.
____ 11. Long, narrow country of four main islands; most thickly populated country in the world; exports majority of the world's electronic products.
____ 12. Recently politically reunified country; one important product is steel.
____ 13. Second-largest country in the world; leading paper exporter.
____ 14. European country for centuries politically repressed; now becoming industrialized; chemicals are one of its leading exports.
____ 15. 96 percent of its people live on 4 percent of the land; much of the world's finest cotton comes from here.
____ 16. African nation has world's largest concentration of gold.
____ 17. Huge, heavily populated country eats most of what it raises but is a major tea exporter.
____ 18. Large country that produces oil and gold; has recently undergone major political and economic changes.
____ 19. Has only about 50 people per square mile but lots of trees; major timber exporter.
____ 20. Sliver of a country on Europe's Atlantic coast; by far the world's largest exporter of cork.

a. Argentina
b. Australia
c. Barbados
d. Canada
e. China
f. Costa Rica
g. Egypt
h. France
i. Germany
j. India
k. Italy
l. Japan
m. Portugal
n. Russia
o. Saudi Arabia
p. South Africa
q. Spain
r. Sweden
s. United States
t. Zaire

Answers: 1–c, 2–o, 3–b, 4–a, 5–f, 6–e, 7–h, 8–t, 9–k, 10–s, 11–l, 12–i, 13–d, 14–q, 15–g, 16–p, 17–j, 18–n, 19–r, 20–m.

EXHIBIT 4 A Foreign Exchange-Rate Table

From the exchange-rate table, you learn how much a dollar is worth in other currencies. For example, on this day, March 2, 1995, one franc would cost 27.36 cents; one British pound would cost 2.2336 dollars.

Source: The *Globe and Mail*, March 3, 1995.

B16

Foreign Exchange

Cross Rates

	Canadian dollar	U.S. dollar	British pound	German mark	Japanese yen	Swiss franc	French franc	Dutch guilder	Italian lira
Canada dollar	—	1.4036	2.2336	0.9624	0.014650	1.1351	0.2736	0.8592	0.000848
U.S. dollar	0.7125	—	1.5913	0.6857	0.010437	0.8087	0.1949	0.6121	0.000604
British pound	0.4477	0.6284	—	0.4309	0.006559	0.5082	0.1225	0.3847	0.000380
German mark	1.0391	1.4584	2.3209	—	0.015222	1.1794	0.2843	0.8928	0.000881
Japanese yen	68.26	95.81	152.46	65.69	—	77.48	18.68	58.65	0.057884
Swiss franc	0.8810	1.2365	1.9678	0.8479	0.012906	—	0.2410	0.7569	0.000747
French franc	3.6550	5.1301	8.1637	3.5175	0.053545	4.1488	—	3.1404	0.003099
Dutch guilder	1.1639	1.6336	2.5996	1.1201	0.017051	1.3211	0.3184	—	0.000987
Italian lira	1179.25	1655.19	2633.96	1134.91	17.275943	1338.56	322.64	1013.21	—

Mid-market rates in Toronto at noon, Mar. 2, 1995. Prepared by the Bank of Montreal Treasury Group.

		$1 U.S. in Cdn.$ =	$1 Cdn. in U.S.$ =
U.S./Canada spot		1.4036	0.7125
1 month forward		1.4062	0.7111
2 months forward		1.4087	0.7099
3 months forward		1.4106	0.7089
6 months forward		1.4158	0.7063
12 months forward		1.4220	0.7032
3 years forward		1.4431	0.6930
5 years forward		1.4776	0.6768
7 years forward		1.5356	0.6512
10 years forward		1.6156	0.6190
Canadian dollar	High	1.3885	0.7202
in 1995:	Low	1.4267	0.7009
	Average	1.4066	0.7109

Country	Currency	Cdn. $ per unit	U.S. $ per unit
Britain	Pound	2.2336	1.5913
1 month forward		2.2372	1.5909
2 months forward		2.2402	1.5902
3 months forward		2.2422	1.5895
6 months forward		2.2459	1.5863
12 months forward		2.2430	1.5773
Germany	Mark	0.9624	0.6857
1 month forward		0.9650	0.6863
3 months forward		0.9699	0.6876
6 months forward		0.9761	0.6894
12 months forward		0.9849	0.6926
Japan	Yen	0.014650	0.010437
1 month forward		0.014725	0.010471
3 months forward		0.014871	0.010542
6 months forward		0.015088	0.010657
12 months forward		0.015490	0.010893
Algeria	Dinar	0.0332	0.0236
Antigua, Grenada and St. Lucia	E.C.Dollar	0.5208	0.3711
Argentina	Peso	1.40360	1.00000
Australia	Dollar	1.0340	0.7367
Austria	Schilling	0.13674	0.09742
Bahamas	Dollar	1.4036	1.0000
Barbados	Dollar	0.7053	0.5025
Belgium	Franc	0.04679	0.03333
Bermuda	Dollar	1.4036	1.0000
Brazil	Real	1.653239	1.177856
Bulgaria	Lev	0.0215	0.0153
Chile	Peso	0.003424	0.002440
China	Renminbi	0.1665	0.1186
Cyprus	Pound	3.0680	2.1858
Czech Rep	Koruna	0.0525	0.0374
Denmark	Krone	0.2426	0.1728
Egypt	Pound	0.4125	0.2939

Country	Currency	Cdn. $ per unit	U.S. $ per unit
Fiji	Dollar	0.9853	0.7020
Finland	Markka	0.3144	0.2240
France	Franc	0.2736	0.1949
Greece	Drachma	0.00604	0.00431
Hong Kong	Dollar	0.1815	0.1293
Hungary	Forint	0.01258	0.00896
Iceland	Krona	0.02136	0.01522
India	Rupee	0.04473	0.03187
Indonesia	Rupiah	0.000634	0.000452
Ireland	Punt	2.2219	1.5830
Israel	N Shekel	0.4701	0.3349
Italy	Lira	0.000848	0.000604
Jamaica	Dollar	0.04373	0.03115
Jordan	Dinar	2.0225	1.4409
Lebanon	Pound	0.000856	0.000610
Luxembourg	Franc	0.04679	0.03333
Malaysia	Ringgit	0.5501	0.3919
Mexico	N Peso	0.2377	0.1693
Netherlands	Guilder	0.8592	0.6121
New Zealand	Dollar	0.8913	0.6350
Norway	Krone	0.2179	0.1552
Pakistan	Rupee	0.04557	0.03247
Philippines	Peso	0.05396	0.03845
Poland	Zloty	0.5795450	0.4128990
Portugal	Escudo	0.00927	0.00660
Romania	Leu	0.0008	0.0006
Russia	Ruble	0.000310	0.000221
Saudi Arabia	Riyal	0.3743	0.2667
Singapore	Dollar	0.9700	0.6911
Slovakia	Koruna	0.0461	0.0329
South Africa	Rand	0.3892	0.2773
South Korea	Won	0.001781	0.001269
Spain	Peseta	0.01093	0.00779
Sudan	Dinar	0.0366	0.0261
Sweden	Krona	0.1918	0.1366
Switzerland	Franc	1.1351	0.8087
Taiwan	Dollar	0.0537	0.0382
Thailand	Baht	0.0565	0.0403
Trinidad, Tobago	Dollar	0.2469	0.1759
Turkey	Lira	0.0000338	0.0000241
Venezuela	Bolivar	0.00827	0.00589
Zambia	Kwacha	0.001755	0.001250
European Currency Unit		1.7910	1.2760
Special Drawing Right		2.1002	1.4963

The U.S. dollar closed at $1.4034 in terms of Canadian funds, up $0.0057 from Wednesday. The pound sterling closed at $2.2644, up $0.0469.

In New York, the Canadian dollar closed down $0.0029 at $0.7126 in terms of U.S. funds. The pound sterling was up $0.0270 to $1.6135.

Unless you collect currencies, the reason you want the currency of another country is that you want to buy something that country produces or an existing asset of that country. Say you want to buy a car which costs 9,684,000 South Korean won. Looking at the table you see that the exchange rate is $1 for 562 won. Dividing 562 into 9,684,000 won tells you that you need $17,231 to buy the car. So before you can buy the car, somebody must go to a foreign exchange market with $17,231 and exchange those dollars for 9,684,000 won. Only then can the car be bought in Canada.

EXHIBIT 5 Canada's Trade Balance

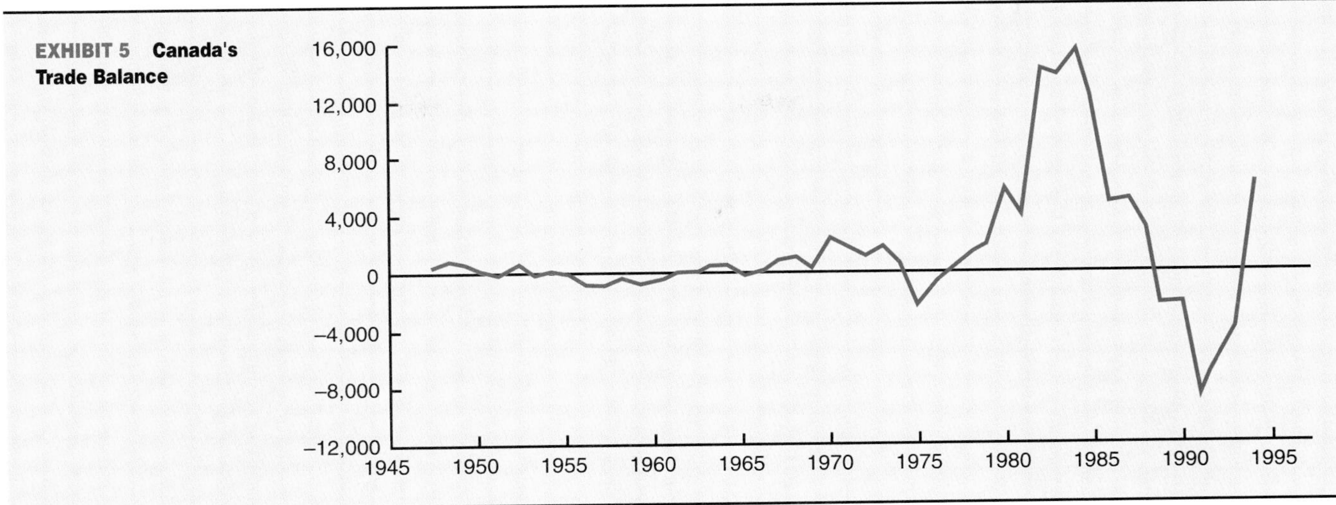

Most final buyers don't do this; the importer does it for them. But whenever a foreign good is bought, someone must trade currencies.

THE CANADIAN INTERNATIONAL TRADE BALANCE

One reason a Canadian economics course must consider international issues early on is the Canadian **balance of trade** (the difference between the value of the goods and services Canada exports and the value of the goods and services it imports). When imports exceed exports, a country is running a **balance of trade deficit;** when exports exceed imports, a country is running a **balance of trade surplus.**[1]

Balance of trade The difference between the value of goods a nation exports and the value of goods it imports.

Balance of trade deficit When a nation imports more than it exports.

Balance of trade surplus When a nation exports more than it imports.

Merchandise trade balance The difference between the goods a nation exports and the goods a nation imports.

Services balance The difference between the services a nation exports and the services a nation imports.

Exhibit 5 shows that Canada ran a trade surplus from 1978 to 1988. In 1984, when the trade surplus was at its peak, Canadian exports of goods and services were about 28.5 percent of gross domestic product (GDP); imports of goods and services were about 25 percent. The 3.5 percent difference meant Canada exported about $15.5 billion worth of goods and services more than it imported. In 1994 Canada ran a trade surplus, partly as a result of the increased world demand for Canadian goods that came from a lower value of the dollar.

We have to be careful about the terminology we use when we look at Canada's international position, since the balance of trade contains two components. The first is the **merchandise trade balance**—it measures the difference between our exports and our imports of goods. The second component is the **services balance**—it captures trade in services. If we took a close look at Canada's trade in merchandise, we'd see that Canada has been a net exporter of goods since at least 1973. The deficit in the balance of trade that we see in Exhibit 5 is due to the fact that Canada has been a net importer of services. It may sound funny, but when your cousin Fred vacations in Florida during spring break, he's really importing the services that the Florida vacation provides. While we export more goods to the rest of the world than we import from the rest of the world, it isn't enough to compensate for the deficit in the services account. That's why the balance of trade is negative even though you might hear on the news or read in the newspaper that Canada just ran a record merchandise trade surplus.

Debtor and Creditor Nations

Running a trade deficit isn't necessarily bad, nor is running a trade surplus. In fact, while you're running a trade deficit, it's rather nice. If you were a country, you probably would be running a trade deficit now since, most likely, you're consuming

[1] We're only interested in the balance of trade right now. There's much more to be said about Canada's international trade position, and we'll come back to this in much greater detail in macroeconomics in a later chapter—as if you haven't had enough already!

ADDED DIMENSION  BLACK AND GREY MARKETS IN CURRENCY

Foreign exchange markets are a good example of supply and demand forces at work. Whenever there's excess supply or demand for something, there's incentive for suppliers and demanders to get together to eliminate the excess.

Let's consider the issue in relation to the former Soviet Union. In 1989, at the official price of 0.64 rubles per U.S. dollar, the quantity of U.S. dollars demanded far exceeded the quantity of U.S. dollars supplied. In the former Soviet Union, adventurous individuals (who weren't worried about the wrath of the invisible foot—that is, about being prosecuted for violating foreign exchange laws) traded in a black market at a higher price, which in the early 1990s reached 30 rubles per U.S. dollar.

A black market, which involves trades of a good that can't legally be traded, is a natural result of government price restrictions. Often the government knows that such trading goes on and chooses, for political reasons, not to enforce its own laws strictly. (There are situations like this in Canada. Here the speed limit is 100 kilometres per hour on many roads, but almost everyone drives at 110 kilometres per hour, which some police tend to accept as a fact of life.)

An unofficially condoned black market is a *grey market*. Trading on it is more open, risk of prosecution and upward pressure on price from the invisible foot are less, and prices on it are usually closer to the supply/demand equilibrium than black market prices.

The Soviet foreign exchange market became a grey market in late 1989. (The grey market price of a U.S. dollar was between 5 and 15 rubles rather than the .64 rubles you'd get at the official rate.) If you went to the former Soviet Union at that time, individuals would come up to you on the street and offer to trade rubles for U.S. dollars at something near the grey market price. In 1991 the Soviet Union broke apart and Russia began to let the ruble be freely tradable. Because of political and economic problems, the ruble's value fell enormously and it took thousands of rubles to get one U.S. dollar.

(importing) more than you're producing (exporting). How can you do that? By living off past savings, getting support from your parents or a spouse, or borrowing.

Countries have the same options. They can live off foreign aid, past savings, or loans. For example, the American economy is currently running a trade deficit, and the United States is financing the trade deficit by selling off assets—financial assets such as shares and bonds, or real assets such as real estate and corporations. Since the assets of the United States total many billions of dollars, it can continue to run trade deficits for decades to come.

Canada hasn't always had a balance of trade deficit. We've had periods of deficits, surpluses, and fairly consistent cyclical patterns around zero, as shown in Exhibit 5. The problem with running a prolonged trade deficit is that a country ends up borrowing more from abroad than it lends abroad. This means it becomes a large debtor nation—and it ends up paying interest on its borrowed money every year without getting anything for it.

Determinants of the Trade Balance

5 Two important determinants of the trade balance are:
(1) A country's competitiveness; and
(2) The relative state of a country's economy.

Competitiveness A country's ability to produce goods and services more cheaply than other countries.

In determining the size of the trade balance, two factors are important:

1. Canadian competitiveness and the value of the Canadian dollar.
2. The state of the Canadian economy compared to that of other countries.

Let's look at each factor.

Canadian Competitiveness Probably the single most important issue in determining whether a country runs a trade deficit or a trade surplus is its **competitiveness** (the ability to produce goods more cheaply than other countries). Competitiveness depends upon productivity—a country's output per worker and its technological innovativeness (its ability to develop new and different products).

In the 1950s and early 1960s, Canada was highly competitive. Even though Canadian workers were paid substantially more than foreign workers, Canadian goods were cheaper, better, and more desired than foreign goods. In the 1950s, the label MADE IN JAPAN was a sign of low-quality, cheap goods. That has changed since the late 1970s. While Canada lost its competitive edge, Japan gained one. Today MADE IN JAPAN is a sign of quality.

Japan's rise from a defeated country after World War II, with few natural resources, little land, and a devastated economy, to an international economic power that outcompetes Canada in almost every aspect of economics, was an important economic story of the 1980s. One reason for Japan's rise was cultural. Another reason was the relative values of the Japanese yen and Canadian dollar. Throughout much of the 1960s, 1970s, and 1980s, the yen's relative value was low. A major determinant of a country's competitiveness is the value of its currency. A currency that is low in value relative to other currencies encourages the country's exports by lowering their prices and discourages its imports by raising their prices. (In 1965, $1 bought about 300 yen; in the mid-1990s, $1 bought less than 60 yen. Conversely, the dollar's relatively high value during the 1960s undermined Canadian competitiveness.)

In the late 1980s, the dollar's value relative to the yen fell substantially, making Canadian goods more competitive. That didn't immediately reduce the Canadian balance of trade deficit, and it became apparent that the problems of Canada in international competitiveness had additional causes. But it did eventually help improve Canadian competitiveness. By 1993, the rise in value of the yen had pushed Japanese car prices up sufficiently so that Canadian cars seemed like bargains, causing a recovery of the Canadian automobile industry in 1994. However, the fall in the dollar's value has a downside: It means that Canadian assets are cheaper for foreigners. They can buy not only the products, but also the firms that make those products, the buildings within which those products are made, and the land upon which those buildings stand. In the 1990s, we'll likely hear much about foreigners "buying up Canada."

Talk of foreign control over Canadian resources isn't new. In 1974, the federal government established the Foreign Investment Review Agency (FIRA) to oversee foreign investment and foreign takeovers of large Canadian firms. There was concern that foreigners were gaining too much power over *what* and *how* Canada produced. Foreign investment has been an important source of Canadian economic growth, and FIRA was directly opposed to overseas investment. In 1985, the federal government replaced FIRA with Investment Canada. Its mandate was to encourage investment without primary concern over the source of funds, since by then it was felt that both foreign and domestic capital were needed to restore growth in the Canadian economy. Today, foreign direct investment in Canada totals over $140 billion. Nevertheless, domestic concerns over foreign control remain, so we shouldn't be surprised to hear about it in the news.

The State of the Canadian Economy A second factor in determining the trade balance is the state of the economy. The level of Canadian income affects the trade balance, and the trade balance affects the level of Canadian income. The reason for the first effect is simple. Say Canada is running a balance of trade deficit. When Canadian income rises, Canada imports more goods and services (you can finally afford that trip to France), so the balance of trade deficit increases.

The second effect—the trade balance's effect on Canadian income—isn't so simple. Say Canada has a balance of trade deficit. When Canada imports more (or exports less), the trade deficit worsens and the rise in imports means Canadian production falls, which means Canadian citizens have less income; they spend less and Canadian income falls even more. So an increase in the trade deficit lowers income. It also works the opposite way: When Canada exports more (imports less), Canadian production rises; as Canadian production rises, Canadian citizens have more income; they spend more and Canadian income rises even more. This effect of exports on domestic income is what economists mean when they say a country has "export-led growth." A country with export-led growth has a balance of trade surplus which stimulates growth in income.

Economists' View of Trade Restrictions

Large trade deficits often inspire politicians to call for trade restrictions prohibiting imports. Most economists, liberal and conservative alike, generally oppose such restrictions. The reason is that even though trade restrictions directly decrease the trade deficit, they also have negative effects on the economy that work in the opposite direction.

One negative effect is that trade restrictions reduce domestic competition. When a group of Canadian producers can't compete with foreign producers—either in price or in quality—that group often pushes for trade restrictions to prevent what they call "unfair" foreign competition. Canadian producers benefit from the trade restrictions, but consumers are hurt. Prices rise and the quality of the goods falls.

A second negative effect is that trade restrictions bring retaliation. If one country limits imports, the other country responds; the first country responds to that . . . The result is called a *trade war,* and a trade war hurts everyone.

Such a trade war occurred in the 1930s and significantly contributed to the Great Depression of that period. To prevent trade wars, countries have entered into a variety of international agreements. The most important is the **World Trade Organization (WTO),** the successor agency to the **General Agreement on Tariffs and Trade (GATT).** Under GATT, countries agreed not to impose new tariffs or other trade restrictions except under certain limited conditions. These agreements are continued under WTO.

World Trade Organization (WTO) World body charged with reducing impediments to trade; it replaced GATT in 1995.

INTERNATIONAL ECONOMIC POLICY AND INSTITUTIONS

Just as international trade differs from domestic trade, so does international economic policy differ from domestic economic policy. When economists talk about Canadian economic policy, they generally refer to what the Canadian federal government can do to achieve certain goals. In theory, at least, the Canadian federal government has both the power and the legal right of compulsion to make Canadian citizens do what it says. It can tax, it can redistribute income, it can regulate, and it can enforce property rights.

There is no international counterpart to a nation's federal government. Any meeting of a group of countries to discuss trade policies is voluntary. No international government has powers of compulsion. Hence, dealing with international problems must be done through negotiation, consensus, bullying, and concessions.

Governmental International Institutions

6 Five important international economies institutions are:

1. The UN;
2. The WTO;
3. The World Bank;
4. The IMF; and
5. The EU.

World Bank A multinational, international financial institution that works with developing countries to secure low-interest loans.

International Monetary Fund (IMF) A multinational, international financial institution concerned primarily with monetary issues.

Group of Five Group that meets to promote negotiations and coordinate economic relations among countries. The Five are Japan, Germany, Britain, France, and the United States.

Group of Seven Group that meets to promote negotiations and coordinate economic relations among countries. The Seven are Japan, Germany, Britain, France, Canada, Italy, and the United States.

To discourage bullying and to encourage negotiation and consensus, governments have developed a variety of international institutions and agreements to promote negotiations and coordinate economic relations among countries. These include the United Nations (UN), World Trade Organization (WTO), World Bank, World Court, International Monetary Fund (IMF), and regional organizations such as the Organization of Petroleum Exporting Countries (OPEC), European Union (EU), and North American Free Trade Agreement (NAFTA).

These organizations have a variety of goals. For example, the **World Bank** works closely with developing countries, channelling low-interest loans to them to foster economic growth. The **IMF** is concerned with international financial arrangements. When developing countries encountered financial problems in the 1970s and had large international debts that they could not pay, the IMF helped work on repayment plans.

In addition to these formal institutions, there are informal meetings of various countries. These include **Group of Five** meetings of Japan, Germany, Britain, France, and the United States; and **Group of Seven** meetings with Japan, Germany, Britain, France, Canada, Italy, and the United States.

Since governmental membership in international organizations is voluntary, their power is limited. When Canada doesn't like a World Court ruling, it simply states that it isn't going to follow the ruling. When Canada is unhappy with what the United Nations is doing, it can withhold some of its dues. Other countries do the same from time to time. Other member countries complain, but can do little to force compliance. It doesn't work that way domestically. If you decide you don't like Canadian policy and refuse to pay your taxes, you'll wind up in jail.

What keeps nations somewhat in line when it comes to international rules is a moral tradition: Countries want to (or at least want to look as if they want to) do what's "right." Countries will sometimes follow international rules to keep international opinion favourable to them. But national self-interest often overrides scruples.

Global Corporations

Chapter 4 introduced you to Canadian corporations and listed the largest corporations in Canada. More and more of these and other corporations are transcending national

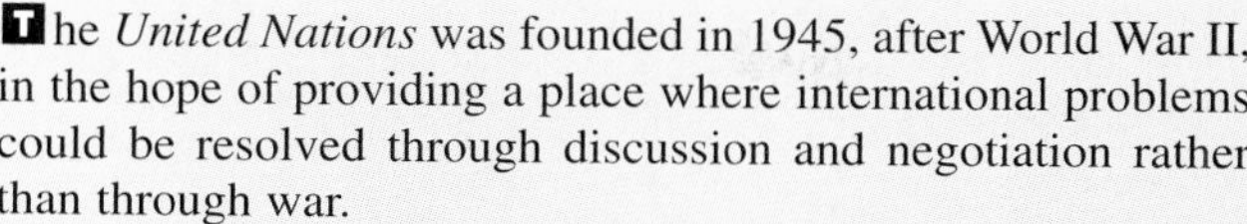

INTERNATIONAL ECONOMIC INSTITUTIONS

A REMINDER

The *United Nations* was founded in 1945, after World War II, in the hope of providing a place where international problems could be resolved through discussion and negotiation rather than through war.

The *World Bank* is a multilateral, international financial institution established in 1944. One of its main objectives is to provide funding to developing countries.

The *International Monetary Fund* (IMF), another international financial institution founded in 1944, lends money to developing countries in the form of "aid" packages which require recipient countries to try to reach certain economic goals.

The *Organization of Petroleum Exporting Countries* (OPEC) consists of 13 major oil-exporting countries in the Middle East, Far East, Africa, and South America. Formed in 1960, the organization promotes its member countries' joint national interests, such as preventing reductions in the price of oil.

The *Organization of Economic Cooperation and Development* (OECD) was set up in 1961 to promote economic cooperation among individual countries. Its 24 members include all major industrial countries and most Western European countries. The OECD is the best source of comparative statistics for Western economies.

boundaries. They have branches on both the production and sales sides throughout the world. As they do, they become global, or multinational, corporations rather than national corporations.

Global corporations offer enormous benefits for countries. They create jobs; they bring new ideas and new technologies to a country, and they provide competition for domestic companies, keeping them on their toes. But global corporations also pose a number of problems for governments. One is their implications for domestic and international policy. A domestic corporation exists within a country and can be dealt with using policy measures within that country. A global corporation exists within many countries and there is no global government to regulate or control it. If it doesn't like the policies in one country—say taxes are too high or regulations too tight—it can shift its operations to other countries.

Countries often compete for these global corporations by changing their regulations to encourage companies to use them as their home base. For instance, firms might register their oil tankers in Liberia to avoid paying Canadian wages, and put their funds in Bahamian banks to avoid Canadian financial disclosure laws.

At times it seems that global corporations are governments unto themselves, especially in relation to poorer countries. Consider Exhibit 6 (a)'s list of some large global corporations and their sales. Then compare it with Exhibit 6 (b)'s list of some small and middle-size economies and their output. In terms of sales, a number of global corporations are larger than the economies of middle-size countries. This comparison is not quite accurate, since sales do not necessarily reflect power; but when a company's decisions can significantly affect what happens in a country's economy, that company has significant economic power.

When global corporations have such power, it is not surprising that they can sometimes dominate a country. The corporation can use its expertise and experience to direct a small country to do its bidding rather than the other way around.

Another problem global corporations present for governments involves multiple jurisdiction. Global corporations can distance themselves from questionable economic activities by setting up *dummy corporations.* A dummy corporation exists only on paper, and is actually controlled by another corporation. Sometimes when a corporation really wants to separate itself from the consequences of certain actions, it creates dummy corporations, in which one paper corporation controls another paper corporation, which in turn controls another paper corporation. Each corporation is incorporated in a different nation, which makes it difficult, if not impossible, to trace who is actually doing what and who can be held accountable.

Before you condemn globals, remember: Globals don't have it so easy either.

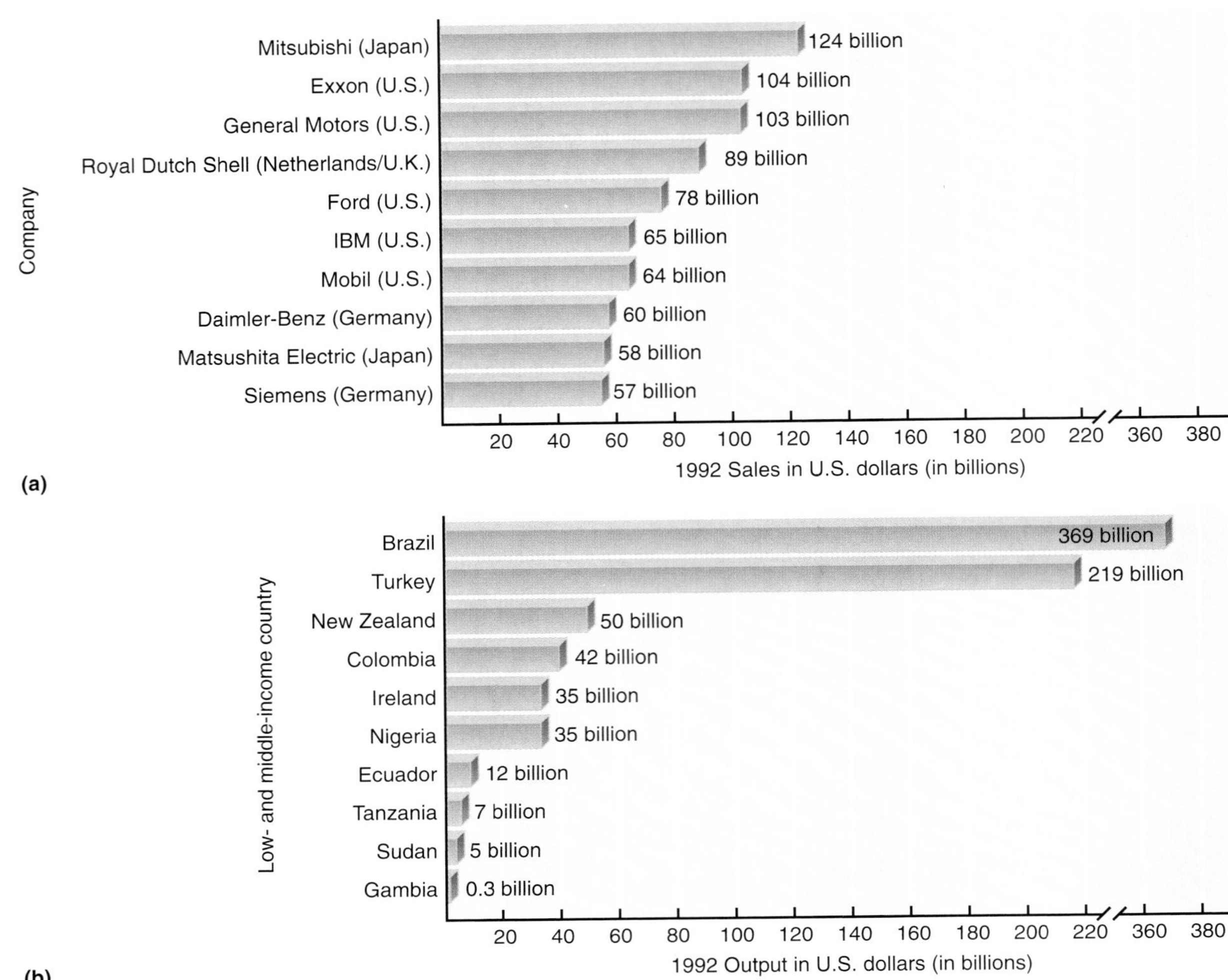

EXHIBIT 6 Global Corporations

As you can see in the charts, a number of global corporations are larger than the economies of some countries in terms of sales. This is important to a small country whose economy can be affected by a decision a global corporation might make.
Source: *CIA World Fact Book,* 1993 and *World Almanac,* 1994.

Customs and laws differ among countries. Trying to meet the differing laws and ambiguous limits of acceptable action in various countries is often impossible. For example, in many countries bribery is an acceptable part of doing business. If you want to get permission to sell a good, you must pay the appropriate officials *baksheesh* (as it's called in Egypt) or *la mordita* (as it's called in Mexico). In Canada, such payments are illegal bribes. Given these differing laws, the only way a Canadian company can do business in some foreign countries is to break Canadian laws.

Moreover, global corporations often work to maintain close ties among countries and to reduce international tension. If part of your company is in an Eastern European country and part in Canada, you want the two countries to be friends. So beware of making judgements about whether global corporations are good or bad. They're both simultaneously.

WHO ARE OUR INTERNATIONAL COMPETITORS?

So far we've given you a brief introduction to the international economic problems Canada faces and to some of the international institutions that exist to coordinate international economic activity. In this section we introduce three of our rivals, the United States, the European Union, and Japan, giving you a brief background of their histories and economic institutions. We also briefly discuss a fourth competitor—the devel-

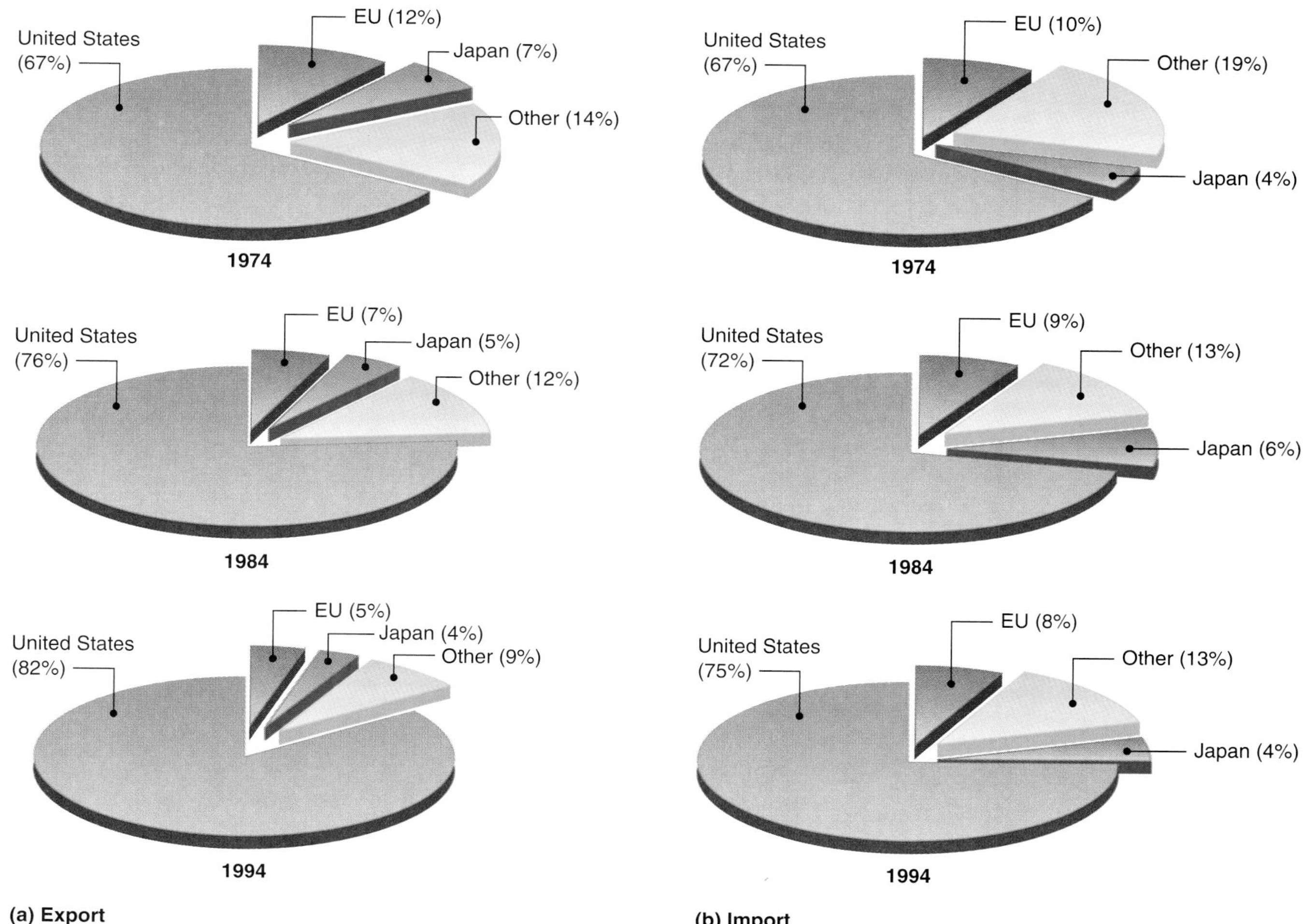

EXHIBIT 7 Geographic Breakdown of Canada's Import and Export Shares for 1974, 1984, 1994

You can see that Canada's share of exports to the United States and imports from the United States have grown substantually over the last 20 years. Trade with the EU (formerly the EEC) has fallen off during this period.

Sources: *Statistics Canada, CANSIM Database,* March 1995.

oping world—and explain why, with the new North American Free Trade Agreement (NAFTA), questions of our economic and political relations with Mexico and the United States are likely to be much in the news in the 1990s.

The United States is by far our most important trading partner. In 1994, Canada exported over $44 billion worth of merchandise to the United States while we imported only $38 billion from the United States. In 1994, trade with the United States represented 82 percent of exports and 75 percent of imports. Exhibit 7 shows how Canada's trade shares have changed over the last 20 years.

The geographic and cultural ties linking Canada and the United States are strong and resilient to changes in the political landscape in both countries. The economies are highly integrated in both trade and financial markets. They are similarly endowed, with Canada relatively resource rich as compared to the industrial machine that drives the United States economy.

That is not to say that trade relations have always been rosy. Disputes over government subsidies and unfair trading practices have been common since Confederation. These were perhaps most apparent during the recession in 1982–83. It saw the United States adopt **protectionist policies**—policies that favour domestic

Protectionist policies Policies that favour domestic products over foreign-produced products.

products over foreign-produced products—in an attempt to shelter domestic firms and workers from foreign competition through the introduction of tariffs, import licenses, and other nontariff barriers (like quality controls over imported agricultural goods) that were to the detriment of Canada. Public debate in Canada led to the view that we might be best served by entering into an agreement with the United States to reduce impediments to the free flow of goods and services across the Canada–U.S. border. Negotiations led to an historic agreement—The Canada–U.S. **Free Trade Agreement** (FTA) came into effect on January 1, 1989. It set into place a schedule for reducing trade barriers and the elimination of many nontariff barriers. Its primary objectives were outlined in the Preamble to the agreement:

Free Trade Agreement (FTA) Trade deal signed by Canada and the United States aimed at reducing barriers to trade. It took effect on January 1, 1989.

> PREAMBLE
>
> The Government of Canada and the Government of the United States of America, resolved:
>
> TO STRENGTHEN the unique and enduring friendship between their two nations;
>
> TO PROMOTE productivity, full employment, and a steady improvement of living standards in their respective countries;
>
> TO CREATE an expanded and secure market for the goods and services produced in their territories;
>
> TO ADOPT clear and mutually advantageous rules governing their trade;
>
> TO ENSURE a predictable commercial environment for business planning and investment;
>
> TO STRENGTHEN the competitiveness of the United States and Canadian firms in global markets;
>
> TO REDUCE government-created trade distortions while preserving the Parties' flexibility to safeguard the public welfare;
>
> TO BUILD on their mutual rights and obligations under the *General Agreement on Tariffs and Trade* and other multilateral and bilateral instruments of cooperation; and
>
> TO CONTRIBUTE to the harmonious development and expansion of world trade and to provide a catalyst to broader international cooperation;
>
> HAVE AGREED as follows: . . .

While few would argue against the objectives outlined in the Preamble, labour groups in Canada were vehemently opposed to the deal. They saw it as an attempt by Canadian firms to break the unions by threatening to move production to low-wage areas of the United States if the Canadian unions didn't make wage and benefit concessions. Business argued that these concessions were necessary if Canadian firms were to compete in the global marketplace and that rationalization would be necessary to increase the efficiency of Canadian industry. Proponents of the FTA argued that only through a process of cooperation would Canada hope to maintain its standard of living during the process of **globalization**—the cross-border spread of goods and services, factors of production, firms, and markets. The FTA was seen as a critical step in revitalizing the Canadian economy.

Globalization The cross-border spread of goods and services, factors of production, firms, and markets.

Have the objectives outlined in the Preamble been accomplished? Is Canada better off as a result of the FTA? It's difficult to say, since the recession of 1990–91 hastened changes to the structure of the Canadian economy, as did the process of globalization that encompassed the United States and Canada. It's fairly safe to say that the agreement provided better Canadian access to United States markets than we would have had in the absence of a trade deal, especially given the recession of the early 1990s and the ensuing wave of United States protectionism. The effects that United States protectionism might have had during this period were minimized. We'll look at our trade relations with the United States later in this chapter and in more detail in the macroeconomic chapters on international trade and finance.

The European Union

In 1957, several governments of Europe formed the European Economic Community. This organization, now called the **European Union (EU),** has undergone many changes since its founding—changes that have strengthened the economic and politi-

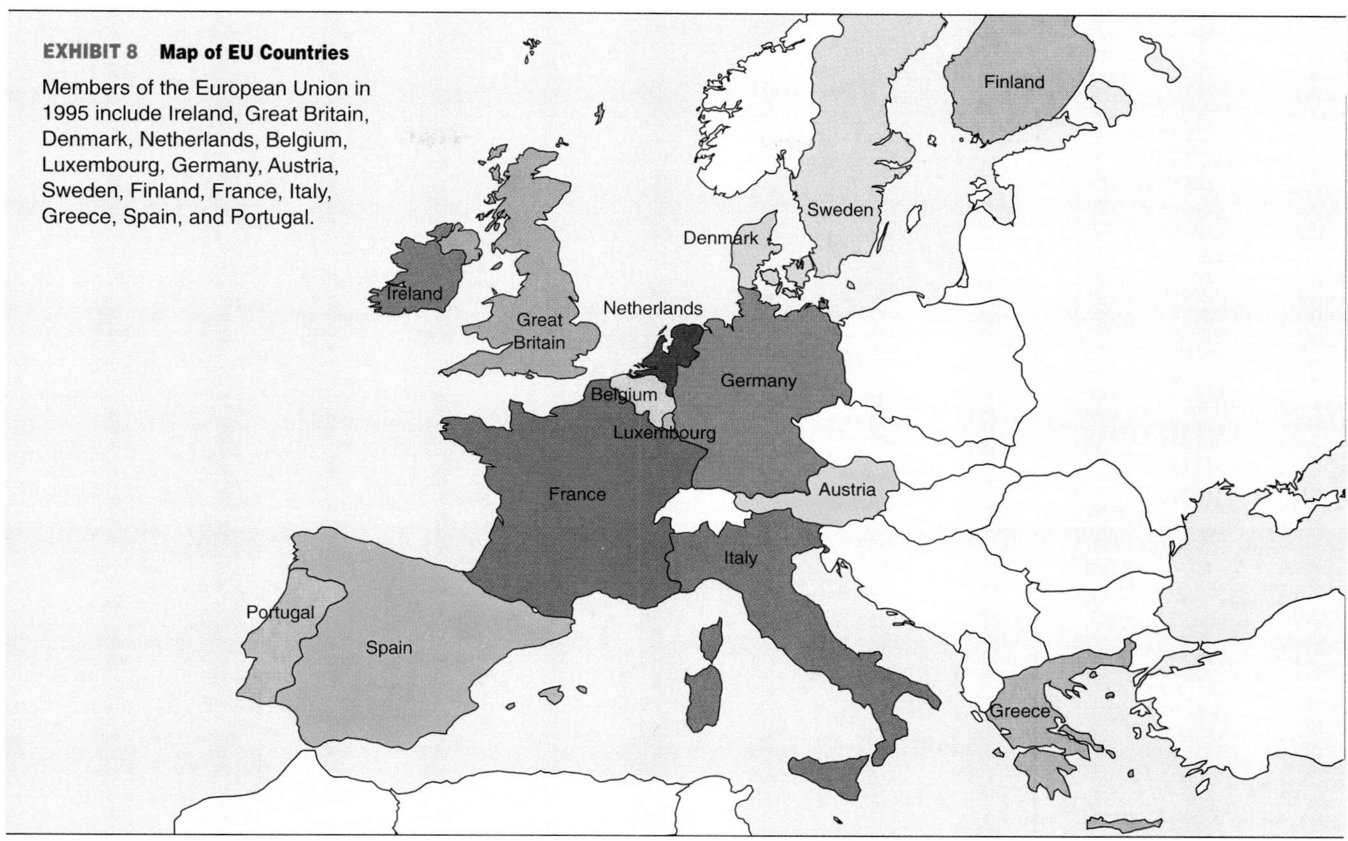

EXHIBIT 8 Map of EU Countries

Members of the European Union in 1995 include Ireland, Great Britain, Denmark, Netherlands, Belgium, Luxembourg, Germany, Austria, Sweden, Finland, France, Italy, Greece, Spain, and Portugal.

cal ties among the countries. In the EU, as in any economic union, members allow free trade among themselves to help their economies by providing a larger marketplace and more competition for their own companies. Over time, the EU has expanded from 6 countries to the 15 shown in Exhibit 8's map. In 1995, Austria, Sweden, Norway, and Finland are scheduled to join.

7A The European Union (EU) is an economic and political union of European countries that allow free trade among countries. It was created to provide larger marketplace for member countries.

The EU's initial goals were:

1. To remove barriers to trade among member nations;
2. To establish a single commercial policy toward nonmember countries;
3. To better coordinate member countries' economic policies; and
4. To promote competitiveness with other countries.

Meeting those goals hasn't been easy, but the EU has made significant progress.

Why did the countries of the EU combine? Two primary reasons were to establish better markets for European companies and to compete better against Canadian and United States goods. In the 1950s and 1960s, when Canada and the United States were highly competitive with other countries and had a trade surplus, they could look beneficently at, and even encourage, such developments. In the 1990s, however, United States and Canadian goods are far less competitive and there are large trade deficits, so the United States and Canada find it much harder to encourage a potential competitor. The EU's gains likely will come at the expense of the United States and Canada.

European Union (EU) An economic and political union of European countries that allow free trade among countries.

These fears have increased as cooperation among EU countries has grown. In 1992, most trade barriers among member nations were removed, and the EU adopted a single commercial policy toward outside nations. The movement toward economic integration has not gone easily, and attempts at further unification have been fraught with political difficulties and confusion. Specifically, the movement toward a common currency—the ECU (European Currency Unit)—and a single monetary policy broke down in the 1990s and now likely won't take place until the 21st century, if at all.

ADDED DIMENSION 

THE NORTH AMERICAN FREE TRADE AGREEMENT

The North American Free Trade Agreement (NAFTA) came into effect on January 1, 1994. It created the world's largest free-trade area—360 million consumers in Mexico, Canada, and the United States. Since Mexico is one of the fastest-growing markets in the world, this gives Canada an excellent opportunity to expand to Mexico.

The NAFTA eliminates a number of tariff and nontariff barriers to trade between the three countries. The Canada–United States Free Trade Agreement has already improved Canadian access to United States markets, and the gains to Canada from NAFTA arise primarily from access to the Mexican market. Until now, Mexico has followed very restrictive trade practices, with import licenses and tariffs all but pricing Canadian goods and services out of the market. Under the new agreement, Mexico will eliminate or substantially lessen trade barriers in agriculture and automobiles. Canada also stands to gain from exporting services in the form of information and communications expertise as well as financial services.

Critics of NAFTA argue that low Mexican wages will attract firms that would otherwise have located in Canada. While it is true that industries that are labour-intensive will gravitate towards Mexico, Mexican wages will increase as productivity in Mexico rises toward United States and Canadian levels. Along the way, income in all three nations should rise, but there may be significant short-run implications for Canadian industry and labour, with competitive pressures forcing firms and workers to become more efficient. The agreement should be much in the news in the 1990s.

The early 1990s saw significant discussions on what the EU's commercial policy will be and whether it will be fair to the United States and Canada. Other European countries are also talking about uniting with the EU countries and forming a larger European trading community.

Regardless of what happens with further European economic and political integration, the EU makes a formidable competitor for Canada and the United States. Its combined production slightly exceeds United States production but is much less than that of Canada and the United States combined. The EU has a strong international economic position, since many member countries enjoy trade surpluses while Canada and the United States have trade deficits.

Developments in the EU have been made even more important by recent events in Eastern Europe. Eastern European countries have changed from socialist to more market-oriented economic systems and are attempting to establish closer economic and political ties with the West. East and West Germany are reunified. These developments will open up new markets for which Canada, the United States, and the EU will all compete. In that competition, the EU has both cultural and geographic advantages over the United States and Canada.

North American Free Trade Agreement (NAFTA) Trade deal signed by Canada, Mexico, and the United States aimed at reducing barriers to North American trade; went into effect January 1, 1994.

In response to the EU's increasing strength, Canada has entered into a free-trade agreement with the United States and Mexico (with Chile set to join in the late 1990s) called the **North American Free Trade Agreement (NAFTA).** Once the agreement is in place (it is to be phased in over 15 years), Canadian firms will be able to produce in Mexico—or vice versa—subject to Mexican regulations and at Mexican wage rates, and ship directly into the United States without international legal hurdles. NAFTA raises significant questions about the short-run effects of free trade, such as: Should goods sold in Canada all be subject to the same regulations regardless of where they are produced? Will free trade with Mexico and the United States increase jobs or decrease jobs in Canada?

The agreement should be much in the news in the 1990s, particularly since the Mexican peso underwent a significant depreciation in late 1994 and 1995. Even though the Canadian and American governments intervened in an attempt to lessen the decline in the value of the peso, serious concerns were raised by international investors who feared Mexican firms and the Mexican government might default on their external obligations. In an attempt to assuage their fears, the Mexican minister of finance went on a whirlwind tour of the world's financial markets in early 1995 to explain how Mexico was going to deal with the depreciation. Given that the Canadian dollar had been steadily losing value against the U.S. dollar in late 1994 and early 1995, the gains to Canada from international trade agreements were no longer as pre-

Japan has become a major player in the world economy.
Reuters/Bettman.

dictable as was once thought. We'll come back to this in a later chapter in macroeconomics on international trade.

Besides entering into NAFTA, Canada and the United States also argued strongly against high EU protective barriers on imports from foreign countries. Since there are no international organizations specifically designed to coordinate and facilitate international trade among trading areas, a new policy problem of the 1990s may be trade wars among "free trading" areas.

"Japan, Inc."

Japan is a little country with a lot of people—about 125 million, over four times as many people as Canada—but it fits them into 146,000 square miles, less than 4 percent of the area of Canada. Almost two-thirds of Japan is covered with forest, and much of the rest of the land has poor soil. It has almost no oil; its coal is very low grade; it must import nearly 100 percent of its petroleum and all of its iron ore (used to make steel) and bauxite (used to make aluminum). It has some copper and other minerals such as zinc, but not enough. Even with heavy forestation, it doesn't have enough lumber for domestic use and must import lumber.

7B Japan is a small, crowded, poorly endowed chain of islands which has been enormously successful economically.

Besides being small, crowded, and poorly endowed, Japan is a chain of islands and has a language that is extremely difficult to learn. These facts have tended, until very recently, to isolate it from the rest of the world. Japan broke its isolation by entering World War II, which it lost, leaving its economy in ruins.

By almost all objective analyses, then, one would expect Japan to be a poor, underdeveloped country. It isn't. Instead, it is one of the most successful and developed economies in the world. In the 1980s, its economic strength earned it the nickname *Japan, Inc.* In the 1990s, while still successful, Japan has had its problems. Its stock market crashed in the early 1990s, and the government has spent considerable resources propping up its financial sector. Moreover, with the rise in the value of the yen in the early 1990s and the subsequent rise in price of its exports, Japanese exports declined and the Japanese economy fell into a recession; unemployment rose because exports fell due to limited demand. With these events, Japan has lost its "supereconomy" status, and has joined the ranks of the other industrialized economies. It is successful, but it is not without its problems.

Cultural Reasons for Japan's Success One reason is cultural. Japan has a social and cultural commitment to hard work. A second cultural trait that has helped Japan's economy is its strong tradition of saving money. These cultural traits are reinforced by social and economic institutions. Japan's educational system is much more demanding than that of Canada. Students go to school longer and are required to work harder than most

ADDED DIMENSION 

GERMANY: THE LEADING EU COUNTRY

The largest European Union economy is Germany. Germany has been on the losing end of two world wars and, nonetheless, has emerged as one of the leading economies of the world. One reason is cultural: German culture reinforces hard work and makes saving a virtue. Also, the country's coal and iron resources helped it establish a strong industrial base as long ago as the early 1900s.

After losing World War II in 1945, Germany was divided into East and West Germany. East Germany, which had a large part of the manufacturing base of prewar Germany, was controlled by a Communist government. West Germany was controlled by the victorious Allied forces, who encouraged it to set up a democratic market economy. The Allies limited West German military spending, while the United States, through the Marshall Plan (an assistance plan for Europe which the United States ran after World War II), pumped in large amounts of money to help the West German economy recover from the war. And recover it did. In the 1960s and 1970s, the West German economy grew so fast that it was called an *economic miracle.*

West Germany's economic story contrasted significantly with East Germany's. East Germany grew more than any of the other Eastern bloc Communist economies, but its growth didn't match West Germany's. To prevent East Germans from emigrating to West Germany, East Germany closed its borders with West Germany in 1961 and built a wall between the two countries. Economic and political changes in East Germany at the end of the 1980s led to the introduction of a market economy in East Germany, an opening of the border, and physical destruction of the wall. In 1990, East and West Germany were reunified.

The problems of economic and political reunification were immense. They placed enormous strains on the German political and economic system. To fund the reunification, the German government borrowed (it ran deficits) and raised taxes. Interest rates rose in Germany, placing significant strains on the European Union. In the 1990s, the German economy remained relatively strong, but it was no longer the economic miracle. It found itself with many of the same difficulties as Canada.

Canadian students. This imposes on children a discipline and a habit of hard work that persists in later life. Many Japanese enjoy work. Their work is their hobby as well as their job. Only in Japan will you find government-sponsored classes teaching people how not to work so hard.

The Japanese savings tradition is also encouraged by government policies that keep prices of consumer goods high, make borrowing for consumer goods comparatively expensive, and maintain a skimpy government pension system. One of the reasons the Japanese save a much higher percentage of their incomes than most other people do is that they worry about supporting themselves in their old age.

Neomercantilist Market economy guided by government.

Japan as a Neomercantilist Country Another reason that some economists cite for Japanese development is its government's strong role in stimulating export-led growth. These economists argue that Japan's economic growth is not an example of the power of the invisible hand, but of the three invisible forces working together to direct an economy toward growth. In many economists' view, the Japanese economic system is as closely related to mercantilism as to capitalism. Some have called it a **neomercantilist** economic system.

The power of Japan's neomercantilist approach is striking. In the late 1940s, with few resources and raw materials and devastated by World War II, Japanese firms, under government direction, borrowed in order to finance the purchase of raw materials from abroad. The Japanese government directed firms to allocate a large portion of output for export. They started with small products, paid workers low wages, saved their profits, and learned about international markets. Then they ploughed back those savings into more raw materials, more manufacturing, and more exports. They continued this process, each time manufacturing more sophisticated products than before.

Japan put off making improvements in housing, transportation, highways, parks, cultural institutions, and public health while it directed its efforts to rebuilding and developing technology. Government policy encouraged and sheltered business.

MITI Japanese agency, the Ministry of International Trade and Industry, that guides the Japanese economy.

The Japanese government developed an aggressive trading policy under the control of its **Ministry of International Trade and Industry (MITI).** It encouraged businesses to cooperate, not compete, with one another in order to be more efficient. The government instituted strong tariffs that are still in force. It prohibits altogether

ECONOMIES THAT DON'T WORK SO WELL

ADDED DIMENSION 

For every economy that works well, there are many more economies that aren't achieving their goals. Considering one of them helps us keep our perspective. Take Pakistan, a country of about 120,000,000 people. Pakistan is poor; the average per capita income is about $400. In Canada the equivalent figure is about $22,000. Its political structure is, in theory, democratic, but the army plays a major role in determining who will rule. Coups d'état (overthrows of the government) and unexplained deaths of high leaders are common. The resulting political instability keeps out most foreign investments.

Pakistan is an Islamic republic which has had significant fights with India ever since the two nations were created out of the former single British commonwealth country. The British commonwealth "India" was divided into "India" and "Pakistan" in 1947 after World War II. In 1971, Pakistan's internal strife led to half the country declaring its independence and forming a separate country, Bangladesh.

Pakistan's economy is primarily agricultural, although it also manufactures textiles and chemicals. One out of every 60 people has a TV; one out of every 165 has a car. In North America the equivalent figures are one TV for every 1.3 people, and one car for every 1.8 people. Housing is poor for the majority of the people, and many barely get enough to eat. Income distribution is highly unequal, with a small group being very rich and a great majority being extremely poor.

Most industry has heavy government involvement and is highly inefficient. Without large tariff barriers, it could not compete. Such dependency on the government's prevention of competition breeds corruption. Most Pakistanis have little faith that their government bureaucracy will work for the benefit of society.

the import of some articles that might compete with Japanese manufacturers. In short, Japan does not follow a laissez-faire policy in either the domestic or the international economy, and it is successful.

Not all economists agree that the government's role in Japanese economic development has been positive. Some economists argue that hard work and high savings led to growth that was partially offset by the government's involvement. They point out that MITI often backed the losing, not the winning, industries. The companies and technologies *it didn't back,* not the ones it did back, were the growth sectors of the Japanese economy. They argue that Japanese growth occurred in spite of, not because of, government involvement.

The Japanese Cooperative Spirit Japan's labour market is remarkably different from that in Canada. Large companies have what are called *permanent employees.* By tradition, a man, once hired, stays with the same company for his entire working life. Women are unlikely to be permanent employees and are expected to resign their jobs when they get married. The relationship between the company and the worker is close—workers are members of the corporate family and their social life revolves around the company. The nature of the Japanese labour market is now changing. Some women can be permanent employees and some employees move to other companies, and downsizing employment has begun to enter corporate strategy, but the traditional system still predominates.

Labour unions exist in Japan, but are organized according to industry. In Canada, unions are more likely to be organized by type of skill. Organization by industry allows Japanese workers to do many different jobs within a firm. Until recently, Canadian organized workers would not work outside their specialty.

Japan's pay structure is also different from that in Canada. Japanese workers know that their bonuses, gifts, and special allowances depend on how well their company is doing. Until recently, most Canadian workers received only a wage or salary and no bonus. Another Japanese characteristic contributing to its economic success is the tradition of cooperation between unions and business; in Canada, labour and management are frequently in conflict.

Another difference is that Japan has few lawyers and is a far less litigious society than Canada. Some cynics have suggested the small number of lawyers is a major reason for Japan's great success. Businesses don't get bogged down by legal maneuvering and litigious behaviour. Less-cynical people downplay this issue, but they agree Japanese people's cooperative spirit contributes to Japan's success.

Inefficient Japanese Traditions Not all Japanese institutions promote efficiency. Some Japanese institutions hinder economic progress. Take its agricultural system. Before the war, most farmland in Japan that was not owned by the government was owned by a few individuals who rented it out in small parcels to others. After the war, the big farmland holdings were broken up by the government and sold off to former tenants at low prices. The result was thousands of small farms, averaging an acre in size. Few are larger than three acres. These small farms are highly inefficient, but are kept in business by large government subsidies and tariffs on foreign agricultural products. Because of the structure of Japanese political institutions, these subsidies are almost untouchable, despite Canadian farmers' complaints about trade restrictions.

In the 1990s, a second inefficient Japanese tradition was being seen more and more. That tradition was political corruption in which Japanese politicians received large payoffs from Japanese businesses for government support. In 1993, this corruption brought down the ruling party, and led to its replacement by a series of coalitions of reformist parties. Whether these changes will improve the system, or whether such corruption is inherent in any neomercantilist system, remains to be seen.

Japan, Inc., versus Canada

Both the Japanese and Canadian economies are successful, but they differ significantly from each other. There is less competition among firms in Japan than in Canada. Japanese firms work closely with government in planning their industrial strategy. Canadian firms often see government as an opponent, not a partner. Similarly with labour and business: In Japan they generally cooperate; in Canada they generally are opponents.

The Japanese Ministry of International Trade and Industry plays a key role in determining what will be produced and who will produce it. MITI's goal has been to establish strong export-led growth, and that goal has been accomplished, although whether it was because of MITI, or in spite of MITI, is debatable. MITI also has an economic planning board that oversees many parts of the Japanese economy. Japan is no laissez-faire economy.

Don't Overestimate the Differences

The differences between the Canadian and Japanese economies are large, but should not be overestimated. Both economies rely on markets. In both, profit incentives motivate production.

As global corporations bridge the gap between these two economies, the differences (once very large) are shrinking. Canadian labour unions and firms are cooperating more, while Japanese firms and labour unions are cooperating less. The Japanese system of permanent employment in large firms is breaking down.

With both systems successful, it is difficult to say that one set of institutions is better than the other. They are merely distinct from each other. The differences reflect social, cultural, and geographic conditions in the two countries. Some people have suggested that Canada should adopt a neomercantilist system like Japan's. Maybe it should, but it is not at all clear that Japanese institutions could be transferred to Canada. What works in one country can bomb in another.

The argument that policies that work in one country cannot necessarily be translated into policies that work in another country doesn't mean Japan's experience is of no relevance to Canada. In itself, the fact that a policy works in one country means that policy deserves consideration by other countries. That's tough for economists with a strong distrust of government to say, but it must be said. An open mind is a necessary attribute of a good economist.

The Developing Countries of the World as Competitors

Japan and the EU have developed industrial economies similar to Canada's economy. There is, however, a much larger group of countries out there that are at various lower levels of industrial development. Many of them are anxious for industrial development and will likely provide significant competition for the Canadian economy. If Japan and the EU can't out-compete Canada, these other countries, with low wage rates and governments eager to give global corporations whatever they want, often can. If Canadian firms don't take advantage of this low-cost labour, Japanese and European firms will, and will export the output to Canada.

Of these developing countries, Mexico is of special interest to Canada. The reason is NAFTA, which will allow easy access into the Canadian market for firms producing in Mexico. As NAFTA brings in freer trade, Canadian companies are likely to experience significant Mexican competition. In return, of course, Canadian companies will have a new open market to sell to—Mexico. As inevitably happens with competition, some people will be helped, and some will be hurt.

CONCLUSION

Knowing about other countries' economies helps us keep our own economy in perspective. We don't have the space here (an example of scarcity) to look at other countries' tax structures, public finances, support of education, labour markets . . . the list is endless. But as you wonder about any of the economic policies that are discussed throughout this book, take a few minutes to ask somebody from a foreign country about its economy, and go to the library and look up another country's way of handling its economy (even if you look no further than an encyclopedia). See how that country compares to Canada. Then try to explain what does or doesn't work in that country and whether it would or would not work in Canada. Doing so will make the course more meaningful and your understanding of economics stronger.

CHAPTER SUMMARY

- To understand the Canadian economy, one must understand its role in the world economy.
- Knowledge of the facts about the world economy is necessary to understand the world economy.
- Countries can be classified in many ways, including industrial, middle-income, and low-income economies.
- International trade differs from domestic trade because (1) there are potential barriers to trade and (2) countries use different currencies.
- The relative value of a currency can be found in an exchange rate table.
- The Canadian trade deficit is large. It is financed by selling Canadian assets to foreign owners.
- Canadian competitiveness and the state of the Canadian economy compared to other countries are important in determining the trade deficit's size.
- International policy coordination must be achieved through consensus among nations.
- Global corporations are corporations with significant operations in more than one country.
- Two important international competitors to Canada are the EU and Japan. In Japan and in many EU nations, government plays a larger role in directing the economy than in Canada.

KEY TERMS

balance of trade *(111)*
balance of trade deficit *(111)*
balance of trade surplus *(111)*
comparative advantage *(107)*
competitiveness *(112)*
European Union (EU) *(119)*
exports *(106)*
foreign exchange market *(108)*
Free Trade Agreement (FTA) *(118)*
General Agreement on Tariffs and Trade (GATT) *(114)*
global corporations *(104)*
globalization *(118)*
Group of Five *(114)*
Group of Seven *(114)*
imports *(106)*
International Monetary Fund (IMF) *(114)*
merchandise trade balance *(111)*
Ministry of International Trade and Industry (MITI) *(123)*
neomercantilist *(122)*
nontariff barriers *(108)*
North American Free Trade Agreement (NAFTA) *(120)*
protectionist policy *(118)*
quotas *(108)*
services balance *(111)*
tariffs *(108)*
World Bank *(114)*
World Trade Organization (WTO) *(114)*

QUESTIONS FOR THOUGHT AND REVIEW

The number after each question represents the estimated degree of critical thinking required. (1 = almost none; 10 = deep thought.)

1. A good measure of a country's importance to the world economy is its area and population. True or false? Why? *(5)*
2. Canada exports wheat while Japan exports cars. Why? *(5)*
3. What are the two ways in which international trade differs from domestic trade? *(3)*
4. Find the exchange rate for Swedish krone in Exhibit 4 and also the most current rate from your newspaper. *(3)*
5. If one Canadian dollar will buy .67 Swiss francs, how many Canadian dollars will one Swiss franc buy? *(5)*
6. The Canadian economy is falling apart because Canada is one of the biggest debtor nations in the world. Discuss. *(7)*
7. What is likely to happen to the Canadian trade deficit if the Canadian economy grows rapidly? Why? *(5)*
8. Why do most economists oppose trade restrictions? *(5)*
9. What effect has the establishment of the EU had on the economy? Why? *(9)*
10. Japan's successful economy is an example of the power of the invisible hand. True or false? Why? *(6)*

PROBLEMS AND EXERCISES

1. This is a library research question.
   a. What are the primary exports of Brazil, Honduras, Italy, Pakistan, and Nigeria?
   b. Which countries produce most of the world's tin, rubber, potatoes, wheat, marble, and refrigerators?
2. This is an entrepreneurial research question. You'd be amazed about the information that's out there if you use a bit of initiative.
   a. Does the largest company in your relevant geographic area (town, city, whatever) have an export division? Why or why not?
   b. If you were an advisor to the company, would you suggest expanding or contracting its export division? Why or why not?
   c. Go to a store and look at 10 products at random. How many were made in Canada? Give a probable explanation why they were produced where they were produced.
3. Assume Canada can produce Toyotas at the cost of $8,000 per car and Chevrolets at $6,000 per car. In Japan, Toyotas can be produced at 1,000,000 yen and Chevrolets at 500,000 yen.
   a. In terms of Chevrolets, what is the opportunity cost of producing Toyotas in each country?
   b. Who has the comparative advantage in producing Chevrolets?
   c. Assume Canadians purchase 500,000 Chevrolets and 300,000 Toyotas each year. The Japanese purchase far fewer of each. Using productive efficiency as the guide, who should most likely produce Chevrolets and who should produce Toyotas, assuming one is going to be produced in one country and one in the other?
4. From 1984 to 1994, the share of Canadian exports to Western Europe fell from 7 percent to 5 percent, while the share going to the United States rose from 76 percent to 82 percent.
   a. What are likely reasons why this change occurred?
   b. What would you predict would happen to these percentages if the Western European economy boomed?
   c. Why would Prime Minister Jean Chretien urge the Western Europeans to stimulate their economy?
5. In one of the boxes, a grey market in Russian rubles is discussed.
   a. Draw the supply and demand curves for rubles in terms of dollars and show where the quantity supplied or demanded would be at an official price of .05 rubles per dollar, which is significantly below the equilibrium price.
   b. In the graph in *a,* show what the grey market price of dollars would be.
   c. In that same graph, show what the black market price of rubles would have likely been if the Russian government had enforced the exchange laws.
6. From your knowledge of current events, are Canada and the United States currently embroiled in a trade dispute? Over what commodity are they arguing? Which country feels it is being harmed? How do trade agreements affect the dispute?
7. What is the current exchange rate of the Canadian dollar against: the Italian lire? the Iranian rial? the Australian dollar? the Jamaican dollar? Why isn't a Canadian dollar equal in value to a Jamaican dollar? A U.S. dollar?

PART 2

Microeconomics

PART

In my vacations, I visited the poorest quarters of several cities and walked through one street after another, looking at the faces of the poorest people. Next I resolved to make as thorough a study as I could of Political Economy.

You may remember having already seen this quotation from Alfred Marshall. It began the first chapter. We chose this beginning for two reasons. First, it gives what we believe to be the best reason to study economics. Second, the quotation is from a hero of ours, one of the economic giants of all times. His *Principles of Economics* was economists' bible in the late 1800s and early 1900s. How important was Marshall? It was Marshall who first used the supply and demand curves as an engine of analysis.

We repeat this quotation here in the introduction to the microeconomics section because for Marshall economics was microeconomics, and it is his vision of economics that underlies this book's approach to microeconomics. For Marshall, economics was an art that was meant to be applied—used to explain why things were the way they were, and what we could do about them. He had little use for esoteric theory that didn't lead to a direct application to a real-world problem. Reflecting on the state of economics in 1906, Marshall wrote to a friend:

> I had a growing feeling in the later years of my work at the subject that a good mathematical theorem dealing with economic hypotheses was very unlikely to be good economics: and I went more and more on the rules—(1) Use mathematics as a shorthand language, rather than as an engine of inquiry. (2) Keep to them until you have done. (3) Translate into English. (4) Then illustrate by examples that are important in real life. (5) Burn the mathematics. (6) If you can't succeed in (4), burn (3). This last I did often. (From a letter from Marshall to A. L. Bowley, reprinted in A. C. Pigou, *Memorials of Alfred Marshall,* p. 427.)

Marshall didn't feel this way about mathematical economics because he couldn't do mathematics. He was trained as a formal mathematician, and he was a good one. But, for him, mathematics wasn't economics, and the real world was too messy to have applied to it much of the fancy mathematical economic work that some of his fellow economists were doing. Marshall recognized the influence of all three invisible forces and believed that all three had to be taken into account in applying economic reasoning to reality.

Since 1906 when Marshall wrote this letter, the economics profession has moved away from its Marshallian roots. The profession has found other heroes who have created a mathematical foundation for economics that's both impressive and stultifying. Mathematical economics that has only the slightest connection to the real world has overwhelmed much of the real-world economics that Marshall followed. That's sad.

Not to worry. You won't see such highfalutin mathematical economics in these microeconomic chapters. The chapters follow the Marshallian methodology and present the minimum of formal theory necessary to apply the concepts of economics to the real world, and then they do just that; they start talking about real-world issues.

Part I (Chapters 6–8) presents that minimum of theory necessary to understand the economic way of thinking. It introduces you to the foundations of economic reasoning. Part II (Chapters 9–13) introduces you to various market structures, providing you with a way of approaching real-world markets. But even in these theoretical chapters the focus is on intuition and putting the economic approach to problems into perspective rather than on presenting technique for the sake of technique.

Part III (Chapters 14–16) looks at a particular set of markets—factor markets. These markets play a central role in determining the distribution of income. These chapters won't tell you how to get rich (you'll have to wait for the sequel for that), but it will give you new insights into perplexing problems. Part IV (Chapters 17–20) integrates economic reasoning with real-world institutions and normative issues to give insight into what's happening, and how they come up with policy proposals. It will explain why economists differ.

Finally, in Part V (Chapters 21–22) we consider international issues. While international issues were considered in earlier chapters, given their importance in modern day economies this specific consideration seems warranted.

CHAPTER

6

Individual Choice and Demand

The theory of economics must begin with a correct theory of consumption.

~Stanley Jevons

After reading this chapter, you should be able to:

1. Discuss the principle of diminishing marginal utility.
2. Summarize economists' analysis of rational choice.
3. Explain how marginal utility accounts for the law of demand.
4. Distinguish a complementary good from a substitute good.
5. Explain why economists can believe there are many explanations of individual choice, but nonetheless focus on self-interest.
6. Define the concept *price elasticity of demand* and explain what it tells us about total revenue.
7. Explain the importance of substitution in determining the elasticity of demand.

No analysis is more important to economics than the analysis of individual choice. It is the foundation of economic reasoning and it gives economics much of its power.

We touched on the analysis of individual choice in Chapters 1 and 2. Chapter 1 introduced you to examples of economic reasoning using individual choice. In Chapter 2 you were introduced to the law of demand: The quantity demanded increases as the price decreases. In this chapter we extend that analysis and explore the formal reasoning that underlies individual choice theory and the law of demand.

This formal economic analysis of choice centres on self-interest: People do what they do because doing so is in their interest. The first part of this chapter shows you that foundation and leads you through some exercises to make sure you understand the reasoning. The second part of the chapter relates that analysis to the real world, giving you a sense of when the model is useful and when it's not. Finally, the third part of the chapter introduces you to elasticity, a term economists use to describe demand curves.

As you go through this chapter, think back to Chapter 1, which set out the goals for this book. One goal was to get you to think like an economist. This chapter, which formally develops the reasoning process behind economists' cost/benefit approach to problems, examines the underpinnings of how to think like an economist.

INDIVIDUAL CHOICE, SELF-INTEREST, AND ECONOMIC REASONING

Why do people do what they do? There are many explanations. Freudian psychology tells us we do what we do because of an internal fight between the id, ego, and super-ego, plus some hangups people have about their bodies. Other psychologists tell us it's a search for approval by our peers; we want to be OK. Economists agree that these are important reasons, but argue that if we want an analysis that's simple enough to apply to problems, these heavy psychological explanations are likely to get us all mixed up. At least to start with, we need an easier underlying psychological foundation. And economists have one—self-interest. People do what they do because it's in their self-interest.

Economists' analysis of individual choice doesn't deny that most of us have our quirks. Each individual is unique and often strange. That's obvious in what we buy. On certain items we're penny-pinchers; on others we're big spenders. For example, how many of you or your parents clip coupons to save 40¢ on cereal but then spend \$20 on a haircut? How many save 50¢ a kilogram by buying a low grade of meat but then spend \$10 on a bottle of wine, \$40 on dinner at a restaurant, or \$30 for a concert ticket?

But through it all comes a certain rationality. Much of what people do reflects their rational self-interest. Thus, a good beginning in understanding individual choice is to focus on the rational part of people's behaviour. That's why economists start their analysis of individual choice with a relatively simple, but powerful, underlying psychological foundation.

Using that simple theory, two factors determine what people do: the pleasure people get from doing or consuming something, and the price of doing or consuming that something. Price is the market's tool to bring the quantity supplied equal to the quantity demanded. Changes in price provide incentives for people to change what they're doing. Through those incentives the invisible hand guides us all. Thus, to understand economics you must understand how price affects our choices. That's why we focus on the effect of price on the quantity demanded. We want to understand the way in which a change in price will affect what we do.

In summary, economists' theory of rational choice is a simple, but powerful, theory that shows how these two things—pleasure and price—are related.

UTILITARIAN FOUNDATIONS OF INDIVIDUAL CHOICE

Let's start with an analysis of what we buy. Why do we buy what we buy? Economists' analysis of individual choice starts with the proposition that individuals try to get as much pleasure as possible out of life. To analyze the choice formally we must measure pleasure.

Measuring Pleasure

How does one measure pleasure? We don't know the answer to that, but back in the 1800s economists such as Jeremy Bentham thought that eventually they would be able to measure pleasure by measuring brain waves. In the expectation of this discovery they even developed a measure of pleasure which they called a *util.* They predicted that someday a machine that could measure utils would be developed. Not surprisingly, they called this machine a *utilometer.* This utilometer was to be connected to people's heads and an economist would read it as people went through their daily activities. Eating broccoli might give 10 utils; eating a hot fudge sundae might give 10,000 utils. (OK, so we're chocoholics.)

Eventually these 19th-century economists gave up hope of developing a utilometer, but economists use the term **utility** as a quaint, shorthand term for the pleasure or satisfaction that one expects to get from consuming a good or service. (And you thought that economists didn't have a sense of humour.) Utility serves as the basis of economists' analysis of individual choice.

Utility A measure of the pleasure or satisfaction one gets from consuming a good or service.

Cardinal and Ordinal Utility

In discussing utility, economists initially used what are called *cardinal measures.* (An example of a cardinal measure is anything that can be measured by an actual number.) But no economist today believes that these actual numbers given to utility have meaning. Economists have gone to great lengths to show that only ordinal measures are necessary. To have an ordinal measure all you need is a ranking of goods that people reveal when they choose one good over another. (That means you can say "a hot fudge sundae gives me more pleasure than a raw turnip," but you don't need to say how much more pleasure it provides.)

It's important to keep in the back of your mind that economists don't need to measure utils, especially if you're going on in economics, but it's not important to keep it in the front of your mind. In introductory economics there's nothing quite as useful as a good old util. It gives one real numbers to work with, rather than all kinds of fancy measure theories. So here's the deal: we will use real numbers in discussing utility and you promise that you will remember they're not really needed. (If you don't accept this deal, see Appendix A where we go through the same analysis without using cardinal measures.)

The Relationship between Total Utility and Marginal Utility

In discussing utility, it's important to distinguish between *total utility* and *marginal utility.* **Total utility** refers to the total satisfaction one gets from one's consumption of a product. **Marginal utility** refers to the satisfaction one gets from the consumption of an incremental or additional product above and beyond what one has consumed up to that point. For example, eating a whole kilo of Beluga caviar might give you 4,700 utils (units of utility).[1] Consuming the first 900 grams may have given you 4,697 utils. Consuming the last 100 grams of caviar might give you an additional 3 utils. The 4,700 is total utility; the 3 is the marginal utility of eating that last 100 grams of caviar.

Total utility The satisfaction one gets from one's entire consumption of a product.

Marginal utility The satisfaction one gets from the consumption of an incremental or additional product above and beyond what one has consumed up to that point.

An example of the relationship between total utility and marginal utility is given in Exhibit 1. Let's say that the marginal utility of the first slice of pizza is 14, and since you've eaten only one slice, the total utility is also 14. Let's also say that the marginal utility of the second slice of pizza is 12, which means that the total utility of two slices of pizza is 26 (14 + 12). Similarly for the third, fourth, and fifth slices of pizza, whose marginal utilities are 10, 8, and 6, respectively. If we add the marginal utilities you get from eating each of these slices, we arrive at the total utility of your eating those pieces of pizza. We do so in column 2 of Exhibit 1 (a).

Notice that marginal utility shows up between the lines. It is the utility of changing consumption levels. Thus, the marginal utility of changing from one to two slices of pizza is 12. The relationship between total and marginal utility can also be seen graphically. In Exhibit 1 (b) we graph total utility (column 2 of Exhibit 1 (a)) on the vertical axis, and number of slices of pizza (column 1 of Exhibit 1 (a)) on the horizontal axis. As you can see, total utility increases up to seven slices of pizza; after eight slices it starts decreasing—after eight pieces of pizza you're so stuffed that you can't stand to look at another slice.

Jeremy Bentham was a 19th-century economist and philosopher who strongly advocated utilitarianism. *The Bettmann Archive.*

[1]We choose specific numbers to make the examples more understandable and to make the points we want to make. A useful exercise is for you to choose different numbers and reason your way through the same analysis.

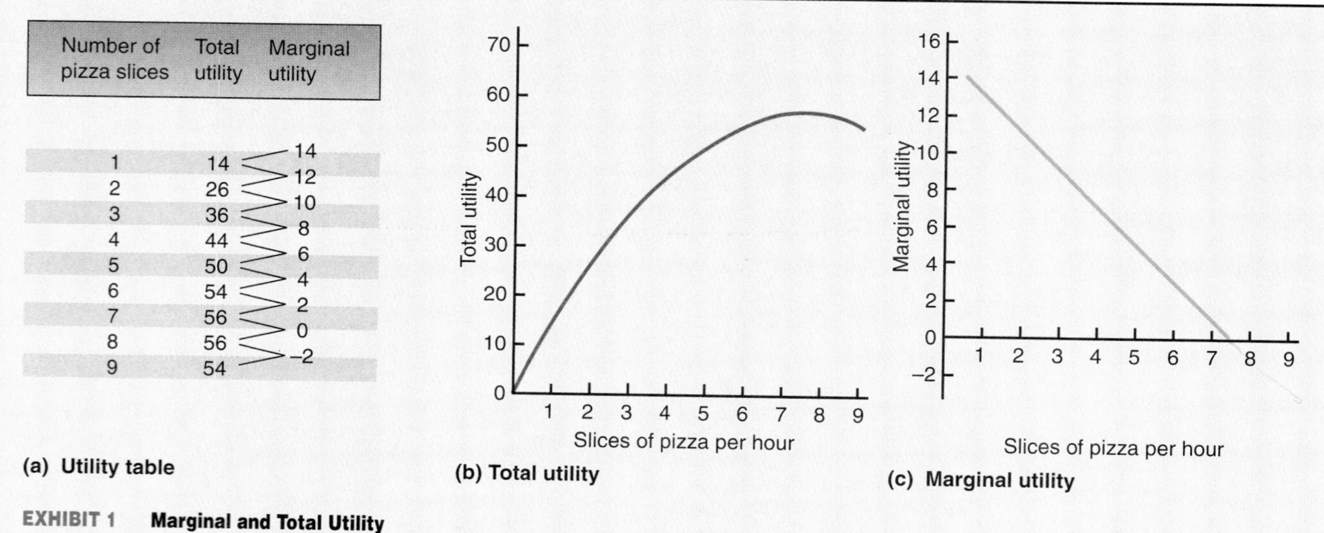

Number of pizza slices	Total utility	Marginal utility
1	14	14
2	26	12
3	36	10
4	44	8
5	50	6
6	54	4
7	56	2
8	56	0
9	54	−2

EXHIBIT 1 Marginal and Total Utility

Marginal utility tends to decrease as consumption of a good increases. Notice how the information in the table (**a**) can be presented graphically in two different ways. The two different ways are, however, related. The downward slope of the marginal utility curve (**c**) is reflected in the total utility curve being bowed downward in (**b**). Notice that marginal utility relates to changes in quantity so the marginal utility line is graphed at the halfway point. For example, in (**c**), between 7 and 8, marginal utility becomes zero.

In Exhibit 1 (c) we graph marginal utility (column 3 of Exhibit 1 (a)) on the vertical axis and slices of pizza (column 1) on the horizontal axis. Notice how marginal utility decreases while total utility increases. When total utility stops increasing (between 7 and 8 slices), marginal utility is zero. Beyond this point total utility would decrease and marginal utility would be negative. An additional slice of pizza will actually make you worse off.

Diminishing Marginal Utility

Diminishing marginal utility At some point, as individuals increase their consumption of a good, consuming another unit of the product will simply not yield as much additional pleasure as did consuming the preceding unit.

Now let's consider the shapes of these curves a bit more carefully: What are they telling us about people's choices? As we've drawn the curves, the marginal utility that a person gets from each additional slice of pizza decreases with each slice of pizza eaten. Economists believe that the shapes of these curves accurately describe the pattern of people's enjoyment. They have given this principle a name: **diminishing marginal utility.** As individuals increase their consumption of a good, at some point consuming another unit of the product will simply not yield as much additional pleasure as did consuming the preceding unit.

Consider, for example, that late-night craving for a double cheese and pepperoni pizza. You order one and bite into it. Ah, pleasure! But if you've ordered a large pizza and you're eating it all by yourself, your additional pleasure is going to decrease with each additional slice that you consume. In other words, after some point, you get fewer utils from each additional slice of pizza that you consume. That's the principle of diminishing marginal utility:

> *As more and more of an item is consumed, eventually each additional unit adds fewer utils than the previous unit. In general:*

$$X \uparrow \rightarrow MU_x \downarrow \text{ and conversely, } (X \downarrow \rightarrow MU_x \uparrow).$$

1 The principle of diminishing marginal utility states that, after some point, the marginal utility received from each additional unit of a good decreases with each unit consumed.

Notice that the principle of diminishing marginal utility does not say that you don't enjoy consuming more of a good; it simply states that as you consume more of the good, you enjoy the additional unit less than you did the previous unit. A fourth slice of pizza still tastes good, but it doesn't match the taste of the third slice. At some point, however, marginal utility can become negative. Say you had two large pizzas and only two hours in which to eat them. Eating the last slice could be pure torture.

But in most situations you have the option *not* to consume any more of a good. When consuming a good becomes torture (meaning its utility is negative), you simply don't consume any more of it. If you eat a slice of pizza (or consume an additional unit of any other good), that's a good indication that its marginal utility is still positive.

Rational Choice and Marginal Utility

The analysis of rational choice is the analysis of how individuals choose goods in order to maximize total utility, and how maximizing total utility can be accomplished by considering marginal utility. That analysis begins with the premise that rational individuals want as much satisfaction as they can get from their available income. How do they achieve that?

Let's start by considering a number of choices. (Answer each choice as you read it.)

Choice 1: Between a $1 slice of pizza giving you 41 utils and a $1 sub sandwich that gives you 30 utils.

Choice 2: Between a Maserati at $170,000 that gives you 120,000 utils and a Yugo at $5,000 that gives you 20,000 utils.

Choice 3: Between reading an additional chapter in this book that gives you an additional 200 utils at a cost of one hour of your time, and reading an additional chapter in psychology that gives you an additional 100 utils at a cost of 40 minutes of your time or 150 utils for a chapter and a half. (Psychology is easier but less fulfilling than economics.)

Choice 4: Between having a date with that awesome guy Jerry, which gives you 2,000 utils and costs you $70, and taking out plain Jeff, which gives you 200 utils and costs you $10.

The correct choices, in terms of marginal utility, are: (1) the pizza, (2) the Yugo, (3) a chapter of this book, and (4) Jerry.

If you answered all four correctly, either you're lucky or you have a good understanding of the principle of rational choice. Now let's explore the principle of rational choice more thoroughly by considering each of the four examples.

Choice 1 Since the slice of pizza and the sub both cost $1, and the pizza gives you more utils than the sub, the pizza is the rational choice. If you spend $1 on the sub rather than the pizza, you're losing 11 utils and not making yourself as happy as you could be. You're being irrational. Any choice (for the same amount of money) that doesn't give you as many utils as possible is an irrational choice.

But now let's say that the price of subs falls to 50¢ so that you can buy two subs for the same price you previously had to pay for only one. Let's also say that two subs would give you 56 utils (not 2 × 30 = 60—remember the principle of diminishing marginal utility). Which would now be the more rational choice? The two subs, because their 56 utils are 15 more than you would get from that dollar spent on one slice of pizza.

Another way of thinking about your choice is to recognize that essentially what you're doing in your choices is buying utils. Obviously you want to get the most for your money, so you make those choices that have the highest util per unit of cost. Let's see how this way of thinking about it works by considering our second choice.

Choice 2 The Maserati costs $170,000 and we get 120,000 utils from it. Per dollar spent we get:

$$\frac{120{,}000 \text{ utils}}{\$170{,}000} = .71 \text{ utils.}$$

With the Yugo, for each dollar spent we get

$$\frac{20{,}000 \text{ utils}}{\$5{,}000} = 4 \text{ utils.}$$

You require more utils per dollar for the Yugo than for the Maserati, so we choose the Yugo. To say something has the highest util per unit of cost is to say that it has the highest marginal utility per dollar. Alternatively, you can decide to choose the cheapest, lowest-cost-per-util item. The Maserati gives you 0.71 utils per dollar, so one util costs about $1.43 ($1 divided by 0.71). The Yugo gives you 4 utils per dollar, so a util costs 25¢. The util from a Yugo is cheaper. Since the cost per util is determined by dividing $1 by the marginal utility per dollar, having the lowest cost per util is equivalent to having the highest marginal utility.

Choice 3 Here the two alternatives have a cost in time, not money. The analysis, however, is the same. You calculate the marginal utility (number of utils) of the choice facing you, and divide that by the cost of the activity; that gives you the marginal utility per dollar. Then choose the activity that has the highest *MU* per dollar or lowest cost per util. When you do that, you see that this chapter gives you 3 1/3 utils per minute (200/60 = 3 1/3), while the psychology chapter gives you 2 1/2 utils per minute. So you choose to read another chapter in this book.[2]

Choice 4 Taking out Jerry gives you 28 1/2 utils per dollar (2,000/$70), while taking out Jeff gives you 20 utils per dollar (200/$10). So you choose to take out Jerry.

Principle of rational choice Spend your money on those goods that give you the most marginal utility per dollar.

2 Principle of rational choice: spend your money on those goods that give you the most marginal utility per dollar.

If $\frac{MU_x}{P_x} > \frac{MU_y}{P_y}$, choose to consume an additional unit of good x.

If $\frac{MU_x}{P_x} < \frac{MU_y}{P_y}$, choose to consume an additional unit of good y.

If $\frac{MU_x}{P_x} = \frac{MU_y}{P_y}$, you're maximizing utility; you cannot increase your utility by adjusting your choices.

The basic **principle of rational choice** is as follows: *Spend your money on those goods that give you the most marginal utility (MU) per dollar.* The principle of rational choice is important enough for us to emphasize.[3]

If $\frac{MU_x}{P_x} > \frac{MU_y}{P_y}$, *choose to consume an additional unit of good x.*

If $\frac{MU_x}{P_x} < \frac{MU_y}{P_y}$, *choose to consume an additional unit of good y.*

If $\frac{MU_x}{P_x} = \frac{MU_y}{P_y}$, *you're maximizing utility; you cannot increase your utility by adjusting your choices.*

By substituting the marginal utilities and prices of goods into these formulas, you can always decide which good it makes more sense to consume. Consume the one with the highest marginal utility per dollar.

Let's apply these formulas by substituting in the numbers from one of our previous examples: the choice between the Maserati and the Yugo. The marginal utility of the Maserati was 120,000; the price was $170,000. The marginal utility of the Yugo was 20,000; the price was $5,000. Substituting,

$$\frac{20{,}000}{\$5{,}000} = 4 \text{ utils per } \$ > \frac{\$120{,}000}{\$170{,}000} = .7 \text{ utils per } \$.$$

So choose the Yugo.

Rational Choice and Maximizing Utility

In each of the previous four examples, there was a clear winner. If in the examples you had been maximizing utility and hence were in equilibrium, there couldn't have been a clear winner. Why? As you make choices, it's important to remember the principle of diminishing marginal utility: As we consume more of an item, the marginal utility we get from the last unit consumed decreases. Conversely as we consume *less* of an item, the marginal utility we get from the last unit consumed *increases.* (The principle of diminishing marginal utility operates in reverse.)

The principle of rational choice tells you to keep adjusting your spending if the marginal utility per dollar (*MU/P*) of two goods differs. The only time you don't adjust your spending is when there is no clear winner. When you've maximized utility, the

[2]As we've pointed out before, we choose the numbers to make the points we want to make. A good exercise for you is to choose different numbers that reflect your estimate of the marginal utility you get from choice, and see what your rational choices are. And remember our deal.

[3]The symbol > means "greater than." The symbol < means "less than."

ratios of the marginal utility to price of the two goods are equal. This insight accounts for the third formula in the principle of rational choice:

$$If \frac{MU_x}{P_x} = \frac{MU_y}{P_y}, \text{ you're maximizing utility; you're in equilibrium.}$$

Rational Choice and Simultaneous Decisions

So far in discussing our examples, we've considered each of the four choices separately. But in real life, choices aren't so neatly separated. Say you were presented with all four choices simultaneously. If you make all four of the decisions given in the examples, are you being rational? The answer is no. Why? The pizza gives you 46 utils per dollar; taking out Jerry gives you 28 utils per dollar; and the Yugo gives you only 4 utils per dollar. You aren't being rational; you aren't maximizing your utility. It would clearly make sense to dump the Yugo and take out Jerry on pizza binges instead (assuming, of course, that he'll go out with you without your Yugo).

But what about the fourth choice: studying psychology or economics? We can't compare the costs of studying to the costs of the other goods because, as we noted earlier, the costs of both studying alternatives are expressed in terms of time, not money. If we can assign a money value to the time, however, we can make the comparison. Let's say you can earn $6 per hour, so the value of your time is 10¢ per minute. This allows us to think about both alternatives in terms of dollars and cents. Since a chapter in economics takes an hour to read, the cost in money of reading a chapter is 60 minutes × 10¢ = $6. Similarly the cost of the 40 minutes you'd take to read the psychology chapter is $4.

With these values we can compare our studying decisions with our other decisions. The value in utils per dollar of reading a chapter of this book is:

$$\frac{200}{\$6} = 33.3 \text{ utils per dollar}$$

So forget about dating Jerry with its value of 28 utils per dollar. Your rational choice is to study this chapter while stuffing yourself with pizza.

But wait. Remember that, according to the principle of diminishing marginal utility, as you consume more of something, the marginal utility you get from it falls. So as you consume more pizza and spend more time reading this book, the marginal utilities of these activities will fall. Thus, as you vary your consumption, the marginal utilities you get from the goods are changing.

When do you stop varying your consumption? When you maximize utility—when the marginal utility per dollar spent on each choice is equal. Achieving equilibrium by maximizing utility (juggling one's choices, adding a bit more of one and choosing a bit less of another) requires more information than we've so far presented. We need to know the marginal utility of alternative amounts of consumption for each choice and how much income we have to spend on all those items. With that information we can choose among alternatives.

An Example of Rational Choice In Exhibit 2 we consider an example in which we have the necessary information to make simultaneous decisions. In this example, we have $7 to spend on ice cream cones and Big Macs. The choice is between ice cream at $1 a cone and Big Macs at $2 apiece. In the exhibit you can see the principle of diminishing marginal utility in action. The marginal utility (*MU*) we get from either good decreases as we consume more of it. Marginal utility (*MU*) becomes negative after five Big Macs or six ice cream cones.

The key columns for your decision are the *MU/P* columns. They tell you the *MU* per dollar spent on each of the items. By following the rule that we choose the good with the higher marginal utility per dollar, we can quickly determine the optimal choice (remember we said that occurs when the marginal utility per dollar spent on each good is equal).

Let's start by considering what we'd do with our first $2. Clearly we'd only eat ice cream. Doing so would give us 29 + 17 = 46 utils, compared to 10 utils if we

EXHIBIT 2 Maximizing Utility

(P = $2)				(P = $1)			
Q	TU	MU	MU/*P*	*Q*	TU	MU	MU/*P*
0	0			0	0		
		20	10			29	29
1	20			1	29		
		14	7			17	17
2	34			2	46		
		10	5			7	7
3	44			3	53		
		3	1.5			2	2
4	47			4	55		
		0	0			1	1
5	47			5	56		
		−5	−2.5			0	0
6	42			6	56		
		−10	−5			−4	−4
7	32			7	52		

spent the $2 on a Big Mac. How about our next $2? Again the choice is clear; the 10 utils per dollar from the Big Mac are plainly better than the 7 utils per dollar we can get from ice cream cones. So we buy one Big Mac and two ice cream cones with our first $4.

Now let's consider our fifth and sixth dollars. The *MU/P* for a second Big Mac is 7. The *MU/P* for a third ice cream cone is also 7, so we could spend the fifth dollar on either—if McDonald's will sell us half a Big Mac. We ask them if they will, and they tell us no, so we must make a choice between either two additional ice cream cones or another Big Mac for our fifth and sixth dollar. Since the marginal utility per dollar of the fourth ice cream cone is only 2, it makes sense to spend our fifth and sixth dollar on another Big Mac. So now we're up to two Big Macs and two ice cream cones and we have one more dollar to spend.

Now how about our last dollar? If we spend it on a third ice cream cone we get 7 additional utils. If McDonald's maintains its position and only sells whole Big Macs, this is our sole choice since we only have a dollar and Big Macs sell for $2. But let's say that McDonald's wants the sale and this time offers to sell us half a Big Mac for $1. Would we take it? The answer is no. The next Big Mac gives us only 5 utils per dollar whereas the third ice cream cone gives us 7 utils per dollar. So we spend the seventh dollar on a third ice cream cone.

With these choices we've arrived at equilibrium—we're maximizing total utility. Our total utility is 34 from two Big Macs and 53 utils from the three ice cream cones, making a total of 87 utils.

Why do these two choices make sense? Because they give us the most utility per dollar and hence the highest total utility. These choices make the marginal utility per dollar equal as between the last Big Mac and the last ice cream cone. The marginal utility per dollar we get from our last Big Mac is:

$$\frac{MU}{P} = \frac{14}{\$2} = 7$$

The marginal utility per dollar we get from our last ice cream cone is:

$$\frac{MU}{P} = \frac{7}{\$1} = 7$$

The marginal utility per dollar of each choice is equal, so we know we can't do any better. For any other choice we would get less total utility, so we could increase our total utility by switching to one of these two choices.

The General Principle of Rational Choice Our example involved only two goods, but the reasoning can be extended to the choice among many goods. Our analysis of rational choice has shown us that the principle of rational choice among many goods is simply an extension of the basic principle of rational choice applied to two goods. That general principle for maximizing utility is to equate, as closely as possible, the marginal utility per dollar of the activities or goods being considered.

When $\frac{MU_x}{P_x} > \frac{MU_y}{P_y}$, *consume more of good x.*

When $\frac{MU_x}{P_x} < \frac{MU_y}{P_y}$, *consume more of good y.*

Stop adjusting your consumption when the marginal utilities per dollar are equal.

So the general principle of rational choice is this:

Choose goods and activities so that the marginal utilities per dollar of the goods consumed are equal:

$$\frac{MU_x}{P_x} = \frac{MU_y}{P_y}$$

When this principle is met, the consumer is in equilibrium; the marginal cost per util is equal for all goods and the consumer is as well off as it is possible to be.

Notice that the rule does not say that the rational consumer should consume a good until its marginal utility reaches zero. The reason is that the consumer doesn't have enough money to buy all she wants. She faces an income constraint and does the best she can under that constraint—that is, she maximizes utility. To buy more goods she has to work more, so she should work until the marginal value of another dollar earned just equals the marginal value of another dollar spent. According to economists' analysis of rational choice, a person's choice of how much to work is made simultaneously with the person's decision of how much to consume. So when you say you want a Porsche but can't afford one, economists ask whether you're working two jobs and saving all your money to buy a Porsche. If you aren't, you're demonstrating that you don't really want a Porsche, given what you would have to do to get it.

Marginal Utility and the Law of Demand

Now that you know the basic rule for maximizing utility, let's bring in the law of demand and see how it relates to marginal utility. The law of demand says that the quantity demanded of a good depends inversely on the relative price of that good. Accordingly when the price of a good goes up, the quantity we consume of it goes down.

Now let's consider the law of demand in relation to our marginal utility rule. When the price of a good goes up, the marginal utility *per dollar* we get from that good goes down. So when the price of a good goes up, if we were initially in equilibrium, we no longer are. Therefore we lower our consumption of that good. The principle of rational choice shows us formally that following the law of demand is the rational thing to do.

3 According to the principle of rational choice, if there is diminishing marginal utility and the price of a good goes up, we consume less of that good. Hence, the principle of rational choice leads to the law of demand.

Let's see how. If:

$$\frac{MU_x}{P_x} = \frac{MU_y}{P_y}$$

and the price of good *y* goes up, then:

$$\frac{MU_x}{P_x} > \frac{MU_y}{P_y}$$

Our condition for maximizing utility is no longer satisfied. Consider the preceding example, in which we were in equilibrium with 87 utils (34 from two Big Macs and 53 from three ice cream cones) with the principle of rational choice fulfilled:

$$\begin{matrix} \text{Big Mac} & & \text{Ice cream} \\ \frac{14 \text{ marginal utils}}{\$2} & = & \frac{7 \text{ marginal utils}}{\$1} = 7 \end{matrix}$$

If the price of an ice cream cone rises from \$1 to \$2, the marginal utility per dollar for one Big Mac (whose price hasn't changed) exceeds the marginal utility per dollar of ice cream cones:

$$\begin{array}{ccc} \text{Big Mac} & & \text{Ice Cream} \\ \frac{14}{\$2} & > & \frac{7}{\$2} \end{array}$$

To satisfy our condition for maximizing utility so that our choice will be rational, we must somehow raise the marginal utility we get from the good whose relative price has risen and lower the *MU* we get from a good whose relative price has fallen. Following the principle of diminishing marginal utility, we can increase marginal utility only by decreasing our consumption of the good whose price has risen. As we consume fewer ice cream cones and more Big Macs, the marginal utility of ice cream rises and the marginal utility of a Big Mac falls.

This example can be extended to a general rule: If the price of a good rises, you'll increase your total utility by consuming less of it. When the price of a good goes up, consumption of that good must go down. Our marginal utility rule underlies the law of demand:

> *Law of demand: The quantity demanded of a good will rise the lower its price, other things constant.*

Or alternatively:

> *The quantity demanded of a good will fall the higher its price, other things constant.*

This discussion of marginal utility and rational choice shows the relationship between marginal utility and the price we're willing to pay. When *MU* is high, as it is with diamonds, the price we're willing to pay is high. When marginal utility is low, as it is with water, the price we're willing to pay is low. Since our demand for a good is an expression of our willingness to pay for it, quantity demanded is related to marginal utility.

Complements, Substitutes, and Shift Factors of Demand In Chapter 2, we spent a lot of time distinguishing between movements along a demand curve—a change in the quantity demanded—and shifts in demand caused by a change in a shift factor. Now that we've studied the foundations of choice theory, it is useful to reconsider those distinctions. A shift factor changes the marginal utility one gets from a good and hence changes how much of a good is desired at all prices. Say, for example, that it rains. That raises the MU of umbrellas and puts people off their rational choice equilibrium. They adjust—buy more umbrellas—and that adjustment shifts the demand for umbrellas out.

Similarly, a change in the price of a good puts people off their rational choice equilibrium and causes them to modify their consumption of that good, and of other goods. They continue to do so until the ratio of marginal utilities is in line with the new price ratios. For example, say the price of pencils goes up; one reduces one's consumption of pencils, raising the marginal utility of pencils.

In the adjusting process, a price change of one good indirectly affects the marginal utility of, and hence the demand for, another good. For example, when the price of a Big Mac goes up, one consumes fewer Big Macs, raising the marginal utility of consuming Big Macs. One then also consumes more of other goods—say, pizza—lowering the marginal utility one gets from pizzas. So, a change in the price of Big Macs will affect the demand for pizzas. That's why price of related goods is a shift factor of demand for a good.

Substitutes Goods that can be used in place of one another.

There are actually two ways in which a price change of a related good can affect the demand for a good. The Big Mac/pizza example is an example in which goods were **substitutes**—goods that can be used in place of one another. When goods *X* and *Y* are substitutes, the rise in price of good *Y* will decrease the marginal utility one gets

ADDED DIMENSION

INCOME AND SUBSTITUTION EFFECTS

In the discussion of the law of demand we didn't say precisely how much the quantity demanded would decrease with a price rise. We didn't because of a certain ambiguity that arises when one talks about changes in nominal prices. To understand the cause of this ambiguity, notice that with $7 we can no longer consume two big Macs and three ice cream cones. We've got to cut back for two reasons: First, we're poorer due to the rise in price. This is called the *income effect.* Second is the change in the *relative* prices. The price of ice cream has risen relative to the price of Big Macs. This is called a *substitution effect.* Technically the law of demand is based only upon the substitution effect.

To separate the two effects, let's assume that somebody compensates us for the rise in price of ice cream cones. Since it would cost $10 [(2 × $2 = $4) + (3 × $2 = $6)] to buy what $7 bought previously, we'll assume that someone gives us an extra $3 to compensate us for the rise in price. This eliminates the income effect. We now have $10 so we can buy two Big Macs and the three ice cream cones as we did before. If we do so, our total utility is once again 87 (34 utils from two Big Macs and 53 utils from three ice cream cones). But will we do so?

We see that Big Macs give us more *MU* per dollar. What happens if we exchange an ice cream cone for an additional Big Mac, so instead of buying three ice cream cones and two Big Macs, we buy three Big Macs and two ice cream cones? The *MU* per dollar of Big Macs falls from 7 to 5 and the *MU* per dollar of the ice cream cone (whose price is now $2) rises from 3.5 to 8.5. Our total utility rises to 44 from three Big Macs and 46 from two ice cream cones, for a total of 90 utils rather than the previous 87. We've increased our total utility by shifting our consumption out of ice cream, the good whose price has risen. The price of ice cream went up and, even though we were given more money so we could buy the same amount as before, we did not; we bought fewer ice cream cones. That's the substitution effect in action: It tells us that when the relative price of a good goes up, the quantity purchased of that good decreases, *even if you're given money to compensate you for the rise.*

from good *Y*, and hence will increase the demand for good *X*. For example, say the price of hot dogs goes up. The demand for hamburgers will increase—hot dogs and hamburgers are substitutes for each other. This is the most common way the price of a related good effect works.

4 A good is a substitute for another good if its consumption goes up when the price of the other good goes up. A good is a complement for another if its consumption goes down when the price of the other good goes up.

It is possible, however, for the price of a related good effect to work in another manner. For example, if the goods are **complements**—goods that are used in conjunction with other goods—a fall in the price of good *Y* will directly increase the marginal utility of good *X*, and hence will *increase* the demand for good *X*. For example, say the price of hot dogs goes up and that people use lots of mustard on hot dogs (but not on hamburgers; on hamburgers they use ketchup). The increase in price and the related decrease in the consumption of hot dogs will directly lower the *MU* one gets from mustard, and hence, will decrease the demand for mustard. The same is true for all complementary goods.

Complements Goods used in conjunction with other goods.

Other shift factors also affect marginal utility, and hence affect demand. An increase in income, for example, increases the total utility one gets from one's income, and thereby increases one's consumption of almost all goods, although the increase may be greater for some goods than for others. Goods whose consumption increases with an increase in income are called **normal goods.** It is, however, possible that an increase in income can affect relative preferences so much that an increase in income can cause a decrease in the consumption of a particular good. Goods whose consumption decreases when income increases are called **inferior goods.** In some instances, potatoes are an example of an inferior good. As income goes up, people might so significantly shift their consumption toward meat and away from potatoes that their total consumption of potatoes decreases.

Normal goods Goods whose consumption increases with an increase in income.

Inferior goods Goods whose consumption decreases when income increases.

Applying Economists' Theory of Choice to the Real World

Understanding a theory involves more than understanding how a theory works; it also involves understanding the limits the assumptions underlying the theory place on the use of the theory. So let us consider some of the assumptions upon which economists' analysis of choice is based. The first assumption we'll consider is the implicit assumption that decisions can be made costlessly.

The Cost of Decision Making and Bounded Rationality The theory of rational choice makes reasonably good intuitive sense when we limit our examples to two or three choices, as we did in this chapter. But in reality, there are hundreds of thousands of choices that we must make simultaneously. It simply doesn't make intuitive sense that we're going to apply rational choice to all those choices simultaneously—that would exceed our decision-making abilities. This cost of decision making means that it is only rational to be somewhat irrational—to do things without applying the rational choice model. Thinking about decisions is one of the things we all economize on.

How real-world people decide in real-world situations is an open question that modern economists are spending a lot of time researching. Following the work of Nobel Prize winner Herbert Simon, a number of economists have come to believe that, to make real-world decisions, most people use **bounded rationality**—rationality based on *rules of thumb*—rather than using the rational choice model. They argue that many of our decisions are made with our minds on automatic pilot. This view of rationality has significant implications for interpreting and predicting economic events. For example, one rule of thumb is that "you get what you pay for," which means that if something has a high price we tend to think it is better than something that has a low price. Put technically, we rely on price to convey information about reality. This reliance on price for information changes the inferences one can draw from the analysis, and can lead to upward-sloping demand curves.

Bounded rationality Rationality based on *rules of thumb* rather than using the rational choice model.

A second rule of thumb that people sometimes use is "follow the leader." When one doesn't know what to do, one does what one thinks smart people are doing. Consider the clothes you're wearing. We suspect many of your choices of what to wear reflect these rules of thumb. Suppliers of these goods certainly think so and spend enormous amounts of money to exploit these rules of thumb. They try to steer your automatic pilot toward their goods. The suppliers emphasize these two rules ("you get what you pay for" and "follow the leader") to convince people their product is the "in" thing to buy. If they succeed, they've got a goldmine; if they fail, they've got a flop. Advertising is designed to mine these rules of thumb.

In technical terms, the "follow the leader" rule leads to **focal point equilibria** in which a set of goods is consumed, not because the goods are objectively preferred to all other goods, but simply because through luck, or advertising, they have become focal points to which people have gravitated. Once some people started consuming a good, others followed.

Focal point equilibrium Equilibrium in which goods are consumed, not because the goods are objectively preferred to all other goods, but simply because through luck or advertising they have become focal points to which people have gravitated.

Herbert Simon was awarded the Nobel Prize in 1978 for work on the importance of institutions and process to economic theory. © *The Nobel Foundation.*

Given Tastes A second assumption implicit in economists' theory of rational choice is that utility functions are given, and are not shaped by society. In reality our preferences are determined not only by nature, but also by our experiences—by nurture. Let's consider an example: Forty percent of major league baseball players chew tobacco, but close to zero percent of your professors chew tobacco. Why? Are major league baseball players somehow born with a tobacco-chewing gene while college professors are not? We doubt it. Tastes often are significantly influenced by society.

Tastes and Individual Choice One way in which economists integrate the above insights into economics is by emphasizing that the analysis is conducted on the assumption of "given tastes." As discussed above, in reality, economists agree that often forces besides price and marginal utility play a role in determining what people demand. They fully recognize that there is a whole other analysis necessary to supplement theirs—an analysis of what determines taste.

Ask yourself what you ate today. Was it health food? Pizza? Foie gras? Whatever it was, it was probably not the most efficient way to satisfy your nutritional needs. The most efficient way to do that would be to eat only soybean mush and vitamin supple-

ADDED DIMENSION

MAKING STUPID DECISIONS

It is hard to make good decisions. You need lots of training—in math, in economics, in logic. Think of kids—do five-year-olds make rational decisions? Some dyed-in-the-wool utilitarians might argue that whatever decision one makes must, by definition, be rational, but such usage makes the concept tautological—true by definition.

When applying the theory of rational choice, most economists agree that some decisions people make can be irrational. For example, they will concede that five-year-olds make a lot of what most parents would call "stupid (or irrational) decisions." By a stupid decision they mean a decision that has expected consequences which, if the child had logically thought about them, would have caused the child not to make that particular decision. But five-year-olds often haven't learned how to think logically about expected consequences, so economists don't assume decisions made by five-year-olds reflect the rational choice model.

In the real world, parents and teachers spend enormous effort to teach children what is rational, reasonable, and "appropriate." Children's decision-making process reflects that teaching. But parents and teachers teach more than a decision-making process; they also teach children a moral code that often includes the value of honour and the value of selflessness. These teachings shape their children's decision-making process (although not always in the way that parents or teachers think or hope) and modify their preferences. So our decision-making process and our preferences are, to some degree, taught to us.

Recognizing that preferences and decision-making processes are, to some degree, taught, not inherent, eliminates the fixed point by which to judge people's decisions: Are they making decisions that reflect their true needs, or are they simply reflecting what they have been taught? Eliminating that fixed point makes it difficult to draw unambiguous policy implications from economists' model of rational choice.

ments at a cost of about $300 per year. That's less than one-tenth of what the average individual today spends on food per year. Most of us turn up our noses at soybean mush. Why? Because tastes are important.

We emphasize this point about the importance of tastes because some economists have been guilty of forgetting their simplifying assumption. An example of this is that some economists in the 1800s thought that society's economic needs eventually would be fully satisfied and that we would enter a golden age of affluence where all our material wants would be satisfied. They thought there would be surpluses of everything. Clearly that hasn't happened. Somehow it seems that whenever a need is satisfied, it's replaced by yet another want, which soon becomes another need.

There are, of course, examples of wants being temporarily satisfied, as a company on a small island in the Caribbean is reported to have discovered. Employees weren't showing up for work. The company sent in a team of efficiency experts who discovered the cause of their problem: The firm had recently raised wages, and workers had decided they could get all they wanted (warm weather, a gorgeous beach, plenty of food, and a little bit of spending money) by showing up for work once, maybe twice, a week. Such a situation was clearly not good for business, but the firm found a solution. It sent in thousands of Sears catalogues, and suddenly the workers were no longer satisfied with what they already had. They wanted more and went back to work to get it. When they were presented with new possibilities, their wants increased. Companies know that tastes aren't constant, and they spend significant amounts of money in advertising to make consumers have a taste for their goods. It works, too.

Tastes are also important in explaining differences in consumption between countries. For example, in Japan one wouldn't consider having a meal without rice. Rice has a ceremonial, almost mystical value there. In many parts of Canada supper means meat and potatoes. In Germany, carp (a large goldfish) is a delicacy; in Canada many people consider carp inedible. In Canada corn is a desirable vegetable; in parts of Europe, until recently, it was pig food.

To say we don't analyze tastes in the core of economic theory doesn't mean that we don't take them into account. Think back to Chapter 2 when we distinguished shifts in demand (the entire demand schedule shifts) from movements along the demand curve. Those movements along the demand curve were the effect of price. Tastes were one of the shift factors of demand. So economists can include tastes in their analysis; a change in tastes makes the demand curve shift.

Individual Choice Theory in Context

5 Economists use their simple self-interest theory of choice because it cuts through many obfuscations, and in doing so often captures a part of reality that others miss.

We began this chapter with a discussion of the simplifying nature of the economists' analysis of rational choice. Now that you've been through it, you may be wondering if it's all that simple. In any case, we're sure most of you would agree that it's complicated enough. When we're talking about formal analysis, we're in total agreement.

But if you're talking about informal analysis and applying the analysis to the real world, most economists would also agree that this theory of choice is in no way acceptable. Economists believe that there's more to life than maximizing utility. We believe in love, anger, and doing crazy things just for the sake of doing crazy things. We're real people.

But, we argue, simplicity has its virtue, and often people hide their selfish motivations. Few people like to go around and say, "I did this because I'm a selfish, calculating person who cares primarily about myself." Instead they usually emphasize other motives. "Society conditioned me to do it"; "I'm doing this to achieve fairness"; "It's my upbringing." And they're probably partially right, but often they hide and obscure their selfish motives in their psychological explanations. The beauty of economists' simple psychological assumption is that it cuts through many obfuscations (that's an obfuscating word meaning smokescreens) and, in doing so, it often captures a part of reality that others miss. Let's consider a couple of examples.

Why does government have restrictions on who's allowed to practice law? The typical layperson's answer is that these restrictions exist to protect the public. The economists' answer is that many of the restrictions do little to protect the public. Instead their primary function is to restrict the number of lawyers and thereby increase the marginal utility of existing lawyers and the price they can charge.

Why do people pollute? The layperson's answer is that people haven't been educated about the importance of the environment. The economists' answer is that people aren't paying enough for their polluting activities.

Why do museum directors almost always want to increase the size of their collections? The layperson's (and museum directors') answer is that they're out to preserve our artistic heritage. The economists' answer is that it often has more to do with maximizing the utility of the museum staff. (Economist William Grampp recently made this argument in a book about the economics of art. He buttressed his argument by pointing out that more than half of museums' art is in storage and not accessible to the public. Acquiring more art will simply lead to more going into storage.)

Now in no way are we claiming that the economic answer based on pure self-interest is always the correct one. But we are arguing that approaching problems by asking the question, "What's in it for the people making the decisions?" is a useful approach that will give you more insight into what's going on than many other approaches. It gets people to ask tough, rather than easy, questions. After you've asked the tough questions, then you can see how to modify the conclusions by looking deeply into the real-world institutions.

ELASTICITY OF DEMAND

6A Price elasticity of demand is defined as a measure of the percent change in the quantity demanded divided by the percent change in the price.

Now that we've examined the foundations of the law of demand, it's time to talk about a term economists use to describe the responsiveness of quantity demanded to changes in price: **price elasticity of demand** (or often just *elasticity of demand*). It's a measure of the percent change in quantity of a good demanded divided by the percent change in the price of that good. Price elasticity of demand is an important concept, so let's write it down formally:

$$E_d = \frac{\text{Percent change in quantity demanded}}{\text{Percent change in price}}$$

Let's consider an example. Say the price of a good goes up by 10 percent and, in response, the quantity demanded falls by 20 percent. The price elasticity of demand would be −2. Alternatively, say the price goes down by 5 percent and the quantity rises by 2 percent. In that case the price elasticity of demand would be −.4.

Two things to remember in thinking about elasticity are:

1. By convention, we ignore the minus sign.
2. It uses percentages, not absolute amounts.

Let's briefly consider each.

Ignoring the Minus Sign

The first point to notice about the discussion of elasticity is that when we said what the price elasticity of demand was, we said −2. This follows because whenever price goes up, quantity demanded falls. This inverse relationship is deeply ingrained in every economist's mind. But negative numbers are a pain, especially when you're comparing two negative numbers, say −2 and −4. Which is larger? (The answer is −2.) To avoid this confusion, generally economists talk about elasticity as a positive number and remember that it's actually negative. (Those of you who remember some math can think of the definition of elasticity as being an absolute value, rather than a simple number.) We'll follow that convention in this book, which means that you've got to remember that the elasticity of demand is actually negative even though we talk about it as positive.

Use of Percentages

The second point to notice is that elasticity uses percentages, not absolute amounts. In describing demanders' responsiveness, we use percentages rather than absolute amounts for two reasons. The first is that percentage changes are unaffected by our choice of units. For example, say the price rises from $1.00 to $1.20 per litre and quantity demanded falls from 400 to 380 litres. Is that highly responsive or not? If we use cents, the change seems relatively responsive, with a change of price of 20 cents bringing about a change in quantity demanded of 20 litres. But if we use dollars, it seems far more responsive—with the change of one-fifth of a dollar bringing about a change in quantity demanded of 20 litres. So there seems to be a difference in responsiveness, depending on the units we're using. Using percentages eliminates this difference caused by the unit we measure in. Measuring in cents or dollars, the percentage change in our price is 20/100 or .20/1.00, both of which are 20 percent. A 20 percent change in price brings about a 5 percent change in quantity demanded.

The second reason for using percentages is that it makes comparisons of responsiveness of different goods easier since the percentage change gives us insight into what will happen to total revenue. Say a $1.00 increase in the price of a $2,000 computer decreases the quantity demanded by one, from 10 to 9. Say also that a $1.00 increase in the price of a pen, from $1.00 to $2.00, decreases quantity demanded by one—from 10,000 to 9,999. Using absolute numbers, the $1.00 price decrease had the same effect on the quantities.

But such a comparison of absolute numbers is not very helpful. To see that, ask yourself which good you'd rather be selling. As a percentage of price, the computer price increase of 1/2,000 of the original price is relatively small, and the decrease in quantity demanded of 1/10 of original sales is large, so total revenue would decrease. As a percentage, the price increase in pens was relatively large—100 percent—and the percentage quantity decrease is small. So, if you raised the price of pens there will be an increase in total revenues. Clearly, if you're raising your price in these examples you'd rather be selling pens than computers. By using percentages, this is made clear: a .05 percent increase in price decreases quantity demanded by 10 percent, so the elasticity is 200. With pens, a 100 percent increase in prices decreases quantity demanded by .01 percent, an elasticity of .001. So the elasticities measure tells us the two situations are substantially different.

Elasticity, Total Revenue, and Description of Demand

The usefulness for sellers of comparing responsiveness to price changes derives from elasticity's relationship with total revenues. (E_d represents price elasticity of demand.)

Elastic Percent change in quantity demanded is greater than percent change in price, $E_d > 1$.

Unitary elasticity Percent change in quantity demanded equals percent change in price, $E_d = 1$.

Inelastic Percent change in quantity demanded is less than percent change in price, $E_d < 1$.

- If E_d is greater than 1, a rise in price lowers total revenue. (Price and total revenue move in opposite directions.) The demand in that price range is described as **elastic.** When demand is elastic, the percent change in quantity demanded is greater than the percent change in price.
- If E_d is equal to 1, a rise in price leaves total revenue unchanged. The demand is described as having **unitary elasticity.** When demand is unit elastic, the percent change in quantity demanded equals the percent change in price.
- If E_d is less than 1, a rise in price increases total revenue. (Price and total revenue move in the same direction.) The demand in that price range is described as **inelastic.** When demand is inelastic, the percent change in quantity demanded is less than the percent change in price.

An Example

Now let's try some real-world examples. The first is a university president thinking of raising tuition. Say that raising tuition by 10 percent will decrease the number of students by only 1 percent. What's the elasticity? The percent change in quantity is 1 percent; the percent change in price is 10 percent. Dividing the percent change in quantity by the percent change in price, we have an elasticity of .1. That's an inelastic demand ($E_d < 1$), so raising tuition will increase the university's total revenue.

6B If demand is inelastic, a rise in price increases total revenue. If demand is elastic, a rise in price lowers total revenue. If demand is unitary elastic, a rise in price has no effect on revenue.

But if a 10 percent rise in tuition will decrease the enrollment by 25 percent, the elasticity will be large (2.5). In response to an increase in tuition, the university's total revenue will significantly decrease. When you have an elastic demand you should hesitate to increase price. (To make sure you're following the argument, explain the likely effect an elastic demand will have on lowering tuition.)

Elasticity and the Demand Curve

Let's now see how to calculate the elasticity in the area around a point on a demand curve. In Exhibit 3 we do so for a hypothetical demand curve facing a university.

Say it's thinking of raising tuition from $900 to $945, an increase of 5 percent (45/900). Doing so will cause it to move along the demand curve from point *A* to point *B*. Extending lines down to the quantity axis we can see that this will cause enrollment to fall from 300 to 255, a decrease of 15 percent (45/300). Remembering that elasticity is defined as the percent change in quantity demanded divided by the percent change in price, we can now calculate the elasticity of the demand curve at point *A*. It's 15% / 5% = 3.

The elasticity at the initial price and initial quantity (point *A*) is 3. But after the price change, we will be at point *B*—the new price of $945 and the new quantity of 255. The elasticity at point *B* is (45/255)/(45/945) which equals 3.71. That's as exact a measure as we can give of elasticity over a range of points on a demand curve. It's somewhere between 3 and 3.71.

These calculations point out an important fact: elasticity changes at different points on a straight-line demand curve. To see this more clearly, let's consider a point further away from points *A* and *B*—point *C*—and, again, a 5 percent tuition increase. What is the elasticity of demand at this point? Extending our lines down to the quantity axis, we can see that quantity will decrease from 900 to 885, a decrease of 15/900 = 1.67%. So the elasticity of point *C* is approximately (15/900)/(15/300) = .33. It's fallen substantially.

Now let's think a bit more about the question of what elasticity was facing the university president who was thinking of raising price from $900 (point *A*) to $945 (point *B*). The elasticity at the initial point was 3 and at the point she would move to it was 3.7. So what do you tell her the elasticity facing her is?

Arc elasticity The average elasticity of a range of points on a demand curve.

Economists, quite reasonably, use an average of the two when describing the elasticity of a section of a demand curve. The average can be calculated using the *arc elasticity method.* **Arc elasticity** is the average elasticity of a range of points on a demand curve. It's calculated in the following manner: Instead of dividing the changes in price and quantity by one end point or the other, you add both end points and divide them by 2. Doing so using the facts in our previous example gives:

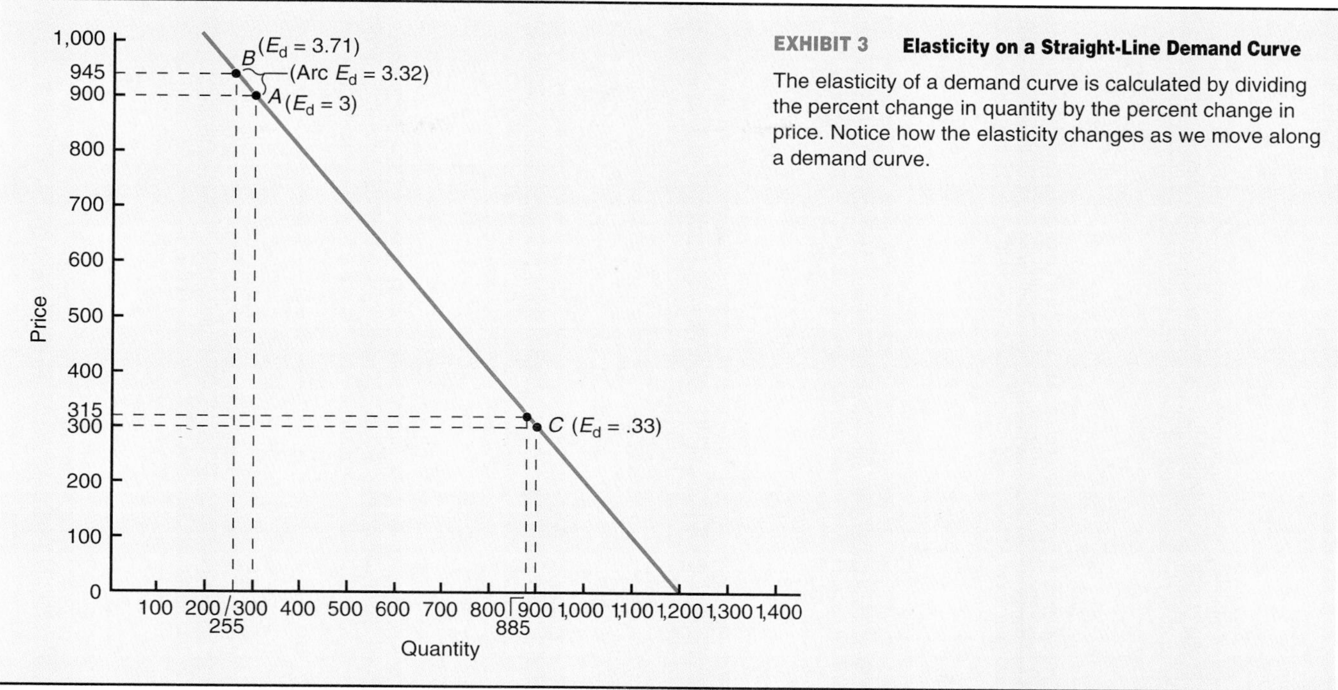

EXHIBIT 3 Elasticity on a Straight-Line Demand Curve

The elasticity of a demand curve is calculated by dividing the percent change in quantity by the percent change in price. Notice how the elasticity changes as we move along a demand curve.

$$\text{Arc } E_d = \frac{\dfrac{45}{(255 + 300)/2}}{\dfrac{45}{(900 + 945)/2}} = 3.32$$

In the real world, elasticities are calculated with statistical techniques, with a great amount of effort devoted to distinguishing between movement along a demand curve and shifts of a demand curve. Because of difficulties in distinguishing these two, our estimates of elasticities are rough and ready and can easily vary by, say, 20 or even 40 percent up or down. Thus, while economists give specific elasticities for demand curves, we interpret those numbers loosely.

Elasticity Is Not a Slope In thinking about elasticity in relation to a demand curve, students make the common mistake of saying *elasticity* but thinking *slope.* Remember that elasticity isn't the same as slope. Slope tells us what will happen to quantity demanded when price changes. In Exhibit 3 the slope of the demand curve is −1. And since it's a straight line, its slope is −1 at every point on that demand curve. That isn't the case for elasticity. Elasticity changes at each point on a straight-line demand curve.

Elasticity and Total Revenue: A Closer Look

Total revenue The amount a firm receives for selling its products; obtained by multiplying price by the quantity supplied.

As a review of elasticity, let's consider more carefully the relationship between elasticity and **total revenue**—the payments firms receive for their goods—and see how it can be demonstrated graphically.

The relationship between elasticity and total revenue is no mystery. There's a very logical reason why they are related, which can most neatly be seen by recognizing that total revenue ($P \times Q$) is represented by the area under the demand curve at that price and quantity. For example, at point *A* on demand curve D_1 in Exhibit 4 (a), the total revenue at price $4 and quantity 6 is the area designated by the *A* and *B* rectangles, $24.

If we increase price to $5, quantity demanded decreases to 5, so total revenue is now $25. Total revenue has increased slightly, so the demand curve at point *A* is slightly inelastic, but close to unit elasticity. The new total revenue is represented by

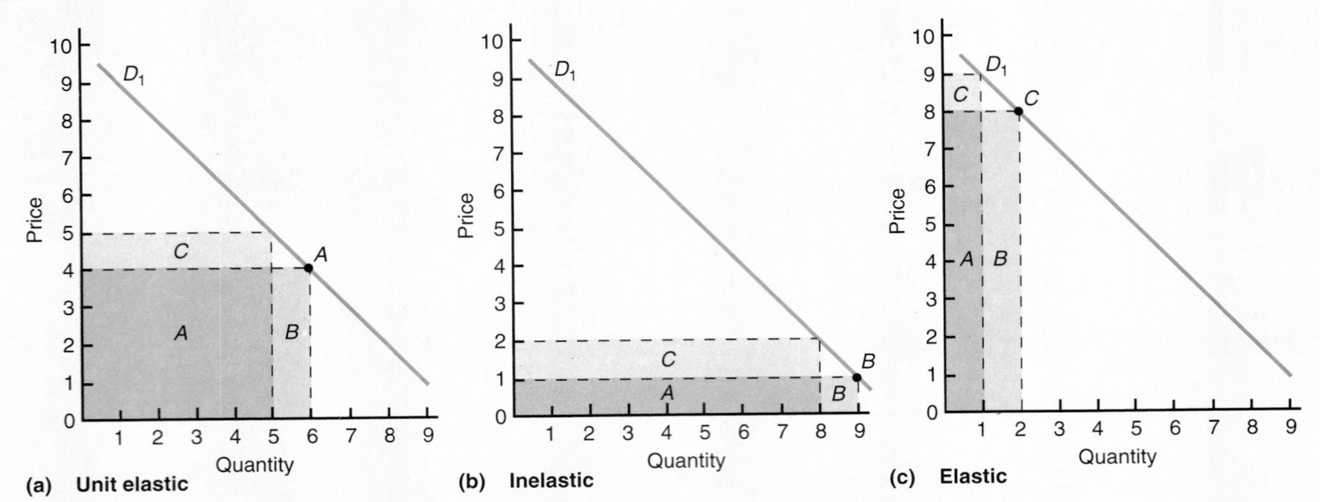

EXHIBIT 4 Elasticity and Total Revenue

Total revenue is measured by the rectangle one gets by extending lines from the demand curve to the price and quantity axes. The change in total revenue resulting from a change in price can be estimated by comparing the size of the before and after rectangles. If price is being raised, total revenue increases by rectangle *C* and decreases by rectangle *B*. As you can see, the effect of a $1 price rise on total revenue differs significantly at different points on a demand curve. (**a**) shows an almost unitary elastic point, (**b**) shows an inelastic point, and (**c**) shows an elastic point.

the *A* and *C* rectangles. The difference between the old total revenue (*A* and *B*) and the new total revenue (*A* and *C*) is the difference between the rectangles *B* and *C*. Comparing these rectangles provides us with a visual method of estimating elasticities. Comparing the size of these two rectangles, let's see what happens to total revenue.

In Exhibit 4 (b) we consider an inelastic point; in Exhibit 4 (c) we consider a highly elastic point. Whereas in Exhibit 4 (b) the slope of the demand curve is the same as in Exhibit 4 (a), we're at a different point on the demand curve (point *B*). If we raise our price from $1 to $2, quantity demanded falls from 9 to 8. The gained area (rectangle *C*) is much greater than the lost area (rectangle *B*). In other words, total revenue increases significantly, so the demand curve at point *B* is highly inelastic.

In Exhibit 4 (c) the demand curve is again the same, but we're at still another point, *C*. If we raise our price from $8 to $9, quantity demanded falls from 2 to 1. The gained area (rectangle *C*) is much smaller than the lost area (rectangle *B*). In other words, total revenue decreases significantly, so the demand curve at point *C* is highly elastic.

Notice that the elasticity of a straight-line demand curve changes as you move along that demand curve. The way in which elasticity changes and its relationship to total revenue can be seen in Exhibit 5.

When output is zero, total revenue is zero; similarly when price is zero, total revenue is zero. That accounts for the two end points of the total revenue curve in Exhibit 5 (b). Let's say we start at a price of zero, where demand is very inelastic. As we increase price (decrease quantity demanded), total revenue increases significantly. As we continue to do so, the increases in total revenue become smaller until finally, after output of Q_0, total revenue actually starts decreasing. It continues decreasing at a faster and faster rate until finally, at zero output, total revenue is zero. These relationships are summarized in Exhibit 5 (c).

Perfectly Elastic and Inelastic Demand Curves Economists have developed terminology other than *elastic* and *inelastic* to describe two special cases; the case in which the demand curve is perfectly horizontal (slope = 0) and the case in which the demand

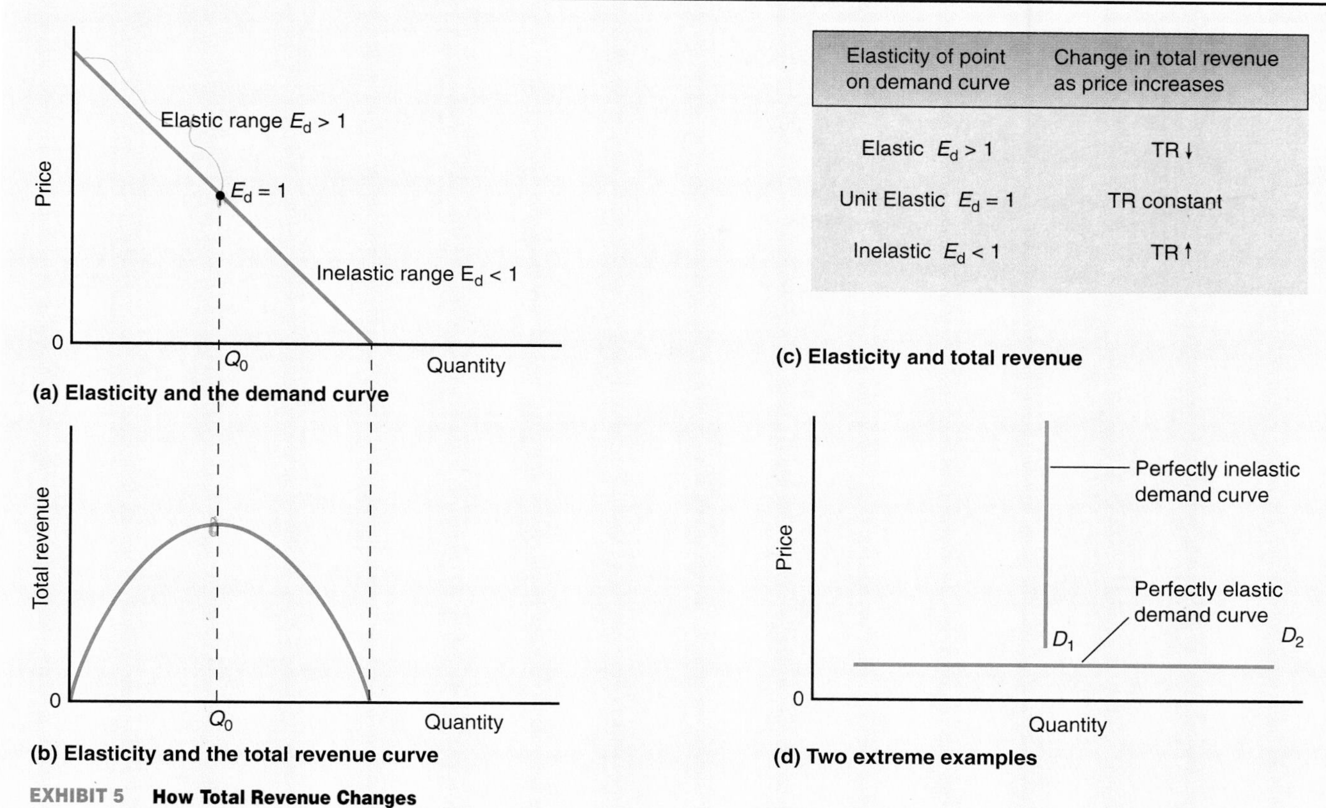

EXHIBIT 5 How Total Revenue Changes

Total revenue is at a maximum when elasticity equals one, as you can see in (**a**) and (**b**). When demand is elastic, total revenue increases with a decrease in price. When demand is inelastic, total revenue decreases with a decrease in price. Two special cases are shown in (**d**). A perfectly inelastic curve is vertical; total revenue will increase substantially with any rise in price. A perfectly elastic curve is horizontal; total revenue will fall to zero with any rise in price.

curve is perfectly vertical (slope = infinity). When the demand curve is perfectly horizontal, the elasticity is infinite. Economists describe such a curve as **perfectly elastic.**

Perfectly elastic Horizontal demand curve, E_d = infinity.

When the demand curve is perfectly vertical, the elasticity is zero. Economists describe such a demand curve as **perfectly inelastic.** If one raises price with a perfectly elastic demand curve, total revenue falls to zero; and if one raises price with a perfectly inelastic demand curve, total revenue increases proportionately. A perfectly elastic (D_2) and a perfectly inelastic (D_1) demand curve are demonstrated in Exhibit 5 (d).

Perfectly inelastic Vertical demand curve, $E_d = 0$.

The Influence of Substitution on the Elasticity of Demand

7 As a general rule, the more substitutes a good has, the more elastic is its demand.

Now that you know how to measure elasticity of demand, let's consider some of the factors that are likely to make demand more or less elastic. The influence of these factors can be summed up in one word: *substitution.* As a general rule, *the more substitutes a good has, the more elastic is its demand.*

The reasoning is as follows: If a good has substitutes, a price rise for that good will cause the demander to shift consumption to those substitute goods. When a satisfactory substitute for a good is available, a rise in that good's price will have a large effect on the quantity demanded, and the demand curve will tend to be elastic. For example, we think a Whopper is a satisfactory substitute for a Big Mac; if most people agree with us, the demand for Big Macs is very elastic.

The number of substitutes a good has is affected by several factors:

1. The larger the time interval considered, or the longer the run, the more elastic is the demand curve for the goods.

2. The less a good is a necessity, the more elastic is its demand curve.
3. The more specifically a good is defined, the more elastic is its demand curve.

These three reasons are derivatives of the substitution factor. Let's consider each to see why.

1. There are more substitutes in the long run than in the short run. That's because the long run provides more options for change. For example, let's consider the World War II period when the price of rubber went up considerably. In the short run, there were few substitutes; the demand for rubber was inelastic. In the long run, however, the rise in the price of rubber stimulated research for alternatives. Many alternatives were found. Today automobile tires, which were all made of rubber at the time World War II broke out, are almost entirely made from synthetic materials. In the long run, the demand curve was very elastic.
2. Necessities, by definition, tend to have fewer substitutes than do luxuries. Insulin for a diabetic is a necessity; the demand is highly inelastic. Chocolate ecstasy cake, however, is a luxury. A variety of other luxuries can be substituted for it (for example, cheesecake, a ball game, or a book).
3. If the good we're talking about is broadly defined (say, transportation), there aren't many substitutes and the demand will be inelastic. If you want to get from *A* to *B,* you need transportation. If the definition of the good is narrowed (say, to "transportation by bus"), there are more substitutes. Instead of taking a bus you can walk, ride your bicycle, or drive your car. In that case the demand curve is more elastic. Another example is beer—the demand for beer is fairly inelastic, yet the demand for a particular brand might be very elastic (because there are many other brands you might drink).

Let's consider how some of the substitution factors affect a specific decision. Let's say you've been hired by two governments (the city of Ottawa, Ontario, and the federal government) to advise them about the effect that raising the gas tax by 10 percent will have on tax revenues.

In your report to the two governments, you would point out that in the short run the demand curve would be less elastic than in the long run, since people aren't going to trade in their gas-guzzling cars for fuel-efficient cars immediately in response to a 10 percent rise in gas taxes—partly because they can't afford to, partly because they don't want to, and partly because not that many fuel-efficient cars are available to buy at the moment. In the long run, however, when the time comes that they would ordinarily purchase a new car, they're likely to switch to cars that are more fuel-efficient than their old cars, and to switch as much as they can to forms of transportation that are more fuel-efficient than cars. Then the demand will be far more elastic.

The second point you'd note is that although many people have had their gasoline cars converted to alternative fuels, gasoline dominates the market and is generally considered a necessity—although not all driving is necessary. However, since fuel is only a small part of what it costs to drive a car, the demand will probably tend to be inelastic.

As for the third factor (how broadly defined the good we're talking about is) you have to be careful. It makes your recommendations for the government of the city of Ottawa and for the federal government quite different from each other. For the federal government, which is interested in the demand for gasoline in the entire country, gasoline has a relatively inelastic demand. A general rule of thumb might be that a 1¢ rise in tax will raise tax revenues by $1 billion. That inelasticity can't be carried over to the demand for gasoline in a city such as Ottawa. Because of the city's size, people in Ottawa have a choice. A large proportion of the people who buy gas in Ottawa could as easily buy gas in Hull. Gasoline in Ottawa is a narrowly defined good and therefore has a quite *elastic* demand. A rise in price will mean a large fall in the quantity of gas demanded.

ADDED DIMENSION

INCOME AND CROSS ELASTICITY OF DEMAND

While price elasticity is the elasticity that economists most often talk about, elasticity is a general concept that relates percent changes in something with percent changes in something else.

One frequently used elasticity is *cross elasticity of demand* (the percent change in quantity of one good divided by the percent change in price of another good). An example of where cross elasticity might be important is a hot dog and mustard. The price of hot dogs can influence the demand for mustard. (Notice we used "demand," not "quantity demanded," to emphasize that in response to a change in anything but the price of that good, the entire demand curve shifts; there's no movement along the demand curve.)

When we look at cross elasticity of demand, we can't ignore signs as we did with the elasticity of demand (to avoid confusion economists refer to the elasticity of demand as the "own-price" elasticity of demand, since it tells us how quantity demanded changes when the "own-price" of a good changes). When goods are substitutes, their cross elasticity of demand is positive (as the price of orange juice rises, the demand for apple juice rises), while goods that are complements (like hot dogs and mustard) have a negative cross elasticity of demand (if the price of a hot dog rises, the demand for mustard might fall).

Another commonly used elasticity term is *income elasticity of demand,* the percent change in demand that will result from a percent change in income.

$$E_1 = \frac{\text{Percent change in demand}}{\text{Percent change in income}}$$

As an example, say your income goes up by 100 percent and your demand for Big Macs goes up by 50 percent. Your income elasticity for Big Macs would be:

$$\frac{50\%}{100\%} = 1/2$$

The following table presents income elasticities measured for some groups of goods.

Commodity	Price Elasticity Short run	Long run
Motion pictures	.81	3.41
Foreign travel	.24	3.09
Household electricity	.14	1.94
Intercity bus transportation	.17	1.89
Tobacco products	.21	0.86
Radio and TV repairs	.64	5.20
Furniture	2.60	0.53
Jewelry and watches	1.00	1.64
Food produced and consumed on farms	.61	—

In the short run, people often save increases in income, so most goods, other than impulse-bought goods, have low income elasticities. To avoid this problem, economists generally focus on long-run income elasticities. Notice that some goods have long-run income elasticities less than 1, which means that their consumption doesn't keep pace with rises in income. These tend to be relative necessities (goods that are necessities compared to other goods). Other goods have long-run elasticities greater than 1; their consumption more than keeps pace with rises in income. They tend to be relative luxuries.

Finally, notice the one good—food produced and consumed on farms—with a negative income elasticity. As mentioned earlier in the text, such goods are called *inferior goods.* As income rises, people not only decrease the proportionate amount they spend on such goods; they decrease the absolute amount they spend.

Source: Hendrik S. Houthakker and Lester D. Taylor, *Consumer Demand in the United States: Analyses and Projections,* 2nd ed. (Cambridge, MA: Harvard University Press, 1970).

EXHIBIT 6 Short-Run and Long-Run Elasticities of Demand

Product	Price Elasticity	
	Short run	Long run
Radio and television repair	0.47	3.84
Tobacco products	0.46	1.89
Electricity (for household consumption)	0.13	1.89
Stationery	0.47	0.56
Medical care and hospitalization insurance	0.31	0.92
Intercity bus trips	0.20	2.17
Toys (nondurable)	0.30	1.02
Movies/motion pictures	0.87	3.67
Foreign travel by U.S. residents	0.14	1.77

Source: Hendrik S. Houthakker and Lester D. Taylor. *Consumer Demand in the United States: Analyses and Projections,* 2nd ed. (Cambridge, MA: Harvard University Press, 1970).

We mention this point because in August 1980 someone forgot about it when the U.S. city of Washington, D.C., raised the tax on a gallon of gasoline by 8¢, a rise at that time of about 5 percent. In response, monthly gasoline sales in Washington, D.C., fell from 16 million gallons to 11 million gallons, a 40 percent decrease! The demand for gas in Washington was not inelastic, as it was for the United States as a whole; it was very elastic ($E_d = 8$). Washingtonians went elsewhere to buy gas. Within four months the city had repealed the tax increase.

The fact that smaller geographic areas have more elastic demands limits how highly provincial and local governments can tax goods relative to their neighbouring localities or provinces. Where there are differences, new stores open all along the border and existing stores expand to entice people to come over that border and save on taxes. For example, the introduction of the GST hurt businesses in many Canadian border towns—Canadians crossed into the U.S. and bought what they needed at a much lower price (even after exchanging Canadian dollars for American dollars). While they were supposed to declare their purchases and pay the appropriate duties and taxes when they reentered Canada, not everyone did—and Canadian border communities suffered (but as the exchange rate changed, it became more expensive to buy U.S. dollars, and cross-border shopping has fallen substantially since the early 1990s).

Exhibit 6 presents empirical estimates of elasticity of demand. Notice that, as expected, different estimates are provided for the short- and long-run elasticities of each good. Also notice that the estimates are for the entire country; if one were doing estimates for a specific region in the country, the estimates could be expected to show more elasticity.

Taking an example from Exhibit 6, notice that the long-run demand for movies is elastic. If movie theatres raise their prices, it's relatively easy for individuals simply to stay home and watch television. Thus, intuitively we consider movies to have close substitutes, so we would expect the demand to be relatively elastic.

As a second example, in the short run the demand for electricity is highly inelastic. People either have electrical appliances or they don't. In the long run, however, it becomes elastic since people can shift to gas for cooking and oil for heating, and can buy more energy-efficient appliances.

As an exercise, you might see if you can explain why each of the other goods listed in the table has the elasticity of demand reported.

Individual and Market Demand Elasticity

In thinking about demand elasticity, keep in mind the point made in Chapter 2: The market demand curve is the horizontal summation of individual demand curves, and some individuals have highly inelastic demands and others have highly elastic demands. A slight rise in the price of a good will cause some people to stop buying the good; the slight increase won't affect other people's demand for the good at all.

Stores conduct short-run sales in order to price discriminate.

Demand elasticity is influenced both by how many people drop out totally and by how much an existing consumer marginally changes his or her quantity demanded.

If a firm can somehow separate the people with less elastic demand from those with more elastic demand, it can charge more to the individuals with inelastic demands and less to individuals with elastic demands. We see examples of firms trying to do just that throughout the economy. Let's consider three:

1. Airlines' Saturday stay-over specials. If you stay over a Saturday night, usually you can get a much lower airline fare than if you don't. The reason is that businesspeople have inelastic demands and don't like to stay over Saturday nights, while pleasure travellers have more elastic demands. By requiring individuals to stay over Saturday night, airlines can separate out businesspeople and charge them more.
2. The phenomenon of selling new cars. Most new cars don't sell at the listed price. They sell at a discount. Salespeople are trained to separate out comparison shoppers (who have more elastic demands) from impulse buyers (who have inelastic demands). By not listing the selling price of cars so that the discount can be worked out in individual negotiations, salespeople can charge more to customers who have inelastic demands.
3. The almost-continual-sale phenomenon. Some items, such as washing machines, go on sale rather often. Why don't suppliers sell them at a low price all the time? Because some buyers whose washing machines break down have inelastic demand. They can't wait, so they'll pay the "unreduced" price. Others have elastic demands; they can wait for the sale. By running sales (even though they're frequent sales), sellers can separate demanders with inelastic demand curves from demanders with elastic demand curves.

CONCLUSION

That's the end of our introduction to individual choice theory. There was a lot to learn, but we hope that the facts and applications that were combined with it made it more palatable. Whether it was or was not palatable, it's a necessary chapter. Economists are continually thinking about, empirically measuring, and applying the analysis and terminology in this chapter. Their conversations are dotted with elastic, inelastic, and applications of the principle of rational choice.

A few years ago there was a survey in which economics graduate students were asked whether they often applied the principle of rational choice in their daily lives. They overwhelmingly answered yes. A few students wrote, "Doesn't everyone?" Even those graduate economics students who didn't like the principle of rational choice and the selfishness it implied about human nature still applied the principle of rational choice in analyzing real-world events. Their comments included, "Yes, I am brainwashed," and "Very often in spite of myself."

One of the goals of the book set forth in Chapter 1 is to get you to think like an economist. If we were to choose one principle that's central to thinking like an economist, the principle of rational choice would be it. Look at the world around you and apply the principle: Look for some phenomenon that doesn't seem as if it could have been a rational choice and then think harder because, from some perspective, it will have an explanation that accords with the principle of rational choice.

The fact that the principle of rational choice can explain everything doesn't mean that it's the best explanation imaginable. It's important to look at as many different explanations as possible, empirically testing when possible to choose among alternative explanations and, when it's impossible to test, keeping in the back of your mind various alternative explanations. Some economists believe that the principle of rational choice provides the best explanation of almost all events. Other economists believe that social and political factors must be built into the explanations of almost all events. But all economists in some way use the principle of rational choice in approaching problems. That's why this chapter is so important.

CHAPTER SUMMARY

- The principle of diminishing marginal utility states that as you consume more of an item, an additional unit of consumption will yield fewer utils than the previous unit.
- The principle of rational choice is:

If $\frac{MU_x}{P_x} > \frac{MU_y}{P_y}$, choose to consume more of good x.

If $\frac{MU_x}{P_x} < \frac{MU_y}{P_y}$, choose to consume more of good y.

If $\frac{MU_x}{P_x} = \frac{MU_y}{P_y}$, you're maximizing utility; you're indifferent between good x and good y.

- The law of demand can be derived from the principle of rational choice.
- To apply economists' analysis of choice to the real world, one must carefully consider, and adjust for, the underlying assumptions, such as costlessness of decision making and given tastes.
- A good is a substitute for another good if its consumption goes up when the price of the other good goes up; a good is a complement for another good if its consumption goes down when the price of the other good goes up.
- Economists describe demand curves by their elasticity.
- If one raises price and has: an elastic demand curve, total revenue falls; an inelastic demand curve, total revenue rises; a unitary elastic demand curve, total revenue is unchanged.
- The more substitutes a good has, the more elastic its demand curve.

KEY TERMS

arc elasticity *(146)*
bounded rationality *(142)*
complements *(141)*
diminishing marginal utility *(134)*
elastic *(146)*
focal point equilibrium *(142)*
inelastic *(146)*
inferior goods *(141)*
marginal utility *(133)*
normal goods *(141)*
perfectly elastic *(149)*
perfectly inelastic *(149)*
price elasticity of demand *(144)*
principle of rational choice *(136)*
substitutes *(140)*
total revenue *(147)*
total utility *(133)*
unitary elasticity *(146)*
utility *(133)*

QUESTIONS FOR THOUGHT AND REVIEW

The number after each question represents the estimated degree of critical thinking required. (1 = almost none; 10 = deep thought.)

1. How would the world be different than it is if the principle of diminishing marginal utility seldom held true? *(8)*
2. It is sometimes said that an economist is a person who knows the price of everything but the value of nothing. Is this statement true or false? Why? *(9)*
3. Assign a measure of utility to the study you are putting into your various courses. Do your study habits follow the principle of rational choice? *(6)*
4. The marginal utility of your consumption of widgets is 40; it changes by 2 with each change in widgets consumed. The marginal utility of your consumption of wadgets is also 40 but changes by 3 with each change in widgets consumed. The price of widgets is $2 and the price of wadgets is $3. How many widgets and wadgets should you consume? *(4)*
5. What key psychological assumptions do economists make in their theory of individual choice? *(7)*
6. Explain your motivation for four personal decisions you have made in the past year, using economists' model of individual choice. *(7)*
7. Determine the elasticity of demand if, in response to an increase in price of 10 percent, quantity decreased by 20 percent. Would it be elastic or inelastic? *(3)*
8. A firm has just increased its price by 5 percent over last year's price, and it found that quantity sold remained the same. The firm comes to you and wants to know its elasticity of demand. How would you calculate it? What additional information would you search for before you did your calculation? *(7)*
9. Why would an economist be more hesitant about making an elasticity estimate of the effect of an increase in price of 1 percent rather than an increase in price of 50 percent? *(6)*
10. Demand for private school education is generally considered to be highly inelastic. What does this suggest about tuition increases at private schools in the future? Why don't private schools raise tuition by amounts even greater than they already do? *(9)*

PROBLEMS AND EXERCISES

1. *a.* The following table gives the price and total utils of three goods: A, B, and C.

		Total utility							
Good	Price	1	2	3	4	5	6	7	8
A	$10	200	380	530	630	680	700	630	430
B	$2	20	34	46	56	64	72	78	82
C	$6	50	60	70	80	90	100	90	80

As closely as possible, determine how much of the three goods you would buy with $20. Explain why you chose what you did.

b. The following table gives the marginal utility of John's consumption of three goods: A, B, and C.

Units of consumption	*MU* of A	*MU* of B	*MU* of C
1	20	25	45
2	18	20	30
3	16	15	24
4	14	10	18
5	12	8	15
6	10	6	12

(1) .Good A costs $2 per unit, good B costs $1, and good C costs $3. How many units of each should a consumer with $12 buy to maximize his or her utility?

(2) How will the answer change if the price of B rises to $2?

(3) How about if the price of C is 50¢ but the other prices are as in part *a*?

2. As your annual income increases from $50,000 to $55,000, your quantity of meat demanded increases from 300 to 350 kilograms.
   a. Calculate your income elasticity of demand for meat.
   b. What additional information would you want to have to ensure that your answer is correct?
   c. If your income falls to $25,000, what would you predict would happen to your quantity of meat demanded?
3. In the "Added Dimension" box on "Income and Cross Elasticity of Demand," the short-run elasticity for furniture was higher than the long-run elasticity. What is a likely explanation for that?
4. Early Classical economists found the following "diamond/water" paradox perplexing: "Why is water, which is so useful and necessary, so cheap, when diamonds, which are so useless and unnecessary, are so expensive?" Using the utility concept, explain why it is not really a paradox.
5. The president of a liberal arts college asked an economist about the effect of a particular proposal on net income, enrollment, and student GPA. The proposal was the following: "For the incoming class: (a) cut tuition for students in the top 10 percent of their high school class by 50 percent; (b) cut tuition for students in the top 10th to 20th percent of their high school class by 33 percent; (c) cut tuition for students in the top 20th to 30th percent of their high school class by 25 percent; (d) leave tuition the same for all

others." He believed the demand was highly elastic.

a. What was the economist's response?

b. What would her response have been if the demand had been highly inelastic?

6. In his memoirs, Nobel Prize-wining economist George Stigler explains how the famous British economist Phillip Wicksteed decided where to live. His two loves were fresh farm eggs, which were more easily obtained the farther from London he was, and visits from friends, which decreased the further he moved away from London. Given these two loves, describe the decision rule that you would have expected Wicksteed to follow.

7. You are buying your spouse, significant other, or close friend a ring. You decide to show your reasonableness, and buy a cubic zirconium ring that sells at 1/50 the cost of a mined diamond and that any normal person could not tell from a mined diamond just by looking at it. In fact, the zirconium will have more brilliance and fewer occlusions (imperfections) than a mined diamond.

   a. How will your spouse (significant other, close friend) likely react?

   b. Why?

   c. Is this reaction justified?

8. Economists William Hunter and Mary Rosenbaum wrote an article in which they estimated the demand elasticity for motor fuel as between .4 and .85.

   a. If the price rises 10 percent and the initial quantity sold is 10 million litres, what is the range of estimates of the new quantity demanded?

   b. In carrying out their estimates, they came up with different elasticity estimates for rises in prices than for falls in prices, with an increase in price having a larger elasticity than a decrease in price. What hypothesis might you propose for their findings?

Indifference Curve Analysis

As we stated in the chapter, analyzing individual choice using cardinal utility (giving utility actual numbers) is unnecessary. In the chapter, we asked you to make a deal with us: You'd remember that cardinal utility is unnecessary and we'd use cardinal numbers. This appendix is for those who didn't accept our deal (and for those whose professors want them to get some practice in graphish). It presents an example of a more formal analysis of individual choice.

Sophie's Choice

Sophie is a junk food devotee. She lives on two goods: chocolate bars, which cost $1 each, and cans of soda, which sell for 50¢ apiece. Sophie is trying to get as much pleasure as possible, given her $10 income. Alternatively expressed, Sophie is trying to maximize her utility, given an income constraint.

By translating this statement of Sophie's choice into graphs, we can demonstrate the principle of individual choice without ever mentioning any specific amount of utility.

The graph we'll use will have chocolate bars on the vertical axis and cans of soda on the horizontal axis, as in Exhibit A1.

Graphing the Income Constraint

Let's begin by asking: How can we translate her income constraint (the $10 maximum she has to spend) into graphish? The easiest way to do that is to ask what would happen if she spent her $10 all on chocolate bars or all on cans of soda. Since a chocolate bar costs $1, if she spends it all on chocolate bars she can get 10 bars (point *A* in Exhibit A1). If she spends it all on cans of soda, she can get 20 cans of soda (point *B*). This gives us two points.

But what if she wants some combination of soda and chocolate bars? If we draw a line between points *A* and *B*, we'll have a graphical picture of her income constraint and can answer that question because that line shows us

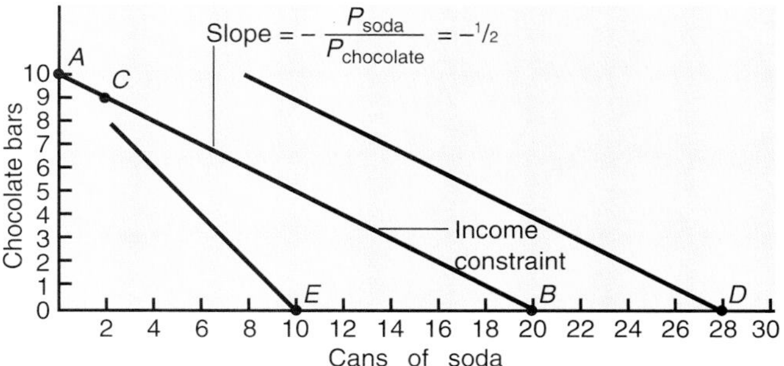

EXHIBIT A1 Graphing the Income Constraint

the various combinations she can buy. The line is her income constraint in graphish.

To see that it is, say Sophie is spending all her money on chocolate bars. She then decides to buy one fewer chocolate bar. That gives her $1 to spend on soda, which, since those cans cost 50¢ each, allows her to buy 2 cans. Point *C* (9 chocolate bars and 2 cans of soda) represents that decision. Notice how point *C* is on the income constraint. Repeat this exercise from various starting points until you're comfortable with the fact that the line does indeed represent the various combinations of soda and chocolate bars Sophie can buy with the $10. It's a line with a slope of $-1/2$ and intersects the chocolate bar axis at 10 and the cans-of-soda axis at 20.

To be sure that you've got it, ask yourself what would happen to the income constraint if Sophie got another $4 to spend on the two goods. Going through the same reasoning should lead you to the conclusion that the income constraint will shift to the right so that it will intersect the cans-of-soda axis at 28 (point *D*), but its slope won't change. (We started the new line for you.) Make sure you can explain why.

Now how about if the price of a can of soda goes up to $1? What happens to the income line? (This is a question many people miss.) If you said the income line becomes steeper, shifting in along the cans-of-soda axis to point E while remaining anchored along the chocolate bar axis until the slope equals -1, you've got it. If you didn't say that, go through the same reasoning we went through at first (if Sophie buys only cans of soda . . .) and then draw the new line. You'll see it becomes steeper. Put another way, the absolute value of the slope of the curve is the ratio of the price of cans of soda to the price of chocolate bars; the absolute value of the slope becomes greater with a rise in the price of cans of soda.

Graphing the Indifference Curve

Now let's consider the second part of Sophie's choice: the pleasure part. Sophie is trying to get as much pleasure as she can from her \$10. How do we deal with this in graphish?

To see, let's go through a thought experiment. Say Sophie had 14 chocolate bars and 4 cans of soda (point A in Exhibit A2). Let's ask her, "Say you didn't know the price of either good and we took away 4 of those chocolate bars (so you had 10). How many cans of soda would we have to give you so that you would be just as happy as before we took away the 4 chocolate bars?"

Since she's got lots of chocolate bars and few cans of soda, her answer is probably "Not too many; say, 1 can of soda." This means that she would be just as happy to have 10 chocolate bars and 5 cans of soda (point B) as she would to have 14 chocolate bars and 4 cans of soda (point A). Connect those points and you have the beginning of a "just-as-happy" curve. But that doesn't sound impressive enough, so, following economists' terminology, we'll call it an *indifference curve.* She's indifferent between points A and B.

If you continue our thought experiment, you'll get a set of combinations of chocolate bars and cans of soda like that shown in the table in Exhibit A2.

If you plot each of these combinations of points on the graph in Exhibit A2 and connect all these points, you have one of Sophie's indifference curves: a curve representing combinations of cans of soda and chocolate bars among which Sophie is indifferent.

Let's consider the shape of this curve. First, it's downward sloping. That's reasonable; it simply says that if you take something away from Sophie, you've got to give her something in return if you want to keep her indifferent between what she had before and what she has now.

Second, it's bowed inward. That's because as Sophie gets more and more of one good, it takes fewer and fewer of another good to compensate for the loss of the good she incurred in order to get more of the other good. The underlying reasoning is similar to that in our discussion of the law of diminishing marginal utility, but notice we haven't even mentioned utility. Technically the reasoning for the indifference curve being bowed inward is called *the law of diminishing marginal rate of substitution.* It

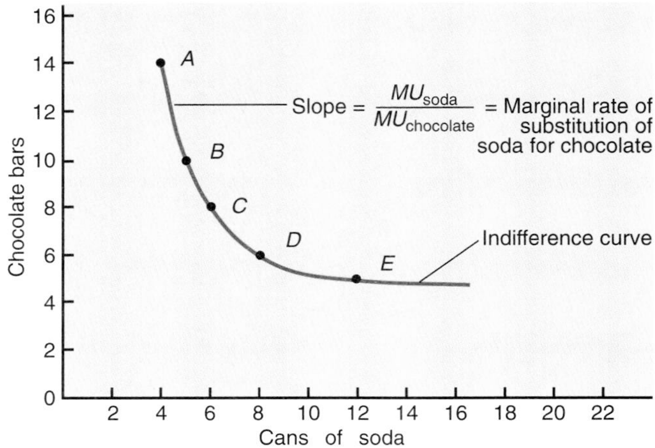

Chocolate bars	Cans of soda	
14	4	*A*
10	5	*B*
8	6	*C*
6	8	*D*
5	12	*E*

EXHIBIT A2 Sophie's Indifference Curve

tells us that as you get more and more of a good, if some of that good is taken away, then the marginal addition of another good you need to keep you on your indifference curve gets less and less.

Even more technically one can say that the absolute value of the slope of the indifference curve equals the ratio of the marginal utility of cans of soda to the marginal utility of chocolate bars:

$$\text{slope} = \left|\frac{MU_{\text{soda}}}{MU_{\text{chocolate}}}\right| = \text{Marginal rate of substitution}$$

That ratio equals the marginal rate of substitution of cans of soda for chocolate bars. Let's consider an example. Say that in Exhibit A2 Sophie is at point A and that the marginal utility she gets from an increase from 4 to 5 cans of soda is 10. Since we know that she was willing to give up 4 chocolate bars to get that 1 can of soda (and thereby move from point A to point B), that 10 must equal the loss of utility she gets from the loss of 4 chocolate bars out of the 14 she originally had. So the marginal rate of substitution of cans of soda for chocolate bars between points A and B must be 4. That's the absolute value of the slope of that curve. Therefore her MU of a chocolate bar must be about 2.5 (10 for 4 chocolate bars).

One can continue this same reasoning, starting with various combinations of goods. If you do so, you can get a whole group of indifference curves like that in Exhibit A3. Each curve represents a different level of happiness. Assuming she prefers more to less, Sophie is better off if she's on Curve II than if she's on Curve I, and even better

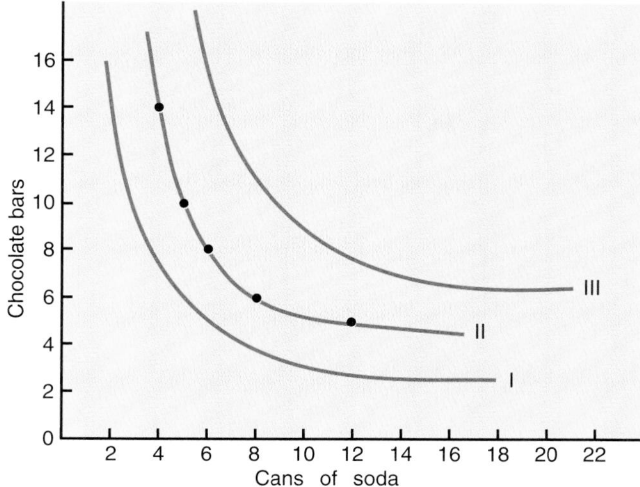

EXHIBIT A3 A Group of Indifference Curves

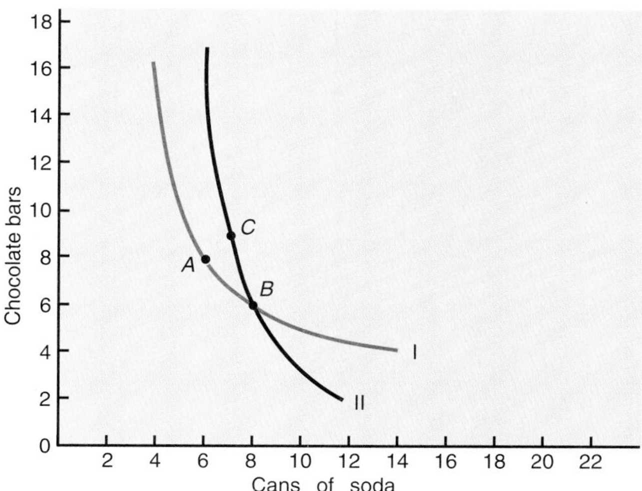

EXHIBIT A4 Why Indifference Curves Cannot Cross

off if she's on Curve III. Her goal in life is to get out to the furthest indifference curve she can.

To see whether you've followed the reasoning, ask yourself the following question: "Assuming Sophie prefers more of a good to less (which seems reasonable), can any two of Sophie's indifference curves cross each other as the ones in Exhibit A4 do?"

The answer is no, no, no! Why? Because they're indifference curves. If the curves were to cross, the "prefer-more-to-less" principle would be violated. Say we start at point *A*: Sophie has 8 chocolate bars and 6 cans of soda. We know that since *A* (8 chocolate bars and 6 sodas) and *B* (6 chocolate bars and 8 cans of soda) are on the same indifference curve, Sophie is indifferent between *A* and *B*. Similarly with points *B* and *C*: Sophie would just as soon have 9 chocolate bars and 7 cans of soda as she would 6 chocolate bars and 8 cans of soda.

It follows by logical deduction that point *A* must be indifferent to *C*. But consider points *A* and *C* carefully. At point *C*, Sophie has 7 cans of soda and 9 chocolate bars. At point *A* she has 6 cans of soda and 8 chocolate bars. At point *C* she has more of both goods than she has at point *A*, so to say she's indifferent between these two points violates the "prefer-more-to-less" criterion. Ergo (that's Latin, meaning "therefore") two indifference curves cannot intersect. That's why we drew the group of indifference curves in Exhibit A3 such that they did not intersect.

Combining Indifference Curves and Income Constraint

Now let's put the income constraint and the indifference curves together and ask how many chocolate bars and cans of soda Sophie will buy if she has $10, given the psychological makeup described by the indifference curves in Exhibit A3.

To answer that question, we must put the income line of Exhibit A1 and the indifference curves of Exhibit A3 together, as we do in Exhibit A5.

As we discussed, Sophie's problem is to get to as high an indifference curve as possible, given her income constraint. Let's first ask if she should move to point *A* (8 chocolate bars and 10 cans of soda). That looks like a good point. But you should quickly recognize that she can't get to point *A*; her income line won't let her. (She doesn't have enough money.) Well then, how about point *B* (7 chocolate bars and 6 cans of soda)? She can afford that combination; it's on her income constraint. The problem with point *B* is the following: She'd rather be at point *C* since point *C* has more chocolate bars and the same amount of soda (8 chocolate bars and 6 cans of soda). But, you say, she can't reach point *C*. Yes, that's true, but she can reach point *D*. And, by the definition of an indifference curve, she's indifferent between point *C* and point *D*, so point *D* (6 chocolate bars and 8 cans of soda), which she can reach given her income constraint, is preferred to point *B*.

The same reasoning holds for all other points. The reason is that the combination of chocolate bars and cans of soda represented by point *D* is the best she can do. It is the point where the indifference curve and the income line are tangent—the point at which the slope of the income line ($-P_s/P_c$) equals the slope of the indifference curve ($-MU_s/MU_c$). Equating those slopes gives $P_s/P_c = MU_s/MU_c$ or:

$$MU_c/P_c = MU_s/P_s$$

This equation, you may remember from the chapter, is the equilibrium condition of our principle of rational choice. So by our graphish analysis we arrived at the same conclusion we arrived at in the chapter, only this time we did it without mentioning cardinal utility. This

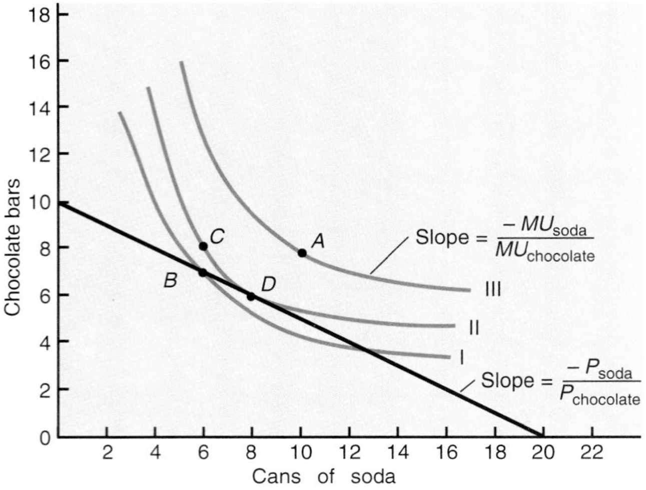

EXHIBIT A5 Combining Indifference Curves and Income Constraint

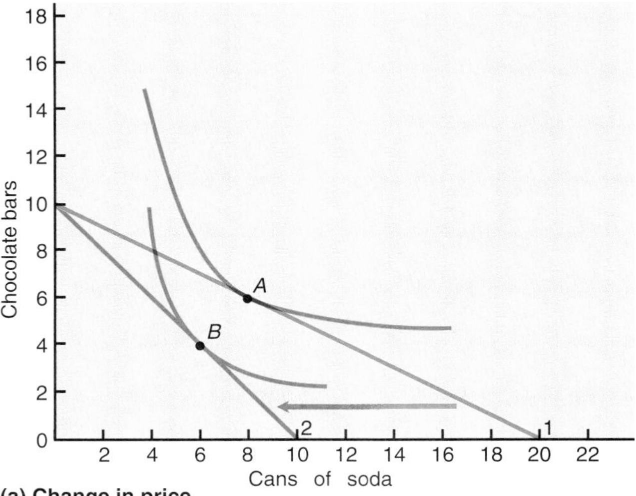

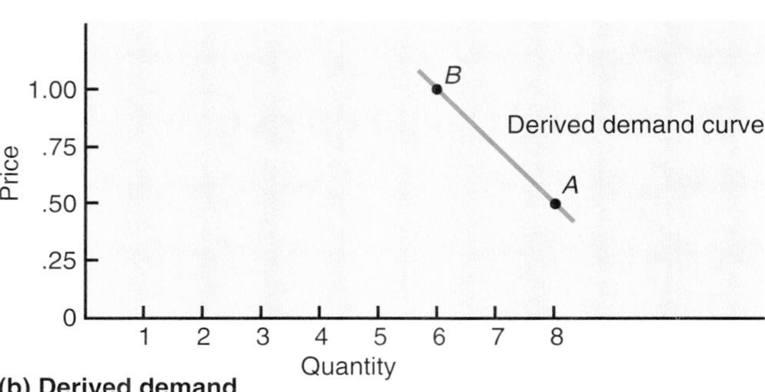

EXHIBIT A6 From Indifference Curves to Demand Curves

means that even without a utilometer, economists' principle of rational choice is internally logical.

Deriving a Demand Curve from the Indifference Curve

Not only can one derive the principle of rational choice with indifference curve/income line analysis, one can also derive a demand curve. To do so, ask yourself what a demand curve is. It's the quantity of a good that a person will buy at various prices. Since the income line gives us the relative price of a good, and the point of tangency of the indifference curve gives us the quantity that a person would buy at that price, we can derive a demand curve from the indifference curves and income lines. To derive a demand curve we go through a set of thought experiments asking how many cans of soda Sophie would buy at various prices. We'll go through one of those experiments.

We start with the analysis we used before when Sophie started with $10 and chose to buy 8 cans of soda when the price of a can of soda was 50¢ (point *A* in Exhibit A6 (a)). That analysis provides us with one point on the demand curve. We present that by point *A* in Exhibit A6 (b). At a price of 50¢, Sophie buys 8 cans of soda.

Now say the price of a can of soda rises to $1. That rotates the income line in, from income line 1 to income line 2 as in Exhibit A6 (a). She can't buy as much as she could before. But we can determine how much she'll buy by the same reasoning we used previously. She'll choose a point at which her lower indifference curve is tangent to her new income line. As you can see, she'll choose point *B*, which means that she buys 6 cans of soda when the price of a can of soda is $1. Graphing that point (6 cans of soda at $1 each) on our price/quantity axis in Exhibit A6 (b), we have another point on our demand curve, point *B*. Connect these two together and you can see we're getting a downward-sloping demand curve, just as the law of demand said we would. To make sure you understand, continue the analysis for a couple of additional changes. You'll see that the demand curve you derive will be downward sloping.

There's much more one can do with indifference curves. One can distinguish income effects and substitution effects. (Remember, when the price of a can of soda rose, Sophie was worse off. So to be as well off as before, as is required by the substitution effect, she'd have to be compensated for that rise in price by an offsetting fall in the price of chocolate bars.) But let's make a deal. You tentatively believe us when we say that all kinds of stuff can be done with indifference curves and income constraints, and we'll leave the further demonstration and the proofs for you to experience in the intermediate microeconomics courses.

CHAPTER

7

Supply, Production, and Costs I

Production is not the application of tools to materials, but logic to work.

~Peter Drucker

After reading this chapter, you should be able to:

1. Explain why opportunity costs underlie the law of supply.
2. Define and use the elasticity of supply concept.
3. Distinguish between the long run and the short run.
4. State the law of diminishing marginal productivity and explain its role in determining the shape of short-run cost curves.
5. Distinguish the various kinds of cost curves and describe the relationships among them.
6. Explain why the marginal cost curve always goes through the minimum point of an average cost curve.

The ability of Western market economies to supply material goods and services to members of their societies makes them the envy of many other societies and is one of the strongest arguments for using the market as a means of organizing society. Somehow markets are able to channel individuals' imagination, creativity, and drive into the production of material goods and services that other people want. They do this by giving people incentives to supply goods and services to the market.

Ultimately all supply comes from individuals. Individuals control the factors of production such as land, labour, and capital. Why do individuals supply these factors to the market? Because they want something in return. This means that industry's ability to supply goods is dependent on individuals' willingness to supply the factors of production they control. This connection became obvious in the formerly socialist countries in the late 1980s and early 1990s when consumer goods were unavailable. People in those countries stopped working (supplying their labour). They reasoned: Why supply our labour if there's nothing to get in return?

The analysis of supply is more complicated than the analysis of demand. In the supply process, people first offer the factors of production they control to the market. Then the factors are transformed by firms, such as Inco or the CBC, into goods and services that consumers want.

Complications are a pain for textbook writers; we want to make the analysis simple for you. (Really we do.) So what we do is to separate out the analysis of the supply of factors of production (considered in detail in later chapters) from the supply of produced goods. This allows us to assume that the prices of factors of production are constant in our analysis of the supply of produced goods, which simplifies the analysis enormously. There's no problem with doing this as long as you remember that behind any produced goods are individuals' factor supplies. Ultimately people, not firms, are responsible for supply.

Even with the analysis so simplified, there's still a lot to cover—so much, in fact, that we devote two chapters (this chapter and the next) to considering production, costs, and supply. In this chapter we introduce you to the production process and short-run cost analysis. Then, in the next chapter, we focus on long-run costs and how cost analysis is used in the real world.

SUPPLY, OPPORTUNITY COST, AND REAL PEOPLE

To emphasize the reality that people, not firms, are responsible for supply, let's talk briefly about individuals' decisions to supply factors of production. How do you decide how much labour, capital, or land to supply? The answer lies in the opportunity cost to you of keeping the factor for yourself. Let's use the most relevant example for most of you—your labour.

Opportunity Costs and the Law of Supply

1 When you supply a factor, you are forgoing its benefits for yourself. The opportunity cost of that forgone pleasure tends to increase the more you supply, which is why opportunity costs underlie the law of supply.

Opportunity cost The forgone pleasure of the next-best alternative.

How much labour will you supply to the market? Think about it using the economic reasoning that is becoming second nature to you (we hope). The answer we're sure you've arrived at is that it depends on how much you value your leisure, because leisure is what you're forgoing when you work. An hour of leisure is the **opportunity cost** (the forgone pleasure of the next-best alternative) of an hour of work. The same holds true for anything else you supply. Supply ultimately depends on the opportunity cost of the supplier.

Let's consider another example: housing. During the 1988 Winter Olympics in Calgary, there wasn't a vacant hotel room in sight. If there weren't enough hotel rooms, where did one stay, you ask? In people's houses. A number of Calgarians determined that, given the right price, they were willing to provide visitors with rooms in their houses. The higher the price, the more rooms supplied. (The same holds true around college campuses and in places that have special events like concerts, or the seventh game of a Stanley Cup series.) As the price rises, the quantity of a factor supplied to a market expands. Still another example involves truck drivers in Canada. Their hourly pay has fallen in the last 10 years as the trucking industry has become more competitive. As this has happened, the quantity of individuals wanting to be truck drivers has decreased.

ADDED DIMENSION

GOODS AND BADS

Some "goods" are actually "bads" because of the costs associated with holding them (for example, garbage, old tires, and broken cars). The opportunity cost of having them is negative. In that case more people want to get rid of the good than want to hold the good, so the good has a negative price.

Whether something has a positive or negative price depends on supply and demand. If it were discovered that garbage made an excellent fuel, people would pay for garbage. If everyone wanted to be a doctor, instead of paying doctors to treat them, people would pay to be allowed to doctor someone. If you could convince people that work is fun, they would pay you to allow them to work for you. Supply and demand determine the price of goods, but underlying supply and demand are social mores, technology, people's tastes, and the availability and usefulness of resources.

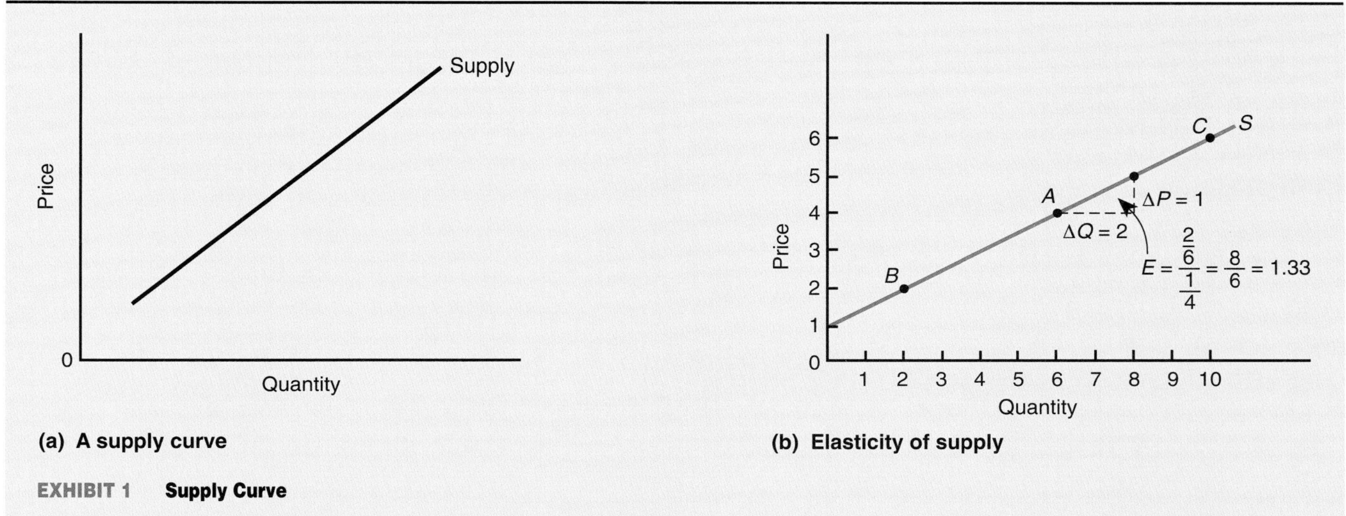

EXHIBIT 1 Supply Curve

The supply curve is upward sloping as in (**a**). This follows from the law of supply: When the price of a good increases, the quantity of that good supplied will increase. In (**b**) you can see how elasticity can be calculated. Using the point elasticity formula, you divide percent change in quantity supplied by percent change in price, and the result is the elasticity at that point.

What this means is that ultimately there's a law of supply, just as there's a law of demand. The law of supply is:

> *When the price of a good increases, the quantity of that good supplied will increase.*

It tells us that the supply curve will be upward sloping as in Exhibit 1.

Elasticity of Supply

Like the shape of demand curves, supply curves' shape is described by the concept of elasticity. **Price elasticity of supply** is the percent change in quantity supplied divided by the percent change in price. In common-sense terms, it measures the relative responsiveness of quantity supplied evoked by a change in price. Because the supply curve slopes upward, the elasticity of supply is positive so you don't need to use the convention of remembering, but not using, the minus sign, as you had to with the elasticity of demand:

Price elasticity of supply The percent change in quantity supplied divided by the percent change in price.

$$E_s = \frac{\text{Percent change in quantity supplied}}{\text{Percent change in price}}$$

2 E_S = Percent change in quantity supplied/Percent change in price

Let's consider an example. Say that the quantity of housing supplied to the rental market in an area increases 20 percent when the price goes up 10 percent. The elasticity of supply would be 2.

ADDED DIMENSION

A QUICK GEOMETRIC TOOL FOR ESTIMATING THE ELASTICITY OF SUPPLY

There's an easy way to estimate the elasticity of any straight-line supply curve. You simply extend it (or a line tangent to it, if it's curved) to one of the axes, as in the accompanying graph. The point at which this extension intersects the axes indicates the elasticity of the supply curve:

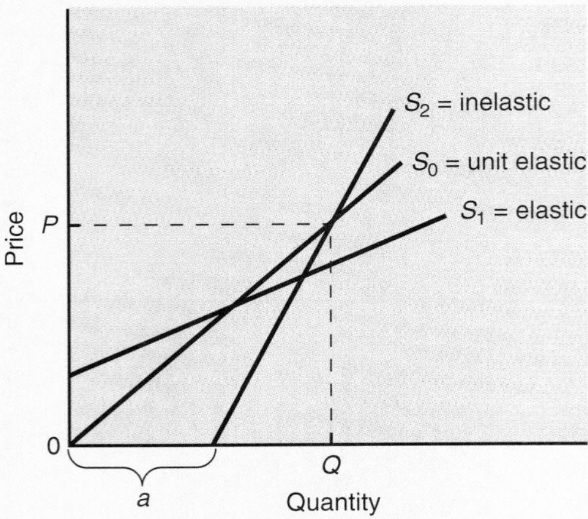

- If the extension intersects the vertical (price) axis, as does S_1, the supply curve has an elasticity greater than 1; this supply curve is elastic.
- If the extension intersects the horizontal (quantity) axis, as does S_2, all points on the supply curve have an elasticity less than 1; the supply curve is inelastic.
- If the extension intersects the two axes at the origin, the supply curve has an elasticity of 1; the supply curve has unit elasticity.

If you combine this trick with a knowledge that a perfectly elastic supply curve is horizontal and a perfectly inelastic supply curve is vertical, you can even remember which is which. If a straight-line supply curve crosses the horizontal axis, all points on it are inelastic; if it crosses the vertical axis, all points on it are elastic.

In Exhibit 1 (b) you can see how elasticity at a point on the supply curve can be calculated graphically. The point we are considering is point A, where $P = \$4.00$ and $Q = 6$. We want to find how much quantity will change when price changes from \$4 to \$5. As you can see, when price rises from \$4 to \$5, the quantity rises by 2. So the percent change in quantity is 2/6 = 33 percent, and the percent change in price is 1/4 = 25 percent. Then we substitute in our formula (percent change in quantity/percent change in price), which gives us (2/6)/(2/8), or 33%/25%, and arrive at our answer: 33%/25% = 1.33. To see if you've got it, try calculating the elasticity at point B. You should come up with an answer of approximately 2.

Terminology Used to Describe Elasticity of Supply The same terminology is used to describe elasticity of supply as is used to describe elasticity of demand:

- If the percent change in quantity supplied is less than the percent change in price, the elasticity of supply is less than 1 and the supply is said to be *inelastic.*
- A supply curve that is perfectly vertical (i.e., for which quantity supplied does not change in response to a change in price) is called *perfectly inelastic.*
- If the percent change in the quantity supplied equals the percent change in the price, the elasticity of supply is equal to 1 and the supply has *unit elasticity.*
- If the percent change in the quantity supplied exceeds the percent change in price, the elasticity of supply is greater than 1 and the supply is *elastic.*
- A supply curve that's perfectly horizontal (i.e., for which there's an infinite, or

ADDED DIMENSION

VALUE ADDED AND THE CALCULATION OF TOTAL PRODUCTION

This book (like all economics textbooks) treats production as if it were a one-stage process—as if a single firm transformed a factor of production into a consumer good. Economists write like that to keep the analysis manageable. (Believe us, it's complicated enough.) But you should keep in mind that reality is more complicated. Most goods go through a variety of stages of production.

For example, consider the production of desks. One firm transforms raw materials into usable raw materials (iron ore into steel); another firm transforms usable raw materials into more usable inputs (steel into steel rods, bolts, and nuts); another firm transforms those inputs into desks, which it sells wholesale to a general distributor, which then sells them to a retailer, which sells them to consumers. Many goods go through five or six stages of production and distribution. As a result, if you added up all the sales of all the firms you would overstate how much total production was taking place.

To figure out how much total production is actually taking place, economists use the concept *value added.* **Value added** is the contribution that each stage of production makes to the final value of a good. A firm's value added is determined by subtracting from the firm's total output the cost of the inputs bought from other firms. For example, if a desk assembly firm spends $4,000 of its revenue on component parts and sells its output for $6,000, its value added is $2,000, or 33 1/3 percent of its revenue.

When you add up all the stages of production, the value added of all the firms involved must equal 100 percent, and no more, of the total output. When we discuss "a firm's" production of a good in this book, to relate that discussion to reality, you should think of that firm as a composite firm consisting of all the firms contributing to the production and distribution of that product.

Why is it important to remember that there are these various stages of production? Because it brings home to you how complicated producing a good is. If any one of those stages gets messed up, the good doesn't get to the consumer. Producing a better mousetrap isn't enough. The firm must also be able to get it out to consumers and let them know that it's a better mousetrap. The standard economic model doesn't bring home this point. But if you're ever planning to go into business for yourself, you'd better remember it. Many people's dreams of supplying a better product to the market have been squashed by this reality.

---

larger than imaginable, quantity response to a change in price) is called *perfectly elastic.*

The Influence of Substitution on the Elasticity of Supply Just as was the case with elasticity of demand, the most important determinant of elasticity of supply is the number of substitutes for the good. If substitution is easy, supply will be elastic; if substitution is difficult, the supply will be inelastic.

Since most of the issues concerning elasticity of supply are parallel to those of elasticity of demand which we discussed at length last chapter, we'll be brief. As was the case with demand, the ease of substitution depends on the time dimension considered. The shorter the time period, the fewer possibilities of substitution, and the less elastic the supply. Some economists distinguish these time periods—the instantaneous period in which the quantity supplied is fixed so the elasticity of supply is perfectly inelastic. This supply is sometimes called the *momentary supply.* In the short run, some substitution is possible, so the short-run supply curve is somewhat elastic. Finally, in the long run, significant substitution is possible—including totally different technologies. The supply curve becomes very elastic and may even become downward sloping.

In determining the elasticity of supply, one must remember that many supplied goods are produced, so we must take into account how easy it is to substitute for existing goods by producing more of that good. And before we can do that we need to talk about the production process in detail.

To make sure you have the general idea, however, let's go through a couple of examples to check whether you can intuitively determine elasticity of supply. Let's first consider land. There's a fixed amount of it; you can't make more of it (at least not easily), so land is very inelastic in supply. (The supply curve is close to vertical.) Now how about ballpoint pens? It's relatively easy to make another pen, so it seems reasonable that the supply of pens will be quite elastic (close to horizontal). As a third example, think about the supply of your labour. How many more hours would you supply if your wage went up by various percentages? Based on that information, determine what your elasticity of labour supply is. (For doing economics, ours are very inelastic.)

THE PRODUCTION PROCESS

With examples like housing and labour, the law of supply is rather intuitive. These goods already exist and their supply to the market depends on people's opportunity costs of keeping them for themselves and for supplying them to the market. But many of the things we buy (such as VCRs, cars, and jackets) don't automatically exist; they must be produced. The supply of such goods depends upon production. So let's now consider production and see how production relates to supply.

The Role of the Firm in Production

Firm Economic institution that transforms factors of production into consumer goods.

Transactions costs Costs of undertaking trades through the market.

A key concept in production is the firm. A **firm** is an economic institution that transforms factors of production into consumer goods. A firm (a) organizes factors of production, (b) produces goods, and/or (c) sells produced goods to individuals.

The firm operates within a market, but, simultaneously, it is a negation of the market in the sense that it replaces the market with command and control. How an economy operates—which activities are organized through markets, and which activities are organized through firms—depends upon **transaction costs**—costs of undertaking trades through the market—and the rent or command over resources that organizers can appropriate to themselves by organizing production in a certain way. Ronald Coase won a Nobel Prize in 1991 for pathbreaking work on the nature of the firm and transactions costs.

In Chapter 4 we talked about the myriad firms that exist in real life. They include sole proprietorships, partnerships, and corporations. These various firms are the production organizations that translate factors of production into consumer goods.

The Long Run and the Short Run

3 The long-run decision is a planning decision in which the firm has maximum flexibility. In the long run the firm can vary whatever inputs it wants. In the short run, some inputs are fixed.

Long-run decision A decision in which the firm can choose among all possible production techniques.

Short-run decision Firm is constrained in regard to what production decisions it can make.

The production process is generally broken down into a *long-run* planning decision, in which a firm chooses the least-expensive method of producing from among all possible methods, and a *short-run* adjustment decision, in which a firm adjusts its long-run planning decision to reflect new information.

In a **long-run decision** a firm chooses among all possible production techniques. This means that it can choose the size of the plant it wants, the type of machines it wants, and the location it wants. In a **short-run decision** the firm has fewer options since it has to produce using current facilities and methods.

The terms *long run* and *short run* do not necessarily refer to specific periods of time independent of the nature of the production process. They refer to the degree of flexibility the firm has in changing the level of output. In the long run, by definition, the firm can vary the inputs as much as it wants. In the long run all inputs are variable. In the short run some of the flexibility that existed in the long run no longer exists. In the short run some inputs are so costly to adjust that they are treated as fixed. *So in the long run all inputs are variable; in the short run some inputs are fixed.*

Production Tables and Production Functions

Production table Table showing the output that will result from various combinations of factors of production or inputs.

How a firm combines factors of production to produce consumer goods can be presented in a **production table** (a table showing the output resulting from various combinations of factors of production or inputs).

Real-world production tables are complicated. They often involve hundreds of inputs, hundreds of outputs, and millions of possible combinations of inputs and outputs. Studying these various combinations and determining which is best requires expertise and experience. Business schools devote entire courses to it (operations research and production analysis); engineering schools devote entire specialties to it (managerial engineering).

Studying the problems and answering the questions that surround the production relationship make up much of what a firm does: What combination of outputs should it produce? What characteristics should those outputs have? What combination of inputs should it use? What combination of techniques should it use? What new techniques should it explore? To answer these questions, the managers of a firm look at a production table.

Ronald Coase won the Nobel Prize in 1991 for work on the theory of firms and markets. ©*The Nobel Foundation.*

Production tables are so complicated that in introductory economics we concentrate on short-run production analysis in which one of the factors is fixed. Doing so allows us to capture some important technical relationships of production without getting too tied up in numbers. The relevant part of a production table of widgets appears in Exhibit 2 (c).[1] In it the number of the assumed fixed inputs (machines) has already been determined. Columns 1 and 2 of the table tell us how output varies as the variable input (the number of workers) changes. For example, you can see that with 3 workers the firm can produce 17 units of output. Column 3 tells us workers' **marginal product** (the additional output that will be forthcoming from an additional worker, other inputs constant). Column 4 tells us workers' **average product** (output per worker).

Marginal product Additional output forthcoming from an additional input, other inputs constant.

Average product Total output divided by the quantity of the input.

It is important to distinguish marginal product from average product. Workers' average product is the total output divided by the number of workers. For example, let's consider the case of five workers. Total output is 28, so average product is 5.6 (28 divided by 5). To find the marginal product we must ask how much additional output will be forthcoming if we change the number of workers. For example, if we change from 4 to 5 workers, the additional worker's marginal product will be 5; if we change from 5 to 6, the additional worker's marginal product will be 3. That's why the marginal products are written between the lines.

The information in a production table is often summarized in a production function. A **production function** is a curve that describes the relationship between the inputs (factors of production) and outputs. Specifically, the production function tells the maximum amount of output that can be derived from a given number of inputs. Exhibit 2 (a) shows us the production function based on the information in the production table in Exhibit 2 (c). The number of workers is on the horizontal axis and the output of widgets is on the vertical axis.

Production function Equation that describes the relationships between inputs and outputs, telling the maximum amount of output that can be derived from a given number of inputs.

The Law of Diminishing Marginal Productivity

Exhibit 2 (b) graphs the workers' average and marginal productivities from the production function in Exhibit 2 (a). (Alternatively you can determine those graphs by plotting columns 3 and 4 from the table in Exhibit 2 (c).) Notice that both marginal and average productivities are initially increasing, but that eventually they both decrease. Between 7 and 8 workers, the marginal productivity actually becomes negative.

This means that initially this production function exhibits increasing marginal productivity and then it exhibits *diminishing marginal productivity.* Eventually it exhibits negative marginal productivity.

The same information can be gathered from Exhibit 2 (a), but it's a bit harder to interpret.[2] Notice that initially the production function is bowed upward. Where it's bowed upward there is increasing marginal productivity, as you can see if you extend a line down to Exhibit 2 (b). Then, between 2.5 and 7.5 workers, the production function is bowed downward but is still rising. In this range there's diminishing marginal

[1]What's a widget? It's a wonderful little gadget that's the opposite of a wadget. (No one knows what they look like or what they are used for.) Why discuss widgets? For the same reason that scientists discuss fruit flies—their production process is simple, unlike most real-world production processes.

[2]Technically the marginal productivity curve is a graph of the slope of the total product curve.

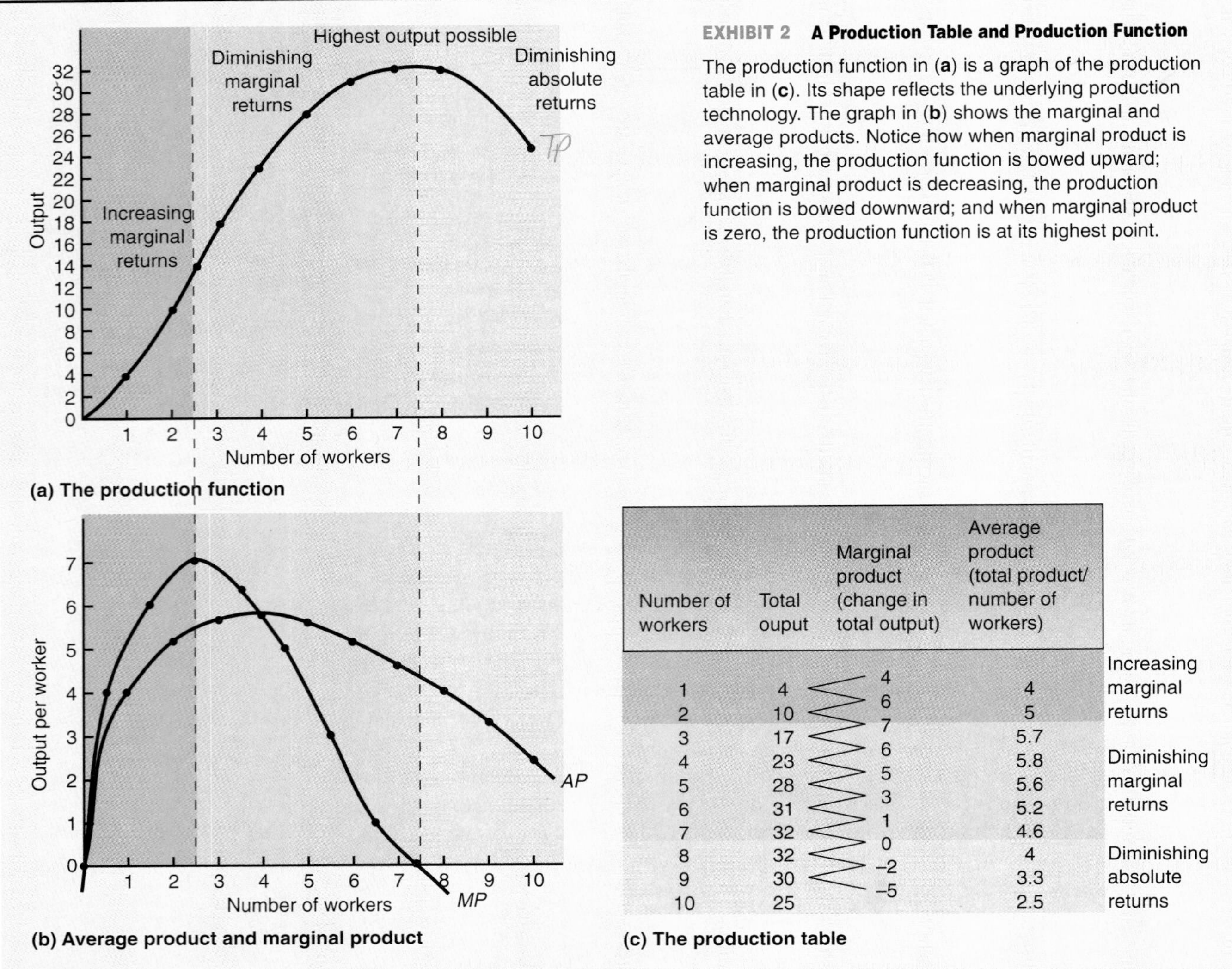

EXHIBIT 2 A Production Table and Production Function

The production function in (**a**) is a graph of the production table in (**c**). Its shape reflects the underlying production technology. The graph in (**b**) shows the marginal and average products. Notice how when marginal product is increasing, the production function is bowed upward; when marginal product is decreasing, the production function is bowed downward; and when marginal product is zero, the production function is at its highest point.

Number of workers	Total ouput	Marginal product (change in total output)	Average product (total product/ number of workers)	
		4		
1	4		4	Increasing marginal returns
		6		
2	10		5	
		7		
3	17		5.7	Diminishing marginal returns
		6		
4	23		5.8	
		5		
5	28		5.6	
		3		
6	31		5.2	
		1		
7	32		4.6	
		0		
8	32		4	Diminishing absolute returns
		−2		
9	30		3.3	
		−5		
10	25		2.5	

(c) The production table

productivity, as you can see by extending a line down to Exhibit 2 (b). Finally there's negative marginal productivity.

The most important area of these relationships is the area of diminishing marginal productivity. Why? Because that's the most likely area for a firm to operate in. For example, if it's in the first range and marginal productivity is increasing, a firm can increase its existing workers' output by hiring more workers; it will have a strong incentive to do so and get out of that range. Similarly if hiring an additional worker actually cuts total output (as it does when marginal productivity is negative), the firm would be crazy to hire that worker. So it stays out of that range. This means that the most relevant part of the production function is that part exhibiting diminishing marginal productivity.

4A The law of diminishing marginal productivity states that as more and more of a variable input is added to an existing fixed input, after some point the additional output one gets from the additional input will fall.

This range of the relationship between fixed and variable inputs is so important that economists have formulated a law that describes what happens in production processes when they reach this range—when more and more of one input is added to a fixed amount of another input. It's called the **law of diminishing marginal productivity,** which states that as more and more of a variable input is added to an existing fixed input, eventually the additional output one gets from that additional input is going to fall.

Let's consider the underlying reasoning for this law a bit more carefully. Within the range of diminishing marginal productivity, as you add more workers, they must

Modern production often involves quite different technology than production formerly did. In this picture we see the status display board in the network operations centre of a large company. © *Cameramann/The Image Works.*

share the existing machines, so the marginal product of the machines increases and the marginal product of the workers decreases.

As we stated in the introductory chapter, the law of diminishing marginal productivity is sometimes called *the flower pot law* because if it didn't hold true, the world's entire food supply could be grown in one flower pot. In the absence of diminishing marginal productivity, one could take a flower pot and keep adding seeds to it, getting more and more food per seed until one had enough to feed the world. In reality, however, a given flower pot is capable of producing only so much food no matter how many seeds you add to it. At some point, as you add more and more seeds, each additional seed will produce less food than did the seed before it. Eventually the pot reaches a stage of diminishing absolute productivity in which the total output, not simply the output per unit of input, decreases as inputs are increased.

THE COSTS OF PRODUCTION

Probably in a firm, far more discussion is about costs than about anything else. Invariably costs are too high and the firm is trying to figure out ways to lower costs. But the concept *costs* is ambiguous; there are many different types of costs and it's important to know these different types. Let's consider some of the most important categories of costs in reference to Exhibit 3, which gives a table of costs associated with making between 4 and 32 pairs of earrings.

Fixed Costs, Variable Costs, and Total Costs

Fixed costs Costs that are spent and cannot be changed in the period of time under consideration.

Fixed costs are costs that are spent and cannot be changed in the period of time under consideration. There are no fixed costs in the long run since all inputs are variable and hence their costs are variable. In the short run, however, a number of costs will be fixed. For example, say you make silver earrings. You buy a machine for working with silver. If consumer tastes change and the demand for silver earrings all but disappears, you're stuck with that machine. The money you spent on it is a fixed cost.

Fixed costs are shown in column 2 of Exhibit 3. Notice that fixed costs remain the same ($50) regardless of the level of production. As you can see, it doesn't matter whether output is 15 or 20; fixed costs are always $50.

Variable costs The costs of variable inputs; they change as output changes.

Besides buying the machine, the silversmith must also hire workers. These workers are the earring maker's **variable costs.** Variable costs are costs that change as output changes. The earring maker's variable costs are shown in column 3. Notice that as output increases, variable costs increase. For example, when she produces 11 pairs of earrings, variable costs are $106; when she produces 17, variable costs rise to $150.

EXHIBIT 3 The Cost of Producing Earnings

Output	Fixed costs (FC)	Marginal costs (MC) Variable costs (VC)	Average Total costs (TC) (FC + VC)	Average variable (change in total costs)	fixed costs (AFC) FC/Output	Average total costs (AVC) VC/Output	costs (ATC) AFC + AVC
4	$50	$50	$100		$12.50	$12.50	$25.00
5	50	60	110	$10	10.00	12.00	22.00
10	50	100	150		5.00	10.00	15.00
11	50	106	156	6	4.54	9.64	14.18
17	50	150	200		2.94	8.82	11.76
18	50	157	207	7	2.78	8.72	11.50
21	50	182	232		2.38	8.67	11.05
23	50	200	250		2.17	8.70	10.87
24	50	210	260	10	2.08	8.75	10.83
28	50	250	300		1.79	8.93	10.72
29	50	265	315	15	1.72	9.14	10.86
32	50	350	400		1.56	10.94	12.50

Total cost Sum of the fixed and variable costs.

All costs are either fixed or variable in the standard model so the sum of her fixed and variable costs equals her **total cost.**

$$TC = FC + VC$$

The earring maker's total costs are presented in column 4. Each entry in column 4 is the sum of the entries in columns 2 and 3 in the same row. For example, to produce 17 pairs of earrings, fixed costs are $50 and variable costs are $150 so total cost is $200.

Average Total Cost, Average Fixed Cost, and Average Variable Cost

5A Total cost curves relate total costs to output. Average costs measure total cost divided by the quantity produced.

Average total cost Total cost divided by the quantity produced. Often called *average cost.*

Average fixed cost Fixed cost divided by quantity produced.

Average variable cost Variable cost divided by quantity produced.

Total cost, fixed cost, and variable cost are important, but much of firms' discussion is of average cost. So the next distinction we want to make is between total cost and average cost. To arrive at the earring maker's average cost, we simply divide the total amount of whatever cost we're talking about by the quantity produced. Each of the three costs we've discussed has a corresponding average cost.

For example, **average total cost** (often called **average cost**) equals total cost divided by the quantity produced. Thus:

$$ATC = TC/Q$$

Average fixed cost equals fixed cost divided by quantity produced:

$$AFC = FC/Q$$

Average variable cost equals variable cost divided by quantity produced:

$$AVC = VC/Q$$

Average fixed cost and average variable cost are shown in columns 6 and 7 of Exhibit 3. The most important average cost concept, average total cost, is shown in column 8. Average total cost can also be thought of as the sum of average fixed cost and average variable cost (remember these are based on a particular level of output):

$$ATC = AFC + AVC$$

As you can see, the average total cost of producing 17 pairs of earrings is $11.76. It can be calculated by dividing total cost ($200) by output (17).

Marginal Cost

All these costs are important to our earring maker, but none of them is the most important cost she considers in her decision as to how many pairs of earrings to produce.

ADDED DIMENSION

THE HISTORY OF THE LAW OF DIMINISHING MARGINAL PRODUCTIVITY

When economists were first formulating their analysis of production, farming was the most important economic activity and most individuals worked on the land. Economists devised their analysis of production to help them structure their ideas about what would happen to total production as the population grew and hence the number of workers increased. In thinking about this issue, they came up with the law of diminishing marginal productivity, which describes what will happen if more and more of a flexible input (labour) is added to a fixed input (land).

The law of diminishing marginal productivity states that eventually, when more and more of a variable input is added to a fixed input, the additional output that results from that additional input decreases.

Initially the law of diminishing marginal productivity was the basis of some gloom-and-doom predictions, which prompted writer Thomas Carlyle to call economics *the dismal science.* The gloom-and-doom predictions were that since the amount of land is fixed, as the population grows, with more workers working the fixed amount of land, eventually the point of diminishing marginal productivity will be reached and the amount of food available per person will decline. Starvation will result, decreasing the population to the subsistence level of output per person. If given any more wages, workers will have more kids and reduce the output per person again to subsistence. This was known as the *iron law of wages:*

Diminishing marginal productivity combined with human beings' uncontrolled sexual drive will result in increases in the supply of labour so that average output and wages will decrease to the subsistence level.

For most Western economies the gloom-and-doom predictions have not come true. Even the originator of the predictions, Thomas Malthus, eliminated them from later editions of *An Essay on Population,* the book in which he first propounded them. Similarly the iron law of wages was soon dropped.

It was not because the law of diminishing marginal productivity doesn't hold true that the gloom-and-doom predictions were dropped. Rather they were dropped because technological changes overwhelmed the law of diminishing marginal productivity. Over time, fewer and fewer individuals have been able to grow more and more output on a smaller amount of land.

While in Canada gloom-and-doom predictions have been overtaken by events, in many developing countries the law of diminishing marginal productivity is very much in effect. In those countries output per individual is decreasing, often to the subsistence level or even below it. Economists in some developing countries believe that not only has the point of diminishing marginal productivity set in, but the point of input saturation has been reached: Output, rather than merely not increasing with additional inputs, actually decreases, and the marginal productivity of additional workers is negative.

Marginal cost The change in cost associated with a change in quantity.

That distinction goes to marginal cost, which appears in column 5.[3] **Marginal cost** is the increased (decreased) total cost of increasing (or decreasing) the level of output by one unit. Let's find marginal cost by considering what happens if our earring maker increases production by one unit—from 10 to 11. Looking again at Exhibit 3, we see that the total cost rises from $150 to $156. In this case the marginal cost of producing the eleventh unit is $6.

The marginal cost concept is extremely important to economic reasoning. But before we get into that, it is important to see how these cost concepts can be presented graphically. It's important for two reasons: First, graphs reinforce your understanding of the cost concepts; and second, one of the most efficient ways of testing whether you understand the cost concepts is with graphs. So let's say that our earring maker is a visually oriented person who asks you (an economics consultant) to show her what all those numbers in the table in Exhibit 3 mean.

[3]Since only selected output levels are shown, not all entries have marginal costs. For a marginal cost to exist, there must be a marginal change, a change by only one unit.

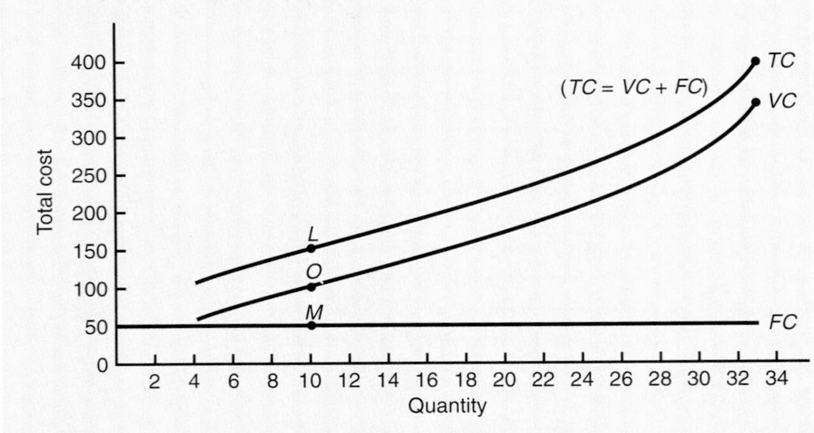

EXHIBIT 4 Total Cost Curves

Total fixed costs are always constant; they don't change with output. All other total costs increase with output. As output gets high the rate of increase has a tendency to increase.

Graphing Cost Curves

To do so, you first draw a graph, putting quantity on the horizontal axis and a dollar measure of various costs on the vertical axis. In this graphical presentation we will focus on average cost curves because that's what economists generally do. But, for completeness, we will also briefly discuss total cost curves, which, since they are directly related to average-cost curves, provide the same information.

Total Cost Curves Exhibit 4 graphs the total cost, total fixed cost, and total variable cost of all the levels of output given in Exhibit 3.[4] Thus, the total cost curve is determined by plotting the entries in column 1 and the corresponding entries in column 4. For example, point *L* corresponds to a quantity of 10 and a total cost of $150. Notice that the curve is upward sloping: Increasing output increases total cost.

The total fixed cost curve is determined by plotting column 1 and column 2 on the graph. The total variable cost curve is determined by plotting column 1 and column 3.

As you can see, the total variable cost curve has the same shape as the total cost curve: Increasing output increases variable cost. This isn't surprising, since the total cost curve is the vertical summation of total fixed cost and total variable cost. For example, at output 10, total fixed cost equals $50 (point *M*); total variable cost equals $100 (point *O*); and total cost equals $150 (point *L*).

Average and Marginal Cost Curves In Exhibit 5, we present the average fixed cost curve, average total cost curve (or average cost curve, as it's generally called), average variable cost curve, and marginal cost curve associated with the cost figures in Exhibit 3. Each point on the four curves represents a combination of two corresponding entries in Exhibit 3. Points on the average variable cost curve are determined by plotting the entries in column 1 and the corresponding entries in column 7. Points on the average fixed cost curve are determined by entries in column 1 and the corresponding entries in column 6. Points on the average total cost curve are determined by entries in column 1 and the corresponding entries in column 8. Finally, the marginal cost curve is determined by plotting the entries in column 1 and the corresponding entries in column 5. As was the case with the total cost curves, all our earring maker need do is look at this graph to find the various costs associated with different levels of output.

5B The marginal cost curve goes through the minimum point of the average total cost curve and average variable cost curve; each of these curves is U-shaped. The average fixed costs curve slopes down continuously.

One reason the graphical visualization of cost curves is important is that the graphs of the curves give us a good sense of what happens to costs as we change output.

[4]To keep the presentation simple, we focus only on the most important part of the total cost curve, that part that follows the simplest rules. Other areas of the total cost curve can be bowed downward rather than bowed upward.

THE $5,000 FLASHLIGHT

ADDED DIMENSION

We've used simple examples in this chapter to keep the terminology clear. Now, let's briefly discuss a more relevant example: LEDs (light-emitting diodes). These diodes are the little electronic gadgets that light up digital watches, calculator displays, and the like. Hewlett Packard is a major producer of LEDs.

As part of the company's development process, it is continually trying to find new uses for these LEDs. The company recently made a technological breakthrough that allowed it to produce a much more powerful version, which lights up brightly enough to illuminate large signs and uses far less electricity than the alternatives. To demonstrate the power of these new LEDs, the company had 200 flashlights built, like the one pictured here.

Because the developmental costs of these LEDs were enormous, the division of the company that worked on them was assigned a large overhead cost, all of which was fixed in relation to output. But only a small number of flashlights were made. If one were to calculate the average costs of these flashlights, that average total cost would be about $5,000 apiece. Hewlett Packard gave them away. Was Hewlett Packard simply being nice? No. These flashlights helped create demand and show the power of the company's technological breakthrough, increasing the demand for LEDs and thereby spreading the fixed costs to a greater number of units, significantly lowering the average cost per unit.

John Thoeming.

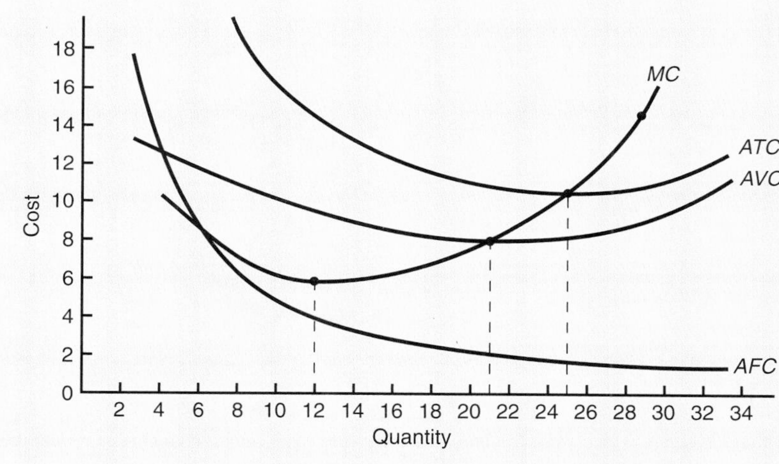

EXHIBIT 5 Per Unit Output Cost Curves

The average fixed cost curve is downward sloping; the average variable cost curve and average total cost curve are U-shaped. The U-shaped *MC* curve goes through the minimum points of the *AVC* and *ATC* curves..

Downward-Sloping Shape of the Average Fixed Cost Curve Let's start our consideration with average fixed cost. Average fixed cost is decreasing throughout. The average fixed cost curve looks like a child's slide: It starts out with a steep decline; then it becomes flatter and flatter. What this tells us about production is straightforward: As output increases, the same fixed cost can be spread over a wider range of output, so average fixed cost falls. Average fixed cost initially falls quickly but then falls more and more slowly. As the denominator gets bigger while the numerator stays the same, the increase has a smaller and smaller effect.

4B As more and more of a variable input is added to a fixed input, the law of diminishing marginal productivity causes marginal and average productivities to fall. As these fall, marginal and average costs rise.

The Law of Diminishing Marginal Productivity and the U-Shape of the Average and Marginal Cost Curves Let's now move on to the average and marginal cost curves. Why do they have the shapes they do? Or expressed another way, how does our analysis of production relate to our analysis of costs? You may have already gotten an idea of how production and costs relate if you remembered Exhibit 2 and recognized the output numbers that we presented there were the same output numbers that we used in the cost analysis. The reason they were the same is that the cost analysis is of that earlier production analysis. The laws governing costs are the same laws governing productivity that we just saw in our consideration of production.

When output is increased in the short run, it can only be done by increasing the variable input. But as more and more of a variable input is added to a fixed input, the law of diminishing marginal productivity enters in. Marginal and average productivities fall. The key insight here is that when marginal productivity falls, marginal cost must rise, and when average productivity of the variable input falls, average variable cost must rise. So to say that productivity falls is the equivalent to saying that cost rises.

It follows that if eventually the law of diminishing marginal productivity holds true, then eventually both the marginal cost curve and the average cost curve must be upward sloping. And, indeed, in our examples they are. It's also generally held that at low levels of production, marginal and average productivities are increasing. This means that marginal cost and average variable cost are initially falling. If they're falling initially and rising eventually, at some point they must be neither rising nor falling. This means that both the marginal cost curve and the average variable cost curve are U–shaped.

The average total cost curve is the vertical summation of the average fixed cost curve and the average variable cost curve, so it's always higher than both of them. As you can see in Exhibit 5, the average total cost curve has the same general U–shape as the average variable cost curve, but its low point is to the right of the low point for the average variable cost curve. We'll discuss why after we cover the shape of the average variable cost curve.

Average total cost initially falls faster and then rises more slowly than average variable cost. If one increased output enormously, the average variable cost curve and the average total cost curve would almost meet. Average total cost is of key importance to our earring maker. She wants to keep it low.

The Relationship between the Marginal Productivity and Marginal Cost Curves In Exhibit 6 (a), we redraw the marginal cost curve and average variable cost curve presented in Exhibit 5. Notice their U–shape. Initially costs are falling. Then there's some minimum point. After that, costs are rising.

In Exhibit 6 (b), we graph the average and marginal productivity curves that we first developed in Exhibit 2 (b), although this time we relate average and marginal productivities to output, rather than to the number of workers. Thus, we know that the average product of two workers is 5, and that two workers can produce an output of 10, so when output is 10, the worker's average productivity is 5. Point *A* corresponds to an output of 10 and average productivity of 5.

Now let's compare the graphs in (a) and (b). If you look at the two graphs carefully, you'll see that one is simply the mirror image of the other. The minimum point of the average variable cost curve (output = 21) is at the same level of output as the maximum point of the average productivity curve; the minimum point of the marginal cost curve (output = 12) is at the same level of output as the maximum point on the marginal productivity curve. When the productivity curves are falling, the corresponding cost curves are rising. Why is that the case? Because as productivity falls, costs per unit increase; and as productivity increases, costs per unit decrease.

6 When marginal cost exceeds average cost, average cost must be rising. When marginal cost is less than average cost, average cost must be falling. This relationship explains why marginal cost curves always intersect the average cost curve at the minimum of the average cost curve.

The Relationship between the Marginal Cost and Average Cost Curves Now that we've considered the shapes of each cost curve, let's consider some of the important relationships among them—specifically the relationships between the marginal cost curve on the one hand and the average variable cost and average total cost curves on the other. These relationships are shown graphically for a different production process in Exhibit 7.

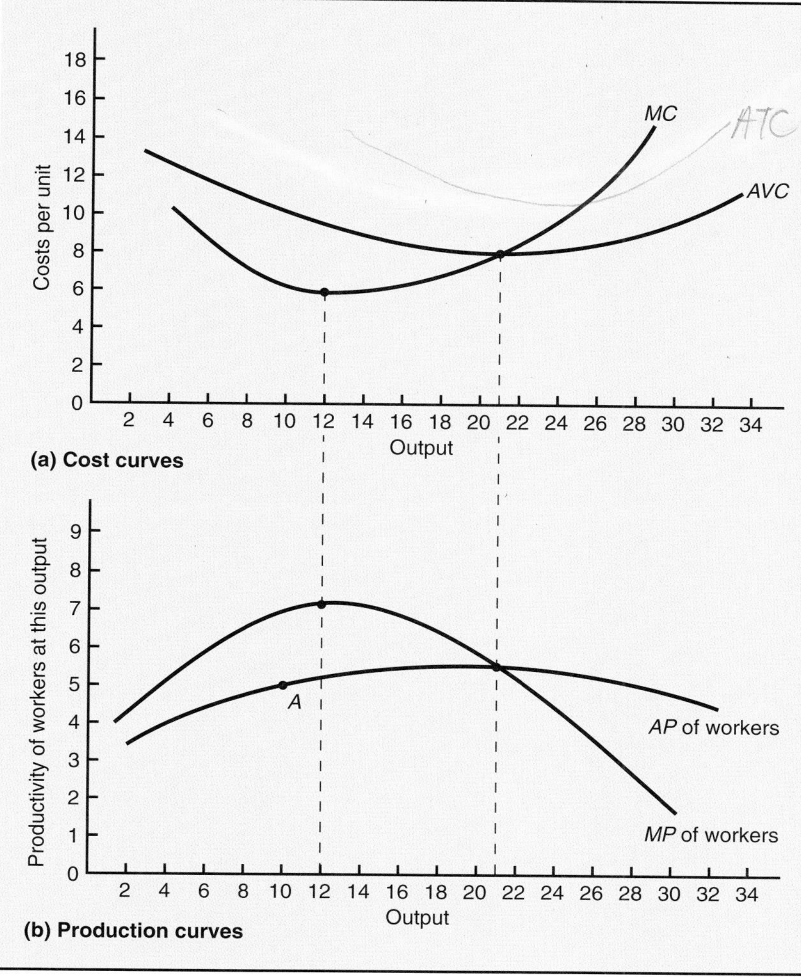

EXHIBIT 6 The Relationship between Productivity and Costs

The shapes of the cost curves are mirror-image reflections of the shapes of the corresponding productivity curves. When one is increasing, the other is decreasing; when one is at a minimum, the other is at a maximum.

Let's first look at the relationship between marginal cost and average total cost. In areas *A* and *B* at output below 5, even though marginal cost is rising, average total cost is falling. Why? Because in areas *A* and *B* the marginal cost curve is below the average total cost curve. At point *B*, where average total cost is at its lowest, the marginal cost curve intersects the average total cost curve. In area *C*, above output 5, where average total cost is rising, the marginal cost curve is above the *ATC* curve.

The positioning of the marginal cost curve is not happenstance. The position of marginal cost relative to average total cost tells us whether average total cost is rising or falling.

If MC > ATC, then ATC is rising.

If MC = ATC, then ATC is at its low point.

If MC < ATC, then ATC is falling.

To understand why this is, think of it in terms of your grade point average. If you have a B average and you get a C on the next test (that is, your marginal grade is a C), your grade point average will fall below a B. Your marginal grade is below your average grade, so your average grade is falling. If you get a C+ on the next exam (that is, your marginal grade is a C+), *even though your marginal grade has risen from a C to a C+,* your grade point average will fall. Why? Because your marginal grade is still below your average grade. To make sure you understand the concept, explain the next two cases:

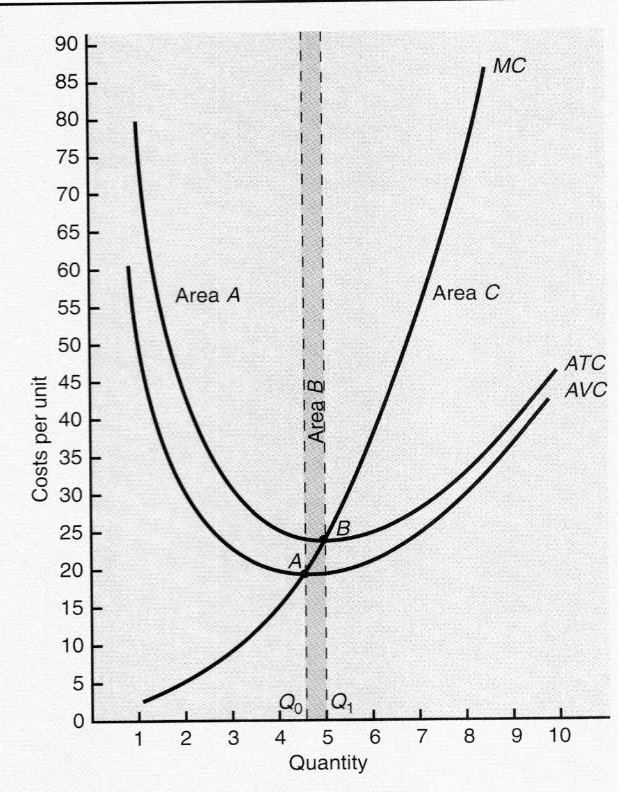

EXHIBIT 7 Relationship of Marginal Cost Curve to Average Variable Cost and Average Total Cost Curves

The marginal cost curve goes through the minimum point of both the average variable cost curve and the average total cost curve. Thus there is a small range where average total costs are falling and average variable costs are rising.

1. If your marginal grade is above your average grade, your average grade will rise.
2. If your marginal grade and average grade are equal, the average grade will remain unchanged.

Marginal and average reflect a general relationship that also holds for marginal cost and average variable cost.

If MC > AVC, then AVC is rising.

If MC = AVC, then AVC is at its low point.

If MC < AVC, then AVC is falling.

This relationship is best seen in area *B* of Exhibit 7 when output is between Q_0 and Q_1. In this area the marginal cost curve is above the average variable cost curve, so average variable cost is rising; but the *MC* curve is below the average total cost curve, so average total cost is falling.

The intuitive explanation for what is represented in this area is that average total cost includes average variable cost, but it also includes average fixed cost, which is falling. As long as short-run marginal cost is only slightly above average variable cost, the average total cost will continue to fall. Put another way: Once marginal cost is above average variable cost, as long as average variable cost doesn't rise by more than average fixed cost falls, average total cost will still fall.

INTERMISSION

At this point we're going to cut off the chapter, not because we're finished with the subject, but because there's only so much that anyone can absorb in one chapter. It's time for a break.

CHAPTER SUMMARY

- No one is going to supply a good to the market unless the price he or she will get for that good equals or exceeds the opportunity cost of that good.
- Price elasticity of supply is the percent change in quantity divided by the percent change in price.
- In the long run a firm can choose among all possible production techniques; in the short run it is constrained in its choices.
- The law of diminishing marginal productivity states that as more and more of a variable input is added to a fixed input, the additional output the firm gets will eventually be decreasing.
- Costs are generally divided into fixed costs, variable costs, and total costs.
- The average variable cost curve and marginal cost curve are mirror images of the average product curve and the marginal product curve, respectively.
- If $MC > ATC$, then ATC is rising.
  If $MC = ATC$, then ATC is constant.
  If $MC < ATC$, then ATC is falling.

KEY TERMS

average fixed cost *(170)*
average product *(167)*
average total cost (often called average cost) *(170)*
average variable cost *(170)*
firm *(166)*
fixed costs *(169)*
law of diminishing marginal productivity *(168)*
long-run decision *(166)*
marginal cost *(171)*
marginal product *(167)*
opportunity cost *(162)*
price elasticity of supply *(163)*
production function *(167)*
production table *(166)*
short-run decision *(166)*
total cost *(170)*
transactions costs *(166)*
value added *(165)*
variable costs *(169)*

QUESTIONS FOR THOUGHT AND REVIEW

The number after each question represents the estimated degree of critical thinking required. (1 = almost none; 10 = deep thought.)

1. State the law of supply and explain how it relates to opportunity cost. *(5)*
2. If the supply curve is perfectly inelastic, what is the opportunity cost of the supplier? *(6)*
3. "There is no long run; there are only short and shorter runs." Evaluate that statement. *(8)*
4. What is the difference between marginal product and average product? *(3)*
5. If average product is falling, what is happening to short-run average variable cost? *(3)*
6. If marginal cost is increasing, what do we know about average cost? *(4)*
7. If average productivity falls, will marginal cost necessarily rise? How about average cost? *(4)*
8. Say that neither labour nor machines are fixed but that there is a 50 percent quick order premium paid to both workers and machines in the short run. Once you buy them, they cannot be returned, however. What do your short-run marginal cost and short-run average total cost curves look like? *(9)*
9. If machines were variable and labour fixed, how would the general shapes of the short-run average cost curve and marginal cost curve change? *(6)*
10. If you increase production to an infinitely large level, the average variable cost and the average total cost will merge. Why? *(4)*

PROBLEMS AND EXERCISES

1. Find and graph the *TC, AFC, AVC, AC,* and *MC* from the following table.

Units	*FC*	*VC*
0	100	0
1	100	40
2	100	60
3	100	70
4	100	85
5	100	130

2. An economic consultant is presented with the following table on average productivity and asked to derive a table for average variable costs. The price of labour is $15 per hour.

Labour	*TP*
1	5
2	15
3	30
4	36
5	40

a. Help him do so.

b. Show that the graph of the average productivity curve and average variable cost curve are mirror images of each other.

c. Show the marginal productivity curve for outputs between 1 and 5.

d. Show that the marginal productivity curve and marginal cost curve are mirror images of each other.

3. In one of the "Added Dimension" boxes in this chapter, there are three statements about the elasticities of straight-line supply curves. One of those statements is that supply curves intersecting the quantity axis are inelastic. Can you prove that that is true by algebraic manipulation of the elasticity formula?

4. A firm has fixed costs of 100 and variable cost of the following:

Output	1	2	3	4	5	6	7	8	9
Variable cost	35	75	110	140	175	215	260	315	390

a. Graph the *AFC, ATC, AVC,* and *MC* curves.

b. Explain the relationship between the *MC* curve and the two average cost curves.

c. Say fixed costs dropped to 50. Graph the new *AFC, ATC, AVC,* and *MC* curves.

d. Which curves shifted in *c?* Why?

5. Say that a firm has fixed costs of 200 and constant variable costs of 25.

a. Graph the *AFC, ATC, AVC,* and *MC* curves.

b. Explain why the curves have the shapes they do.

c. What law is not operative for this firm?

d. Say that instead of increasing by a constant 25, variable costs increase by 5 for each unit, so that the cost of 1 is 25, the cost of 2 is 30, the cost of 3 is 35, and so on. Graph the *AFC, ATC, AVC,* and *MC* curves associated with these costs.

e. Explain how costs would have to increase in *d* in order for the curves to have the "normal" shapes of the curves presented in the text.

6. Answer the following questions given the production/cost data in the table below:

Number of workers	Total output	Marginal product of labour	Average product of labour	Total labour cost	Marginal cost	Average variable cost
0	0					
1	20					
2	44					
3	72					
4	96					
5	116					
6	132					
7	144					
8	152					
9	156					
10	156					

a. Fill in the average and marginal products of labour. How did you arrive at your answers?

b. Assume each worker costs the firm $60. Fill in total labour costs, and the rest of the table. Explain how you calculated your answers.

c. If the marginal product of labour is rising, what's happening to marginal cost? If the marginal product of labour is falling, what happens to marginal cost?

d. What is the relationship between changes in the average product of labour and changes in average variable cost? Explain.

7. Some short-run cost information for Pete's Pizza Parlour is given in the following table:

Quantity	Fixed cost	Variable cost	Marginal cost	Average fixed cost	Average variable cost	Average total cost
0	$100	$0				
2		12				
4		20				
6		20				
8		43				
10		58				
12		78				
14		105				
16		160				

a. Complete the table.

b. Indicate whether each of the following is True or False:

T F Whenever *MC* is rising, average total cost must be rising.

T F Whenever *MC* is rising, average variable cost must be rising.

T F Whenever *MC* is above average total cost, average total cost must be rising.

T F Whenever *MC* is above average variable cost, average variable cost must be rising.

T F Whenever *MC* is above average fixed cost, average fixed cost must be rising.

CHAPTER

8

Supply, Production, and Costs II

Economic efficiency consists of making things that are worth more than they cost.

~J. M. Clark

After reading this chapter, you should be able to:

1. Distinguish technical efficiency from economic efficiency.
2. Explain how economies of scale influence the shape of long-run cost curves.
3. Differentiate diminishing marginal productivity from diseconomies of scale.
4. State the envelope relationship between short-run cost curves and long-run cost curves.
5. Explain the central role of opportunity costs in all supply decisions.
6. Discuss some of the problems of using cost analysis in the real world.
7. Apply the marginal cost concept to decisions facing you.

Welcome back. We hope you've reestablished your relationship with the real world and are ready to return, with renewed vigour, to the world of economics. When we took our intermission last chapter we had worked our way through the various short-run costs. That short run is a time period in which some inputs are fixed. A key determinant of the shape of the short-run cost curve is marginal productivity. If those last two sentences don't ring some bells and create images of cost curves dancing in your head, you may have been intermissioning before intermission, so a review of the last chapter is in order. If those bells are ringing, then we can continue and consider firms' long-run decisions and the determinants of the long-run cost curves. We'll do that in the first part of this chapter. Then in the second part we'll talk about applying cost analysis to the real world.

MAKING LONG-RUN PRODUCTION DECISIONS

In the long run, firms have many more options than they do in the short run. They can change any input they want. Plant size is not given; neither is the technology available given.

To make their long-run decisions, firms look at the costs of the various inputs and the technologies available for combining those inputs, and then decide which combination offers the lowest cost.

Say you're opening a hamburger stand. One decision you'll have to make is what type of stove to buy. You'll quickly discover that many different types are available. Some use more gas than others but cost less to buy; some are electric; some are self-cleaning and hence use less labour; some are big; some are little; some use microwaves; some use convection. Some have long-term guarantees; some have no guarantees. Each has a colourful brochure telling you how wonderful it is. After studying the various detailed specifications and aspects of the production technology, you choose the stove that has the combination of characteristics that you believe best fits your needs.

Next you decide on workers. Do you want bilingual workers, college-educated workers, part-time workers, experienced workers . . . ? You get the idea: Even simple production decisions involve complicated questions. These decisions are made on the basis of the expected costs, and expected usefulness, of inputs.

Technical Efficiency and Economic Efficiency

1 Technical efficiency is efficiency that does not consider cost of inputs. The least-cost technically efficient process is the economically efficient process.

Technical efficiency A situation in which as few inputs as possible are used to produce a given output.

Economically efficient Using the method of production that produces a given level of output at the lowest possible cost.

One important distinction to keep in mind in considering firms' long-run production decisions is the distinction between technical efficiency and economic efficiency. The production process transforms inputs into outputs. Any firm will want to choose a technically efficient production process. **Technical efficiency** in production means that as few inputs as possible are used to produce a given output.

Many different production processes can be technically efficient. For example, say you know that to produce 100 tons of wheat you can use 10 workers and 1 acre or use 1 worker and 100 acres. Which of these two production techniques is more efficient? Both can be technically efficient since neither involves the use of more of both inputs than the other technique. But that doesn't mean that both are equally efficient. That question can't be answered unless you know the relative costs of the two inputs. If an acre of land rents for $1,000,000 and each worker costs $10 a day, our answer likely will be different than if land rents for $40 an acre and each worker costs $100 a day. This is no longer a technical question; this is an economic question whose answer depends upon the costs of production. Which of the variety of technically efficient methods of production is *economically efficient?* The **economically efficient** method of production is that method that produces a given level of output at the lowest possible cost.

In long-run production decisions, firms will look at all available production technologies and choose the technology that, given the available inputs and their prices, is the economically efficient way to produce. These choices will reflect the prices of the various factors of production. Those prices, in turn, will reflect the factors' relative scarcities.

Consider the use of land by firms in Canada and firms in Japan. Canada has large amounts of land—1/3 km^2 per person—so the price of land is lower than in Japan, which has only .003 km^2 per person. An acre of rural land in Canada might cost about \$700; in Japan it costs about \$15,000. Because of this difference in price of inputs, production techniques use land much more intensively in Japan than in Canada. Similarly with China: Labour is more abundant so production techniques are more labour-intensive than in Canada. Whereas China would utilize hundreds of people to build a road, primarily using human labour, Canada would use three or four people along with three machines. Both countries are being economically efficient, but because costs of inputs differ, the economically efficient method of production differs. Thus, the economically efficient method of production is that technically efficient method of production that has the lowest cost.

Determinants of the Shape of the Long-Run Cost Curve In the last chapter we saw that the law of diminishing marginal productivity accounted for the shape of the short-run cost curve. That followed since we kept adding more of a variable input to a fixed input. The law of diminishing marginal productivity doesn't apply to the long run since in the long run all inputs are variable. The most important determinants of what is economically efficient in the long run are economies and diseconomies of scale. Let's consider each of these in turn and see what effect they will have on the shape of the long-run average cost curve.

Economies of Scale When the per-unit output cost of all inputs decreases as output increases, we say that there are **economies of scale** in production. For example, if producing 40,000 VCRs costs the firm \$16,000,000 (\$400 each), but producing 200,000 VCRs costs the firm \$40,000,000 (\$200 each), there are significant economies of scale associated with choosing to produce 200,000 rather than 40,000.

Economies of scale A decrease in per-unit cost as a result of an increase in output.

One of the ways that economists measure economies of scale is by looking at what happens to output as input usage changes. For example, if we double all inputs, and output doubles, we say there are **constant returns to scale.** If we double all inputs and output more than doubles, we say there are **increasing returns to scale,** while if output less than doubles, we say there are **decreasing returns to scale.**

Constant returns to scale When output rises by the same proportionate change in inputs. For example, when a firm uses twice as much labour and capital and obtains twice as much output.

Increasing returns to scale When a firm's output rises by proportionately more than the change in its inputs; for example, if a firm uses twice as much capital and labour and obtains three times as much output.

Decreasing returns to scale When output rises by proportionately less than the change in input usage; for example, when a firm uses three times as much capital and labour and only doubles its output.

In real-world production processes, at low levels of production economies of scale are extremely important. The reason is that many production techniques are indivisible—they must be used at a certain minimum level before they begin to become useful. For example, say you want to produce a kilogram of steel. You can't just build a mini blast furnace, stick in some coke and iron ore, and come out with your single kilogram of steel. Technology requires that technically efficient blast furnaces be of a minimum size with a production capacity that is measured in metric tonnes per hour, not kilograms per year. The cost of the blast furnace is said to be an **indivisible setup cost** (the cost of an indivisible input for which a certain minimum amount of production must be undertaken before the input becomes economically feasible to use).

Indivisible setup cost The cost of an indivisible input for which a certain minimum amount of production must be undertaken before the input becomes economically feasible to use.

Indivisible setup costs are important because they create many real-world economies of scale: As output increases, the costs per unit of output decrease (there are increasing returns to scale). As an example, consider this book. Setting the type for it is an indivisible setup cost; it is a cost that must be incurred if any production is to take place, but it is not a cost that increases with the number of books produced. That means that the more copies of the book that are produced, the lower the typesetting cost per book. That's why it costs more per book to produce a textbook for an upper-level, low-enrollment course than it does for a lower-level, high-enrollment course. The same amount of work goes into both (both need to be written, edited, and set into type), and the printing costs differ only slightly.

The actual print run costs of printing a book are only about \$1 to \$8 per book. The other costs are indivisible setup costs. Because of these indivisible setup costs, large economies of scale are possible in printing books. Prices of produced goods, including books, reflect their costs of production. As you move to upper-level academic courses, you'll likely discover that the books are smaller and less colourful but cost as much as, or more than, this introductory text.

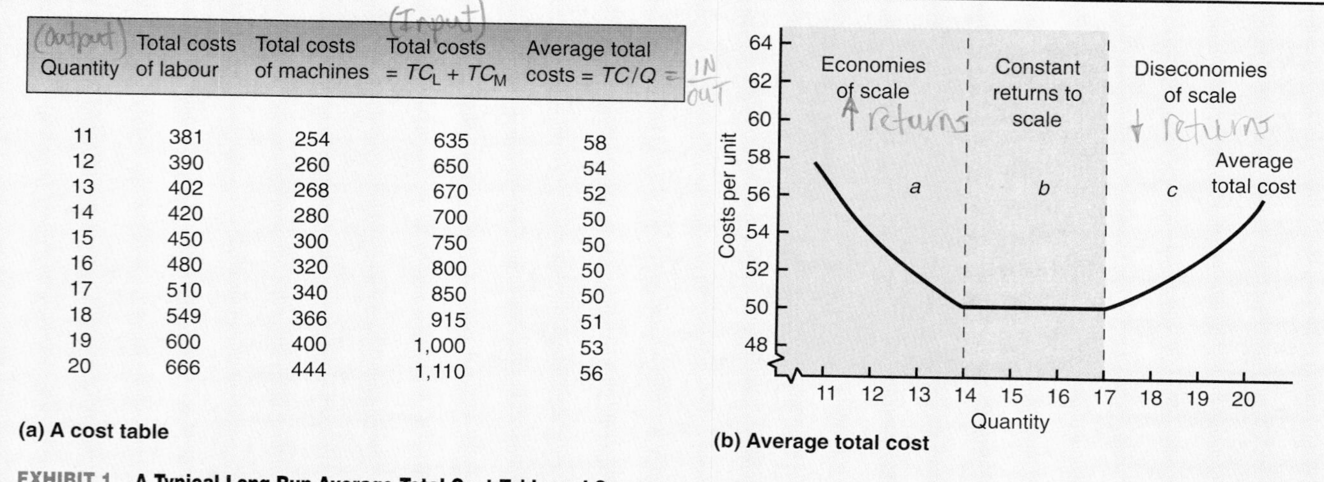

Quantity	Total costs of labour	Total costs of machines	Total costs $= TC_L + TC_M$	Average total costs $= TC/Q$
11	381	254	635	58
12	390	260	650	54
13	402	268	670	52
14	420	280	700	50
15	450	300	750	50
16	480	320	800	50
17	510	340	850	50
18	549	366	915	51
19	600	400	1,000	53
20	666	444	1,110	56

(a) A cost table

(b) Average total cost

EXHIBIT 1 A Typical Long-Run Average Total Cost Table and Curve

In the long run, average costs initially fall because of economies of scale; then they are constant for a while, and finally they tend to rise due to diseconomies of scale.

2 In the longer run all inputs are variable, so only economies of scale can influence the shape of the long-run curve.

In the long-run planning decisions about the cost of producing this book, the expected number of copies to be sold was an important element. That figure influenced the number of books produced, which in turn affected the expected cost per unit. This will be the case any time there are economies of scale. With economies of scale, cost per unit of a small production run is higher than cost per unit of a large production run.

Exhibit 1 (a) demonstrates a normal long-run production table; Exhibit 1 (b) shows the related typical shape of a long-run average cost curve. (Notice that there are no fixed costs. That's because we're in the long run so all costs are variable.) Economies of scale account for the downward-sloping part. Cost per unit of output is decreasing.

Minimum efficient level of production The amount of the production run that spreads out setup costs sufficiently for a firm to undertake production profitably.

Because of the importance of economies of scale, businesspeople often talk of a minimum efficient level of production. What they mean by **minimum efficient level of production** is that, given the price at which they expect to be able to sell a good, the indivisible setup costs are so high that production runs of less than a certain size don't make economic sense. Thus, the minimum level of production is the amount of production that spreads setup costs out sufficiently for a firm to undertake production profitably.

Let's look at a real-world example. Several years ago one of us thought it would be a good idea to buy a franchise for a Baskin-Robbins Ice Cream store (so we love ice cream . . .). In talking it over together, we recognized that in the relatively small city we were considering, we get heavy tourist traffic during the summer, and we were sure people would be willing to pay for a premium treat on our hot summer days. When we looked into the cost of obtaining a franchise, we learned that there were a number of conditions we'd have to meet—some relating to the size of store we would have to run. Experience from selling other franchises had shown the owners of the franchise rights the minimum efficient level of production.

Diseconomies of scale An increase in per-unit cost as a result of an increase in output.

Diseconomies of Scale Notice that on the right side of Exhibit 1 (b) the long-run average cost curve is upward sloping. Average cost is increasing. When the per-unit cost of all inputs increases as a result of an increase in output, we say that there are **diseconomies of scale** in production (alternatively, we could say there are decreasing returns to scale). For example, if producing 200,000 VCRs costs the firm $40,000,000 ($200 each) and producing 400,000 VCRs costs the firm $100,000,000 ($250 each), there

ADDED DIMENSION

PRODUCING THE MAZDA MIATA

The normal production run of an automobile is about 200,000 units per year. Why is it so high? Because of indivisible setup costs. In order to reduce those indivisible setup costs to an acceptable level, the production level per year must equal at least 200,000 or the car is considered an economic failure. The Pontiac Fiero, a sporty two-seater, was dropped in 1988 because it didn't sell well enough to sustain that production level.

But what is an indivisible setup cost depends on the structure of production. Japanese companies structure production differently from North American companies and have a much lower level of indivisible setup costs. For example, at just about the same time as Pontiac dropped the Fiero, a Japanese company, Mazda, entered the market with the Miata, another sporty two-seater. Because Mazda's assembly line is designed to handle different sizes and shapes of vehicles (which permits economies of scope discussed later in the text), its minimum profitable production level for the Miata is about 30,000, not 200,000. This alternative structure of production made it possible for the Miata to do well in a market that buys a total of about 40,000 two-seater sports coupes annually.

are diseconomies of scale associated with choosing to produce 400,000 rather than 200,000. Diseconomies of scale usually, but not always, start occurring as firms get large.

3 Diminishing marginal productivity refers to the decline in productivity caused by increasing units of a variable input being added to a fixed input. Diseconomies of scale refer to decreases in productivity which are brought about because of increases of all inputs equally.

Diseconomies of scale could not occur if production relationships were only technical relationships. If that were the case, the same technical process could be used over and over again at the same cost. In reality, however, production relationships have social dimensions, which introduce the potential for important diseconomies of scale into the production process in two ways:

1. As the size of the firm increases, monitoring costs generally increase.
2. As the size of the firm increases, team spirit or morale generally decreases.

Monitoring costs are the costs incurred by the organizer of production in seeing to it that the employees do what they're supposed to do. If you're producing something yourself, the job gets done the way you want it done; monitoring costs are zero. However, as the scale of production increases, you have to hire people to help you produce. This means that if the job is to be done the way you want it done, you have to monitor (supervise) your employees' performance. The cost of monitoring can increase significantly as output increases; it's a major contributor to diseconomies of scale. Most big firms have several layers of bureaucracy devoted simply to monitoring others. The job of middle managers is, to a large extent, monitoring.

Monitoring costs Costs incurred by the organizer of production in seeing to it that employees do what they are supposed to do.

The other social dimension that can contribute to diseconomies of scale is the loss of **team spirit** (the feelings of friendship and being part of a team that bring out people's best efforts). Most types of production are highly dependent on team spirit. When that team spirit or morale is lost, production slows considerably. A good example is the former Soviet Union in its earlier transition from capitalism to socialism and its ongoing transition from socialism to capitalism. During both transitions, people lost faith in the system; whatever team spirit had existed fell apart, and production decreased by 25 percent or more.

Team spirit The feelings of friendship and being part of a team that bring out people's best effort.

An important reason diseconomies of scale can come about is that the bigger things get, the more checks and balances are needed to ensure that the right hand and the left hand are coordinated. The larger the organization, the more checks and balances and the more paperwork.

Some large firms manage to solve these problems and thus avoid diseconomies of scale by having a number of modest-sized plants rather than a single large plant. But as a firm's size increases, it's much harder to maintain that team spirit effectively and to monitor employees. So, often these problems of monitoring and loss of team spirit limit the size of firms. They underlie diseconomies of scale in which relatively less output is produced for a given increase in inputs, so that per-unit costs of output increase.

ADDED DIMENSION

REVIEW OF COSTS

We've covered a lot of costs and cost curves quickly, so a review is in order. First, let's list the cost concepts and their definitions.

1. Marginal cost: the additional cost resulting from a one-unit change in output.
2. Total cost: all costs.
3. Average total cost: total cost divided by total output (*TC/Q*).
4. Fixed cost: cost that is already spent and cannot be recovered. (It exists only in the short run.)
5. Average fixed cost: fixed cost divided by total output (*FC/Q*).
6. Variable cost: cost of variable inputs. Variable cost does not include fixed cost.
7. Average variable cost: variable cost divided by total output (*VC/Q*).

Each of these costs can be represented by a curve. A number of these curves have specific relationships to the other cost curves.

1. *MC: MC* intersects *AVC* and *ATC* at their minimum points.
2. If *MC* > *AVC,* then *AVC* is rising. If *MC* < *AVC,* then *AVC* is falling.
3. If *MC* > *ATC,* then *ATC* is rising. If *MC* < *ATC,* then *ATC* is falling.
4. *ATC:* a U–shaped curve.
5. *AVC:* a U–shaped curve lower than the *ATC,* with the minimum point slightly to the left.
6. *AFC:* a downward-sloping curve that starts high, initially decreases rapidly, and then decreases slowly.
7. The long-run *ATC* curve is a U–shaped curve which forms an envelope around the various short-run *ATC* curves.

The Importance of Economies and Diseconomies of Scale Economies and diseconomies of scale play important roles in real-world long-run production decisions. Economies of scale underlie firms' attempts to expand their markets either at home or abroad. If they can make and sell more at lower per-unit costs, they will make more profits. Diseconomies of scale prevent a firm from expanding and can lead corporate raiders to buy the firm and break it up in the hope that the smaller production units will be more efficient, thus eliminating some of the diseconomies of scale.

The long-run and the short-run average cost curves have the same U–shape. But it's important to remember that the reasons why they have this U–shape are quite different. The assumption of initially increasing and then eventually diminishing marginal productivity (as a variable input is added to a fixed input) accounts for the shape of the short-run average cost curve. Economies and diseconomies of scale account for the shape of the long-run average cost curve.

The Relationship between Short-Run Average Total Cost and Long-Run Average Total Cost

4 The envelope relationship is the relationship explaining that, at the planned output level, short-run average total cost equals long-run average total cost, but at all other levels of output, short-run average total cost is higher than long-run average total cost.

Since in the long run all inputs are flexible, while in the short run some inputs are not flexible, long-run cost will always be less than or equal to short-run cost. To see this, let's consider a firm that had planned to produce 100 but now adjusts its plan to produce more than 100. We know that in the long run the firm chooses the lowest-cost method of production. In the short run it faces an additional constraint: All expansion must be done using only the variable input. That constraint must increase average cost (or at least not decrease it) compared to what average cost would have been had the firm planned to produce that level to begin with. If it didn't, the firm would have chosen that new combination of inputs in the long run. Additional constraints increase cost. This relationship between long-run and short-run average total costs is known as the **envelope relationship,** shown in Exhibit 2.

Why it's called an *envelope relationship* should be clear from the exhibit. Each short-run average total cost curve touches the long-run average total cost curve at one, and only one, output level; at all other output levels, short-run average cost exceeds long-run average cost. The long-run average total cost curve is an envelope of short-run average total cost curves. The **minimum efficient scale** of plant is determined by the short-run average total cost curve that intersects the long-run average total cost curve at its minimum. In Exhibit 2, that's the plant size associated with $SATC_3$.

Minimum efficient scale The plant size which minimizes both short-run and long-run average total cost.

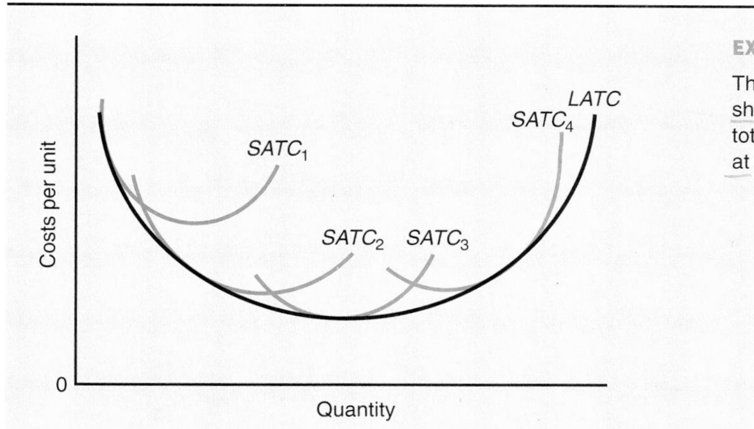

EXHIBIT 2 Envelope of Short-Run Average Total Cost Curves

The long-run average total cost curve is an envelope of the short-run average total cost curves. Each short-run average total cost curve touches the long-run average total cost curve at only one point.

COSTS, ENTREPRENEURIAL ACTIVITY, AND THE SUPPLY DECISION

In this chapter and the last we have discussed the technical nature of costs and production. In the next chapter we will formally relate costs of production to the supply of goods. As a bridge between the two chapters, let's conclude this chapter with a consideration of the entrepreneur, who establishes the relationship between costs and the supply decision, and of some of the problems of using cost analysis in the real world.

Price Must Be Expected to Exceed Cost for a Good to Be Supplied

5 The difference between the expected price of a good and the expected average total cost of producing it—the good's opportunity cost—is the supplier's expected economic profit per unit. The opportunity cost must be below price for a good to be supplied.

In thinking about the connection between cost and supply, one fundamental insight is that the revenue received for a good must be greater than the planned cost of producing it. Otherwise why would anyone supply it? The difference between the expected price of a good and the expected average total cost of producing it (the good's opportunity cost) is the supplier's expected economic profit per unit. It's profit that underlies the dynamics of production in a market economy.

Let's return to our example of a Baskin-Robbins Ice Cream store. The initial cost of the franchise and "setup" costs were estimated to be about $144,000, with monthly expenses on the order of $10,000. If we wanted to pay down the bank loan used to finance the business in one year, how much ice cream would we have to sell each month?

Over a year the total cost would have been about $264,000 (12 × $10,000 + $144,000). That means we'd have to sell an average of $22,000 each month! If we couldn't produce at least $22,000 in sales each month, we'd be better off not opening the store—and would sales in the summer make up for the seasonal decline we'd expect to see during the winter? At, say, a price of $2.00 a cone, we'd have to sell 11,000 cones a month (on average) just to break even!

Even if we extended our horizon to pay off the bank loan over two years, we probably wouldn't have satisfied the $16,000 in monthly sales that would have been required (be sure you can figure out how we obtained this figure . . . maybe a nice dish of double chocolate supreme would help your thinking right now . . .). Needless to say, we didn't go ahead with the project (much to the delight of our cholesterol count).

Entrepreneur Individual who sees an opportunity to sell an item at a price higher than the average cost of producing it.

An **entrepreneur** is an individual who sees an opportunity to sell an item at a price higher than the average cost of producing it. The entrepreneur is the organizer of production and the one who visualizes the demand and convinces the individuals who own the factors of production that they want to produce that good. Similarly, the entrepreneur also must convince demanders that what the entrepreneur is producing is what the demanders want. Cost enters into these decisions as a cutoff. Entrepreneurs who don't cover their cost generally don't stay in business.

The Entrepreneur and Supply

Cost curves do not become supply curves through some magic process. To move from cost to supply, entrepreneurial initiative is needed. The entrepreneur analyzes costs and supplies output. An entrepreneur must organize people to do something that he or she wants them to do. He or she must be a psychologist, a cheerleader, a boss, a confessor, and an engineer, to name just a few of the skills an entrepreneur needs. It's these dynamic, driven individuals who underlie supply and who instigate production. They're people who get other people off their behinds.

By allowing entrepreneurs to earn profit, market economies encourage people to channel their drive into supplying material goods. Entrepreneurs create production and hence supply. Without entrepreneurs there would be little supply because there would be no one to recognize and act on demand potential.

The greater the difference between price and average total cost, the greater the entrepreneur's incentive to tackle the organizational problems and supply the good. That insight underlies the dynamic laws of supply discussed in Chapter 2.

USING COST ANALYSIS IN THE REAL WORLD

6 Some of the problems of using cost analysis in the real world include:

1. Economies of scope;
2. Learning by doing and technological change;
3. Many dimensions;
4. Unmeasured costs;
5. Joint costs;
6. Indivisible costs;
7. Uncertainty;
8. Asymmetries; and
9. Multiple planning and adjustment periods with many different short runs.

All too often students walk away from an introductory economics course thinking that cost analysis is a relatively easy topic. Memorize the names, shapes, and relationships of the curves, and you're home free. In the textbook model, that's right. In real life, it's not, because actual production processes are marked by:

1. Economies of scope;
2. Learning by doing and technological change;
3. Many dimensions;
4. Unmeasured costs;
5. Joint costs;
6. Indivisible costs;
7. Uncertainty;
8. Asymmetries; and
9. Multiple planning and adjustment periods with many different short runs.

The general model provides a nice framework with which to approach production, but before the model can be really applied it must be expanded to incorporate these complications. Alas, in introductory economics we don't have time to discuss these complications in detail, but we do have time to give you a sense of their importance. We'll do so by briefly considering four qualifications.

Economies of Scope

Economies of scope The costs of producing products are interdependent, so that producing one good lowers the cost of producing another.

The cost of production of one product often depends on what other products a firm is producing. When the costs of producing products are interdependent, so that it's less costly for a firm to produce one good when it's already producing another, economists say that there are **economies of scope** in the production of the two goods. For example, once a firm has set up a large marketing department to sell cereal, the department might be able to use its expertise in marketing a different product—say, laundry detergent. A firm that sells gasoline can simultaneously use its gas station attendants to sell soda, milk, and incidentals. The minimarts so common along our highways and neighbourhood streets developed because gasoline companies became aware of economies of scope.

Economies of scope play an important role in firms' decisions of what combination of goods to produce. They look for both economies of scope and economies of scale. When you read about firms' mergers, think about whether the combination of their products will generate economies of scope. Many otherwise unexplainable mergers between seemingly incompatible firms can be explained by economies of scope.

Learning by Doing and Technological Change

Learning by doing Becoming more proficient at doing something by actually doing it; in the process, learning what works and what doesn't.

The production terminology that we've been discussing is central to the standard economic models. In the real world, however, other terms and concepts are also important. The production techniques available to real-world firms are constantly changing because of *learning by doing* and *technological change.* These changes occur over time and cannot be accurately predicted.

Unlike events in the standard economic model, all events in the real world are influenced by the past. That's why learning by doing is important in the real world, but isn't a part of the standard economic model. **Learning by doing** simply means that as we do something, we learn what works and what doesn't, and over time we become more proficient at it. Practice may not make perfect, but it certainly makes better and more efficient. Many firms estimate that output per unit input will increase by 1 or 2 percent a year, even if no changes in inputs or technologies occur, as employees learn by doing.

The concept of learning by doing emphasizes the importance of the past in trying to predict performance. Let's say a firm is deciding between two applicants for the job of managing its restaurant. One was a highly successful student but has never run a restaurant; the other was an OK student who has run a restaurant that failed. Which one does the firm hire? The answer is unclear. The first applicant may be brighter, but the lack of experience will likely mean that the person won't be hired. Businesses give enormous weight to experience. So this firm may reason that in failing, the second applicant will have learned lessons that make her the better candidate. Canadian firms faced such a choice when they were invited to expand into the new market economies of Eastern Europe in the early 1990s. Should they hire the former communist managers who had failed to produce efficiently, or should they hire the reformers? (Generally they decided on the former communist managers, hoping they had learned by failing.)

Technological change offers an increase in the known range of production techniques. Technological change provides brand new ways of producing goods. For example, at one point automobile tires were made from rubber, clothing was made from cotton and wool, and buildings were made of wood. As a result of technological change, many tires are now made from petroleum distillates, much clothing is made from synthetic fibres (which in turn are made from petroleum distillates), and many buildings are constructed from steel.

Technological change An increase in the range of production techniques that provides new ways of producing goods.

Technological change can fundamentally alter the nature of production cost. Say, for instance, that physicists discovered a new method of cold fusion (combining atoms to produce energy). That discovery would greatly reduce the need for oil and other increasingly scarce and expensive sources of energy, and it would have far-reaching effects on the costs of production of almost all goods. Other possibilities for technological change with significant effects exist in the new field of genetic engineering.

Technological changes that are far less drastic in their consequences are occurring every day. A new fertilizer is developed that increases crop yield per acre; a new machine is designed that does the work of two people. These technological changes can lower costs enormously. Whenever technological change (or learning by doing) occurs, the cost curve shifts down since the same output can be produced at a lower cost.

Many Dimensions

The only dimension in the standard model is the level of output. Many, if not most, decisions that firms make are not the one-dimensional decisions of the standard model, such as "Should we produce more or less?" They're multidimensional questions like "Should we change the quality? Should we change the wrapper? Should we improve our shipping speed? Should we increase our inventory?" Each of these questions relates to a different dimension of the production decision and each has its own marginal costs. Thus, there isn't just one marginal cost; there are 10 or 20 of them. Good economic decisions take all relevant margins into account.

The reason that the standard model is important is that each of these questions can be analyzed using the same reasoning used in the standard model. But you must remember, *in applying the analysis, it's the reasoning, not the specific model, that's important.*

Unmeasured Costs

If one were to ask, "In what area of decision making do businesses most often fail to use economic insights?" the answer most economists would give is costs. The relevant costs are generally not the costs you'll find in a firm's accounts.

Why the difference? Economists operate conceptually; they include in costs exactly what their theory says they should. Accountants who have to measure firms' costs in practice and provide the actual dollar figures take a much more pragmatic

Production then—The nature of production has changed considerably in the last 60 years. This picture shows a 1933 production line in which people did the work as the goods moved along the line. *UPI/Bettmann.*

approach; their concepts of costs must reflect only those costs that are reasonably precisely measurable.

Economists Include Opportunity Cost Let's take a few examples. First, say that a business produces 1,000 widgets that sell at $3 each for a total revenue of $3,000. To produce these widgets the business had to buy $1,000 worth of widgetgoo, which the owner has hand-shaped into widgets. An accountant would say that the total cost of producing 1,000 widgets was $1,000 and that the firm's profit was $2,000. That's because an accountant uses explicit costs that can be measured. Thus,

Accounting profit Definition of profit used by accountants that states profit is total revenue minus explicit measurable costs.

Accounting profit = *Total revenue* − Explicit measurable costs.

Economic profit is different. An economist, looking at that same example, would point out that the accountant's calculation doesn't take into account the time and effort that the owner put into making the widgets. While a person's time involves no explicit cost in money, it does involve an *opportunity cost,* the forgone income that the owner could have made by spending that time working in another job. If the business takes 400 hours of the person's time and the person could have earned $6 an hour working for someone else, then the person is forgoing $2,400 in income. Economists include that implicit cost in their concept of cost. When that implicit cost is included, what looks like a $2,000 profit becomes a $400 economic loss.

Economic profit Definition of profit used by economists that states profit is total implicit and explicit revenues minus total implicit and explicit costs.

Economic profit = *Implicit and explicit revenues* − Implicit and explicit costs.

Economic Depreciation versus Accounting Depreciation Now let's take a second example. Say a firm buys a machine for $10,000 that's meant to last 10 years, but after one year, machines like that become in short supply so instead of falling, its value rises to $12,000. An accountant, looking at the firm's costs that year, would use **historical cost** (what the machine cost in terms of money actually spent) depreciated at, say, 10 percent per year, so the machine's cost for each of its 10 years of existence would be $1,000. An economist would say that since the value of the machine is rising, the machine has no cost; in fact, it provides a revenue of $2,000 to the firm. The standard

Historical cost Cost in terms of money actually spent.

Production now—The nature of production has changed considerably in the last 60 years. This picture shows a modern production line. Robots do much of the work. *© Keystone/The Image Works.*

model avoids such messy, real-world issues of measuring costs and instead assumes that all costs are measurable in a single time period.

The Standard Model as a Framework

We suspect that even with its simplifications, the standard model has been more than enough to learn in an introductory course. Learning the standard model, however, only provides you with the rudiments of cost analysis, in the same way that learning the rules of mechanics only provides you with the basics of mechanical engineering. In addition to a knowledge of the laws of mechanics, building a machine requires years of experience. Similarly for economics and cost analysis. Introductory economics provides you with a superb framework for starting to think about real-world cost measurement, but it can't make you an expert cost analyst.

Cost Considerations in Everyday Life: Two Examples

Let's now consider two examples of cost considerations in everyday life. Let's first consider an example of an incorrect decision often made by individuals that they would not make if they correctly specified cost; and, second, let's consider an example of a firm's pricing policy that makes sense if one understands marginal cost.

7 Marginal cost analysis can be applied to just about every decision facing you. For example, the marginal benefit of reading these marginal notes must exceed the marginal cost, or you shouldn't read them.

An Individual's Decision about Which of Two Stocks to Sell Say you bought two stocks: one at \$100, one at \$10. You have a chance to sell either stock at \$50. Which should you sell? Many people would answer that you should sell the stock you bought at \$10 because you'll make a profit of \$40, and if you sell the \$100 stock, you'll sustain a loss of \$50. But that reasoning is wrong. After you spent the money to buy the two stocks in the first place, that expenditure became a fixed cost and shouldn't enter into your decision about which stock to sell. You make a profit or loss when the price of the shares goes up or down, not when you sell the stock. Since you have the option of selling, the market valuation of the stock at each moment in time is used to determine your profit, not the valuation of the stock when you sell it.

The economist's answer to the question of which of the two stocks you should sell is "It depends on what you expect to happen to the price of the stocks in the future." Decisions should not be based on the past, except to the degree that the past can be used to predict the future. Variations of this "mistake" occur all the time in business. Firms often set their prices based on invoice costs of the goods they sell, not on the current replacement or opportunity costs.

ADDED DIMENSION 

NEW APPROACHES IN COST ANALYSIS

Factories run by numbers. Numbers to calculate profit and losses; to analyze the costs of new products; and to chart corporate strategy. But a lot of managers are relying on the wrong numbers.

As they adopt new manufacturing techniques like computer-aided design, just-in-time stock management, and total quality control, many firms are discovering that their existing account systems also need dragging into the 1990s. Unless the bean-counters join the manufacturing revolution, traditional cost accounting will have little place in the factory of the future.

The two previous paragraphs introduced an article in *The Economist* (March 3, 1990, p. 61) describing a conference on strategic manufacturing. This conference focused on managerial or cost accounting (the application of cost analysis to managerial decisions). Unlike *financial accounting* (which involves keeping track of income, assets, and liabilities), managerial accounting is used to help managers determine the cost of producing products and plan future investment. It's the direct application of microeconomics to production.

In the 1980s and 1990s there has been an enormous change in cost accounting. The leaders of this change—such as Robert Kaplan of the Harvard Business School—argue that cost accounting systems based on traditional concepts of fixed and variable costs lead firms consistently to make the wrong decisions. They argue that in today's manufacturing, direct labour costs have fallen substantially—in many industries to only 2 or 3 percent of the total cost—and overhead costs have risen substantially. This change in costs facing firms requires a much more careful division among types of overhead costs, and a recognition that what should and should not be assigned as a cost to a particular product differs with each decision.

These developments in managerial accounting require an even deeper understanding of costs than accountants have previously needed. As one firm's director of manufacturing was quoted in *The Economist* article, "Unless management accountants move fast [to incorporate these new concepts], they will be almost without use to the manufacturing manager of 1995."

A Firm's Pricing Policy Based on Marginal Cost Let's consider another example of cost and the many dimensions of output. Electric utilities often argue that they should be allowed to charge higher rates for electricity used during times of peak demand and lower rates during off-peak times. Many people argue against such a pricing policy because they believe that a firm's prices should be based on its costs. They argue that the costs of producing electricity are the same at 7 P.M. as at 4:30 A.M. and the utility should charge the same price at all times.

Understanding marginal cost and recognizing that output has multiple dimensions sheds a different light on the issue. The cost of supplying electricity consists primarily of the overhead cost that must be incurred to build facilities large enough to meet demand in the peak period. After that capacity is built, the marginal cost of supplying electricity at any point other than at the peak load is low. However the marginal cost of supplying peak load power is high. By setting different rates for peak and off-peak usage, electric companies are actually reflecting their cost structure. Economists generally support "peak load pricing" because it's based on the relevant marginal cost.

CONCLUSION AND A LOOK AHEAD

We've come to the end of our discussion of production, cost, and supply. The two chapters we spent on them weren't easy; there's tons of material here, and, quite frankly, it will likely require at least two or three reads and careful attention to your professor's lecture before your mind can absorb it. So if you're planning to sleep through a lecture, the ones on these chapters aren't the ones for that.

These chapters, in combination with our discussion of individual choice, will provide the framework for most of the later chapters, which really do get into interesting real-world issues. But you've got to know the basics to truly understand those issues. So, now that you've come to the end of these two chapters, unless you really feel comfortable with the analysis, it's probably time to review them from the beginning. (Sorry, but remember, there's no such thing as a free lunch.)

CHAPTER SUMMARY

- An economically efficient production process must be technically efficient, but a technically efficient process need not be economically efficient.
- Production is a social, as well as a technical, phenomenon; that's why concepts like team spirit are important.
- The long-run average total cost curve is U–shaped. Economies of scale initially cause average total cost to decrease; diseconomies eventually cause average total cost to increase.
- There is an envelope relationship between short-run average cost curves and long-run average cost curves.
- An entrepreneur is an individual who sees an opportunity to sell an item at a price higher than the average cost of producing it.
- Once one starts applying cost analysis to the real world, one must include a variety of other dimensions of costs that the standard model does not cover.

KEY TERMS

accounting profit *(189)*
constant returns to scale *(181)*
decreasing returns to scale *(181)*
diseconomies of scale *(182)*
economic profit *(189)*
economically efficient *(180)*
economies of scale *(181)*
economies of scope *(186)*
entrepreneur *(185)*
envelope relationship *(184)*
historical cost *(189)*
increasing returns to scale *(181)*
indivisible setup cost *(181)*
learning by doing *(186)*
minimum efficient level of production *(182)*
minimum efficient scale *(184)*
monitoring costs *(183)*
team spirit *(183)*
technical efficiency *(180)*
technological change *(187)*

QUESTIONS FOR THOUGHT AND REVIEW

The number after each question represents the estimated degree of critical thinking required. (1 = almost none; 10 = deep thought.)

1. Distinguish technical efficiency from economic efficiency. *(2)*
2. A student has just written on an exam how in the long run fixed cost will make the average total cost curve slope downward. Why will the professor mark it incorrect? *(3)*
3. What inputs do you use in studying this book? What would the long-run average total cost and marginal cost curves for studying look like? Why? *(8)*
4. Why could diseconomies of scale never occur if production relationships were only technical relationships? *(7)*
5. When economist Jacob Viner first developed the envelope relationship, he told his draftsman to make sure that (1) all the marginal cost curves went through both the minimum point of the short-run average cost curve and (2) the point where the short-run average total cost curve was tangent to the long-run average total cost curve. The draftsman told him it couldn't be done. Viner told him to do it anyhow. Why was the draftsman right? *(8)*
6. What is the role of the entrepreneur in translating cost of production into supply? *(4)*
7. Your average total cost is 40; the price you receive for the good is 12. Should you keep on producing the good? Why? *(5)*
8. A student has just written on an exam that technological change will mean that the cost curve is downward sloping. Why did her teacher mark it wrong? *(6)*
9. Distinguish economic profit from accounting profit. *(3)*
10. If you were describing the marginal cost of an additional car driving on a road, what costs would you look at? What is the likely shape of the marginal cost curve? *(9)*

PROBLEMS AND EXERCISES

1. Visit a nearby company and ask it what would happen to its per-unit costs if sales increased by 10 percent. Try to figure out how its answer relates to the concepts in the last two chapters, remembering especially the discussion about using cost analysis in the real world.
2. Find out the total budget of your college or university. (It often takes a bit of sleuthing, but almost all college and university budgets are in the public record.) Find out the number of students. What is the total cost per student? What is the relevant marginal cost of an additional student?

   Now say you're on a planning committee charged with eliminating an expected 2 percent budget deficit next year.

Using the budget figures, make some suggestions. Explain why presidents of universities and colleges don't last long.

3. A pair of shoes that wholesale for $32.50 has approximately the following costs:

Manufacturing labour	$2.25
Materials	4.95
Factor overhead, operating expenses, and profit	8.50
Sales costs	4.50
Advertising	2.93
Research and development	2.00
Interest	.33
Net income	3.33
Total	32.50

   a. Which of these costs would likely be a variable cost?

   b. Which would likely be a fixed cost?

   c. If output were to rise, what would likely happen to average total costs? Why?

4. Peggy-Sue's cookies are the best in the world, or so we hear. She has been offered a job by Cookie Monster, Inc., to come to work for them at $125,000 per year. Currently, she is producing her own cookies, and she has revenues of $260,000 per year. Her costs are $40,000 for labour, $10,000 for rent, $35,000 for ingredients, and $5,000 for utilities. She has $100,000 of her own money invested in the operation, which, if she left, could be sold for $40,000 that she could invest at 10 percent per year.

   a. Calculate her accounting and economic profits.

   b. Advise her as to what she should do.

5. A major issue of contention at many colleges concerns the cost of meals that are rebated if someone does not sign up for the meal plan. The administration usually says that it should rebate only marginal cost of the food alone, which it calculates at, say, $1.25 per meal. Students say that the marginal cost should include more costs such as the saved space from fewer students using the facilities and the reduced labour expenses on food preparation. This can raise the marginal cost to $6.00.

   a. Who is correct, the administration or the students?

   b. How might your answer differ if this argument was being conducted in the planning stage, before the dining hall is built?

   c. If one accepts the $1.25 figure of a person not eating, how could one justify using a higher figure of about $6.00 for the cost of feeding a guest at the dining hall, as many schools do?

6. The following table provides details on a firm's total costs and total revenue, using technology that involves a fixed expenditure on capital of $300.

Q	*TC*	*AC*	*MC*
0	300		
10	350		
20	380		
30	420		
40	480		
50	600		
60	780		
70	980		
80	1200		
90	1710		
100	2300		

   a. Fill in the columns for *AC* and *MC*. Graph the *AC* and *MC* curves on the same diagram. Graph the TC cost on a different diagram.

   b. At what point does *MC* cross *AC*? Is this what you expect?

   c. If a different technology is used to produce output, fixed capital expenditures rise by $200. Repeat parts *a* and *b*. Explain your answers.

CHAPTER

9

Perfect Competition

There's no resting place for an enterprise in a competitive economy.

~Alfred P. Sloan

After reading this chapter, you should be able to:

1. List the seven conditions for perfect competition.
2. Explain why producing an output at which marginal cost equals price maximizes total profit for a perfect competitor.
3. Demonstrate why the marginal cost curve is the supply curve for a perfectly competitive firm.
4. Determine the output and profit of a perfect competitor graphically and numerically.
5. Explain why perfectly competitive firms make zero economic profit in the long run.
6. Use supply and demand curves to discuss real-world events.
7. Discuss the Pareto optimal criterion and state three criticisms of it.

In physics when you study the laws of gravity, you initially study what would happen in a vacuum. Perfect vacuums don't exist, but talking about what would happen if you dropped an object in a perfect vacuum makes the analysis easier. So too with economics. Our equivalent of a perfect vacuum is perfect competition. In perfect competition the invisible hand of the market operates unimpeded. In this chapter we'll consider how perfectly competitive markets work and see how the cost analysis developed in the previous chapters can be applied.

PERFECT COMPETITION

Perfectly competitive Market in which economic forces operate unimpeded.

A **perfectly competitive** market is a market in which economic forces operate unimpeded. For a market to be called *perfectly competitive,* it must meet some stringent conditions:

1. Buyers and sellers are price takers.
2. The number of firms is large.
3. There are no barriers to entry.
4. Firms' products are homogeneous (identical).
5. Exit and entry are instantaneous and costless.
6. There is complete information.
7. Selling firms are profit-maximizing entrepreneurial firms.

These conditions are needed to ensure that economic forces operate instantaneously and are unimpeded by other invisible or visible forces. For example, say that there weren't a large number of firms. The few firms in the industry would then have an incentive to get together and limit output so they could get a higher price. They would stop the invisible hand from working. Similarly for the other conditions, although the reasoning why they're necessary can get rather complicated.

The Necessary Conditions for Perfect Competition

1 Seven conditions for a market to be perfectly competitive are:

1. Both buyers and sellers are price takers.
2. Large number of firms.
3. No barriers to entry.
4. Homogeneous product.
5. Instantaneous exit and entry.
6. Complete information.
7. Profit-maximizing entrepreneurial firms.

Price taker Firm or individual who takes the market price as given.

Barrier to entry A social, political, or economic impediment that prevents firms from entering a market.

Homogeneous product A product such that each firm's output is indistinguishable from any other firm's output.

To give you a sense of these conditions, let's consider them a bit more carefully.

1. *Both buyers and sellers are price takers.* A **price taker** is a firm or individual who takes the market price as given. When you buy, say, toothpaste, you go to the store and find that the price of toothpaste is, say, \$1.38 for the medium-size tube; you're a price taker. The firm, however, is a price maker since it set the price at \$1.38. So even though the toothpaste industry is highly competitive, it's not a perfectly competitive market. In a perfectly competitive market, supply and demand determine the price; both firms and consumers take the market price as given.
2. *The number of firms is large.* It's almost self-explanatory to say that the number of firms is large. Large means sufficiently large so that any one firm's output compared to the market output is imperceptible, and what one firm does has no influence on what other firms do.
3. *No barriers to entry.* **Barriers to entry** are any things that prevent other firms from entering a market. They might be legal barriers such as exist when firms acquire a patent to produce a certain product. Barriers might be technological, such as exist when the minimum efficient scale of production allows only one firm to produce at the lowest average total cost. Or barriers might be created by social forces, such as when bankers will lend only to certain types of people and not to other types. Perfect competition can have no barriers to entry.
4. *Homogeneous product.* A **homogeneous product** is a product such that each firm's output is indistinguishable from any other firm's output. Corn bought by the bushel is relatively homogeneous. One kernel is indistinguishable from every other kernel. On the other hand, you can buy 30 different brands of many goods—soft drinks, for instance: Pepsi, Coke, 7-Up, and so on. Each is slightly different from the other and thus not homogeneous.
5. *Instantaneous exit and entry.* Say all the grocery stores in your neighbour-

Commodity, currency, and stock exchanges provide the closest real-world analogue to competitive markets.
© *David Wells/The Image Works.*

hood raised their prices by 30 percent without their costs having gone up. What would happen in the next week or month? Probably nothing, other than customers getting mad. You'd still shop there until a new store opened in a convenient place with more reasonable prices. In a perfectly competitive market, the new store would open immediately upon hearing that the prices in the existing stores had gone up. It wouldn't wait a week, or even an hour.

6. *Complete information.* In a perfectly competitive market, not only would the store open up immediately; you'd also know about it instantaneously. So too would other firms. Similarly, if any firm experienced a technological breakthrough, all firms would know about it and would be able to use the same technology instantaneously.
7. *Profit-maximizing entrepreneurial firms.* Firms can have many goals and be organized in a variety of ways. For perfect competition to exist, firms' goals must be profit and only profit, and the people who make the decisions must receive only profits and no other form of income from the firms.

The Necessary Conditions and the Definition of Supply

These are strict, but necessary, conditions for a perfectly competitive market to exist. Combined, they create an environment in which each firm, following its own self-interest, will offer goods to the market in a predictable way. If these conditions hold, we can talk formally about the supply of a produced good. If they aren't met, then our formal definition of supply of produced goods dissolves; we can still talk informally about supply of produced goods and cost conditions, but we cannot use our formal concept of supply and how it relates to costs. This follows from the definition of **supply:**

Supply A schedule of quantities of goods that will be offered to the market at various prices.

> *Supply is a schedule of quantities of goods that will be offered to the market at various prices.*

This definition requires the supplier to be a price taker (our first condition). In almost all other market structures (frameworks within which firms interact economically), firms are not price takers; they are price makers, and the question "How much should I supply, given a price?" will not be asked. Instead the question asked is "Given a demand curve, how much should I produce and what price should I charge?" In other

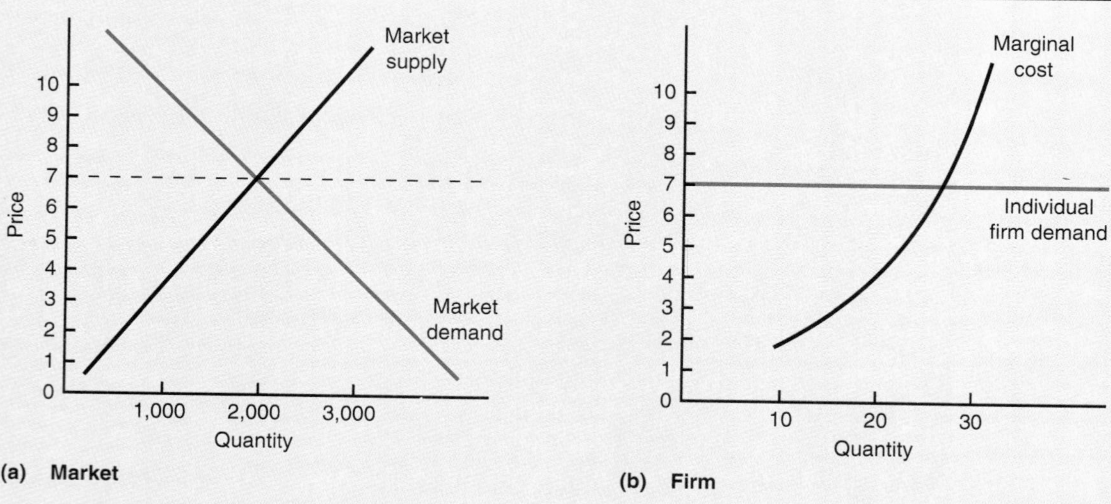

EXHIBIT 1 Market Demand Curve versus Individual Firm Demand Curve

Even though the demand curve for the market is downward sloping, the perceived demand curve of an individual firm is perfectly elastic because each firm is so small relative to the market.

market structures, the supplier sets the quantity and price, based on costs, at whatever level is best for it.[1]

The second condition—that the number of firms is large—is necessary so that firms have no ability to *collude* (to operate in concert so that they can get more for themselves). Conditions 3 through 6 are closely related to the first two; they make it impossible for any firm to forget that there are hundreds of other firms out there just waiting to supply a good if it doesn't. Condition 7 lets us specify a firm's goals. If we didn't know the goals, we wouldn't know how firms would react when faced with the given price.

What's nice about these conditions is that they allow us to formally relate supply to the cost concept that we developed in the last chapter: marginal cost. If the conditions hold, a firm's supply curve will be that portion of the firm's short-run marginal cost curve above the average variable cost curve, as we'll see shortly.

Of course, as later chapters will reveal, even if we can't technically specify a supply function, and even if the conditions for perfect competition don't fully exist, supply forces are still strong and many of the insights of the competitive model carry over. That's why it's important to know that competitive model well.

Demand Curves for the Firm and the Industry

Now that we've considered the competitive supply curve for the industry, let's turn our attention to the competitive demand curve for the firm. Here we must recognize that the demand curve for the industry is downward sloping as in Exhibit 1 (a), but the perceived demand curve for the firm is perfectly elastic as in Exhibit 1 (b). (Remember, we told you those terms would be important.)

Why the difference? It's a difference in perception. Each firm in a competitive industry is so small that it perceives its own demand curve as perfectly elastic even though the demand curve for the industry is downward sloping. Think of it as removing one piece of sand from a beach. Does that lower the level of the beach? For all practical, and even most impractical, purposes, we can assume it doesn't. Similarly for

[1]A firm's ability to set price doesn't mean that it can choose just any price it pleases. Other market structures can be highly competitive, so the range of prices a firm can charge and still stay in business is often limited. Such highly competitive firms are not perfectly competitive because they still set price, rather than supply a certain quantity and accept whatever price they get.

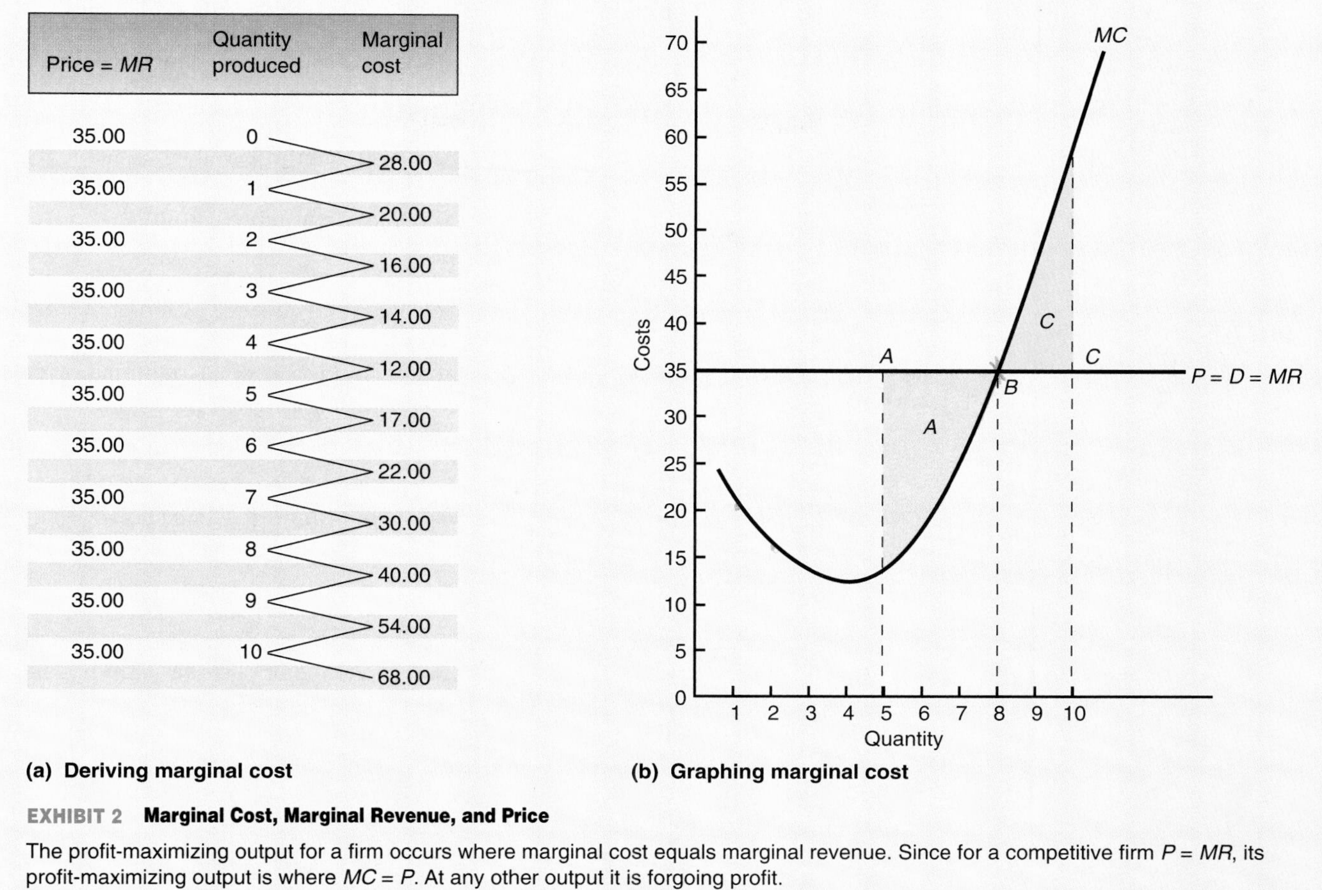

Price = MR	Quantity produced	Marginal cost
35.00	0	
		28.00
35.00	1	
		20.00
35.00	2	
		16.00
35.00	3	
		14.00
35.00	4	
		12.00
35.00	5	
		17.00
35.00	6	
		22.00
35.00	7	
		30.00
35.00	8	
		40.00
35.00	9	
		54.00
35.00	10	
		68.00

(a) Deriving marginal cost **(b) Graphing marginal cost**

EXHIBIT 2 Marginal Cost, Marginal Revenue, and Price

The profit-maximizing output for a firm occurs where marginal cost equals marginal revenue. Since for a competitive firm $P = MR$, its profit-maximizing output is where $MC = P$. At any other output it is forgoing profit.

a perfectly competitive firm: Its demand curve is perfectly elastic even though the demand curve for the market is downward sloping.

This difference in perception is extremely important. It means that firms will increase their output in response to an increase in demand even though that increase in output will cause price to fall and can make all firms collectively worse off. But since, by the assumptions of perfect competition, they don't organize collectively, each firm follows its self-interest. Let's now consider that self-interest in more detail.

PROFIT MAXIMIZATION AND EQUILIBRIUM OF A COMPETITIVE FIRM

Marginal cost The change in cost associated with a change in quantity.

Marginal revenue The change in revenue associated with change in quantity.

The goal of a firm is to maximize profits—to get as much for itself as possible. To do so, it should produce where **marginal cost** (the change in total cost associated with a change in quantity) equals **marginal revenue** (the change in total revenue associated with a change in quantity). Any other output level will yield lower profits. Thus, the marginal cost curve is a competitive firm's supply curve because, given a price, the firm can do no better (its profits are the highest possible) than producing the quantity at which marginal cost equals price which in turn equals marginal revenue.

To see that this is the case, consider Exhibit 2 (a), which lists both marginal cost and marginal revenue. The information in Exhibit 2 (a) is generally presented graphically, as we do in Exhibit 2 (b).

A firm is interested in maximizing profit, so in its decision about what quantity to produce it will continually ask the question: What will changes in quantity do to profit? Profit is the difference between total revenue and total cost. What happens to profit in response to a change in output is determined by *marginal revenue (MR)* and *marginal cost (MC)*. That's why marginal revenue and marginal cost are key concepts in determining the profit-maximizing or loss-minimizing level of output of any firm.

To emphasize the importance of *MR* and *MC*, those are the only cost and revenue figures we show in Exhibit 2. Notice that we don't list profit at all. This is because to calculate profit you must know average total cost *(ATC)* and average revenue. But you don't need to know what *ATC* is to determine the profit-maximizing output. All you need know is *MC* and *MR*. When marginal revenue and marginal cost are equal, the firm is maximizing profit. You only need *ATC* if you want to know what that level of profit will be.

Since *MC* and *MR* are so important, let's look at them more carefully.

Marginal Revenue

Let's first consider marginal revenue (the additional revenue the firm gets from selling another unit of output). For a competitive firm marginal revenue is simple to determine—it's the price it gets for the good. For example, if the firm increases output from 2 to 3, the price it receives for each additional unit sold is $35 so its marginal revenue is $35, the price of the good. At a price of $35 it can sell as much as it wants. So:

For a competitive firm, $MR = P$.

Marginal revenue is given in column 1 of Exhibit 2 (a). As you can see, *MR* equals $35 for all levels of output. But that's what we saw in Exhibit 1 which showed that the demand curve for a perfect competitor is perfectly elastic and equal to its marginal revenue curve.

Marginal Cost

Now let's move on to marginal cost. We'll be brief since we discussed marginal cost in detail in an earlier chapter. Marginal cost is that change in cost that accompanies a change in output. Exhibit 2 (a) shows marginal cost in column 3. Notice that initially in this example, marginal cost is falling, but by the fifth unit of output, it's increasing. This is consistent with our discussion in earlier chapters.

Notice also that the marginal cost figures are given for movements of one quantity to another. That's because marginal concepts tell us what happens when there's a change in something, so marginal concepts are best defined between numbers. The numbers in the shaded rows are the marginal costs. So the marginal cost of increasing output from 1 to 2 is 20, and the marginal cost of increasing output from 2 to 3 is 16. The marginal cost right at 2 (which the marginal cost graph shows) would be between 20 and 16 at approximately 18.

Profit Maximization: $MC = MR$

We just stated that, to maximize profit, a firm should produce where marginal cost equals marginal revenue. Looking at Exhibit 2 (b), we see that a firm following that rule should produce at an output of 8 where $MC = MR = 35$. Now let us try to convince you that 8 is indeed the profit-maximizing output. To do so, let's consider three different possible quantities the firm might look at.

Let's say that initially it decides to produce 5, placing it at point *A* in Exhibit 2 (b). At output *A*, the firm gets $35 for each widget but its marginal cost of increasing output is $17. We don't yet know the firm's profit (the difference between its total revenue and its total cost), but we do know what effect changing output will have on profit. For example, say the firm increases production from 5 to 6. Its revenue will rise by $35. (In other words, its marginal revenue is $35.) Its marginal cost of increasing output is $17. So if it increases production by one unit, profit increases by $18 (the difference between *MR*, $35, and *MC*, $17), so at an output of 5 it makes sense (meaning the firm can increase its profit) to increase output. This reasoning holds true as long as the marginal cost is below the marginal revenue. The blue shaded area *(A)* represents the entire increase in profit the firm can get by increasing output.

Now let's say that the firm decides to produce 10 widgets, placing it at point *C*. Here the firm gets $35 for each widget, but the marginal cost of decreasing to 9 is greater than that at $54. If the firm decreases production by one unit, its cost decreases by $54 and its revenue decreases by $35. Profit increases by $19 ($54 − $35 = $19), so at point *C*, it makes sense to decrease output. This reasoning holds true as long as the marginal cost is above the marginal revenue. The red shaded area *(C)* represents the increase in profits the firm can get by decreasing output.

At point *B* (output = 8) the firm gets \$35 for each widget, and its marginal cost is \$35 as you can see in Exhibit 2 (b). If it increases output by one unit, its cost will rise by \$40 and its revenue will increase by \$35, so its profit falls by \$5. If the firm decreases output by one unit, its cost falls by \$30 and its revenue falls by \$35, so its profit falls by \$5. Either increasing or decreasing production will decrease profit, so point *B*, at an output of 8, where marginal cost equals marginal revenue (price), is the **profit-maximizing condition** for a perfectly competitive firm. This leads us to the following conclusion:

Profit-maximizing condition Marginal cost equals marginal revenue (price), $MR = P = MC$.

The profit-maximizing condition of a competitive firm is $MC = MR = P$.

You should commit this profit-maximizing condition to memory. You should also be sure that you understand the intuition behind it. If marginal revenue isn't equal to marginal cost, a firm obviously can increase profit by changing output. If that isn't obvious, the marginal benefit of an additional hour of thinking about this condition will exceed the marginal cost (whatever it is), meaning that you should . . . right, you guessed it . . . study some more.

2 If marginal revenue does not equal marginal cost, a firm obviously can increase profit by changing output. Therefore, profit is maximized when MC = MR = P.

The Marginal Cost Curve Is the Supply Curve

Now let's consider again the definition of the supply curve as a schedule of quantities of goods that will be offered to the market at various prices. Notice that the marginal cost curve fits that definition. It tells how much the firm will supply at a given price. If the price is \$35, we showed that the firm would supply 8. If the price had been \$20, the firm would have supplied 6; if the price had been \$61, the firm would have supplied 10. Because the marginal cost curve tells us how much of a produced good a firm will supply at a given price, the marginal cost curve is the firm's supply curve. The *MC* curve tells the competitive firm how much it should produce at a given price. (As you'll see later, there's an addendum to this statement. Specifically, the marginal cost curve is the firm's supply curve only if price exceeds average variable cost.)

3 Because the marginal cost curve tells us how much of a produced good a firm will supply at a given price, the marginal cost curve is the firm's supply curve.

The Broader Importance of the $MR = MC$ Equilibrium Condition

This marginal revenue = marginal cost equilibrium condition is simple, but it's enormously powerful. As we'll see, it carries over to other market structures. If you replace revenue with benefits, it also forms the basis of economic reasoning. With whom should you go out? What's the marginal benefit? What's the marginal cost? Should you marry Pat? What's the marginal benefit? What's the marginal cost? As we discussed in Chapter 1, thinking like an economist requires thinking in these marginal terms and applying this marginal reasoning to a wide variety of activities. Understanding this condition is to economics what understanding gravity is to physics. It gives you a sense of if, how, and why prices and quantities will move.

Economic Profit, Accounting Profit, and Normal Profit

In earlier chapters we emphasized that the concept of cost that economists use isn't necessarily cost as measured by accountants, but is instead *opportunity cost* (the value of forgone opportunities) of using an input in its next-best alternative use. The meaning of the $MR = MC$ equilibrium condition must be interpreted in reference to this definition.

The goal of a competitive firm is to maximize profit (the residual left over after all the factors of production have been paid). *Profit* is defined:

$$\textit{Profit} = \textit{Total revenue} - \textit{Total costs}$$

A profit-maximizing firm tries to hold down cost and get as much as it can for the goods it sells. A firm whose goal is profit maximization can be analyzed as an independent entity, analogous to the individual in consumer theory, but instead of maximizing utility as the individual does, the firm maximizes profit. Because profits are the difference between total revenue and total cost, the fact that there are two alternative concepts of cost means that there are two alternative concepts of profit: accounting profit and economic profit. **Accounting profit** is the profit one arrives at using the accountants' definition of cost. **Economic profit** is the profit one arrives at using the economists' definition of cost. In this discussion of the competitive firm, we're interested in *economic* profit.

Accounting profit Definition of profit used by accountants that states profit is total revenue minus explicit measurable costs.

Economic profit Definition of profit used by economists that states profit is total implicit and explicit revenues minus total implicit and explicit costs.

EXHIBIT 3 Accountants' versus Economists' Concepts of Profit

Accountants' concept		
Total revenue		$1,000
Costs		
Labour	$100	
Materials	600	
Rent	80	
Total costs		780
Accounting profit		$ 220

Economists' concept			
Total revenue			$1,000
Explicit costs			
Labour	$100		
Materials	600		
Rent	80		
Total explicit costs		780	
Implicit costs			
Owner's salary	100		
Normal profit	80		
Total implicit costs		180	
Total costs			960
Economic profits			$ 40

Unfortunately, as we discussed in the last chapter, in applying the analysis to the real world often there's no measure of economic profit. Accountants do the measuring and economists are stuck with using accountants' measurements and trying to relate the unmeasured economic profit to the measured accounting profit. In doing so, economists have found that accountants consistently leave out one cost that economists believe should be included: the implicit cost of owners of business. This includes the implicit interest that owners could have received from the funds had they invested those funds in another business (the opportunity cost of capital) and the wages they could have earned if they had spent their time working as employees for someone else as opposed to managing their own business (the opportunity cost of their time).

Exhibit 3 gives an example that distinguishes the accountants' and the economists' concepts of cost and profit. Notice that the economists' costs include implicit costs. Thus, economists' profits are lower than accountants' profits. Because accounting profits leave out these two costs, accounting profits are often higher than economic profits, which do include these costs. To distinguish between the two, economists sometimes call implicit costs *normal profits*. **Normal profits** are the returns to the owners of business for the opportunity cost of their implicit inputs. To an economist, normal profits are actually included as a cost and are not included in *economic profit*. As we'll see later, a competitive firm earns normal profits (a normal return for the work and capital its owner puts in), but it does not earn economic profit in the long run.

Normal profits Payments to entrepreneurs as the return on their risk taking.

Setting $MC = MR$ Maximizes Total Profit

We've spent great effort emphasizing that all you need to know is *MC* and *MR* to determine profit-maximizing output. Now that you know that, let's turn our attention to profit. How do we determine profit? Notice that when you talk about maximizing profit, you're talking about maximizing total profit, not profit per unit. Profit per unit would be maximized at a much lower output level than is total profit. Firms don't care about profit per unit; as long as an increase in output will increase total profits, a profit-maximizing firm should increase output. That's difficult to intuit, so let's consider a concrete example.

Say two people are selling T-shirts that cost $4 each. One sells 2 T-shirts at a price of $6 each and makes a profit per shirt of $2. His total profit is $4. The second person sells the T-shirts at $5 each, making a profit per unit of only $1 but selling 8. Her total profit is $8, twice as much as the fellow who had the $2 profit per unit. In this case, $5 (the price with the lower profit per unit), not $6, yields more total profit.

Determining Profit and Loss

In the discussion of the firm's choice of output, given price, we carefully presented only marginal cost and price. We talked about maximizing profit, but nowhere did we mention what profit, average total cost, average variable cost, or average fixed cost is. We mentioned only marginal cost and price to emphasize that marginal cost is all that's needed to determine a competitive firm's supply curve (and a competitive firm is the only firm that has a supply curve) and the output that will maximize profit.

ADDED DIMENSION

PROFIT MAXIMIZATION AND REAL-WORLD FIRMS

Most real-world firms do not have profit as their only goal. The reason is that, in the real world, the decision maker's income is part of the cost of production. For example, a paid manager has an incentive to hold down costs, but has little incentive to hold down his income which, for the firm, is a cost. Alternatively, say that a firm is a worker-managed firm. If workers receive a share of the profits, they'll push for higher profits, but they'll also see to it that in the process of maximizing profits they don't hurt their own interests—maximizing their wages.

A manager-managed firm will push for high profit, but will see to it that it doesn't achieve those profits by hurting the manager's interests. Managers' pay will be high. In short, real-world firms will hold down the costs of factors of production *except* the cost of the decision maker.

In real life, this problem of the lack of incentives to hold down costs is important. For example, firms' managerial expenses often balloon even as firms are cutting "costs." Similarly, CEOs and other high-ranking officers of the firm often have enormously high salaries. How and why the lack of incentives to hold down costs affects the economy is best seen by first considering the nature of an economy with incentives to hold down all costs. That's why we use as our standard model the profit-maximizing firm.*

*Standard model means the model that economists use as our basis of reasoning; from it, we branch out.

EXHIBIT 4 Costs Relevant to a Firm

Price = Marginal revenue	Quality produced	Total fixed cost	Average fixed cost	Total variable cost	Average variable cost	Total cost	Average total cost	Marginal cost	Total revenue	Total profit
$35.00	0	$40.00	—	0	—	$ 40.00	—		0	$−40.00
35.00	1	40.00	$40.00	$ 28.00	$28.00	68.00	$68.00	$28.00	$ 35.00	−33.00
35.00	2	40.00	20.00	48.00	24.00	88.00	44.00	20.00	70.00	−18.00
35.00	3	40.00	13.33	64.00	21.33	104.00	34.67	16.00	105.00	1.00
35.00	4	40.00	10.00	78.00	19.50	118.00	29.50	14.00	140.00	22.00
35.00	5	40.00	8.00	90.00	18.00	130.00	26.00	12.00	175.00	45.00
35.00	6	40.00	6.67	107.00	17.83	147.00	24.50	17.00	210.00	63.00
35.00	7	40.00	5.71	129.00	18.43	169.00	24.14	22.00	245.00	76.00
35.00	8	40.00	5.00	159.00	19.88	199.00	24.88	30.00	280.00	81.00
35.00	9	40.00	4.44	199.00	22.11	239.00	26.56	40.00	315.00	76.00
35.00	10	40.00	4.00	253.00	25.30	293.00	29.30	54.00	350.00	57.00

Determining Profit from a Table of Costs The $P = MR = MC$ condition tells us how much output a competitive firm should produce to maximize profit. It does not tell us what level of profit the firm makes. The level of profit is determined by total revenue minus total cost. Exhibit 4 expands Exhibit 2 (a) and presents a table of costs with all the costs relevant to the firm. Going through each of the columns and reminding yourself of the definition of each is a good review of the last chapter. If the definitions don't come to mind immediately, you need a review. [We pause here to allow you to review; if you don't know the definitions of *MC, AVC, ATC, FC,* and *AFC,* go back and reread the previous two chapters.]

Pause

The firm is interested in maximizing profit. Looking at Exhibit 4, you can quickly see that the profit-maximizing position is 8, as it was before, since at an output of 8, total profit is highest.

4 The profit-maximizing output can be determined in a table (as in Exhibit 4) or in a graph (as in Exhibit 5).

The maximum profit the firm can earn is $81, which we calculated by subtracting total cost of $199 from total revenue of $280. Notice also that average total cost is lowest at an output of about 7, and the average variable cost is lowest at an output of about 6.[2] Thus, the profit-maximizing position (which is 8) is not necessarily a posi-

[2]We say "about 6" and "about 7" because the table gives only whole numbers. The actual minimum point occurs at 5.55 for average variable cost and 6.55 for average total cost. The nearest whole numbers to these are 6 and 7.

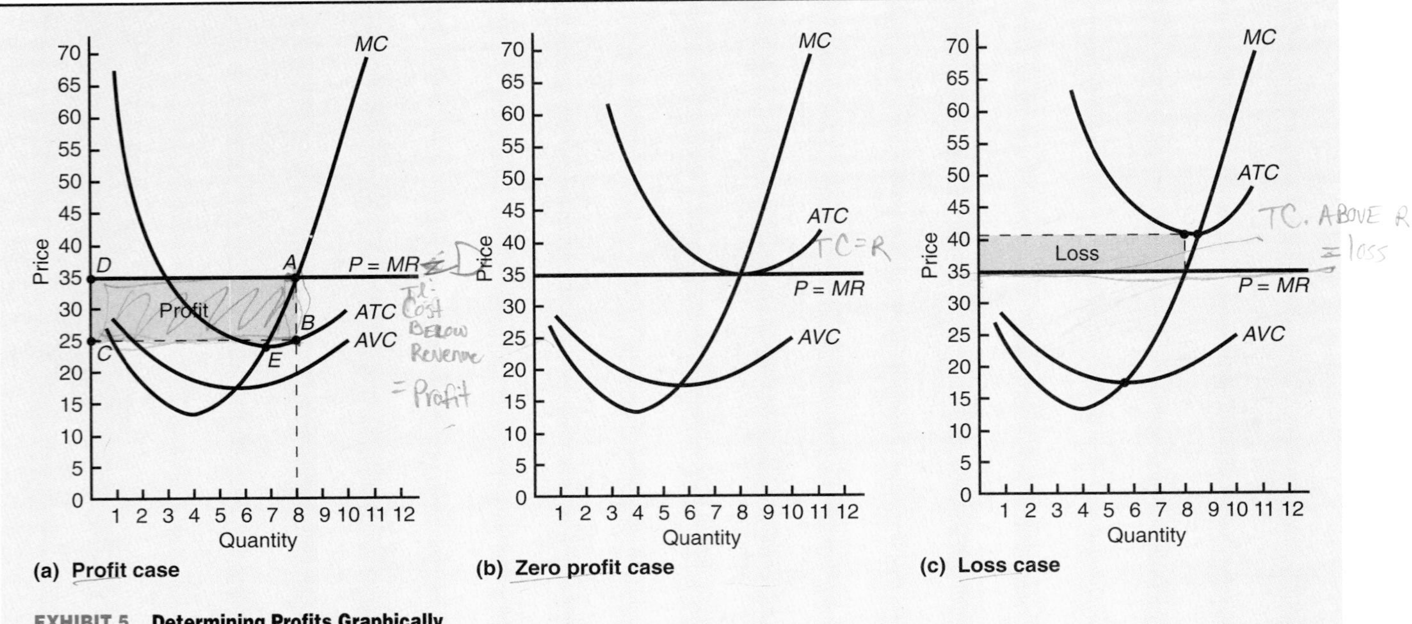

EXHIBIT 5 Determining Profits Graphically

The profit-maximizing output depends *only* on where the *MC* and *MR* curves intersect. The total amount of profit or loss that a firm makes depends on the price it receives and its average total cost of producing the profit-maximizing output. This exhibit shows the case of (**a**) a profit, (**b**) zero profit, and (**c**) a loss.

tion that minimizes either average variable cost or average total cost. It is only the position that maximizes total profit. Notice the relationship between marginal cost and the price of \$35 (which equals marginal revenue) at output level 8. Increasing output from 7 to 8 has a marginal cost of \$30, which is less than \$35, so it made sense to do so. Increasing output from 8 to 9 has a marginal cost of \$40, which is more than \$35, so it does not make sense to do so. The output 8 is the profit-maximizing output.

Determining Profit from a Graph These relationships can be seen in a graph. In Exhibit 5 (a) we add the average total cost and average variable cost curves to the graph of marginal cost and price first presented in Exhibit 2. Notice that the marginal cost curve goes through the lowest points of both average cost curves. (If you don't know why, it would be a good idea to go back again and review the previous chapter.)

The way you find profit graphically is first to find the point where $MC = MR$ (point A). That intersection determines the quantity the firm will produce if it wants to maximize profit. Why? Because the vertical distance between a point on the marginal cost curve and a point on the marginal revenue curve represents the additional profit the firm can make by increasing output. For example, if it increases production from 6 to 7, its marginal cost is \$22 and its marginal revenue is \$35. By increasing output it can increase profit by \$13 (from \$63 to \$76). The same reasoning holds true for any output less than 8. For outputs higher than 8, the opposite reasoning holds true. Marginal cost exceeds marginal revenue, so it pays to decrease output. So to maximize profit, the firm must see that there is no distance between the two curves—it must see where they intersect.

After having determined that quantity, drop a vertical line down to the horizontal axis and see what average total cost is at that output level (point B). Doing so determines the profit per unit at the profit-maximizing output because it's the distance between the price the firm receives (its average revenue) and its average cost. Since the firm will earn that profit on each unit sold, you next extend a line back to the vertical axis (point C). Next go up the price axis to the price that, for a competitive firm, is the marginal revenue (point D). That gives us the shaded rectangle, $ABCD$, which is the total profit earned by the firm (the total quantity times the profit per unit).

Notice that at the profit-maximizing position, the profit per unit isn't at its highest because average total cost is not at its minimum point. Profit per unit of output would be highest at point *E*. A common mistake that students make is to draw a line up from point *E* when they are finding profits. That is wrong. It is important to remember: *To determine maximum profit you must first determine what output the firm will choose to produce by seeing where MC equals MR and then determine the average total cost at that quantity by dropping a line down to the ATC curve.* Only then can you determine what maximum profit will be.

Notice also that as the curves in Exhibit 5 (a) are drawn, *ATC* at the profit-maximizing position is below the price, and the firm makes a profit per unit of a little over $10. The choice of short-run average total cost curves was arbitrary and doesn't affect the firm's profit-maximizing condition: $MC = MR$. It could have been assumed that fixed cost was higher, which would have shifted the *ATC* curve up. In Exhibit 5 (b) it's assumed that fixed cost is $81 higher than in Exhibit 5 (a). Instead of $40, it's $121. The appropriate average total cost curve for a fixed cost of $121 is drawn in Exhibit 5 (b). Notice that in this case economic profit is zero and the marginal cost curve intersects the minimum point of the average total cost curve at an output of 8 and a price of $35. In this case the firm is making zero economic profit. (Remember, although economic profit is zero, all resources, including entrepreneurs, are being paid their opportunity cost, so they're getting a normal return.)

In Exhibit 5 (c), fixed cost is much higher—$169. Profit-maximizing output is still 8, but now at an output of 8 the firm is making an economic loss of $6 on each unit sold, since its average total cost is $41. The loss is given by the shaded rectangle. In this case, the profit-maximizing condition is actually a loss-minimizing condition. So $MC = MR = P$ is both a profit-maximizing condition and a loss-minimization condition.

We draw these three cases to emphasize to you that determining the profit-maximizing output level doesn't depend on fixed cost or average total cost. It depends only on where marginal cost equals price.

Total Revenue and Total Cost

Throughout this chapter we've emphasized the determination of profit by equating marginal cost and price. That focuses the analysis on the relevant issues since marginal changes highlight the relevant considerations in choosing the profit-maximizing output.

An alternative method to see how the firm maximizes profit, which helps distinguish between profit per unit and total profit, is to look at total revenue and total cost, as Exhibit 6 does. In it we plot the firm's total revenue and total cost curves. The total revenue curve is a straight line; each additional good sold increases revenue by the same amount, $35. The total cost curve is bowed upward at most quantities, reflecting the changing marginal cost at different levels of output. The firm's profit is represented by the distance between the total revenue curve and the total cost curve. For example, at output 5, the firm makes $45 in profit.

Total profit is maximized where the vertical distance between total revenue and total cost is greatest. In this example total profit is maximized at output 8, just as in the alternative approach. At that output, marginal revenue (the slope of the total revenue curve) and marginal cost (the slope of the total cost curve) are equal.

The Shutdown Point

Supply Curve = part MC ABOVE AVC

Earlier we stated that the supply curve of a competitive firm is its marginal cost curve. More specifically, as mentioned in footnote 2, the supply curve is the part of the marginal cost curve that is above the average variable cost curve. Considering why this is the case should help the analysis stick in your mind.

Let's consider Exhibit 7 (a reproduction of Exhibit 5 (c)) and the firm's decision at various prices. At a price of $35, it's incurring a loss of $6 per unit. If it's making a loss, why doesn't it shut down? The answer lies in the fixed costs. There's no use crying over spilt milk. In the short run a firm knows it must pay these fixed costs regardless of whether or not it produces. The firm only considers the costs it can save

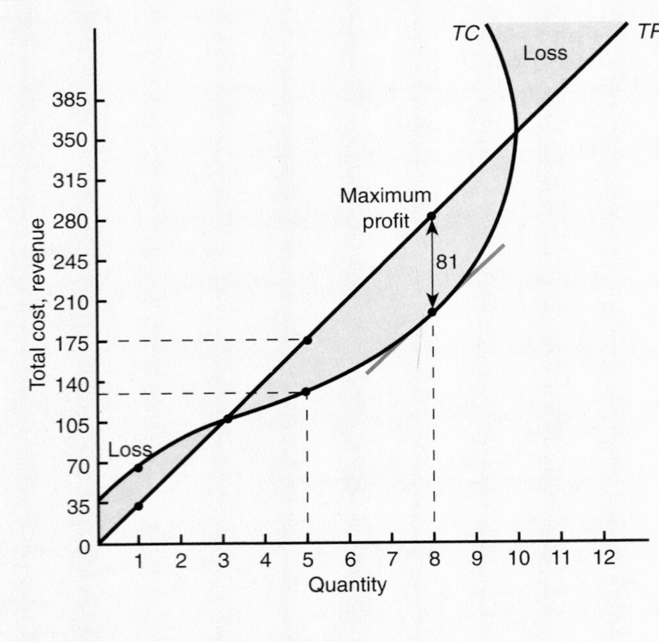

(a) Profit maximization: A graph

EXHIBIT 6 Determination of Profits by Total Cost and Total Revenue Curves

The profit-maximizing output level can also be seen by considering the total cost curve and the total revenue curve. Profit is maximized at the output where total revenue exceeds total cost by the largest amount. This occurs at an output of 8.

Quantity	Total revenue	Total cost	Profit	
0	0	40	–40	
1	35	68	–33	
2	70	88	–18	
3	105	104	1	
4	140	118	22	
5	175	130	45	
6	210	147	63	
7	245	169	76	
8	280	199	81	← profit maximization
9	315	239	76	
10	350	293	57	

(b) Profit maximization: A table

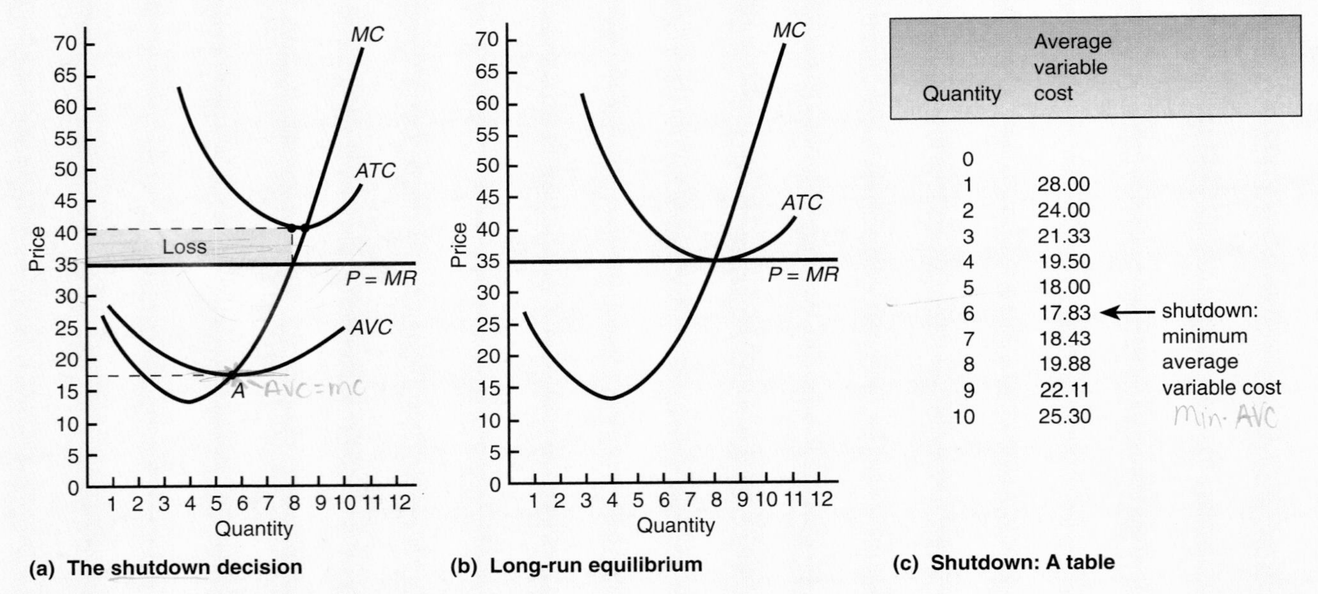

Quantity	Average variable cost	
0		
1	28.00	
2	24.00	
3	21.33	
4	19.50	
5	18.00	
6	17.83	← shutdown: minimum average variable cost
7	18.43	
8	19.88	
9	22.11	
10	25.30	

(a) The shutdown decision **(b) Long-run equilibrium** **(c) Shutdown: A table**

EXHIBIT 7 The Shutdown Decision and Long-Run Equilibrium

A firm should continue to produce as long as price exceeds average variable cost. Once price falls below that, the firm will do better by temporarily shutting down and saving the variable costs. This occurs at point *A* in (**a**). In (**b**), the long-run equilibrium position for a marginal firm in an industry is shown. In that long-run equilibrium, only normal profits are made.

by stopping production, and those costs are its variable costs. As long as a firm is covering its variable costs, it pays to keep on producing. By producing, its loss is $48; if it stopped producing, its loss would be all the fixed costs ($169). So it makes a smaller loss by producing.

However, once the price falls below average variable costs (below $17.80), it will pay to shut down (point *A* in Exhibit 7 (a)). In that case the firm's loss from producing would be more than $169, and it would do better to simply stop producing temporarily and save the variable cost. Thus, the point at which *MC* equals *AVC* is the **shutdown point** (that point at which the firm will gain more by temporarily shutting down than it will by staying in business). When price falls below the shutdown point, the average variable costs the firm can save by shutting down exceed the price it would get for selling the good. When price is above average variable cost, in the short run a firm should keep on producing even though it's making a loss. As long as a firm's total revenue is covering its total variable cost, temporarily producing at a loss is the firm's best strategy because it's making less of a loss than it would make if it were to shut down.

Shutdown point Point at which the firm will gain more by shutting down than it will by staying in business.

Shutdown: AVC = MC

LONG-RUN COMPETITIVE EQUILIBRIUM

5 Since profits create incentives for new firms to enter, output will increase, and the price will fall until zero profits are being made.

The analysis of the competitive firm consists of two parts: the short-run analysis just presented, and a long-run analysis. The essence of the long-run analysis is that profits and losses are inconsistent with long-run equilibrium. In the long run, only the zero-profit equilibrium shown in Exhibit 7 (b) is possible. The existence of above-normal profits would cause firms to enter the industry, raising industry output, which causes the price to fall until the marginal firm can expect zero economic profit. Similarly, the existence of losses will cause firms to exit the industry until the marginal firm can expect only the normal profit. The requirement that in the long run zero profits exist is called the **zero profit condition.**

Zero profit condition In the long run, zero profits exist.

Why is that the case, and how does it come about? Let's say that the average firm in an industry is making an economic profit. Because entry is open to anyone, the existence of profit will entice new firms to enter, putting downward pressure on the price due to the increase in output. The price will continue to fall until no new firms have an incentive to enter, which means that the average firm in the industry is not making a profit. Only at zero profit does entry stop.

Now let's say that the average firm in the industry is making a loss. It will stay in business in the short run, as long as the price it receives exceeds the *AVC,* but in the long run, as its machines wear out and as its fixed costs become variable, it will get out of the business.

As some firms get out of business, the price will rise. So when firms are making a loss there is pressure for the price in that industry to rise. Price will continue to rise until firms are no longer making a loss.

Summarizing: In the long run only one of the three total average cost curve positions is an equilibrium—the one in which there is neither an economic profit nor an economic loss (the position in which long-run average total cost equals the price, which equals marginal cost). This is known as the *zero profit condition.* It defines the long-run equilibrium of a competitive industry.

We should point out once again that *zero profit* does not mean that the entrepreneur doesn't get anything for her efforts. The entrepreneur is an input like any other input. In order to stay in the business she must receive her opportunity cost or normal profit (the amount she would have received in the next-best alternative). That normal profit is built into the costs.

Another aspect of the zero profit position deserves mention. What if one firm has superefficient workers or machinery? Won't the firm make a profit in the long run? The answer is, again, no. Other firms will see the value of those workers or machines and will bid up the price of any specialized input until all profits are eliminated. As we'll discuss later, those inputs receive what are called *rents* to their specialized ability. A **rent** is an income received by a specialized factor of production. For example, say the average worker receives $400 per week but Sarah, because she's such a good worker, receives $600. So $200 of the $600 she receives is a rent to her specialized ability.

Rent An extra income received by a specialized factor of production. (Ex worker)

Remember, the costs that we use in our marginal cost curve analysis are *opportunity costs* (the amount that the input would be paid in its next-best option). Thus, if the profits exist because of specialized inputs, they'll be squeezed out by rents; if the profits exist because of a sudden increase in demand, they'll be squeezed out by new entry. For example, say that a restaurant opens and does wonderfully because it has a super chef. The restaurant makes a large profit, but it will also discover that other restaurants will be offering to hire this super chef at double or triple her current wage. Either the first restaurant matches those offers, losing its above-normal profit, or it loses the chef, losing its above-normal profits. One way or the other, the restaurant is squeezed.

The zero profit condition is enormously powerful; it makes the analysis of competitive markets far more applicable to the real world than can a strict application of the assumption of perfect competition. If economic profit is being made, firms will enter and compete that profit away. Price will be pushed down to cost of production as long as there are no barriers to entry. As we'll see in later chapters, in their analysis of whether markets are competitive many economists focus primarily on whether barriers to entry exist.

Convergence to Equilibrium and Experimental Economics

Experimental economics A branch of economics that gains insights into economic issues by conducting controlled experiments.

In the last 20 years a new branch of economics—experimental economics—has developed. **Experimental economics** is that branch of economics that tests the validity of economic hypotheses by controlled experiments. Experiments are run that simulate market structures and predictions of theories. One of the results experimental economics has arrived at is that double auction markets—a certain type of competitive market in which price is established by individuals bidding without communication with one another—tend to converge relatively quickly to a competitive equilibrium (where $MC = P = MR$) when trading is repeated with the same underlying cost structure. After getting to a competitive equilibrium, price stays there even though market participants have no idea what the competitive equilibrium is (although the experimenters know precisely where it is since they set up the experiment).

These experiments have given economists some additional support for believing that certain structures of competitive markets will converge to equilibrium. But the experiments have also shown the importance of the assumptions and institutions. For example, when the experiment was changed from a double auction market to a posted price market in which sellers stated the price at which they would sell, the price converged to equilibrium much more slowly.

The Supply and Demand Curves for the Industry

Market supply curves Horizontal sum of all firms' marginal cost curves, taking account of any changes in input prices that might occur.

Most of the preceding discussion has focused on firm supply and demand analysis. Now let's consider supply and demand in an industry. We've already discussed industry demand. Even though the firm's demand curve is perfectly elastic, the industry demand curve is downward sloping.

How about the industry supply curve? We previously demonstrated that the supply curve for a competitive firm is that firm's marginal cost curve (above the average variable cost curve). To move from individual firms' marginal cost curves or supply curves to the **market supply curve,** we must sum up all the firms' marginal cost curves horizontally *and* take account of any changes in input prices that might occur. As we sum them up, the market supply curve becomes more elastic than the individual supply curves. This means that there is a larger quantity-supplied response to an increase in price for the entire market than there is for an existing individual firm. The reason is that the supply response comes from two sources:

1. Increase in output of existing firms.
2. Entrance of new firms into the market.

To arrive at the market supply curve, we cannot simply add all the individual firms' supply curves together. When there are industry-wide changes in demand, factor prices are likely to change, which would force costs up or down for each individual firm. For example, if there were an increase in demand for the industry's output that raised the price of that industry's input, there would be an upward shift in each of the individual firms' marginal costs (their supply curves) and the market supply curve would be less elastic than the horizontal summation of the individual firms' supply curves. In the extreme case where all firms in an industry are competitively supplying

ADDED DIMENSION

THE SHUTDOWN DECISION AND THE RELEVANT COSTS

The two previous chapters emphasized that it is vital to choose the relevant costs to the decision at hand. Discussing the shutdown decision gives us a chance to demonstrate the importance of those choices. Say the firm leases a large computer which it needs to operate. The rental cost of that computer is a fixed cost for most decisions, if, as long as the firm keeps the computer, the rent must be paid whether or not the computer is used. However, if the firm can end the rental contract at any time, and thereby save the rental cost, the computer is not a fixed cost. But neither is it your normal variable cost. Since the firm can end the rental contract and save the cost only if it shuts down, that rental cost of the computer is an *indivisible setup cost.* For the shutdown decision, the computer cost is a variable cost. For other decisions about changing quantity, it's a fixed cost.

The moral: The relevant cost can change with the decision at hand, so when you apply the analysis to real-world situations, be sure to think carefully about what is the *relevant cost.*

a perfectly inelastic resource or factor input, the market supply would be perfectly inelastic. Any increase in demand would increase the price of that factor. Costs would rise in response to the increase in demand; output would not.

As a check on whether you understand the ideas behind summing up supply curves, consider the following case: There are constant returns to scale but diminishing marginal product. Input prices are fixed. What does the market supply curve look like? If you answered "perfectly elastic," you've got it! You recognized that constant returns to scale and fixed input prices mean that an infinite number of firms can enter at the market price, so output can expand without limit at the existing price. If you didn't get it, a review probably is in order.

SUPPLY AND DEMAND TOGETHER

Now that we've been through the basics of the competitive supply and demand curves, we're ready to consider the two together and to see how adjustment will likely take place in the firm and in the market.

An Increase in Demand

First, in Exhibit 8 (a) and (b), let's consider a market that's in equilibrium, but that suddenly experiences an increase in demand. Exhibit 8 (b) shows the market reaction. Exhibit 8(a) shows a representative firm's reaction. Originally market equilibrium occurs at a price of $7 and market supply of 700 thousand units (point *A* in (b)), with each firm producing 10 units (point *A* in (a)). Firms are making zero profit because they're in long-run equilibrium. If demand increases from D_0 to D_1, the firms will see the market price increasing and will increase their output until they're once again at a position where $MC = P$. This occurs at point *B* at a market output of 840 thousand units in (b) and at a firm output of 12 in (a). In the short run the existing firms make an economic profit (the shaded area in Exhibit 8 (a)). Price has risen to $9 but average cost is only $7.10, so if the price remains $9 the firm is making a profit of $1.90 per unit. But price cannot remain at $9 since each firm will have an incentive to expand and new firms will have an incentive to enter the market. This will push the price down.

As existing firms expand and new firms enter, there is a movement along the long-run market supply curve. Output increases and market price falls. Eventually the new long-run market equilibrium is reached. If there are no specialized inputs at that new long-run equilibrium, the price will fall back to the original price, $7. The entry of new firms or expansion of existing firms will provide the additional output. The final equilibrium will be at a higher output but the same price. If there had been specialized inputs, or if there were diseconomies of scale, the costs to the firms would have risen and the new equilibrium price would have been higher. Then the long-run supply curve would not have been perfectly elastic; it would have been upward sloping.[3]

[3]To check your understanding, ask yourself the following question: What if there had been economies of scale? If you answered, "There couldn't have been," you're really into economic thinking. (For those of you who aren't all that heavily into economic thinking, the reason is that if there had been economies of scale, the market structure would not have been perfectly competitive. One firm would have kept expanding and expanding, and as it did, its costs would have kept falling.)

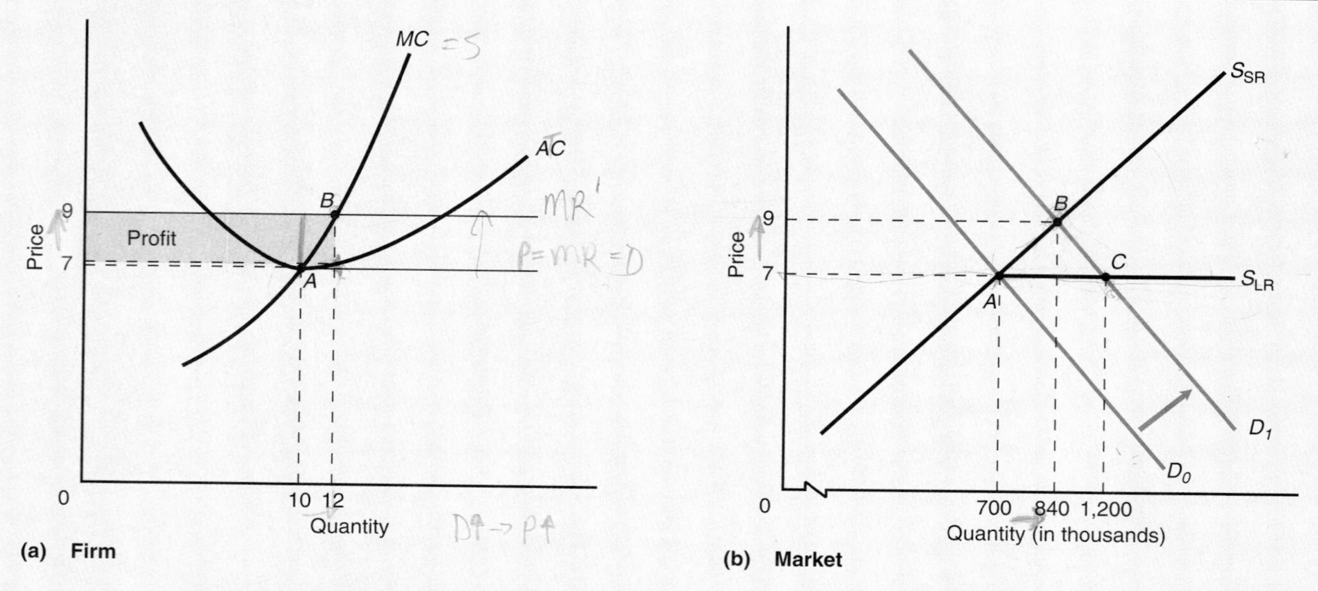

EXHIBIT 8 Market Response to an Increase in Demand

Faced with an increase in demand which it sees as an increase in price and hence profits, a competitive firm will respond by increasing output (from *A* to *B*) in order to maximize profit. A firm's response is shown in (**a**); the market reponse is shown in (**b**). As all firms increase output and as new firms enter, price will fall until all profit is competed away. Thus the long-run supply curve will be perfectly elastic as is S_{LR} in (**b**). The final equilibrium will be at the original price but a higher output. The original firms return to their original output (*A*) but since there are more firms in the market, the market output increases to (*C*).

Notice that in the long-run equilibrium, once again there is zero profit being made. Long-run equilibrium is defined by zero economic profit. Notice also that the long-run supply curve is much more elastic than the short-run supply curve. That's because output changes are much less costly in the short run than in the long run. *In the short run, the price does more of the adjusting. In the long run, more of the adjustment is done by quantity.*

A Technological Improvement

Next, in Exhibit 9 let's consider the effect of a technological improvement available to all firms. The initial equilibrium is at point *A*. The technological improvement lowers the marginal cost (from MC_0 to MC_1) and the average cost (from AC_0 to AC_1) for all firms. In the short run, existing firms make a profit equal to the distance between the market price and their average cost. If price would remain constant, they would increase output to point *B*. However, firms expand output and as new firms enter the market price is forced down, causing existing firms to change output to point *C* and finally to point *D*. Price falls from P_0 to P_1 to P_2 and quantity increases from Q_0 to Q_1 to Q_2, as shown in Exhibit 9 (b).

As before, the increase in output eventually does not come from a movement along the short-run marginal cost curve, but instead comes from the entry of new firms or expansion by existing firms—movement along the long-run industry supply curve.

A Decrease in Demand

Now, in Exhibit 10, let's consider a market that suddenly experiences a decrease in demand. Only this time let's also take into account the possibility of specialized inputs. Market equilibrium initially occurs at a price of $7 and market supply of 700,000 units, with each firm providing 10 units (point *A* in both (a) and (b)). Initially firms are in long-run equilibrium so there is no economic profit. Now suddenly demand decreases from D_0 to D_1. In the short run, total output falls to 560,000 units and market price falls to $5 (point *B*).

As the price falls to $5, individual firms cut output to where $MC = \$5$ at 8 units of output (point B). Average total cost rises to $7.40, so individual firms will experi-

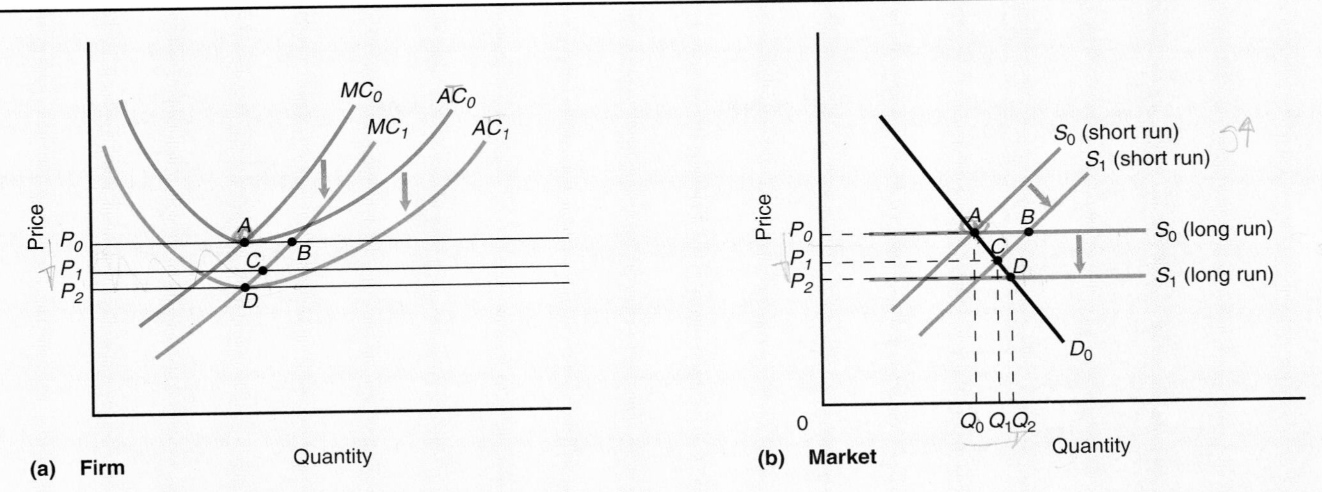

EXHIBIT 9 Market Response to a Technological Improvement

A technological improvement will shift the AC and MC curves down, creating short-run profits. As existing firms expand output and as new firms enter, this profit will be competed away until the price has once again fallen to equal average total costs. The long-run equilibrium is shown by point D in both (**a**) and (**b**). The additional output is supplied by new firms.

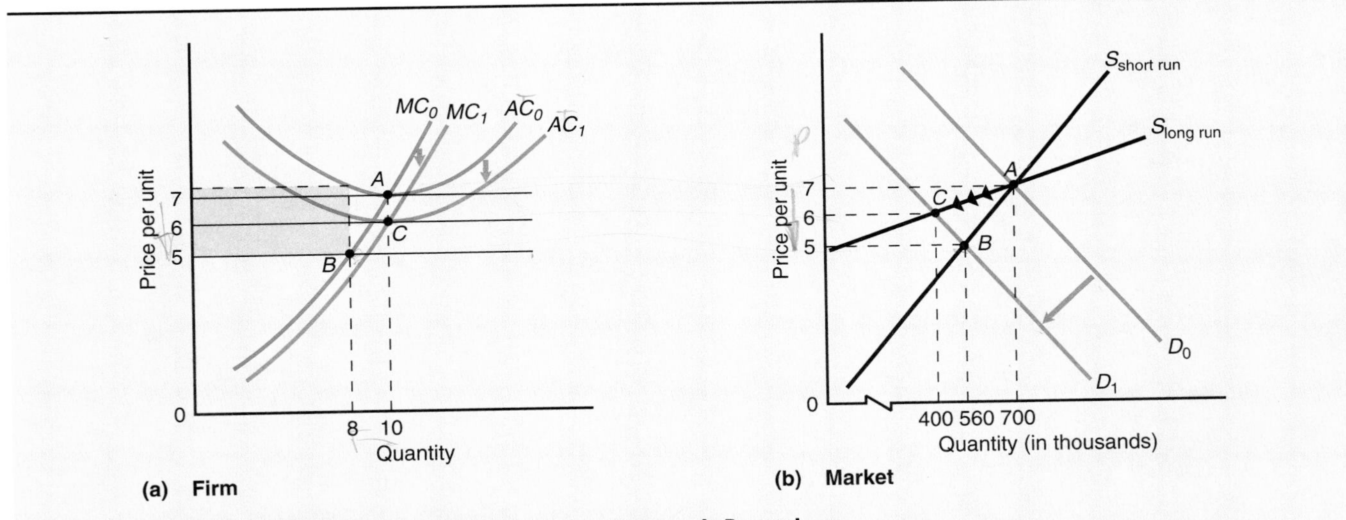

EXHIBIT 10 Market with Specialized Inputs Response to a Decrease in Demand

Faced with a decrease in demand which it sees as a fall in price and hence profit, a competitive firm will respond by decreasing output in order to minimize losses. Firm output and market output will fall. In (**b**) we see the market response: as all firms decrease output, the demand for specialized inputs will fall, causing the firm's cost in (**a**) to fall from AC_0 to AC_1. The long-run equilibrium price will be lower than the original price, and the long-run supply curve S_{LR} will be upward sloping, rather than perfectly elastic.

ence losses, as shown in the shaded region of Exhibit 10 (a). Those firms for whom price falls below average variable cost will exit the market.

As firms exit, there is a movement along the long-run market supply curve in Exhibit 10 (b), which is more elastic than the short-run supply, but is not perfectly elastic. The reason is that as output decreases, the demand for, and hence the price of, specialized inputs will fall, decreasing marginal cost and average cost. Eventually a new long-run market equilibrium at a price of \$6 (point C) will be reached at a lower quantity and lower price than the original equilibrium, but at a lower quantity and higher price than the short-run equilibrium.

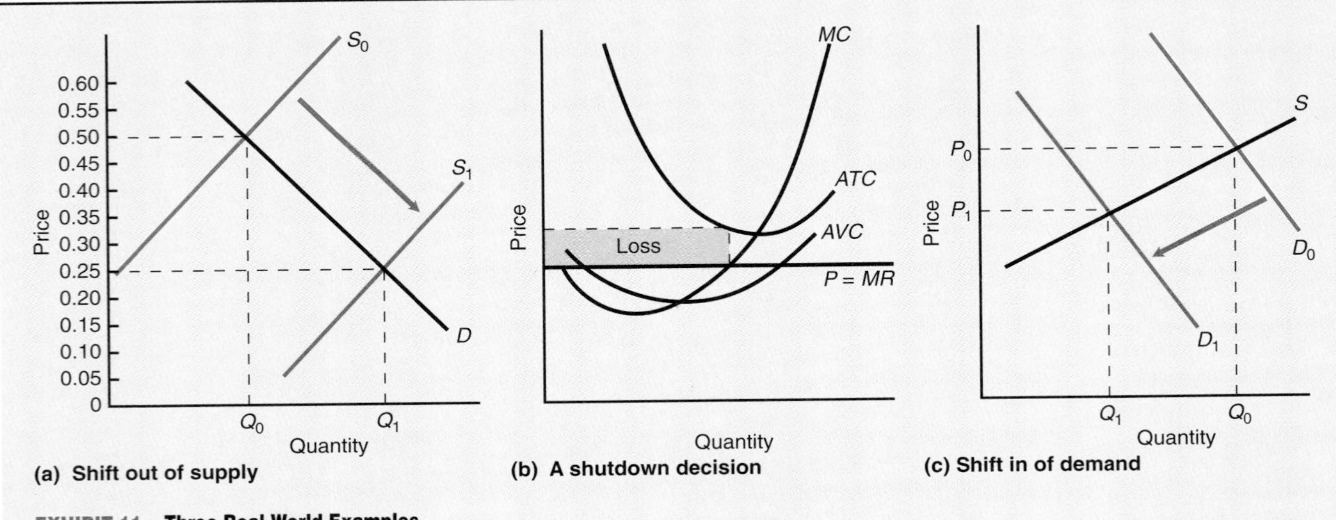

EXHIBIT 11 Three Real-World Examples

Supply-demand analysis can be applied to a wide variety of real-world examples. This exhibit shows three, but there are many more. As you experience life today, a good exercise is to put on your supply-demand glasses and to interpret everything you see in a supply-demand framework.

Other Examples in the Real World

6 Supply and demand curves can be used to describe most real-world events.

The perfectly competitive model and the reasoning underlying it are extremely powerful. With them you have a simple model to use as a first approach to predict the effect of, or to explain why, an event occurred in the real world. For example, consider the following events, all of which were reported in the newspapers recently.

1. Blueberry harvest is double what was predicted.
2. Owners of a chain of department stores decide to close over 100 stores after experiencing two years of losses.
3. Tourism in Vietnam is only half of what was projected.

Exhibit 11 shows these three cases. Let's briefly go through how each of them fits in with the perfectly competitive story.

In the first, the supply increases enormously so the supply curve shifts out from S_0 to S_1. In response, the price of blueberries is expected to fall. The newspaper reported that the wholesale price fell from 50¢ a kilo to 25¢ a kilo, as shown in Exhibit 11 (a), so the event is consistent with the model.

In the second example (Exhibit 11 (b)), we see a shutdown decision evolving into a long-run decision to stop producing. Initially, the department store chain saw the losses it was suffering as temporary. It was covering average variable cost, so it continued producing even while it was making a loss. So in the two years prior to the shutdown decision, the chain's cost curves look like those in Exhibit 11 (b). Since price exceeded average variable cost, the department chain continued to produce even though it was making a loss.

But after two years of losses the firm's perspective changed. The company moved from the short run to the long run. It began to believe that the demand wasn't temporarily low, but that it was permanently low. It began to ask: What costs are truly fixed and what costs are simply indivisible costs that we can save if we close down completely, selling our buildings and reducing our overhead? Since in the long run all costs are variable, the *ATC* became its relevant *AVC*. The company recognized that demand had fallen below these long-run average costs. At that point, it shut down those stores for which $P < AVC$.

The third case is an example of a fall in demand. Because demand fell from D_0 to D_1, as shown in Exhibit 11 (c), we would expect that the price of tourist services in Vietnam fell—which it did. Vietnamese hotels were cutting prices by 25 percent, and Vietnam was offering special tourist packages with reduced rates.

There are hundreds of other real-world examples to which the perfectly competitive model adds insight. That's one reason why it's important to keep it in the back of your mind.

PERFECT COMPETITION, PARETO OPTIMALITY, AND JUDGING ECONOMIC SYSTEMS

Two other related reasons why perfect competition is important are that:

1. It provides an understanding of how the invisible hand works to guide self-interest into society's interest; and
2. It provides a benchmark by which to judge economic systems.

From our earlier discussions you should have an informal sense of how the invisible hand translates self-interest into society's interest, but we haven't yet discussed that issue formally. Unfortunately, a formal sense of how the invisible hand guides self-interest into society's interest is not easy to provide, nor is it easy even to define what is meant by *society's interest.* As economists struggled with these issues, eventually they posed the following question: Can one show that a perfectly competitive equilibrium meets the **Pareto optimal criterion** that no person can be made better off without another being made worse off? This problem is one that many economists have worked on, but it was only in 1959 that Gerard Debreu succeeded in formally proving that a competitive economy met the Pareto optimal criterion under a specific set of conditions. For his work he was given a Nobel prize in 1983.

Pareto optimal criterion Criterion that no person can be made better off without another being made worse off.

Let's briefly consider what Debreu proved. He showed that if there were a complete set of markets (a market for every possible good) now and in the future, and if all market transactions had no side effects on anyone not involved in those transactions, then if the economy were perfectly competitive, the invisible hand would guide the economy to a Pareto optimal result. In this case the supply curve (which represents the marginal cost to the individual supplier) would represent the marginal cost to society, while the demand curve would represent the marginal benefit to society. In a supply/demand equilibrium, not only would an individual be as well off as he or she possibly could be, given where he or she started from, so too would society. A perfectly competitive market equilibrium would be Pareto optimal.

A Geometric Representation of the Welfare Loss of Deviations from Perfect Competition

Debreu's formal proof allows economists to use perfect competition as a benchmark. Since perfect competition is Pareto optimal, then any deviation from perfect competition would represent a welfare loss to society. Exhibit 12 considers an example, showing the welfare loss of a deviation from equilibrium.

As was stated earlier, the demand curve represents the marginal benefit to society; the supply curve represents the marginal cost to society. If that's the case at the competitive equilibrium, the marginal benefit equals the marginal cost and society is in a Pareto optimal position. Since the demand curve slopes downward and the supply curve slopes upward, many people are doing quite well in this competitive equilibrium. They would have been willing to pay a lot more for the good, and to supply the good at a much lower price than they actually end up doing in a competitive equilibrium. They get a surplus.

Not surprisingly, economists have developed names for the benefits consumers and producers get. Those names are *consumer surplus* and *producer surplus.* **Consumer surplus** is the difference between what consumers would have been willing to pay and what they actually pay. In Exhibit 12, at a competitive equilibrium consumer surplus is the triangle composed of areas *A, B,* and *C.* **Producer surplus** is the difference between the price at which producers would have been willing to supply a good and the price they actually receive. In Exhibit 12 it's the triangle composed of areas *D, E,* and *F.* The competitive equilibrium maximizes producer and consumer surpluses.

Consumer surplus The additional amount that consumers would be willing to pay for a product above what they actually pay.

Producer surplus The difference between the price at which producers would have been willing to supply a good and the price they actually receive.

To fix the ideas of consumer and producer surplus in your mind, let's consider a couple of real-world examples. Think about the water you drink. What does it cost? Almost nothing. At the margin, that's how much it's worth to you, but since you'd die of thirst if you had no water, you are getting an enormous amount of consumer surplus from that water. Next, consider a hockey player who loves the game so much he'd play

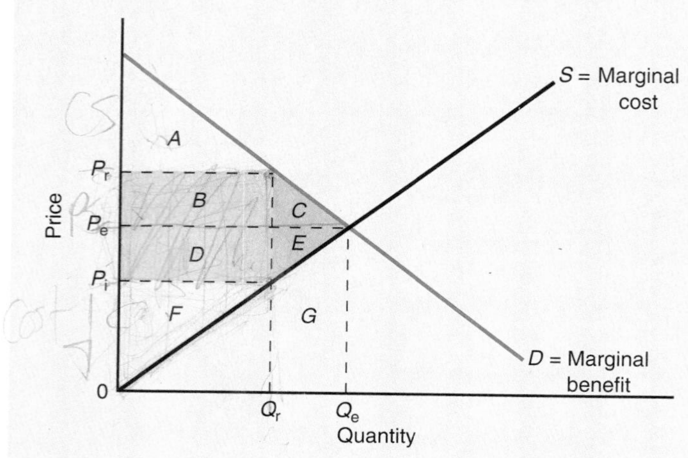

EXHIBIT 12 Welfare Loss from Deviation from Competition

The area between the equilibrium price and the demand curve (the triangle composed of areas *A*, *B*, and *C*) is the consumer surplus. The area between the equilibrium price and the supply curve (the triangle composed of areas *D*, *E*, and *F*) is the producer surplus. If producers can restrict supply to Q_r, they can charge price P_r and transfer area *B* from consumer surplus to producer surplus. Doing so creates a welfare loss of the areas *C* and *E*.

Gerard Debreu won the Nobel prize in 1983 for work on competitive equilibrium theory. *©The Nobel Foundation.*

for free. But he finds that people are willing to pay to see him and that he can receive $10,000 a game. He is receiving producer surplus.

Now let's say that someone places a restriction on the quantity supplied at Q_r. The price that demanders pay now rises to P_r and some consumer surplus is transferred to producer surplus. Those suppliers who are lucky enough to sell in the market receive price P_r even though they'd be willing to supply that quantity at price P_i. Producers who leave the market lose the rectangle represented by the areas *E* and *G* but gain back area *G*, the opportunity cost of their inputs, as they use those inputs in other pursuits, leaving *E* as a net loss. Producers still in the market benefit by area *B*. But that benefit comes at the cost of consumers who are hurt by that same area *B*. The restriction causes a transfer of benefits from consumers to producers. Consumers who leave the market are hurt by the triangle represented by the area *C*.

Notice that this transfer from consumer to producer surplus is not a total wash. The triangular area composed of areas *C* and *E* represents benefits that the excluded producers and excluded consumers won't get. That triangle is the welfare cost of a restriction on the market—the welfare cost of a deviation from perfect competition.

Because of its welfare implications, perfect competition has been used as a benchmark by which to judge the cost of deviating from competition. For example, as we'll see in later chapters, anti-combines legislation—legislation limiting monopolies and determining market structure—is often designed to make markets more competitive, and the costs of government restrictions are often measured by their deviation from a competitive equilibrium.

Criticism of the Pareto Optimality Benchmark

7 The Pareto optimal criterion is that no person can be made better off without another being made worse off. Three criticisms of the Pareto optimal criterion are:

1. The Nirvana criticism.
2. The second-best criticism.
3. The normative criticism.

Nirvana criticism Comparing reality to a situation that cannot occur (*i.e.*, to Nirvana).

Second-best criticism If the economy is not currently at the competitive equilibrium, it is not at all clear that particular moves toward a competitive equilibrium will be in society's interest.

The Pareto optimality benchmark has been the subject of much controversy. Critics offer a number of criticisms of using perfect competition as a benchmark:

1. The **Nirvana criticism:** A perfectly competitive equilibrium is highly unstable. It's usually in some person's interest to restrict entry by others, and, when a market is close to a competitive equilibrium, it is in few people's interest to stop such restrictions.

   To compare reality to a situation that cannot occur (i.e., to Nirvana) is an unfair and unhelpful comparison because it leads to attempts to achieve the unachievable. A better benchmark would be a comparison with workable competition—a state of competition that one might reasonably hope could exist.

2. The **second-best criticism:** The conditions leading to the conclusion that perfect competition leads to a Pareto optimality are so restrictive that they are never even closely met in reality. If the economy deviates in hundreds of ways from perfect competition, how are we to know whether a movement toward a competitive equilibrium in one of those ways will make the economy closer to perfect competition?

3. The **normative criticism:** Even if the previous two criticisms didn't exist, the competitive benchmark still isn't appropriate because there is nothing necessarily wonderful about Pareto optimality. A Pareto optimal position could be a horrendous position, depending on the starting position. For example, say the starting position is the following: One person has all the world's revenues and all the other people are starving. If that rich person would be made worse off by having some money taken from him and given to the starving poor, that starting position would be Pareto optimal. By most people's normative criteria, it would also be a lousy position.

Normative criticism The desirability of a Pareto optimal position depends on the desirability of the starting position.

Critics of the use of the Pareto optimality goal argue that society has a variety of goals. Pareto optimality may be one of them, but it's only one. They argue that economists should take into account all of society's goals—not just Pareto optimality—when determining a benchmark for judging policies.

The Importance of the Competitive Model for All Economists

The debate between supporters and critics of the Pareto optimality benchmark is an ongoing one. Supporters argue that it's the appropriate benchmark, and that competitive equilibrium achieves Pareto optimality. Critics contend that Pareto optimality is just one of many of society's goals. But even critics agree that the forces the perfectly competitive model describes—the pressure on prices to gravitate toward costs of production and the pressure for prices to change as long as supply and demand are not in equilibrium—are strong and show themselves in a variety of real-world markets. Even critics of Pareto optimality believe there is a purpose in studying perfect competition. So, for all economists, it's absolutely necessary that everybody trained in economics understands the perfectly competitive model.

CONCLUSION

We've come to the end of the presentation of perfect competition. It was challenging, but if you went through it carefully, it will serve you well, both as a basis for later chapters and as a reference point for how real-world economies work. But like many good things, a complete understanding of the chapter doesn't come easy.

CHAPTER SUMMARY

- The necessary conditions for perfect competition are that buyers and sellers be price takers, the number of firms be large, there be no barriers to entry, firms' products be homogeneous (identical), exit and entry be instantaneous and costless, there be complete information, and sellers be profit-maximizing entrepreneurial firms.
- The supply curve of a competitive firm is its marginal cost curve. Only competitive firms have supply curves.
- The profit-maximizing position of a competitive firm is where marginal revenue equals marginal cost.
- In the short run, competitive firms can make a profit or loss. In the long run, they make zero profits.
- The shutdown price for a perfectly competitive firm is a price below the minimum point of the average variable cost curve.
- The Pareto optimal criterion is that no one can be made better off without another being made worse off.
- Three criticisms of the Pareto optimality benchmark include the Nirvana criticism, the second-best criticism, and the normative criticism.

KEY TERMS

accounting profit *(199)*
barriers to entry *(194)*
consumer surplus *(211)*
economic profit *(199)*
experimental economics *(206)*
homogeneous product *(194)*
marginal cost *(197)*
marginal revenue *(197)*
market supply curve *(206)*
Nirvana criticism *(212)*
normal profits *(200)*
normative criticism *(213)*
Pareto optimal criterion *(211)*
perfectly competitive *(194)*
price taker *(194)*
producer surplus *(211)*
profit-maximizing condition *(199)*
rent *(205)*
second-best criticism *(212)*
shutdown point *(205)*
supply *(195)*
zero profit condition *(205)*

QUESTIONS FOR THOUGHT AND REVIEW

The number after each question represents the estimated degree of critical thinking required. (1 = almost none; 10 = deep thought.)

1. If a firm is owned by its workers but otherwise meets all the qualifications for a perfectly competitive firm, will its price and output decisions differ from the price and output decisions of a perfectly competitive firm? Why? *(9)*
2. A profit-maximizing firm has an average total cost of $4 but gets a price of $3 for each good it sells. What would you advise it to do? *(3)*
3. How would your answer to Question 2 differ if you knew the average variable cost was $3.50? *(4)*
4. You're thinking of buying one of two firms. One has a profit margin of $8 per unit; the other has a profit margin of $4 per unit. Which should you buy? Why? *(4)*
5. Say that half of the cost of producing wheat is the rental cost of land (a fixed cost) and half is the cost of labour and machines (a variable cost). If the average total cost of producing wheat is $8 and the price of wheat is $6, what would you advise a farmer to do? ("Grow something else" is not allowed.) *(5)*
6. If marginal cost is four times the quantity produced and the price is $20, how much should the firm produce? Why? *(3)*
7. Find three events in the newspaper that can be explained or interpreted with supply/demand analysis. *(7)*
8. Show graphically the welfare loss that would occur if government established a requirement that everyone consume 10 percent more beets than he or she is currently consuming. *(9)*
9. If one can show that the welfare loss in Question 8 is small—say 1/2 of 1 percent of the cost of the beets—and that eating beets makes people healthy, would you support a beet-eating requirement? Why? *(9)*
10. State what is wrong with each of the graphs. *(3)*.

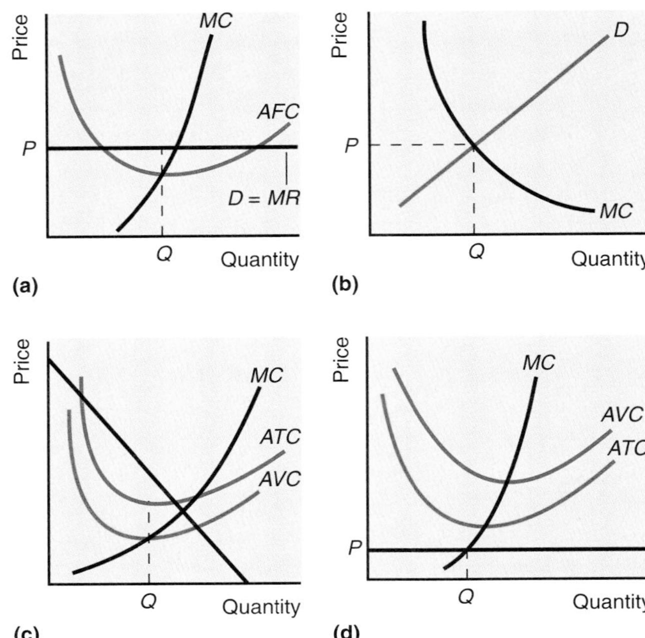

PROBLEMS AND EXERCISES

1. *a.* Based on the following table, what is the profit-maximizing output?

Output	Price	Total costs
0	$10	$ 30
1	10	40
2	10	45
3	10	48
4	10	55
5	10	65
6	10	80
7	10	100
8	10	140
9	10	220
10	10	340

   b. How would your answer change if, in response to an increase in demand, the price of the good increased to $15?
2. Economan has been infected by the free-enterprise bug. He sets up a firm on extraterrestrial affairs. The rent of the building is $4,000, the cost of the two secretaries is $40,000, and the cost of electricity and gas comes to $5,000. There's a great demand for his information, and his total revenue amounts to $100,000. By working in the firm, though, Economan forfeits the $50,000 he could earn by working for the Friendly Space Agency and the $4,000 he could have earned as interest had he saved his funds instead of putting them in this business. Is he making a profit or loss by an accountant's definitions of profit and loss? How about by an economist's definition?
3. Graphically demonstrate the quantity and price of a perfectly competitive firm.
   a. Explain why a slightly larger quantity would not be preferred.
   b. Explain why a slightly lower quantity would not be preferred.
   c. Label the shutdown point in your diagram.
   d. You have just discovered that shutting down means that you would lose your land zoning permit which is required to start operating again. How does that change your answer to c?
4. According to a newspaper article, generally the price of live worms was $1.17 a dozen. Then there was a drought.

a. Demonstrate graphically what will happen to the price and quantity of worms sold.

b. If the price rose to $1.75 and the quantity sold fell from 90,000 to 60,000, what would your estimate of the elasticity of demand be?

5. A biotechnology firm has just announced it has created a tomato that will not rot for weeks. It designed such a fruit by changing the genetic structure of the tomato (it's called gene-wrecking). If this development proves successful, what effect will this technological change have

   a. On the price of tomatoes?

   b. On farmers who grow tomatoes?

   c. On the geographic areas where tomatoes are grown?

   d. On where tomatoes are generally placed on salad bars in winter?

6. Currently central banks (banks of governments) hold 35,000 tons of gold—one-third the world's supply. This is the equivalent of 17 years' production. In the 1990s there has been discussion about the central banks selling off their gold, since it is no longer tied to money supplies. Assuming they did sell it:

   a. Demonstrate, using supply and demand analysis, the effect on the price of gold in the long run and the short run.

   b. If you were an economist advising the central banks and you believed that selling off the gold made sense, would you advise them to do it quickly or slowly? Why?

7. In a perfectly competitive industry the market demand and supply are given by the following functions:

   $Q^d = 15{,}000 - 400\ P$

   $Q^s = 5{,}000 + 600\ P$

   a. What is the equilibrium price and industry output?

   Be sure to draw a diagram to support your answer.

   Now assume that a new firm is considering entering the industry. It has the following marginal cost function:

   $MC = -10 + 4\ Q$

   b. If it does enter the industry, what output should it produce to maximize profits? (Remember—draw a diagram.)

   c. How much profit will it make? (Draw a diagram.)

   d. Should it enter the industry? Why? (Draw a diagram.)

8. Helen's Haircut Emporium is a price taker.

Output (haircuts/hour)	Total cost ($/hour)	*VC*	*AVC*	*ATC*	*MC*
0	20				
1	24				
2	32				
3	44				
4	60				
5	80				

   a. Complete the cost table. (What are the units at the top of each column?)

   b. Construct a graph presenting *MC, AVC,* and *ATC* curves.

   c. If haircuts sell for $18, what is the profit-maximizing output per hour? Illustrate your answer.

   d. Show Helen's supply curve on your diagram.

   e. What is Helen's shutdown point (to the nearest $0.50)?

   f. Below what price (approximately) would Helen leave the industry in the long run? Why?

9. A perfectly competitive industry consists of 100 equal-sized firms. The firms fall into three categories according to their cost structures. Their short-run marginal costs are shown below:

Output per day	40 Firms (Type A) *MC* per firm	30 Firms (Type B) *MC* per firm	30 Firms (Type C) *MC* per firm
1	$20	$40	$20
2	25	45	30
3	30	50	40
4	35	55	50
5	40	60	60
6	45	65	70
7	50	70	80
8	60	75	90
9	70	80	100
10	80	85	110
11	90	90	120

   a. How much will a type A firm supply at a price of $40?

   b. How much will total supply of type B firms be at a price of $80?

   c. What will total industry supply be at a price of $50?

   d. Assuming that marginal cost is above average variable cost for all firms at levels of output, compile the total industry supply table at $10 intervals between $10 and $90.

P	$20	$30	$40	$50	$60	$70	$80	$90
Q^s	—	—	—	—	—	—	—	—

   e. Assume that the demand curve facing the industry is given by:

   $Q^d = 1{,}100 - 5\ P$

   Complete the industry demand table given below.

P	$20	$30	$40	$50	$60	$70	$80	$90
Q^d	—	—	—	—	—	—	—	—

   f. What are equilibrium price and quantity?

CHAPTER

10

Monopoly

Monopoly is business at the end of its journey.
~Henry Demarest Lloyd

After reading this chapter, you should be able to:

1. Summarize how and why the decisions facing a monopolist differ from the collective decisions of competing firms.
2. Explain why $MC = MR$ maximizes total profit for a monopolist.
3. Determine a monopolist's price, output, and profit graphically and numerically.
4. Show why a perfectly price-discriminating monopolist will produce the same output as a perfect competitor.
5. Show graphically the welfare loss from monopoly and explain why it may underestimate people's view of the loss from monopoly.
6. Explain why, without barriers to entry, there would be no monopoly.
7. Explain why economists generally favour having government charge for monopolies.

In the previous chapter we considered perfect competition. We now move to the other end of the spectrum: monopoly. **Monopoly** is a market structure in which one firm makes up the entire market. It is the polar opposite to competition. It is a market structure in which the firm faces no competitive pressure from other firms.

Monopoly A market structure in which one firm makes up the entire market.

Monopolies exist because of barriers to entry into a market that prevent competition. These can be legal barriers (as in the case where a firm has a patent that prevents other firms from entering), sociological barriers where entry is prevented by the invisible handshake, or natural barriers where the firm has a unique ability to produce what other firms can't duplicate.

A key question we want to answer in this chapter is: How does a monopolist's decision differ from the collective decision of competing firms (i.e., from the competitive solution)? Answering that question brings out a key difference between a competitive firm and a monopoly. Since a competitive firm is too small to affect the price, it does not take into account the effect of its output decision on the price it receives. A competitive firm's marginal revenue (the additional revenue it receives from selling an additional unit of output) is its price. Since a monopolistic firm's output decision can affect price, it does take that effect into account; its marginal revenue is not its price. A monopolistic firm will reason: "If I increase production, the price I can get for each unit sold will fall, so I had better be careful about how much I increase production."

1 For a competitive firm, marginal revenue equals price. For a monopolist, it does not. The monopolist takes into account the fact that its decision can affect price.

Let's consider an example. Say your two children love to draw, and some of their works are seen by a travelling art critic who decides they're the greatest thing since Rembrandt, or at least since The Group of Seven. Carefully she tears each page out of their artbooks, mounts them on special paper, and numbers them: Bill Number 1 (Chaos on the Green), Jenny Number 2 (One View), and so on.

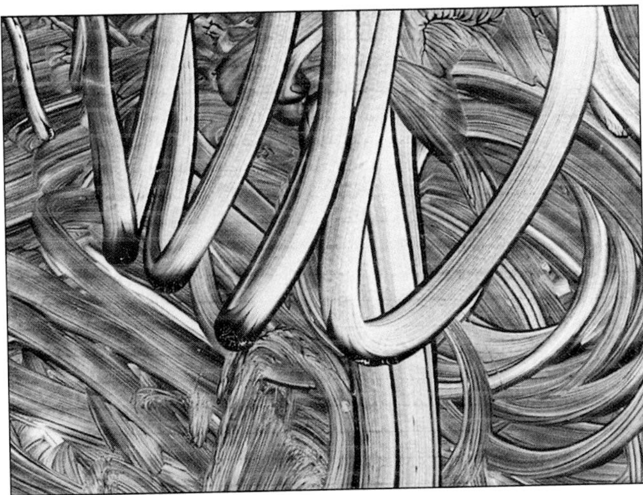

All told, she has 100. She figures, with the right advertising and if your kids are a hit on the art circuit, she'll have a monopoly in your children's art. She plans to sell each piece for $20,000: She gets 50 percent, your kids get 50 percent. That's $1 million for your children. You tell her, "Hey! I can show you a whole drawer full of artwork my kids have given me. I must have 500 altogether. Then my kids get $5 million and you get $5 million."

The art critic has a pained look on her face. She says, "You've been thinking of your kids' artwork when you should have been studying. Their drawings are valued at $20,000 each only if they're rare. If there are more than 500, they're worth $1,000 each. And if it becomes known that you have a desk full of their drawings, they'll be worth nothing, I won't be able to limit quantity at all, and my monopoly will be lost. So obviously we must figure out some way to limit the number of pictures your kids draw. Why don't you hide their artbooks?" Knowing your children as you do, at that point you decide to forget about their fortune and you start studying. You tell yourself

EXHIBIT 1 Monopolistic Profit Maximization

1 Quantity	2 Price	3 Total revenue	4 Marginal revenue	5 Total cost	6 Margial cost	7 Average total cost	8 Profit
0	$36	0	—	$47			$−47
			$33		$1		
1	33	33		48		$48.00	−15
			27		2		
2	30	60		50		25.00	10
			21		4		
3	27	81		54		18.00	27
			15		8		
4	24	96		62		15.50	34
			9		16		
5	21	105		78		15.60	27
			3		24		
6	18	108		102		17.00	6
			−3		40		
7	15	105		142		20.29	−37
			−9		56		
8	12	96		198		24.75	−102
			−15		80		
9	9	81		278		30.89	−197

to always remember that increasing production doesn't necessarily make suppliers better off.

As we saw in the last chapter, competitive firms do not take advantage of that insight. Each individual competitive firm, responding to its self-interest, is not doing what is in the interest of the firms collectively. In competitive markets, as one supplier is pitted against another, the demanders benefit. In monopolistic markets, the firm faces no competitors and does what is in its best interest. Monopolists see to it that the monopolists, not the demanders, benefit.

A MODEL OF MONOPOLY

How much should the monopolistic firm choose to produce if it wants to maximize profit? To answer that we have to consider more carefully the effect that changing output has on the monopoly. That's what we do in this section. First, we consider a numerical example; then we consider that same example graphically. The relevant information for our example is presented in Exhibit 1.

Determining the Monopolist's Price and Output Numerically

Marginal revenue The change in revenue associated with change in quantity.

Exhibit 1 shows the price, total revenue, marginal revenue, total cost, marginal cost, average total cost, and profit at various levels of production. It's similar to the table in Exhibit 4 of the last chapter where we determined a competitive firm's output. The big difference is that marginal revenue changes as output changes and is not equal to the price. Why?

First, let's remember the definition of marginal revenue. **Marginal revenue** is the change in total revenue that occurs as a firm changes its output. In this example, if a monopolist increases output from 4 to 5 by lowering its price from $24 to $21, its revenue increases from $96 to $105, so marginal revenue is $9. That $9 can be divided into two elements: the $21 the firm got for selling another unit minus the $3-per-unit fall in the price that occurred on the other four units as the firm had to lower its price in order to sell the additional unit. That's $21 − $12 = $9.

As you can tell from the table, profits are highest ($34) at 4 units of output at a price of $24. At 3 units of output and a price of $27, the firm has total revenue of $81 and a total cost of $54, yielding a profit of $27. At 5 units of output and a price of $21, the firm has a total revenue of $105 and a total cost of $78, also for a profit of $27. The highest profit it can make is $34, which the firm does when it produces 4 units. This is its profit-maximizing level.

At that profit-maximizing output of 4 units, marginal revenue equals marginal cost, just as it did for the competitive firm. This cannot be seen precisely in the table

ADDED DIMENSION

A QUICK TOOL FOR GRAPHING THE MARGINAL REVENUE CURVE

Here's a quick way to help you graph the marginal revenue curve. *MR* is a line that starts at the same point on the price axis as does a linear demand curve, but that intersects the quantity axis at a point half the distance from where the demand curve intersects the quantity axis. (If the demand curve isn't linear, you can use the same trick if you use lines tangent to the curved demand curve.) So you can extend the demand curve to the two axes, and draw a line from where the demand curve intersects the price axis to that halfway mark on the quantity axis (3 in the figure below). That line is the marginal revenue curve. (*Yes,* there is a mathematical proof that shows this works, but we'll leave it for you to learn in an upper-level microeconomics course).

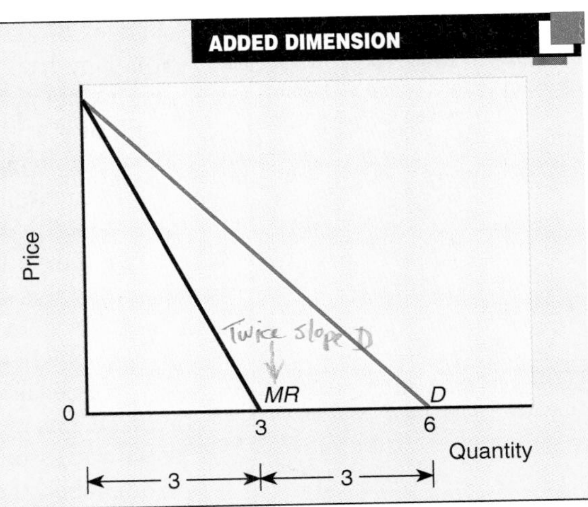

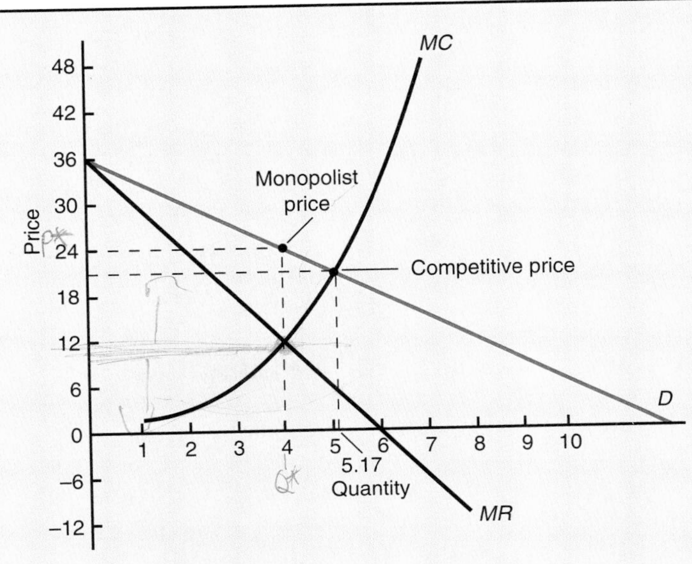

EXHIBIT 2 Determining the Monopolist's Price and Output Graphically

The profit-maximizing output is determined where the *MC* curve intersects the *MR* curve. To determine the price (at which *MC* = *MR*) the monopolist would charge, one first finds that output and then extends a line to the demand curve, in this case finding a price of $24. This price is higher than the competitive price, $20.50, and the quantity, 4, is lower than the competitor's quantity, 5.17.

since the table is for discrete jumps and does not tell us the marginal cost and marginal revenue exactly at 4; it only tells us the marginal cost and marginal revenue of moving from 3 to 4 ($8 and $15 respectively) and the marginal cost and marginal revenue of moving from 4 to 5 ($16 and $9 respectively). If small adjustments (1/100 of a unit or so) were possible, the marginal cost and marginal revenue precisely at 4 would be 12. Because drawing the curve implicitly assumes we can make very small changes, the graphs of the marginal revenue curve and marginal cost curve will intersect at an output of 4 and a marginal cost and marginal revenue of $12.

This is the general rule that any firm must follow to maximize profits: Produce at an output level at which *MC* = *MR*. What's different is that for a monopolist, marginal revenue does not equal price; marginal revenue is below price.

If you think about it, it makes sense that the point where marginal revenue equals marginal cost determines the profit-maximizing output. If the firm increases output beyond the quantity (4) where *MC* > *MR*, the additional revenue it gets ($9) is below the additional cost it incurs ($16). If it decreases output to 3 from 4 where *MC* < *MR*, the revenue it loses ($15) exceeds the additional cost it saves ($8).

2 If a monopolist deviates from the output level at which marginal cost equals marginal revenue, profits will decline.

Determining the Monopolist's Price and Output Graphically

The monopolist's output decision can also be seen graphically. Exhibit 2 graphs the table's information into a demand curve, a marginal revenue curve, and a marginal cost curve. The marginal cost curve is a graph of the change in a firm's cost as it

Marginal Revenue Curve Graphical measure of the change in revenue that occurs in response to a change in price and output.

changes output. It's the same curve as we saw in our discussion of perfect competition. The **marginal revenue curve** is a graph of the change in total revenue. It is graphed by plotting and connecting the points given by quantity and marginal revenue in Exhibit 1. The marginal revenue curve tells us the change in total revenue when there is a change in price and output.

The marginal revenue curve is new, so let's consider it a bit more carefully. It tells us the additional revenue the firm will get by expanding output. It is a downward-sloping curve that begins at the same point as the demand curve but then decreases faster. In this example, marginal revenue is positive up until the firm produces six units. Then marginal revenue is negative; after six units the firm's total revenue decreases when it increases output.

3A The monopolist's price and output are determined as follows:

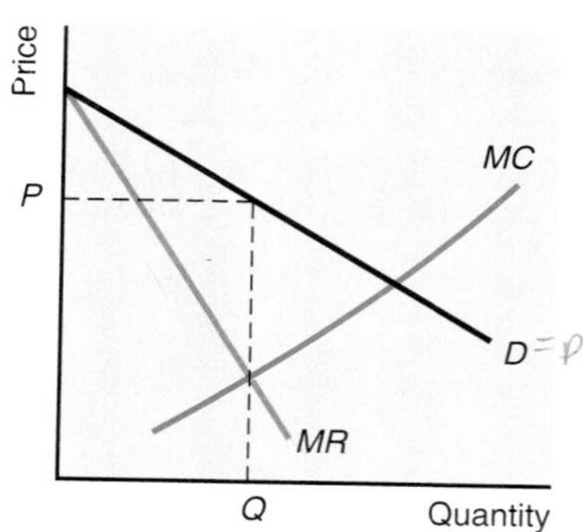

Notice specifically the relationship between the demand curve (which is the average revenue curve) and the marginal revenue curve. Since the demand curve is downward sloping, the marginal revenue curve is below the average revenue curve. (Remember, if the average curve is falling, the marginal curve must be below it.)

Having plotted these curves, let's ask the same question as we did before: What output should the monopolist produce, and what price should it charge? To answer those questions, the key curves to look at are the marginal cost curve and the marginal revenue curve.

We can tell from the graph what will happen to profit by looking at the positions of the marginal revenue curve and the marginal cost curve at the output and price we're considering. At the output where the demand curve intersects the marginal cost curve, marginal cost is significantly above the marginal revenue curve. Whenever that's the case, profits will increase when output is reduced since the saving in cost (the area under the relevant part of the marginal cost curve) is greater than the lost revenue (the area under the relevant part of the marginal revenue curve). So at an output where the demand curve intersects the marginal cost curve (5.17 in Exhibit 2) it definitely pays for the firm to restrict output.

If restricting output a little bit helps that much, how about if the monopolist restricts output some more, to 4 units? Since marginal cost exceeds marginal revenue, doing so makes sense. Well then, how about decreasing output by another unit, from 4 to 3? If you look at the graph, you'll see that doing so doesn't make sense since at all output levels below 4, marginal revenue is above marginal cost. That means that the lost revenue from reducing output will exceed the saving from reducing marginal cost.

MR = MC Determines the Profit-Maximizing Output for a Monopolist From the preceding discussion you should have a good sense of what determines whether the monopolist's profit will rise or fall with a change in output, and what output it should choose. You simply compare the marginal revenue curve to the marginal cost curve at the different output levels being considered. If the marginal revenue is below the marginal cost, it makes sense to reduce production. Doing so decreases marginal cost and increases marginal revenue. If marginal cost is below marginal revenue you should increase production. If the marginal revenue is equal to marginal cost, it does not make sense to increase or reduce production. So the monopolist should produce at the output level where $MC = MR$. As you can see, the output the monopolist chooses is 4 units, the same output that we determined numerically. This leads to the following insights:

If $MR > MC$, *the monopolist gains profit by increasing output.*

If $MR < MC$, *the monopolist gains profit by decreasing output.*

If $MC = MR$, *the monopolist is maximizing profit.*

MR = MC Marginal revenue curve equals marginal cost; the condition under which a monopolist is maximizing profit.

Thus $\boldsymbol{MR = MC}$ is the profit-maximizing rule for a monopolist.

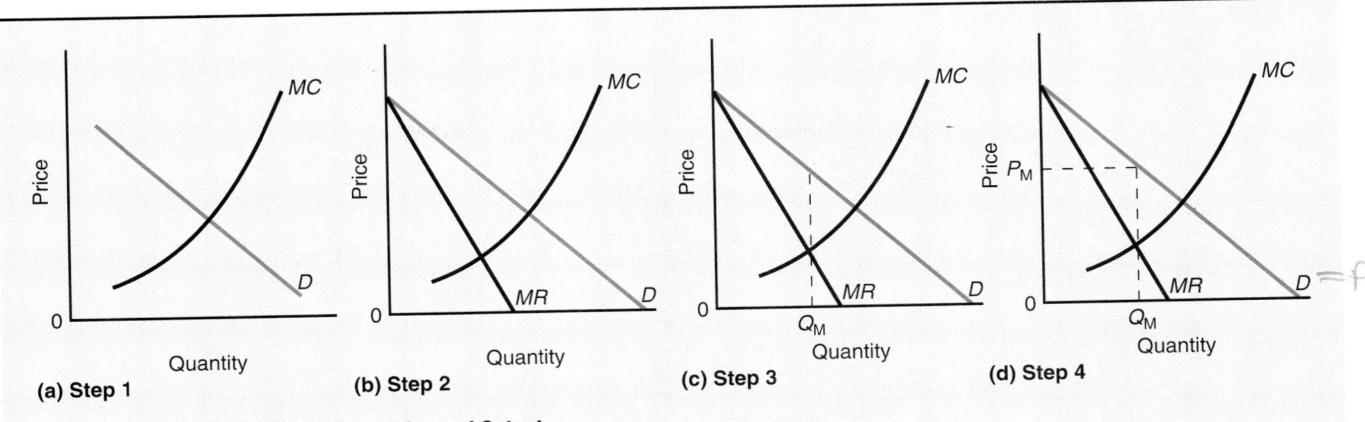

EXHIBIT 3 Finding the Monopolist's Price and Output

Determining a monopolist's price and output can be tricky. In the text there is a full discussion of the steps shown in this exhibit. To make sure you understand, try to go through the steps on your own, and then check your work with the text.

Determining the Price a Monopolist Will Charge The $MR = MC$ condition determines the quantity a monopolist produces; in turn, that quantity determines the price the firm will charge. Since the demand curve tells us what consumers will pay for a given quantity, to find the price a monopolist will charge you must extend the quantity line up to the demand curve. We do so in Exhibit 2 and see that the profit-maximizing output level of 4 allows a monopolist to charge a price of \$24.

Comparing a Monopolist's and a Perfectly Competitive Firm's Outputs and Prices For a competitive industry, the summations of firms' marginal cost curves is the industry supply curve. (The above statement has some qualifications which are best left to intermediate classes.) The competitive level of output would be at 5.17 at a price of \$20.50, as Exhibit 2 shows. The monopolist's output was 4 and its price was \$24. So, if a monopolistic market can be made competitive, you can see that output is lower and price is higher in a monopoly than in a competitive market. The reason is that the monopolist takes into account the effect restricting output has on price.

Equilibrium output for the monopolist, like equilibrium output for the competitor, is determined by the $MC = MR$ condition, but because the monopolist's marginal revenue is below its price, its equilibrium output is different from a competitive market.

Example We've covered a lot of material quickly, so it's probably helpful to go through an example slowly and carefully to review the reasoning process. Here's the problem:

> Say that a monopolist with marginal cost curve MC faces a demand curve D in Exhibit 3 (a). Determine the price and output the monopolist would choose.

The first step is to draw the marginal revenue curve, since we know that a monopolist's profit-maximizing output level is determined where $MC = MR$. We do that in Exhibit 3 (b), remembering the trick of extending our demand curve back to the vertical and horizontal axes and then bisecting the horizontal axis.

The second step is to determine where $MC = MR$. Having found that point, we extend a line up to the demand curve and down to the quantity axis to determine the output the monopolist chooses, Q_M. We do this in Exhibit 3 (c).

A REMINDER

MONOPOLISTS DON'T HAVE SUPPLY CURVES

In comparing monopoly and competition, it's important to remember the definition of a supply curve: It's the quantity that will be supplied at various prices. A supply curve shows the quantity response of *price takers*.

A monopolist is not a price taker; hence it cannot have a supply curve. A monopolist looks at its marginal cost, looks at its demand schedule, and decides what price to charge based on the intersection of its marginal revenue and marginal cost curves. It chooses output and price in a way that gives it the highest possible profit.

Finally we see where the quantity line intersects the demand curve. Then we extend a horizontal line from that point to the price axis, as in Exhibit 3 (d). This determines the price the monopolist will charge, P_M.

PROFITS AND MONOPOLY

determined by ATC & P= ATR

So far we've talked about the output and pricing decisions of a monopolist. We haven't said anything about whether the monopolist makes a profit.[1] As was the case with the perfect competitor, that can be determined only by comparing average total cost to price. So before we can determine profit, we need to add another curve: the average total cost curve. As we saw with a perfect competitor, it's important to follow the correct sequence when finding profit.

- First, determine the output the monopolist will produce by the intersection of the marginal cost and marginal revenue curves.
- Second, determine the price the monopolist will charge for that output.
- Third, determine average cost at that level of output.
- Fourth, determine the monopolist's profit (loss) by comparing average revenue (= *P*) to average total cost.

If price exceeds average cost at the output it chooses, the monopolist will make a profit. If price equals average cost, the monopolist will make no profit (but it will make a normal profit). (Forgotten what *normal profits* are? Then it's back to Chapter 9 for you.) If price is less than average cost, the monopolist will incur a loss: Total cost exceeds total revenue.

An Example of a Monopolist Making a Profit

3B A monopolist's profit is determined by the difference between ATC and price, as in the following diagram:

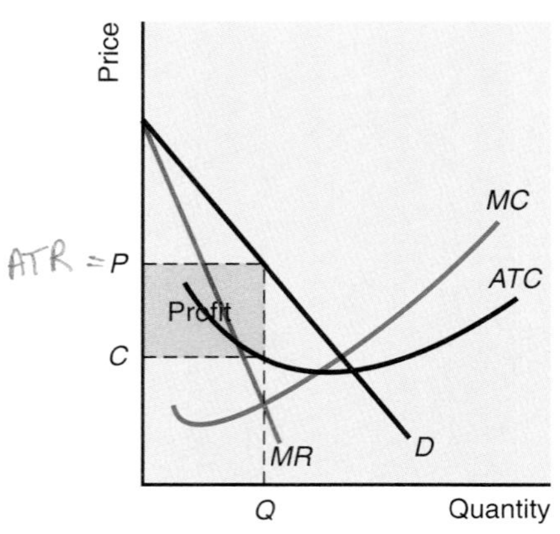

We consider the case of a profit in Exhibit 4, going through the steps slowly. The monopolist's demand, marginal cost, and average total cost curves are presented in Exhibit 4 (a). Our first step is to determine output, which we do by drawing the marginal revenue curve and finding the output level at which marginal cost equals marginal revenue. From that point draw a vertical line to the horizontal (quantity) axis. That intersection tells us the monopolist's output, Q_M in Exhibit 4 (b). The second step is to find what price the monopolist will charge at that output. We do so by extending the vertical line to the demand curve (point *A*) and then extending a horizontal line over to the price axis. Doing so gives price, P_M. Our third step is to determine the average cost at that price. We do so by seeing where our vertical line at the chosen output intersects the average total cost curve (point *B*). That tells us the monopolist's average cost at its chosen output.

To determine profit, we extend lines from where the quantity line intersects the demand curve (point *A*) and the average total cost curve (point *B*) to the price axis in Exhibit 4 (c). The resulting shaded rectangle represents the monopolist's profit.

[1]Remember the distinction between economic profit and accounting profit. This chapter's discussion of profit considers economic profit.

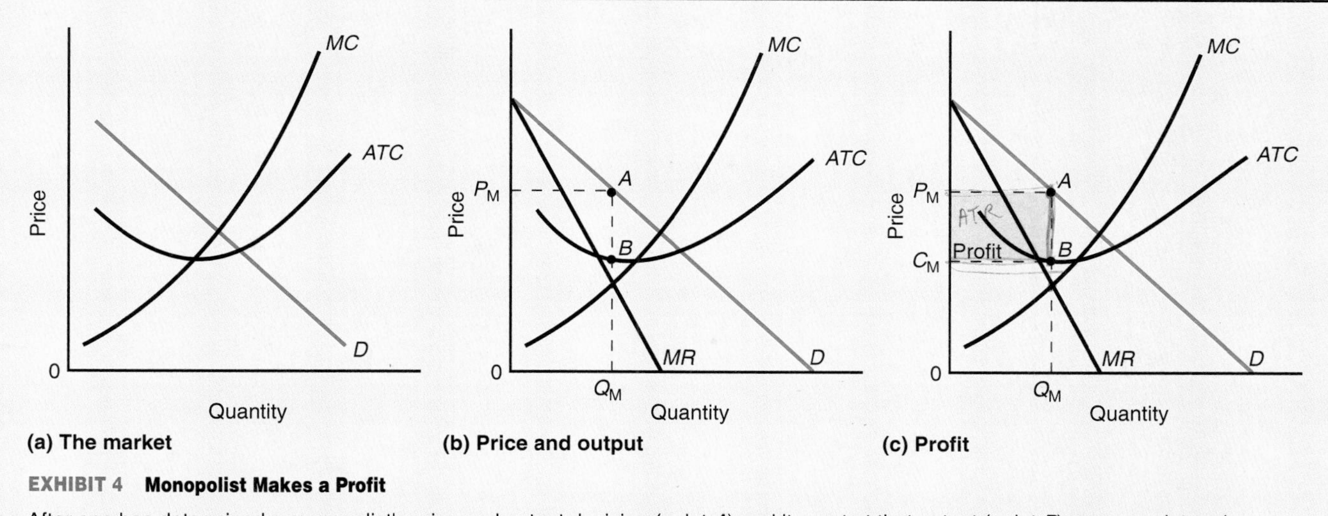

EXHIBIT 4 Monopolist Makes a Profit

After one has determined a monopolist's price and output decision (point *A*) and its cost at that output (point *B*), one can determine the profit by extending a line from point *A* to point *B* to the price axis and back to point *A*. The resulting rectangle represents the monopolist's profit.

An Example of a Monopolist Breaking Even and Making a Short-Run Loss

In Exhibit 5 (a) and (b) we consider two other average total cost curves to show you that in the short run, a monopolist may make a loss or no profit as well as an economic profit. In Exhibit 5 (a) the monopolist is making zero profit; in Exhibit 5 (b) it's making a loss. So clearly in the short run a monopolist can be making either a profit or a loss, or it can be breaking even. If a monopolist is making a loss in the short run, it will attempt to lower its average costs of production by adopting new technologies, or it can try to use advertising to increase the demand for its product with a view to increasing the price it is able to charge for its goods. If that doesn't work, the monopolist will shut down. It won't operate if there are losses in the long run.

A Monopolist with a Zero Marginal Cost

Just to make sure that you really understand what's going on, let's consider an extreme case—a monopolist that has no cost of production. What will it charge and what will its profits be? Consider Exhibit 5 (c). Since marginal cost is zero, marginal cost is coincidental with (lies on top of) the horizontal axis. The marginal revenue curve intersects that marginal cost at Q_M. The price the monopolist charges is P_M. Total revenue is given by the shaded area. Assuming fixed costs are also zero, and since by assumption there is no cost, total revenue is equal to profit.

As a review of the elasticity concept, ask yourself what is the elasticity at that point. If you said it's 1, you're right. If not, we're sorry to say, you'd better review the discussion of elasticity in the chapter on demand before the next exam. We pause for you to review.

Now that you're back, we've got another question for you. Will the elasticity at the price that the normal monopolist charges be elastic (greater than 1) or inelastic (less than 1)? If you answered without hesitation that it's always elastic, you're in good shape on elasticity. If not, you've had your warnings. Remember, life is tough; no one ever said that learning difficult concepts is easy.

The Price-Discriminating Monopolist

Price discriminate To charge different prices to different individuals.

The better to cement into your mind your understanding of the profit-maximizing condition $MC = MR$, let's consider what would happen if our monopolist suddenly gained the ability to **price discriminate**—to charge different prices to different individuals or groups of individuals (for example, students as compared to businesspeople). This means that individuals high up on the demand curve could be charged a high price;

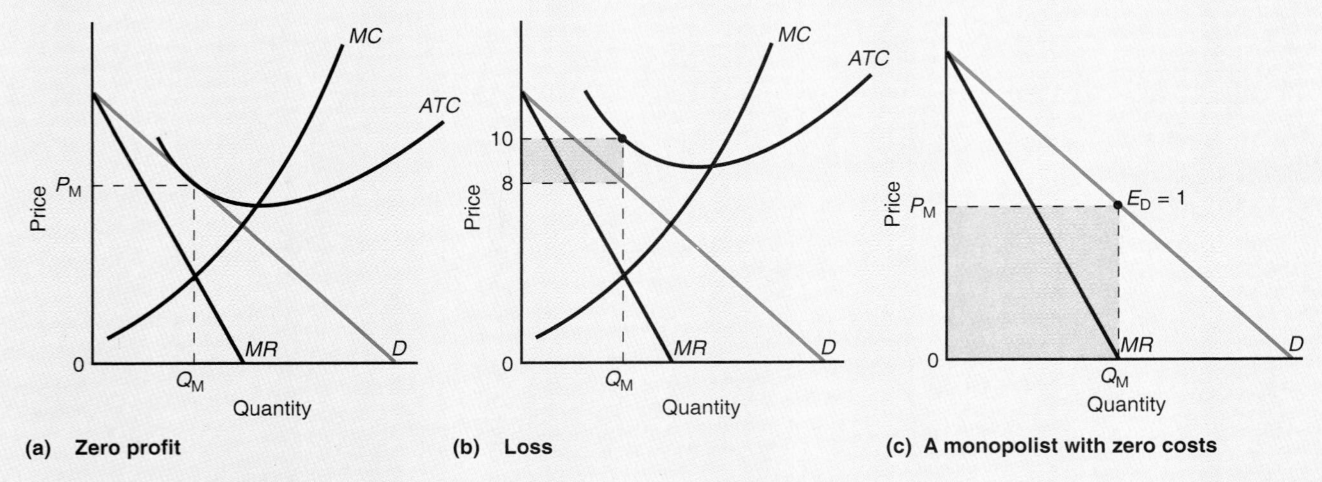

EXHIBIT 5 Three Other Monopoly Cases

Depending on where the *ATC* curve falls, a monopolist can make a profit, break even (as in (**a**)), or make a loss (as in (**b**)) in the short run. In the long run, a monopolist who is making a loss will get out of business. (**c**) shows the equilibrium for a monopolist with zero marginal cost. When a monopolist has a zero marginal cost, the marginal cost curve is coincidental with the quantity axis. Thus, it produces an output at which the *MR* curve intersects the quantity axis and charges a price P_M. At the corresponding point on its demand curve, the elasticity is 1 because that maximizes total revenue. Assuming fixed costs are zero, *ATC* are also zero and total revenue equals total profit.

individuals low on the demand curve could be charged a lower price without affecting the price charged to other individuals.

Consumer surplus The additional amount that consumers would be willing to pay for a product above what they actually pay.

A firm that price discriminates captures demanders' **consumer surplus** (the difference between the price demanders would have been willing to pay and the price they must actually pay). A normal monopolist, by assumption, must charge all individuals the same price. Thus, the price-discriminating firm is giving a good deal to some individuals who would have been willing to pay more. If a monopolist can price discriminate, it doesn't have to give any demanders a good deal. It can extract the maximum consumer surplus from each demander.

When Would a Monopolist Engage in Price Discrimination? Under what conditions can a monopolist—the only seller of a product—engage in price discrimination? When can it charge different prices for the same good? Common sense suggests that price discrimination is feasible only when the people who buy at a low price are prevented from reselling the good to people who face a higher price. There are many real-world examples. A movie ticket for a child costs less than an adult's ticket—because there's no way for the child to resell the ticket to an adult. Similarly, when utility rates (water, sewer, electric, gas) are higher for businesses than for residential customers, it is because there's no way for households to resell the service to firms.

Preventing resale isn't the only condition conducive to price discrimination. The monopolist would have to be able to identify different "markets" for its goods—whether these differences are based on the number of items sold (where quantity discounts apply and hence price is lower relative to the case in which only a few items are sold), differences in age (the movie ticket example, or student discounts at grocery stores), gender (think of haircuts), or affluence (more affluent customers might face a higher price—think of legal fees in a one-lawyer town). These different markets reflect differences in the elasticity of demand for the good. If it is going to consider engaging in price discrimination, a monopolist would have to be able to identify buyers in terms of their elasticities, and price accordingly.

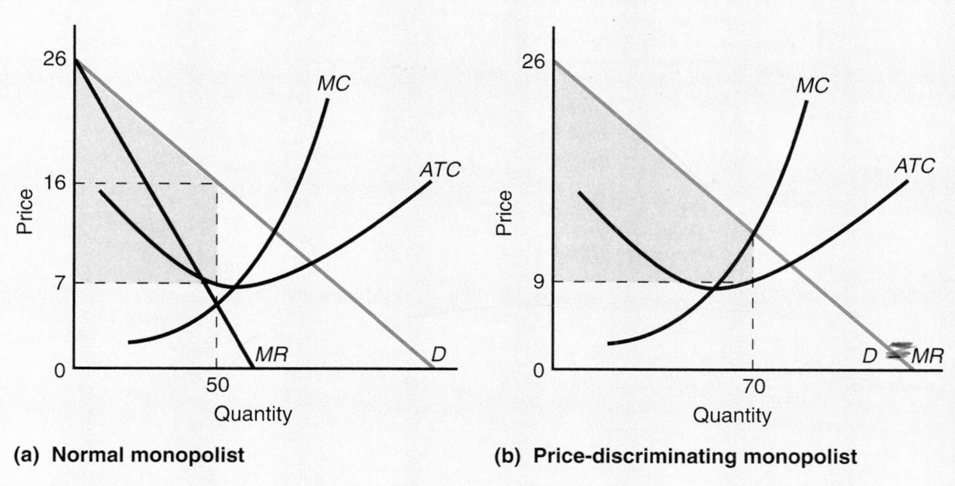

(a) Normal monopolist

(b) Price-discriminating monopolist

EXHIBIT 6 A Normal versus a Perfectly Price-Discriminating Monopolist

If a monopolist can perfectly discriminate among buyers and can charge them all as much as they are willing to pay, her marginal revenue curve will equal her demand curve. She will produce at the same output level as does a competitive firm. On average, however, she will charge a much higher price than would a competitive firm.

A Normal Monopolist versus a Price-Discriminating Monopolist Exhibit 6 (a) graphs the decisions facing a normal monopolist. A normal monopolist will choose to produce 50 units at a price of $16 and a cost per unit of $7, making a profit of $450, the shaded rectangle. The shaded triangle is the remaining consumer surplus.

The perfectly price-discriminating monopolist is able to charge a different price to each customer. When she sells more, she doesn't have to lower her price to other customers willing to pay high prices. So she can extract the full consumer surplus. Since she doesn't have to lower her price to sell more, her marginal revenue isn't the same as the normal monopolist's. Since she doesn't need to lower the price for other customers when she sells more, her *MR*—marginal revenue—is the same as her *AR*—average revenue (total revenue divided by quantity), which is simply her demand curve. So, for a perfectly price-discriminating monopolist: $P = AR = MR$.

4 A price discriminating monopolist does not lose revenue on previously sold products, so its marginal revenue curve equals its demand curve. Thus, it will produce the same quantity as will a perfectly competitive firm.

In Exhibit 6 (b) we consider the decision facing a price-discriminating monopolist. For a price-discriminating monopolist, we find that she will produce at an output of 70, a far higher output than the normal monopolist's, and will make a profit of $700, the shaded region, almost twice the profit of the normal monopolist. She produces the same output that a perfectly competitive industry would have. There is no monopolistic restriction on output.

Price Discrimination in the Real World The price discrimination just discussed is mainly of theoretical interest. It's presented to bring home the point that a price-discriminating monopolist will have an output more like a competitive firm than will a normal monopolist. In the real world it's highly unlikely that a monopolist will be able to charge everyone a different price. However, as discussed in the chapter on demand, price discrimination occurs all the time. There we pointed out the following examples:

1. *All airline Super Saver fares include Saturday night stayovers.* This is a method of price discrimination. Businesspeople who have highly inelastic demands generally aren't willing to stay over a Saturday night, so they're charged a high price while tourists and leisure travellers who have a far more elastic demand curve and who are willing to stay over a Saturday night are charged a low price.
2. *Automobiles are seldom sold at list price.* Once again we have an example of price discrimination. Salespeople can size up the customer and determine the customer's elasticity. People who haven't done the research and don't know that selling at 10 percent off list is normal (i.e., people with inelastic demand) pay higher prices than people who search out all the alternatives (people with elastic demand).

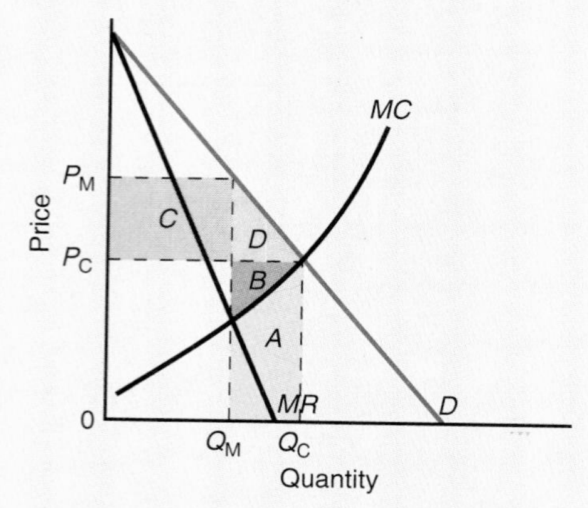

EXHIBIT 7 The Welfare Loss from Monopoly

The welfare loss of a monopolist is represented by the triangles *B* and *D*. The rectangle *C* is a transfer from consumer surplus to the monopolist. The area *A* represents the opportunity cost of diverted resources. This is not a loss to society since the resources will be used in producing other goods.

Now that you've analyzed price-discriminating monopolies, you should understand them better. To see whether you do, try to provide a price discrimination explanation for the following:

1. Theatres have Monday/Tuesday-night special rates.
2. Retail tire companies run special sales about half the time.
3. Restaurants generally make most of their profit on alcoholic drinks and just break even on food.

THE WELFARE LOSS FROM MONOPOLY

In the previous two sections, two conclusions should have started you thinking. The first is that there is no necessary reason why a monopolist must make a short-run profit. The second is that if a monopolist is a price discriminator (which means it makes more profit than a normal monopoly), then its output is closer to the competitive output. From these two conclusions we can reason that profits aren't the primary reason that the economic model we're using sees monopoly as being inferior to perfect competition. If not because of profits, then why does the economic model have such a negative view of monopoly?

A Partial Equilibrium Presentation of the Welfare Loss

5 The welfare loss from monopoly is a triangle as in the graph below. It is not the loss that most people consider. They are often interested in normative losses that the graph does not capture.

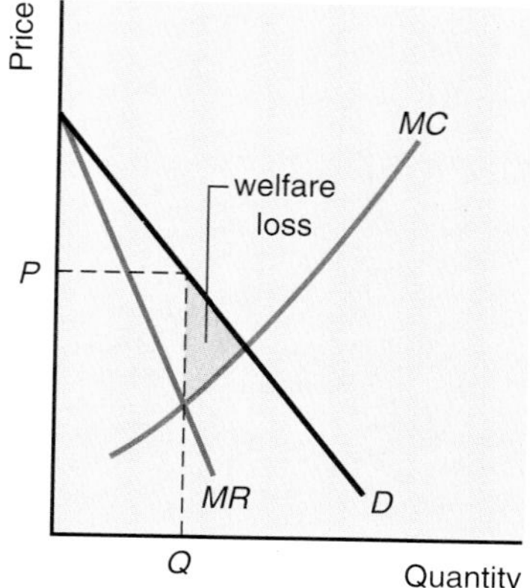

One reason can be seen by looking more carefully at the normal monopolist's equilibrium in Exhibit 7. A monopolist produces at Q_M at price P_M; a competitive market produces a higher quantity Q_C at a lower price P_C. Now let's consider what the benefits to society would be if the monopolist would increase output. The cost to society of increasing output from Q_M to Q_C is measured by the area under the marginal cost curve, the shaded area labelled *A*. This cost is the opportunity cost of the resources—the value of the resources in their next-best use. The benefit to society of increasing output from Q_M to Q_C is the area under the demand curve between those two quantities: areas *A, B,* and *D*. (Area *C* is neither a gain nor a loss to society. It represents a transfer of income from the monopolist to the consumer that would occur if there were a fall in price. Since both monopolist and consumer are members of society, the gain and loss net out.)

The triangular areas *B* and *D* are the net gain to society of eliminating monopoly. Thus, these triangular areas are also a measure of the welfare loss to society from the existence of monopoly. Thinking about consumer surplus (which we discussed previously) may help you to see what's going on here. As defined before, consumer surplus is the additional amount consumers would have been willing to pay for a good, but didn't have to. In a competitive market consumers would have received the areas *C* and *D* as part of their consumer surplus. But they didn't. The monopoly extracts *C* from them as its profit (that's a redistributional effect), so the consumer loses, but the monopolist gains. But the triangle *D* is lost to society; the consumer loses it but the monopolist doesn't get it. It's the cost of the monopoly restriction. The same argument

ADDED DIMENSION

THE SECOND-BEST AND SOME QUALIFICATIONS TO THE WELFARE LOSS

The welfare loss argument just presented requires an addendum. The loss shown in the partial equilibrium diagram is caused by relative prices being changed from competitive prices by a monopolist. But what if monopoly already exists in some other sectors and existing prices aren't competitive prices? When a monopolist changes relative prices, will that cause a similar welfare loss? The answer depends on how the demands are interrelated and whether the new complete set of relative prices is closer to the competitive set of prices than is the old set of relative prices.

Such issues were briefly introduced in the last chapter. They are called *second-best issues.* Second-best issues are issues related to determining the welfare loss due to restrictions on output if the rest of the world isn't characterized by perfect competition. In general, second-best questions can only be answered by using a complicated set of equations—such a complicated set that when we were in graduate school we could hardly work our way through them, so there's no way we're going to foist them on you.

There's one case, however, that captures the essence of the argument and shows whether you're following the problem raised by second-best issues. Say that *all* the markets in an economy, except one, are monopolistic, and the prices in these monopolistic markets are 10 percent higher than the competitive price. Now say that the one competitive price rises by 10 percent, while all other prices remain constant. Now all markets are equally monopolized. Will the monopolization of that last market create a welfare loss? The answer is no. In fact it will create a welfare gain, since the rise in the last competitive price toward a monopolistic price must make the overall relative prices closer to the relative competitive prices. If all prices exceed the competitive prices by 10 percent, the monopolistic relative prices are identical to the competitive relative prices.

The preceding argument was worked out way back in 1926 by a brilliant mathematical economist named Frank Ramsey. Because of his work, the name *Ramsey rule* has been given to the argument that if all prices rise by an equal percentage, it's like no relative price having risen at all, and hence there's no welfare loss.

---

can be made about the triangle *B,* only this time replace *consumer* with *producer. B* is the lost producer surplus.

As discussed in the previous chapter, this area designated by *B* and *D* is often called the *deadweight loss* or **welfare loss triangle;** it is a geometric representation of the welfare cost in terms of misallocated resources that are caused by monopoly. That welfare cost of monopoly is one of the reasons economists oppose monopoly. That cost can be summarized as follows: Because monopolies distort relative prices, people's decisions don't reflect the true cost to society. Price doesn't equal marginal cost. Because price doesn't equal marginal cost, people's choices are distorted; they choose to consume less of the monopolist's output and more of some other output than they would if there were competitive markets. That distinction means that the marginal cost of increasing output is lower than the marginal benefit of increasing output, so there's a welfare loss.

Welfare loss triangle Geometric representation of the welfare cost in terms of the resource misallocation caused by monopoly.

Measuring the Welfare Loss from Monopoly

If the welfare loss from monopoly is large, it would seemingly make sense for the government to enter into the market and prevent monopoly. If, on the other hand, the welfare loss from monopoly is small, it would make sense for the government not to worry about monopoly. Thus, the size of the welfare loss from monopoly and other restrictions on supply is an important economic question.

To answer this question, economists have spent a fair amount of time trying to measure the welfare loss from monopoly. Almost all measurements of that welfare loss as a percentage of GDP have been rather small. One early attempt was made by Arnold Harberger (which is why welfare triangles are sometimes called *Harberger triangles*). Harberger estimated the demand elasticities for a variety of goods produced by monopolies and thereby estimated the welfare loss from monopoly. He found that the welfare loss from monopoly was only about 1/2 of 1 percent of total GDP. Later estimates have differed slightly from the Harberger estimates and have shown monopoly to be more of a problem, but they too have been relatively small. Thus, at least

Airlines typically offer many different fares in an attempt to price discriminate. *Ray Stott/The Image Works.*

from the welfare loss point of view, it would seem that while monopolies are a problem, they aren't an enormous problem to society when compared to issues such as unemployment or drugs.

Government Policy and Monopoly

The empirical estimates of the welfare loss due to monopoly suggest that monopolies are a relatively minor problem. But society has consistently been concerned about monopoly. Public dislike for monopolies has forced government to create laws preventing monopoly. It seems that the public opposes monopoly much more vehemently than one would expect it to, based on the measurement of the welfare loss from monopoly.

There are two explanations for this difference between the layperson's view of monopoly (he or she doesn't like monopoly) and the view that follows from empirical work based on the standard economic model (monopoly isn't much of a problem). One explanation is that society is wrong—that if society understood the economic model, it wouldn't be as concerned about monopoly as it is. A second explanation is that the monopolistic model isn't capturing some of people's normative arguments against monopoly. Both explanations have some validity.

Most economists would agree that the lay public often expresses a knee-jerk reaction to monopoly, not a reasoned judgment. Knee-jerk reactions are often wrong, so the argument that society is wrong to be so concerned about monopoly has a ring of truth. Knee-jerk reactions often don't hold true when subjected to careful scrutiny.

But, as discussed in the previous chapter, there are questions whether the economists' competitive equilibrium is an appropriate benchmark from which to judge welfare. The competitive benchmark doesn't take into account income distributional effects and issues of fairness. The public's judgments about real-world events do take these additional welfare considerations into account. Therefore the second explanation—that the monopolistic model isn't capturing some of people's normative arguments against monopoly—is also reasonable.

These two explanations aren't necessarily contradictory. They can complement one another. In certain instances the public might oppose monopoly because it doesn't understand the costs of monopoly, while in other instances it might dislike monopoly based on broader normative criteria that the standard model doesn't capture.

The economist's job is to help separate these two views. Doing so makes the analysis of monopoly a more complicated undertaking than simply drawing and understanding welfare triangle losses.

The standard model of monopoly just presented is elegant, but, like many things elegant, it hides some issues, and these issues could help explain the difference between the standard model of monopoly (which suggests monopoly isn't much of a problem) and the public's dislike of monopoly.

A BROADER VIEW OF MONOPOLY

6 If there were no barriers to entry, profit-maximizing firms would always compete away monopoly profits.

Barrier to entry A social, political, or economic impediment that prevents firms from entering a market.

One issue the standard model of monopoly hides is: What prevents other firms from entering the monopolist's market? You should be able to answer that question relatively quickly. If a monopolist exists, it must exist due to some type of **barrier to entry** (a social, political, or economic impediment that prevents firms from entering the market). Three important barriers to entry are natural ability, increasing returns to scale, and government restrictions. In the absence of barriers to entry, the monopoly would face competition from other firms, which would erode its monopoly.

This recognition is one of the main reasons why economists generally support free international trade and oppose tariffs. Tariffs are a barrier to entry to foreign firms and thus provide monopoly power to Canadian firms, allowing them to charge the consumer more than they otherwise could.

Types of Barriers to Entry and the Public's View of Monopoly

Studying how these barriers to entry are established, and what the costs of establishing them are, enriches the standard model and lets us distinguish different types of monopoly. For example, a barrier to entry might exist because a firm is better at producing a good than anyone else. It has unique qualities that make it more efficient than all other firms. The barrier to entry in this case is the firm's ability.

Such monopolies based on ability usually don't provoke the public's ire. Often in the public's mind such monopolies are "just monopolies." The standard economic model doesn't distinguish between a "just" and an "unjust" monopoly. The just/unjust distinction raises the question of whether a firm has acquired a monopoly based on its ability, or based on certain unfair positions such as initially pricing low to force competitive companies out of business but then pricing high. Many public debates over monopoly focus on such normative issues, about which the economists' standard model has nothing to say.

An alternative reason why a barrier to entry might exist is that there are significant economies of scale. If sufficiently large economies of scale exist, it would be inefficient to have two producers since if each produced half of the output, neither could take advantage of the economies of scale. Monopolies that exist because economies of scale create a barrier to entry are called **natural monopolies.** Where natural monopoly exists, the perfectly competitive solution is impossible, since average total costs are not covered where $MC = P$. Some output restriction is necessary in order for production to be feasible.

Natural monopolies Monopolies that exist because economies of scale create a barrier to entry.

Examples of natural monopolies include federal and provincial **crown corporations**—firms whose major shareholder is the government. These firms usually report to the government through a cabinet minister, who is also the chairperson of the public enterprize—although in some cases the corporation is headed by an unelected official (for example, the New Brunswick Power Commission recently named a University of New Brunswick engineering professor to be its chairman). Exhibit 8 lists the top 10 provincial and the top 10 federal crown corporations in 1994 (rated by revenue).

Crown corporation Firms whose major shareholder is a provincial or federal government.

A third reason monopolies can exist is that they're created by government. The support of laissez-faire by Classical economists such as Adam Smith and their opposition to monopoly arose in large part in reaction to those government-created monopolies, not in reaction to any formal analysis of welfare loss from monopoly.

Normative Views of Monopoly

Many laypeople's views of government-created monopoly reflect the same normative judgements that Classical economists made. Classical economists considered, and much of the lay public considers, such monopolies unfair and inconsistent with liberty. Monopolies prevent people from being free to enter whatever business they want and are undesirable on normative grounds. In this view, government-created monopolies are simply wrong.

EXHIBIT 8 Largest Federal and Provincial/Municipal Crown Corporations: 1994

	Sales ($000s)	Assets ($000s)
Federal		
Canadian National Railway Co.	$4,670,000	$7,809,000
Canada Post	4,115,554	2,612,837
The Canadian Wheat Board	3,873,441	8,858,583
Canadian Commercial Corp.	880,565	390,631
Via Rail Canada Inc.	451,113	790,351
Atomic Energy of Canada Ltd.	375,673	848,400
Canadian Broadcasting Corp.	374,410	1,582,041
Cape Breton Development Corp.	231,800	379,926
Marine Atlantic Inc.	110,439	396,083
The St. Lawrence Seaway Authority	71,876	577,770
Provincial		
Ontario Hydro	8,732,000	44,085,000
Hydro Québec	7,297,000	51,608,000
B.C. Hydro and Power Authority	2,185,000	10,453,000
Liquor Control Board of Ontario	2,054,990	201,204
Société des alcools du Québec	969,800	194,900
Manitoba Hydro	924,800	5,928,500
N.B. Power Corp.	895,667	4,358,681
Sask. Power Corp.	836,770	3,270,000
Toronto Electric Commissionairs	764,290	684,700
Sasktel	626,443	1,154,608

Source: The Financial Post 500, May 1995.

This normative argument against government-created monopoly doesn't extend to all types of government-created monopolies. The public accepts certain types of government-created monopoly that it believes have overriding social value. Examples include the provision of electric power, the sale of alcoholic beverages (in some provinces), and the licensing of certain professionals (physicians, dentists, lawyers, etc.). When you go to your dentist with a sore tooth, you can rest assured that your dentist has met some minimum standard set by the professional licensing body in conjunction with provincial and federal regulations over the provision of dental services (although much like a driver's license, they may have obtained a license to practice long, long ago). Another example is patents. A **patent** is a legal protection of a technical innovation which gives the person holding the patent a monopoly on using that innovation. To encourage research and development of new products, government gives out patents for a wide variety of innovations, such as genetic engineering, Xerox machines, and cans that can be opened without a can opener.

Patent A legal protection of a technical innovation that gives the person holding the patent a monopoly on using that innovation.

A second normative argument against monopoly is that the public doesn't like the income distributional effects of monopoly. Although, as we saw in our discussion of monopoly, monopolists do not always earn an economic profit, they often do, which means that the existence of monopoly might transfer income in a way that the public (whose normative views help determine society's policy toward monopoly) doesn't like. This distributional effect of monopoly based on normative views of who deserves income is another reason many laypeople oppose monopoly: They believe it transfers income from "deserving" consumers to "undeserving" monopolists.

A third normative reason people oppose government-created monopoly that isn't captured by the standard model of monopoly is that the possibility of government-created monopoly encourages people to spend a lot of their time in political pursuits trying to get the government to favour them with a monopoly, and less time doing "productive" things.

This third normative argument against monopoly has been integrated into the standard model of monopoly by a group of political economists called **public choice economists** (economists who integrate an economic analysis of politics with their analysis of the economy). Public choice economists argue that if the government

Public choice economists Economists who integrate an economic analysis of politics with their analysis of the economy.

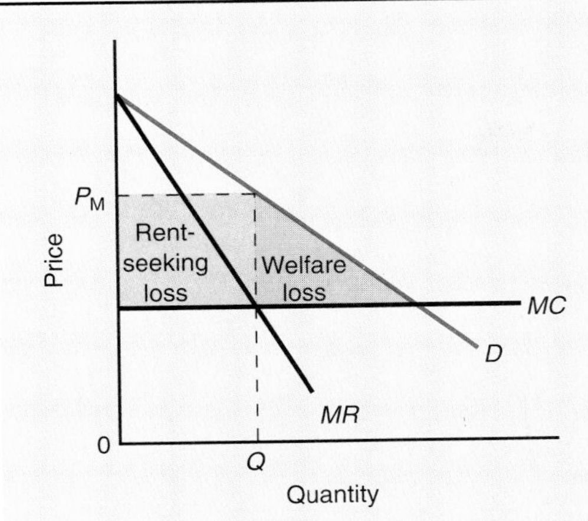

EXHIBIT 9 The Rent-Seeking Loss from Monopoly

If monopolies compete and spend money to achieve their monopoly profits, there will be an additional waste of resources to society, which will approximately equal the total expected profits. Thus rent-seeking analysis sees a second loss to society from monopoly.

doesn't charge for a monopoly, individuals will spend large amounts of money in **rent seeking** (attempting to influence the structure of economic institutions in order to create rents for themselves). They do so by lobbying and otherwise trying to persuade government to give them the monopoly. Public choice economists further argue that the resources people spend on trying to get their monopoly is a waste of resources (that's the normative judgement) and that this waste is much larger than the traditionally incurred welfare loss from monopoly. Public choice economists argue that if there is competition for monopolies, people will spend up to the total expected amount of profit from a monopoly.

Rent seeking Attempting to influence the structure of economic institutions in order to create rents for oneself.

The **rent-seeking loss from monopoly** is shown in Exhibit 9. The possible profits from monopoly create a desire for monopoly and lead potential monopolists to spend resources to gain that monopoly. The resources spent are a waste (unless they serve other purposes) and hence, according to these economists who analyze rent seeking, the welfare cost of monopoly is not only the Harberger triangle, it's also the Tullock rectangle, so-named for Gordon Tullock who first made this argument back in 1967. That **Tullock rectangle** equals the entire profit of the monopolist, and its size often dwarfs the Harberger welfare triangle. According to Tullock, monopolists spend all their profits on rent seeking.

Rent-seeking loss from monopoly Waste caused by people spending money trying to get government to give them a monopoly.

Tullock rectangle Graphical measure from monopoly that results when potential monopolists spend resources to gain monopoly. The waste equals the entire profit of the monopoly.

Each of these arguments probably plays a role in the public's dislike of monopoly. As you can see, these real-world arguments blend normative judgements with objective analysis, making it difficult to arrive at definite conclusions. Most real-world problems require this blending, making applied economic analysis difficult. The economist must interpret the normative judgements about what people want to achieve and explain how public policy can be designed to achieve those desired ends.

Let's now consider how economic theory might be used to analyze monopoly and to suggest some alternative policies. We first look at a debate about charging for monopolies. Then we look at a more specific example involving AIDS and AZT.

Should Government Charge Firms if It Gives Them a Monopoly Right?

Should the government charge for a monopoly that it gives out? One group argues that if the government charges, it will increase the monopolist's cost, and hence its price, so the government shouldn't charge. The other side's normative argument is that it's only fair to charge a monopolist. Let's now see where economists come out in this debate.

7 Economists generally favour government charging for monopolies because those charges do not raise the price the monopolist charges, and they tend to reduce the rent-seeking expenditures spent to get that monopoly.

The first question an economist will ask is how the government will charge for the monopoly. Let's say that, if it is to charge, it will auction off the monopoly right to the highest bidder. In Exhibit 10, if the expected profits are $120, we can predict that the bidding for the monopoly right will approach that $120 economic profit. (Remember, economic profit considers the entrepreneur's effort as a cost.)

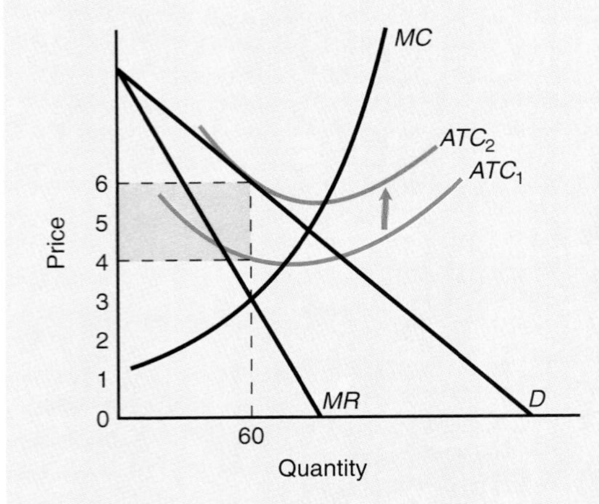

EXHIBIT 10 Selling Monopoly Rights

If the government charges a fixed fee for a monopoly, it will not affect the price, but will raise the fixed costs and hence reduce the profit (the shaded area).

Let's say a firm buys a monopoly to sell hot dogs on the highway, paying $119.99 for that monopoly. The $119.99 is a cost that some people say will push up the monopolist's price. Let's now consider how the economic model says this cost will affect the firm's decision on how many hot dogs to sell and what to charge for them. The economic model directs us to ask the following question: "What does the expenditure of $119.99 do to marginal cost or marginal revenue?" The answer is that it doesn't affect marginal cost or marginal revenue, so it doesn't affect the quantity or the price that the monopolist charges because both of those are determined only by where marginal cost and marginal revenue intersect.

What *does* it affect? It increases fixed cost (which is why the change has no effect on marginal cost), and in doing so it shifts up the average total cost curve to a point where the monopolist makes almost no profit. Thus, according to the economic model, the result of an auction for a monopoly is to transfer most of the monopoly profit from the monopolist to the government. It will not raise price and therefore, in regard to the two arguments posed at the beginning of this section, the economist would come out in favour of charging the full value for a monopoly. Charging for a monopoly has an additional advantage. To the degree that it eliminates profit from the monopoly, it reduces rent-seeking expenditures to get that monopoly. So in this case economic analysis supports charging for a monopoly, if you're going to have a monopoly.

AIDS, AZT, and Monopoly

As a final example of how knowledge of economics helps deal with real-world monopoly problems, let's consider the problem of AIDS and the medicinal drug AZT. AZT is believed to slow the onset of AIDS. The drug was developed by Burroughs Wellcome, which has a patent on it. That patent gives Burroughs Wellcome a monopoly. Patents are given on medicine to encourage firms to find cures for various diseases. The monopoly the patent gives them lets them charge a high price so that the firms can expect to make a profit from their research. Whether such patents are in the public interest isn't an issue since the patent has already been issued.

What is at issue is what to do about AZT. Currently demand for AZT is highly inelastic, so the price Burroughs Wellcome can charge is high even though its marginal cost of producing it is low. Whether Burroughs Wellcome is making a profit on AZT depends on its cost of development. But since that cost is already spent, that's irrelevant to the current marginal cost; development cost affects Burroughs Wellcome's *ATC* curve, not its marginal cost curve. Thus, Burroughs Wellcome is charging an enormously high price for a drug that may help save people's lives and that costs Burroughs Wellcome a very small amount to produce.

What, if anything, should the government do? Some people have suggested that the government come in and regulate the price Burroughs Wellcome charges, requiring the firm to charge only its marginal cost. Doing so would make the marginal cost

ADDED DIMENSION

THE WINNER'S CURSE

In the discussion about the hot dog monopoly, we were careful to specify a bid of $119.99, not $120. That still left a whole penny of economic profit. Normal profit is sufficient to keep a monopoly in a market, but, assuming a monopoly is already making a normal profit, some expected economic profit is needed to induce it to enter a new market. So some small above-normal profit has to be left to the monopolist to entice it to enter the business. Clearly a penny isn't enough, but it's enough to make the point to you: Disequilibrium adjustment from equilibrium requires the expectation of economic profit.

In real life, often there's great uncertainty about the value of a monopoly right. Individuals have differing views of what the monopoly is worth, and depending on the actual auction and the interdynamics during the bidding, the bid for a monopoly right will be higher or lower than the actual profit.

Often it's higher because of what's called the *winner's curse.* The person who wins at the auction is the person who values the monopoly right most highly, which means that the average bidder's estimate of the value of the monopoly right was lower than the amount the winner paid. If people on average are right, that means the winner paid too much and will make a loss on operating the monopoly. That's why her victory imposes the winner's curse.

of producing AZT equal to the price people pay, which would make society better off. But most economists have a problem with that policy. They point out that doing so will have significant disincentive effects on drug companies. One reason drug companies spend billions of dollars for drug research is their expectation that they'll be able to make large profits if they're successful. If drug companies expect the government to come in and take away their monopoly when they're successful, they won't search for cures. So forcing Burroughs Wellcome to charge a low price for AZT would help AIDS victims, but it would hurt people suffering from diseases that are currently being researched and that might be researched in the future in the expectation of profits. So there's a strong argument not to regulate.

But the thought of people dying when a cheap cure—or at least a partially effective treatment—is available is repulsive to us and to many others. Indeed, Burroughs Wellcome has felt the pressure and has made AZT available to HIV-positive children (children infected with the AIDS virus but not yet suffering from actual AIDS) at a much lower price than it does to others (an example of price discrimination). In 1989 it lowered the price of AZT for everyone by 20 percent.

An alternative policy suggested by economic theory is for the government to buy the patent from Burroughs Wellcome and allow anyone to make AZT so the price would approach its marginal cost. Admittedly this would be expensive. It would cause negative incentive effects, and the government would have to increase taxes to cover the buyout's costs. But this approach would avoid the problem of the regulatory approach and achieve the same ends. However, it would also introduce new problems, such as determining which patents the government should buy.

Whether such a buyout policy makes sense remains to be seen, but in debating such issues the power of the simple monopoly model becomes apparent.

CONCLUSION

We've come to the end of the presentation of the formal models of perfect competition and monopoly. Working through the models takes a lot of effort, but, as our health club instructors used to say, "No pain, no gain." In an earlier chapter, we quoted Einstein: "A theory should be as simple as possible, but not more so." This chapter's analysis isn't simple; it takes repetition, working through models, and doing thought experiments to get it down pat. But it's as simple as possible. Even so, it's extremely easy to make a foolish mistake, as one of us did in his Ph.D. oral examination when he was outlining an argument on the blackboard. ["*What* did you say the output would be for this monopolist, Mr. Colander?"] As he learned then, it takes long hours of working through the models again and again to get them right.

CHAPTER SUMMARY

- The price a monopolist charges is higher than that of a competitive market due to the restriction of output; a monopolist can make a profit in the long run.
- A monopolist's profit-maximizing output is where marginal revenue equals marginal cost.
- To determine a monopolist's profit, first determine its output (where $MC = MR$). Then determine its price and average total cost at that output level.
- A perfectly price-discriminating monopolist sells more and makes a higher profit than a normal monopolist.
- The welfare loss to society from monopoly, as measured by Harberger and others, is relatively small. Normative measures of the welfare cost can increase that loss significantly.
- The public often opposes monopoly, based on normative reasons that the economic model doesn't capture.
- Three important barriers to entry are natural ability, increasing returns to scale, and government restrictions.
- Selling rights to monopoly will eliminate profit to a degree and reduce the time and money spent on rent seeking.

KEY TERMS

barrier to entry *(229)*
consumer surplus *(224)*
crown corporation *(229)*
marginal revenue *(218)*
marginal revenue curve *(219)*
monopoly *(217)*
$MR = MC$ *(221)*
natural monopolies *(229)*
patent *(230)*
price discriminate *(223)*
public choice economists *(230)*
rent seeking *(231)*
rent-seeking loss from monopoly *(231)*
Tullock rectangle *(231)*
welfare loss triangle *(227)*

QUESTIONS FOR THOUGHT AND REVIEW

The number after each question represents the estimated degree of critical thinking required. (1 = almost none; 10 = deep thought.)

1. Demonstrate graphically the profit-maximizing positions for a perfect competitor and a monopolist. How do they differ? *(3)*
2. Monopolists differ from perfect competitors because monopolists make a profit. True or false? Why? *(4)*
3. Explain the effects on college education of the development of a teaching machine that you plug into a student's brain and that makes the student understand everything. How would your answer differ if a college could monopolize production of this machine? *(9)*
4. Say you place a lump sum tax (a tax that is treated as a fixed cost) on a monopolist. How will that affect her output and pricing decisions? *(4)*
5. A monopolist is selling fish. But if the fish don't sell, they rot. What will be the likely elasticity at the point on the demand curve at which the monopolist sets the price? *(6)*
6. Provide a price discrimination argument for the existence of the three unexplained examples of price discrimination in the text. *(6)*
7. Will the welfare loss from a monopolist with a perfectly elastic marginal cost curve be greater or less than the welfare loss from a monopolist with an upward-sloping marginal cost curve? *(5)*
8. Copyrights provide authors with a monopoly. What effect would eliminating copyrights have on the price and output of textbooks? Should copyrights be eliminated? *(8)*
9. Some authors believe that they should get a fee whenever someone borrows their books from the library. What effect would such a fee have on the price and quantity of books demanded? Why? Should such fees be charged? (8)
10. If people had to pay for monopoly, they would buy less monopoly, so the Tullock rectangle overestimates the rent-seeking loss from monopoly. True or false? Why? *(9)*

PROBLEMS AND EXERCISES

1. A monopolist with a straight-line demand curve finds that it can sell two units at $12 each or 12 units at $2 each. Its fixed cost is $20 and its marginal cost is constant at $3 per unit.
   a. Draw the *MC, ATC, MR,* and demand curves for this monopolist.
   b. At what output level would the monopolist produce?

c. At what output level would a perfectly competitive firm produce?

2. State what's wrong with the following graphs:

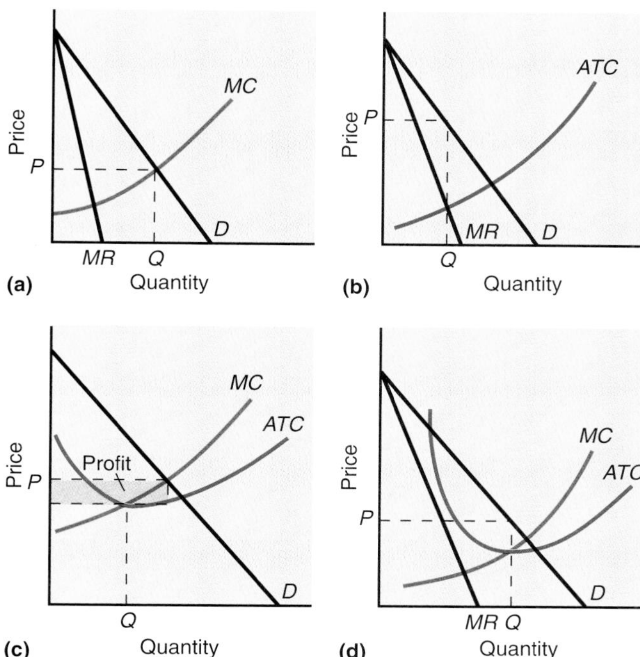

3. Wyeth-Ayerst Laboratories developed Norplant, a long-acting contraceptive, in the early 1990s. In the United States, the firm priced the contraceptive at $350, and in other countries, the firm priced it at $23.
   a. Why would the firm price it differently in different countries?
   b. Was the pricing fair?
   c. What do you think will happen to the price over time? Why?
4. Demonstrate:
   a. The welfare cost of monopoly.
   b. The rent-seeking cost of monopoly.
   c. If creating monopoly had a constant marginal cost (in other words, restricting output costs money), how would that cost affect your answer to *b*?
   d. How would your answer to *c* differ if there were a lump sum cost to creating monopoly?
5. New York City has issued 11,787 taxi licenses, called medallions, and has not changed that number since 1937.
   a. What does that limitation likely do to the price of taxi medallions?
   b. In the early 1990s, the New York City Taxi Commission promulgated a rule that required single-cab medallion owners to drive their cabs full time. What will that rule do to the price of the medallion?
   c. If New York City increased the number of medallions by 1,000, selling the additional 1,000 at the market rate, and gave half the proceeds to owners of existing medallions, what would happen to the price of medallions?
   d. What would happen to the wealth of existing medallion owners?
6. The following information relates to a monopolist:

Output *Q*	Total cost *TC*	Price *P*	Quantity demanded	*MC*	*MR*	*TR*	Profit
0	$22	$22	0				
1	26	20	1				
2	30	18	2				
3	35	15	3				
4	43	13	4				
5	53	11	5				
6	65	9	6				

   a. Complete the table.
   b. Using graph paper, plot the *MC* and *MR* curves in one diagram, and the *TC* and *TR* curves in another diagram.
   c. What is the (approximate) profit-maximizing output level?
   d. At what price (approximately) will the monopolist sell the product?
   e. What are the monopolist's profits (approximately) at the answers of *c* and *d* above?
7. The table below shows the costs and revenues of a monopolist producer of armour-plated all-terrain amphibious stretched limousines:

Quantity (limos/day)	*AR* = *P*	*TR*	*MR* ($000)	*AC*	*TC*	*MC*
1	$100			$110		
2	95			90		
3	90			80		
4	85			75		
5	80			74		
6	75			76		
7	70			81		

   a. Complete the table.
   b. At what daily output of limos will the monopolist maximize profits?
   c. How much profit will be made?
   d. If the government wanted to provide a tax (to reduce profits to 1) or a subsidy (to provide profits of 1, if the firm is making a loss), what would that fixed tax/payment be? Why?

CHAPTER 11

Monopolistic Competition, Oligopoly, and Strategic Pricing

Competition, you know, is a lot like chastity. It is widely praised, but alas, too little practiced.

~Carol Tucker

After reading this chapter, you should be able to:

1. Interpret a concentration ratio
2. List the four distinguishing characteristics of monopolistic competition.
3. Demonstrate graphically the equilibrium of a profit-maximizing monopolistic competitor.
4. Show how advertising affects the firm in monopolistic competition.
5. State why an oligopoly has a strong desire to form a cartel.
6. Explain why the contestable market theory would lead to determining competitiveness by performance rather than structure.
7. Summarize the important elements of various market structures.

As soon as economists start talking about real-world competition, market structure becomes a focus of the discussion. **Market structure** is the set of physical characteristics of the market within which firms interact. It involves the number of firms in the market, the barriers to entry, and the communication among firms. Monopoly and competition are the two polar cases of market structure that economists generally focus on. Real-world markets generally fall in between, and it is useful to introduce briefly two market structures between perfect competition and monopoly: monopolistic competition and oligopoly. They not only provide you with a sense of how the models can apply to the real world; they also help cement the concepts learned in the last chapter into your mind.

Market structure The physical characteristics of the market within which firms interact.

Perfect competition has an almost infinite number of firms; monopoly has one firm. **Monopolistic competition** and oligopoly fall between these two extremes. Monopolistic competition is a market structure in which there are many firms selling differentiated products. Because there are many firms, any one firm's decision is independent of other firms' decisions. Monopolistic competition falls closer to perfect competition; it has many firms, but not an uncountable number. **Oligopoly** is a market structure in which there are a few interdependent firms. Oligopoly falls closer to monopoly; it has only a few firms, but more than one firm. Exhibit 1 shows the spectrum of market structures, with the number of firms on the horizontal axis and market share as a percentage on the vertical axis. You should be aware that most Canadian firms fall almost entirely between perfect competition and monopoly—in oligopoly and monopolistic competition. Using precise definitions, perfectly competitive and monopolistic industries are nearly nonexistent in Canada.

Monopolistic competition A market structure in which many firms sell different products.

Oligopoly A market structure with a few independent firms.

THE PROBLEMS OF DETERMINING MARKET STRUCTURE

Any estimate of the distribution of market structures must be treated with care. Defining an industry is a complicated task—inevitably numerous arbitrary decisions must be made. Similarly, defining the relevant market of a given industry is complicated. For example, there are hundreds of banks in Canada, and banking is considered reasonably competitive. However there may be only one or two banks in a particular small town, so there will be a monopoly or oligopoly with respect to banks in that town. Is Canada, or the town, the relevant market? The same care must be taken when we think of international competition. Many firms sell in international markets and, while a group of firms may compose an oligopoly within Canada, the international market might be more accurately characterized by monopolistic competition.

Another dimension of the definitional problem concerns deciding what is to be included in an industry. If you define the industry as "the transportation industry," there are many firms. If you define it as "the automobile industry," there are fewer firms; if you define it as "the sports car industry," there are still fewer firms. Similarly with the geographic dimension of industry. There's more competition in the global market than in the local market. The narrower the definition, the fewer the firms.

Determining Industry Structure

1 A concentration ratio is the percentage of industry output that a specific number of the largest firms have.

To measure industry structure, economists look at the **concentration ratio.** It is the percentage of the total industry output that the top firms of the industry have. Concentration ratios in Canada are typically based on the largest four or the largest eight firms—these are referred to as the **four-firm concentration ratio** and the **eight-firm concentration ratio.** The higher the ratio, the closer to an oligopolistic or monopolistic type of market structure. For example, a four-firm concentration ratio of 60 tells you that the top four firms in the industry produce 60 percent of the industry's output. The classification of industries as monopolistically competitive or oligopolistic that you saw in Exhibit 1 was organized in large part around concentration ratios. If the four-firm concentration ratio was below 40 percent, the presumption was that the industry was monopolistically competitive. If the four-firm concentration ratio was between 40 and 80 percent, the presumption was that it was oligopolistic. If the four-firm concentration ratio was greater than 80 percent, the industry was considered monopolistic.

Four-firm concentration ratio The percentage of industry output of the largest four firms.

Eight-firm concentration ratio The percentage of industry output of the largest eight firms.

Exhibit 2 presents the four-firm and eight-firm concentration ratios of selected industries in Canada as of 1988. For example, you can see that the top four tobacco

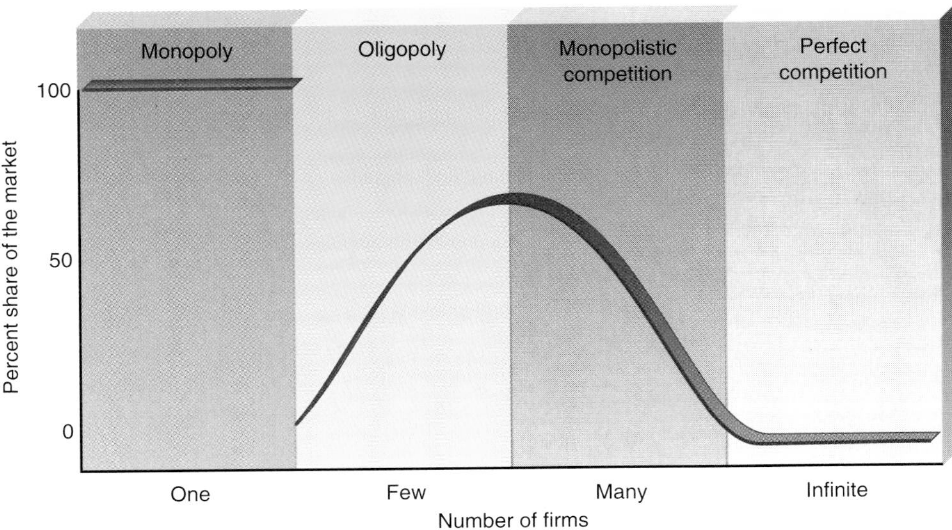

EXHIBIT 1 The Spectrum of Market Structures

There are many types of market structures, ranging from a market with one firm (monopoly) to a market with an almost infinite number of firms (perfect competition). Real-world markets generally fall between the two. Oligopoly is a market structure with a few *interdependent* firms. Monopolistic competition is a market structure in which there are more firms and their decisions are *independent*. Most industries are either oligopolistically or monopolistically competitive. Both monopoly and perfect competition are almost non-existent.

firms enjoyed almost 99 percent of total tobacco product sales in 1988. The next-largest four firms in that sector accounted for 1 percent of total tobacco product sales. At the other end of the spectrum, the top four construction firms accounted for only 2.2 percent of total construction revenues, and the next four added only an additional 1.3 percent. From this we can deduce that the tobacco products industry was monopolistic while the construction industry was monopolistically competitive.

Conglomerate Firms and Bigness

Conglomerate A large corporation whose activities span various unrelated industries.

The four-firm concentration ratio doesn't really give us a picture of a corporation's bigness. That's because many corporations are **conglomerates** (companies that span a variety of unrelated industries). For example, a conglomerate might produce both shoes and automobiles.

To see that concentration ratios are not an index of bigness, say there were only 11 firms in the entire country, each with a 9 percent share of each industry. The concentration ratio would classify the Canadian economy as reasonably competitive, but many people would seriously doubt whether that were the case. Little work has been done on classifying conglomerates or in determining whether they have any effect on an industry's competitiveness.

The Importance of Classifying Industry Structure

Now that we've talked about the classifications of industries, we need to ask why it's important to classify them in market structures such as monopolistic competition and oligopoly. The reason is that the greater the number of sellers, the greater the likelihood that an industry is competitive.

In terms of formal modelling it's important to classify industries because the number of firms in an industry plays an important role in determining whether firms explicitly take other firms' actions into account. In monopolistic competition, there are so many firms that individual firms do not explicitly take into account rival firms' likely responses to their decisions. In oligopoly there are fewer firms, and each firm explicitly takes into account other firms' expected reactions to its decisions. Taking explicit account of a rival's expected response to a decision you are making is called **strategic decision making.** In oligopolies all decisions, including pricing decisions, are strategic decisions. Thus, one distinguishes between monopolistic competition and

Strategic decision making Taking explicit account of a rival's expected response to a decision you are making.

ADDED DIMENSION

FOREIGN COMPETITIVE OLIGOPOLIES

Market structures change over time. Take, for instance, the automobile industry, which has always been used as the classic oligopoly model. Starting in the 1970s, however, foreign auto makers have made large inroads into the North American market and have added new competition to it. Foreign companies such as Honda, Nissan, and Toyota have entered the market, as seen in the accompanying pie chart which lists major automobile companies and their market shares.

As you can see, the four-firm concentration ratio is about 75 percent, so the industry is still classified as an oligopoly. GM still considers what Ford and Chrysler's reactions will be, but with the addition of foreign competition, there are getting to be too many firms for one firm to consider the reactions of all the other firms. The auto industry is becoming more monopolistically competitive.

Such change in industry structure is to be expected. Monopoly and oligopoly allow firms to make above-normal profits. Above-normal profits invite entry, and unless there are entry barriers, the result will likely be a breakdown in that monopoly or oligopoly.

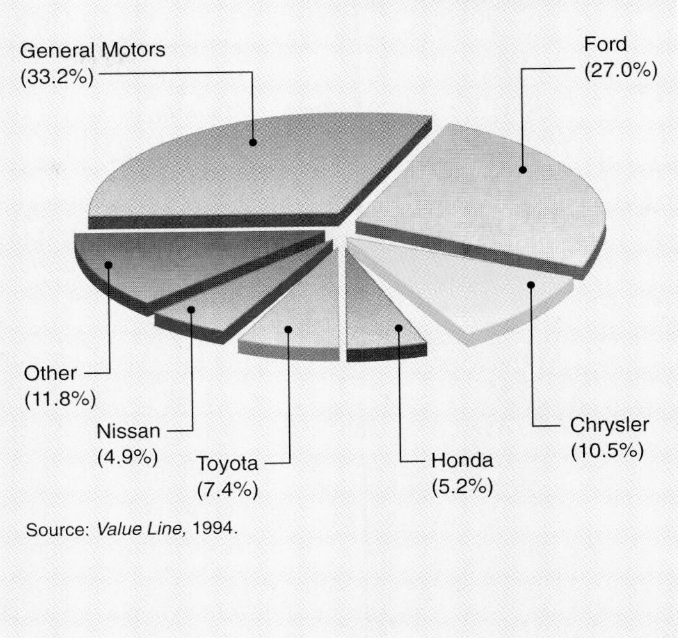

Source: *Value Line*, 1994.

EXHIBIT 2 Four- and Eight-Firm Concentration Ratios in Canada: 1988

	Percent of revenue	
Industry	Top 4	Top 8
Tobacco products	98.9%	100.0%
Petroleum and coal products	74.5	90.8
Storage	71.7	79.0
Beverages	59.2	77.6
Primary metals	63.3	76.6
Communications	64.8	76.4
Rubber products	51.2	74.5
Transport equipment	68.4	74.4
Public utilities	58.4	73.9
Metal mining	58.9	73.0
Mineral fuels	38.6	54.4
Paper and allied industries	38.9	52.6
Non-metalic mineral products	30.6	44.1
Transportation	36.4	43.3
Electrical products	32.1	40.9
Textile mills	32.5	40.9
Printing, publishing, and allied industries	25.7	37.4
Chemicals and chemical products	25.5	35.4
Finance	16.4	28.9
Food	19.6	28.7
Leather products	16.9	26.2
Wood industries	17.8	25.2
Other mining	14.1	21.9
Knitting mills	11.4	21.5
Machinery	11.3	18.6
Metal fabricating	11.4	18.1
Retail trade	9.7	14.8
Miscellaneous manufacturing	10.2	14.2
Furniture industries	7.6	13.4
Wholesale trade	7.4	12.5
Clothing industries	6.6	9.9
Services	4.5	6.9
Agriculture, forestry, and fishing	2.6	4.4
Construction	2.2	3.5

Source: *Statistics Canada* 61–210, CANSIM Database, 1993.

oligopoly by whether or not they explicitly take into account competitors' reactions to their decisions.

Why is the distinction important? Because it determines whether economists can model and predict the price and output of an industry. Nonstrategic decision making can be predicted relatively accurately if individuals behave rationally. Strategic decision making is much more difficult to predict, even if people behave rationally. Consistent with this distinction, economists' model of monopolistic competition has a definite prediction. A model of monopolistic competition will tell us: Here's how much will be produced and here's how much will be charged. Economists' model of oligopoly doesn't have a definite prediction. There are no unique price and output decisions at which an oligopoly will rationally arrive; there are a variety of rational oligopoly decisions.

MONOPOLISTIC COMPETITION

The four distinguishing characteristics of monopolistic competition are:

1. Many sellers in a highly competitive market;
2. Differentiated products, but firms still act independently;
3. Multiple dimensions of competition; and
4. Easy entry of new firms in the long run so there are no long-run profits.

Let's consider each in turn.

Many Sellers

2 Four distinguishing characteristics of monopolistic competition are:

1. Many sellers in a highly competitive market;
2. Differentiated products, but firms still act independently.
3. Multiple dimensions of competition; and
4. Easy entry of new firms in the long run so there are no long-run profits.

When there are a few sellers, it's reasonable to explicitly take into account your competitors' reactions to the price you set. When there are many sellers, it isn't. In monopolistic competition one doesn't take into account rivals' reactions. Here's an example. There are many types of soap: Ivory, Irish Spring, Zest, and so on. So when Ivory decides to run a sale, it won't spend a lot of time thinking of Zest's reaction. There are so many firms that one firm can't concern itself with the reaction of any specific firm. The soap industry is characterized by monopolistic competition. On the other hand, there are only a few major automobile firms, so when GM sets its price, it will explicitly consider what Ford's reaction may be. If GM raises its price, will Ford go along and also raise price? Or will it hold its price at its current level and try to sell its cars on the basis of lower prices? The automobile industry is an oligopoly.

The fact that there are many sellers in monopolistic competition also makes collusion difficult since, when there are many firms, getting all of them to act as one is difficult. Monopolistically competitive firms act independently.

Product Differentiation

The "many sellers" characteristic gives monopolistic competition its competitive aspect. Product differentiation gives it its monopolistic aspect. In a monopolistically competitive market, the goods that are sold aren't homogeneous as in perfect competition; they are differentiated slightly. Irish Spring soap is slightly different from Ivory which in turn is slightly different from Zest.

So in one sense each firm has a monopoly in the good it sells. But that monopoly is fleeting; it is based upon advertising to let people know, and to convince them, that one firm's good is different from the goods of competitors. The good may or may not really be different. Bleach differs little from one brand to another, yet buying Clorox makes many people feel "safe" that they're getting pure bleach. The authors themselves generally don't buy it; we buy generic bleach. Ketchup, on the other hand, while made from the same basic ingredients no matter what the brand, differs among types (in our view). We buy only Heinz and would never think of getting any other type—to us, other types aren't true ketchup.

Because a monopolistic competitor has some monopoly power, advertising to increase that monopoly power (and hence increase the firm's profits) makes sense as long as the marginal benefit of advertising exceeds the marginal cost. Despite the fact that their goods are similar but differentiated, to fit the monopolistically competitive model, firms must make their decisions as if they had no effect on other firms; they must not act strategically or interdependently—that would make the industry an oligopoly.

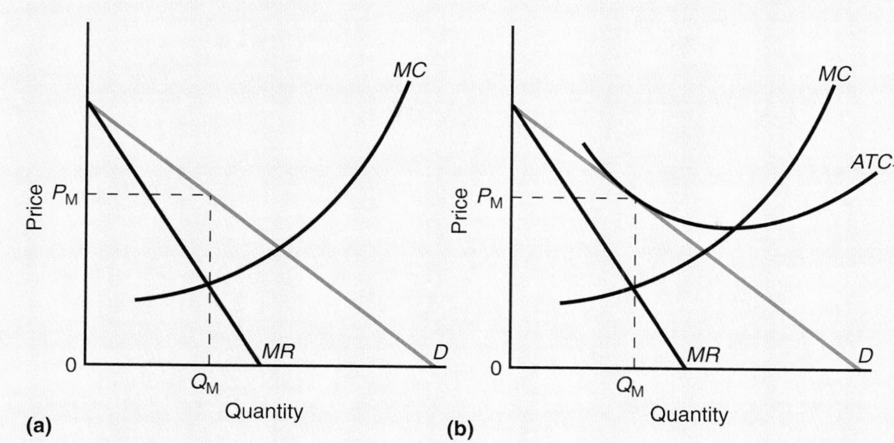

EXHIBIT 3 Monopolistic Competition

In (**a**) you can see that a monopolistically competitive firm prices in the same manner as a monopolist. It sets price where marginal revenue equals marginal cost. In (**b**) you can see that the monopolistic competitor is not only a monopolist but also a competitor. Competition implies zero economic profit in the long run. Economic profits are determined by the average total cost (*ATC*) curve. At equilibrium, *ATC* must be equal to price. It will be equal to price only if the *ATC* curve is tangent to the demand curve at the output the firm chooses.

Multiple Dimensions of Competition

In perfect competition, price is the only dimension on which firms compete; in monopolistic competition, competition takes many forms. Product differentiation reflects firms' attempt to compete on perceived quality; advertising is another form competition takes. Other dimensions of competition include service and distribution outlets. These multiple dimensions of competition make it much harder to analyze a specific industry, but these alternative methods of competition follow the same general decision rules as price competition:

- Compare marginal costs and marginal benefits; and
- Change that dimension of competition until marginal costs equal marginal benefits.

Ease of Entry of New Firms in the Long Run

The last condition for a market to be considered monopolistically competitive is that entry must be relatively easy and there must be no significant barriers to entry. The absence of barriers to entry means that there can be no long-run economic profits; in monopolistic competition if there were long-run economic profits, other firms would enter. Barriers to entry create the potential for long-run economic profit and prevent competitive pressures from pushing price down to cost. When no barriers to entry exist, firms enter until no economic profit exists.

Graphical Representation of Monopolistic Competition

3 The equilibrium of a monopolistic competitor is different from that of a perfectly competitive firm and a monopolist.

Although a full analysis of the multiple dimensions of monopolistic competition cannot be compressed into a two-dimensional graph, a good introduction can be gained by considering it within the standard graph.

To do so we simply consider the four propositions of monopolistic competition and see what implication they have for our curves. First, we recognize that the firm has some monopoly power; therefore the firm in monopolistic competition faces a downward-sloping demand curve. The downward-sloping demand curve means that in making decisions about prices, the monopolistic competitor will, as will a monopolist, use a marginal revenue curve that is below price. So at its profit-maximizing output, marginal cost will be less than price (not equal to price as it would be for a perfect competitor). We consider that case in Exhibit 3 (a).

The monopolistic competitor faces the demand curve *D,* marginal revenue curve *MR,* and marginal cost curve *MC*. This demand curve is its portion of the total market demand curve. Using the $MC = MR$ rule discussed in the last chapter, you can see that the firm will choose output level Q_M (because that's the level of output at which marginal revenue intersects marginal cost). Having determined output, we extend a dotted line up to the demand curve and see that the firm will set a price equal to P_M. This price exceeds marginal cost. So far all we've done is to reproduce the monopolist's decision.

Where does the competition come in? Competition implies zero economic profit in the long run. (If there's profit, a new competitor will enter the market, decreasing

Gasoline stations watch the competition carefully, and their prices often move together. *Michael Polselli.*

the existing firms' demand [shifting it to the left].) In long-run equilibrium a perfect competitor makes only a normal profit. Economic profits are determined by *ATC*, not by *MC*, so the competition part of monopolistic competition tells us where the average total cost must be at the long-run equilibrium output. It must be equal to price, and it will be equal to price only if the *ATC* curve is tangent to the demand curve at the output the firm chooses. We add that average total cost curve to the *MC*, *MR*, and demand curves in Exhibit 3 (b). Profit or loss, we hope you remember, is determined by the difference between price and average total cost at the quantity the firm chooses.

To give this condition a little more intuitive meaning, say, for instance, that the monopolistic competitive firm is making a profit. This profit would set two adjustments in motion. First, it would attract new entrants. Some of the firm's customers would defect and its portion of the market demand curve would decrease. Second, to try to protect its profits the firm would likely increase expenditures on product differentiation and advertising to offset that entry. (There would be an All New, Really New, Widget Campaign.) These expenditures would shift its average total cost curve up. These two adjustments would continue until the profits disappeared and the new demand curve was once again tangent to the average cost curve. A monopolistically competitive firm can make no long-run economic profit.

Comparing Monopolistic Competition with Perfect Competition

If both the monopolistic competitor and the perfect competitor make zero economic profit in the long run, it might seem that, in the long run at least, they're identical. They aren't, however. The perfect competitor perceives its demand curve as perfectly elastic, and the zero economic profit condition means that it produces at the minimum of the average total cost curve where the marginal cost curve equals price. We demonstrate that case in Exhibit 4 (a).

The monopolistic competitor faces a downward-sloping demand curve. It produces where the marginal cost curve equals the marginal revenue curve, and not where *MC* equals price. In equilibrium, price exceeds marginal cost. The average total cost curve of a monopolistic competitor is tangent to the demand curve at that output level, which cannot be at the minimum point of the average total cost curve since the demand curve is sloping downward. The minimum point of the average total cost curve (where a perfect competitor produces) is at a higher output (Q_C) than that of the monopolistic competitor (Q_M). We demonstrate the monopolistically competitive equilibrium in Exhibit 4 (b) to allow you to compare monopolistic competition with perfect competition.

As you can see, the difference between a monopolist and a monopolistic competitor is in the position of the average total cost curve in long-run equilibrium. For a monopolist, the average total cost curve can be, but need not be, at a position below price so that the monopolist makes a long-run economic profit. The average total cost curve of a monopolistic competitor must be tangent to the demand curve at the price

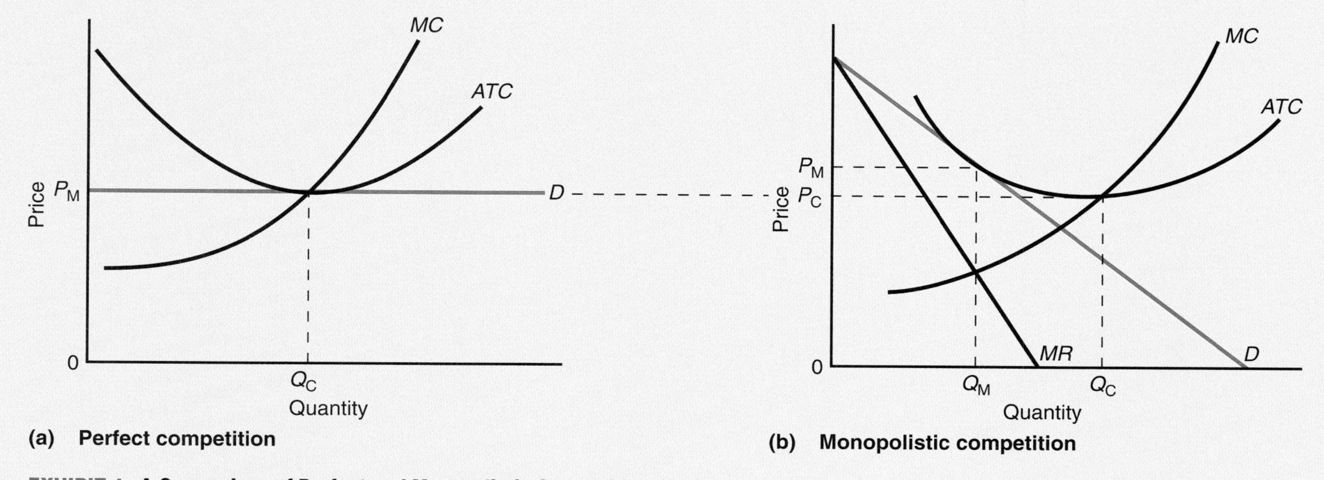

EXHIBIT 4 A Comparison of Perfect and Monopolistic Competition

The perfect competitor perceives its demand curve as perfectly elastic, and zero economic profit means that it produces at the minimum of the *ATC* curve, as represented in (**a**). A monopolistic competitor, on the other hand, faces a downward-sloping demand curve and produces where marginal cost equals marginal revenue, as represented in (**b**). The *ATC* curve is tangent to the demand curve at that level, which is *not* at the minimum point of the *ATC* curve. The monopolistic competitor produces Q_M at price P_M. A perfect competitor with the same marginal cost curve would produce Q_C at price P_C.

and output chosen by the monopolistic competitor. No long-run economic profit is possible.

The difference between a perfect competitor and a monopolistic competitor is that the perfect competitor in long-run equilibrium produces at a point where $MC = P = ATC$. At that point, ATC is at its minimum.

A monopolistic competitor produces at a point where $MC = MR$. Price is higher than marginal cost. For a monopolistic competitor in long-run equilibrium:

$$(P = ATC) \geq (MC = MR)$$

At that point, ATC is not at its minimum.

What does this distinction between a monopolistically competitive industry and a perfectly competitive industry mean in practice? It means that for a monopolistic competitor, since increasing output lowers average cost, increasing market share is a relevant concern. If only the monopolistic competitor could expand its market, it could do better. For a perfect competitor, increasing output offers no benefit in the form of lower average cost. A perfect competitor would have no concern about market share (the firm's percentage of total sales in the market).

Advertising and Monopolistic Competition

4 Advertising allows a firm to differentiate its products from those of its competitors.

While firms in a perfectly competitive market have no incentive to advertise (since they can sell all they want at the market price), monopolistic competitors have a strong incentive. That's because their products are differentiated from the others; advertising plays an important role in providing that differentiation.

A primary goal of advertising is to shift the firm's demand curve to the right to increase demand for its product. That allows the firm to sell more, to charge a higher price, or to enjoy a combination of the two. It is advantageous to the firm if the marginal revenue of advertising exceeds the marginal cost of advertising. Advertising has two effects: It shifts the demand curve out, and it shifts the average total cost curve up.

When many firms are advertising, the advertising might be done less to shift the demand curve out than to keep the demand curve where it is—to stop demanders from shifting to a competitor's product. In either case, firms advertise to move the demand curve further out than where it would be if the firms weren't advertising. Advertising

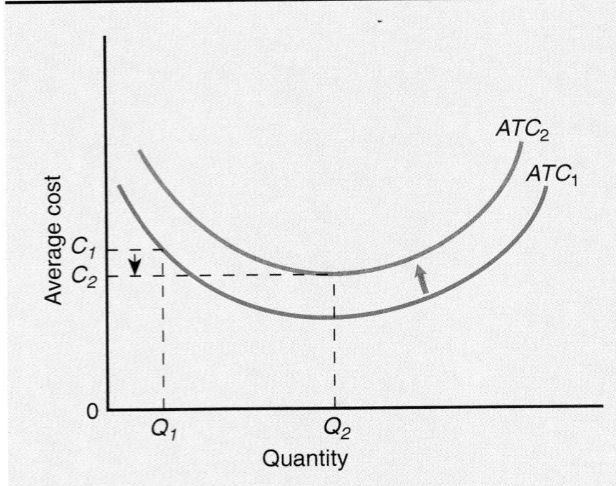

EXHIBIT 5 Advertising and Economies of Scale

Advertising shifts the average total cost curve up from ATC_1 to ATC_2, as shown here. Since more consumers hear about the product, the producer can increase output from Q_1 to Q_2. In the example, even though the average cost curve shifts up, the firm's cost per unit falls from C_1 to C_2.

is often designed to increase the firm's market share. Market share is especially important when there are economies of scale.

Advertising and Economies of Scale Advertising shifts the average total cost curve up (and under some conditions the marginal revenue and marginal cost curves too), but where there are economies of scale in production, advertising can result in lower average total costs, as Exhibit 5 shows. In it we see that advertising shifts the *ATC* curve upward from ATC_1 to ATC_2. (Advertising on television can cost over $1 million per minute.) However, since more consumers hear about the product, the firm can increase output, say from Q_1 to Q_2. In such a case, cost per unit declines from C_1 to C_2 because of economies of scale. The lower cost from economies of scale more than offsets the cost of advertising.

Does Advertising Help or Hinder Us? Our perception of products (the degree of trust we put in them) is significantly influenced by advertising. Think of the following pairs of goods:

Rolex	Timex
Cheerios	Oat Circles
Clorox bleach	generic bleach

Each of these names conveys a sense of what it is and how much trust we put in the product, and that determines how much we're willing to pay for it. For example, most people would pay more for Cheerios than for Oat Circles. Each year firms spend billions on advertising. That advertising increases firms' costs but it also differentiates their products.

Are we as consumers better off or worse off with differentiated products? That's difficult to say. There's a certain waste in much of the differentiation that occurs. It shows up in the graph by the fact that monopolistic competitors don't produce at the minimum point of their average total cost curve. But there's also a sense of trust that we get from buying names we know and in having goods that are slightly different from one another. We're sophisticated consumers who know that there's little difference between Clorox bleach and a no-name store brand of bleach, or between generic aspirin and Bayer aspirin. Yet sometimes we buy Clorox bleach and Bayer aspirin even though they cost more.

Edward Chamberlin, one of the originators of the description of monopolistic competition, believed that the difference between the cost of a perfect competitor and the cost of a monopolistic competitor was the cost of what he called "differentness."[1]

[1]About the same time as Chamberlin developed his theory of monopolistic competition, Joan Robinson, a Cambridge, England, economist, developed a theory of imperfect competition. Her theory is similar to Chamberlin's, and the two economists are generally seen as the originators of the idea.

Enormous amounts of product differentiation occur in the aggregate economy. Firms spend large amounts of money to convince people that their product is better. © *Mark Antman/The Image Works.*

If consumers are willing to pay that cost, then it's not a waste but, rather, it's a benefit to consumers.

One must be careful about drawing any implications from this analysis. Average total cost for a monopolistically competitive firm includes advertising and costs of differentiating a product. Whether we as consumers are better off with as much differentiation as we have, or whether we'd all be better off if all firms produced a generic product at a lower cost, is debatable.

OLIGOPOLY

The central element of oligopoly is that there are a small number of firms in an industry so that, in any decision it makes, each firm must take into account the expected reaction of other firms. Oligopolistic firms are mutually interdependent and therefore use strategic decision making.

Most industries in Canada have some oligopolistic elements. If you ask almost any businessperson whether he or she directly takes into account rivals' likely response, the answer you'll get is, "In certain cases, yes; in others, no."

Most retail stores that you deal with are oligopolistic in your neighbourhood or town, although by national standards they may be quite competitive. For example, how many grocery stores do you shop at? Do you think they keep track of what their competitors are doing? You bet. They keep a close eye on their competitors' prices and set their own accordingly. In fact, many times we've seen local shops "escort" some of their competitors out of the store. It seems the competition had come armed with portable computers that were being used to record prices.

Models of Oligopoly Behaviour

No single general model of oligopoly behaviour exists. The reason is that there are many possible ways in which an oligopolist can decide on pricing and output strategy, and there are no compelling grounds to characterize any of them as the oligopoly strategy. Although there are five or six formal models, we'll focus on two informal models of oligopoly behaviour that give you insight into real-world problems rather than exercise your reasoning and modelling abilities as our earlier discussion did. The two models we'll consider are the cartel model and the contestable markets model. These two models, combined with the case study of pricing by a jewelry firm should give you a sense of how real-world oligopolistic pricing takes place.

Why, you ask, can't economists develop a simple formal model of oligopoly? The reason lies in the interdependence of oligopolists. Since there are so few competitors, what one firm does specifically influences what other firms do, so an oligopolist's plan must always be a contingency or strategic plan: "If my competitors act one way, I'll do X, but if they act another way, I'll do Y." Strategic interactions have a variety of potential outcomes rather than a single outcome such as shown in the formal models we discussed. An oligopolist spends enormous amounts of time guessing what its competitors will do, and it develops a strategy of how it will act, depending on what its competitors do.

Cartel A combination of firms that acts like a single firm.

Cartel model of oligopoly Model that assumes that oligopolies act as if they were a single monopoly.

The Cartel Model A **cartel** is a combination of firms that acts as if it were a single firm; a cartel is a shared monopoly. If oligopolies can limit entry by other firms, they have a strong incentive to cartelize the industry and to act as a monopolist would, restricting output to a level that maximizes profit to the combination of firms. Thus, the **cartel model of oligopoly** is a model that assumes that oligopolies act as if they were monopolists that have assigned output quotas to individual member firms of the oligopoly so that total output is consistent with joint profit maximization. All firms follow a uniform pricing policy which serves their collective interest.

Since a monopolist makes the most profit that can be squeezed from a market, the cartelization strategy is the best an oligopoly can do. That strategy requires each oligopolist to hold its production below what would be in its own interest were it not to collude with the others. Such explicit formal collusion is against the law in Canada, but informal collusion is allowed and oligopolies have developed a variety of methods to collude implicitly. Thus, the cartel model has some relevance.

There are problems with it, however. For example, various firms' interests often differ, so it isn't clear what the collective interest of the firms in the industry is. In many cases a single firm, often the largest or dominant firm, takes the lead in pricing and output decisions, and the other firms (which are often called *fringe firms*) follow suit, even though they might have preferred to adopt a different strategy.

5 If oligopolies can limit the entry of other firms and form a cartel, they increase the profits going to the combination of firms in the cartel.

This dominant-firm cartel model works only if there are barriers to entry to the smaller firms, or the dominant firm has significantly lower cost conditions. If that were not the case, the smaller firms would pick up an increasing share of the market, eliminating the dominant firm's monopoly. An example of such a dominant firm market was the copier market in the 1960s and 1970s in which Xerox set the price and other firms followed. That copier market also shows the temporary nature of such a market. As the firms became more competitive on cost and quality, Xerox's market share fell, and it lost its dominant position. In the 1990s, the copier market is far more competitive than it used to be.

In other cases the various firms meet, sometimes only by happenstance, at the golf course or at a trade association gathering, and arrive at a collective decision. In Canada meetings for this purpose are illegal, but they do occur. In yet other cases the firms just happen to come to a collective decision, even though they have never met. Such collective decisions are known as **implicit collusion.**

Implicit collusion Multiple firms making the same pricing decisions even though they have not consulted with one another.

Implicit Price Collusion Implicit price collusion, in which firms just happen to charge the same price but didn't meet to discuss price strategy, isn't against the law. Oligopolies often operate as close to the fine edge of the law as they can. For example, many oligopolistic industries allow a price leader to set the price, and then the others follow suit. The airline and steel industries take that route. Firms just happen to charge the same price or very close to the same price.

It isn't only in major industries that you see such implicit collusion. In small towns, you'll notice that most independent carpenters charge the same price. There's no explicit collusion, but were a carpenter to offer to work for less than the others, the invisible handshake wouldn't be extended to her at morning coffee.

Or let's take another example: the fish market where sport fishermen sell their catch at the dock. When near the ocean we often go to the docks to buy fresh fish. There are, on average, about 20 stands, all charging the same price. Prices fluctuate by subtle agreement, and close to the end of the day the word goes out that prices can be reduced (usually for good reason—there's only so long a fish looks good out of water).

We got to know some of the sellers and asked them why they priced like that when it would be in their individual interest to set their own price. Their answer: "We like

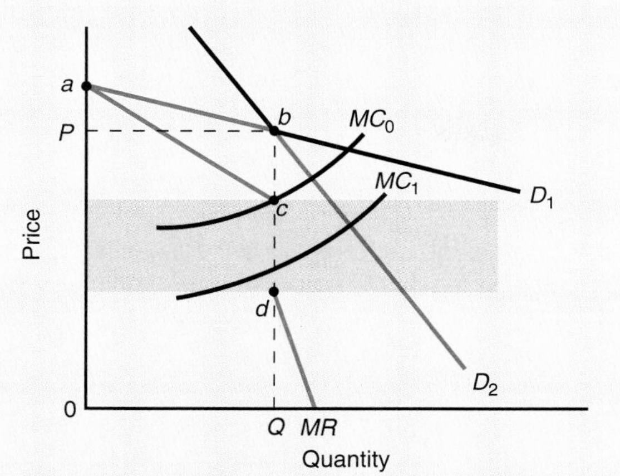

EXHIBIT 6 The Kinked Demand Curve

One explanation of why prices are sticky is that firms face a kinked demand curve. Say a firm is producing output *Q* at price *P*. If it tries to raise its price, other firms will not follow, so the demand curve is very elastic (shown by demand curve D_1). If the firm decides to decrease its price, all other firms will immediately follow suit, so demand is less elastic, as represented by demand curve D_2. To the firm, the relevant portions of D_1 and D_2 are the blue portion of D_1 and the red portion of D_2. Thus the firm's perceived demand has a kink in it. When we draw the relevant marginal revenue curve for this kinked demand we see that the corresponding *MR* curve is discontinuous. There is a gap in it. Shifts in marginal costs between c and d (the shaded area) will not change the price or the output that maximizes profits since they do not change the intersection of marginal cost and marginal revenue.

our boat and don't want it burned." They may have been talking in hyperbole, but the invisible handshake plays an important role in stabilizing prices in an oligopoly.

Cartels and Technological Change Even if all firms in the industry cooperate, other firms, unless they are prevented from doing so, can always enter the market with a technologically superior new product at the same price or with the same good at a lower price. It is important to remember that technological changes are constantly occurring, and that a successful cartel with high profits will provide incentives for significant technological change, which can eliminate demand for its monopolized product. For example, record players gave way to cassettes and cassettes are giving way to CDs. Technologies are constantly changing, and as they do, industries, and the goods produced, must change.

Why Are Prices Sticky? Informal collusion happens all the time in Canadian businesses. One characteristic of informal collusive behaviour is that prices tend to be sticky. They don't change frequently and so the existence of informal collusion is an important reason why prices are sticky. But it's not the only reason.

Another reason is that firms don't explicitly collude, but they have certain expectations of other firms' reactions, which changes their perceived demand curves. Specifically, they perceive a kinked demand curve (not kinky, but kinked) facing them. This kinked demand curve is used especially to explain why firms often do not use lower-price strategies to increase sales.

Let's go through the reasoning behind the kinked demand curve. If a firm increases its price, and the firm believes that other firms won't go along, its perceived demand curve for increasing price will be very elastic (D_1 in Exhibit 6). It will lose lots of business to the other firms that haven't raised their price. The relevant portions of its demand curve and its marginal revenue curve are shown in blue in Exhibit 6.

The kinked demand curve assumes, however, that the firm's perception of how other firms would respond if it decreased its price is different. It assumes that all other firms would immediately match that decrease, so it would gain very few, if any, additional sales. A large fall in price would result in only a small increase in sales, so its demand is very inelastic (D_2 in Exhibit 6). This inelastic portion of the demand curve and the corresponding marginal revenue curve are shown in red in Exhibit 6.

Notice that when you put these two curves together you get a rather strange demand curve (it's kinked) and an even stranger marginal revenue curve (one with a gap). We didn't make a mistake in drawing the curves; that's the way they come out given the assumptions. When there's a kink in the demand curve there has to be a gap in the marginal revenue curve.

If firms do indeed perceive their demand curves as kinked at the market price, we have another explanation of why prices tend to be sticky. Shifts in marginal cost in the shaded area (such as MC_0 to MC_1) will not change the firm's profit maximization position. A large shift in marginal cost is required before firms will change their price. Why should this be the case? The intuitive answer lies in the reason behind the kink. If the firm raises its price, other firms won't go along, so it will lose lots of market share. However, when the firm lowers price, other firms will go along and the firm won't gain market share. Thus, there are strong reasons for the firm not to change its price in either direction.

We should emphasize that the kinked demand curve is not a theory of oligopoly pricing. It does not say why the original price is what it is; the kinked demand curve is simply a theory of sticky prices.

6 In the contestable market model of oligopoly, pricing and entry decisions are based only on barriers to entry and exit, not on market structure. Thus, even if the industry contains only one firm, it could still be a competitive market if entry is open.

The Contestable Market Model A second model of oligopoly is the contestable market model. The **contestable market model** is a model of oligopoly in which barriers to entry and barriers to exit, not the structure of the industry, determine a firm's price and output decisions. Thus, it places the emphasis on entry and exit conditions, and says that the price that an oligopoly will charge will exceed the cost of production and be dependent only on the entry and exit barriers to new firms. The higher the barriers, the more the price exceeds cost. If there are no barriers to entry or exit, the price an oligopolist sets will be equivalent to the competitive price. Thus, an industry that structurally looks like an oligopoly could set highly competitive prices and output levels.

Contestable market model A model that bases pricing and output decisions on entry and exit conditions, not on market structure.

Comparison of the Contestable Market Model and the Cartel Model Because of the importance of the invisible handshake in determining strategies of oligopolies, no one "oligopolistic model" exists. The stronger the ability of oligopolies to collude (i.e., the more the invisible handshake can prevent entry), the closer to a monopolist solution the oligopoly can reach. The weaker the invisible handshake and the harder it is to prevent new entry, the closer to the competitive solution the oligopoly solution is. That's as explicit as one can be.

There are two extremes that an oligopoly model can take: (1) the cartel model in which an oligopoly sets a monopoly price; and (2) the contestable market model in which an oligopoly with no barriers to entry sets a competitive price. Thus, we can say that an oligopoly's price will be somewhere between the competitive price and the monopolistic price. Other models of oligopolies give results in between these two.

Much of what happens in oligopoly pricing is highly dependent on the specific legal structure within which firms interact. In Japan, where large firms are specifically allowed to collude, we see Japanese goods selling for a much higher price than those same Japanese goods sell for in Canada. For example, you may well pay twice as much for a Japanese television in Japan as you would in Canada. From the behaviour of Japanese firms, we get a sense of what pricing strategy Canadian oligopolists would follow in the absence of the restrictions placed on them by law.

Strategic Pricing and Oligopoly

Strategic pricing Firms set their price based upon the expected reactions of other firms.

Notice that both the cartel model and the contestable market model use **strategic pricing** decisions. They set their price based upon the expected reactions of other firms, which means that strategic pricing is a central characteristic of oligopoly.

One can see the results of strategic decision making all the time. For example, consider a firm that announces that it will not be undersold—that it will match any competitor's lower price and will even go under it. Is that a pro-competitive strategy, leading to a low price? Or is it a strategy to increase collusive information and thereby prevent other firms from breaking implicit pricing agreements? Recent work in economics suggests that it is the latter.

Let's now see how a specific consideration of strategic pricing decisions shows that the cartel model and the contestable market model are related.

New Entry as a Limit on the Cartelization Strategy One of the things that limits oligopolies from acting as a cartel is the threat from outside competition—competition from a firm that's a potential competitor but isn't part of the social network and therefore doesn't care about the invisible handshake pressure. Often this outside competitor is much larger than the firms in the oligopoly.

For example, regional financial institutions have a tendency to collude (implicitly, of course), offering lower interest to savers and charging higher interest to borrowers than institutions in large centres charge, even though their average costs aren't significantly higher. When we ask small-town credit unions, trust companies, and caisses populaires why this is, they tell us that our perceptions are faulty and that we should mind our own business. But if a big bank, which could care less about increasing the wealth of small-town financial institutions, enters the town and establishes a branch office, interest rates to savers seem to go up and interest rates to borrowers seem to go down. The big bank can add significant competition—competition that couldn't come from within the town.

On a national scale, the outside competition often comes from international firms. For example, implicit collusion among North American automobile firms led to foreign firms' entry into the North American automobile market. There are many such examples of this outside competition breaking down cartels with no barriers to entry. Thus, a cartel with no barriers to entry faces a long-run demand curve that's very elastic. This means that its price will be very close to its marginal cost and average cost. This is the same prediction that came from the contestable market theory.

Price Wars Whenever there's strategic decision making there's the possibility of a war. Price wars are the result of strategic pricing decisions gone wild. Thus, in any oligopoly it's possible that firms can enter into a price war where prices fall below average total cost.

The reasons for such wars are varied. Since oligopolistic firms know their competitors, they can personally dislike them; sometimes a firm's goal can be simply to drive a disliked competitor out of business, even if that process hurts the firm itself. Passion and anger play roles in oligopoly pricing because interpersonal and interfirm relations are important.

Alternatively, a firm might impersonally push the price down temporarily to drive the other firm out of business, whereupon it can charge an even higher price because potential entrants know that the existing firm will drive them out if they try to enter. It's this continual possibility that strategies can change that makes oligopoly prices so hard to predict.

A CASE STUDY

Once one gets to real-life situations, one sees that most pricing is done according to rules of thumb that exist in each industry. These rules of thumb base prices upon costs. Let's consider the pricing strategy of a real-world retail firm and discuss how it fits into our model.

Setting Retail Prices

Most goods go through a variety of stages before they're finally sold to you, the consumer. The good is produced by a company; then it's often sold through a wholesaler to retail outlets who sell it to you. Thus, the stages are:

$$\text{Manufacturer} \rightarrow \text{Wholesaler} \rightarrow \text{Retailer} \rightarrow \text{Consumer}$$

Manufacturers' outlet stores supposedly eliminate the wholesaler and retailer, but in fact they've become simply a new type of discount retailing.

When you talk about pricing of a retail good, you actually have to divide it up into its parts. How does the manufacturer price? How does the wholesaler price? How does the retailer price? Most of our previous discussion was mainly relevant to pricing by manufacturers. In this section we focus on pricing by wholesalers and retailers.

Neither wholesalers nor retailers have a cost of physical production. They simply buy a product and sell that same product. Their value added is their getting the product from the manufacturer to the individuals who want it.

Cost Markup Pricing

How do these firms price? Most businesses price according to rules of thumb. They add on a percentage markup over their cost to determine their selling price. These markups have evolved over time. The percentage markup is influenced by supply and demand factors so that, if entry is free, the returns to wholesaling and retailing in the long run are normal returns—enough to cover costs and wages plus a return to the firm's inputs. Thus, the markup varies considerably among industries. In supermarkets, because of high volume relative to inventory, the markup is low—often below 10 percent. In jewellery, where inventory is high relative to volume, the markup is high—60 to 100 percent. These markups aren't fixed; they change according to supply and demand pressures. If a good isn't selling, a firm will lower its markup. If a firm wants to take an aggressive expansion stance, it will lower its markup and expand its market share.

To give you an idea of how markups work, let's consider the pricing policy of a small jewellery store. It follows what's known as a *modified Hamilton markup* as shown in the following table.

Wholesale cost	Markup
0–$25	100%
$25–$50	66
$50–$100	60
$100–$200	55
$200–$300	50
$300–$1,000	40
$1,000–special order	20

Notice that the markup falls as the price rises. That's justified because direct selling cost (salesperson's time) is as high (or higher) on a $2 item as on a $200 item. Repairs, which are sent out to a jeweller who specializes in that work, are priced at cost because they bring in customers. Thus, for repairs there is no markup. New sales cover all overhead: direct and indirect costs.

While the formula markup is set, it's not fixed in stone. When wholesale prices are rising, the owner will recalculate prices on old inventory to the latest price. He'll also walk around town, looking into competitors' windows, checking their prices, and matching his prices to theirs. Notice that in doing so he's taking supply and demand into account and serving the function of an auctioneer because he knows if his goods are priced significantly higher than competitors', he'll lose sales. If his prices are lower than theirs, he'll check his markup policy to see that he hasn't made a mistake.

When goods don't sell in a year's time, he'll lower the price on them every week until they do sell. Again the forces of supply and demand are at work.

He doesn't stock expensive items (those selling for over $1,000), but he has a supplier who'll send them to him in a day. To these items he adds only a 20 percent markup because they don't contribute to his inventory costs (and this price keeps them competitive with those at the other jewellery stores in town).

He never runs a sale. He says, "It's bad for business because people will simply wait for a sale." He's disdainful of jewellery stores that do run so-called sales when what they, in fact, do is bring in a whole new set of merchandise marked up at a 250 percent rate and sell it at "half price," bringing the actual price down close to his own normal marked-up price. Such sales aren't really sales, but are simply advertising gimmicks which he feels lower the quality of the store holding the sale and hurt total sales in the long run. (Were we to ask the other stores, we'd hear a different view.) This case isn't unique. If you went to most retail stores you'd find a similar rule-of-thumb pricing procedure.

What's relevant about the markup rules of thumb that most firms use in pricing is that they aren't inconsistent with our models. The rules develop so as to reflect the forces of supply and demand, and they change over time. To understand the economy, a blend of institutional and theoretical knowledge is required.

Game theory The application of economic principles to interdependent situations.

GAME THEORY, OLIGOPOLY, AND STRATEGIC DECISION MAKING

The lack of ability to come to an explicit conclusion about what price and quantity an oligopoly will choose doesn't mean that economic reasoning and principles don't apply to oligopoly. They do. Most oligopolistic strategic decision making is carried out with the implicit or explicit use of **game theory** (the application of economic prin-

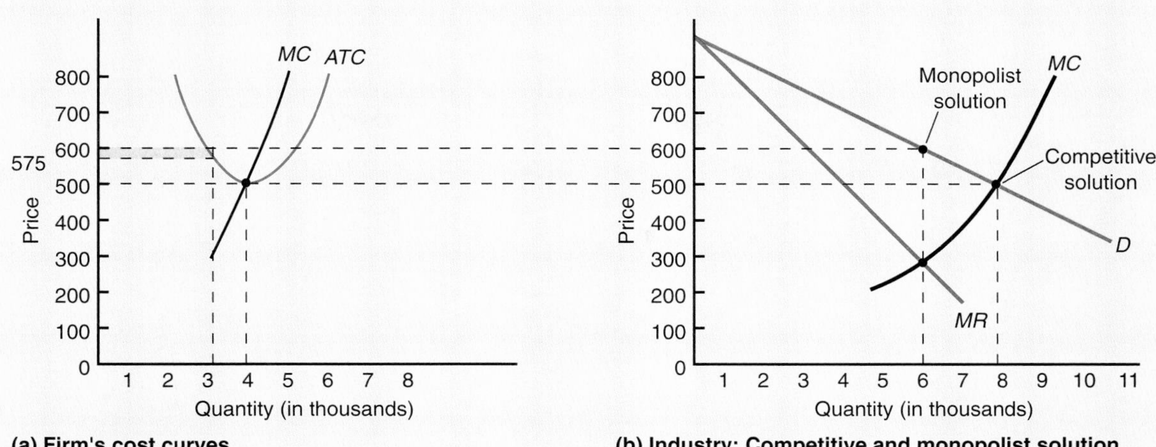

EXHIBIT 7 Firm and Industry Duopoly Cooperative Equilibrium

In (**a**) We show the marginal and average total cost curve for either firm in the duopoly. Thus to get the average and marginal cost for the industry, you double each. In (**b**) the industry marginal cost curve (the horizontal sum of the individual firms' marginal cost curves) is combined with the industry demand and marginal revenue curves. At the competitive solution for the industry, output is 8,000 and price is $500. As you can see in (**a**), at that price economic profits are zero. At the monopolist solution, output is 6,000 and price is $600. As you can see in (**a**), *ATC* are $575 at an industry output of 6,000 (firm output of 3,000), so each firm's profit is 25 x $3,000 = $75,000 (the shaded area in (**a**)).

ciples to interdependent situations). Game theory is economic reasoning applied to decision making.

To give you a sense of game theory, we'll present a well-known game called the **prisoner's dilemma** and show how game theory works. The standard prisoner's dilemma can be seen in the following example: Two suspects are caught and are interrogated separately. Each prisoner is offered the following options:

Prisoner's dilemma A well-known game that nicely demonstrates the difficulty of cooperative behaviour in certain circumstances.

> If neither prisoner confesses, each will be given a 6-month sentence on a minor charge.
>
> If one prisoner confesses and the other does not, the one who confesses will go free and the other will be given a 10-year sentence.
>
> If they both confess, they'll each get a 5-year sentence.

What strategy will they choose? If the invisible handshake is weak, and neither can count on the other not to confess, the optimal strategy (the one that maximizes expected benefits) will be for each to confess, because it is the best choice regardless of what the other does. Confessing is the rational thing for each prisoner to do. That's why it's called the *prisoner's dilemma.* Trust gets one out of the prisoner's dilemma. If the prisoners can trust one another, the optimal strategy is not to confess, and they both get only a light sentence. But trust is a hard commodity to come by without an explicit enforcement mechanism.

The prisoner's dilemma has its simplest application to oligopoly when the oligopoly consists of only two firms. So let us consider the strategic decisions facing a "foam peanut" (packing material) **duopoly**—an oligopoly with only two firms. Let us assume that the average total cost and marginal cost of producing foam peanuts are the same for both firms, and are such that only two firms can exist in the industry. These costs are shown in Exhibit 7 (a).

Duopoly An oligopoly with only two firms.

Assume that a production facility with a minimum efficient scale of 4,000 tonnes is the smallest that can be built. In Exhibit 7 (b), the marginal costs are summed and the industry demand curve is drawn in a way that the competitive price is $500 per tonne and the competitive output is 8,000 tonnes. The relevant industry marginal revenue curve is also drawn.

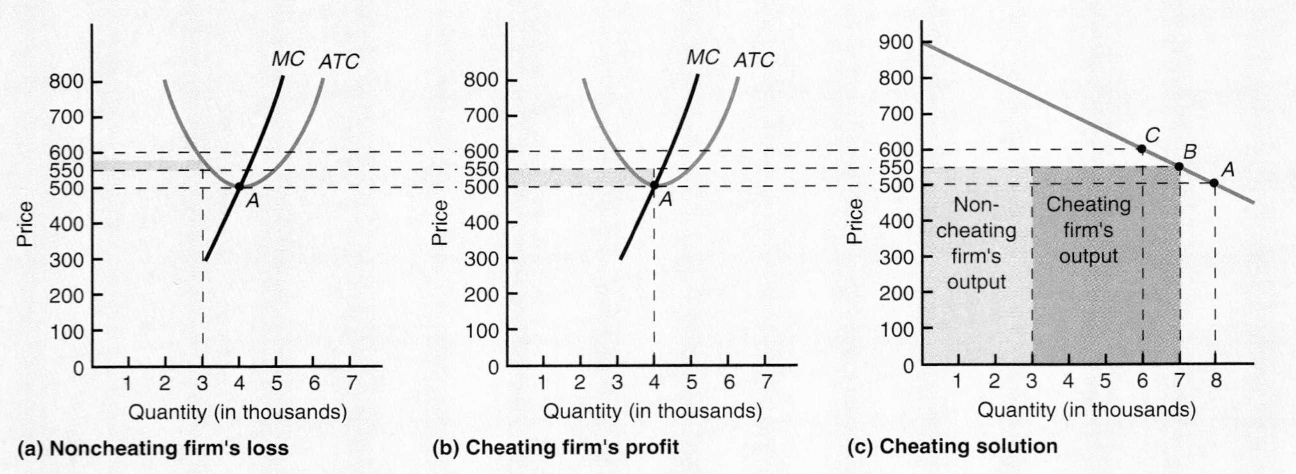

EXHIBIT 8 Firm and Industry Duopoly Equilibrium when One Firm Cheats

In this Exhibit we demonstrate the three different outcomes. Exhibits (**a**) and (**b**) show the noncheating and the cheating firm's output and profit, respectively, while (**c**) shows the industry output and price.

Say they both cheat. The price is $500 and output is 8,000 (4,000 per firm) (point *A* in (**c**)). Both firms make zero profit since their average total costs of $500 equal the price they receive.

If neither cheats, the industry output is 6,000, the price is $600, and their *ATC* is $575 as before. This outcome gives them a profit of $75,000 each and would place them at point *C* in (**c**). This outcome was considered in Exhibit 7.

If one firm cheats and the other does not, the output is 7,000 and the industry price is $550 (point *B* in (**c**)). The noncheating firm's loss is shown by the shaded area in (**a**); its costs are $575, its output is 3,000, the price it receives is $550, and its loss is $75,000. The cheating firm's profit is shown by the shaded area in (**b**). Its average total costs are $500, the price it receives is $550, and its output is 4,000, so its profit is the shaded area in (**b**)—$200,000. So if one firm is cheating, it pays to be that firm; it doesn't pay to be honest when the other firm cheats.

If there is full collusion, the firms will act as a joint monopolist setting total output at 6,000 tonnes where $MR = MC$ (3,000 tonnes each). This gives them a price of $600 with a cost of $575 per tonne, for a joint economic profit of $150,000, or $75,000 each. The firms prefer this equilibrium to the competitive equilibrium where they earn zero economic profit.

If they can ensure that they will both abide by the agreement, the monopolist output will be the joint profit maximizing output. But what if one firm cheats? What if one firm produces 4,000 tonnes (1,000 tonnes under the counter)? The additional 1,000 tonnes in output will cause the price to fall to $550 per tonne. The cheating firm's average total costs fall to $500 as its output rises to 4,000, so its profit rises to $200,000. The noncheating firm's profit moves in the opposite direction. Its average total costs remain $575, but the price it receives falls to $550, so it loses $75,000 instead of making $75,000. This gives it a large incentive to cheat also. The division of profits and output split is shown in Exhibit 8. If the noncheating firm decides to become a cheating firm, it eliminates its loss and the other firm's profit, and the duopoly moves to a zero profit position.

In Exhibit 8 (a), you can see that the firm that abides by the agreement and produces 3,000 units makes a loss of $75,000; its average total costs are $575 and the price it receives is $550. In Exhibit 8 (b) you can see that the cheating firm makes a profit of $200,000; its average costs are $500, so it is doing much better than when it did not cheat. The combined profit of the cheating and the noncheating firms is $200,000 − $75,000 = $125,000, which is lower than if they cooperated. By cheating, the firm has essentially transferred $125,000 from the other firm to itself and has reduced their combined profit by $25,000. Exhibit 8 (c) shows the output split between the two firms. If both firms cheat, the equilibrium output moves to the competitive output, 8,000, and both the firms make zero profit.

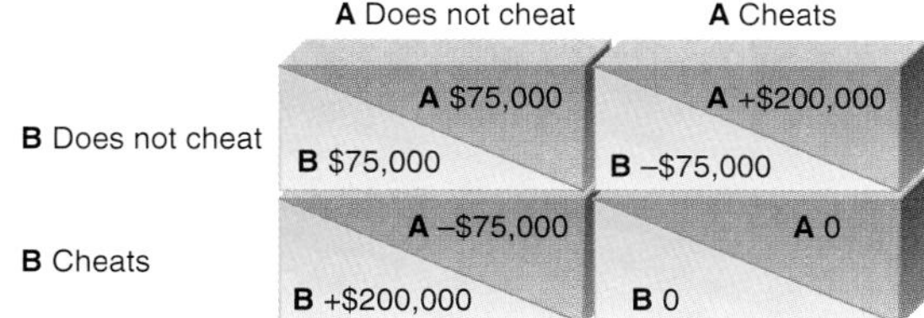

EXHIBIT 9 The Payoff Matrix of Strategic Pricing Duopoly

The strategic dilemma facing each firm in a duopoly can be shown in a payoff matrix that captures the four possible outcomes. **A**'s strategies are listed horizontally; **B**'s strategies are listed vertically. The payoffs of the combined strategies for both firms are shown in the four boxes of the matrix, with **B**'s payoff shown in the gold shaded triangles and **A**'s payoff shown in the blue shaded triangles. For example, if **A** cheats but **B** doesn't, **A** makes a profit of $200,000 but **B** loses $75,000.

Their combined optimal strategy is to cartelize and achieve the monopoly payoff, with both firms receiving a profit of $75,000. However, each must expect that if it doesn't cheat and the other does cheat, it will lose $75,000. To avoid losing that $75,000, both firms will cheat, which leads them to the payoff in the lower right hand corner—the competitive solution with zero profit for each firm.

It is precisely to provide insight into this type of strategic situation that game theory was developed. It does so by analyzing the strategies of both firms under all circumstances and placing the combinations in a **payoff matrix**—a box that contains the outcomes of a strategic game under various circumstances.

Payoff matrix A box that contains the outcomes of a strategic game under various circumstances.

The duopoly presented above is a variation of the prisoner's dilemma game. The results can be presented in a payoff matrix that captures the essence of the prisoner's dilemma discussed above. In Exhibit 9, each square shows the payoff from a pair of decisions listed in the columns and rows. The *blue* rectangles show A's profit; the *red* rectangles show B's profit. For example, if neither cheats, the result for both is shown in the upper-right-hand square, and if they both cheat, the result is shown in the lower-left-hand square.

Notice the dilemma they are in if detecting cheating is impossible. If they can't detect whether the other one cheated and each believes the other is maximizing profit, each must expect the other one to cheat. But if Firm A expects Firm B to cheat, the relevant payoffs are in the second row. Given this expectation, if Firm A doesn't cheat, it loses $75,000. So Firm A's optimal strategy is to cheat. Similarly for Firm B. If it expects Firm A to cheat, its relevant payoffs are in the second column. Firm B's optimal strategy is to cheat. But if they both cheat they end up in the lower-right-hand square with zero profit.

In reality, of course, cheating is partially detectable, and even though explicit collusion and enforceable contracts are illegal in Canada, implicit collusive contracts are not. Moreover, in markets where similar conditions hold time after time, the cooperative solution is more likely since each firm will acquire a reputation based on its past actions, and firms can retaliate against other firms who cheat. But the basic dilemma remains for firms and pushes oligopolies toward a zero-profit competitive solution.

Game Theory and Experimental Economics

Game theory has offered significant insight into the structure of economic problems but arrives at the conclusion that a number of alternative solutions are possible. A new branch of economics—**experimental economics**—has developed that offers insight into which of several results will be forthcoming. Let's consider an example.

Experimental economics A branch of economics that gains insights into economic issues by conducting controlled experiments.

When game theorists have done experiments, they have found that people believe that the others in the game will work toward a cooperative solution. Thus, when the gains from cheating are not too great, often people do not choose the individual profit-maximizing position, but instead choose a more cooperative strategy, at least initially. Such cooperative solutions tend to break down, however, as the benefits of cheating become larger. Additionally, as the number of participants gets larger, the less likely it is that the cooperative solution will be chosen and the more likely it is that competitive solutions will be chosen.

Experimental economists have also found that the structure of the game plays an important role in deciding the solution. For example, posted price markets, in which the prices are explicitly announced, are more likely to reach a collusive result than are nonposted or uncertain price markets, where actual sale prices are not known.

Oligopoly Models, Structure, and Performance

The fourfold division of markets that we've considered so far has all been based on the structure of the markets. By *structure* we mean the number, size, and interrelationship of firms in an industry. A monopoly (one firm) is the least competitive; perfectly competitive industries (an almost infinite number of firms) are the most competitive. Classification by structure is easy for students to learn and accords nicely with intuition. The cartelization model fits best with this classification system because it assumes the structure of the market (the number of firms) is directly related to the price a firm charges. It predicts that oligopolies charge higher prices than do monopolistic competitors.

The contestable market model gives far less weight to market structure. According to it, markets that look structurally highly oligopolistic could actually be highly competitive—much more so than markets that structurally look less competitive. This contestable market model view of judging markets by performance, not structure, has had many reincarnations. Close relatives of it have previously been called the *barriers-to-entry* model, the *stay-out pricing* model, and the *limit-pricing* model. These models provide a view of competition that doesn't depend on market structure.

To see the implications of the contestable market approach, let's consider an oligopoly with a four-firm concentration ratio of 60 percent. Using the structural approach we would say that, because of the multiplicity of oligopoly models, we're not quite sure what price firms in this industry would charge, but that it seems reasonable to assume that there would be some implicit collusion and that the price would be closer to a monopolist price than to a competitive price. If that same market had a four-firm concentration ratio of 30 percent, the industry would be more likely to have a competitive price.

A contestable market model advocate would disagree. She would argue that barriers to entry and exit are what's important. If no significant barriers to entry exist in the first case but significant barriers to entry exist in the second case, the second case would be more monopolistic than the first. An example is the type of fish market mentioned earlier, where there were 20 sellers (none with a large percentage of the market) and significant barriers to entry (only fishermen from the pier were allowed to sell fish there and the slots at the pier were limited). Because of those entry limitations, the pricing and output decisions would be close to the monopolistic price. If you took that same structure but had free entry, you'd get much closer to competitive decisions.

As we presented the two views, we emphasized the differences in order to make the distinction clear. However, we must also point out that there's a similarity in the two views. Often barriers to entry are the reason there are only a few firms in an industry. And when there are many firms, that suggests that there are few barriers to entry. In such situations, which make up the majority of cases, the two approaches come to the same conclusion.

CONCLUSION

7 Exhibit 10 gives a summary of the central differences among the four various market structures.

As you can see, the real world gets very complicated very quickly. We'll show you just how complicated in the next chapter. But don't let the complicated real world get you down on the theories presented here. It's precisely because the real world is so complicated that we need some framework, such as the one presented in this chapter. That framework lets us focus on specific—hopefully the most important—issues. Because the framework is so important, as a conclusion to this chapter we summarize the primary market structures in a final exhibit, Exhibit 10.

Structure / Characteristics	Monopoly	Oligopoly	Monopolistic competition	Perfect competition
Number of firms	1	Few	Many	Almost infinite
Pricing decisions	$MC = MR$	Strategic pricing, between monopoly and perfect competition	$MC = MR$	$MC = MR = P$
Output decisions	Most output restriction	Output somewhat restricted	Output restricted somewhat by product differentiation	No output restriction
Interdependence	Only firm in market, not concerned about competitors	Interdependent strategic pricing and output decision	Each firm acts independently	Each firm acts independently
Profit	Possibility of long-run economic profit	Some long-run economic profit possible	No long-run economic profit possible	No long-run economic profit possible

EXHIBIT 10 A Comparison of Various Market Structures

This table captures the central differences among various market structures.

CHAPTER SUMMARY

- Industry structures are measured by concentration ratios across four- and eight-firm levels.
- Conglomerates operate in a variety of different industries. Industry concentration measures do not assess the bigness of these conglomerates.
- In monopolistic competition, firms act independently; in an oligopoly, they take account of each other's actions.
- Monopolistic competitors differ from perfect competitors in that the former face a downward-sloping demand curve.
- A monopolistic competitor differs from a monopolist in that a monopolistic competitor makes zero long-run economic profit in long-run equilibrium.
- An oligopolist's price will be somewhere between the competitive price and the monopolistic price.
- Game theory and the prisoner's dilemma can shed light on strategic pricing decisions.
- A contestable market theory of oligopoly judges an industry's competitiveness more by performance and barriers to entry than by structure.

KEY TERMS

cartel *(246)*
cartel model of oligopoly *(246)*
concentration ratio *(237)*
conglomerate *(238)*
contestable market model (of oligopoly) *(248)*
duopoly *(251)*
eight-firm concentration ratio *(237)*
experimental economics *(253)*
four-firm concentration ratio *(237)*
game theory *(250)*
implicit collusion *(246)*
market structure *(237)*
monopolistic competition *(237)*
oligopoly *(237)*
payoff matrix *(253)*
prisoner's dilemma *(251)*
strategic decision making *(238)*
strategic pricing *(248)*

QUESTIONS FOR THOUGHT AND REVIEW

The number after each question represents the estimated degree of critical thinking required. (1 = almost none; 10 = deep thought.) Questions 1 and 2 require library research.

1. You're working for a company that buys up other companies. The company assigns you to find out whether the college textbook publishing industry is highly concentrated. Is it or isn't it? *(8)*
2. Now your company tells you to find information on the following industries: (a) light bulbs, (b) robes and nightgowns, (c) chewing gum. You do what you are asked. *(6)*
3. Which industry is more-highly concentrated: one with a four-firm concentration ratio of 55 percent or one with an eight-firm concentration ratio of 82 percent? *(6)*
4. Does the product differentiation in monopolistic competition make us better or worse off? Why? *(8)*
5. If a monopolistic competitor has a constant marginal cost of $6 and the following demand table, what output will it choose? *(5)*

Q	20	18	16	14	12	10
P	$2	$4	$6	$8	$10	$12

6. In Question 5, what will be the monopolistic competitor's average fixed cost at the output it chooses? Why? *(8)*
7. What did Adam Smith mean when he wrote, "Seldom do businessmen of the same trade get together but that it results in some detriment to the general public"? *(6)*
8. Private schools of the same calibre generally charge roughly the same tuition. Would you characterize these colleges as a cartel type of oligopoly? *(9)*
9. What are some of the barriers to entry in the restaurant industry? In the automobile industry? *(5)*
10. Describe a situation you have faced in your lifetime which can be characterized as a prisoner's dilemma situation. *(7)*

PROBLEMS AND EXERCISES

1. A firm is convinced that if it lowers its price, no other firm in the industry will change price; however, it believes that if it raises its price, all other firms will match its increase. The current price is $8 and its marginal cost is constant at $8.
   a. Sketch the general shape of the firm's *MR*, *MC*, and demand curves.
   b. If the marginal cost falls to $6, what would you predict would happen to price?
   c. If the marginal cost rises to $10, what would you predict would happen to price?
   d. Do a survey of five or six firms in your area. Ask them how they believe other firms would respond to their increasing and decreasing price. Based on that survey, discuss the relevance of this kinked demand model compared to the one presented in the book.
2. You're the manager of a firm that has constant marginal cost of $6. Fixed cost is zero. The market structure is monopolistically competitive. You're faced with the following demand curve:

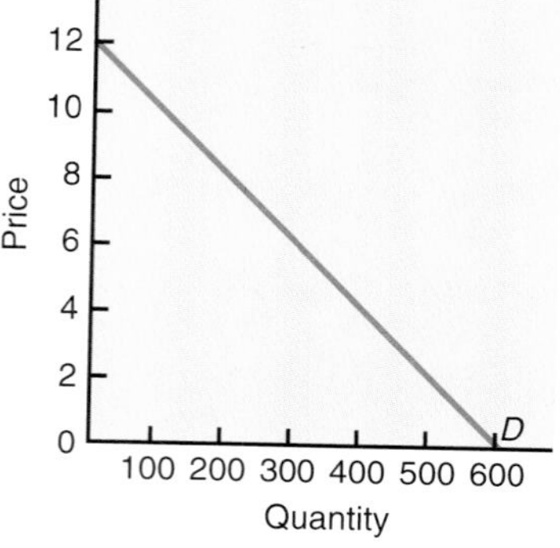

   a. Determine graphically the profit-maximizing price and output for your firm in the short run. Demonstrate what profit or loss you'll be making.
   b. Do the same for the long run.
   c. Thanks to a technological innovation, you have zero marginal cost. Demonstrate the new profit-maximizing price and output in the short run. Demonstrate graphically the short-run profit at that new profit-maximizing output.
3. Suppose the pizza market is divided as follows:

Pizza Hut	20.7%
Pizza Twice	17.0
McDonald's	6.7
Pizza Inn	2.2
Pizza Delight	2.0
All others	51.4

   a. How would you describe its market structure?
   b. What is the 4-firm concentration ratio?
4. Suppose Klondyck Airlines was experiencing difficulties, so its CEO called the CEO of its major rival, Great White North Air, and said, "Raise your prices 20 percent and I'll raise ours the next morning."
   a. Why would he make this suggestion?
   b. If you were the chairman of Great White North Air, would you have gone along?
   c. Why should the chairman of Klondyck Airlines not have done this?
5. Two firms, TwiddleDee and TwiddleDum, make up the entire market for wodgets. They have identical costs. They are currently colluding and are making $2 million each. TwiddleDee has a new CEO, Mr. Notsonice, who is considering cheating. He has been informed by his able assis-

tant that if he cheats he can increase the firm's profit to $3 million, but that cheating will reduce TwiddleDum's profit to $1 million. You have been hired to advise Mr. Notsonice.

a. Construct a payoff matrix for him that captures the essence of the decision.

b. If the game is only played once, what strategy would you advise?

c. How would your answer to *b* change if the game were to be played many times?

d. What change in the profit made when colluding (currently $2 million) would be needed to change your advice in *b*?

6. Say that in 1995, the infant/preschool toy market four-firm concentration ratio was 72 percent. Assume that with 8 percent of the market, Mattel was the fourth-largest firm in that market, and that Fisher Price was the market leader with 27 percent. Now say that Mattel is wondering whether to buy Fisher Price and has hired you as a consultant. Your assignment is to help Mattel decide by answering questions *a* through *d*.

a. Why would Mattel want to buy Fisher Price?

b. What arguments can you think of in favour of making this acquisition?

c. What arguments can you think of against making this acquisition?

d. How do you think the four-firm concentration ratio for the entire toy industry would compare to this infant/preschool toy market concentration ratio?

CHAPTER 12

Competition in the Real World

It is ridiculous to call this an industry. This is rat eat rat; dog eat dog. I'll kill 'em, and I'm going to kill 'em before they kill me. You're talking about the . . . survival of the fittest.

~Ray Kroc (founder of McDonald's)

After reading this chapter, you should be able to:

1. Define the monitoring problem and state its implications for economics.
2. Explain how corporate takeovers can improve firms' efficiency.
3. Discuss why competition should be seen as a process, not a state.
4. Show graphically what a natural monopoly is.
5. List three ways in which firms protect their monopoly.

In earlier chapters we've seen some nice, neat models, but as we discussed in the last chapter, these models don't fit reality directly. Real-world markets aren't perfectly monopolistic; they aren't perfectly competitive either. They're somewhere between the two. The monopolistic competition and oligopoly models in that last chapter come closer to reality and provide some important insights into the "in-between" markets, but, like any abstract discussion, they, too, lose dimensions of the real-world problem. In this chapter we remedy that shortcoming and give you a sense of what real-world firms, markets, and competition are like.

THE GOALS OF REAL-WORLD FIRMS

Maybe the best place to start is with the assumption that firms are profit maximizers. There's a certain reasonableness to this assumption; firms definitely are concerned about profit, but are they trying to maximize profit? The answer is: It depends.

The first insight is that if firms are profit maximizers, they aren't just concerned with short-run profit; most are concerned with long-run profit. Thus, even if they can, they may not take full advantage of a potential monopolistic situation now, in order to strengthen their long-run position. For example, many stores have liberal return policies: "If you don't like it, you can return it for a full refund." Similarly, many firms spend millions of dollars improving their reputations. Most firms want to be known as "good citizens." Such expenditures on reputation and goodwill can increase long-run profit, but reduce short-run profit. These policies are inconsistent with short-run profit maximization; they aren't inconsistent with long-run profit or wealth maximization.

The Problem with Profit Maximization

A second insight into how real-world firms differ from the model is that the decision makers' income is often a cost of the firm. Most real-world production doesn't take place in owner-operated businesses; it takes place in large corporations with eight or nine levels of management, thousands of shareholders whose stock is often held in trust for them, and a board of directors, chosen by management, overseeing the company by meeting two or three times a year. Signing a proxy statement is as close as most shareowners get to directing "their company" to maximize profit.

Why is the structure of the firm important to the analysis? Because economic theory tells us that, unless someone is seeing to it that they do, self-interested decision makers have little incentive to hold down their pay. But their pay is a cost of the firm. And if their pay isn't held down, the firm's profit will be lower than otherwise. Most firms manage to put some pressure on managers to make at least a predesignated level of profit. (If you ask managers, they'll tell you that they face enormous pressure.) So the profit motive certainly plays a role—but to say that profit plays a role is not to say that firms maximize profit. Having dealt with many companies, we'll go out on a limb and say that there are enormous wastes and inefficiencies in many Canadian businesses.

This structure presents a problem in applying the model to the real world. The general economic model assumes individuals are utility maximizers—that they're self-seeking. Then, in the standard model of the firm, the assumption is made that firms, composed of self-seeking individuals, are profit-seeking firms, without explaining how self-seeking individuals who manage real-world corporations will find it in their interest to maximize profit for the firm. Economists recognize this problem; it's an example of the **monitoring problem** introduced in an earlier chapter.

1 The monitoring problem is that employees' incentives differ from the owner's incentives. Because monitoring these employees is expensive, some economists are studying ways to change the situation.

Monitoring problem Problem that employees' incentives differ from the owner's incentives and that monitoring the employees is expensive.

The general monitoring problem is that employees' incentives differ from the owner's incentives, and it's costly to see that the employee does the owner's bidding. The monitoring problem is now a central problem focused on by economists who specialize in industrial organization. They study internal structures of firms and look for an **incentive-compatible contract** which managers can be given. An incentive-compatible contract is one in which the incentives of each of the two parties to the contract correspond as closely as possible. The incentive structure is such that the firm's goals and the manager's goals match. The specific monitoring problem relevant to firm structure is that often owners find it too costly to monitor the managers to ensure that managers do what's in the owners' interest. And self-interested managers are only

Incentive-compatible contract An agreement in which the incentives and goals of both parties match as closely as possible.

EXHIBIT 1 **Pay of Top 10 High-Level Managers, 1993**

Chief executive	Company	1993 total pay (in millions)
1. Lawrence Bloomberg	First Marathon, Inc	$6.9
2. Stephen E. Bachand	Canadian Tire Corp., Ltd.	3.2
3. Robert B. Schultz	Midland Walwyn, Inc.	2.9
4. W. Galen Weston	George Weston, Ltd.	2.1
5. Peter Munk	Horsham Corp.	1.9
6. Edgar Bronfman, Sr.	The Seagram Co., Ltd.	1.8
7. Matthew Barrett	Bank of Montreal	1.8
8. Purdy Crawford	Imasco, Ltd.	1.7
9. Edgar Bronfman, Jr.	The Seagram Co., Ltd.	1.6
10. Paul Demarais	Power Corp.	1.6

Source: *MacLean's,* May 9, 1994.

interested in maximizing the firm's profit if the structure of the firm requires them to do so.

When appropriate monitoring doesn't take place, high-level managers can pay themselves very well. Canadian managers are very well paid, as can be seen in Exhibit 1; many receive multimillion-dollar salaries. But are these multimillion-dollar salaries too high? That's a difficult question. Most of the high salaries are not pure salaries, but include stock options and bonuses for performance. There are, of course, other perspectives. When one considers what some sports, film, and music stars receive, the high salaries of Canadian managers are placed in a different light.

One way to get an idea about an answer is to compare Canadian managers' salaries with those in Japan, where the structure of control of firms is different. Banks in Japan have significant control, and they closely monitor performance. The result is that, in Japan, high-level managers on average earn much less than what their Canadian counterparts make, while wages of low-level workers are comparable to those of low-level workers in Canada. Given Japanese companies' success in competing with Canadian companies, this suggests that high managerial pay in Canada reflects a monitoring problem inherent in the structure of corporations.

What Do Real-World Firms Maximize?

If firms don't maximize profit, what do they maximize? What are their goals? The answer again is: It depends.

Real-world firms often have a set of complicated goals that reflect the organization structure and incentives built into the system. Clearly, profit is one of their goals. Firms spend a lot of time designing incentives to get managers to focus on profit.

But often other intermediate goals become the focus of firms. For example, many real-world firms focus on growth in sales; at other times they institute a cost-reduction program to increase long-run profit. At still other times they may simply take it easy and not push hard at all, enjoying the position they find themselves in—being what Joan Robinson (a British economist who studied intermediate market structures and who developed the reasoning behind marginal revenue curves) called **lazy monopolists,** a term descriptive of many, but not all, real-world corporations.

Lazy monopolist Firm that does not push for efficiency, but merely enjoys the position it is already in.

The Lazy Monopolist and X-Inefficiency

X-inefficiency Operating less efficiently than technically possible.

Lazy monopolists see to it that they make enough profit so that the stockholders aren't squealing; they don't push as hard as they can to hold their costs down. They do their jobs as inefficiently as is consistent with keeping their jobs. The result is what economists call **X-inefficiency** (firms operating far less efficiently than they could technically). Such firms have monopoly positions, but they don't make large monopoly profits. Instead, their costs rise because of inefficiency, and they simply make a normal level of profit.

The standard model avoids dealing with the monitoring problem by assuming that the owner of the firm makes all the decisions. The owners of firms who receive the profit, and only the profit, would like to see that all the firm's costs are held down.

EXHIBIT 2 True Cost Efficiency and the Lazy Monopolist

A monopolist producing efficiently would have costs C_M and would produce at price P_M and quantity Q_M. A lazy monopolist, on the other hand, would let costs rise until the minimum level of profit is reached, at C_{LM}. Profit for the monopolist is represented by the entire shaded area, whereas profit for the lazy monopolist is squeezed down to area B.

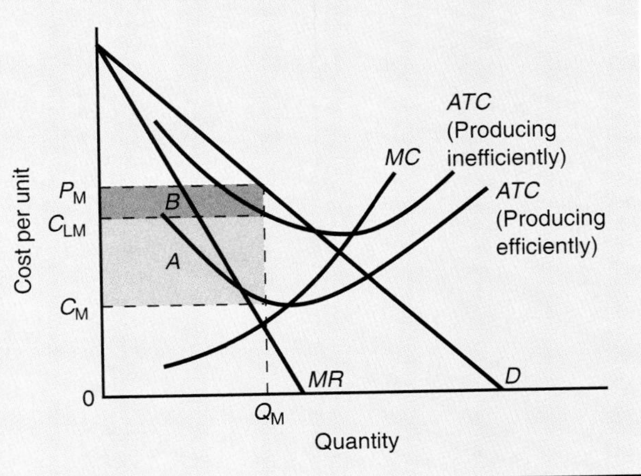

Unfortunately, very few real-world firms operate that way. In reality owners seldom make operating decisions. They hire or appoint managers to make those decisions. The managers they hire don't have that same incentive to hold costs down. Therefore it isn't surprising to many economists that managers' pay is usually high and that high-level managers see to it that they have "perks" such as chauffeurs, jet planes, ritzy offices, and assistants to do as much of their work as possible.

The equilibrium of a lazy monopolist is presented in Exhibit 2. A monopolist would produce at price P_M and quantity Q_M. Average total cost would be C_M, so the monopolist's profit would be the entire shaded rectangle (areas A and B). The lazy monopolist would allow cost to increase until the firm reached its normal level of profit. In Exhibit 2, cost rises to C_{LM}. The profit of the lazy monopolist is area B. The remainder of the potential profit is eaten up in cost inefficiencies.

What places a limit on firms' laziness is the degree of competitive pressures they face. All economic institutions must have sufficient revenue coming in to cover costs, so all economic institutions have a limit on how lazy and inefficient they can get—a limit imposed by their monopoly position. They can translate the monopoly profit into X-inefficiency, thereby benefiting the managers and workers in the firm, but once they've done so, they can't be more inefficient. They would go out of business.

How Competition Limits the Lazy Monopolist If all individuals in the industry are lazy, then laziness becomes the norm and competitive pressures don't reduce their profits. Laziness is relative, not absolute. But if a new firm comes in all gung-ho and hard working, or if an industry is opened up to international competition, the lazy monopolists can be squeezed, and they must undertake massive restructuring to make themselves competitive. Many Canadian firms have been undergoing such restructuring in order to make themselves internationally competitive.

A second way in which competitive pressure is placed on a lazy monopolist is by a **corporate takeover** in which another firm or a group of individuals issues a tender offer (that is, offers to buy up the stock of a company to gain control and to install its own managers). Usually such tender offers are financed by large amounts of debt, which means that if the takeover is successful, the firm will need to make large profits just to cover the interest payments on the debt.

Corporate takeover A firm or a group of individuals issues an offer to buy up the stock of a company to gain control and to install its own managers.

2 Corporate takeovers, or simply the threat of a takeover, can improve firms' efficiency.

Managers don't like takeovers. A takeover may mean losing their jobs and the perks that go along with the jobs, so they'll often restructure the company on their own. Such restructuring frequently means incurring large amounts of debt to finance a large payment to stockholders. These payments place more pressure on management to operate efficiently. Thus, the threat of a corporate takeover provides competitive pressure on firms to maximize profits.

Were profit not a motive at all, one would expect the lazy monopolist syndrome to take precedence. Thus, it's not surprising that nonprofit organizations often display these lazy monopolist tendencies. For example, some colleges, schools, and libraries have a number of rules and ways of doing things that, upon reflection, benefit the employees of the institution rather than the customers. At most colleges, students aren't polled as to what time they would prefer classes to meet; instead, the professors and administrators decide when they want to teach. We leave it to you to figure out whether your college exhibits these tendencies and whether you'd prefer that your college or library change to a for-profit institution. Studying these incentive-compatible problems is what management courses are all about.

Motivations for Efficiency Other than the Profit Incentive

We're not going to discuss management theory here other than to stimulate your thinking about the problem. However, we'd be remiss in presenting you this broad outline of the monitoring problem without mentioning that the drive for profit isn't the only drive that pushes for efficiency. Some individuals derive pleasure from efficiently run organizations. Such individuals don't need to be monitored. Thus, if administrators are well intentioned, they'll hold down costs even if they aren't profit maximizers. In such cases, monitoring (creating an organization and structure that gives people profit incentives) can actually reduce efficiency! It's amazing to some economists how some nonprofit organizations operate as efficiently as they do—some libraries and colleges fall into that category. Their success is built on their employees' pride in their jobs, not on their profit motive.

Most economists don't deny that such inherently efficient individuals exist, and that most people derive some pleasure from efficiency, but they believe that it's hard to maintain that push for efficiency year in, year out, when some of your colleagues are lazy monopolists enjoying the fruits of your efficiency. Most people derive some pleasure from efficiency, but, based on their observation of people's actions, economists believe that holding down costs without the profit motive takes stronger willpower than most people have.

THE FIGHT BETWEEN COMPETITIVE AND MONOPOLISTIC FIRMS

3 When competitive pressures get strong, individuals often fight back through social and political pressures. Competition is a process—a fight between the forces of monopolization and the forces of competition.

Real-world competition A fight between the forces of monopolization and the forces of competition.

Even if all the assumptions for perfect competition could hold true, it's unlikely that real-world markets would be perfectly competitive. The reason is that perfect competition assumes that individuals accept a competitive institutional structure, even though there are generally significant gains to be made by changing that structure. The simple fact is that *self-seeking individuals don't like competition for themselves* (although they do like it for others), and when competitive pressures get strong and the invisible hand's push turns to shove, individuals often shove back, using either social or political means. That's why you can only understand real-world competition if you understand how the three invisible forces (the invisible hand, foot, and handshake) push against each other to create real-world economic institutions. **Real-world competition** should be seen as a process—a fight between the forces of monopolization and the forces of competition.

How Monopolistic Forces Triumph over Perfect Competition

Let's consider some examples. During the Depression of the 1930s, competition was pushing down prices and wages. What was the result? Individuals socially condemned firms for unfair competition, and numerous laws were passed to prevent it. Unions were strengthened politically and given monopoly powers so they could resist the pressure to push down wages.

As another example, consider agricultural markets, which have many of the conditions for almost perfect competition. To our knowledge, not one country in the world allows a competitive agricultural market to exist! As you'll see in later chapters, Canada has a myriad of laws, regulations, and programs that prevent agricultural markets from working competitively. Canadian agricultural markets are characterized by price supports, acreage limitations, and quota systems. Thus, where perfectly competitive markets could exist, they aren't allowed to. An almost infinite number of other examples can be found. Our laws and social mores simply do not allow perfect competition to work because government emphasizes other social goals besides efficiency. When competition negatively affects these other goals (which may or may not be

EXHIBIT 3 Movement Away from Competitive Markets

In the case where suppliers of $0L$ can restrict suppliers of LM from entering the market, they can raise the price of the good from P_M to P_L, giving the suppliers of $0L$ area A in additional income. The suppliers kept out of the market lose area C in income. The demanders, on the other hand, lose both areas A and B, giving them strong incentive to fight collusion. Often the costs of organizing for demanders are higher than the costs for the suppliers, so demanders accept the market restrictions.

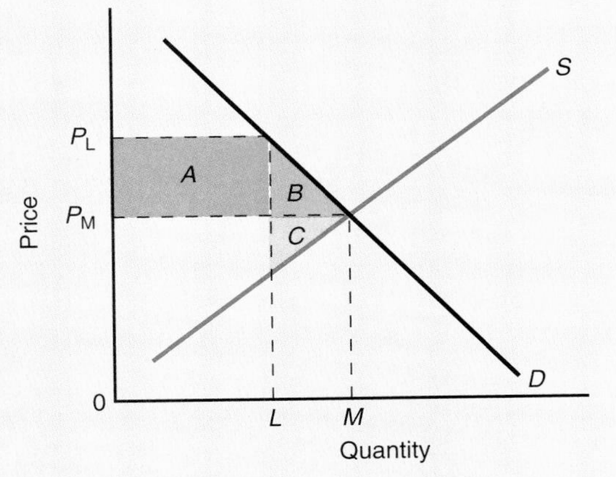

goals that most people in society hold), government prevents competition from operating.

Economic Insights and Real-World Competition

The nonexistence of perfectly competitive markets *should not* make you think that economics is irrelevant to the real world. Far from it. In fact, the movement away from perfectly competitive markets could have been predicted by economic theory!

Consider Exhibit 3. Competitive markets will exist only if suppliers or demanders don't collude. If the suppliers producing OL can get together and restrict entry, preventing suppliers who would produce LM from entering the industry, the remaining suppliers can raise their price from P_M to P_L, giving them the shaded area, A, in additional income. If the cost of their colluding and preventing entry is less than that amount, economic theory predicts that these individuals will collude. The suppliers kept out of the market lose only area C so they don't have much incentive to fight the restrictions on entry. The demanders lose the areas A plus B so they have a strong incentive to fight. However, often their cost of organizing a protest is higher than the suppliers' cost, so the demanders accept the restrictions.

Suppliers introducing restrictions on entry seldom claim that the reason for the restrictions is to increase their incomes. Usually they couch the argument for restrictions in terms of the general good but, while their reasons are debatable, the net effect of restricting entry into a market is to increase suppliers' income to the detriment of demanders. In a later chapter, we'll consider the cases of licensing doctors and lawyers as examples of such restrictions. For now, all we want to point out is that economic theory predicts that there will be strong pressures away from perfectly competitive markets in the real world.

How Competitive Forces Triumph over Monopoly

Don't think that because perfect competition doesn't exist, competition doesn't exist. In the real world, competition is fierce; the invisible hand is no weakling. It holds its own against the other invisible forces.

Competition is so strong that it makes the other extreme (perfect monopolies) as rare as perfect competition. For a monopoly to exist, other firms must be prevented from entering the market. In reality it's almost impossible to prevent entry, and therefore it's almost impossible for perfect monopoly to exist. Monopoly profits send out signals to other firms. Those signals cause competition from other firms who want to get some of that profit for themselves. To get some of that profit, they break down the monopoly through political or economic means. If the monopoly is a legal monopoly, high profit will lead potential competitors to lobby to change the law underpinning that monopoly. If the law can't be changed—say the monopolist has a **patent** (a legal right to be the sole supplier of a good)—potential competitors will generally get around the obstacle by developing a slightly different product or by working on a new technology that avoids the monopoly but satisfies the relevant need.

Patent A legal protection of a technical innovation that gives the person holding the patent a monopoly on using that innovation.

Say, for example, that you've just discovered the proverbial better mousetrap. You patent it and prepare to enjoy the life of a monopolist. But to patent your mousetrap, you must submit the technical drawings of how your better mousetrap works to the patent office. That gives all potential competitors (some of whom have better financing and already-existing distribution systems) a chance to study your idea and see if they can think of a slightly different way (a way sufficiently different to avoid being accused of infringing on your patent) to achieve the same end. They often succeed—so often, in fact, that many firms don't apply for patents on new products because the information in the patent application spells out what's unique about the product. That information can help competitors more than the monopoly provided by the patent hurts competitors. Instead many firms try to establish an initial presence in the market and rely on inertia to protect what little monopoly profit they can extract.

Going to the patent office isn't the only way competitors gather information about competing products. Firms routinely buy other firms' products, disassemble them, figure out what's special about them, and then copy them within the limits of the law. This process is called **reverse engineering.**

Reverse engineering Firm buying up other firms' products, disassembling them, figuring out what's special about them, and then copying them within the limits of the law.

Variations on reverse engineering and cloning go on in all industries. Consider the clothing industry. One firm we know of directs its secretaries to go to top department stores on their lunch hour and to buy the latest fashions that they like. The secretaries bring the clothes back and, that afternoon, the seamstresses and tailors dismantle each garment into its component parts, make a pattern of each part, and sew the original up again. The next day the secretary who chose that garment returns it to the department store, saying "I don't really like it."

Meanwhile the firm has express-mailed the patterns to its Hong Kong office, and two weeks later its shipment of garments comes in—garments that are almost, but not perfectly, identical to the ones the secretaries bought. The firm sells this shipment to other department stores at half the cost of the original.

Another example is the production of textbooks. This text (and every other text) was written only after a careful examination of all other successful—and a few of the not-so-successful—competitors. Then we got together with the publisher and tried to determine what we liked and didn't like in the competitors' books; reviewers were asked what they liked and disliked in them too. Not until we had all that information did we sit down and write this book. There were lots of things we and the reviewers didn't like in the competitors' books, so this book significantly differs from those books. But many new books are clones of existing successful books. They have similar sections and similar discussions in slightly different words. Success breeds competition.

If you ask businesspeople, they'll tell you that competition is fierce and that profit opportunities are fleeting—which is a good sign that competition does indeed exist in the Canadian economy.

Natural Monopolies and Competition

4 A natural monopoly is an industry with strong economies of scale so that average cost is continually falling. It can be demonstrated graphically that as the number of firms in a natural monopoly increases, the average cost of producing a fixed number of units also increases.

Certain industries enjoy strong economies of scale so average costs are continually falling. Such industries are called **natural monopolies** because it is less costly for one firm to operate than for more than one firm to operate. We demonstrate that in Exhibit 4.

If one firm produces Q_1, its cost per unit is C_1. If two firms each produce half that amount, $Q_{1/2}$, so that their total production is Q_1, the cost per unit will be C_2, which is significantly higher than C_1. In cases of natural monopoly, as the number of firms in the industry increases, the average cost of producing a fixed number of units increases. For example, if there were three firms in the industry and they each had a third of the market, each firm would have average cost C_3. It follows that, in the case of natural monopoly, even if a single firm makes some monopoly profit, the price it charges may still be lower than the price two firms making no profit would charge.

Fair Price Doesn't Necessarily Mean Low Price

If the natural monopoly has a relatively inelastic demand over the range of production, it will have an incentive to charge a high price (at which price the demand will no longer be inelastic) and will make substantial profit.

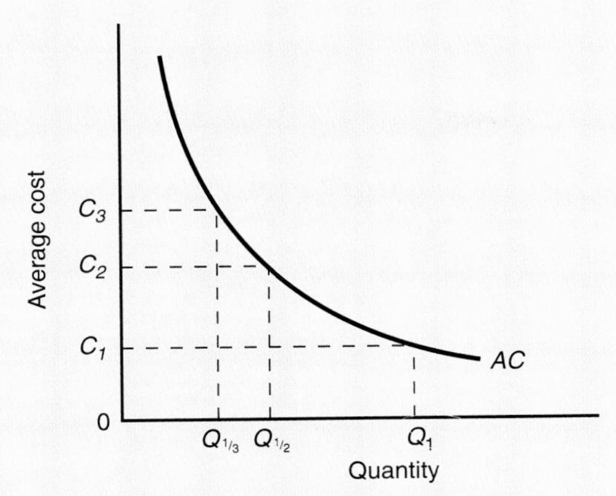

EXHIBIT 4 Efficiency and Regulation of Natural Monopolies

This graph shows the average cost curve for a natural monopoly. One firm producing Q_1 would have average cost of C_1. If total production remains at Q_1 and another firm enters the market, sharing quantity produced, each firm would produce $Q_{1/2}$ goods at average cost C_2. If three firms each produced $Q_{1/3}$, the average cost for each would be C_3. In a case of a natural monopoly, as the number of firms in the industry increases, the average cost of producing a fixed number of units increases.

Examples of natural monopoly are telephone service, cable TV provision, and electric utilities. But even in these cases of natural monopoly, competition works in other ways. High monopoly profits generate research on alternative ways of supplying the product, such as sending TV signals through electrical lines or sending phone messages by satellite. When this competition doesn't work fast enough, people direct their efforts toward government, and political pressure is brought to bear either to control the monopoly through regulation or to break up the monopoly.

Canadian Business magazine reports on business and economic trends.

In the past, the pressure to regulate these natural monopolies has been stronger than competitive pressure to lower prices. Firms have been given the exclusive right to operate in the industry but, in return, they've had to agree to have the price they charge and the services they provide regulated by regulatory boards. Regulatory boards control the price that natural monopolies charge so it will be a "fair price," which they generally define as a price that includes all costs plus a normal return on capital investment (a normal profit, but no excess profit). Most provinces have a number of regulatory boards.

When firms are allowed to pass on all cost increases to earn a normal profit on those costs, they have little or no incentive to hold down costs. In such cases, X-inefficiency develops with a passion, and such monopolies look for capital-intensive projects that will increase their rate bases. To fight such tendencies, regulatory boards must screen every cost and determine which costs are appropriate and which aren't—an almost impossible job. For example, nuclear power is an extremely capital-intensive method of producing electric power, and regulated electric companies favoured nuclear power plants until they were told that some nuclear power plant construction costs could not be passed on.

Once regulation gets so specific that it's scrutinizing every cost, the regulatory process becomes extremely bureaucratic, which itself increases the cost. Moreover to regulate effectively, the regulators must have independent information and must have a sophisticated understanding of economics, cost accounting, and engineering. Often regulatory boards are made up of volunteer laypeople who start with little expertise; they are exhausted or co-opted by the political infighting they have had to endure by the time they develop some of the expertise they need. As is often the case in economics, there's no easy answer to the problem.

Because of the problems with regulation, some economists argue that even in the case of natural monopoly, no regulation is desirable, and that society would be better off relying on direct competitive forces. They argue that regulated monopolies inevitably inflate their costs so much and are so inefficient and lazy that a monopoly right should never be granted.

How Firms Protect Their Monopolies The image we've presented of competition being engendered by profits is a useful one. It shows how a market economy adjusts to ever-changing technology and demands in the real world. Competition is a dynamic, not a static, force.

5 Firms protect their monopolies by (1) advertising and lobbying, (2) producing products as nearly unique as possible, and (3) charging low prices.

Firms do not sit idly by and accept competition. They fight it. How do monopolies fight real-world competition? By spending money on maintaining their monopoly. By advertising. By lobbying. By producing products that are difficult to copy. By not taking full advantage of their monopoly position, which means charging a low price which discourages entry. Often firms could make higher short-run profits by charging a higher price, but they forgo the short-run profits in order to strengthen their long-run position in the industry.

Firms also spend an enormous amount of money on patenting their products, and establishing trademarks that bring instant recognition to the good (see if you can think of some). It costs serious money to protect those patents. When a fly-by-night operation starts producing and selling "knock-offs"—cheap imitations of a product covered by a patent or trademark—the legal wheels start churning. That's good for lawyers (one of us has a brother who's a patent lawyer), but it's not so good for the firm. It is one of the costs of protecting a monopoly.

Cost-Benefit Analysis of Creating and Maintaining Monopolies

Preventing real-world competition costs money. Monopolies are expensive to create and maintain. Economic theory predicts that if firms have to spend money on creating and protecting their monopoly, they're going to "buy" less monopoly than if it were free. How much will they buy? They will buy monopoly until the marginal cost of monopoly equals the marginal benefit. Thus, they'll reason:

- Does it make sense for us to hire a lobbyist to fight against this law which will reduce our monopoly power? Here is the probability that a lobbyist will be effective; here is the marginal cost; and here is the marginal benefit.
- Does it make sense for us to buy this machine? If we do, we'll be the only one to have it and are likely to get this much business. Here is the marginal cost and here is the marginal benefit.
- Does it make sense for us to advertise to further our market penetration? Here are the likely various marginal benefits; here are the likely marginal costs.

COMPETITION AND STUDYING DYNAMIC ECONOMIC PROCESSES

As you can see, even in those cases where the standard models of monopoly and perfect competition don't fit reality well, the reasoning process they're meant to teach (how self-seeking individuals try to structure real-world institutions based upon a decision rule relating marginal benefit and marginal cost) is a useful way to look at many real-world problems. It provides insights and often clarifies events that would otherwise be unintelligible. That doesn't mean that it will explain everything; some people aren't self-seeking. But considering how the self-seeking view of human nature explains reality is often helpful. It's how economists look at the world.

Studying economics is an unending process. The study doesn't stop with reading the textbook. By keeping your eyes and ears open, and following the economic news, you'll find that your understanding of how real-world markets work is deepened year after year.

CHAPTER SUMMARY

- The goals of real-world firms are many. Profit plays a role, but the actual goals depend upon the incentive structure embodied in the organizational structure of the firm.
- Competition limits the amount of X-inefficiency in a firm.
- The competitive process involves a continual fight between monopolization and competition.
- In a natural monopoly, because of economies of scale it is cheaper for one firm to produce a good than for two or more firms to produce it.
- Firms protect their monopolies by such means as advertising, lobbying, and producing products that are difficult for other firms to copy.
- Firms will spend money on monopolization until the marginal cost equals the marginal benefit.

KEY TERMS

corporate takeover *(261)*
incentive-compatible contract *(259)*
lazy monopolist *(260)*
monitoring problem *(259)*
natural monopoly *(264)*
patent *(263)*
real-world competition *(262)*
reverse engineering *(264)*
X-inefficiency *(260)*

QUESTIONS FOR THOUGHT AND REVIEW

The number after each question represents the estimated degree of critical thinking required. (1 = almost none; 10 = deep thought.)

1. Are managers and high-level company officials paid high salaries because they're worth it to the firm, or because they're simply extracting profit from the company to give themselves? How would you tell whether you're correct? *(9)*
2. Some have argued that competition will eliminate X-inefficiency from firms. Will it? Why? *(7)*
3. Nonprofit colleges must be operating relatively efficiently. Otherwise for-profit colleges would develop and force existing colleges out of business. True or false? Why? *(9)*
4. If it were easier for demanders to collude than for suppliers to collude, there would often be shortages of goods. True or false? Why? *(9)*
5. If it were easier for demanders to collude than for suppliers to collude, the price of goods would be lower than the competitive price. True or false? Why? *(9)*
6. Monopolies are bad; patents give firms monopoly; therefore patents are bad. True or false? Why? *(7)*
7. Suppose Canada adopts a new health care system in which price controls are a central feature, aimed at making health care affordable. Would economists oppose such a plan? What would be their likely reasoning?
8. Natural monopolies should be broken up to improve competition. True or false? Why? *(6)*
9. Technically competent firms will succeed. True or false? Why? *(6)*

PROBLEMS AND EXERCISES

1. Econocompany is under investigation for violating competition laws. The government decides that Econocompany has a natural monopoly and that, if it is to keep its business, it must sell at a price equal to marginal cost. Econocompany says that it can't do that and hires you to explain to the government why it can't.
   a. You do so in reference to the following graph.

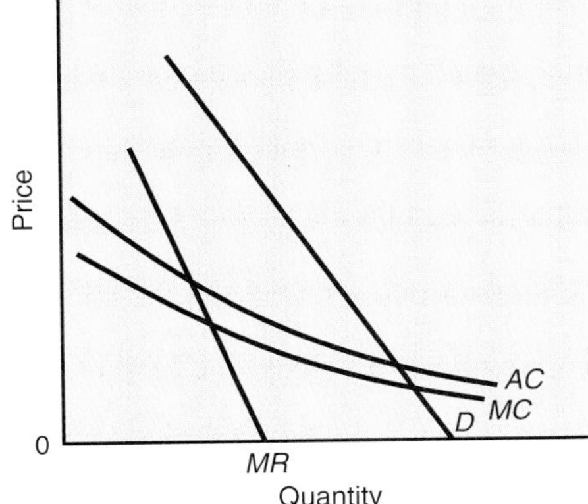

   b. What price would it charge if it were unregulated?
   c. What price would you advise that it should be allowed to charge?
2. Demonstrate graphically the net gain to producers and the net loss to consumers if suppliers are able to restrict their output to Q_r in the following graph. Demonstrate the net deadweight loss to society.

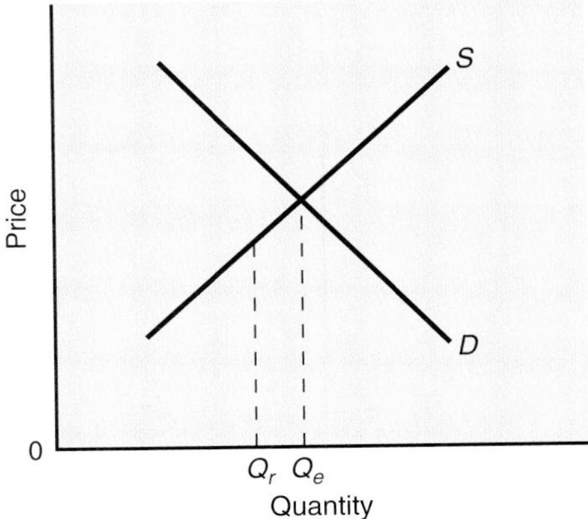

3. The title of an article in *The Wall Street Journal* was "Pricing of Products Is Still an Art, Often Having Little Link to Costs." In the article, the following cases were cited:
   - Vodka pricing: All vodkas are essentially indistinguishable—colourless, tasteless, and odourless—and the cost

of producing vodka is independent of brand name, yet prices differ substantially.

- Perfume: A $100 bottle of perfume may contain $4–$6 worth of ingredients.
- Jeans and "alligator/animal" shirts: The "plain pocket" jeans and the Lacoste knockoffs often cost 40 percent less than the brand name items, yet the knockoffs are essentially identical to the brand name items.

a. Discuss whether these differences undermine economists' analysis of pricing.

b. What do each of these examples imply about fixed costs and variable costs?

c. What do they likely imply about costs of production versus costs of selling?

d. As what type of market would you characterize each of the above examples?

4. Airlines and hotels have many frequent flier and frequent visitor programs in which individuals who fly the airline or stay at the hotel receive bonuses that are the equivalent of discounts.

   a. Give two reasons why these companies have such programs rather than simply offering lower prices.

   b. Can you give other examples of such programs?

   c. What is a likely reason why firms don't monitor these programs?

   d. Should the benefits of these programs be taxable to the recipients?

CHAPTER

13

Competition and Industrial Policies

People of the same trade seldom meet together, even for merriment and diversion, but the conversation ends in a conspiracy against the public, or in some contrivance to raise prices.

~Adam Smith

After reading this chapter, you should be able to:

1. Give a brief history of Canadian anticombines policy.
2. Discuss the three areas of anticompetitive behaviour addressed in the Competition Act of 1986: price-fixing, merger, and the "abuse of a dominant position."
3. Describe four ways of abusing a dominant position.
4. Differentiate between horizontal, vertical, and conglomerate mergers and provide several reasons why firms might want to merge.
5. Discuss seven reasons to object to a merger proposal.
6. Outline eight restrictive practices that are prohibited under the Competition Act.
7. Discuss Nationalization and Privatization.
8. Define the term *industrial policy.*
9. Give reasons for and against an activist industrial policy.

Competition policy The government's policy toward the competitive process.

Competition policy is the government's policy toward the competitive process. It's the government's rulebook for carrying out its role as referee.[1] In volleyball, for instance, a rulebook would answer such questions as: When should a foul be called? When has a person caught and thrown rather than hit the ball over the net? In business a referee is needed for such questions as: When can two companies merge? What competitive practices are legal? When is a company too big (what is big?)? To what extent is it fair (and what does that mean?) for two companies to coordinate their pricing policies? When is a market sufficiently competitive or too monopolistic? What kind of industry-specific rules—called direct regulation—should the government adopt?

Canada has seen wide swings in economists' prescriptions concerning such questions, but the dominant view today is based on "judgement by performance": we should judge the competitiveness of markets by the performance of firms in that market. That sounds easy enough, but just what constitutes the appropriate "market" and the definition of a "firm" are open to some debate. That's particularly true given the degree to which international trade affects the Canadian economy. The market concept that might be most appropriate for competition policy could span international borders; the firm under investigation could be involved in the production of many different products, only one of which is under review. These complications highlight just some of the difficulties in the regulation of competition in Canada.

Anti-combines legislation/policy Government's policy toward the competitive process.

Combine A combination of firms that acts as if it were a single firm.

To show how the Canadian government has applied the performance criterion on refereeing the economy, in this chapter we consider the government's application of anti-combines legislation to regulate business. **Anti-combines legislation** is the legislation by which the government carries out its competition policy. A **combine** is a combination of firms that acts as if it were a single firm—it's a shared monopoly and it acts to restrict output to a level that maximizes profit to the combination. After we discuss this referee function of the government, we consider how recent changes in the economy are changing the government's role as economic referee.

HISTORY OF CANADIAN ANTI-COMBINES LEGISLATION

The National Policy and Beyond

1 Canadian anti-combines policy has evolved since the late 1800s.

National Policy An 1879 policy that defined supportive roles for domestic Canadian companies within which they competed.

Protective tariffs Taxes on imports of goods similar to domestic goods aimed at sheltering domestic producers from foreign competition.

Capital intensive Methods of production that use proportionately more capital than any other factor input.

In 1879 the federal government introduced a policy called the **National Policy.** This was a policy which defined supportive rules for domestic Canadian companies within which they competed. Among other things, this National Policy created **protective tariffs**—taxes on imports of goods that are similar to domestic goods—to shelter domestically produced goods. These protective tariffs of 1879 sheltered Canadian manufacturers, located primarily in Ontario and Quebec, from cheaper products produced abroad.

The 1870s and 1880s were a period of profound economic change. Significant economies of scale followed from lower transportation costs (due to railway and seaway expansion) and the introduction of **capital intensive** production techniques—techniques using machines rather than labour. These economies of scale led to an increase in the average size of firms. Despite the decreased costs of the new technology, these large Canadian firms engaged in manufacturing were not particularly efficient, and they were not passing on the gains of increased productivity to the Canadian consumer; they didn't have to since the protective tariff all but excluded foreign imports.

These developments led both the public and politicians to reconsider the National Policy, and in 1889 the government decided that the protective tariffs were limiting needed competition to these large firms. This decision was made easier by the fact that many of these firms were foreign owned.

Revised Legislation

In 1888 a Select Committee of the House of Commons was charged with investigating the behaviour of a number of industries that appeared to exhibit restrictive business practices. By 1889 a law was passed that subsequently made it a criminal offence to limit competition. The law was the first of many that forms the legal basis of Canada's **anti-combines policy**—government's policy towards limiting monopoly,

[1]The government has two roles: it's an actor, but it's also a referee.

and regulating market structure. Specifically, that 1889 law made it a criminal offence to stifle competition by "unduly" limiting competition or "unreasonably" enhancing price. Unfortunately the wording of the Act was ambiguous and it had little effect on the way that business operated. To see the ambiguity, consider the following section:

> Every one is guilty of an indictable offence and liable to a penalty not exceeding four thousand dollars and not less than two hundred dollars, or two years imprisonment, and if a corporation is liable to a penalty not exceeding ten thousand dollars and not less than one thousand dollars, who conspires, combines, agrees or arranges with any other person, or with any railway, steamship, steamboat, or transportation company, unlawfully—
>
> (a) to unduly limit the facilities for transporting, producing, manufacturing, supplying, storing, or dealing in any article or commodity which may be a subject of trade or commerce: or—
> (b) to restrain or injure trade or commerce in relation to any such article or commodity; or—
> (c) to unduly prevent, limit, or lessen the manufacture or production of any such article or commodity, or to unreasonably enhance the price thereof; or—
> (d) to unduly prevent or lessen competition in the production, manufacture, purchase, barter, sale, transportation or supply of any such article or commodity, or in the place of insurance upon person or property.

They are strong-sounding statements, but there is enormous ambiguity about what "unduly prevents and limits" or what "unreasonably enhances" means. When a law contains such ambiguity, it's often weak in practice, and this law was no exception.

Subsequent revisions of the 1889 law led to the first Anti-Combines Act in 1910. It established procedures for investigating **restrictive business practices**—practices that prevent or make it difficult for other businesses to enter the same kinds of fields. These practices ranged from forming monopolies and mergers to other agreements that the legislation considered to be to the detriment of the public (we discuss mergers and their regulation later in this chapter). The Act was revised again in 1919; and in 1923 a permanent position was created to investigate allegations of restrictive behaviour. Changes to the Act in 1935, 1937, 1952, and 1960 led to a number of additions to the list of activities that attracted criminal charges. The 1952 revision saw the introduction of the Restrictive Trade Practices Commission to investigate complaints and provide reports.

Restrictive business practices Practices that prevent or make it difficult for other businesses to enter the same kinds of fields

Did the Anti-Combines Policy Work?

The government had very little success in court actions dealing with merger and monopoly since the burden of proof in a criminal proceeding has to satisfy "proof beyond a reasonable doubt." For other offences such as **price-fixing**—combining together with other firms and setting a uniform price—there were many convictions, since the evidence was easy to find—there were "smoking guns" everywhere. In 1976 the Act was revised to allow the regulatory authorities to take civil action against firms engaged in what were alleged to be restrictive practices, such as exclusive dealing, tied selling, and refusal-to-sell practices—practices which restrict a firm's options.

The most recent modification of Canada's anti-combines policy occurred in 1986 when the **Competition Act** was passed. This Competition Act placed "merger and monopoly" under civil law, where the standards of proof are much easier to meet than those under criminal law. Since then there have been a number of successful challenges in the courts.

We now turn to a discussion of the 1986 Act and the activities the government views as being harmful to competition.

Price-fixing Combining with other firms to set a uniform price.

Competition Act 1986 legislation setting Canadian anti-combines policy.

Competition Tribunal The body charged with adjudicating Canada's competition policy.

Prohibition orders These tell a firm that it must stop engaging in an offensive practice or risk a penalty if it does not stop.

THE 1986 COMPETITION ACT

The 1986 Competition Act included sweeping changes to the way that restrictive practices were defined, and it provided a vehicle to the authorities for intervention—the **Competition Tribunal** (which replaced the Restrictive Trade Practices Commission). The Tribunal has the power to issue **prohibition orders** and impose other remedies when adjudicating a case. Prohibition orders tell a company that it must stop engaging in the offensive practice or risk a penalty if it does not stop.

2 Three areas of anti-competitive behaviour addressed in the Competition Act of 1986 include: price-fixing, merger, and the "abuse of a dominant position".

The 1986 Act revised competition policy so that its focus was not primarily on market structure, e.g., monopoly or perfect competition. The criteria on which to intervene now rely on the concept of **anti-competitive behaviour.** This can take one of many forms: monopolistic or abusive behaviour, mergers, and restrictive practices. We will look at each of these in this chapter.

Abuse of Dominant Position

Anti-competitive behaviour Forms the basis of intervention and can be either monopolistic or abusive behavior, merger, or restrictive policies.

Abuse of a dominant position The new concept of monopolistic or abusive behaviours, it defines a number of anti-competitive acts.

3 There are four ways of abusing a dominant position.

The new concept of monopolistic or abusive behaviour involves the **abuse of a dominant position,** which defines a number of specific anti-competitive acts, including:

1. Fighting brands, which occurs when a firm has two similar goods and it provides a discount on one to capture the market and drive out competition.
2. The withholding of resources required by competitors, which might arise if a firm bought and hoarded the raw materials that their competition needed to bring their product to market.
3. The adoption of product specifications that would prevent competitors from entering the market or that would be incompatible with those of their competitors.
4. Pricing below cost in an effort to drive out the competition.

Predator A firm that attempts to drive out its competitors.

Some see these laws as anti-business. They point out that, using these definitions of anti-competitive acts, they are "damned if they do, and damned if they don't." A firm that raises price is seen as a monopolist, while one that lowers price is accused of being a **predator.** And if a firm fixes price, it is seen as colluding! Another concern is that in some cases these activities might arise as a result of "superior competitive performance"—that is, the firm may actually just be running its business in an extremely efficient manner and only taking advantage of circumstances that legally exist in the economy. A very competitive firm that aggressively seeks to enter and secure a market may be able to argue that its actions are the result of the invisible hand. Supporters of the policy point out that the Act also specifies that the Director of Investigations must show that there was intent to behave in an anti-competitive manner and that the practices under review will substantially lessen competition.

Recent Cases

Discussion of two recent cases should give you a sense of how the policy is being applied in the 1990s. In the summer of 1994 the Bureau of Competition Policy accused the A.C. Nielsen Co. of Canada Ltd. of engaging in anti-competitive behaviour through an abuse of dominant position. Nielsen's main competitor in the United States wanted to move to Canada and provide research to firms using grocery chain scanner data, but it was alleged that Nielsen's marketing research arm had control over the market-share data in the grocery sector through a network of exclusive contracts for the purchase of the scanner data. The Competition Tribunal is set to hear arguments. This action will likely take several years before it is finally concluded.

The summer of 1994 also brought a settlement in a case involving the Interac system. Interac was established in 1985, and, according to press reports, its purpose was to allow customers access to their financial accounts through a network of automated teller machines (ATMs). The founders of the system—the charter members—included six large chartered banks, a trust company, a credit union, and a caisse populaire. Other financial institutions could obtain access to the network after being sponsored by one of the charter members and paying an appropriate fee. American Express Canada Inc. and the Trust Companies Association of Canada complained of exorbitant fees to the Bureau of Competition Policy, leading to a three-year investigation. In late 1994 a settlement was imminent, but the details of the settlement were a closely guarded secret. One can be sure that part of the deal involved opening up banking machine networks to a larger number of institutions.

Policy towards Mergers

Merger The act of combining two firms.

The 1986 Act also dealt with mergers. The term **merger** is a general term meaning the combination of firms. The picture it conveys is of two firms combining to form one firm. For many mergers, that picture isn't appropriate. For example, often the firm buying another company is essentially a **shell corporation,** a structure that exists primarily to buy up other firms. When a shell corporation buys another firm, the resulting combination, while technically a merger, is called a **takeover** to emphasize that little true merging is taking place. Such takeovers change the control over the firm but do not affect market concentration.

Shell corporation A structure that exists primarily to buy up other firms.

Takeover Purchase of a firm by another firm that then takes direct control over its operations.

A term often used in place of merger is **acquisition.** In an acquisition, two firms merge by one firm buying out the other. It is a merger, but it is not a merger of equals and the acquiring firm may not take over direct control of the acquired firm's operations. In a merger of equals, neither firm takes over the other, and it's not clear who'll be in charge after the merger. Sometimes acquisitions become complicated and small companies buy up large companies.

Acquisition A company buys another company; the buyer has direct control of the resulting venture, but does not necessarily exercise that direct control.

Takeovers and acquisitions are said to be *friendly* or *hostile.* A **friendly takeover** is one in which one corporation is willing to be acquired by the other. A **hostile takeover** is one in which the firm being taken over doesn't want to be taken over. How can a hostile takeover happen? Remember our earlier discussion of corporations. Corporations are owned by shareholders, but are managed by a different group of individuals. The two groups' interests do not necessarily coincide. When it is said that a corporation doesn't want to be taken over, that means that the corporation's managers don't want the company to be taken over. In a hostile takeover the management of each corporation presents its side to the shareholders of both corporations. The shareholders of the corporation that is the takeover target ultimately decide whether or not to sell their shares. If enough shareholders sell, the takeover succeeds.

Friendly takeover When one corporation is willing to be acquired by another.

Hostile takeover A merger in which one company buys another that does not want to be bought.

In a form of hostile takeover (known as *double Pac Man*) two firms try to swallow each other; or alternatively the target of a hostile takeover bid tries to make itself unpalatable—the *poison pill* strategy. In the poison pill strategy, the firm that doesn't want to be taken over agrees before the merger to do something stupid if it's taken over so that this firm is no longer desirable to potential taking-over firms. For example, say that Stubborn, Ltd., doesn't want to be taken over. So Stubborn borrows billions of dollars and uses that money to buy some company worth about half what Stubborn pays for it. That's a stupid move. After that move Stubborn isn't a desirable firm to be taken over. (So it wasn't so stupid, right?) Of course, after Stubborn isn't taken over, it's stuck with the company it paid too much for, and it's also stuck with the interest it has to pay on the multibillion dollar loan it took out. Stubborn has provided itself with a poison pill to keep invaders away, but it has to live with the poison pill itself. (So maybe it was a stupid move after all.)

In other cases the company taking over doesn't really want to take over the other company. Instead it's hoping for *greenmail* (a payment from the potential victim to halt the takeover bid).

The specific nature of a merger is of interest to people working for the corporations involved. It determines whether employees will move up or down in the corporate pecking order, or even whether they'll keep their jobs at all. When a firm is threatened by a hostile takeover, top management is likely to hunt for another firm, a friendly one that will be a "white knight" coming to the rescue. The white knight firm, it is hoped, will keep all the management employees in their jobs. When their jobs are at stake, it is often questionable whether management searches out the firm that will pay shareholders the best price. Management's interest is likely to be in keeping their jobs, not in making money for the shareholders.

Strategies have been developed to protect shareholders from management's interest overriding shareholders' interest. One such strategy is the *golden parachute.* The board of directors of the corporation provides that if the corporation should be acquired by another corporation, people holding top management jobs are guaranteed large payments of money—as high as $40 or $50 million in some cases. This is a golden parachute. It means that management can feel comfortable when the corporation is approached by a potential buyer and will make decisions based on the shareholders' interests, not on whether management jobs will be left undisturbed.

Golden parachutes afford shareholders some assurance that if their firm receives an acquisition or takeover offer, management will consider it. Golden parachutes protect top management because either they'll keep their jobs or, if they lose their jobs, their pain will be soothed by compensation in big bucks. Golden parachutes do nothing for low-level management and ordinary workers, who may suffer demotions or layoffs after two firms have merged.

All this financial gamesmanship has led some to believe that the government should enact laws restricting takeovers because of their effect on managerial incentives. The disadvantage of takeovers for the economy is that managers spend too much time playing the takeover game and too little time overseeing the truly productive activities of the firm. But many economists oppose the passage of such legislation, arguing that fear of a takeover keeps managers on their toes—adding competitive pressure to the economy. To prevent takeovers would be to eliminate that competitive pressure.

4 Mergers can be horizontal, vertical, or conglomerate, and there are many reasons why firms might want to merge.

Horizontal merger A merger of companies in the same industry.

Vertical merger Combination of two companies, one of which supplied inputs to the other's production.

Mergers are also classified by the types of businesses that are merging. A merger of two companies in the same industry is a **horizontal merger.** This might occur when both firms recognize the efficiency gains from economies of scale in management, production, and distribution. An example would be when one apple juice producer purchases another apple juice producer. When a firm merges with the supplier of one of its inputs, that is called a **vertical merger.** The gains to this union appear obvious, but are more subtle than they appear. If you run a feed mill, a large chicken farm may want to vertically merge with your firm to reduce its costs. While you gain a stable market for your feed from the vertical merger, the operators of the chicken farm may not want you to supply your product to their competitors, or they may want you to focus exclusively on chicken feed. Any gains you perceive from the merger must be balanced against potential losses from losing effective control over your firm's activities.

Conglomerate merger Combination of unrelated businesses.

If two firms in unrelated industries merge, this is called a **conglomerate merger.** Why would two unrelated firms want to merge? Why would one want to be bought out by another? There are five general reasons:

1. *To achieve economies of scope.* Although the businesses are unrelated, some overlap is almost inevitable, so economies of scope are likely. For example, one firm's technical or marketing expertise may be helpful to the other firm, or the conglomerate's increased size may give it better bargaining power with its suppliers. One firm may also have specific assets that cannot be fully exploited in one product line—say computer software.
2. *To get a good buy.* Firms are always on the lookout for good buys. If a firm believes that another firm's stock is significantly undervalued, it can buy that stock at its low price and then sell it at a profit later when the stock is no longer undervalued.
3. *To diversify.* Many industries have a cyclical nature. In some parts of the business cycle they do poorly; in other parts of the business cycle they do just fine. Buying an unrelated company allows a firm to diversify and thereby to even out the cyclical fluctuation in its profits.
4. *To ward off a takeover bid.* Firms are always susceptible to being bought out by someone else. Sometimes they prevent an unwanted buyout by merging with another firm in order to become so large that they're indigestible. For example, in 1989 Time, Inc., merged with Warner Communications to reduce the likelihood that Time would be taken over by a third firm, Paramount.
5. *To strengthen their political-economic influence.* The bigger you are, the more influence you have. Individuals who run companies like to have and use influence. Merging can increase their net influence considerably.

5 There are at least seven reasons to object to a merger proposal.

Prenotification When a firm must advise the Director of Investigations of its intentions before its plans take place.

The number of mergers in Canada has been rising steadily, with the vast majority being between competitors—that is, horizontal mergers.

Under certain conditions, firms planning to merge must inform the Director of Investigations of their plans before they take place. This is called **prenotification** and is required when the combined Canadian assets or revenues of the merging parties

ADDED DIMENSION

WHEN A FIRM WISHES IT HADN'T MERGED

In the late 1980s Canadian Pacific (now Canadian Airlines International) and Air Canada agreed to merge their computer reservation systems into one system called Gemini. The Director of Investigations decided to act against the merger since it appeared to lessen competition. A negotiated settlement was reached, and the parties were initially content with the outcome of the merger.

Then in the early 1990s, Canadian Airlines decided they wanted to merge with American Airlines, and a necessary condition of the deal was that they dissolve their relationship with Air Canada. The first request to the Competition Tribunal was rejected, only to be appealed to the Supreme Court of Canada. The result was that Canadian Airlines has been released from the merger with Air Canada.

exceed $400 million, and if the assets or revenues of the acquired firm exceed $35 million. The 1986 Act provides a number of reasons for the Director of Investigations to object to any proposed merger. All focus on the extent to which competition may be substantially reduced as a result of the merger. They include:

1. The extent of foreign competition;
2. Whether one of the parties to the merger is "failing";
3. The availability of close substitutes;
4. The existence of barriers to entry;
5. How competitive the industry will be after the merger;
6. The likelihood that the merger would remove an effective competitor; and
7. The nature and extent of innovation in the relevant market.

There are ways around the prenotification requirement. The Director of Investigations can issue what are called **Advance Ruling Certificates,** telling the parties proposing a merger that, on the basis of the information available, the Director will not challenge the transaction. If the merger exceeds the prenotification limits, these Advance Ruling Certificates provide an exemption from the prenotification requirements.

Advance Ruling Certificates Issued by the Director of Investigations, these tell the parties proposing to merge that on the basis of available information, the merger will not be challenged.

Some Evidence on Mergers

During the first three years of the new Act, over 369 mergers were examined, and only 19 were opposed. In seven cases, plans to merge were abandoned—the other nine were able to restructure their plans to meet the objections of the Director. In 1992–93 there were 627 mergers and 238 examinations were ongoing at the end of the year. In that same period there were 101 Advance Ruling Certificates issued, 4 mergers were monitored, and 2 examinations were concluded by means of contested proceedings. Only 3 transactions were abandoned. In 1994–95 the Department budgeted for 650 merger transactions and 205 examinations.

When making a determination to allow a proposed merger to take place, the Director must consider whether the plan will improve economic efficiency. The Director can then allow the merger to take place, or allow a partial consummation of the parties' plans. For example, in 1987 Nabisco Brands, Ltd., wanted to sell three regionally based coffee-supply divisions to Nestle Enterprises, Ltd. The Director concluded that the acquisition would unduly restrain competition in the Western provinces and allowed the sale of only the Ontario-based firm. Nabisco revised its merger plans to make them acceptable to the Tribunal.

Restrictive Practices

6 A number of restrictive practices are prohibited under the Competition Act.

Price discrimination To charge different prices to different individuals.

There are several other practices that are prohibited under the Competition Act. The first relates to **price discrimination,** in which firms charge different customers different prices. If price differences do not reflect differences in the costs of servicing the different markets, the firm is engaging in an illegal activity. Note that this refers to price discrimination that affects competition—when the local supermarket offers a 10 percent discount for senior citizens on Wednesdays, that's not price discrimination. If it charges people who speak English a different price than those who speak another

Predatory pricing Charging low prices with the aim of driving out the competition.

language, that is discrimination. A related activity involves **predatory pricing:** charging low prices with the aim of driving out the competition (this is also covered under the "abuse of a dominant position").

An example of a case of predatory pricing involved a leading pharmaceutical firm, Hoffman-LaRoche. It was charged with selling its tranquilizer Valium at an unreasonably low price—it even gave it away to hospitals for a year—with the aim of driving other drug companies out of the tranquilizer market. It was found guilty of predatory pricing.

Resale price maintenance When a manufacturer dictates the retail price of its goods to a retailer.

Another illegal practice is known as **resale price maintenance.** This can take many forms, but perhaps the most common involves a manufacturer dictating the retail price of its goods to the retailer. If at the point of final sale the retailer does not abide by the demands of the manufacturer, its supply of the product is cut off. This could happen when suppliers try to stop retailers both from raising price and lowering price, although the courts have allowed firms to stop supplying retailers who use their goods as "loss leaders" in an attempt to generate business. Except for loss leading, retail price maintenance is per se illegal; that is, there is no room for the Director or the parties involved to come to a satisfactory solution to the problem. Resale price maintenance is illegal. No ifs, ands, or buts.

A good example of a case involving resale price maintenance involved the refusal of a supplier (H. D. Lee) to continue to sell jeans to a department store chain (Army and Navy) that sold the jeans at a price below that specified by the supplier. The supplier was found guilty of resale price maintenance. Another involved a case in which an appliance manufacturer (Moffats) picked up half of the advertising costs of its dealers as long as they advertised a price that was at or above a price specified by the manufacturer. This manufacturer was also found guilty.

Other Illegal Practices

Bid rigging Potential suppliers coordinate their bids to ensure an equitable distribution of successful bids.

Misleading advertising Statements that another firm's product or service is inferior or that one's own product or service has some unique advantage that, in fact, it does not have.

Deceptive marketing Marketing strategies that make consumers think that they are getting something they are not.

There are a number of other illegal practices that restrict competition, such as bid rigging, misleading advertising, and deceptive marketing. **Bid rigging** typically involves a public tender for goods and services. Potential suppliers meet to coordinate their activities to ensure that there is an "equitable" distribution of the work. This behaviour is illegal since it substantially lessens competition.

Misleading advertising involves a firm making statements that another firm's product or service is inferior or that one's own product or service has some unique advantage that, in fact, it does not have.

Deceptive marketing is similar to misleading advertising; it involves marketing strategies that make consumers think they are getting something they are not. Marketing of time-share resort ownership often borders on, or is, deceptive marketing.

Let's consider examples of how these policies work in practice. In November 1992 a case involving bid rigging in the biological insecticide industry was settled. The company involved, Abbott Laboratories Limited, agreed to pay a fine of $2 million. Popsicle Industries, Ltd., was recently convicted of misleading representation relating to a promotional contest and paid a $200,000 fine.

Exclusive dealing A manufacturer supplies its goods on the condition that the retailer cannot carry a competitor's product.

Tied selling Access to one product is conditional on the purchase of another product.

Exclusive dealing and tied selling are also prohibited under the Competition Act, if they substantially lessen competition. **Exclusive dealing** occurs when a manufacturer supplies its product on the condition that the retailer cannot carry a competitor's product. **Tied selling** refers to a situation in which a business can have access to another firm's product only as long as it buys a second product from that firm. Classic examples include copying machines and the paper used to make the copies: if you buy our machine, you must buy our paper. Difficulties in proving that competition is reduced by exclusive dealing and tied selling have led to a "rule of reason": objections must apply to major suppliers and must clearly be based on the potential for a substantial reduction in competition.

NATIONALIZATION AND PRIVATIZATION

In the last chapter, "Competition in the Real World," we saw that some activities might be characterized as natural monopolies—postal services, power generation and distribution, transportation, and certain financial services. Economies of scale allow the natural monopolist to produce at a lower average cost than if the market were perfectly

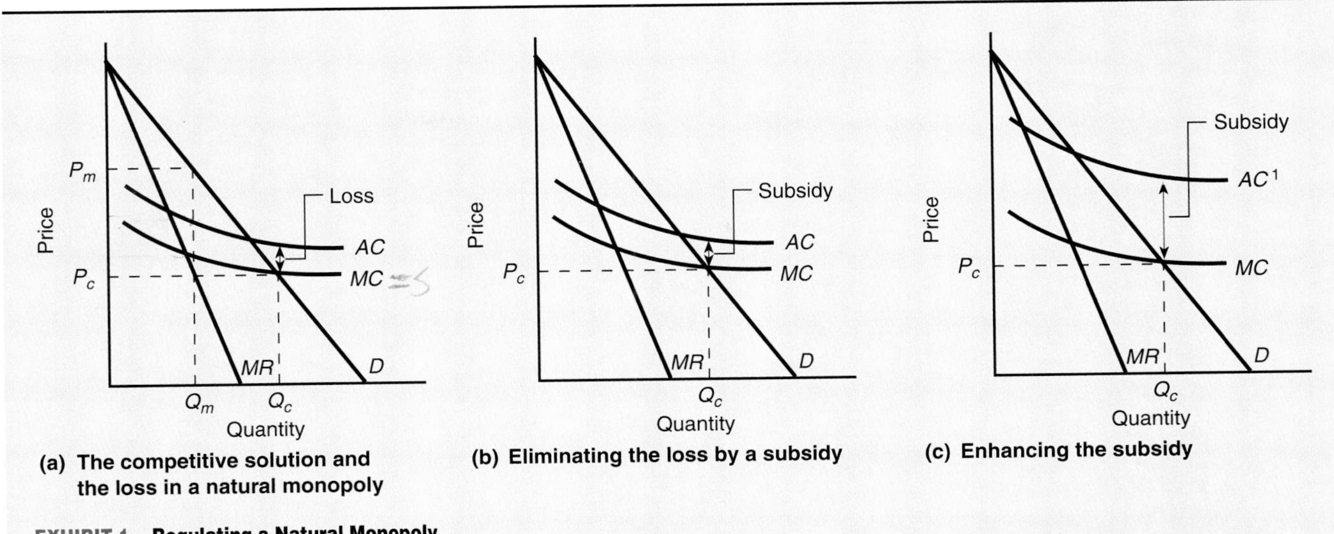

(a) The competitive solution and the loss in a natural monopoly

(b) Eliminating the loss by a subsidy

(c) Enhancing the subsidy

EXHIBIT 1 Regulating a Natural Monopoly

In panel (**a**) the monopolist will incur a loss at the competitive price P_c and output Q_c. One solution is to provide a subsidy, as shown in panel (**b**). If the managers inflate their costs—perhaps by paying themselves hefty salaries—the required subsidy rises, with the managers of the firm the beneficiaries.

competitive. Exhibit 1 (a) shows us that a monopolist will set marginal cost equal to marginal revenue and charge the price the market will bear. The problem with regulating the monopolist is that if we enforce a competitive solution and set price equal to marginal cost, the monopolist will incur a loss. Price is below average unit cost at that level of output. One solution, illustrated by Exhibit 1 (b), is to provide a subsidy to the monopolist so that it breaks even.

7 Nationalization and privatization might lead to greater economic efficiency.

This may be the case for many **crown corporations**—publicly owned firms like Canada Post, the CBC, CN (soon to be transferred to the private sector), and Atomic Energy of Canada. These are federally owned firms, and there are a host of provincially owned crown corporations in telecommunications, broadcasting, and public utilities. These operate at *arm's length* from the government—that is, they are essentially independent. They offer one solution to the problem of natural monopolies. We know that a natural monopoly will set price to maximize its profits and that this creates a deadweight loss to society. By nationalizing the monopoly, the government can exercise control over pricing decisions and make more output available than the unregulated monopoly does. The difficulty in nationalizing a natural monopoly arises when the bureaucrats charged with running the firm decide to inflate costs in the pursuit of their own interests. If managers know they will be allocated a budget of 90 percent of what they ask for, human nature almost all but guarantees they'll ask for more than they need. As Exhibit 1 (c) shows us, this raises the subsidy the government is required to offer to the firm, with the managers of the firm the beneficiaries.

Crown corporation Businesses whose major shareholder is the federal, provincial, or municipal government; usually natural monopolies in which economies of scale create a barrier to entry.

The Problem of Impacted Information

Another problem that frequently plagues crown corporations is that managers fail to minimize costs, since they are insulated from competitive pressures—there is no incentive to constantly search out the least-cost procedures. Moreover, regulators are forced to accept the information they are provided, and in some circumstances the picture they are presented may be more consistent with managements' views and desires than with reality. This kind of information is called **impacted information** because it is skewed to deliver only the impact that the "informer" wants to convey. Some economists argue that, because regulators can never be sure they are getting the whole picture, there is impacted information. Regulatory vigilance cannot substitute for the discipline of the competitive market.

Impacted information Information that does not convey the whole story—more likely to support one point of view.

ADDED DIMENSION

EXCESSIVE EXPENSES PLAGUE NB WORKERS' COMPENSATION BOARD

The following article reports on revelations that the Chairman of the Workers' Compensation Board spent funds on entertainment at local area resorts during a period of fiscal restraint, and that the Premier was not happy.

WCB TO EXAMINE POLICIES

By Elizabeth Hanton
Staff Writer

The chairman of the Workers' Compensation Board has recommended making changes to the expense policies of board members and other employees.

In a news release issued Friday afternoon, John Roushorne said he will be making that recommendation to the WCB's corporate board.

The statement came three days after the WCB chairman's appearance before the legislature's Standing Committee on Crown Corporations. When the committee met on Tuesday, New Democratic Party Leader Elizabeth Weir questioned Mr. Roushorne about money spent on meetings held at a fishing lodge on the Restigouche River and at the Algonquin Hotel in St. Andrews. The expenses included fishing licences, bar tabs and greens fees for golf. These two week-ends cost approximately $12,000.

Yesterday, Mr. Roushorne had separate private meetings with Premier Frank McKenna and with Vaughn Blaney, the minister of advanced education and labor.

The disclosures didn't sit well with the premier, who said on Thursday he felt the allegations of excessive expenses at a time of ongoing restraint throughout government, was inconsistent with good management. Premier McKenna said he would meet privately with Mr. Roushorne.

When it came to power in 1987, the McKenna government cracked down on expenses. While expenses incurred by line departments were targeted, the WCB was not included because, as a Crown corporation, it operates at arm's length from government and is funded by employers.

During yesterday's sitting of the committee on Crown corporations, Ms. Weir put forward a motion calling for a member of the committee to be present at the meeting between Mr. Roushorne and the premier—and volunteered for the task.

She withdrew the motion when committee member Reg MacDonald (L–Bay du Vin) told her that meeting had already taken place. However, the NDP leader said the issue isn't over.

"A behind-the-scenes slap on the fingers won't solve the problem at the Workers' Compensation Board," Ms. Weir said.

In his statement, Mr. Roushorne said the premier and Mr. Blaney both felt the WCB should comply with government policies regarding personal expenses, particularly as they pertain to the purchase of alcoholic beverages.

"The concerns of the government are legitimate, appropriate and no doubt represent those of the average New Brunswicker," Mr. Roushorne said.

Source: *The Daily Gleaner.*

Is Privatization the Key?

Privatization Finding private buyers for publicly owned government businesses.

One response to the rising costs of maintaining crown corporations is **privatization**—finding private buyers for publicly owned government businesses. Government is not terribly efficient as a producer, and we know there are incentives to inflate costs to maximize budget allocations to one's department. This has led to a rising tide of selling off crown corporations to the private sector. The federal government has already sold Air Canada, and more crown corporations and government activities are up for sale (legislation to sell CN Rail was introduced in early 1995). The need to reduce costs in a period of fiscal restraint puts pressure on the managers of crown corporations to become more efficient, but with limited resources governments are becoming less and less interested in subsidizing activities that might be better handled by the private sector. Government must also balance the costs of continuously reviewing management decisions against the benefits that might be accrued.

Critics of privatization suggest that a more competitive environment might force crown corporations to be more efficient, and that the government does not need to privatize firms operating under these conditions. Others argue that managers of crown corporations are so set in their ways that they are incapable of reducing costs, so we need even more privatization. These are topical issues in economic policy that are the subject of ongoing debate.

DEREGULATION AND INDUSTRIAL POLICY

We end this chapter with a discussion of deregulation, and in doing so, look to the future of industrial policy in Canada. In a previous chapter we introduced the concentration ratio—it gives a measure of industrial concentration, that is, the proportion of total industrial activity that is attributable to the largest four or eight firms. In the United States, competition policy allows measures of industrial concentration a large role in determining the appropriate response to a proposed merger, but that is not true in Canada. With smaller markets than those in the United States to capture relevant economies of scale, we may need fewer firms and a higher degree of concentration. As we've already seen, in some Canadian industries (look back and find the ones we mean) there may only be eight firms!

Industrial Concentration

We know that industrial concentration can have deleterious effects on economic efficiency, and it may adversely affect the distribution of income. Think of one-industry towns where workers are forced to buy at the company store and bank at the "company" bank. Think of the political influence the firm might have over local affairs. There may be a reason for the government to intervene and regulate an industry. On the other hand, some economists would argue that regulation has increased the costs of doing business so substantially that only the big players can afford, in former Prime Minister Mulroney's words, to "roll the dice." Regulation may have actually given firms market power.

Deregulation

A number of industries have been deregulated in an attempt to foster competition and allow domestic firms a chance to compete against foreign firms on a level playing field. These effects are easiest to see in the transportation industry with airline and trucking deregulation. In these cases prices actually dropped after the industry was deregulated, and the free market worked to identify uncompetitive routes and business practices. While some small areas did not benefit from deregulation since they lost the services the government had been forcing the industry to provide, most other areas gained. While there may have been an accompanying reduction in the services provided by the industry, the changes were beneficial to society as a whole. As long as the authorities stand watch for anticompetitive behaviour, the gains to deregulation will be long-lived. In other words, competition law can be an effective substitute for regulation.

Industrial Policy

Industrial policy A government's formal policy toward business.

8 Industrial policy refers to the government's role in actively determining the structure of industry in Canada.

This has led some economists to argue that the government needs to adopt a detailed plan for industrial development. **Industrial policy** refers to the government's role in actively determining the structure of industry in Canada. Advocates claim that this will result in gains from cooperation and increased international competitiveness as funds are channelled to high-growth industries. Should the government try to pick the industrial "winners" and the "losers," and implement policies that are consistent with these choices?

Advocates of an activist industrial policy point to Japan's Ministry of International Trade and Industry (MITI) as an example of how an activist industrial policy would work. MITI is generally credited with engineering Japan's economic growth over the past 40 years, although there is dispute about how successful MITI has actually been. The ministry provided money and research, and saw to it that companies focused on international, rather than domestic, competition. It smoothed the flow of capital to certain industries it wanted to promote, such as the electronics industry. It did this by taking such measures as consulting with banks and encouraging loans. MITI would say "So-and-So is a good company" and that statement was a code to banks that they should approve So-and-So's loan application.

9 Economists can find reasons for and against an activist industrial policy. Most would probably come out against an activist role for government, given the invisible feet of politics and law.

Does an Activist Stance Have Any Problems?

Japan's success did not come without problems. Its activism involved government in business decisions. This opened up significant possibilities for graft. In the late 1980s a major scandal erupted in Japan when it was revealed that some Japanese corporations had given many politicians in the ruling Liberal Democratic Party options to buy shares in the companies at low prices.

Such problems are likely to arise under an activist industrial policy. Because government decisions can mean a difference of hundreds of millions of dollars to firms, companies will inevitably spend money to influence those decisions, either legally through lobbying or illegally through bribery and graft. The exposure of the scandals in Japan has already changed the face of Japanese politics. Whether the scandals will change Japan's industrial policy remains to be seen.

Any time economic decisions are made on a political basis, waste is inevitable. It's the cost of an activist industrial policy in a democratic government. But there are also benefits. Competition can be wasteful, especially in research. That's why scientific conventions (rules limiting scientists' behaviour) exist that support openness and sharing of scientific knowledge. Cooperation by firms with government and universities can lead to more productive research.

In weighing these costs and benefits, a majority of economists come out on the side of opposing an activist industrial policy for Canada. This includes most conservative economists who generally oppose activist government policies plus a number of liberal economists who are concerned about the politics of an industrial policy. They believe that a formal activist industrial policy would probably lead to more inefficiency and waste as the invisible foot of politics and of law extended their influence over the invisible hand of the marketplace, yielding more costs than benefits. On top of all of the other problems there is also the problem of "impacted information"—where do you get the information for the right decisions?

To argue against an activist industrial policy is not to argue against an informal government policy of encouraging research in certain areas. This can be done by fostering connections between universities and business, by directly subsidizing private industry's basic research, or by loosening rules over anticompetitive behaviour and restrictive practices. All of these actions carry the potential for positive externalities (benefits that accrue to those other than the buyers and sellers of a particular commodity). Many economists support such policies in particular cases even as they oppose a general activist industrial policy being extended to all businesses.

CHAPTER SUMMARY

- Canadian anti-combines policy has changed substantially since Confederation.
- Three areas of anti-competitive behaviour addressed in the 1986 Competition Act include price-fixing, mergers, and the abuse of a dominant position.
- There are four ways of abusing a dominant position.
- Mergers can be horizontal, vertical, or conglomerate, and the reasons behind a merger can be varied. There are at least seven reasons to object to a proposed merger.
- The Director of Investigations launches actions against firms who appear to be involved in anti-competitive activities.
- A number of restrictive practices are prohibited under the Competition Act. These include tied selling, resale price maintenance, exclusive dealing, bid rigging, misleading advertising, deceptive marketing, price discrimination, and predatory pricing.
- Nationalizing a natural monopolist would allow the government to control pricing and production decisions.
- Privatization involves selling crown corporations to the private sector in the hope that the profit motive will encourage economic efficiency.
- An active industrial policy for Canada would involve the government picking the winner and the losers. This might lead to inefficiency and waste when we think about the invisible feet of politics and law.

KEY TERMS

abuse of a dominant position *(272)*
acquisition *(273)*
Advance Ruling Certificates *(275)*
anti-combines legislation *(270)*
anti-combines policy *(270)*
anti-competitive behaviour *(272)*
bid rigging *(276)*
capital intensive *(270)*
combine *(270)*
Competition Act *(271)*
competition policy *(270)*
Competition Tribunal *(271)*
conglomerate merger *(274)*
crown corporation *(277)*
deceptive marketing *(276)*
exclusive dealing *(276)*
friendly takeover *(273)*
horizontal merger *(274)*
hostile takeover *(273)*
impacted information *(277)*
industrial policy *(279)*
merger *(272)*
misleading advertising *(276)*
National Policy *(270)*
predator *(272)*
predatory pricing *(276)*
prenotification *(274)*
price discrimination *(275)*
price-fixing *(271)*
privatization *(278)*
prohibition orders *(271)*
protective tariffs *(270)*
resale price maintenance *(276)*
restrictive business practices *(271)*
shell corporation *(273)*
takeover *(273)*
tied selling *(276)*
vertical merger *(274)*

QUESTIONS FOR THOUGHT AND REVIEW

The number after each question represents the estimated degree of critical thinking required. (1 = almost none; 10 = deep thought.)

1. Specifically, of which anticompetitive behaviour was H. D. Lee convicted? *(2)*
2. Colleges and universities require that certain courses be taken at that institution in order to get a degree. Is that an example of a tie-in contract that limits consumers' choices? If so, should it be against the law? *(7)*
3. Some students receive financial aid in the form of scholarships and bursaries. Is that price discrimination? If so, should it be against the law? *(7)*
4. Why did the 1986 Competition Act redefine some activities from criminal offences to civil offences? *(5)*
5. If you were an economist for a Canadian tobacco firm that wanted to merge, would you rely on eight-firm concentration ratios? Why? *(5)*
6. Has airline service to your area improved as a result of deregulation? *(6)*
7. Should Canada adopt an activist industrial policy? *(7)*
8. What would be the benefits to privatization of crown corporations? *(6)*
9. Is there any way around the prenotification requirements for a merger? *(4)*
10. Why was A.C. Neilsen Co. of Canada, Ltd., accused of anticompetitive behaviour? *(3)*

PROBLEMS AND EXERCISES

1. You're working at the Bureau of Competition Policy. Ms. Ecofame has just brought in a new index, the Ecofame Index, which she argues is preferable to the eight-firm concentration ratio. The Ecofame Index is calculated by cubing the concentration ratio of the top 10 firms in the industry.

   State the advantages and disadvantages of the Ecofame Index as compared to the eight-firm concentration ratio.
2. Using a monopolistic competition model, a cartel model of oligopoly, and a contestable market of oligopoly, discuss and demonstrate (graphically where possible) the effect of anti-combines policy.
3. In 1993 Mattel proposed acquiring Fisher-Price for $1.1 billion. In the toy industry, Mattel is a major player with 11 percent of the market. Fisher-Price has 4 percent. The other two large firms are Tyco, with a 5 percent share, and Hasbro, with a 15 percent share. In the infant/preschool toy market, Mattel has an 8 percent share and Fisher-Price has a 27 percent share, the largest. The other two large firms are Hasbro, with a 25 percent share, and Rubbermaid, with a 12 percent share.
   a. What is the approximate four-firm concentration ratio for these firms in each industry?
   b. Give an argument why the merger might decrease competition.
   c. Give an argument why the merger might increase competition.
4. Demonstrate graphically how regulating the price of a monopolist can both increase quantity and decrease price.
   a. Why did the regulation have the effect it did?
   b. How relevant to the real world do you believe this result is in the "contestable markets" view of the competitive process?
   c. How relevant to the real world do you believe this result is in the "cartel" view of the competitive process?

CHAPTER

14

Work and the Labour Market

Work banishes those three great evils: boredom, vice, and poverty.
~Voltaire

After reading this chapter, you should be able to:

1 Apply rational choice theory to derive the supply of labour.

2 Explain why an increase in the marginal tax rate is likely to reduce the quantity of labour supplied.

3 Determine a firm's derived demand for labour.

4 Explain why a monopolist's demand for labour will be lower than a competitive firm's demand for labour.

5 Define *monopsonist* and *bilateral monopoly.*

6 Discuss real-world characteristics of labour markets in terms of the invisible forces.

7 List three types of discrimination.

Most of us earn our living by working. We supply labour (get a job) and get paid for doing things that other people tell us they want done. Even before we get a job, work is very much a part of our lives. We spend a large portion of our school years preparing for work. Probably many of you are taking this economics course because you've been told that it will help to prepare you for a job—or that it will get you more pay than you're getting in your present job. For you, this course is investment in "human capital." If work isn't already familiar to you, once you get out of school (unless you're sitting on a hefty trust fund or marry somebody who is), work in the marketplace will become very familiar to you.

Your job will occupy at least a third of your waking hours. To a great extent, it will define you. When someone asks, "What do you do?" you won't answer, "I clip coupons, go out on dates, visit my children . . ." Instead you'll answer, "I work for the Blank Company" or "I'm an economist" or "I'm a teacher." Defining ourselves by our work means that work is more than the way we get income. It's a part of our social and cultural makeup. If we lose our jobs, we lose part of our identity.

There's no way we can discuss all the social, political, cultural, and economic dimensions of work and labour in one chapter, but it's important to begin by at least pointing them out in order to put our discussion of labour markets in perspective. A **labour market** is a factor market in which individuals supply labour services for wages to other individuals and to firms that need (demand) labour services. The labour market is a market in which social and political pressures are particularly strong, and we can understand the nature of labour markets only by considering how the three invisible forces interact to determine our economic situation.

Labour market Factor market in which individuals supply labour services for wages to firms that demand labour services.

To do that, we first ask the question: What would labour markets be like if only economic forces—the invisible hand—operated on them? Then we examine how the other invisible forces interact with economic forces to produce existing labour market institutions. Finally, we consider the implications of the analysis for you and your future in the job market.

THE INVISIBLE HAND AND THE LABOUR MARKET

If the invisible hand were the only force that was operating, wages would be determined entirely by supply and demand. There's more to it than that, as you'll see, but it shouldn't be surprising to you that our discussion of the invisible hand and the labour market is organized around the concepts of supply and demand.

The Supply of Labour

The labour supply choice facing an individual (that is, the decisions of whether, how, and how much to work) can be seen as a choice between nonmarket activities and legal market activities. Nonmarket activities include sleeping, dating, studying, playing, cooking, cleaning, gardening, and black market trading. Legal market activities include taking some type of paid job or working for oneself, directly supplying products or services to the consumer.

Many considerations are involved in individuals' choice of whether and how much to work and what kind of job to work at. Social background and conditioning are especially important, but the factor economists focus on is the **incentive effect** (how much a person will change his or her hours worked in response to a change in the wage rate). The incentive effect is determined by the value of supplying one's time to legal market activities relative to the value of supplying one's time to nonmarket activities. The normal relationship is:

Incentive effect How much a person will change his or her hours worked in response to a change in the wage rate.

The higher the wage, the higher the quantity of labour supplied.

1 Applying rational choice theory to the supply of labour tells us that the higher the wage, the higher the quantity of labour supplied.

This relationship between the wage rate and the quantity of labour supplied is shown in Exhibit 1. The wage rate is measured on the vertical axis; the quantity of labour supplied is measured on the horizontal axis. As you can see, the upward slope of the supply of labour indicates that as the wage rate increases, the quantity of labour supplied increases. Why is that the normal relationship? Because work involves opportunity cost. By working one hour more, you have one hour less to devote to nonmarket activities. Alternatively, if you devote the hour to nonmarket activities, you lose one hour's worth of income from working.

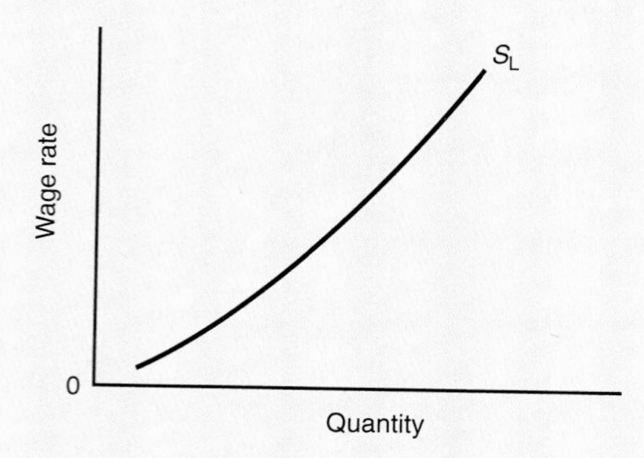

EXHIBIT 1 The Supply of Labour

The supply of labour is generally considered to be upward sloping because the opportunity cost of not working increases as wages get higher.

Say, for example, that by working you would have made \$10 per hour. If you decide to work two hours less, you'll have \$20 less to spend, but two hours more available for other activities (including spending the smaller amount of money). When the wage rises, say to \$12 per hour, an hour of leisure has a higher opportunity cost. As the cost of leisure goes up, you buy less of it, meaning that you work more.

As we noted in our general discussions of supply and demand, the incentive effects represented by the market supply curve come from individuals' either/or decisions to enter, or leave, the labour market; and from individuals' decisions to work more, or fewer, hours. Given the institutional constraints in the labour market which require many people to work a fixed set of hours if they work at all, much of the incentive effect of higher wages works on the either/or decisions of individuals. This affects the labour force participation rate rather than adjusting the number of hours worked. For example, when wages rise, retired workers may find it worthwhile to go back to work, and many teenagers may choose to find part-time jobs.

Real Wages and the Opportunity Cost of Work The upward-sloping supply curve of labour tells you that, other things equal, as wages go up, the quantity of labour supplied goes up. But if you look at the historical record, you see real wages in Canada increasing and the average number of hours worked per person falling. This difference is partly explained by the income effect, which is discussed below. Higher real incomes make people better off, and able to choose more leisure.

Given that people are far richer today than they were 50 or 100 years ago, it isn't surprising that they work less. What's surprising is that they work as much as they do—eight hours a day rather than the four or so hours a day that would be enough to give people the same income that they had a century ago.

The explanation of why people haven't reduced their hours of work more substantially can be found in the type of leisure taken. A century ago, conversation was an art. People could use their time for long, leisurely conversations. Letter writing was a skill all educated people had, and cooking dinner was a three-hour event. Leisure was time-intensive. If today people were satisfied with leisure consisting of long conversations, whittling, and spending quality time with their families rather than skiing, golfing, or travelling, they could get by with working perhaps only four or five hours per day instead of eight hours. But that isn't the case.

Today leisurely dinners, conversations about good books, and witty letters have been replaced by "efficient" leisure: a fast-food supper, a home video, and the instant analysis of current events. Microwave ovens, frozen dinners, Pop-Tarts, cellular telephones, fax machines—the list of gadgets and products designed to save time is endless. All these gadgets that increase the "efficiency" of leisure (increase the marginal utility per hour of leisure spent) cost money, which means people today must work more to enjoy their leisure! In Canada, one reason people work hard is so that they can play hard (and expensively).

ADDED DIMENSION

INCOME AND SUBSTITUTION EFFECTS

Because labour income is such an important component of most people's total income, other things often do not stay equal, and at times the effect can seem strange. For example, say that you earn $10 an hour and you decide to work eight hours per day. Suddenly demand for your services goes up and you find that you can receive $40 an hour. Will you decide to work more hours? According to the rational choice rule, you will, but you might also decide that at $40 an hour you'll work only six hours a day—$240 a day is enough; the rest of the day you want leisure time to spend your money. In such a case a higher wage means working less.

Does this violate the rational choice rule? The answer is no, because other things—specifically your income—do not remain equal. The higher wage makes you decide to work more—as the rational choice rule says; but the effect of the higher wage is overwhelmed by the effect of the higher income that allows you to decide to work less.

To distinguish between these two effects, economists have given them names. The decision, based on the rational choice rule, to work more hours when your pay goes up is called the *substitution effect.* You substitute work for leisure because the price of leisure has risen. The decision to work fewer hours when your pay goes up, based on the fact that you're richer and therefore can live a better life, is called the *income effect.*

It's possible that the income effect can exceed the substitution effect, and a wage increase can cause one to work less (giving the "backward bending" portion of the labour supply curve in the exhibit), but that possibility does not violate the rational choice rule, which refers to the substitution effect only. For those of you who didn't make a deal with us in the chapter on demand, a good exercise is to show the income and substitution effects with indifference curves and to demonstrate how it might be possible for an increase in the wage to lead to a decline in hours of work.

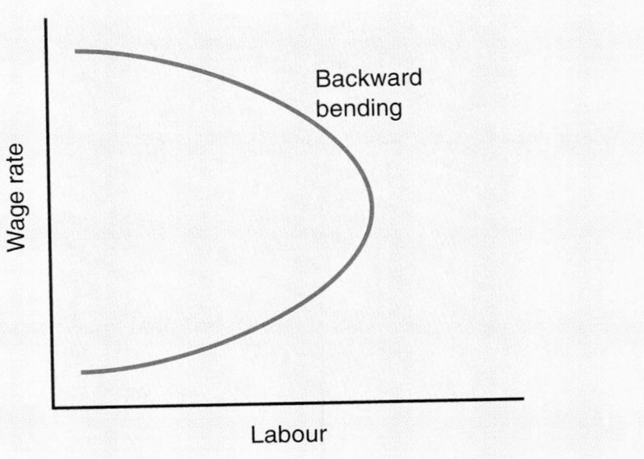

The fast pace of modern society has led a number of people to question whether we, as a society, are better off working hard to play hard. Are we better off or simply more harried? Some people have recently suggested that Canadians adopt a four-day workweek. Proponents of this view argue the plan would increase employment (since the plant/firm in which you work would operate up to seven days a week, but any one employee would only work four days a week—leaving up to three days for new workers). Other proposals for legally limiting the amount of overtime an individual could work in a year are also aimed at forcing people to consume more leisure (and presumably reduce unemployment). Economists don't try to answer the "are we better off working hard to play hard" normative question; but they do point out that people are choosing their harried lifestyle, so to argue that people are worse off, one must argue that people are choosing something they don't really want. That may be true, but it's a tough argument to prove.

The Supply of Labour and Nonmarket Activities In addition to leisure, there are other nonmarket activities in which labour supply issues and market incentives play an important role. For example, there's a whole set of illegal activities, such as selling illegal drugs, which are alternatives to taking a legal job.

Let's say that an 18-year-old street kid figures he has only two options: Either he can work at a $5-an-hour job or he can deal drugs illegally. Dealing drugs involves enormous risks of getting arrested or shot, but it also means earning $50 or $75 an hour. Given that choice, many risk takers opt to sell drugs. When an emergency room doctor asked a shooting victim in Toronto why he got involved in selling drugs, he responded, "I'm not going to work for chump change. I make $2,000 a week, tax free. What do they pay you, sucker?" The doctor had to admit that even she wasn't making that kind of money.

For middle-class individuals who have prospects for good jobs, the cost of being arrested can be high—an arrest can destroy their future prospects. For poor street kids with little chance of getting a good job, an arrest makes little difference to their future. For them the choice is heavily weighted toward selling drugs. This is especially true for the entrepreneurial types—the risk takers—the movers and shakers who might have become the business leaders of the future. We've asked ourselves, had we been in their position, what decision we would have made. And we suspect we know the answer.

Prohibiting certain drugs leads to high income from selling those drugs and has significant labour market effects. The incentive effects that prohibition has on the choices facing poor teenagers in their choice of jobs is a central reason why some economists support the legalization of currently illegal drugs.

Marginal tax rate The tax you pay on an additional dollar.

Income Taxation, Work, and Leisure It is after-tax income, not before-tax income, that determines how much you work. Why? Because after-tax income is what you give up by not working. The government, not you, forgoes what you would have paid in taxes if you had worked. This means that when the government raises your **marginal tax rate** (the tax you pay on an additional dollar), it reduces your incentive to work. The reason is that leisure and other nonmarket activities aren't taxed, so their relative price falls. When the marginal tax rate gets really high—say 60 or 70 percent—it can significantly reduce individuals' incentive to work and earn income.

In Canada marginal tax rates have been on the rise for some time, mainly because government deficits and debts have been rising at historically high rates. European countries also have high marginal tax rates, and like Canada, they are struggling with the problem of providing an incentive for people to work. This is especially true given the European network of relatively generous public assistance programs, which create a disincentive to work. Reforms to Canadian social security programs like unemployment insurance and social assistance (welfare) aim at reducing or eliminating similar dependency effects. Reducing generosity (cutting benefits) provides a motive for people to become more self-sufficient and less reliant on government. For example, in Ontario and New Brunswick, individuals on social assistance must show a willingness to work if offered employment.

Reducing the marginal tax rate won't completely eliminate the problem of negative incentive effects on individuals' work effort. The reason is that the amounts one receives from many other programs are tied to earned income. When your earned income goes up, your benefits from these other programs go down.

2 An increase in the marginal tax rate is likely to reduce the quantity of labour supplied because it reduces the net wage of individuals and hence, via individuals' incentive effect, causes them to work less.

Say, for example, that you're getting welfare and you're deciding whether to take a $5-an-hour job. Let's also assume that income taxes and other deductions reduce the amount you take home from the job by 20 percent, to $4 an hour. If the welfare system is such that your welfare benefits are reduced by 50¢ for every dollar you take home, this means that you lose another $2 per hour, so the marginal tax rate on your $5-an-hour job isn't 20 percent; it's 60 percent. By working an hour, you've increased your net income by only $2. When you consider the transportation cost of getting to and from work, the expense of getting new clothes to wear to work, and other job-associated expenses, the net gain in income is often minimal. Your implicit marginal tax rate is almost 100 percent! At such rates, there's an enormous incentive either not to work or to work off the books (get paid in cash so you have no recorded income that the government can trace).

The negative incentive effect can sometimes be even more indirect. For example, college scholarships are generally given on the basis of need. A family that earns more gets less in scholarship aid; the amount by which the scholarship is reduced as a family's income increases acts as a marginal tax on individuals' income. Why work hard to provide for yourself if there's a program to take care of you if you don't work hard? Hence, the irony in any need-based assistance program is that it reduces people's incentive to prevent themselves from being needy. These negative incentive effects on labour supply that accompany any need-based program present a public policy dilemma for which there is no easy answer.

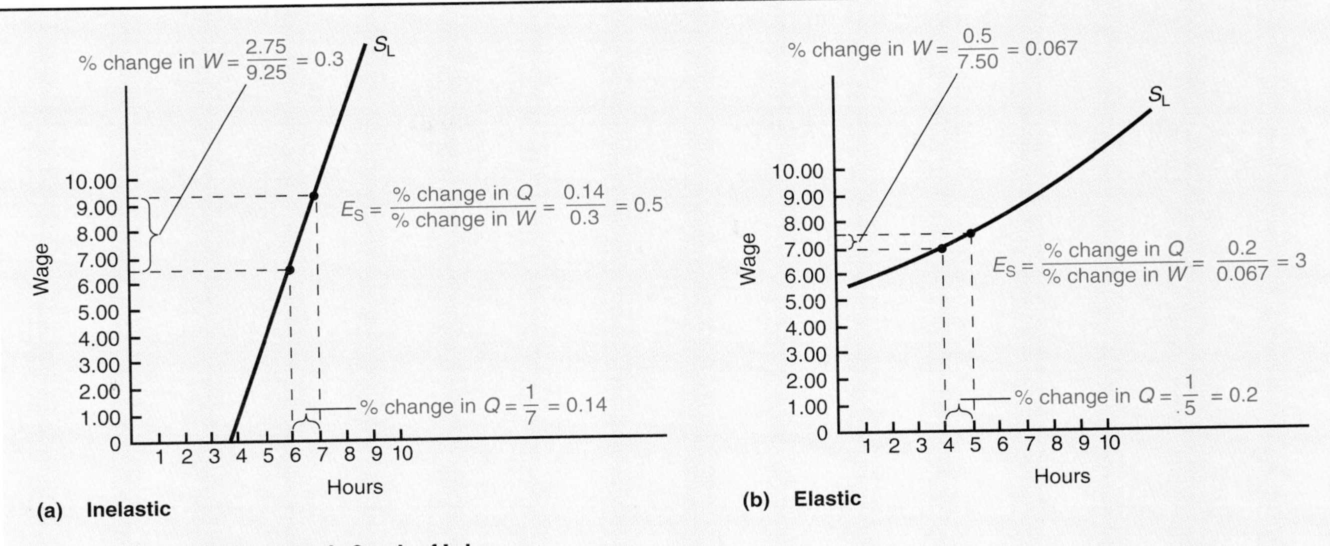

EXHIBIT 2 Inelastic and Elastic Supply of Labour

The elasticity of an individual's supply of labour determines to what extent various incentives affect the amount of labour an individual supplies. In (**a**), the individual has a highly inelastic supply of labour curve: a 30 percent drop in wages would make him work one hour less, whereas an individual with an elastic supply of labour curve, as in (**b**), would work one hour less if his wage were to drop only 6.7 percent.

The Elasticity of the Supply of Labour Exactly how these various incentives affect the amount of labour an individual supplies is determined by the elasticity of the individual's supply curve of labour. Exhibit 2 shows two possible supply curves of labour.[1] The supply curve of labour in Exhibit 2 (a) is inelastic. (The percent change in quantity supplied divided by the percent change in wage is less than one.) The incentive effects cause little change in the number of hours an individual works. The supply curve in Exhibit 2 (b) is elastic; the incentive causes a large change in the number of hours of labour supplied.

The elasticity of the market supply curve is determined by the elasticity of individuals' supply curves and by individuals entering and leaving the labour force. If a large group of people are willing to enter the labour market when wages rise, then the market labour supply will be highly elastic even if individuals' supply curves are inelastic.

The elasticity of supply also depends on the type of market being discussed. For example, the elasticity of labour supply facing one firm in a small town will likely be far greater than the elasticity of the labour supply of all firms in that town. If only one firm raises its wage, it will attract workers away from other firms; if all the firms in town raise their wages, any increase in labour must come from increases in labour force participation, increases in hours worked per person, or in-migration (the movement of new workers into the town's labour market).

Existing workers prefer inelastic labour supplies because that means an increase in demand for labour will raise their wage. Employers prefer elastic supplies because that means an increase in demand for labour doesn't require large wage increases. These preferences can be seen in news reports about Canadian immigration laws, their effects, and their enforcement. Businesses such as restaurants often oppose strict immigration laws. Their reason is that jobs such as janitor, chambermaid, and busper-

[1]Our discussion of supply curves focuses on the incentive effect. Since wages are an important determinant of one's income, there can also be an income effect of changes in the wage: Higher wages make one richer. That income effect can also influence the elasticity of the measured supply curve. For example, higher income might lead one to work less. In certain instances, remember that the income effect can actually make the supply curve of labour backward-bending.

son are frequently filled by new immigrants or illegal aliens who have comparatively low wage expectations.

Because of the importance of the elasticity of labour supply, economists have spent a great deal of time and effort estimating it. Their best estimates of labour supply elasticities to market activities are about 0.1 for heads of households and 1.1 for secondary workers in households. These elasticity figures mean that a wage increase of 10 percent will increase the supply of labour by 1 percent for heads of households (an inelastic supply) and 11 percent for secondary workers in households (an elastic supply). Why the difference? Institutional factors. Hours of work are only slightly flexible. Since most heads of households are employed, they cannot significantly change their hours worked. Many secondary workers in households are not employed, and the higher elasticity reflects new secondary workers entering the labour market.

Immigration and the International Supply of Labour The above elasticities of labour supply are themselves based on other institutional realities, one of the most important of which is international limitation on the flow of people, and hence on labour. In many industries, wages in developing countries are one-tenth or one-twentieth the rate of wages in Canada. This large wage differential means that many people from those low-wage countries would like to move to Canada to earn the higher wages. They cannot always meet the legal immigration restrictions that limit the flow in, but in addition to about 200,000 legal immigrants to Canada per year, thousands more come into Canada illegally, and illegally take a variety of jobs at lower wages and worse conditions than legal residents and Canadian citizens are willing to take. The result is that the actual supply of labour is more elastic than the measured supply, especially in those jobs that cannot be easily policed.

In 1993, the European Union introduced open borders among member countries. That institutional change will likely bring about a more open flow of individuals into higher-wage EU countries from lower-wage EU countries, although other institutionalized restrictions on flows of people, such as language and culture barriers, should prevent the EU from being a unified labour market through the 1990s.

The Derived Demand for Labour

When individuals are self-employed (work for themselves), the demand for their labour is the demand for the product or service they supply—be it cutting hair, shampooing rugs, or filling teeth. You have an ability to do something; you offer to do it at a certain price; and you see who calls. You determine how many hours you work, what price you charge, and what jobs you take. The income you receive depends upon the demand for the good or service you supply and your decision about how much labour you want to supply. In analyzing self-employed individuals, one can move directly from demand for the product to demand for labour.

When a person is not self-employed, determining the demand for labour isn't as direct. It's a two-step process: Consumers demand products from firms; firms, in turn, demand labour and other factors of production to produce those products. The demand for labour by firms is a **derived demand;** it's derived from the consumer's demand for the goods that the firm sells. Thus, you can't think of demand for a factor of production such as labour separately from demand for goods. Firms translate consumers' demands into a demand for factors of production.

Derived demand The demand for factors of production by firms; the nature of this derived demand depends upon the demand for the firms' products.

Factors Influencing the Elasticity of Demand for Labour The elasticity of the derived demand for labour, or for any other factor of production, depends upon a number of factors. We designate one of the most important as number (1), and it is *the elasticity of demand for the firm's good.* The more elastic the final demand, the more elastic the derived demand. Other factors influencing the elasticity of derived demand include: (2) *the relative importance of the factor in the production process* (the more important the factor, the less elastic is the derived demand); (3) *the possibility of, and cost of, substitution in production* (the easier substitution is, the more elastic is the derived demand); and (4) *the degree to which the marginal productivity falls with an increase in the factor* (the faster productivity falls, the less elastic is the derived demand).

Each of these relationships follows from the definition of elasticity (the percent change in quantity divided by the percent change in price) and a knowledge of production. To be sure you understand, ask yourself the following question: "If all I knew about two firms was that one was a perfect competitor and the other was a monopolist, which firm would I say is likely to have the more elastic derived demand for labour?" If your answer wasn't automatically "the competitive firm" (because its demand curve is perfectly elastic and hence more elastic than a monopolist's), we would suggest that at this point you review the discussion of factors influencing demand elasticity in the chapter on demand and relate that to this discussion. The two discussions are similar and serve as good reviews for each other.

Labour as a Factor of Production The traditional factors of production are land, labour, capital, and entrepreneurship. When economists talk of the labour market, they're talking about two of these factors: labour and entrepreneurship. **Entrepreneurship** is a type of creative labour.

Entrepreneurship Labour services that involve high degrees of organizational skills, concern, and creativity.

The reason for distinguishing between labour and entrepreneurship is that an hour of work is not simply an hour of work. If high degrees of organizational skill, concern, and creativity are exerted (which is what economists mean by *entrepreneurship*), one hour of such work can be the equivalent of days, weeks, or even years of simple labour. That's one reason that pay often differs between workers for doing what seems to be the same job. It's also why one of the important decisions a firm makes is what type of labour to hire. Should the firm try to hire high-wage entrepreneurial labour or low-wage nonentrepreneurial labour?

We'll talk about the other two factors of production (land and capital) in the next chapter, but you should note that the formal analysis of the firm's derived demand, presented in this chapter as the derived demand for labour, is quite general and carries over to the derived demand for capital and for land. Firms translate consumers' demands for goods into derived demands for any and all of the factors of production.

The Firm's Decision to Hire What determines a firm's decision to hire someone? The answer is simple. A profit-maximizing firm hires someone if it thinks there's money to be made by doing so. Unless there is, the firm won't hire the person. So for a firm to decide whether to hire someone, it must compare the worker's **marginal revenue product (MRP)** (the marginal revenue it expects to earn from selling the additional worker's output) with the wage that it expects to pay the additional worker. For a competitive firm (for which $P = MR$), that marginal revenue product equals the worker's **value of marginal product**—the worker's **marginal physical product (MPP)**—which is the additional units of output that hiring an additional worker will bring about—times the price (P) at which the firm can sell the additional product.

Marginal revenue product (MRP) The additional revenue a firm receives when it hires an additional worker.

Value of marginal product Marginal physical product times the price for which the firm can sell that product.

Marginal physical product (MPP) Additional units of output that hiring an additional worker will bring about.

$$\text{Marginal revenue product} = MPP \times P$$

Say, for example, that by hiring another worker a firm can produce an additional six widgets an hour, which it can sell at $2 each. That means the firm can pay up to $12 per hour and still expect to make a profit. Notice that a key question for the firm is: How much additional product will we get from hiring another worker? A competitive firm can increase its profit by hiring another worker as long as the value of the worker's marginal product (which also equals her marginal revenue product) ($MPP \times P$) is higher than her wage.

To see whether you understand the principle, consider the example in Exhibit 3 (a). Column 1 shows the number of workers, all of whom are assumed to be identical. Column 2 shows the total output of those workers. Column 3 shows the marginal physical product of an additional worker. This number is determined by looking at the change in the total product due to this person's work. For example, if the firm is currently employing 30 workers and it hires one more, the firm's total product or output will rise from 294 to 300, so the marginal product of moving from 30 to 31 workers is 6.

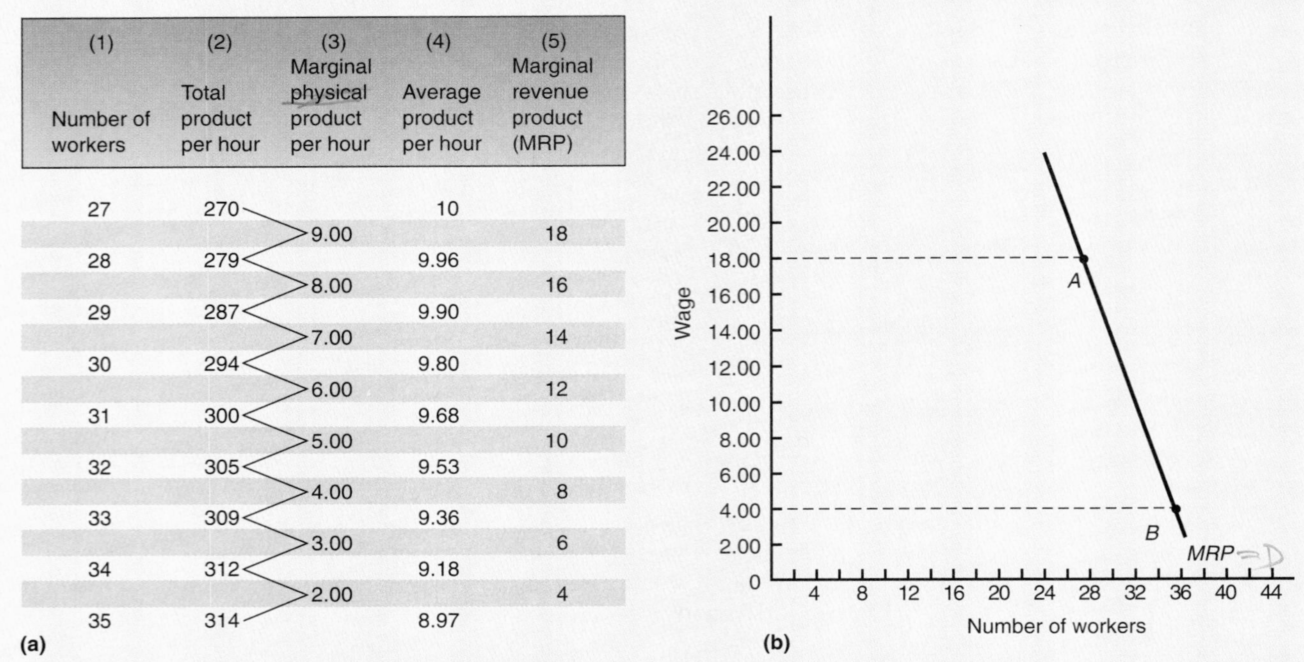

(1) Number of workers	(2) Total product per hour	(3) Marginal physical product per hour	(4) Average product per hour	(5) Marginal revenue product (MRP)
27	270		10	
		9.00		18
28	279		9.96	
		8.00		16
29	287		9.90	
		7.00		14
30	294		9.80	
		6.00		12
31	300		9.68	
		5.00		10
32	305		9.53	
		4.00		8
33	309		9.36	
		3.00		6
34	312		9.18	
		2.00		4
35	314		8.97	

(a)

(b)

EXHIBIT 3 Determining How Many Workers to Hire and the Firm's Derived Demand for Labour

The marginal revenue product is any firm's demand curve for labour. Since for a competitive firm *P=MR*, a competitive firm's derived demand curve is its value of the marginal product curve (*P* x *MPP*). This curve tells us the additional revenue the firm gets from having an additional worker. From the chart in (**a**) we can see that when the firm increases from 27 to 28 workers, the marginal product per hour for each worker is 9. If the product sells for $2, then marginal revenue product is $18, which is one point on the demand curve for labour (point *A* in (**b**)). When the firm increases from 34 to 35 workers, the value of the marginal product decreases to $4. This is another point on the firm's derived demand curve (point *B* in (**b**)). By connecting the two points, as we have done in (**b**), you can see that the firm's derived demand curve for labour is downward sloping.

Notice that workers' marginal product decreases as more workers are hired. Why is this? Remember the assumption of fixed capital: More and more workers are working with the same amount of capital and there is diminishing marginal productivity.

Labour productivity Average output per worker.

Column 4 shows the average output per worker (**labour productivity**), a statistic commonly referred to in economic reports. It's determined by dividing the total output by the number of workers. Column 5 shows the additional worker's marginal revenue product, which, since the firm is assumed to be competitive, is determined by multiplying the price the firm receives for the product it sells ($2) by the worker's marginal physical product.

3 To determine a firm's derived demand curve for labour, you look at the marginal revenue product, because that tells you how much additional money the firm will make from hiring an additional worker.

Column 5, the marginal revenue product, is of central importance to the firm. It tells the firm how much additional money it will make from hiring an additional worker. That marginal revenue product represents a competitive firm's demand for labour.

Derived demand curve for labour The curve describing the demand for labour by firms; it depends on the marginal revenue product of labour—how much additional money the firm will make from hiring additional workers.

Exhibit 3 (b) graphs the firm's derived demand for labour, based on the data in column 5 of Exhibit 3 (a). The resulting curve is the firm's **derived demand curve for labour.** It shows the maximum amount of labour, measured in labour hours, that a firm will hire. To see this, let's assume that the wage is $9 and that the firm is hiring 30 workers. If it hires another worker so it has 31 workers, workers' marginal revenue product of $12 exceeds their wage of $9, so the firm can increase profits by hiring another worker. It increases output and profits, since the additional revenue the firm gets from increasing workers from 30 to 31 is $12 and the additional cost the firm incurs is the wage of $9.

Now say the firm has hired 4 additional workers so it has 34 workers. As the firm hires more workers, the marginal product of workers declines. As you can see from the graph in Exhibit 3 (b), the marginal revenue product of increasing from 34 to 35 workers is $4. Since the workers' marginal revenue product of $4 is less than their wage of $9, now the firm can increase profits by laying off some workers. Doing so decreases output but increases profit, because it significantly increases the average product of the remaining workers.

Only when workers' wage of $9 equals the marginal revenue product does the firm have no incentive to change the number of employees. In this example, the wage ($9) equals workers' marginal revenue product at 32 workers. When the firm is employing 32 workers, either hiring another worker or laying off one worker will decrease profits. Decreasing from 32 to 31 workers loses $10 in revenue, whereas increasing from 32 to 33 workers gains $8 in revenue but costs $9 in wages. Since the marginal revenue product curve tells the firm, given a wage, how many workers it should hire, *the marginal revenue product curve is the firm's demand curve for labour.*

The fact that the demand for labour curve is downward sloping means that as more workers are hired, workers' marginal product falls. This might tempt you to think that the last worker hired is inherently less productive than the first worker hired. But that simply can't be because, by assumption, the workers are identical. Thus, the marginal product of any worker must be identical to the marginal product of any other worker, given that a specified number of workers are working. What the falling marginal product means is that *when 30 rather than 25 workers are working,* the marginal product of any one of those 30 workers is less than the marginal product of any one of 25 of those workers when only 25 are working. When the other inputs are constant, hiring an additional worker lowers the marginal product not only of the last worker but also of any of the other workers.

To understand what's going on here you must remember that when marginal product is calculated, all other inputs are held constant—so if a firm hires another worker, that worker will have to share machines or tools with other workers. When you share tools, you start running into significant bottlenecks, which cause production to fall. That's why the marginal product of workers goes down when a new worker is hired. This assumption that all other factors of production are held constant is an important one. If all other factors of production are increased, it is not at all clear that workers' productivity will fall as output increases.

Why does a firm hire another worker if doing so will lead to a fall in other workers' productivity and, possibly, a fall in the average productivity of all workers? Because the firm is interested in total profit, not productivity. As long as hiring an extra worker increases revenue by more than the worker costs, the firm's total profit increases. A profit-maximizing firm would be crazy not to hire another worker, even if by doing so it lowers the marginal product of the workers.

Factors Affecting the Demand for Labour There are many technical issues that determine how the demand for products is translated through firms into a demand for labour (and other factors of production), but we need not go into them in detail. We will, however, state four general principles and give examples of each. The four general principles are:

1. Changes in the demand for a firm's product will be reflected in changes in its demand for labour.
2. The structure of a firm plays an important role in determining its demand for labour.
3. A change in the other factors of production that a firm uses will change its demand for labour.
4. A change in technology will change its demand for labour.

Let's consider each of these principles in turn.

ADDED DIMENSION

DIFFICULTIES IN DETERMINING MARGINAL PRODUCTIVITIES

The economic model of labour markets assumes that marginal productivities can be determined relatively easily. In reality they can't. They require guesses and estimates which are often influenced by a worker's interaction with the person doing the guessing and estimating. Thus, social interaction plays a role in determining wages. If you get along with the manager, his estimate of your marginal productivity is likely to be higher than if you don't. And for some reason, managers' estimates of their own marginal productivity tend to be high. In part because of difficulties in estimating marginal productivities, actual pay can often differ substantially from marginal productivities.

Changes in the Firm's Demand The first principle is almost self-evident. An increase in the demand for a product leads to an increase in demand for the labourers who produce that product. The increase in demand pushes the price of the firm's goods up, raising the marginal revenue product of labour (which, you'll remember, for a competitive firm is the price of the firm's product times the marginal physical product of labour).

The implications of this first principle, however, are not so self-evident. Often people think of firms' interests and workers' interests as being counter to one another, but this principle tells us that in many ways they are not. What benefits the firm also benefits its workers. Their interests are in conflict only when it comes to deciding how to divide up the total revenues among the owners of the firm, the workers, and the other inputs. Thus, it's not uncommon to see a firm and its workers fighting each other at the bargaining table, but also working together to prevent imports that might compete with the firm's product or to support laws that may benefit the firm.

An example of such cooperation occurred when union workers at a solar energy firm helped fight for an extension of government subsidies for solar energy. Why? Because their contract included a clause that if the solar energy subsidy was extended, the union workers' wages would be significantly higher than if it didn't. This cooperation between workers and firms has led some economists to treat firms and workers as a single entity, out to get as much as they can as a group. These economists argue that it isn't helpful to separate out factor markets and goods markets. They argue that bargaining power models, which combine factor and goods markets, are the best way to analyze at what level wages will be set. In other words, the cost of labour to a firm should be modeled as if it is determined at the same time that its price and profitability are determined, not separately.

The Structure of the Firm and Its Demand for Labour The way in which the demand for products is translated into a demand for labour is determined by the structure of the firm. For example, let's consider the difference between a monopolistic industry and a competitive industry. For both, the decision about whether to hire is based on whether the wage is below or above the marginal revenue product. But the firms which make up the two industries calculate their marginal revenue products differently.

The price of a competitive firm's output remains constant regardless of how many units it sells. Thus, its marginal revenue product equals the value of the marginal product. To calculate its marginal revenue product we simply multiply the price of the firm's product by the worker's marginal physical product. For a competitive firm:

Marginal revenue product of a worker = Value of the worker's marginal product

= MPP × Price of product

4 Because a monopolist's marginal revenue is below a competitive firm's price, its demand for labour will be lower, assuming all else equal.

The price of a monopolist's product decreases as more units are sold since the monopolist faces a downward-sloping demand curve. The monopolist takes that into account. That's why it focuses on marginal revenue rather than price. As it hires more labour and produces more output, the price it charges for its product will fall. Thus, for a monopolist:

EXHIBIT 4 The Effect of Monopoly and Firm Structure on the Demand for Labour

Number of workers	Wage *P*	Price	Marginal revenue (monopolist) *MR*	Marginal physical product *MPP*	Marginal revenue product: Competitive *MPP* × *P*	Marginal revenue product: Monopolist *MPP* × *MR*
5	$ 2.85	$ 1.00	$ .75	5	$ 5.00	$ 3.75
6	2.85	.95	.65	3	2.85	1.95
7	2.85	.90	.55	1	.90	.55

$$\textit{Marginal revenue product of a worker} = MPP \times \textit{Marginal revenue}$$

Since a monopolist's marginal revenue is always less than price, a monopolistic industry will always hire fewer workers than a comparable competitive industry, which is consistent with the result we discussed in the chapter on monopoly: that a monopolistic industry will always produce less than a competitive industry, other things equal.

To ensure that you understand the principle, let's consider the example in Exhibit 4, a table of prices, wages, marginal revenues, marginal physical products, and marginal revenue products for a firm in a competitive industry and a firm in a monopolistic industry.

A firm in a competitive industry will hire up to the point where the wage equals *MPP* × *P* (columns 5 × 3). This occurs at six workers. Hiring either fewer or more workers would mean a loss in profits for a firm in a competitive industry.

Now let's compare the competitive industry with an equivalent monopolistic industry. Whereas the firm in the competitive industry did not take into account the effect an increase in output would have on prices, the monopolist will do so. It takes into account the fact that in order to sell the additional output of an additional worker, it must lower the price of the good. The relevant marginal revenue product for the monopolist appears in column 7. At six workers, the worker's wage rate of $2.85 exceeds the worker's marginal revenue product of $1.95, which means that the monopolist would hire fewer than six workers—five full-time workers and a part-time worker.

As a second example of how the nature of firms affects the translation of demand for products into demand for labour, consider what would happen if workers, rather than independent profit-maximizing owners, controlled the firms. You saw before that whenever another worker is hired, other inputs constant, the marginal physical product of all similar workers falls. That can contribute to a reduction in existing workers' wages. The profit-maximizing firm doesn't take into account that effect on existing workers' wages. It wants to hold its costs down. If existing workers are making the decisions about hiring, they'll take that wage decline into account. If they believe that hiring more workers will lower their own wage, they have an incentive to see that new workers aren't hired. Thus, like the monopolist, a worker-controlled firm will hire fewer workers than a competitive profit-maximizing firm.

There aren't many worker-controlled firms in Canada, but a number of firms include existing workers' welfare in their decision processes. Moreover, with the growth of the team concept discussed in the chapter on production, existing workers' input into managerial decision making is increasing. In many Canadian firms, workers have some say in whether additional workers will be hired and at what wage they will be hired. Other firms have an implicit understanding or a written contract with existing workers that restricts hiring and firing decisions. Some firms, such as (until recently) IBM, had never laid off a worker; if they had to reduce their workforce, they created early retirement incentives. Ultimately, however, if their business gets bad enough, the invisible hand wins out over the invisible handshake, and they lay off workers. That happened for IBM, and many large Canadian businesses, in the early 1990s.

Why do owner-controlled firms consider existing workers' welfare? To be seen as a "good employer," which makes it easier for them to hire in the future. Given the strong social and legal limitations on firms' hiring and firing decisions, one cannot simply apply marginal productivity theory to the real world. One must first understand the institutional and legal structures of the labour market. However, the existence of these other forces doesn't mean that the economic forces represented by marginal productivity don't exist. Rather, it means that firms struggle to find a wage policy that accommodates both economic and social forces in their wage-setting process. For example, in the 1980s and 1990s, a number of firms (such as airlines and automobile firms) negotiated two-tier wage contracts. They continued to pay their existing workers a higher wage, but paid new workers a lower wage, even though old and new workers were doing identical jobs. These two-tier wage contracts were the result of the interactions of the social and market forces.

Changes in Other Factors of Production A third principle determining the derived demand for labour is the amount of other factors of production that the firm has. Given a technology, an increase in other factors of production will increase the marginal physical product of existing workers. For example, let's say that a firm buys more machines so that each worker has more machines with which to work. The workers' marginal physical product increases, and the cost per unit of output for the firm decreases. The net effect on the demand for labour is unclear; it depends on how much the firm increases output, how much the firm's price is affected, and how easily one type of input can be substituted for another—or whether one type of input must be used in conjunction with others.

While we can't say what the final effect on demand will be, we can determine the firm's cost minimization position. When a firm is using resources as efficiently as possible, and hence is minimizing costs, the marginal product of each factor of production divided by the price of that factor must equal that of all the other factors. Specifically, the **cost minimization condition** is:

Cost minimization condition The ratio of marginal product to the price of an input is equal for all inputs.

$$MP_L/w = MP_m/P_m = MP_x/P_x$$

where

w = Wage rate

L = Labour

m = Machines

x = Any other input.

If this cost minimizing condition is not met, the firm could hire more of the input with the higher marginal product and less of other inputs, and produce the same amount of output at a lower cost.

Let's consider a numerical example. Say the marginal product of labour is 20 and the wage is \$4, while the marginal product of machines is 30 and the rental price of machines is \$4. You're called in to advise the firm. You say, "Fire one worker, which will decrease output by 20 and save \$4; spend that \$4 on machines, which will increase output by 30." Output has increased by 10 while costs have remained constant. As long as the marginal products divided by the prices of the various inputs are unequal, you can make such recommendations to lower cost.

Changes in Technology Our fourth and final principle governing the demand for labour concerns the effect of changes in technology. What effect will a change in technology have on the demand for an input? This question has often been debated, and it has no unambiguous answer. What economists do know is that the simple reasoning often used by laypeople when they argue that the development of new technology will decrease the demand for labour is wrong. That simple reasoning is as follows: "Technology makes it possible to replace workers with machines, so it will decrease the demand for labour." This is sometimes called *Luddite reasoning* because it's what

ADDED DIMENSION

THE LUDDITES

In the early 1800s, a group of British textile workers revolted against the introduction of a machine to produce cloth called a *wide frame,* which they said resulted in an inferior product. By all accounts, the wide frame produced textiles faster and reduced demand for textile workers. Angered by the introduction of these machines, a group of textile workers masked themselves and went around breaking up wide frame machines. They threatened any employee who used a wide frame. They were known as *Luddites* in memory of Ned Ludd, a worker who, 30 years earlier, had attacked stocking frames because he thought those devices were replacing workers in the manufacture of stockings.

In 1812, after a number of people had been killed, the British government stepped in and ended the movement, hanging some of the Luddite leaders and sending others to the colonies (which in those days was regarded as a severe punishment). By the 1820s, the wide frame was used throughout the British textile industry. But the term *Luddite* has remained part of the English language and is used to describe people who, in fear of losing their jobs, strongly oppose the introduction of new technology.

drove the Luddites to go around smashing machines in early nineteenth-century England.

What's wrong with Luddite reasoning? First, look at history. Technology has increased enormously, yet the demand for labour has not decreased; instead, it has increased as output has increased. In other words, Luddite reasoning doesn't take into account the fact that total output can change. A second problem with Luddite reasoning is that labour is necessary for building and maintaining the machines, so increased demand for machines increases the demand for labour.

Luddite reasoning isn't *all* wrong. Technology can sometimes decrease the demand for certain types of skills. The computer has decreased demand for calligraphers; the automobile reduced demand for carriage makers. New technology changes the types of labour demanded. If you have the type of labour that will be made technologically obsolete, you can be hurt by technological change. However, technological change hasn't reduced the overall demand for labour; it has instead led to an increase in total output and a need for even more labourers to produce that output.

In the 1990s, we're likely to see an enormous increase in the use of robots to do many repetitive tasks that blue-collar workers formerly did. Thus, demand for manufacturing labour will likely decrease, but it will be accompanied by an increase in demand for service industry labour—designing and repairing robots and designing activities that will fill up people's free time.

International Competitiveness and a Country's Demand for Labour The demand for labour in a country is determined by the relative wage of labour in that country compared to the relative wage of labour in other countries. Multinational corporations are continually making decisions about where to place production facilities, and labour costs—wage rates—play an important role in those decisions. That means the country's exchange rate plays an important role in determining the demand for labour in a country. For example, in the early 1990s many foreign automobile companies switched their production of cars to be sold in Canada from production facilities abroad to facilities in Canada. Why? Because the rise in value of foreign currencies, and fall in value of the Canadian dollar, meant that the hourly rate of labour in Canada was much lower than the hourly rate in some foreign countries (Japan, for example).

But why produce in Canada when the hourly rate in Mexico is only a fraction of that in Canada? Or in Malaysia, where the hourly rate is only about one-tenth that in North America? The reasons are complicated, but include: (1) differences in workers—Canadian workers may be more productive; (2) transportation costs—producing in the country to which you're selling keeps transportation costs down; (3) potential trade restrictions—Japan was under enormous pressure to reduce its trade surplus, and to produce in North America helped them avoid future trade restrictions; (4) compatibility of production techniques with social institutions—production tech-

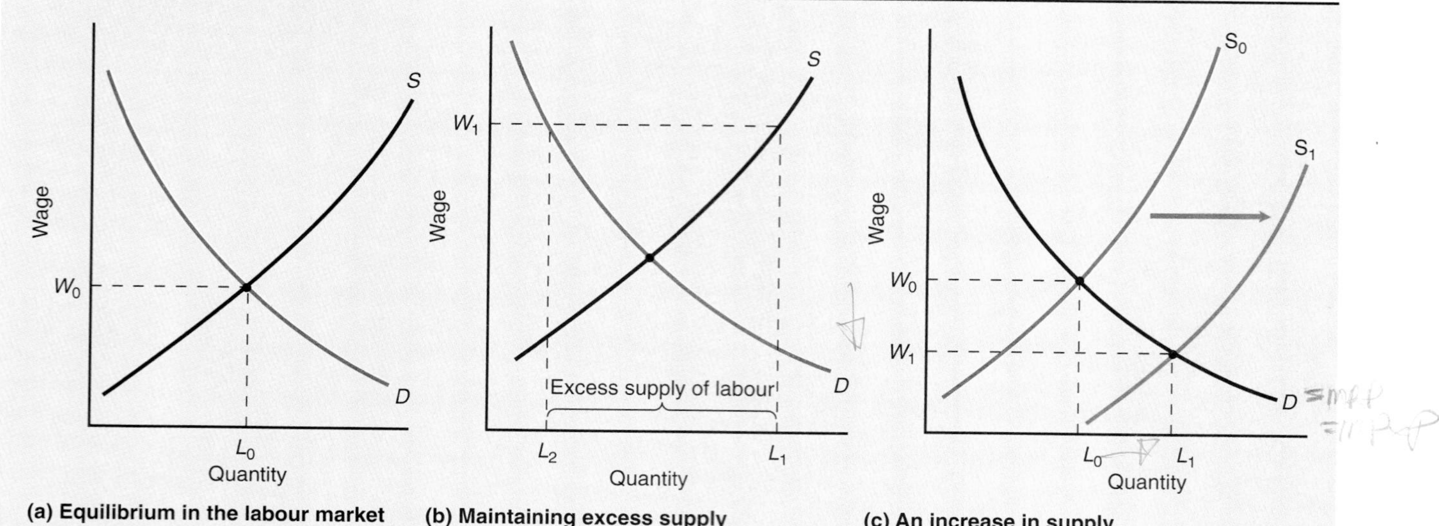

EXHIBIT 5 The Supply of and Demand for Labour and the Effect of an Increase in its Supply
When the supply and the demand curves for labour are placed on the same graph, the equilibrium wage, W_0, is where the supply equals demand as in (**a**). At this wage, L_0 labourers are supplied. We see the effect of an above-equilibrium wage: In order for workers to increase their wages, they must increase the demand for their services or limit the quantity of workers supplied. If they force the firm to pay them a wage of W_1 instead of the equilibrium wage, there will be more workers supplied (L_1) than demanded (L_2). With an excess supply of labour, jobs must be rationed. With an increase in the supply of labour—for example, because of liberalization in the immigration laws—the supply of labour curve shifts outward from S_0 to S_1 as shown in (**c**). Assuming the demand for labour remains the same, the increase in the supply of labour will cause the wage level to drop from W_0 to W_1.

Focal point phenomenon
Phenomenon where a country focuses on another country as a site for business primarily because it knows the conditions in that country, while ignoring other countries that may be just as good but about which it has little knowledge.

niques must fit with a society's social institutions. If they don't, production will fall significantly. Number (5) is the **focal point phenomenon**—a company can't consider all places, and it costs a lot of money to explore a country's potential as a possible host country. Japanese businesses know what to expect when they open a plant in Canada; in many other countries they don't know. So Canada, and other countries that Japanese businesses have knowledge about, become focal points. They are considered by Japanese businesses as potential sites for business, while other, possibly equally good, countries are not. Combined, these reasons lead to a "follow the leader" system in which countries fall in and out of global companies' production plans. The focal-point countries expand and develop; the others don't.

The Supply of and Demand for Labour

Exhibit 5 (a) puts the supply of and demand for labour on the same graph. The equilibrium wage occurs at the point where the quantity of labour supplied equals the quantity of labour demanded. The equilibrium wage is W_0 and the equilibrium quantity of labour is L_0.

Supply and demand forces strongly influence wages, but they do not fully determine wages. Real-world labour markets are filled with examples of suppliers or demanders who resist these supply and demand pressures through organizations such as labour unions, professional associations, and agreements among demanders. But, as we've emphasized throughout the book, supply and demand analysis is a useful framework for considering such resistance.

For example, say that you're advising a firm's workers on how to raise their wages. You point out that if workers want to increase their wages, they must figure out some way either to increase the demand for their services or to limit the labour supplied to the firm. One way to limit the number of workers the firm will hire (and thus keep existing workers' wages high) is to force the firm to pay an above-equilibrium wage, as in Exhibit 5 (b). Say that in their contract negotiations the workers get the firm to agree to pay a wage of W_1. At wage W_1, the quantity of labour supplied is L_1 and the quantity of labour demanded is L_2. The difference, $L_1 - L_2$, represents the

ADDED DIMENSION

WHY SOME WHITE COLLARS SING THE BLUES

By Bruce Little
Economics Reporter

While the recession killed off blue-collar jobs, white-collar employment increased substantially. But paradoxically that wasn't enough to spare white-collar workers from the economy's setbacks in the 1990s.

Between 1989 and 1992, the number of white-collar workers receiving regular benefits under Canada's unemployment-insurance program increased by 33 percent. For blue-collar workers, the increase was 31 percent.

Hardest hit of all among the white-collar crowd were the managers and professionals who sit at the apex of the occupational tree, as the accompanying chart shows. By the time the recession ended in 1992, 158,000 of them were drawing UI, up 46 percent from 1989, the year before the recession began.

In relative terms, that exceeds the 44 percent rise in the number of (former) manufacturing workers who swelled the UI rolls as plants closed or cut their work forces during the recession. In 1992, 180,000 people in what Statistics Canada calls "processing, machining, and fabricating" occupations—the heart of factory work—were drawing UI, up from 125,000 three years earlier.

Yet there's a huge paradox. During that period, the number of managerial and professional jobs *grew* by 233,000 (a gain of 7 percent), while the number of paid factory workers *fell* by 276,000 (a drop of 17 percent).

What's going on here?

The puzzle of the professionals breaks down into two parts. The number of jobs kept growing because many of them are in fields like health, education, and social services, which don't contract just because there's a recession. (Some are shrinking now as governments try to reduce their deficits, but that process hadn't begun in 1992.)

At the same time, companies were laying off middle managers in an attempt to cut costs and make themselves more efficient. That pushed up the number of such people on UI.

Blue- and white-collar workers felt the sting of the recession at different times. The blue-collar workers took their hit first: jobs in manufacturing, construction, and transport (truck drivers, for example) disappeared early as the economy went into its nosedive.

Companies hung onto their white-collar work forces during that period, hoping the 1990s recession—like the one a decade earlier—would be short and sharp. When it turned instead into a protracted period of stagnation, they turned their pruning shears to the office staff.

This breakdown can be found in a fascinating article by Statscan's André Picard in the summer issue of the agency's publication *Perspectives on Labour and Income*. Statscan has been conducting what amounts to a continuing autopsy on the 1990s recession and Mr. Picard's study is the latest contribution.

The growth of managers and professionals getting UI is certainly striking, but it's worth keeping in context. Those groups accounted for one-third of the country's paid workers in 1992 (3.7 million out of 11 million), but less than 14 percent of all UI recipients (158,000 out of 1,150,000).

They were incomparably better off than construction workers, for example, who accounted for 5 percent of the workforce but 17 percent of the UI beneficiaries.

That is characteristic of the entire blue- and white-collar workforces. Blue-collar workers accounted for 41 percent of all paid workers in the 1989–92 period but 60 percent of the UI recipients. White-collar workers accounted for the other 59 percent of workers and only 36 percent of the UI beneficiaries. (Four percent of UI recipients couldn't be classified by occupation.)

Mr. Picard suggests one reason that the managers and professionals—who make up over half of all white-collar workers—fared relatively well despite their increased use of UI: They had the best educations of the lot (four in 10 had a university degree in 1992), which reduced their chance of being unemployed in the first place. Their jobless rate was less than 6 percent in 1992, compared with 14.5 percent among blue-collar workers.

The fact that the recession had a huge impact on the manufacturing, construction and transportation industries also shows up in another of Mr. Picard's figures. The number of men getting UI benefits rose 39 percent, to 682,000, while the number of women on UI climbed by only 17 percent to 466,000. One reason may be that more women work part time, making them ineligible for the kind of UI benefits that go to full-timers.

Regionally, Ontario is the main reason for the big increase in UI recipients between 1989 and 1992. It accounts for only two-fifths of the population, but of the extra 259,000 people drawing regular UI benefits in 1992, 155,000—60 percent of the total—lived in Ontario. That province's jobless rate went from the lowest in the country to more than the national average.

Yet there's another way to keep Ontario's woes in perspective. In 1989, Ontario had the country's highest average personal incomes, 11.4 percent above the national average; in 1992, they were only 7.9 percent above the Canadian norm, but still the highest in the country.

Source: *The Globe and Mail*, June 13, 1994.

number of people who want jobs at wage W_1 compared to the number who have them. In such a case, jobs must be rationed. Whom you know, where you come from, or the colour of your skin may play a role in whether you get a job with that firm.

As a second example, consider what would happen if Canadian immigration laws were liberalized. If you say the supply curve of labour would shift outward and the wage level would drop, you're right, as shown in Exhibit 5 (c). In it the supply of labour increases from S_0 to S_1. In response, the wage falls from W_0 to W_1 and the quantity of labour demanded increases from L_0 to L_1.

EXHIBIT 6 Monopsony, Union Power, and the Labour Market

A monopsonist hires fewer workers and pays them less than would a set of competitive firms. The monopsonist determines the quantity of labour, Q_m, to hire at the point where the marginal factor cost curve intersects the demand curve. The monopsonist pays a wage of W_m. A union has a tendency to push for a higher wage, W_u, and a lower quantity of workers, Q_u.

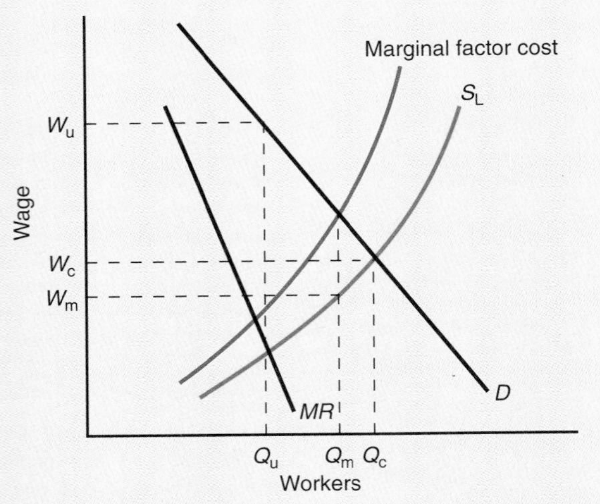

In analyzing the effect of such a major change in the labour supply, however, remember that supply and demand are partial equilibrium tools, and that they're relevant only if the change in the supply of labour doesn't also affect the demand for labour. In reality, a change in Canadian immigration laws might increase the demand for products, thereby increasing the demand for labour and raising wages. Looking at the overall effects of a change, rather than just at the partial equilibrium effects, often makes the final result less clear-cut. That's why it's important always to remember the assumptions behind the model you're using. Those assumptions often add qualifications to the simple "right" answer.

We hope we've given you a sense of how supply and demand analysis can be applied to the labour market. It's applied to the labour market just as it is to any other market: It leads one to consider the incentives of the relevant decision makers, to pinpoint each decision maker's best strategy, and then to see how the various strategies interact within the framework of supply and demand.

Whenever you look at labour markets, thinking about supply, demand, incentives, and strategies is an important first step in figuring out what's going on. However, it's only a first step. As was stated in the introduction to this chapter, the invisible handshake and invisible foot play key roles in determining the wages people receive. In the remainder of this chapter, we discuss some of these issues.

Imperfect Competition and the Labour Market

5 A monopsony is a market in which only a single firm hires labour. A bilateral monopoly is a market in which a single seller faces a single buyer.

Just as product markets can be imperfectly competitive, so too can labour markets. For example, there might be a **monopsony** (a market in which only a single firm hires labour). Alternatively, labourers might have organized together in a union that allows workers to operate as if there were only a single seller. In effect, the union could operate as a monopoly. Alternatively again, there might be a **bilateral monopoly** (a market with only a single seller and a single buyer). Let's briefly consider these three types of market imperfections.

Monopsony

When there's only one buyer of labour services, it makes sense for that buyer to take into account the fact that if it hires another worker, the equilibrium wage will rise and it will have to pay more for all workers. The choice facing a monopsonist can be seen in Exhibit 6. In it, the supply curve of labour is upward sloping so that the **marginal factor cost** (the additional cost to a firm of hiring another worker) is above the supply curve since the monopsonist takes into account the fact that hiring another worker will increase the wage rate it must pay to all workers.

Marginal factor cost The additional cost to a firm of hiring another worker.

Instead of hiring Q_c workers at a wage of W_c, as would happen in a competitive labour market, the monopsonist hires Q_m workers and pays them a wage of W_m. (A good exercise to see that you understand the argument is to show that where there's a

ADDED DIMENSION

DEMOCRACY IN THE WORKPLACE

In Canada, slavery is illegal. One cannot sell oneself to another, even if one wants to. It's an unenforceable contract. But work, which might be considered a form of partial slavery, is legal. We can sell our labour services for a specific, limited period of time.

Is there any inherent reason that such partial slavery should be seen as acceptable? The answer to that question is complicated. It deals with the rights of workers, and is based on value judgements. You must answer it for yourself. We raise it because it's a good introduction to Karl Marx's analysis of the labour market (which deals with alienation) and to some recent arguments about democracy in the workplace.

Marx saw selling one's labour as immoral, just as slavery was immoral. He believed that capitalists exploited workers by alienating them from their labour. The best equivalent we can think of is the way most people today view the selling of sex. Most people see selling sex as wrong because it alienates a person from his or her body. Marx saw all selling of labour that same way. A labour market makes one see oneself as an object, not as a human being.

The underlying philosophical issues of Marx's concern are outside of economics. Most people in Canada don't agree with Marx's philosophical underpinnings. But it's nonetheless a useful exercise to think about this issue and ask yourself whether it helps explain why we somehow treat the labour market as different than other markets and limit by law the right of employers to discriminate in the labour market.

Some of Marx's philosophical tenets are shared by the modern democracy-in-the-workplace movement. In this view, a business isn't owned by a certain group, but is an association of individuals who have come together to produce a certain product. For one group—the owners of shares—to have all the say as to how the business is run, and for another group—the regular workers—to have no say, is immoral in the same way that not having democracy in deciding on government is immoral. According to this view, work is as large a part of people's lives as is national or local politics, and a country can call itself a democracy only if it has democracy in the workplace.

For those of you who say, "Right on!" to the idea of increasing workers' rights, let us add a word of caution. Increasing workers' rights has a cost. It makes it less likely that firms and individuals who can think up things that need doing will do so, and thus will decrease the number of jobs available. It will also enormously increase firms' desire to discriminate. If you know you must let a person play a role in decisions once you hire that person, you're going to be much more careful whom you hire.

None of these considerations mean that democracy in the workplace can't work. There are examples of somewhat democratic "firms." Universities are run as partial democracies, with the faculty deciding what policies should be set. (There is, however, serious debate about how well universities are run.) But as soon as you add worker democracy to production, more questions come up: What about consumers? Shouldn't they, too, have a voice in decisions? What about the community within which the firm is located?

Economics can't answer such questions. Economics can, however, be used to predict and analyze some of the difficulties such changes might bring about.

---

monopsonist, a minimum wage simultaneously can increase employment and raise the wage.)

Union Monopoly Power When a union exists, it will have an incentive to act as a monopolist, restricting supply so as to increase its members' wage. To do so it must have the power to restrict both supply and union membership. The equilibrium wage and employment would depend on who is allowed to be a union member and what methods of redistributing income among union members exist. But there would be a strong tendency for the union to act like a monopolist and to move to an equilibrium somewhat similar to the monopsonist case, except for one important difference. The wage the union would set wouldn't be set below the competitive wage; instead, the wage would be above the competitive wage at W_u, as in Exhibit 6. Faced with a wage of W_u, competitive firms will hire Q_u workers. Thus, with union monopoly power, the benefits of restricting supply accrue to the union members, not to the firm as they did in the monopsonist case.

Bilateral Monopoly As our final case, let's consider a bilateral monopoly in which a monopsonist faces a union with monopoly power. In this case, we can say that the equilibrium wage will be somewhere between the monopsonist wage, W_m, and the union monopoly power wage, W_u, and the equilibrium quantity will be somewhere between Q_u and Q_m in Exhibit 6. Where in that range the wage and equilibrium quantity will be depends on the negotiating skills of the two sides, and other noneconomic forces.

THE OTHER INVISIBLE FORCES AND THE LABOUR MARKET

Let's now consider some real-world characteristics of labour markets. For example:

1. English teachers are paid close to what economics teachers are paid even though the quantity of English teachers supplied significantly exceeds the quantity of English teachers demanded, while the quantity of economics teachers supplied is approximately equal to the quantity demanded.
2. On average, women earn about 78 cents for every $1 earned by men.
3. The relative pay of many kinds of jobs seems to fall into a pattern in which one is always the same percentage of another. This pattern is called a wage contour, and it often remains constant despite shifts in supply and demand among the various jobs.
4. Certain types of jobs are undertaken primarily by members of a single ethnic group. For example, Mohawk Indians make up a large percentage of construction workers on high-rise buildings. They have an uncanny knack for keeping their balance on high, open building frames.
5. Firms often pay higher than "market" wages.
6. Firms often don't lay off workers even when there is a decrease in the demand for their product.
7. Wages don't fluctuate very much as unemployment rises.
8. It often seems that there are two categories of jobs: dead-end jobs and jobs with potential for career advancement. Once in a dead-end job, a person finds it almost impossible to switch to a job with potential.

6 Real-world labour markets are complicated and must be explained by all three invisible forces: the invisible hand, the invisible handshake, and the invisible foot.

Supply and demand analysis alone doesn't explain these phenomena. Each of them can, however, be explained as the result of a combination of invisible forces. Thus, to understand real-world labour markets it is necessary to broaden the analysis of labour markets to include other invisible forces that limit the use of the market. These include the invisible handshake (which creates social limitations on the self-seeking activities of firms and individuals) and the invisible foot (which creates legal limitations on the self-seeking behaviour of firms and individuals). Let's consider a couple of the central issues of interaction among the invisible forces and see how they affect the labour market.

Fairness and the Labour Market

People generally have an underlying view of what's fair. That view isn't always consistent among individuals, but it's often strongly held. The first lesson taught in a personnel or human resources course is that people aren't machines. They're human beings with feelings and emotions. If they feel good about a job, if they feel they're part of a team, then they will work hard; if they feel they're being taken advantage of, they can be highly disruptive.

On some assembly-line jobs, effort is relatively easy to monitor, so individuals can be—and in the past often were—treated like machines. Their feelings and emotions were ignored. Productivity was determined by the speed of the assembly line; if workers couldn't or wouldn't keep up the pace, they were fired.

Efficiency Wages Most modern jobs, however, require workers to make decisions and to determine how best to do a task. Today's managers are aware that workers' emotional state is important to whether they make sound decisions and do a good job. So most firms, even if they don't really care about anything but profit, will try to keep their workers happy. It's in their own interest to do so. That might mean paying workers an above-average wage, not laying them off even if layoffs would make sense economically, providing day care so the workers aren't worried about their children, or keeping wage differentials among workers small to limit internal rivalry. Such actions can often make long-run economic sense, even though they might cost the firm in the short run. They are common enough that they have acquired a name—**efficiency wages**—wages paid above marginal revenue in order to keep workers happy and productive.

Efficiency wages An above-average wage paid to a worker for bringing forth better effort.

Views of fairness also enter into wage determination through political channels. Social views of fairness influence government, which passes laws to implement those views. Minimum wage laws, pay equity laws, and antidiscrimination laws are examples.

Job Discrimination and the Labour Market

Discrimination is an important noneconomic factor that helps explain why labour markets don't operate as supply and demand analysis suggests they should. Managers, like many other people, have prejudices that are reflected (consciously or unconsciously) in their hiring decisions. When one group (in our society, white males) generally controls the hiring for most of the jobs, their prejudices can, and do, affect their hiring decisions. Whether prejudice should be allowed to affect the hiring decision is a normative question for society to settle.

In answering these normative questions, our society has passed laws making it illegal for employers to discriminate on the basis of race, religion, sex, age, disability, or national origin. The reason society has made it illegal is its ethical belief in equal opportunity for all individuals.

Economics cannot provide answers to the normative questions of whether society should allow discrimination. Economics can, however, provide insight into how discrimination, and society's attempts to eliminate it, will affect the economy, so that if society passes laws that prevent market forces from operating, it realizes the cost of doing so.

Three Types of Direct Discrimination In analyzing discrimination, it's important to distinguish three types of direct discrimination. One type of discrimination is based on individual characteristics that will affect job performance. For example, restaurants might discriminate against applicants with sourpuss personalities. Another example of this might be a firm trying to hire young salespeople because its clients like to buy from younger rather than older employees. A second type of discrimination is based on correctly perceived statistical characteristics of a group. A firm may correctly perceive that young people in general have a lower probability of staying on a job than do older people and therefore discriminate against younger people. A third type of discrimination is based on individual characteristics that don't affect job performance or are based on incorrectly perceived statistical characteristics of groups. A firm might not hire people over 50 because the supervisor doesn't like working with older people, even though older people may be just as productive as, or even more productive than, younger people.

Of the three types, the third will be easiest to eliminate; it doesn't have an economic motivation. In fact, discrimination based on individual characteristics that don't affect job performance is costly to a firm, and market forces will work toward eliminating it. An example of the success of a firm's policy to reduce discrimination is the decision by McDonald's to create a special program to hire staff who are mentally challenged, as well as the learning-disabled. These groups make good employees. They have lower turnover rates and follow procedures better than do many of the other people McDonald's hires who view the job as temporary. Moreover, through advertising, McDonald's helped change people's negative view about being served by an exceptional person into a positive view of such service. So in this case market forces and political forces are working together.

7 Three types of discrimination are: (1) discrimination based on individual characteristics that will affect job performance; (2) discrimination based on correctly perceived statistical characteristics of the group; and (3) discrimination based on individual characteristics that don't affect job performance or are incorrectly perceived.

If the discrimination is of either of the first two types and is based on characteristics that do affect job performance, either directly or statistically, the discrimination will be harder to eliminate. Not discriminating can be costly to the firm, so political forces to eliminate discrimination will be working against market forces to keep discrimination.

Whenever discrimination saves the firm money, the firm will have an economic incentive to use subterfuges to get around an antidiscrimination law. These subterfuges will make the firm appear to be meeting the law, even when it isn't. For example, a firm will find another reason to explain why it isn't hiring an older person and will avoid using age as the reason.

Institutional Discrimination Direct discrimination is not the only type of discrimination that can exist. There can also be institutional demand-side discrimination, in which the structure of the job makes it difficult or impossible for certain groups of individuals to succeed. Consider the policies of colleges and universities. To succeed as a professor, administrator, or other professional in the academic market, one must devote an enormous amount of effort during one's 20s and 30s. But these years are precisely the years when, given genetics and culture, many women have major family responsibilities that make it difficult for them to succeed in the academic market. Were academic institutions different—say, a number of positions at universities were designed for high-level, part-time work during this time period—it would be easier for women to advance. Thus, one can argue that women face institutional demand-side discrimination in universities. Of course, one might also argue that it is the supply-side institutions where the discrimination occurs because in relationships, women get more child-rearing responsibility than men. When, for instance, parents have a sick child, someone must stay home, and in the majority of relationships, the woman, not the man, stays home and jeopardizes her advancement potential.

Clearly, we have only touched on the issues; a thorough consideration is beyond the scope of the course. But it is important to note that discrimination can be deeply embedded in institutions and that the lack of direct discrimination actions does not necessarily mean that discrimination does not exist.

Labour Markets in the Real World

Now that we've briefly considered how noneconomic forces can influence labour markets, let's turn our attention to real-world labour markets so you can have a sense of how they developed and how they might affect you.

Labour markets as we now know them developed in the 1700s and 1800s. Given the political and social rules that operated at the time, the invisible hand was free to push wage rates down to subsistence level. Work weeks were long and working conditions were poor. Labourers began to turn to other ways—besides the market—of influencing their wage. One way was to use political power to place legal restrictions on employers in their relationship with workers. A second way was to organize together—to unionize. Let's consider each in turn.

Evolving Labour Laws Over the years, government has responded to workers' political pressure with a large number of laws that limit what can and what cannot be done in the various labour markets. For example, in many areas of production, laws limit to eight the normal number of hours a person can work on one job in a day. The laws also prescribe the amount of extra pay an employee who works more than the normal number of hours must receive. (Generally it's time-and-a-half.)

Similarly, the number and length of coffee breaks workers get are defined by law (one 15-minute coffee break every four hours). Child labour laws mandate that a person must be a certain age in order to be hired. The safety and health conditions under which a person can work are regulated by laws. (For example, on a construction site all workers are required to wear hard hats.) Workers can be fired only for cause, and employers must show that they had cause to fire a worker. (For example, a 55-year-old employee cannot be fired simply because he or she is getting old.) Employers must not allow sexual harassment in the workplace. (Bosses can't make sexual advances to employees and firms must make a good-faith attempt to see that some employees don't sexually harass other employees.)

Pay-equity laws Regulations that attempt to provide similar compensation for comparable jobs.

Pay-equity laws provide for "equal pay for equal work without discrimination on the basis of gender," but that doesn't mean women always receive the salary men get for the same job. It's at this point that the invisible handshake and the invisible foot assert their influence on the market.

One of the problems with pay-equity laws is that they fail to take into account differences in productivity—so if a woman is more productive than a man at a certain task, economic theory says she should be paid more. But compensation schemes rarely account for differences in productivity across workers, let alone across gender—it's much easier for a firm to set a standard wage structure than it is to assess each individual's abilities.

In the continuing evolution of labour legislation, a much broader concept of pay equity has gained increasing support. **Equal pay for work of equal value** attempts to provide the same compensation for different jobs that require approximately the same level of training and skills (such as school bus driver or delivery van driver). This approach still doesn't provide compensation for differences in productivity, but it does try to match compensations across comparable occupations. The main problem with this scheme is that it involves normative decisions such as "a nurse and a teacher should be paid similar salaries," or "an economics professor should earn the same amount of money as an electrician." Given the depth of the normative issues involved, we should expect to see much of this in the news in the 1990s.

Equal pay for work of equal value Providing the same compensation for different jobs that require approximately the same level of training and skill.

What you need to understand is that these laws play an enormously important role in the functioning of the labour market.

Unions and Collective Bargaining Some of the most important labour laws concern workers' right to organize together in order to bargain collectively with employers. These laws also specify the tactics workers can use to achieve their ends. Printers organized in Quebec City and crafts unions organized in Toronto and Hamilton in the early 1800s. The Knights of Labour was formed in 1869, and by 1886 it had approximately 800,000 members (many of whom were in Quebec). But a labour riot in the United States in 1886 turned public opinion against these workers and led to the organization's breakup. After the riot, the American Federation of Labour developed in the United States, while in Canada the Dominion Trades and Labour Congress (later the Trades and Labour Congress of Canada) began to organize strikes to achieve higher wages.

Business opposed unions' right to strike, and initially the government supported business. Police and sometimes the army were sent in to break up strikes. A big strike occurred in 1919: the Winnipeg General Strike. Under the then-existing legal structure of the economy, unions were seen as monopolistic restraints on trade and an intrusion into management rights.

In the 1920s and 1930s, society's view of unions changed, and businesses became more sensitive to allowing workers an input into production decisions. Internal dissension in the U.S. labour movement spilled over into Canada, and in 1936 many Canadian workers affiliated with the newly formed U.S. Congress of Industrial Organizations and, as one consequence, were expelled from the Trades and Labour Congress of Canada. They formed their own body, the Canadian Congress of Labour.

In the United States, businesses weren't happy with unions' increasing strength, and in 1947 they managed to get the Taft-Hartley Act passed. That act placed limitations on U.S. union activities. It allowed states to pass "right-to-work" laws, forbidding union membership to be made a requirement for continued employment. Moreover, it made **closed shops** illegal. In a closed shop the union controls hiring; before anyone can be hired he or she must be a member of the particular union. In **union shops,** which U.S. federal law does permit, individuals are required to join a union after working for the firm for a period of time. A number of states, though, have right-to-work laws that make union shops illegal.

Closed shop A firm in which the union controls hiring.

Union shop A firm in which all workers must join the union.

The story in Canada was very different. In 1939 it became a criminal offence to fire a worker just because the worker belonged to a union. In 1945 a Supreme Court of Canada ruling (sometimes called the *Rand formula*) forced all employees to pay union dues (whether or not they were union members). There were a number of other

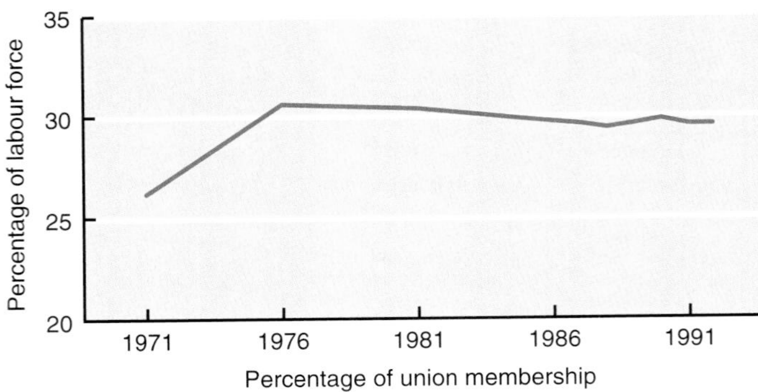

EXHIBIT 7 Union Membership as a Percentage of the Civilian Labour Force

Membership as a proportion of the civilian labour force peaked in the late 1970s and early 1980s.

Source: Canada Yearbook 1994, Statistics Canada.

measures that actually encouraged the union movement: for example, a government-supervised vote had to be held before workers could strike; and penalties were introduced in the event that workers undertook illegal strikes. Both of these provisions, paradoxically, strengthened the union movement because it made union members listen to what union leaders had to say.

In 1950 the two Canadian labour groups (the Trades and Labour Congress and the Canadian Congress of Labour) joined to form the Canadian Labour Congress. As we see in Exhibit 7, since the 1970s, although total membership in unions has been on the rise, union membership as a proportion of the civilian labour force has been declining. (That's because the size of the civilian labour force has been increasing faster than has the number of individuals who have joined a labour union.)

Part of the reason, ironically, is unions' success. By pressuring the government to pass laws that protected workers, unions made themselves less necessary. Another part of the reason is the changing nature of production in North America. Labour unions were especially strong in manufacturing industries. As manufacturing has declined in importance in Canada and the service sector has increased in importance, the base of union membership has been reduced.

That doesn't mean that unions don't have a say in how firms operate. Think of the 1994–95 baseball and hockey seasons—if "seasons" is what they could be called. Players and management disagreed over a number of issues, and for the NHL, only a last-minute deal "saved" the season. The players' union didn't get all that it wanted, nor did the team owners. It's an important lesson to remember that strikes and work stoppages rarely lead to a situation in which everyone is happy and gets what they want.

THE LABOUR MARKET AND YOU

This chapter is meant to give you a sense of how the labour market works. But what does it all mean for those of you who'll soon be getting a job or are in the process of changing jobs? We'll try to answer that question in this section.

One of the major problems you will face is that unemployment falls heavily on youth—from 1989 to 1992 there was a drop in youth employment of about 26 percent. Part-time employment has grown at a much faster rate than full-time work, with the average workweek for part-time workers being only about 16 hours, while full-time workers average about 42 hours per week. Needless to say, you'd prefer a full-time job, unless you highly value your nonmarket activites.

Education levels are playing a more important role than ever before in the labour market. Unemployment rates of those who are between 15 and 24 years old and who have failed to complete high school are over twice as high as unemployment rates for those who complete a university degree. There's a good reason for you to invest in your human capital.

Exhibit 8 shows a variety of potentially useful statistics about the labour market. Let's consider how some of them might affect you. For example, consider relative pay of jobs requiring a university or college degree compared to jobs requiring only high school degrees. Jobs requiring a university or college degree pay significantly more, on average, than do jobs requiring only a high school degree. In recent years the

EXHIBIT 8 Some typical salaries: 1995

Occupation	Salary
Law (3 years of post-graduate study)	
High-ranked school	$80,000
Intermediate-ranked school	40,000
Low-ranked school	25,000
Engineering	
Bachelor's degree	34,000
Master's degree	47,000
Business	
Bachelor's degree	30,000
M.B.A. (2 years of post-graduate study)	45,000
M.D. (at least 5 years of training after the B.A.)	80,000
Ph.D. (5 years of post-gradute study)	
Economics	43,000
Humanities	40,000
Secondary school teacher (at least a B.A.)	30,000
Janitor (high school graduate)	20,000
Retail sales (high school graduate)	18,000
Fast food sales (high school graduate)	12,000

Source: Authors' estimates based on informal surveys.

income gap between the two groups has noticeably increased. So the answer to the question whether it's worthwhile to stick university or college out for another couple of years and get a degree is probably "yes." That's especially true given that recent research has found that the average Canadian will change jobs as many as five times during his or her working life. Having a wide variety of skills—investing in your human capital—is even more important than ever.

Next, consider the salaries of Ph.D.s compared to the salaries of M.B.A.s. A Ph.D. is a person who has gone to graduate school after university or college, usually for a number of years, and earned an advanced degree called a Doctorate of Philosophy—even though there are many subjects besides philosophy (such as economics) in which one can earn a Ph.D. As you can see, starting salaries of Ph.D.s are considerably lower than starting salaries of M.B.A.s and almost all professionals with other kinds of advanced degrees. Does this mean that Ph.D.s are discriminated against? Not necessarily. It's possible that the lower pay of Ph.D.s suggests that Ph.D.s derive a "psychic income" from their work in addition to the amount of money they earn.

Since Ph.D.s are often quite smart, their presumed willingness to accept psychic income as a substitute for higher pay tells you that there's probably much more to consider in a job than the salary. What's most important about a job isn't the wage, but whether you like what you're doing and the life that job is consistent with. (Of course, their lower salaries also could imply that Ph.D.s really aren't so smart.)

So our advice to you is definitely to finish university or college, especially if you enjoy it. (And with books like this, how can you help but enjoy it?) But go to graduate school only if you really enjoy learning. In picking your job, first and foremost pick a job that you enjoy (as long as it pays you enough to live on). Among jobs that you like, choose a job in a field in which the supply of labour is limited, or the demand for labour is significantly increasing. Either of those trends is likely to lead to higher wages. After all, if you're doing something you like, you might as well get paid as much as possible for it.

Jobs in which the supply will likely be limited are those on which the invisible foot has placed restrictions on entry or jobs requiring special abilities. If you have some special ability, try to find a job you enjoy in which you can utilize that ability. You might also look for a job in a field to which entry is restricted, but beware: Jobs

In the late 1800s, many workers worked in sweatshops; they often had quotas that required them to work 60 or more hours a week. Fines were imposed for such indiscretions as talking or smiling. *The Bettmann Archive.*

that are restricted in supply must be rationed, so while such jobs pay higher wages, you may need personal connections to obtain one of them.

We're sure most of you are aware that your choice of jobs is one of the most important choices you'll be making in your life. So we're sure you feel the pressure. But you should also know that a job, unlike marriage, isn't necessarily supposed to be for life. There's enormous flexibility in the Canadian labour market. Many people change jobs even more often than the average five times—say six or seven times—in their lifetime. Thus while the choice is important, a poor choice can be remedied, so don't despair if the first job you take isn't perfect. Good luck.

CHAPTER SUMMARY

- Incentive effects are important in labour supply decisions.
- The demand for labour by firms is a derived demand determined by labour's marginal revenue product.
- A firm's demand for labour is affected by the demand for a firm's product, the firm's internal structure, the price of other factors of production, and technology.
- A monopsony is a market in which only a single firm hires labour; a bilateral monopoly is a market in which there is a single seller and a single buyer.
- In the labour market, the invisible handshake and the invisible foot are very active.
- Labour laws have evolved and will continue to evolve.
- Since the 1980s, labour unions have been declining in importance.
- Discrimination is an important factor that hinders the invisible hand. It has many dimensions.
- Discrimination based on characteristics that affect job performance is hardest to eliminate.
- To be happy, finish university or college and choose a job you enjoy.

KEY TERMS

bilateral monopoly *(297)*
closed shop *(302)*
cost minimization condition *(294)*
derived demand *(288)*
derived demand curve for labour *(290)*
efficiency wages *(300)*
entrepreneurship *(289)*
equal pay for work of equal value *(302)*
focal point phenomenon *(296)*
incentive effect *(283)*
labour market *(283)*
labour productivity *(290)*
marginal factor cost *(297)*
marginal physical product (MPP) *(289)*
marginal revenue product

(MRP) *(289)*
marginal tax rate *(286)*
monopsony *(297)*
pay-equity laws *(302)*
union shop *(303)*
value of marginal product *(289)*

QUESTIONS FOR THOUGHT AND REVIEW

The number after each question represents the estimated degree of critical thinking required. (1 = almost none; 10 = deep thought.)

1. Why are the invisible handshake and the invisible foot more active in the labour market than in most other markets? *(4)*
2. Welfare laws are bad, not for society, but for the people they are meant to help. Discuss. *(8)*
3. Which would you choose: selling illegal drugs at $75 an hour (20 percent chance per year of being arrested) or a $6-an-hour factory job? Why? *(9)*
4. If the wage goes up 20 percent and the quantity of labour supplied increases by 5 percent, what's the elasticity of labour supply? *(3)*
5. A competitive firm gets $3 per widget. A worker's average product is 4 and marginal product is 3. What is the maximum the firm should pay the worker? *(5)*
6. How would your answer to Question 5 change if the firm were a monopolist? *(6)*
7. Why might it be inappropriate to discuss the effect of immigration policy using supply and demand analysis? *(5)*
8. Pay-equity laws require employers to pay the same wage scale to workers who do comparable work or have comparable training. What likely effect would these laws have on the labour market? *(9)*
9. One of the authors has a brother who was choosing between being a carpenter and being a plumber. He was advised to take up plumbing. Why? *(6)*
10. What was the Winnipeg General Strike about? (Requires some research.) *(10)*

PROBLEMS AND EXERCISES

1. Fill in the following table relating number of workers to total product *(TP)*, marginal physical product *(MPP)*, average product *(AP)*, and marginal revenue product *(MRP)*. Assume the competitive firm faces a price of $2 for its good.

Number of workers	*TP*	*MPP*	*AP*	*MRP*
0	10			
2	19			
3		8		
4			8.5	
5				12

2. Your manager comes in with three sets of proposals for a new production process. Each process uses three inputs: land, labour, and capital. Under Proposal A, the firm would be producing an output where the *MPP* of land is 30, labour is 42, and capital is 36. Under Proposal B, at the output produced the *MPP* would be 20 for land, 35 for labour, and 96 for capital. Under Proposal C, the *MPP* would be 40 for land, 56 for labour, and 36 for capital. Inputs' costs per hour are $5 for land, $7 for labour, and $6 for capital.
   a. Which proposal would you adopt?
   b. If the price of labour rises to $14, how will your answer change?
3. A study done by economists Daniel Hamermesh and Jeff Biddle found that people who are perceived as good looking earn an average of 10 percent more than those who are perceived as "homely" and 5 percent more than people who are perceived as "average looking." The pay differential for "homely" *men* was 9 percent greater than for homely *women,* so the poor appearance penalty was found to be greater for men than for women.
   a. What conclusions can one draw from these findings?
   b. Do the findings necessarily mean that there is a "looks" discrimination?
   c. What might explain the larger "looks" pay penalty for males?
4. Suppose in the late 1990s a teen subminimum training wage law were passed by which employers were allowed to pay teenagers less than the prevailing minimum wage.
   a. What effect would you predict this law would have, based on standard economic theory?
   b. Evidence from similar laws passed in other countries suggests that few businesses would use it, and that it would have little effect. What explanation can you give for such evidence?
5. Economists Mark Blaug and Ruth Towse did a study of the market for economists in Britain. They found that the quantity demanded was about 150–200 a year, and that the supply was about 300 a year.
   a. What did they predict would happen to economists' salaries?
   b. What likely happens to the excess economists?
   c. Why doesn't the price change immediately to bring the quantity supplied and the quantity demanded into equilibrium?
6. This question requires some research. Use the methods we've developed in this chapter to explain the 1994–1995 baseball, hockey, and basketball strikes/lockouts. Be sure to describe the market in which the owners and the players operated. Was there perfect competition?

CHAPTER

15

Nonwage and Asset Income: Rents, Profits, and Interest

The first man to fence in a piece of land, saying "This is mine," and who found people simple enough to believe him, was the real founder of civil society.

~Jean-Jacques Rousseau

After reading this chapter, you should be able to:

1. Define rent and explain why landowners bear the entire burden of a tax on land.
2. Explain rent seeking and its relationship to property rights.
3. Differentiate between normal profits and economic profits.
4. Summarize the reasons an entrepreneur searches out market niches.
5. Define interest and explain the loanable funds theory of interest.
6. Demonstrate how interest rates are used in determining present value.
7. Use the annuity rule and the rule of 72 to determine present value.
8. Explain the marginal productivity theory of income distribution.

The four traditional categories of income are wages, rent, profits, and interest. Wages, discussed in the last chapter, are determined by economic factors (the forces of supply and demand), with strong influences by political and social forces that often restrict entry or hold wages at non-market-clearing levels.

The same holds true for nonwage income: rent, profits, and interest. These forms of income are determined by the forces of supply and demand. But, as we have emphasized throughout the book, supply and demand are not necessarily the end of the story. Supply and demand determine price and income, given an institutional structure that includes **property rights** (the rights given to people to use specified property as they see fit) and the **contractual legal system** (the set of laws that govern economic behaviour) of the society. If you change property rights, you change the distribution of income. Thus, in a larger sense, supply and demand don't determine the distribution of income; the distribution of property rights does.

Property rights The rights to use specified property as one sees fit.

Contractual legal system The set of laws that govern economic behaviour.

The system of property rights and the contractual legal system that underlie the Canadian economy evolved over many years. Many people believe that property rights were unfairly distributed to begin with; if you believe that, you'll also believe that the distribution of income and the returns to those property rights are unfair. In other words, you can favour markets but object to the underlying property rights. Many political fights about income distribution concern fights over property rights, not fights over the use of markets.

Such distributional fights have been going on for a long time. In Europe in feudal times much of the land was held communally; it belonged to everyone, or at least everyone used it. It was common land—a communally held resource. As the economy evolved into a market economy, that land was appropriated by individuals, and these individuals became landholders who could determine the use of the land and could receive rent for allowing other individuals to use that land. Supply and demand can explain how much rent will accrue to a landholder; it cannot explain the initial set of property rights.

The type of issues raised by looking at the underlying property rights are in large part academic for Western societies. The property rights that exist, and the contractual legal system under which markets operate, are given. You're not going to see somebody going out and introducing a new alternative set of property rights in which the ownership of property is transferred to someone else. The government may impose shifts at the margin; for example, new **zoning laws** (laws that set limits on the use of one's property) will modify property rights and create fights about whether society has the right to impose such laws. But there will be no wholesale change in property rights. That's why most economic thinking simply takes property rights as given.

Zoning laws Limits on the use of one's property.

But taking property rights as given isn't a reasonable assumption for the developing countries or the formerly socialist countries now in the process of establishing markets. They must decide what structure of property rights they want. Who should be given what was previously government land and property? Who should own the factories? Do those societies want land to be given to individuals in perpetuity, or do they want it given to individuals for, say, 100 years? As these questions have been raised, economists have redirected their analysis to look more closely at the underlying legal and philosophical basis of supply and demand. As they do so they are extending and modifying the economic theory of income distribution, as we'll discuss shortly.

Despite the changes that are taking place, it's helpful to consider the three traditional income categories besides wages (rent, profits, and interest) because doing so provides useful insight into forces that make our economy work and that determine who gets what.

RENT

Rent An income received by a specialized factor of production.

Rent is the income from a factor of production that is in fixed supply. Traditionally rent was associated with land, which was assumed to be a totally fixed factor of production. When the supply of a factor is fixed, all we need to know to determine what the price of land (rent) will be is the amount of land there is and the demand curve.

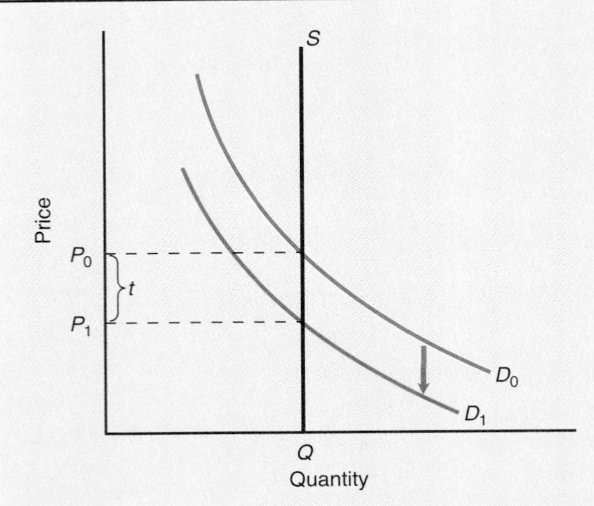

EXHIBIT 1 Rent

A tax on any factor with a perfectly inelastic supply will fall only on the supplier. A tax of t will shift the demand curve down from D_0 to D_1, leaving the after-tax price that the demander pays constant but lowering the after-tax price that the supplier receives by t—from P_0 to P_1.

Exhibit 1 shows how the price of land is determined. In it you can see that since the supply of land is perfectly inelastic, the level of demand determines the rent on land.

The Effect of a Tax on Land

1A Rent is the income from a factor of production that is in fixed supply.

1B As long as land is perfectly inelastic in supply, landowners will pay the entire burden of a tax on land, as in the graph below.

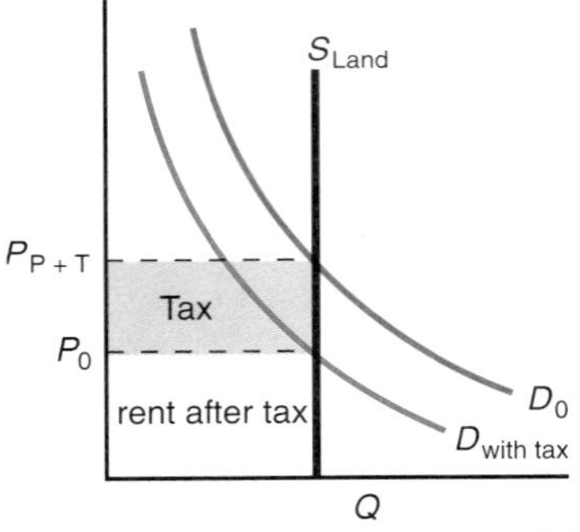

Henry George was a 19th-century economist who advocated the land tax. *Historical Pictures Service.*

To check whether you understand the concept of rent, let's try a couple of questions. Say the government places a tax on the user of land. What will that tax do to the quantity of land supplied? What will that tax do to the price of the land? And who will end up bearing the burden of that tax? (Before proceeding, think, and try to answer these questions.)

The answers you should have given are that the quantity of land supplied will not change, the price of the land will not change, and the owner of the land will bear the entire burden of the tax even though the user of the land will actually pay the tax. In technical terms, the tax shifts the demand curve for land down from D_0 to D_1. Now the user simply pays part of the rental payment (t) to the government. So if the landowner were getting \$100 per year in rent, after a tax of \$30 per year the landowner would get only \$70 per year. This follows immediately from the diagram: Given the quantity of land supplied, demanders will pay no more than the equilibrium price. By assumption, suppliers will supply the same amount of land regardless of the price they receive, so they must bear the entire burden of the tax. If they didn't, the price of land would have to rise and it cannot; demanders won't pay more for that quantity.

If you've followed the analysis, the preceding conclusion was obvious, but now let's extend it to the real world. Say the government increases the property tax. Should tenants who rent apartments worry that such a tax is going to raise rents? The analysis tells us no, they shouldn't; in reality, they do worry about it a lot. Part of the reason is that the assumptions don't fit reality. The supply of land isn't perfectly inelastic; new land can be created by landfills and land can be converted from useless land to useful land by a variety of methods. The supply of apartments is even more elastic since rental apartments have other uses. So the consumers are partially right.

But the model is partially right, too, because even taking these provisos into account, most economists see the supply of apartments as rather inelastic. And as long as the supply of apartments is less elastic than the demand for apartments, most of the property tax will fall on the apartment owner and most of an increase in the property tax won't be passed on to the consumer. It can look as if it's being passed on since actual rents are determined only at periodic intervals, and often the actual rent paid can deviate from the supply/demand-determined rent. Property owners often find it convenient to blame raises in rent on increased costs, even though they would have increased rent even if there had been no tax. Blaming the government is much easier than saying, "Look, apartments are in tight supply. Somebody else will pay me more, so I'm increasing your rent."

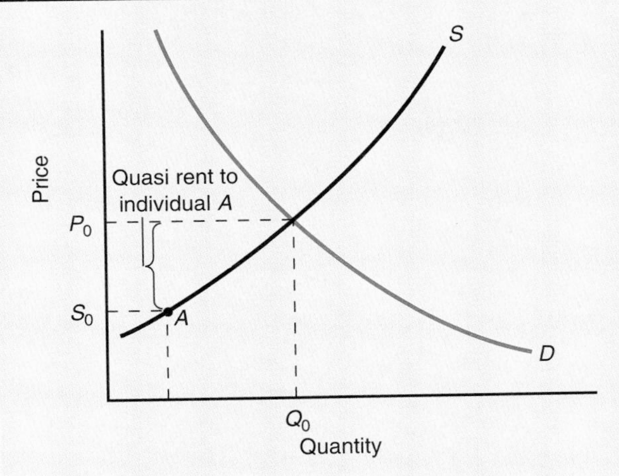

EXHIBIT 2 Quasi Rent

Quasi rent is the payment to a supplier above his or her opportunity cost. In this example an individual represented by point *A* on the supply curve would be willing to supply the good at S_0 but the market equilibrium price is P_0. The difference P_0–S_0 is his or her quasi rent.

The inelastic supply of land and the knowledge that ultimately most of the tax on land will be paid by the owner has led to a number of taxing proposals. One such proposal was put forward by Henry George, who argued that the government should replace all other taxes with a land tax. His proposal enjoyed significant political influence in the late 19th century; an economic institute dedicated to his ideas still exists today.

Quasi Rents

The concept of rent was extended in the 1900s to include any payment to a resource above its opportunity cost—that is, above the amount it would receive in its next-best use. This broader concept of rent is shown in Exhibit 2. In it you can see that the supply curve is upward sloping. Equilibrium is at price P_0 and quantity Q_0. Consider a person on the supply curve at point *A*. That person will receive price P_0, but would have been willing to supply his or her resource at S_0. The difference, $P_0 - S_0$, is the person's rent. (Sometimes this difference is called **quasi rent** or *producer surplus* to distinguish it from pure rent, in which the opportunity cost of supplying the factor is zero.)

Quasi rent Any payment to a resource above the amount that the resource would receive in its next-best use (also called *producer surplus*).

Let's consider an example: Patrick Roy. The demand for his services as a hockey player is high so he earns a multimillion dollar salary. His salary likely significantly exceeds his opportunity cost (the wage he could get at the next-best job). The difference between the two would be the quasi rent component of his salary.

This broader concept of rent applies to all types of income. For example, wage income can include a considerable rent component, as can profits and interest. As long as a supply curve is upward sloping, some suppliers are receiving some rent.[1]

Rent Seeking and Institutional Constraints

Rent seeking Attempting to influence the structure of economic institutions in order to create rents for oneself.

2 Rent seeking is the restricting of supply in order to increase its price. It is an attempt to change the institutional structure and hence the underlying property rights.

The broadened definition of rent led to the insight that if individuals could somehow restrict supply, the rent they received would be higher. Restricting supply in order to increase the price suppliers receive is called **rent seeking.** The concept of rent seeking ties back into our earlier discussion of property rights. If you own something, you can get a rent for owning it. Thus, rent seeking is an attempt to create either ownership rights or institutional structures that favour you. Rent seeking is an activity in which self-interest doesn't necessarily lead to societal interest. The property rights you get might simply take away property rights from another person.

Let's consider an example: high-resolution television. For technical reasons, every country must choose a design (the number and structure of dots per inch on a

[1]One could also say that as long as the demand curve is downward sloping, some demander is receiving rent. One doesn't say that, however. The difference between what a demander would be willing to pay and what the demander actually pays is called *consumer surplus*. As was discussed in earlier chapters, consumer surplus is the demand-side equivalent of rent.

television) for broadcasting. The United States made such a decision for the late 1990s when large-screen television will probably be standard. The firms that got the law defined in a way that favoured their design, rather than a competitor's, received a rent. Thus, firms expended great effort and money to lobby government to adopt their design. When they did so they were rent seeking.

Alternatively, if a group of individuals (workers and firms) can get a tariff imposed on goods that are similar to those that they produce, they'll be able to receive a higher price for their good; a component of that price will be rent, which is why the activity of getting that tariff adopted is another example of rent seeking.

Of course, it is a legitimate activity for people to try to structure property rights to benefit themselves. Sometimes it can have positive social consequences, so there's no easy answer about what is the appropriate social policy to deal with rent seeking. All rent seeking isn't bad, but there's no simple way to separate the bad from the good.

Let's consider a final hypothetical example, from the biotechnology field, which demonstrates one of the problems in making value judgements about rent seeking. Say a firm has created a new organism (a new life form) that eats nuclear waste and transforms it into humus soil. (OK, so we're dreamers; it could happen.) The firm will likely spend enormous amounts of money on trying to ensure that it will "own" that life form, because otherwise it won't make any income from it. In other words it will engage in rent seeking. But the rent seeking has a positive side. Unless a firm can expect to own the life form, it is unlikely to expend money on developing such a life form. Society may well be better off if property rights in such life forms exist.

PROFIT

3 Normal profits are the amount that an entrepreneur can get by supplying entrepreneurship to the market. Economic profits are the entrepreneur's return above and beyond normal profits.

Profit A return on entrepreneurial activity and risk taking.

Normal profits Payments to entrepreneurs as the return on their risk taking.

A second component of nonwage income is profit. **Profit** is a return on entrepreneurial activity and risk taking. As discussed in earlier chapters, profits are generally divided into normal profits and economic profits. **Normal profits** are payments to entrepreneurs as the return on their risk taking. They are an amount that an entrepreneur could get if he or she supplied entrepreneurship to the market. It is the marginal entrepreneur—the entrepreneur whose opportunity cost equals his or her expected gain—who receives a normal profit. Others receive a quasi rent in addition to profit.

Because normal profits include returns on risk taking, profits aren't normally normal. Sometimes normal profits are high; sometimes they're nonexistent; and sometimes they're negative (that is, there are losses). Normal profits should be judged in reference to expectations, not in reference to what they actually are in any one year.

Profit, Entrepreneurship, and Disequilibrium Adjustment

Economic profits are a return on entrepreneurship above and beyond normal profits. Economic profits are a sign of disequilibrium and are a signal to other entrepreneurs that it may be worthwhile to enter that market. Economic profits are the driving force of the invisible hand. The expectation of economic profit leads to innovation and creates incentives for entrepreneurs to enter into new markets. As entrepreneurs enter, they drive the price to an equilibrium price and eliminate economic profits. In this way the expectations of profits are the dynamic force in the economy, unleashing the competitive forces that will eliminate the profits.

To drive this important point home, let's relate this discussion of profit to our earlier analysis. One of the lessons you have learned (or should have learned) from the theoretical analysis of supply and demand is that competition drives the price in a market down to equal average total costs. In the long run, suppliers make normal returns on their investments—that is, zero economic profits. To remind you of that point, we show a firm in long-run equilibrium in Exhibit 3 (a).

Economic profits Definition of profit used by economists that states profit is total implicit and explicit revenues minus total implicit and explicit costs.

Equilibrium isn't something that just exists. It's brought about by competition—by other suppliers entering into the market. Entrepreneurs avoid highly competitive markets that are in equilibrium. Why? Because there aren't a whole lot of profits to be made in such markets. What they look for are not-so-competitive markets—markets in disequilibrium with price greater than average cost. In disequilibrium, you *can* make a lot of profits. Consider Exhibit 3 (b). It represents a market in disequilibrium. Notice that the price is P_0 but the costs per unit are only C_0, which means that the supplier makes an economic profit represented by the shaded rectangle.

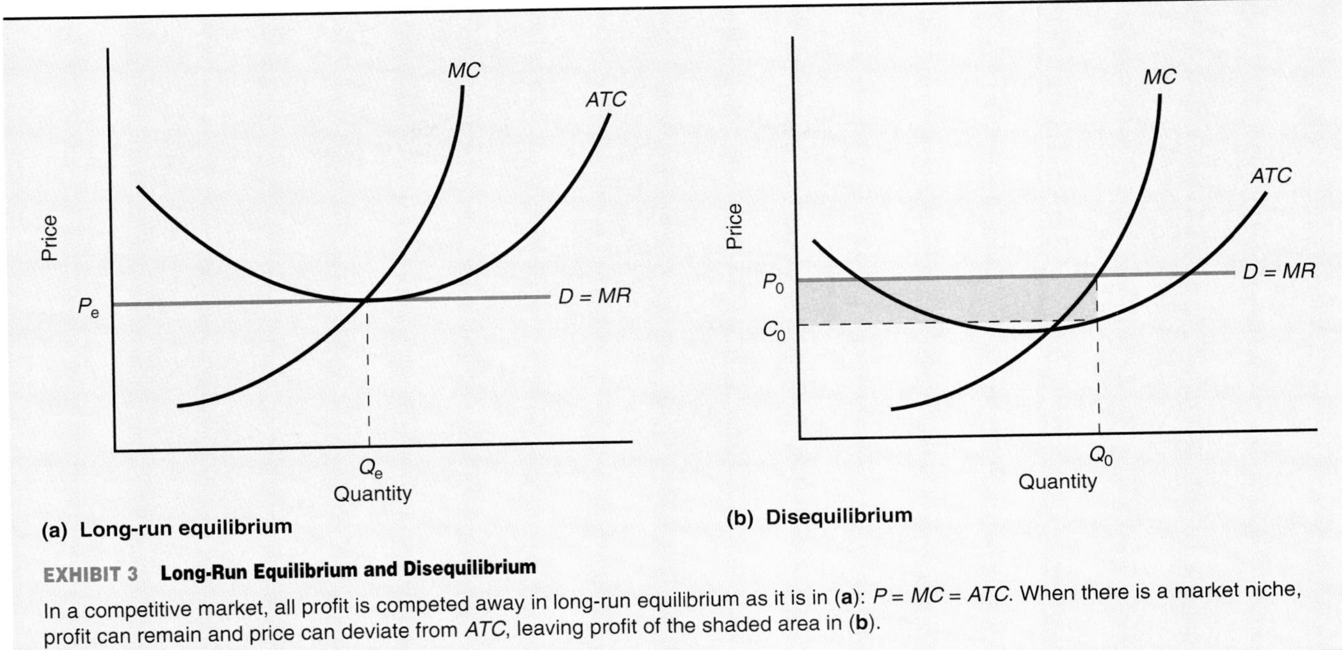

(a) Long-run equilibrium (b) Disequilibrium

EXHIBIT 3 Long-Run Equilibrium and Disequilibrium

In a competitive market, all profit is competed away in long-run equilibrium as it is in (**a**): $P = MC = ATC$. When there is a market niche, profit can remain and price can deviate from *ATC*, leaving profit of the shaded area in (**b**).

Market Niches, Profit, and Rent

Market niche An area in which competition is not working.

What kind of markets are in disequilibrium? Ones in which competition isn't working or is working slowly. An area in which competition is not working is called a **market niche.** Entrepreneurs search for market niches. The best type of market niche to have is a monopoly, in which you're the sole supplier and you face no competition.

Such pure monopolies are rare, but temporary disequilibrium is not rare. In fact, the competitive conditions that push economic profit all the way down to zero often don't exist. For example, if no one knows you're making a profit, competitors won't enter the market to drive the price down; a disequilibrium can continue indefinitely. Bright entrepreneurs who have found a profitable market niche don't advertise the fact.

4 An entrepreneur seeks market niches because within those niches lie economic profits.

Often after an entrepreneur has made an innovation and is enjoying his above-normal economic profits, his income can look a lot like rent. This leads some people to think that society can simply tax it away with no consequence; the entrepreneur's actions won't change. That's true—if one considers those above-normal profits without historical perspective. But with historical perspective, there is a major difference. One of the driving forces behind the entrepreneur was probably the expectation of future profit. That's an important reason why she did her entrepreneurial thing.

It's true that after she's done her entrepreneurial thing, if you take what she got for doing it away from her, it won't change the past. But it will most likely change the future. Other entrepreneurs will draw the inference that their profits will be taken away from them and they won't do their entrepreneurial thing. But entrepreneurial activity is what drives the economy to equilibrium and leads to many of the innovations. If entrepreneurial incentives are removed, society may well be worse off.

INTEREST

Interest The income paid to savers—individuals who produce now but do not consume now.

5A Interest is the income paid to savers—individuals who produce now but do not consume now.

The third traditional component of nonwage income is interest. **Interest** is the income paid to savers—individuals who produce now but don't consume now. Instead they lend out the proceeds of their production, allowing others to invest or consume now. In return they get a promise to pay back that loan, together with whatever interest they negotiated. Whereas profits and rents accrue to the individuals who are supplying some resource to the economy, interest is what businesses and entrepreneurs pay to those who make loans to them. High profits encourage entrepreneurial action; high interest rates discourage it.

Sun Microsystems, founded in 1982, on the vision that "the network is the computer," has rapidly established itself as a leading innovator and global supplier of information technology. One of the leaders of the "open systems" movement, Sun's SPARC workstations and multiprocessing servers rank number 1 in the UNIX market. They found their market niche. © *Sun Microsystems, Inc.*

Alternative Theories of Interest

All economists agree that the interest rate is determined by the supply of and demand for something, but they don't agree on what that something is. Classical economists see the interest rate as determined by the supply of and demand for savings; that is, the interest rate depends primarily upon how much people want to save and how much they want to borrow. Keynesian economists see the interest rate as determined by the supply of and demand for money: how much money is in the economy and how much money people want to hold.

One way to partially reconcile these differences is to distinguish a short-term interest rate from a long-term interest rate. When firms or people borrow for very short periods (less than a year), the interest rate they pay is called a short-term rate. When they borrow for long periods (say, more than 10 years), the interest rate they pay is called a long-term rate.

All economists agree that the supply of and demand for money significantly affects the short-term interest rate. They differ in how they see that short-term interest rate affecting long-term rates.

Keynesians see it as having a much larger effect than do Classicals. For Keynesians, a change in the short-term interest rate will lead to an equivalent long-term interest rate change. Classicals see a changing short-term interest rate often causing the long-term interest rate to move in the opposite direction. Why the difference? Because of differences in views of how quickly, if at all, changes in the money supply are reflected in changes in the price level—changes that require inflation adjustments to the interest rates.

These two theories also agree that, in macroequilibrium, the supply of and demand for both savings and investment will be equal. But they disagree about how that equilibrium is brought about. Keynesians believe that aggregate level of income fluctuates to bring about equilibrium of savings and investment. Classical economists believe that income reflects individuals' desires, and that interest rate changes reflect those desires. For Classicals, any change in the money supply will cause an equivalent change in the price level, which will offset the initial money supply change. Thus only real changes matter.

5B The loanable funds theory of interest says the interest rate is determined by the forces of demand and supply.

Loanable funds theory of interest A theory that suggests the interest rate is determined by the demand for and supply of funds available for investment.

There's no way we have time to do justice to either of these theories; all theories of interest rates are complicated (there are even whole courses devoted to the study of interest rates). To give you an idea of how interest rates are determined in a very simple model, we'll briefly consider the loanable funds theory of interest.

The **loanable funds theory of interest** is based on the idea that the demand for and the supply of loanable funds determine the equilibrium interest rate. Consider Exhibit 4 (a). The demand for loanable funds comes from businesspeople who want to borrow funds for capital expansion—building new plants, obtaining new machin-

ADDED DIMENSION

WHERE TO FIND A MARKET NICHE

Many kinds of market niches exist, and competition works because people search out these market niches and exploit them. In doing so, they eliminate the niches. That's what competition is.

The most likely place to find a temporary market niche may be at your current job. Say you're working for a construction firm and notice that the firm is having trouble reaching high places where it needs to work. The firm doesn't often work on high places, so it isn't worthwhile for it to buy an aerial lift truck; but when it does need to work up high, it could save enormous amounts of time and money if it had such a lift. You check out other construction firms and find they're in a similar situation. You quit your job, buy an aerial lift truck, and start your own firm, renting out your services. For a while, at least, you'll have a market niche.

That is the strategy we followed with this book. Most of the other introductory economics textbooks we read were staid and boring. We believed there was room in the market for a book with pizzazz—a book in which the authors wouldn't be afraid to allow their true style to show through. This book exists in part because of market incentives that led us to exploit a market niche. It's the invisible hand at work.

But market incentives aren't the only reason we wrote this book. We wrote this book because we didn't like the way we were taught introductory economics. Given our egos, we thought we could do better—that we could make economics come alive. The desire to "do it right" was the most important reason we wrote this book. (That isn't to say that the expectation of profit didn't play a role.)

The lesson is simple: To understand the economy it's important to remember that, while the profit motive drives people, so too do other motives.

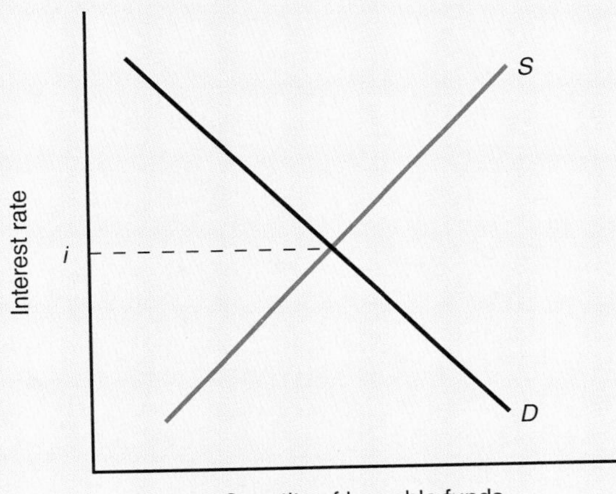

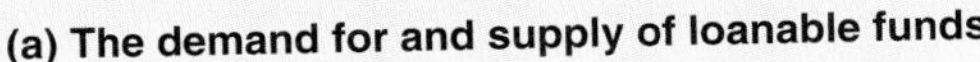
(a) The demand for and supply of loanable funds

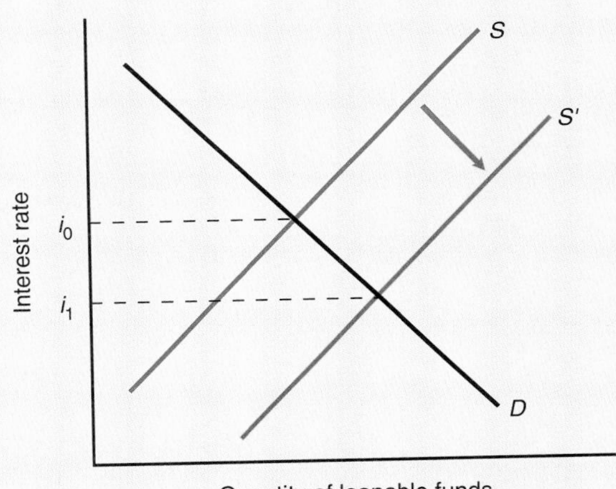

(b) An increase in the supply of loanable funds reduces the interest rate

EXHIBIT 4 The Loanable Funds Theory of Interest

ery, and purchasing new technologies. The demand curve is downward sloping since the lower the cost of borrowing, the more willing are firms to borrow funds. Think of this either in terms of it costing the firm less to borrow, or alternatively, in terms of comparing the interest rate to the rate of return on an investment project—sometimes referred to as the **internal rate of return.** Say the firm believes that it will receive a 4 percent return from building a new plant. If the borrowing costs exceed 4 percent the project isn't attractive, whereas if the borrowing costs are lower than 4 percent, it might make sense to go ahead with the project. When interest rates rise, the cost of borrowing goes up, and, given a fixed internal rate of return, the rise leads to less borrowing. That's because the proposed project no longer offers an attractive rate of return.

Internal rate of return The rate of return on an investment project.

The supply side of the market is based on how households save. When the return from saving is high, households are willing to save more of their incomes. If they are saving more, they are consuming less. The benefit they receive from doing so is the higher consumption they will enjoy in the future when they receive the principal and the interest on the funds they lent. This suggests that *the interest rate can be viewed as the opportunity cost of current consumption*—if you give up some consumption today, the best alternative use of your funds is to save them, and for that you'll receive interest on every dollar you save. That means the supply of loanable funds is a positive function of the interest rate.

The equilibrium interest rate is determined by the intersection of the demand and supply curves. When they shift, equilibrium interest rates change. Consider, for example, a reduction in taxes on the interest earnings that households receive. That would, other things constant, raise the supply of loanable funds, thereby lowering the interest rate. This is shown in Exhibit 4 (b).

As you can see, this is a very simple model of interest rate determination. Others are much more complex, explaining short-term interest rates and long-term interest rates, and how they are related. But one aspect of the interest rate is absolutely essential: its role in allowing us to determine the present value of future income flows and the future values of income in the present.

Present value Method of translating a flow of future income or savings into its current worth.

Present Value **Present value** is a method of translating a flow of future income or savings into its current worth. For example, say a smooth-talking, high-pressure salesperson is wining and dining you. "Isn't that amazing?" the salesman says. "My company will pay $10 a year not only to you, but also to your great-great-great-grandchildren, and more, for 500 years—thousands of dollars in all. And I will sell this annuity—this promise to pay money at periodic intervals in the future—to you for a payment to me now of only $800, but you must act fast. After tonight the price will rise to $2,000."

Do you buy it? Our rhetoric suggests that the answer should be no—but can you explain why? And what price *would* you be willing to pay?

To decide how much an annuity is worth, you need some way of valuing that $10 per year. *You can't simply add up the $10 five hundred times.* Doing so is wrong. Instead you must *discount* all future dollars by the interest rate in the economy. Discounting is required because a dollar in the future is not worth a dollar now.

If you have $1 now, you can take that dollar, put it in the bank, and in a year you will have that dollar plus interest. If the interest rate you can get from the bank is 5 percent, that dollar will grow to $1.05 a year from now. That means also that if the interest rate in the economy is 5 percent, if you have 95¢ now, in a year it will be worth $.9975 (1.05% × $.95 = $.9975). Reversing the reasoning, $1 one year in the future is worth 95¢ today. So the present value of $1 one year in the future at a 5 percent interest rate is 95¢.

6 Interest plays an essential role in the present value formula.

A dollar *two* years from now is worth even less today. Carry out that same reasoning and you'll find that if the interest rate is 5 percent, $1 two years from now is worth approximately 90¢ today. Why? Because you could take 90¢ now, put it in the bank at 5 percent interest, and in two years have $1.

The Present Value Formula Carrying out such reasoning for every case would be a real pain. But luckily, there's a formula and a table that can be used to determine the present value (*PV*) of future income. The formula is:

$$PV = A_1/(1 + i) + A_2/(1 + i)^2 + A_3/(1 + i)^3 + \ldots + A_n/(1 + i)^n$$

where

A_n = the amount of money received n periods in the future

i = the interest rate in the economy (assumed constant).

Solving this formula for any time period longer than one or two years is complicated.

EXHIBIT 5 Sample Present Value and Annuity Tables

Year	Interest Rate						
	3%	4%	6%	9%	12%	15%	18%
1	0.97	0.96	0.94	0.92	0.89	0.87	0.85
2	0.94	0.92	0.89	0.84	0.80	0.76	0.72
3	0.92	0.89	0.84	0.77	0.71	0.66	0.61
4	0.89	0.85	0.79	0.71	0.64	0.57	0.52
5	0.86	0.82	0.75	0.65	0.57	0.50	0.44
6	0.84	0.79	0.70	0.60	0.51	0.43	0.37
7	0.81	0.76	0.67	0.55	0.45	0.38	0.31
8	0.79	0.73	0.63	0.50	0.40	0.33	0.27
9	0.77	0.70	0.59	0.46	0.36	0.28	0.23
10	0.74	0.68	0.56	0.42	0.32	0.25	0.19
15	0.64	0.56	0.42	0.27	0.18	0.12	0.08
20	0.55	0.46	0.31	0.18	0.10	0.06	0.04
30	0.41	0.31	0.17	0.08	0.03	0.02	0.01
40	0.31	0.21	0.10	0.03	0.01	0.00	0.00
50	0.23	0.14	0.05	0.01	0.00	0.00	0.00

(a) Present value table
The present value of a future dollar converts a known future amount into a present amount.

Number of years	Interest Rate						
	3%	4%	6%	9%	12%	15%	18%
1	0.97	0.96	0.94	0.92	0.89	0.87	0.85
2	1.91	1.89	1.83	1.76	1.69	1.63	1.57
3	2.83	2.78	2.67	2.53	2.40	2.28	2.17
4	3.72	3.63	3.47	3.24	3.04	2.85	2.69
5	4.58	4.45	4.21	3.89	3.60	3.35	3.13
6	5.42	5.24	4.92	4.49	4.11	3.78	3.50
7	6.23	6.00	5.58	5.03	4.56	4.16	3.81
8	7.02	6.73	6.21	5.53	4.97	4.49	4.08
9	7.79	7.44	6.80	6.00	5.33	4.77	4.30
10	8.53	8.11	7.36	6.42	5.65	5.02	4.49
15	11.94	11.12	9.71	8.06	6.81	5.85	5.09
20	14.88	13.59	11.47	9.13	7.47	6.26	5.35
30	19.60	17.29	13.76	10.27	8.06	6.57	5.52
40	23.11	19.79	15.05	10.76	8.24	6.64	5.55
50	25.73	21.48	15.76	10.96	8.30	6.66	5.55

(b) Annuity table
The present value of a yearly stream of income converts a known stream of income into a present amount.

To deal with it, people either use a business computer or a present value table like that in Exhibit 5 (a).

Exhibit 5 (a) gives the present value of a single dollar at some time in the future at various interest rates. Notice a couple of things about the chart. The further into the future one goes and the higher the interest rate, the lower the present value. At a 12 percent interest rate, $1 fifty years from now has a present value of essentially zero.

Exhibit 5 (b) is an annuity chart; it tells us how much a constant stream of income for a specific year is worth. Notice that as the interest rate rises, the value of an annuity falls. At an 18 percent interest rate, $1 per year for 50 years has a present value of $5.55. To get the value of amounts other than $1, one simply multiplies the entry in the table by the amount. For example, $10 per year for 50 years at 18 percent interest is 10 × $5.55, or $55.50.

As you can see, the interest rate in the economy is a key to present value. *You must know the interest rate to know the value of money over time.* The higher the current (and assumed constant) interest rate, the more a given amount of money in the present will be worth in the future. Or alternatively, the higher the current interest rate, the less a given amount of money in the future will be worth in the present.

Some Rules of Thumb for Determining Present Value Sometimes you don't have a present value table or a business computer handy. For those times, there are a few rules of thumb and highly simplified formulas for which you don't need either a present-value table or a calculator. Let's consider two of them: the infinite annuity rule and the rule of 72.

7A $PV = X/i$ states the annuity rule: Present value of any annuity is the annual income it yields divided by the interest rate.

The Annuity Rule To find the present value of an annuity that will pay $1 for an infinite number of years in the future (more appropriately termed a *perpetuity*) when the interest rate is 5 percent, we simply divide $1 by 5 percent (.05). Doing so gives us $20. So at 5 percent, $1 a year paid to you forever has a present value of $20. Our general **annuity rule** for any annuity is:

$$PV = X/i$$

That is, the present value of an infinite flow of income, X, is that income divided by the interest rate, i.

Most of the time, people don't offer to sell you annuities for the infinite future. A typical annuity runs for 30, 40, or 50 years. However, the annuity rule is still useful. As you can see from the present-value table, in 30 years at a 9 percent interest rate, the present value of $1 isn't much (it's 8¢), so we can use this infinite flow formula as an approximation of long-lasting, but less than infinite, flows of future income. We simply subtract a little bit from what we get with our formula. The longer the time period, the less we subtract. For example, say you are wondering what $200 a year for 40 years is worth when the interest rate is 8 percent. Dividing $200 by .08 gives $2,500, so we know the annuity must be worth a bit less than $2,500. (It's actually worth $2,411.)

The annuity rule allows us to answer the question posed at the beginning of this section: How much is $10 a year for 500 years worth right now? The answer is that it depends on the interest rate you could earn on a specified amount of money now. If the interest rate is 10 percent, the maximum you should be willing to pay for that 500-year $10 annuity is $100:

$$\$10/.10 = \$100$$

If the interest rate is 5 percent, the most you should pay is $200 ($10/.05 = $200). So now you know why you should have said no to that supersalesman who offered it to you for $800.

7B The Rule of 72 states that 72 divided by the interest rate is the number of years in which a certain amount of money will double in value.

The Rule of 72 A second rule of thumb for determining present values of shorter time periods is the **rule of 72.** The rule of 72 states:

> *The number of years it takes for a certain amount to double in value is equal to 72 divided by the rate of interest.*

Say, for example, that the interest rate is 4 percent. How long will it take for your $100 to become worth $200? Dividing 72 by 4 gives 18. So the present value of $200 at a 4 percent interest rate 18 years in the future is about $100. (Actually it's $102.67.)

Alternatively, say that you will receive $1,000 in 10 years. Is it worth paying $500 for that amount now if the interest rate is 9 percent? Using the rule of 72, we know that at a 9 percent interest rate it will take about eight years for $500 to double:

$$72/9 = 8$$

so the future value of $500 is more than $1,000. It's probably about $1,200. (Actually, it's $1,184.) So if the interest rate in the economy is 9 percent, it's not worth paying $500 now in order to get that $1,000 in 10 years. By investing that same $500 today at 9 percent, you can have $1,184 in 10 years.

The Importance of Present Value Many business decisions require such present value calculations. In almost any business, you'll be looking at flows of income in the future and comparing them to present costs or to other flows of money in the future. That's why understanding present value is a necessary tool.

ADDED DIMENSION

THE PRESS AND PRESENT VALUE

The failure to understand the concept of present value often shows up in the popular press. Here are three examples.

Headline: **COURT SETTLEMENT IS $40,000,000**
Inside story: The money will be paid out over a 40-year period.
Actual value: $11,925,000 (8 percent interest rate).
Headline: **DISABLED WIDOW WINS $25 MILLION LOTTERY**
Inside story: The money will be paid over 20 years.
Actual value: $13,254,499 (8 percent interest rate).
Headline: **BOND ISSUE TO COST TAXPAYERS $68 MILLION**
Inside story: The $68 million is the total of interest and principal payments. The interest is paid yearly; the principal won't be paid back to the bond purchasers until 30 years from now.
Actual cost: $20,000,000 (8 percent interest rate).

Such stories are common. Be on the lookout for them as you read the newspaper or watch the evening news.

THE MARGINAL PRODUCTIVITY THEORY OF INCOME DISTRIBUTION

We've completed our brief survey of rent, profits, and interest. Let's now consider how these categories of income combine with wage income to fit into a theory of income distribution.

The traditional economic theory of the distribution of income is **marginal productivity theory.** This theory states that factors are paid their marginal revenue product (what they contribute at the margin to revenue). We saw how marginal revenue product of labour was determined in the last chapter. In marginal productivity theory, that same reasoning is used to explain the income going to the other three factors. If that factor is entrepreneurship, then the income the person receives can be called *profit;* if that factor is a fixed factor, the income the person receives can be called *rent;* if the factor is current production that is not consumed, the income that person receives can be called *interest.* Marginal productivity theory essentially says that supply and demand determine who gets what.

8 Marginal productivity theory states that factors of production are paid their marginal revenue product.

Modern economists are in the process of extending this functional theory. One extension is to look at the theory of income distribution more abstractly than did early Classical economists. Modern-day economists focus their analysis on what "unspecified" factors of production will be paid, not on what labour or capital or entrepreneurs will be paid. Whether an unspecified factor income is interest, rent, profits, or wages doesn't matter to the analysis since the forces of supply and demand are the same in each case. Modern economists argue that what factors will be paid depends upon (1) the supply of that factor and (2) the derived demand for that factor, which in turn depends upon the marginal productivity of that factor. Thus, they still use the marginal productivity theory, but they use it more abstractly.

Modern-day economists stopped looking at the functional distribution of income among rent, profits, interest, and wages, and started to look at the issue more abstractly because the social reality had changed. The marginal productivity theory of the functional distribution of income was developed to reflect a social reality that had distinct classes of people. One class represented the workers; another represented a group of gentrified landowners who received rent; another represented a group of energetic industrialists; and the fourth represented a group who controlled much of the financial wealth of the society. The wage, rent, profits, and interest categories fit that social reality nicely.

Society's view of individuals who receive their income from investments has often been less than admiring, as seen in the 18th-century etching by Brichet of "The Financier." *Bleichroeder Print Collection, Baker Library, Harvard Business School.*

Modern society is much more complicated and far less class-oriented, which means that the wage/rent/profits/interest components of income are often mixed. When the president of a huge corporation earns $1,000,000 a year, few economists would see that as wage income. Even the terminology describing income forms that modern economists use is different. They often don't talk about labour income as wage income. Instead they use the concept *human capital* for "labour" to emphasize the profit and rent component of wages income.

A second extension modern economists are making to the marginal productivity theory of the functional distribution of income is that they are looking behind it. Marginal productivity theory explains the distribution of income, *given property rights.* It does not explain why property rights are what they are. As we discussed in the beginning of this chapter, modern economists are going beyond the marginal productivity theory of income and are trying to explain why property rights are what they are. This doesn't mean that modern economists don't accept marginal productivity theory; it simply means that they are trying to get at a deeper understanding of the distribution of income.

CONCLUSION

Despite the fact that modern economists are currently expanding the theory of income distribution and are viewing the traditional categories of factors as less important, there is still much to be gained from a knowledge of the traditional theory of income distribution. For example, it tells us that factors in inelastic supply will bear the burden of a large portion of any tax on users of that factor. Similarly it highlights some key elements of the economic forces that determine who gets what—how the forces of supply and demand work. The trick is to understand that and simultaneously to understand the role that political and social forces play in determining what the underlying property rights are, and how those forces interact with economic forces. These questions are high on modern economists' research agendas. Their analysis of rent seeking will likely yield new insights in the years to come.

CHAPTER SUMMARY

- Rent is the income paid to a factor of production that is perfectly inelastic in supply.
- Rent seeking is an attempt to create ownership rights and institutional structures that favour you.
- Normal profits are payments to entrepreneurs and the return on their risk taking. Economic profits are a return on entrepreneurship above and beyond normal profits.
- Entrepreneurs search out market niches in order to earn above-normal profits. Successful search by entrepreneurs tends to eliminate those above-normal profits.
- Interest is the income paid to savers—individuals who produce now but do not consume now.
- The annuity rule and the rule of 72 are useful rules of thumb for determining present value.
- The marginal productivity theory of distribution is the theory that factors of production are paid their marginal revenue product.
- Property rights determine the distribution of income; supply and demand forces distribute income, given property rights.

KEY TERMS

annuity rule *(318)*
contractual legal system *(309)*
economic profits *(312)*
interest *(313)*
internal rate of return *(315)*
loanable funds theory of interest *(314)*
marginal productivity theory *(319)*
market niche *(313)*
normal profits *(312)*
present value *(316)*
profit *(312)*
property rights *(309)*
quasi rent *(311)*
rent *(309)*
rent seeking *(311)*
rule of 72 *(318)*
zoning laws *(309)*

QUESTIONS FOR THOUGHT AND REVIEW

The number after each question represents the estimated degree of critical thinking required. (1 = almost none; 10 = deep thought.)

1. List the four traditional categories of income and explain why they have become less important to modern economic analysis. *(2)*
2. Some people argue that zoning laws are immoral. Based on your understanding of property rights, explain how these people likely justify this position. *(8)*
3. Which would an economist normally recommend taxing: an elastic supply or an inelastic supply? Why? *(4)*
4. Differentiate normal profits from economic profits. *(3)*

5. Explain how technological change might affect the equilibrium interest rate under the loanable funds theory of interest. *(5)*
6. "In perfect competition no one would get rich quick, but the economy would stagnate." Evaluate this statement. *(8)*
7. A salesperson calls you up and offers you an annuity that will pay $200 a year for life. If the interest rate is 7 percent, how much should you be willing to pay for that annuity? *(3)*
8. The same salesperson offers you a lump sum of $20,000 in 10 years. How much should you be willing to pay? (The interest rate is still 7 percent.) *(4)*
9. Define human capital and explain why modern economists' use of the term makes the functional distribution of income analysis less useful. *(5)*
10. "If all people were paid their marginal product, there would be true justice in the economy." Evaluate this statement. *(9)*

PROBLEMS AND EXERCISES

1. Demonstrate graphically how the price of land is determined.
   a. Show the effect of a tax on that land.
   b. Explain why that tax won't cause the price of land to rise.
   c. Based on this analysis, would you support more extensive use of land and property taxes in Canada? Why?
2. What is the present value of a cash flow of $100 per year forever (a perpetuity), assuming:
   The interest rate is 10 percent.
   The interest rate is 5 percent.
   The interest rate is 20 percent.
   a. Working with those same three interest rates, what are the future values of $100 today in one year? How about in two years?
   b. Working with those same three interest rates, how long will it take you to double your money?
3. A team of scientific engineers has designed a new method of generating electricity and of desalinating water. It's a desert wind tower—a hollow cylinder 1,000 metres high (about twice the height of the CN Tower in Toronto). Sea water is pumped into the top of the tower, where it evaporates rapidly. As the air in the tower is cooled by the evaporation, the water falls faster and faster (much like the downdraft of a chimney) and by the time it reaches the bottom of the tower it is going hundreds of miles per hour—fast enough to power turbines. The cost of electricity from this process is predicted to be 2 cents per kilowatt hour—one fourth the cost of generating electricity by oil. The evaporated water could also be condensed and used as fresh water, since the salt will have been removed.
   a. If this concept proves feasible, what would likely happen to the value of desert land near an ocean?
   b. What effect would it have on the price of oil?
   c. If you were advising a major oil-producing country, would you encourage development of this new technology? Why or why not?
4. Taxes on goods with elastic supply have negative incentive effects, so in the late 1980s, following the advice of some economists, Margaret Thatcher, who was then Prime Minister of Great Britain, changed the property tax—in which a person's tax depended on the amount of property the person owned (a tax that had negative incentive effects)—to a poll tax—a tax at a set rate that every individual had to pay. The poll tax had no negative incentive effect.
   a. Show why the poll tax on a perfectly inelastic supply is "theoretically" preferable to a property tax in which the supply is somewhat elastic.
   b. State what you think the real-life consequences of the introduction of the poll tax were.
5. In 1986, all the land in Japan had a total market value of over three times the total market value of the land in Canada, even though there is much more usable land in Canada than there is in Japan. How could there be this difference in total land value between the two countries?
6. In divorce cases, a common debate concerns whether an advanced degree (such as a Ph.D.) should be considered marital property in which the academic advanced degree-holder's spouse should be given an interest.
   a. What are the arguments in favour of seeing it as marital property?
   b. What are the arguments against?
7. In divorce cases, when marital property is divided, it is common for spouses to make cross claims against each other's pension incomes (even if they won't be paid for many years). What are the arguments in favour of, and against, this practice?

CHAPTER

16

Who Gets What? The Distribution of Income

"God must love the poor," said Lincoln, "or he wouldn't have made so many of them." He must love the rich, or he wouldn't divide so much mazuma among so few of them.

~H. L. Mencken

After reading this chapter, you should be able to:

1. State what a Lorenz curve is.
2. Explain what has happened to the Canadian Lorenz curve over time.
3. State the official definition of low income.
4. Summarize the statistical findings on income distribution.
5. Explain three problems in determining whether an equal income distribution is fair.
6. List three side effects of redistributing income.
7. Summarize Canadian expenditure programs to redistribute income.

In 1988, Michael Milken, the junk bond king who was later convicted of insider trading, earned $550 million; that's $10,576,923 per week. Assuming he worked 70 hours per week (you have to work hard to earn that kind of money), that's $151,099 per hour.

In the mid-1990s, the average doctor earned $150,000; that's $2,885 per week. Assuming she worked 70 hours per week (she's conscientious, makes house calls, and spends time with her hospitalized patients), that's $41 per hour.

In the mid-1990s, Joe Smith, a cashier in a fast-food restaurant, earned $22,100, or $425 per week. His base wage was $5.00 per hour. But to earn enough for his family to be able to eat, he worked a lot of overtime, for which he was paid time and a half, or $7.50 per hour. So he made $425 per week by working 70 hours a week.

In the mid-1990s, Nguyen, a peasant in Vietnam, earned $260; that's $5 per week. Assuming he worked 70 hours per week (you have to work hard at that rate of pay just to keep from starving), that's 7¢ per hour.

Are such major differences typical of how income is distributed among people in general? Are such differences fair? And if they're unfair, what can be done about them? This chapter addresses such issues.

WAYS OF CONSIDERING THE DISTRIBUTION OF INCOME

There are several different ways to look at income distribution. In the 1800s, economists were concerned with how income was divided among the owners of business (for whom profits were the source of income), the owners of land (who received rent), and workers (who earned wages). That concern reflected the relatively sharp distinctions among social classes that existed in capitalist societies at that time. Landowners, workers, and owners of businesses were distinct groups. Few individuals moved from one group to another.

Time has changed that, as the social divisions that were once important have faded. Today workers, through their pension plans and investments in financial institutions, are owners of billions of dollars worth of shares issued on the Toronto Stock Exchange. Their percentage of all shares will likely rise well into the next century. Landowners as a group receive only a small portion of total income. Companies are run not by capitalists, but by managers who are, in a sense, workers. In short, the social lines have blurred.

But this blurring of the lines between social classes doesn't mean that we can forget the question: "Who gets what?" It simply means that our interest in who gets what has a different focus. We no longer focus on classification of income by source. Instead we look at the relative distribution of total income. How much income do the top 5 percent get? How much do the top 15 percent get? How much do the bottom 10 percent get? This relative division is called the **size distribution of income.**

A second distributional issue economists are concerned with is the **socioeconomic distribution of income** (the allocation of income among relevant socioeconomic groupings). How much do the old get compared to the young? How much do women get compared to men?

Size distribution of income The relative division or allocation of total income among income groups.

Socioeconomic distribution of income The relative division or allocation of total income among relevant socioeconomic groups.

The next three sections consider these distributional categories. Then the last three sections of the chapter ask whether the distribution of income is fair and, if it isn't, what can be done to change it?

THE SIZE DISTRIBUTION OF INCOME

The Canadian size distribution of income measures aggregate family income, from the poorest segment of society to the richest. It ranks families by their income and tells how much the richest 20 percent (a quintile) and the poorest 20 percent receive. For example, the poorest 20 percent might get 5 percent of the income and the richest 20 percent might get 40 percent.

The Lorenz Curve

Exhibit 1 (a) presents the size distribution of income for Canada in 1993. In it you can see that the 20 percent of Canadian families receiving the lowest level of income got 4.7 percent of the total income. The top 20 percent of Canadian families received 43.9 percent of the total income. The ratio of the income of the top 20 percent compared to the income of the bottom 20 percent was about ten to one (10:1).

Income quintile	Percentage of total family income	Cumulative percentage of total family income 1993
Lowest fifth	4.7	4.7
Second fifth	10.2	14.9
Third fifth	16.5	31.4
Fourth fifth	24.8	56.2
Highest fifth	43.9	100.0

(a)

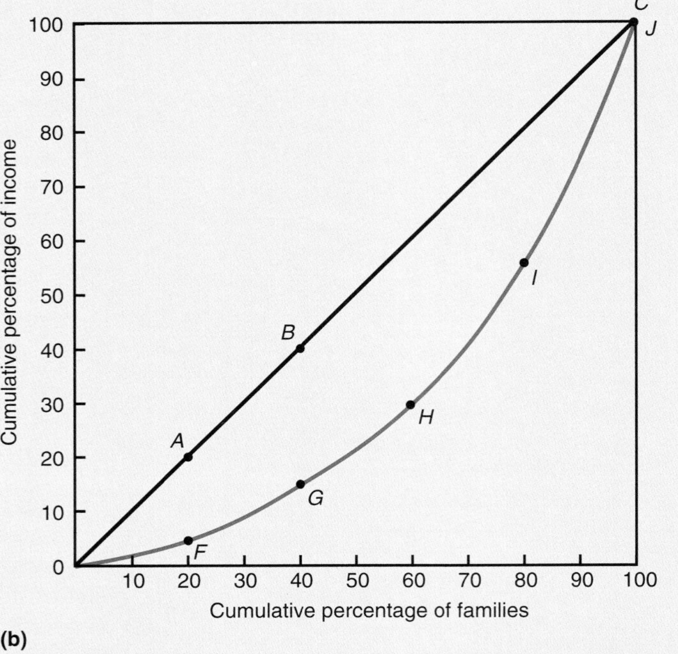

(b)

EXHIBIT 1 A Lorenz Curve of Canadian Income (1993)

If income were perfectly equally distributed, the Lorenz curve would be a diagonal line. In (**b**) we see the Canadian Lorenz curve based on the numbers in (**a**) compared to a Lorenz curve reflecting a perfectly equal distribution of income.
Source: Statistics Canada 13-207 1993, p. 146 (numbers may not add to 100 due to round up).

Lorenz curve A geometric representation of the size distribution of income among families in a given country at a given time.

A **Lorenz curve** is a geometric representation of the size distribution of income among families in a given country at a given time. It measures the percentage of *families* on the horizontal axis, arranged from poorest to richest, and the cumulative percentage of *family income* on the vertical axis. Since the exhibit presents cumulative percentages (all of the families with income below a certain level), both axes start at zero and end at 100 percent.

A perfectly equal distribution of income would be represented by a diagonal line like the one in Exhibit 1 (b). That is, the poorest 20 percent of the families would have 20 percent of the total income (point *A*); the poorest 40 percent of the families would have 40 percent of the income (point *B*); and 100 percent of the families would have 100 percent of the income (point *C*). An unequal distribution of income is represented by a Lorenz curve that's below the diagonal line. All real-world Lorenz curves are below the diagonal because income is always distributed unequally in the real world.

1 A Lorenz curve is a geometric representation of the size distribution of income among families in a given country at a given time.

The coloured line in Exhibit 1 (b) represents a Lorenz curve of the Canadian income distribution presented in Exhibit 1 (a)'s table. From Exhibit 1 (a) you know that, in 1993, the bottom 20 percent of the families in Canada received 4.7 percent of the income. Point *F* in Exhibit 1 (b) represents that combination of percentages (20 percent and 4.7 percent). To find what the bottom 40 percent received, you must add the income percentage of the bottom 20 percent and the income percentage of the next 20 percent. Doing so gives us 14.9 percent (4.7 plus 10.2 percent from column 2 of Exhibit 1 (a)). Point *G* in Exhibit 1 (b) represents the combination of percentages (40 percent and 14.9 percent). Continuing this process for points *H, I,* and *J,* you get a Lorenz curve that shows the size distribution of income in Canada in 1993.

Canadian Income Distribution over Time

Lorenz curves are most useful in visual comparisons of income distribution over time and between countries. Exhibit 2 presents Lorenz curves for Canada in 1965, 1980, and 1993. They show that from 1965 to 1980 the size distribution of income became

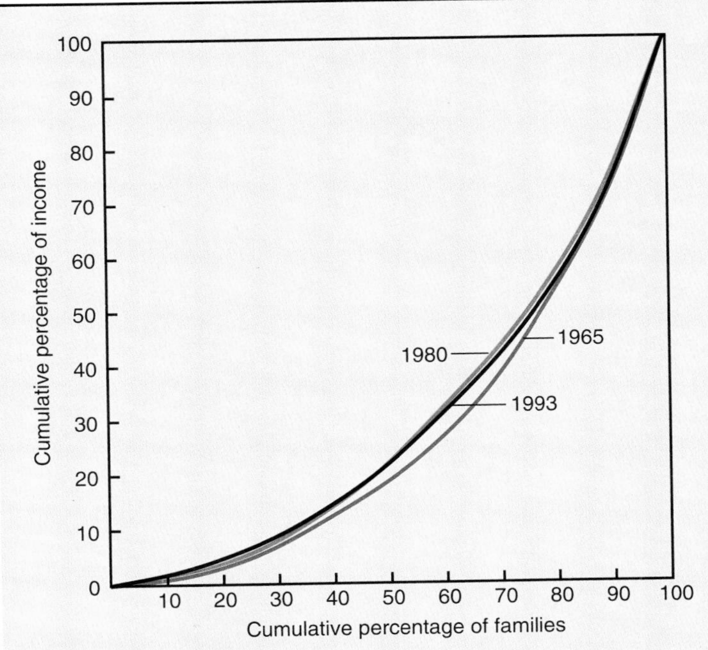

EXHIBIT 2 A Lorenz Curve of Canadian Income: 1965, 1980, and 1993

The distribution of income has changed slightly over the last 30 years.

more equal. (The curve for 1980 is closer to being diagonal than the curve for 1965.) Income of the bottom fifth of families rose by a much higher proportion than did income of the top fifth. That was a continuation of a trend that had begun in the 1950s. In the late 1980s and early 1990s that trend changed. As you can see, from 1980 to 1993 income distribution became more equal at low levels of income while it became less equal at higher levels of income. (The curve for 1993 is closer to the diagonal at low levels of income than is the curve for higher levels of income.)

2 From 1965 to 1980, income inequality in Canada decreased. From 1980 to 1992, it increased at higher levels of income and it fell at lower levels of income.

Important reasons for the initial increase in equality are the redistribution measures instituted by the Canadian government between the 1930s and the 1970s, including welfare programs, unemployment insurance, social security, progressive taxation (taxation of higher income at higher rates, lower income at lower rates), and improved macroeconomic performance of the economy.

The trend back toward greater equality at low levels of income in the 1980s and 1990s was caused by a fall in the real income of the middle class. This was due to wage increases that didn't keep up with price increases during that period, a movement towards progressive taxation, and changes in government funding for some social programs in the 1980s and 1990s. In the early 1990s, the pendulum of social reform swung again: Tax reform is ongoing, fiscal restraint is upon us, yet government funding for some social programs was increased. The effects of these changes on the distribution of income won't be known for a few years.

The distribution of income over time is also affected by demographic factors. Many families have relatively low income in their early years, relatively higher income in their middle years, and then relatively low income again in their retirement years. The Lorenz curve reflects these differences, so even if lifetime income were equally distributed, income in any one year would not be. Moreover, when the baby boom generation retires and is no longer working, its members' income will fall from what it was when they were working. That decline in income relative to the income of the smaller number of working families will affect the Lorenz curve.

Defining Poverty

Much of the government's concern with income distribution has centred on the poorest group—those in poverty. It's tough to say exactly where poverty begins. If poverty were defined as some absolute amount of real income and that amount had been determined 50 or 60 years ago, few in Canada would be in poverty in the 1990s.

Most poor families today have real incomes higher than did the middle class 50 or 60 years ago. If a relative concept of poverty were chosen, whether a family would be classified as being in poverty would depend on what percentage of the average income it received. Poverty would then be impossible to eliminate, because some proportion of people would always be classified as poor.

Poverty A relative measure that attempts to describe individuals whose income does not meet their basic needs.

Low-income cut-off The income level at which families spend at least 20 per cent more than the average family on the necessities of life. Used by Statistics Canada to define low-income families.

There's No Official Definition of Poverty Canada doesn't have an official definition of **poverty.** That's because poverty is a relative measure, depending on a family's size, composition, and location (urban or rural). Statistics Canada has established a **low-income cutoff** that is used to study the incidence of poverty in Canada. This cutoff is based on periodic surveys of family expenditures and incomes. There are two bases currently in use: one using 1986 expenditure patterns and one using 1992 expenditure patterns. The 1986 cutoffs were selected on the basis that families and unattached individuals with incomes below these levels spent, on average, at least 56.2 percent of their income on food, shelter, and clothing. The 1992 cutoffs use a 54.7 percent figures.

A number of interesting issues regarding poverty are debated. Considering them briefly will give you a good sense of the types of statistical and data problems that economists must consider as they analyze the economy. As you might expect, the cost of living in rural areas is considerably different from the cost of living in a large urban area. That means we should take the rural/urban dimension into account when we try to measure poverty. Similarly, Canadian poverty figures include the after-tax income of the poor and the cash assistance that the poor receive. However, they don't take the underreporting of income into account. If one makes adjustments for **in-kind transfers**—transfers of goods rather than money—and underreporting of income, the number of people said to be in poverty decreases below the number calculated without the adjustments. Moreover, since in-kind transfers grew enormously in the 1970s, the official low-income cutoffs underestimate the decline in poverty during that period. So, as is the case with most economic statistics, poverty statistics should be used with care.

In-kind transfer Transfers of goods rather than money.

This is even more apparent when you consider that Statistics Canada periodically updates their estimates of household expenditure patterns. As these figures change, so do all calculations based on the estimates. For example, a 1978 base year was once in use (using a figure of 58.5 percent). Low-income cutoffs based on 1978 estimates of expenditure shares differ from those using either 1986 or 1992 expenditure shares. Exhibit 3 shows the low-income cutoffs using 1978, 1986, and 1992 expenditure weights. The number of people in poverty decreased in the late 1980s and then began increasing in the early 1990s. In 1993 there were almost 5 million people living below the 1992 based low-income cutoff line. That's about one-sixth of Canada's total population!

3 The low-income cut-off is defined by Statistics Canada as the level at which 56.2 percent of income is spent on food, clothing, and shelter given 1986 family expenditure and income data.

In an attempt to provide figures that aren't sensitive to these effects, Statistics Canada also reports poverty statistics based on a **low income measure (LIM).** The LIM is calculated as 50 percent of "adjusted median family income." This adjustment attempts to correct median family income for the differential effects of adults and children in family expenditures. For example, the current practice is to assume that each additional adult increases basic family needs by 60 percent of the needs of the first adult in the family. Each child is assumed to increase basic needs by 40 percent of the needs of the first adult. The choice of these values is applied only to the calculation of median family income to correct for different sizes of families, but it is argued that estimates of poverty based on these measures are less sensitive to changes in family expenditures than are other methods of measurements, and they provide an alternative view of poverty in Canada. (When we use LIMs, there's no distinction between rural and urban estimates of poverty. Some see this as a drawback to using LIMs.)

Low income measure (LIM) A level of income used to measure poverty in Canada—based on 50 percent of adjusted median family income.

Exhibit 4 presents estimates of the number of persons living in poverty based on an income cutoff of 50 percent of adjusted family income. Estimates of the number of persons and the incidence of poverty are similar to those in Exhibit 3. The Low Income Measures are significantly different from the estimated low-income cutoffs.

EXHIBIT 3 Poverty in Canada and Low-Income Cutoffs, 1981–1993

Year	Number of persons (1992 base) (in millions)	Incidence (1992 base)	Low-Income Cutoff, Family of 4 (1992 base) Urban	(1992 base) Rural	(1986 base) Urban	(1986 base) Rural	(1978 base) Urban	(1978 base) Rural
1981	3.7	15.7%	—	—	—	—	$16,361	$12,035
1982	4.1	17.1	—	—	—	—	15,963	11,607
1983	4.5	18.5	—	—	—	—	19,176	14,106
1984	4.6	18.7	—	—	—	—	20,010	14,720
1985	4.3	17.5	—	—	—	—	20,812	15,310
1986	4.1	16.4	—	—	—	—	21,663	15,936
1987	4.0	16.1	—	—	$23,501	$15,999	22,612	16,634
1988	3.9	15.2	—	—	25,525	17,377	23,528	17,308
1989	3.6	14.0	—	—	26,803	18,247	24,706	18,175
1990	4.0	15.2	—	—	28,081	19,117	25,884	19,042
1991	4.4	16.5	—	—	29,661	20,192	27,340	20,113
1992	4.5	16.8	$30,460	$21,050	30,105	20,494	—	—
1993	4.9	17.9	31,017	21,435	30,655	20,869	—	—

Source: Statistics Canada 13-207, various issues.

EXHIBIT 4 Poverty in Canada and Low-Income Measures, 1981–1993

	Number of persons (in millions)	Incidence	Low-income measure 2 Adults and 2 Children
1981	3.6	15.3%	$14,288
1982	3.7	15.6	15,328
1983	3.9	16.0	15,548
1984	3.8	15.8	16,492
1985	3.7	14.9	17,594
1986	3.7	14.7	18,700
1987	3.6	14.2	19,584
1988	3.6	14.3	20,978
1989	3.6	13.9	22,702
1990	3.8	14.7	23,676
1991	3.9	14.6	23,792
1992	3.9	14.5	24,296
1993	4.0	14.7	23,934

Source: Statistics Canada 13-207, 1993, pp. 186–87.

Alternative Views on the Increase in Poverty People who favour policies aimed at achieving equality of income argue that this increase in poverty is a significant cost to society. One reason is that society suffers when some of its people are in poverty, just as the entire family suffers when one member doesn't have enough to eat. Most people derive pleasure from knowing that others are not in poverty.

A second reason society as a whole benefits from a decrease in poverty is that the incentives for crime are decreased. As people's incomes increase, they have more to lose by committing crimes, and, therefore, fewer crimes are committed. In short, poverty breeds problems for society. Eliminating poverty helps to eliminate those problems. Those who favour equality of income argue that the increased poverty in the late 1970s and 1980s represents a failure of the economic policies of that period.

Others respond that the widening gap between rich and poor is not the result of government tax and spending policies. It has more to do with demographic changes. For example, the number of single-parent families increased dramatically during this period, while rapid growth of the labour force depressed wages for young, unskilled workers.

Advocates of reducing poverty respond that this argument is unconvincing. They argue that the tax cuts of the 1980s favoured the rich while decreased funding for gov-

EXHIBIT 5 Canadian Income Distribution Compared to Other Countries

Among countries of the world, Canada has neither the most equal nor the most unequal distribution of income.
Source: The World Bank.

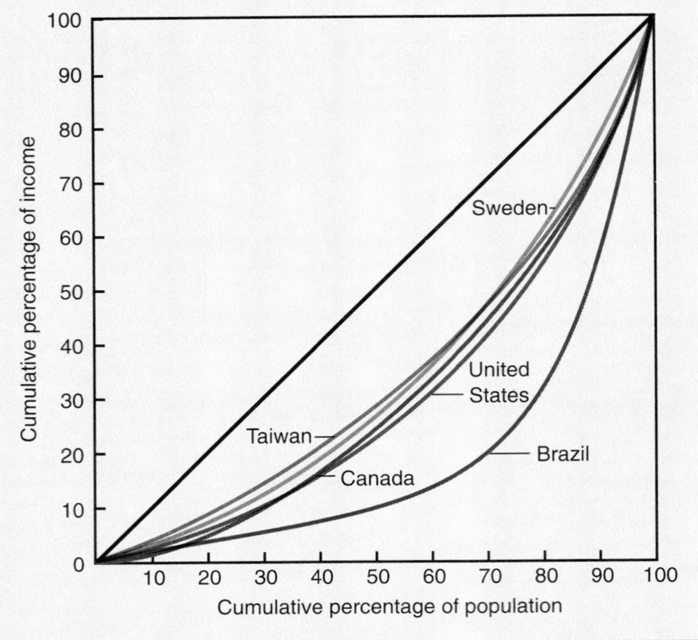

ernment programs hurt the poor. To compensate, they argue, free day care should be provided for children so that heads of single families can work full time, and the low wages of the working poor should be supplemented by government. They hold that demographic changes are not a valid excuse for ducking a question of morality.

International Dimensions of Income: The Income Distribution Question

When considering income distribution, one usually is looking at conditions within a single country. For example, the richest 20 percent of Canadian families gets approximately 10 times what the poorest 20 percent of Canadian families get.

There are other ways to look at income. One might judge income inequality in Canada relative to income inequality in other countries. Is the Canadian distribution of income more or less equal than another country's? One could also look at how income is distributed among countries. Even if income is relatively equally distributed within countries, it may be unequally distributed among countries. Finally one can ask about the total level of world income. If the poorest people in the world had incomes of $100,000 per year, would it matter that some people had incomes of $300,000 a year?

4 Canada's income distribution is similar to that of other industrialized nations.

Comparing Canadian Income Distribution with That in Other Countries

Exhibit 5 gives us a sense of how the distribution of income in Canada compares to that in other countries. We see that Canada has significantly more income inequality than Sweden, but significantly less than Brazil (or most other developing and newly industrialized countries).

An important reason why Canada has more income inequality than Sweden is that Sweden's tax system is more progressive. Until recently (when Sweden's socialist party lost power), the top marginal tax rate on the highest incomes in Sweden was 80 percent, compared to about 50 percent in Canada. Given this difference, it isn't surprising that Sweden has less income inequality. In a newly industrialized country like Brazil, where a few individuals earn most of the income and, to a large degree, control the government, the government is not likely to begin redistributing income to achieve equality.

Income Distribution among Countries

When one considers the distribution of world income, the picture becomes even more unequal than the picture one sees when

ADDED DIMENSION

THE GINI COEFFICIENT

A second measure economists use to talk about the degree of income inequality is the Gini coefficient of inequality. The Gini coefficient is derived from the Lorenz curve by comparing the area between the (1) Lorenz curve and the diagonal (area *A*) and (2) the total area of the triangle below the diagonal (areas *A* and *B*). That is:

Gini coefficient = Area $A/(\text{Areas } A + B)$

A Gini coefficient of zero would be perfect equality, since area *A* is zero if income is perfectly equally distributed. The highest the Gini coefficient can go is 1. So all Gini coefficients must be between zero and one. The lower the Gini coefficient, the closer income distribution is to being equal.

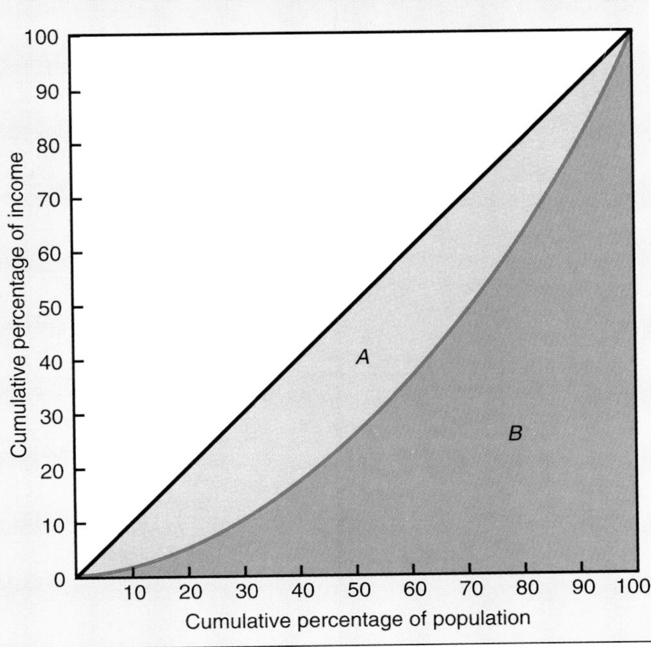

considering the distribution of income within countries. The reason is clear: Income is highly unequally distributed among countries. The average per capita income of the richest 5 percent of the countries of the world is more than 100 times the average income of the poorest 5 percent of the countries of the world. Thus, a Lorenz curve of world income would show much more inequality than the Lorenz curve for a particular country. Worldwide, income inequality is enormous. A minimum level in Canada would be a wealthy person's income in a poor country like Bangladesh.

The Total Amount of Income in Various Countries

To give you a better picture of income distribution problems, you need to consider not only the division of income, but also the total amounts of income in various countries. Exhibit 6 presents per capita GDP for various countries. Looking at the enormous differences of income among countries, we must ask which is more important: the distribution of income or the absolute level of income? Which would you rather be: one of four members in a family that has an income of $3,000 a year, which places you in the top 10 percent of Bangladesh's income distribution, or one of four members of a family with an income of $12,000 (four times as much), which places you in the bottom 10 percent of the income earners in Canada?

SOCIOECONOMIC DIMENSIONS OF INCOME INEQUALITY

The size distribution of inequality is only one of the dimensions that inequality of income and wealth can take. As we mentioned before, the distribution of income according to source of income (wages, rents, and profits) was once considered important. Today's focus is on the distribution of income based on race, ethnic background, geographic region, and other socioeconomic factors such as gender and type of job.

Income Distribution according to Socioeconomic Characteristics

Exhibit 7 gives an idea of the distribution of income according to socioeconomic characteristics.

You can see that income differs substantially by type of job, leading some economists to argue that a new professional/nonprofessional class distinction is arising in Canada. There are also substantial differences between the incomes of women and men. Some of these variations are explained by sociological and cultural differences, but a substantial fraction of that variation is the result of **discrimination** (differential treatment of individuals because of physical or social characteristics).

Discrimination Differential treatment of individuals because of physical or social characteristics.

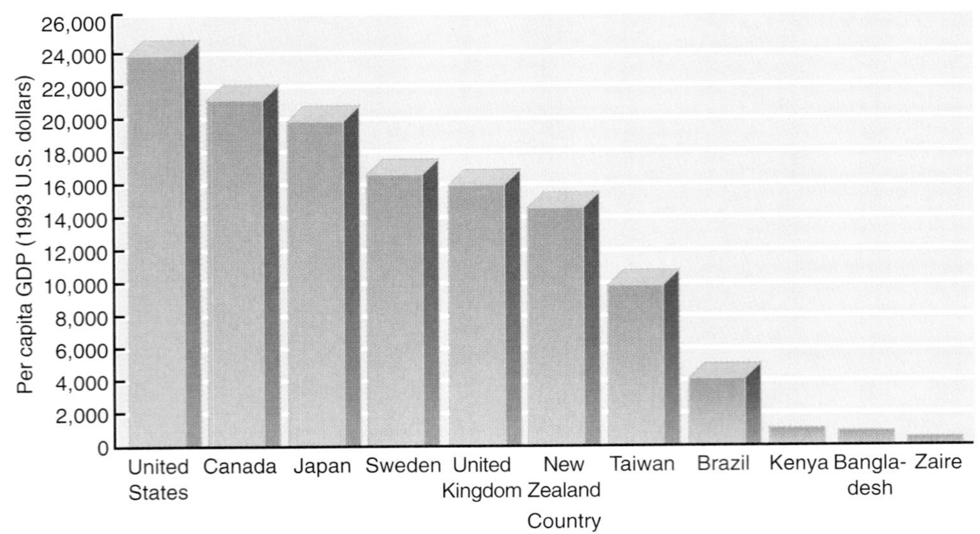

EXHIBIT 6 Per Capita GDP in Various Countries, 1993

Income is unequally distributed among the countries of the world.
Source: CIA, *World Fact Book*, 1994

EXHIBIT 7 Various Socioeconomic Income Distribution Designations (Average Income) (Constant 1990 Canadian dollars)

	1985		1990	
	Men	Women	Men	Women
Managerial, administrative, and related occupations	$45,634	$31,353	$44,879	$32,700
Teaching and related occupations	41,005	37,275	40,600	37,804
Medicine and health	57,907	30,697	57,424	31,557
Clerical and related occupations	22,503	22,622	22,549	23,258
Sales occupations	27,068	21,394	27,562	23,328
Farming, horticultural, and animal husbandry occupations	14,640	12,075	15,278	12,956
Construction trades and occupations	24,527	28,175	26,352	26,276
All occupations	28,918	24,890	29,847	26,033

Source: Statistics Canada 93–332, "Employment Income by Occupation (1991 Census)."

What Are the Causes of Discrimination?

Discrimination exists in all walks of life: Women are paid less than men, and minorities are often directed into lower-paying jobs. Economists have done a lot of research in order to understand the facts about discrimination and what can be done about it. The first problem is to measure the amount of discrimination and get an idea of how much discrimination is caused by what. Let's consider discrimination against women.

On average, women receive somewhere around 78 percent of the pay that men receive to do the same kind of job. That has increased from about 60 percent in the 1970s. This pay gap suggests that discrimination is occurring. The economist's job is to figure out how much of this is statistically significant, and, of that portion that is caused by discrimination, what is the nature of that discrimination.

Analyzing those data, economists have found that somewhat more than half of this difference can be explained by other causes, such as length of time on the job. But that still leaves a relatively large difference that can be attributed to discrimination.

Is it direct demand-side workplace discrimination by employers? Or is it supply-side sociological discrimination that occurs in the general social interactions between men and women? It's clear what direct demand-side workplace discrimination by employers is: When an employer hires a man rather than an equally qualified woman, or pays a woman less for doing a job than the employer pays a man for that job, that's demand-side discrimination.

Supply-side sociological discrimination and demand-side institutional discrimination are more complicated. For example, sociologists have found that in personal relationships women come out on the short end. For instance, women tend to move to be with their partners more than men move to be with their partners. In addition, women in two-parent relationships do much more work around the house and take a greater responsibility for child rearing than men do even when both the man and the woman are employed.

These observations suggest that there is sociological supply-side discrimination. Such discrimination can lead to the same pay statistics as can demand-side discrimination. The more an employer can count on an employee's total dedication to the job, the more likely the employer is to pay that employee a high wage. When a woman gives up a promotion possibility because it would require her to move away from her partner, or resigns a good job to move to be with her partner, she's lowering her average pay. Similarly when she misses a key meeting to stay with a sick child who has a 40°C temperature, she may be behaving admirably, but she is lowering her advancement and pay possibilities. The fact that women, on average, take personal relationships more seriously than do men means that women, on average, will be paid less than men even if there is no demand-side discrimination.

How important are these sociological observations? In discussing discrimination we ask the members of our classes to state if they expect their personal relationships with their partners to be fully equal. The usual result is the following: 80 percent of the women expect a fully equal relationship; 20 percent expect their partner to come first. Eighty percent of the men expect their careers to come first; 20 percent expect an equal relationship. We then point out that somebody's expectations aren't going to be fulfilled. Put simply, most observers believe that supply-side discrimination that occurs in interpersonal relationships is significant.

The issues become even more complicated when one allows for indirect demand-side institutional discrimination. Must careers be structured so that they require enormous time commitment at precisely the time when women's home responsibilities are greatest? Couldn't many careers be structured so that the peak time commitment occurred later, when supply-side sociological discrimination is less intensive? When one considers such issues, supply-side and demand-side factors become intertwined.

Economists have made adjustments for these sociological factors, and have found that supply-side and demand-side institutional factors explain a portion of the lower pay but that direct workplace discrimination also explains a portion. How big a portion to attribute to demand-side factors and how big a portion to attribute to supply-side factors is undetermined, even though the question has been subject to considerable debate. One reason for this continued debate is that the two types of discrimination interact. Say a firm doesn't have an inherent bias against women but expects that women will be less-committed employees. The firm will likely assign women to the less critical jobs. The firm is discriminating against women, but that discrimination is a reflection of its expectation of supply-side discrimination.

A final point: Even if women *in general* are less likely than men to be "fully committed employees," that does not mean that any *individual* woman will be less committed. The question of whether it is appropriate to accept discrimination against particular individuals on the basis of group characteristics is a normative issue that society, not economists, must resolve. What economists can do is identify the nature of the discrimination and point out the consequences of policies intended to eliminate it.

International Male/Female Pay Gaps and Comparable Worth Laws

The male/female pay gap is not consistent across countries. University of Illinois economists Francine Blau and Lawrence Kahn did a study in the early 1990s and found significant differences. In Australia, France, New Zealand, and the Scandinavian countries, women earned about 85 percent of what men earned. In the United States, women earned about 70 percent of what men earned. Why the difference?

The answer most likely is in the institutional structure. The United States had less unionization or direct government involvement in the pay-setting process, and was otherwise less centralized. In Australia, for example, minimum wages are set in various occupations (as opposed to having a general minimum wage as in Canada, and an almost-general federal minimum wage as in the United States); that pulls up the pay of some female workers.

Comparable worth laws Laws in which government groups will determine "fair" wages for specific jobs.

Institutional modifications such as **comparable worth laws**—laws in which government groups will determine "fair" wages for specific jobs—have been suggested as a way of helping eliminate the pay gap, but many economists oppose such laws, feeling that they are incompatible with existing wage-setting institutions in Canada.

The provinces and the federal government have passed laws that require "equal pay for equal work without discrimination on the basis of sex," and the trend in women's pay is now on the rise. For example, Statistics Canada reports that in 1991 single women earned 91 percent of what single men earned. **Pay equity laws** are helping to close the wage gaps based solely on gender.

Pay equity laws Regulations that attempt to provide similar compensation for comparable jobs.

Deciding What to Do about Economic Discrimination

The supply-side/demand-side distinction is important in deciding what to do about discrimination. If the primary cause is on the supply side, it can be strongly argued that if one wants to end discrimination, the fight is best directed at the discrimination that occurs in male/female relationships. Why do women allow themselves to be "exploited" by men, and can that exploitation be reduced? If the discrimination is on the demand side because employers are reluctant to hire women, equal opportunity laws will be more successful than if the discrimination is on the supply side.

As you can see from this brief summary, discussions of discrimination quickly get complicated and intertwined with normative issues. Pointing out that seemingly simple issues are actually very complicated is something that economists often do. It's a logical conclusion of economic thinking.

Income Distribution according to Class

Early economists focused on the distribution of income by wages, profits, and rent because that division corresponded to their class analysis of society. Landowners received rent, capitalists received profit, and workers received wages. Tensions among these classes played an important part in economists' analyses of the economy and policy.

As class divisions by income source have become blurred, they've become only a tiny part of mainstream economists' analysis of the economy. That doesn't mean that other types of socioeconomic classes no longer exist. They do. The United States has a kind of upper class. In fact, there is a company in the United States that publishes the *Social Register,* containing the names and pedigrees of about 35,000 socially prominent people who might be categorized "upper-class." Similarly, it is possible to further divide the U.S. population into a middle class and a lower class.

The difference today is that class divisions are no longer determined by income source. For example, upper-class people do not necessarily receive their income from rent and profits. Today we have "upper-class" people who derive their income from wages and "lower-class" people who derive their income from profits (usually in the form of pensions, which depend upon profits from the investment of pension funds in stocks and bonds). Nowadays in Canada classification is based on characteristics other than source of income. For example, upper-class people don't bowl and lower-class people don't like opera—or so the classes have been stereotyped.

In acknowledging that classes exist, we want to make it clear that in no way are we condoning such stereotyping of individuals. Many people don't fit into any category; their interests, occupations, and activities fit into no class. But to pretend that classes and such stereotyping don't exist when they do, and to fail to deal with the implications of socioeconomic classes in our society, isn't going to make such stereotyping go away.

The Importance of the Middle Class

What has made the most difference is today's class structure in Canada compared to its class structure in earlier periods and to the

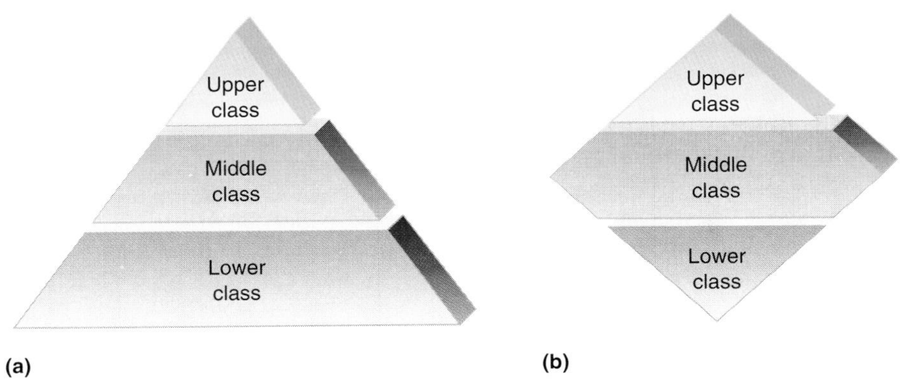

EXHIBIT 8 The Class System as a Pyramid and as a Diamond

The class system in underdeveloped countries is a pyramid; in Canada the class system is more diamond shaped.

structure in today's developing countries is the tremendous growth in the relative size of the middle class. Economists used to see the class structure as a pyramid. From a base composed of a large lower class, the pyramid tapered upward through a medium-sized middle class to a peak occupied by the upper class (Exhibit 8 (a)). The class structure is still pyramidal in developing countries. In Canada and other developed countries, the pyramid has bulged out into a diamond, as shown in Exhibit 8 (b). The middle class has become the largest class, while the upper and lower classes are smaller in relative terms.

This enormous increase in the relative size of the middle class in developed countries has significantly blurred the distinction between capitalists and workers. In early capitalist society, the distributional fight (the fight over relative income shares) was largely between workers and capitalists. In modern capitalist society, the distributional fight is among various types of individuals. Union workers are pitted against nonunion workers; salaried workers are pitted against workers paid by the hour. The old are pitted against the young; women are pitted against men; blacks are pitted against Hispanics and Asians, and all three groups are pitted against whites.

Distributional Questions and Tensions in Society While mainstream economists tend to focus on the size distribution of income, nonmainstream economists tend to emphasize class and group structures in their analysis. Radical economists emphasize the control that the upper class has over the decision process and the political process. Conservative economists emphasize the role of special interests of all types in shaping government policy. Both radical and conservative analyses bring out the tensions among classes in society much better than does the mainstream, classless analysis.

When people feel they belong to a particular class or group, they will often work to further the interests of that class or group. They also generally have stronger feelings about inequalities among classes or groups than when they lack that sense of class or group identity. Using a classless analysis means overlooking the implications of class and group solidarity in affecting the tensions in society.

Those tensions show up every day in political disputes over the tax system, in the quiet fuming of individuals as they see someone else earning more for doing the same job, and in strikes and even riots. Such tensions exist in all countries. In some transitional and developing countries they break out into the open as armed insurrections or riots over food shortages (or soap shortages, as we saw in the former USSR in the early 1990s).

Those tensions have been kept to a minimum in Canadian society. A majority of Canadians believe that income distribution is sufficiently fair for them to accept their share more or less contentedly. To remedy the unfairness that does exist, they don't demand that the entire system be replaced. Instead they work for change within the present system. They look to affirmative action laws, pay equity laws, minimum-wage laws, and social welfare programs for any improvement they perceive to be necessary or desirable. There's much debate about whether these government actions have achieved the desired ends, but the process itself reduces tensions and has worked toward the maintenance of the entire system.

People's acceptance of the Canadian economic system is based not only on what the distribution of income is but also on what people think it should be, what they consider fair. It is to that question that we now turn.

INCOME DISTRIBUTION AND FAIRNESS

Judgements about whether the distribution of income is fair, or whether it should be changed, are normative ones, based on the values one applies to the situation. Value judgements necessarily underlie all policy prescriptions.

Philosophical Debates about Equality and Fairness

Depending on one's values, any income distribution can be justified. For example, Friedrich Nietzsche, the 19th-century German philosopher, argued that society's goal should be to support its supermen—its best and brightest. Lesser individuals' duty should be to work for the well-being of these supermen. Bertram de Juvenal, a 20th-century philosopher, argued that a high level of income inequality is necessary to sustain the arts, beauty, education, and civilization. He and others say that a world of equally distributed income would be a world without beauty. Even if we don't personally own beautiful, expensive homes or aren't devoted opera fans, these philosophers argue, our lives are improved because some people do own such homes and because opera performances exist. Inequality creates diversity in our lives, and that diversity enriches the lives of others.

Other philosophers disagree strongly. They argue that equality itself is the overriding goal. And for many people the inherent value of equality is not open to question—it is simply self-evident.

Believing that equality is an overriding goal does not necessarily imply that income should be equally distributed. For example, John Rawls (a Harvard University professor who believes that equality is highly desirable and that society's goal should be to maximize the welfare of the least well-off) agrees that to meet that goal some inequality is necessary. Rawls argues that if, in pursuing equality, you actually make the least well-off worse off than they otherwise would have been, then you should not pursue equality any further. For example, say under one policy there will be perfect equality and everyone receives $10,000 per year. Under another policy, the least well-off person receives $12,000 per year and all others receive $40,000. Rawls argues that the second policy is preferable to the first even though it involves more inequality.

Economists, unlike philosophers, are not concerned about justifying any particular distribution of income. In their objective role, economists limit themselves to explaining the effects that various policies will have on the distribution of income; they let the policymakers judge whether those effects are desirable.

However, in order to judge economic policies, you, in your role as a citizen who elects policymakers, must make certain judgements about income distribution because all real-world economic policies have distribution effects. Accordingly, a brief discussion of income distribution and fairness is in order.

Fairness and Equality

The Canadian population has a strong general tendency to favour equality—equality is generally seen as fair. Most people share that view, as do we. However, there are instances when equality of income is not directly related to people's view of fairness. For example, consider this distribution of income between John and Fred:

John gets $50,000 a year.

Fred gets $12,000 a year.

Think a minute. Is that fair? The answer we're hoping for is that you don't yet have enough information to make the decision.

Here's some more information. Say that John gets that $50,000 for holding down three jobs at a time, while Fred gets his $12,000 for sitting around doing nothing. At this point, many of us would argue that it's possible that John should be getting even more than $50,000 and Fred should be getting less than $12,000.

But wait! What if we discover that Fred is disabled and unless his income increases to $15,000 a year he will die? Most of us would change our minds again and argue that Fred deserves more, regardless of how much John works.

But wait! How about if, after further digging, we discover that Fred is disabled because he squandered his health on alcohol and drugs? In that case some people would likely change their minds again as to whether Fred deserves more.

By now you should have gotten our point. Looking only at a person's income masks many dimensions that most people consider important in making value judgements about fairness.

5 Three problems in determining whether an equal income distribution is fair are: (1) people don't start from equivalent positions; (2) people's needs differ; and (3) people's efforts differ.

Fairness as Equality of Opportunity

When most people talk about believing in equality in income, they mean they believe in equality of opportunity for comparably endowed individuals to earn income. If equal opportunity of equals leads to inequality of income, that inequality in income is fair. Unfortunately, there's enormous latitude for debate on what constitutes equal opportunity of equals.

In the real world, needs differ, desires differ, and abilities differ. Should these differences be considered relevant differences in equality? You must supply the answers to those questions before you can judge any economic policy because to make a judgement on whether an economic policy should or should not be adopted, you must make a judgement about whether a policy's effect on income is fair. In making those judgements, most people rely on their immediate gut reactions. We hope what you have gotten out of this discussion about John and Fred and equality of opportunity is the resolve to be cautious about trusting your gut reactions. The concept of fairness is crucial and complicated, and it deserves deeper consideration than just a gut reaction.

THE PROBLEMS OF REDISTRIBUTING INCOME

Let's now say that we have considered all the issues discussed so far in this chapter and have concluded that some redistribution of income from the rich to the poor is necessary if society is to meet our ideal of fairness. How do we go about redistributing income?

To answer that question, we must consider what programs exist and what their negative side effects might be. The side effects can be substantial and they can subvert the intention of the program so that far less overall money is available for redistribution and equality is reduced less than one might think.

Three Important Side Effects of Redistributive Programs

6 Three side effects of redistribution of income include the labour/leisure incentive effect, the avoidance and evasion incentive effects, and the incentive effect to look more needy than you are.

Three important side effects that economists have found in programs to redistribute income are:

1. The incentive effects of a tax may result in a switch from labour to leisure.
2. The effects of taxes may include attempts to avoid or evade taxes, leading to a decrease in measured income.
3. The incentive effects of distributing money may cause people to make themselves look as if they're more needy than they really are.

Appendix A provides a numerical example of each of these, showing that these effects can be substantial and make income redistribution costly in terms of reduced total income.

All economists believe that the incentive effects of taxation are important and must be taken into account in policymaking. But they differ significantly in the importance they assign to incentive effects, and empirical evidence doesn't resolve the question. Some economists believe that incentive effects are so important that little taxation for redistribution should take place. They argue that when the rich do well, the total pie is increased so much that the spillover benefits to the poor are greater than the proceeds they would get from redistribution. For example, supporters of this view argue that the growth in capitalist economies was made possible by entrepreneurs. Because those entrepreneurs invested in new technology, there was more growth in society. Moreover, those entrepreneurs paid taxes. The benefits resulting from entrepreneurial action spilled over to the poor, making the poor far better off than any redistribution would. The fact that some of those entrepreneurs became rich is irrelevant because all society was better off due to their actions.

Other economists believe that there should be significant taxation for redistribution. While they agree that sometimes the incentive effects are substantial, they see the goal of equality as overriding these effects.

Politics, Income Redistribution, and Fairness

We began this discussion of income distribution and fairness by making the assumption that our value judgements determine the taxes we pay—that if our values led us to the conclusion that the poor deserved more income, we could institute policies that would get more to the poor. Reality doesn't necessarily work that way. Often politics, not value judgements, plays the central role in determining what taxes individuals will pay. The group that has the most votes will elect lawmakers who will enact tax policies that benefit that group at the expense of groups with fewer votes.

On the surface, the democratic system of one person/one vote would seem to suggest that the politics of redistribution would favour the poor, but it doesn't. One would expect that the poor would use their votes to make sure income was redistributed to them from the rich. Why don't they? The answer is complicated.

One reason is that many of the poor don't vote because they reason that "one vote won't make much difference." As a result, poor people's total voting strength is reduced. A second reason is that the "poor" aren't seen by most politicians as a solid voting block. There's no organization of the poor that can deliver votes to politicians. A third reason is that those poor people who do vote often cast their votes with other issues in mind. An anti-income-redistribution candidate might have a strong view on abortion as well, and for many the abortion view is the one that decides their vote.

A fourth reason is that elections require financing. Much of that financing comes from the rich. The money is used for advertising and publicity aimed at convincing the poor that voting for a person who supports the rich is actually in the best interests of the poor. Poor people are often misled by that kind of publicity, but not necessarily because they are dumb. In our view they do as well as anyone else could in processing the information they receive. The trouble is that information on the redistributive effect of a policy is often biased.

The issues are usually sufficiently complicated that a trained economist must study the information about them for a long time to determine which arguments make sense. Reasonable-sounding arguments can be made to support just about any position, and the rich have the means to see that the arguments that support their positions get the publicity.

REAL-WORLD POLICIES AND PROGRAMS FOR INCOME REDISTRIBUTION

The preceding discussion provided you with a general sense of the theoretical difficulty of redistributing income. In this section we give you a sense of how income redistribution policies and programs have worked in the real world. As you've seen, there are two direct methods through which government redistributes income: taxation (policies that tax the rich more than the poor) and expenditures (programs that help the poor more than the rich).

Taxation to Redistribute Income

The Canadian federal government gets its revenue from a variety of taxes. The two largest sources of revenue are the personal income tax and indirect sales taxes (like the GST).

Provincial and local governments get their revenue from income taxes, sales taxes, and property taxes. The rates vary among provinces.

Progressive tax Average tax rate increases with income.
Proportional tax Average tax rate is constant with income.
Regressive tax Average tax rate decreases with income.

Tax systems can be progressive, proportional (sometimes called flat rate) or regressive. A **progressive tax** is one in which the average tax rate increases with income. It redistributes income from the rich to the poor. A **proportional tax** is one in which the average rate of tax is constant regardless of income level. It is neutral in regard to income distribution. A **regressive tax** is one in which the average tax rate decreases with income. It redistributes income from poor to rich.

EXHIBIT 9 Government Expenditures on Redistribution

	1990 ($ million)	1991
Canada Assistance Plan		
General assistance	$7,146.3	$8,882.8
Senior Citizens Benefits		
OAS	11,803.8	12,705.2
GIS	3,873.2	3,975.7
Canada Pension Plan		
Retirement pensions	8,159.0	9,134.1
Disability pensions	1,799.2	1,955.9
Survivors' pensions	2,215.8	2,434.3
Children's benefits	245.0	257.9

Source: *Canada Yearbook 1994,* p. 268.

Provincial and local governments, as we said, get most of their income from the following sources:

1. Income taxes, which are generally somewhat progressive.
2. Sales taxes, which tend to be proportional (all people pay the same tax rate on what they spend) or slightly regressive. (Since poor people often spend a higher percentage of their incomes than rich people, poor people pay a higher average tax rate as a percentage of their income than rich people.)
3. Property taxes, which are taxes paid on the value of people's property (usually real estate, but sometimes also personal property like cars). Since the value of people's property is related (although imperfectly related) to income, the property tax is considered to be roughly proportional.

When all the taxes paid by individuals to all levels of governments are combined, the conclusion that most researchers come to is that little income redistribution takes place on the tax side. The progressive taxes are offset by the regressive taxes, so the overall tax system is roughly proportional. That is, on average the tax rates individuals pay are roughly equal. Recent changes in the tax laws have increased the rate that high-income people pay and lowered the rate that lower-income people pay. These changes may make the effective tax structure slightly more progressive, but meaningful statistics won't be available for a few years.

Expenditure Programs to Redistribute Income

Since taxes don't redistribute income significantly, if the government does redistribute income, it must do so through expenditure programs. Exhibit 9 presents the federal government's expenditures on some programs that contribute to redistribution.

Canada Pension Plan The **Canada Pension Plan** (Quebec Pension Plan for residents of Quebec) is funded by employee and employer contributions. It provides monthly benefits to retired contributors, as well as disability and survivor's benefits. In 1994 the maximum employee contribution was $806, up more than 7 percent from the previous year.

As the accompanying box illustrates, there's some doubt over whether contribution rates and population growth are high enough to guarantee that in 40 years you'll actually receive a pension. The population is aging, the death rate is going down, and the birth rate has been low. These demographic facts mean that fewer and fewer active workers are contributing to the fund while more and more people are becoming eligible for benefits. Without changes, a Canada Pension crunch can be expected within the next 20 years.

7 Expenditure programs to redistribute income include the Canada Pension Plan, Old Age Security, the Guaranteed Income Supplement, and public assistance (welfare) programs.

Canada Pension Plan (CPP) Funded by employee and employer contributions, it provides monthly benefits to retired contributors, as well as disability and survivor's benefits.

ADDED DIMENSION

WILL YOU RECEIVE A PENSION?

CPP DIPS INTO SURPLUS FUND

Higher Payouts a Result of Rising Disability Claims, Aging Population

By Alan Freeman
Parliamentary Bureau

OTTAWA—The Canada Pension Plan has been forced to dip into its accumulated surplus for the first time in its 28-year history, as an aging population and burgeoning disability claims are resulting in big increases in CPP benefit payouts.

Government officials insist the decline in the surplus was foreseen and doesn't represent a threat to the plan.

Preliminary financial results for the fiscal year ended March 31 show the plan's surplus declined $1.1 billion over the year to $41 billion.

Expenditures by the plan, including administrative costs, rose 9.1 percent to $14.6 billion in 1993–94, while revenue from contributions from employees and employers and interest on investments was flat at $13.51 billion.

The CPP operates in every province but Quebec, which has its own plan that mirrors the CPP.

The drop in the surplus highlights the plan's continuing requirement for higher contributions as the population ages. CPP contributions are collected as a payroll tax from all workers and their employers.

"The main concern that I have is that future contribution rates will be high," said Bernard Dussault, an actuary at the Office of the Superintendent of Financial Institutions who tracks CPP. "Whether it's CPP or a private plan, pensions are expensive."

Ian Markham, a partner at KPMG Actuarial Benefits & Compensation Inc., said the higher contribution rates required to keep CPP solvent pose huge generational issues.

"Will the next generation pay my pension?" asked Mr. Markham, 42, who chairs the Toronto Board of Trade's employee benefits committee. "Will my kids want to pay my pension?"

"There may come a stage where employers and employees say, 'enough is enough.'"

In a recent report, the board of trade suggested several possible reforms to the CPP, including raising the retirement age from 65, as is being done in other countries, or limiting indexation of pensions.

The contribution rate for CPP and for its fellow plan, the Quebec Pension Plan, is set at 5.2 percent of contributory earnings for 1994, split 50–50 between employers and employees. The maximum employee contribution this year is $806, up 7.1 percent from 1993.

After being frozen at 3.6 percent of earnings from 1966 to 1986, the contribution rate has been creeping up since 1986.

The Globe and Mail, April 21, 1994.

Old Age Security Benefits paid to every resident of Canada at age 65.

Old Age Security and the Guaranteed Income Supplement **Old Age Security** benefits are paid to every resident of Canada at age 65. Payments are made for as long as 40 years. The **Guaranteed Income Supplement** is also paid to recipients of Old Age Security benefits, subject to a means test—this is a test that examines expenditure needs and determines whether the supplement is actually required. Together, these two programs work much the way your parents provided what you *needed* and your allowance was for your *wants.*

Unemployment Insurance Program Short-term financial assistance, regardless of need, to eligible individuals who are temporarily out of work.

Unemployment Insurance The **Unemployment Insurance Program** is funded by employer and employee contributions. It was originally designed to provide short-term insurance to workers who experienced short periods of unemployment, although it has gradually evolved to provide benefits to those leaving the labour force due to illness, pregnancy, newborn care, and for those participating in job training and work-sharing programs. In December 1993 over 12 million persons were covered by the program—over a million people received benefits averaging more than $260 per week.

The Chretien government introduced a number of changes to the Unemployment Insurance Program in 1994. These changes were aimed at removing the disincentive to work. They were also aimed at restoring the insurance aspects of the program. Unemployment insurance had become more than an insurance program—it had become a way of life for many Canadians. The Economic Council of Canada reported that nearly 80 percent of the claims in 1989 were made by repeat users, with the highest proportion of repeat users residing in the Atlantic provinces. Many claimants had short-term positions in the fishing industry. Stories of job-sharing within families were widespread. One individual would work the minimum weeks required to qualify for unemployment insurance benefits. That worker would then quit, only to be replaced by a family member who continued the cycle.

The Canada Assistance Plan The **Canada Assistance Plan** provides federal assistance to the provinces for welfare programs. These welfare programs help in covering the basic necessities—food, shelter, clothing, fuel, utilities, and other special needs (like nursing homes, hostels for battered women and children, and child-care facilities). Funding for these programs is shared by the provinces and the federal government.

Canada Assistance Plan A federal program providing assistance to the provinces for welfare programs.

Some preliminary work on reforming the social safety net is currently under way in New Brunswick. NB Works is a national demonstration program that offers training, education, and work experience to clients on social assistance. The aim is to allow them to complete their high school studies and provide them with skills that will increase the likelihood of employment. Similarly, the Self Sufficiency Project is a national program that investigates the effectiveness of a financial subsidy in encouraging people to leave social assistance and become self-sufficient. Preliminary results suggest both of these programs can be successful, but it is too soon to tell whether these types of incentive packages will be part of a revised social security system. The Chretien government is committed to change, but it has deferred making important statements on the future of social policy on at least two occasions. These issues will be much in the news in the 1990s.

The Negative Income Tax Some economists suggest that the solution to income maintenance is the **negative income tax (NIT).** Under this program the government would subsidize households as long as household income fell below some predetermined threshold. In essence, the government would provide a **guaranteed annual income.** As the household earned income from employment, the government subsidy would be reduced (at a rate that might be less than one dollar in subsidy for every dollar earned). The level of employment income at which the subsidy would be completely lost is referred to as the **break-even level of income.** The key to this kind of a program is to set that break-even level of income at the right level (relative to the guaranteed annual income). By doing so, the government can reduce dependency, thereby encouraging self-sufficiency. A simple variant of this program is currently in practice in New Brunswick. The NB Job Corps consists of people close to retirement age who are on social assistance. The government pays each participant $12,000 per year, and in return those who were once on social assistance contribute to the community in a variety of ways, from maintaining public parks to community service.

Negative Income Tax (NIT) A program in which the government would subsidize households as long as their incomes fell below a certain threshold level.

Guaranteed annual income The level of income the government would provide under a negative income tax program.

Break-even level of income The level of employment income at which government subsidy would be completely lost.

Overall Effects of Income Redistribution Programs While the tax system has not proven to be an effective means of redistributing income, the government expenditure system has been quite effective. Exhibit 10 shows approximate Lorenz curves before and after analyzing the effect of both taxes and government programs on the redistribution of income. As you can see, the after-transfer income is significantly closer to being equally distributed. But because of the incentive effects of collecting and distributing the money, that redistribution has come at the cost of a reduction in the total amount of income earned by society. The debate about whether the gain in equality of income is worth the cost in reduction of total income is likely to continue indefinitely.

CONCLUSION

Much more could be said about the issues involved in income redistribution. But limitations of time and space pressure us to move on. We hope this and the last two chapters have convinced you that income redistribution is an important but difficult question. Specifically, we hope we have given you the sense that income distribution questions are integrally related with questions about the entire economic system.

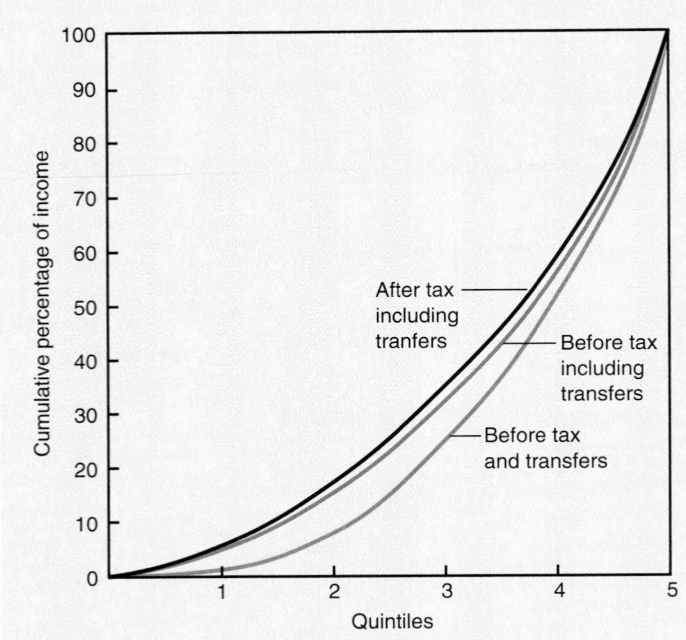

EXHIBIT 10 A Lorenz Curve, Taxes, and Transfers

Taxes and transfers tend to make income more evenly distributed in society.

Source: Statistics Canada 13-210, 1992.

Supply and demand play a central role in the determination of the distribution of income, but they do so in an institutional and historical context. Thus, the analysis of income distribution must include that context as well as one's ethical judgements about what is fair.

CHAPTER SUMMARY

- The Lorenz curve is a measure of the inequality of income.
- There are alternative views about government's role in reducing poverty.
- Fairness is a philosophical question. Each person must judge a program's fairness for him- or herself.
- Income is difficult to redistribute because of incentive effects of taxes, avoidance and evasion effects of taxes, and incentive effects of redistribution programs.
- On the whole, the Canadian tax system is roughly proportional, so it is not very effective as a means of redistributing income.
- Government expenditure programs are more effective than tax policy in reducing income inequality in Canada.

KEY TERMS

break-even level of income *(339)*
Canada Assistance Plan *(339)*
Canada Pension Plan *(337)*
comparable worth laws *(332)*
discrimination *(329)*
guaranteed annual income *(339)*
Guaranteed Income Supplement *(338)*
in-kind transfer *(326)*
Lorenz curve *(324)*
low-income cutoff *(326)*
low income measure (LIM) *(326)*
negative income tax (NIT) *(339)*
Old Age Security *(338)*
pay equity laws *(332)*
poverty *(326)*
progressive tax *(336)*
proportional tax *(336)*
regressive tax *(336)*
size distribution of income *(323)*
socioeconomic distribution of income *(323)*
Unemployment Insurance Program *(338)*

QUESTIONS FOR THOUGHT AND REVIEW

The number after each question represents the estimated degree of critical thinking required. (1 = almost none; 10 = deep thought.)

1. Why are we concerned with the distribution of income between men and women, but not between redheads and blonds? *(8)*
2. The Lorenz curve for Bangladesh looks like this:

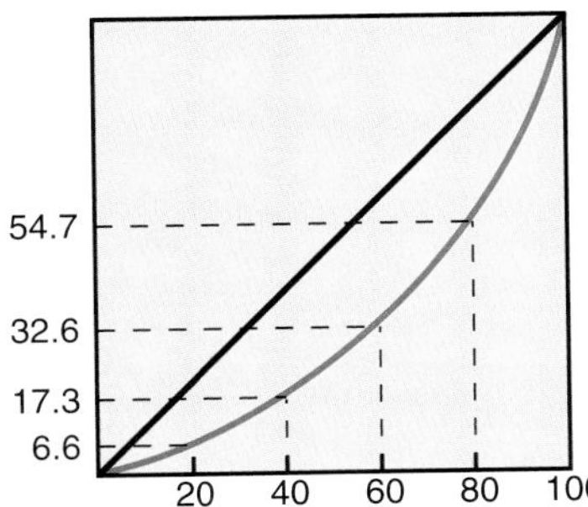

   How much income do the top 20 percent of individuals in Bangladesh receive? *(2)*
3. If one were to draw a Lorenz curve for lawyers, what would it represent? *(5)*
4. Should poverty be defined absolutely or relatively? Why? *(6)*
5. Some economists argue that a class distinction should be made between managerial decision makers and other workers. Do you agree? Why or why not? *(8)*
6. If a garbage collector earns more than an English teacher, does that mean something is wrong with the economy? Why or why not? *(8)*
7. Is it ever appropriate for society to:
   Let someome starve?
   Let someone be homeless?
   Forbid someone to eat chocolate? *(8)*
8. If you receive a paycheque, what percentage of it is withheld for taxes? What incentive effect does that have on your decision to work? *(5)*
9. Give four reasons why women earn less than men. Which reasons do you believe are most responsible for the difference? *(6)*
10. There are many more poor people than there are rich people. If the poor wanted to, they could exercise their power to redistribute as much money as they please to themselves. They don't do that, so they must see the income distribution system as fair. Discuss. *(6)*

PROBLEMS AND EXERCISES

1. The accompanying table shows income distribution data for three countries.

	Percentage of total income		
Income quintile	India	South Korea	Mexico
Lowest 20%	7.0%	5.7%	2.9%
Second quintile	9.2	11.2	7.0
Third quintile	13.5	15.1	12.0
Fourth quintile	20.5	22.4	20.4
Highest 20%	49.8	45.6	57.7

   a. Using this information, draw a Lorenz curve for each country.
   b. Which country has the most-equal distribution of income?
   c. Which country has the least-equal?
   d. By looking at the three Lorenz curves, can you tell which country has the most-progressive tax system? Why or why not?
2. In Taxland, a tax exemption is granted for the first $10,000 earned per year. Between $10,000.01 and $30,000, the tax rate is 25 percent. Between $30,000.01 and $50,000, it's 30 percent. Above $50,000, it's 35 percent. You're earning $75,000 a year.
   a. How much in taxes will you have to pay?
   b. What is your average tax rate? Your marginal tax rate?
   c. Taxland has just changed to a tax credit system in which, in lieu of any exemption, eligible individuals are given a cheque for $4,000. The two systems are designed to bring in the same amount of revenue. Would you favour or oppose the change? Why?
3. Some economists have argued against need-based scholarships because they work as an implicit tax on parents' salaries and hence discourage savings for university or college.
   a. If the marginal tax rate parents face is 20 percent, and 5 percent of parents' assets will be deducted from a student's financial aid each year for four years a child is in university or college, what is the implicit marginal tax on that portion of income that is saved? (For simplicity assume the interest rate is zero and that the parent's contribution is paid at the time the child enters university or college.)
   b. How would your answer differ if parents had two children, with the second entering university or college right after the first one graduated? (How about three?) (Remember that the assets will likely decrease with each child graduating.)
   c. When parents are divorced, how should the contribution of each parent be determined? If your school has need-based scholarships, how does it determine the expected contributions of divorced parents?
   d. Given the above, would you suggest moving to an ability-based scholarship program? Why or why not?
4. Interview three female and three male professors with sig-

nificant others of the opposite sex (i.e., spouses) at your college, asking them what percentage of work in the professor's household each adult household member does.

a. Assuming your results can be extended to the population at large, what can you say about the existence of supply-side institutional discrimination?

b. If gender-related salary data for individuals at your college are available, determine whether women or men of equal rank and experience receive higher average pay.

c. Relate your findings in *a* and *b*.

d. Does the existence of supply-side institutional discrimination suggest that no demand-side discrimination exists? Why or why not?

5. Some economists have proposed making the tax rate progressively depend on the wage rate rather than the income level. Thus, an individual who works twice as long as another but who receives a lower wage would face a lower marginal tax rate.

a. What effect would this change have on incentives to work?

b. Would this system be fairer than our current system? Why or why not?

c. If, simultaneously, the tax system were made regressive in hours worked so that individuals who work longer hours faced lower marginal tax rates, what effect would this change have on hours worked?

d. What would be some of the administrative difficulties of instituting the above changes to our income tax code?

A Numerical Example of the Problems of Redistributing Income

To give you a better sense of the problems of redistributing income, let's consider a numerical example. In this appendix we'll once again consider our John and Fred example. This time we'll say that John and Fred are each working, one job apiece, and that they're roughly equal in ability and needs. Because they're equals, we've decided that, according to our values, it's unfair that John earns more than four times as much as Fred. We believe that Fred should get more than the $12,000 he's currently getting and John should get less than the $50,000 he's currently getting. We decide that, ideally, the income ratio between these two should be one to one. Each should get $31,000:

$$\$12{,}000 + \$50{,}000 = \$62{,}000/2 = \$31{,}000$$

One way to accomplish this end would be to institute a tax on John and give the proceeds to Fred. But in Canada a tax must treat people who are equally situated equally, so our government cannot simply impose a tax on John and give the proceeds to Fred. Instead, in order to treat equals equally, the government must relate the tax to income rather than to individuals. The tax must be such that two people earning the same amount pay the same amount of tax.

Incentive Effects of Taxation

Let's say we impose a tax of 40 percent on everyone's income, hoping that the tax will bring in $20,000 from John and $4,800 from Fred for total revenue of $24,800 available for redistribution. But will our hopes be met? Probably not. Taxes have incentive effects. Both John and Fred, faced with a 40 percent tax rate, will reduce the amount of income that they earn, preferring instead to take more leisure than before. If the government is going to tax away 40 percent of your hard-earned dollars, why work so hard?

Say John reduces his income by 30 percent and Fred reduces his by 20 percent. John's after-tax income is $21,000. (He reduced his income from $50,000 to $35,000, of which the 40 percent tax takes $14,000). Fred's after-tax income is $5,760. (He reduced his income from $12,000 to $9,600, of which the 40 percent tax takes $3,840). Now society's total income (John's plus Fred's) falls from $62,000 to $44,600, so our total tax revenue isn't the $24,800 we hoped for, but only $17,840. As government collects tax revenue to redistribute, incentive effects shrink the total amount of income earned by the society.

Incentive Effects of Distributing Income

The next problem is how to give out the revenue we've collected for redistribution. Since our goal is to redistribute the money to Fred, we might simply give it all to Fred. But doing so would violate the law requiring equal treatment of equally situated individuals, so our redistribution system must be related to income levels and not to the characteristics of particular individuals. Let's say we decide to give the proceeds to persons who have less than $20,000 in after-tax income. We distribute this $17,840 to Fred, pulling his after-tax income up to $5,760 + $17,840 = $23,600, a level slightly higher than John's after-tax income.

But now John, seeing what we've given Fred, figures out a way to work "off the books." He works out a deal so that he's paid $5,000 of his income in cash under the table. He takes a chance by breaking the law and failing to report this $5,000 on his income tax return. That means it looks as if he's earning only $18,000 in after-tax income. He's below the $20,000 cutoff, so he can share in our income redistribution program and get back some of the tax money we collected from him. (His pretax income is still $35,000, but $5,000 of it isn't reported to the government, so he pays the 40 percent tax on only $30,000, which means that his tax is $12,000 and he's left with reported after-tax income of $18,000.) If working off the books doesn't accomplish this goal, he can simply choose to work less in order to make his after-tax income fall below the $20,000 cutoff.

Thus, there's an incentive effect of redistributing income as well as an incentive effect of collecting the money to be redistributed. As income is redistributed, individuals have an incentive to make it look as if they earn less income than they do, or to actually earn less income, in order to get a share of the redistributed income.

The negative incentive effects of redistribution further reduce the size of the income pie. In this case, if John reduces his before-tax income to $30,000, his 40 percent tax is only $12,000—and now the redistribution pot is only $15,840 ($12,000 from John and $3,840 from Fred). At the same time, the number of people eligible to share in the redistribution has doubled. Before only Fred was eligible; now both John and Fred are eligible. Now Fred receives only $7,920 from the government instead of $17,840. So his total before-tax income is $9,600 + $7,920 = $17,520. If John got his reported taxable income down to $30,000 by taking $5,000 under the table, this means that John's after-tax income is $30,920:

$30,000	total reported income
−12,000	taxes
$18,000	after-tax income
+5,000	under-the-table income
$23,000	
+7,920	half share of redistribution pot
$30,920	

The effect of our redistribution program on the total income in our two-person society is an aggregate reduction in income from $62,000 to $39,600 of total reported income (assuming John does take that $5,000 under the table). The initial inequality of measured income was approximately 4.2:1 (John's $50,000 to Fred's $12,000). The higher-income person earned about four times as much as the lower-income person. Now the inequality of measured before-tax income is approximately 3:1 (John's reported $30,000 to Fred's $9,600), an improvement from the 4.2:1 it was before. The inequality of after-tax income is $18,000 (John) to $5,760 (Fred), which is also approximately a 3:1 ratio.

The absolute increase in Fred's income is $1,680 (his income is now $5,760 after-tax income plus $7,920 in redistribution proceeds), and the absolute decrease in John's income is $19,080. The net after-tax, after-redistribution positions are:

John: $30,920

Fred: $13,680

That's approximately a ratio of 2.3:1. Clearly some improvement in equality has been achieved (from 4.2:1 to 2.3:1), but it has come at a high cost in total income of the society, which has fallen from $62,000 to $44,600.

CHAPTER 17

The Role of Government in the Economy

You've got to distinguish between a politician using economics and using economics.

~Charles Schultze

After reading this chapter, you should be able to:

1. State two insights that form the basis of most economists' support of markets.
2. Explain what an externality is.
3. State four arguments in favour of government intervention in the economy.
4. State four arguments against government intervention in the economy.
5. Define a sin tax and state why Milton Friedman would likely disapprove of it.
6. List the arguments for and against licensure.
7. Answer just about every question posed to you with, "It depends on the costs and benefits."

Should the government intervene in the private affairs of individuals? If the government does intervene, what should the nature of that intervention be? Throughout this book, these questions have been at the bottom of policy discussions. In this chapter we address these questions directly, tying together the policy discussions of the earlier chapters. We consider four justifications for government intervention in markets: to prevent restraints on trade; to offset problems of information and rationality; to correct externalities; and to prevent unfairness.

Most activities of real-world markets contain elements to which each of these reasons might apply. Thus, in most cases there's legitimate debate about whether the government should intervene, and, if it should, what form the intervention should take. Such decisions generally can be made only on the basis of specific knowledge about institutions and normative judgements, both of which are beyond the scope of an introductory economics textbook. What this book can provide you with is a framework for making such decisions. That's the purpose of this chapter.

Before you address the issues of government intervention, you must consider the question: What is government? In Canada we're all fairly clear about what we mean by **government.** It's the combination of federal, provincial, and municipal agencies whose officials are elected by the people, or are appointed by officials who are elected by the people. The federal government handles the economic matters of defence, income security, national economic regulation, and macroeconomic stability. Provincial and local governments handle matters of education, roads, welfare, and provincial and local economic regulation.

Government The combination of federal, provincial, and municipal agencies whose officials are elected by the people or appointed by elected officials.

Not all countries are organized like this. Many governments, especially in developing countries, are autocracies in which the leaders are not subject to elections, but hold office on the basis of power or historical precedent. The division of responsibilities among levels of authority also differs. For example, in some countries educational policy is set on the national, rather than the provincial or municipal level.

The discussion in this chapter assumes that the government either is a functioning democracy in which the people elect their leaders or else is a beneficent autocracy in which the unelected leader tries to do what's in the people's best interests. Faced with nonbeneficent autocracies in which the leaders worry only about their own benefit, not society's benefit, and in which the leaders pursue their own self-interests, almost all economists become supporters of government nonintervention or **laissez-faire** (the philosophy that government should intervene in the economy as little as possible).

Laissez-faire Economic policy of leaving coordination of individuals' wants to be controlled by the market.

THE ARGUMENTS FOR AND AGAINST GOVERNMENT INTERVENTION

1 Two insights behind economists' support of markets are: (1) if people voluntarily trade, that trade must be making them better off; and (2) excess profit generates competition and the price falls.

A good way to consider the arguments for and against government intervention is to consider a debate between two imaginary economists: Paul, who favours intervention, and Milton, who opposes it. We, the authors, jointly take the role of moderator. There's one rule: Each will be allowed to present his case without interruption.

As background for the debate, let us state two general insights that form the basis of most economists' support of markets.

1. If two individuals trade in a market, one can presume that they're both better off after the trade; otherwise they wouldn't have traded.
2. If individuals are free to produce whatever goods they want, then when excess profit is being made, more people will enter into the production of that good and consumers will benefit as the price is pushed down.

Both economists in the debate accept these two insights but differ as to how many qualifications they make to them. In the imaginary debate that follows, Milton takes the position that few qualifications should be made. Paul takes the position that many qualifications should be made. The debate begins with Milton having stated the two general propositions, after which he draws the following conclusions:

Milton: *All government intervention can be seen as intervention in free trade among people. Government intervention prevents individuals from making trades that will make them both better off. Thus, government intervention can only hurt society. So let's get the government off our backs.*

ADDED DIMENSION

LAISSEZ-FAIRE IS NOT ANARCHY

Most reasons for government intervention discussed in this chapter are debatable.

There is, however, one governmental role that even the strongest laissez-faire advocates generally accept. That role is for government to set up an appropriate institutional and legal structure within which markets can operate.

The reason there's little debate about this role is that all economists recognize that markets do not operate when there is anarchy. They require institutional structures that determine the rules of ownership, what types of trade are allowable, how contracts will be enforced, and what productive institutions are most desirable.

Before anyone conducts business, he or she needs to know the rules of the game and must have a reasonable expectation that those rules will not be changed. The operation of the modern economy requires that contractual arrangements be made among individuals. These contractual arrangements must be enforced if the economy is to operate effectively.

Economists differ significantly as to what the rules for such a system should be and whether any rules that already exist should be modified. Even if the rules are currently perceived as unfair, it can be argued that they should be kept in place. Individuals have already made decisions based on those rules, and it's unfair to them to change the rules in the middle of the game.

Stability of rules is a benefit to society. When the rules are perceived as unfair and changing them is also perceived as unfair, the government must find a balance between these two degrees of unfairness. Government often finds itself in that difficult position. Thus, while there's little debate about government's role in providing some institutional framework, there's heated debate about which framework is most appropriate.

Paul: *Oh, come on, Milton! I'm not naive. Your argument, while it sounds nice, doesn't stand up to close scrutiny. I can list four arguments for government intervention.*

Four Arguments for Government Intervention

1. Preventing Restraints on Trade

Paul: *The first insight argues that all agreements freely entered into should be allowed. But what if two people agree to limit supply and prevent others from entering the market? That would violate the second insight since individuals would not be free to produce whatever goods they want. You'll certainly want to amend your argument against intervention to rule out certain agreements that restrain trade. Thus, one argument for government intervention is to defend competition and to prevent restraint of trade.*

2. Correcting Informational and Rationality Problems

Paul: *A second argument for intervention is an informational and rationality argument. Your free trade argument assumes that people are rational and have all the information they need to make a rational decision. What if they aren't or don't? Say two individuals make a trade: A 3-year-old says to a 17-year-old, "I'll give you my future inheritance if you'll let me play with your toy." In my view that trade is unfair because the 3-year-old isn't yet able to make rational decisions.*

Milton: *OK, I'll grant you that 3-year-olds don't fit my argument, but I'm talking about adults.*

Paul: *I am too. I only presented the argument about the 3-year-old to establish the point. Let's consider another example where the same principle applies. Let's say that your car breaks down and you have it towed to a garage where the mechanic tells you that your differential is sloppy and your clutch is chattering and that they both need to be replaced at a total cost of $1,600. Or suppose a surgeon tells you that you can have a quadruple coronary artery bypass which will make you feel better—and she'll receive only the standard Medicare fee of $2,000. Both of these cases have a potential for useful government intervention because the two sides in each transaction don't have equal access to information, meaning that the trades aren't necessarily fair. It could well be that all your car really needed was a $10 adjustment, and that you had no need for bypass surgery. How can you be sure if the mechanic and the surgeon are advising what's best for you, or if they just want the money? When both sides of a trade don't have equal access to information, the argument for nonintervention breaks down.*

ADDED DIMENSION

ECONOMIC DEBATES

An intellectual inquiry like economics is a debate of ideas. It's not a set of facts or truths. To understand arguments in economics, one must understand both sides of the arguments and the context within which a particular argument is made.

In a debate of ideas, usually a relatively simple idea is presented first. That simple idea provokes responses that can only be understood if the participants and the audience recognize that the responses are reactions to that initial idea. In order to understand ideas properly, one must know the arguments to which they are a response. These arguments require an understanding of the debate that has preceded them. For example, to understand the externality argument in favour of government intervention, one must understand the basic argument in favour of free trade to which the externality argument is a response.

There are higher and higher levels of arguments. Such higher-level arguments are the grist of academic journals and are one of the reasons many academic arguments seem unintelligible to students who don't know the history of the debate. (Another reason is that sometimes academic arguments are indeed unintelligible.)

We present this chapter as a debate to emphasize, first, that learning economics is like listening in on a conversation in which arguments build on one another, and second, that one can expect that there will always be a rebuttal to any argument. Picturing economics as such as unending clash of ideas gives one a good perspective on many economic issues.

Similarly for rationality. People aren't always rational. Say some fast-talking salesperson convinces a 70-year-old couple to invest all their savings in a partnership to turn water into gold. They might do it voluntarily, but in our view that doesn't make it rational. Government intervention is necessary to prevent such injustices.

3. Correcting for Externalities

Paul: *Let's now consider another case. Say that we agree that I'll produce steel for you. I'll build my plant on land I own, and start producing. Who can complain? It's a fair trade freely entered into by both of us, right? It's fair for the two of us—but what about my plant's neighbours? I suspect that they'll complain, and rightfully so. The resulting smoke will pollute the air they breathe; the sulphur smell will drive all the tourists away; and the factory will be an eyesore. So there's an agreement freely entered into by rational individuals that it may be better for government to prevent because the agreement affects third parties.*

Externalities Results of a decision that are not taken into account by the decision maker.

Such third-party effects are called ***externalities*** *(effects of decisions not taken into account by the decision makers). Externalities provide a potential role for government intervention. I can demonstrate the effect of an externality with the simple supply/demand graph in Exhibit 1.*

The supply curve, S, represents the marginal private cost to society of producing steel. It represents my opportunity cost. The demand curve, D, represents the marginal social benefit to demanders of my steel. When there are no externalities, the marginal private costs and benefits represent the marginal social costs and benefits, so the supply/demand equilibrium (P_0, Q_0) represents the point where the marginal social benefit equals the marginal social cost. At that point society is as well off as possible.

2 Externalities are effects of decisions not taken into account by the decision makers.

But now consider what happens when there are externalities in production, as in this steel plant example. In that case other people must bear part of the cost of our agreement. This means that the marginal social cost is different from the marginal private cost. I represent this case by adding a curve to Exhibit 1 which can be called the marginal social cost curve (to distinguish it from the marginal private cost curve). In my example, this marginal social cost curve would include all the marginal costs that my neighbours bear from my production of steel, as well as all the marginal private costs associated with that production.

When free trade is allowed, these costs aren't taken into account, and the supply/demand equilibrium is at too high a quantity, Q_0, and too low a price, P_0. The combination of price and quantity that takes into account all social costs and benefits occurs at P_1, Q_1, where the marginal social benefit equals the marginal social cost. Some type of intervention to reduce production from Q_0 to Q_1 and raise price from P_0 to P_1 is needed. Government is the logical agency to make that intervention.

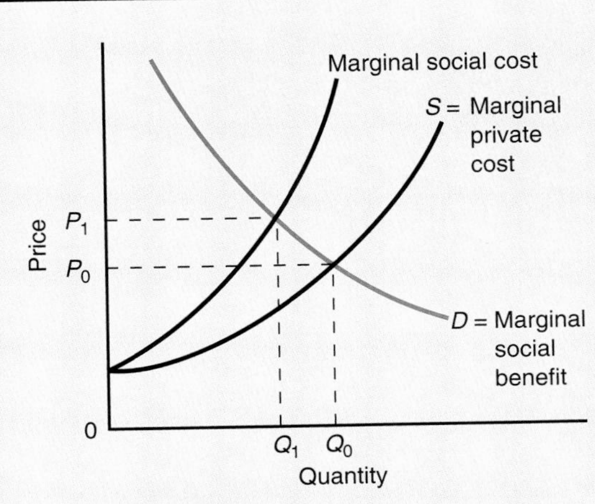

EXHIBIT 1 The Effect of an Externality

When there is a negative externality, the marginal private cost will be below the marginal social cost and the competitive price will be too low to maximize social welfare.

Milton: *I can't let you continue. Your arguments make sense, but they're missing an essential point. And I'm not getting equal time—these boxes are extending the time allotted to Paul. I appeal to the authors to let me respond.*

Authors: *We're sorry, Milton, but rules are rules; besides, good teaching requires presentation of all the arguments. So we'll let Paul state his final argument and then turn the pages over to you.*

4. Preventing Unfairness

Paul: *Thank you, Authors. I'll try to be brief. My final argument is in some ways the most subtle, but in other ways is the most obvious. It goes like this: Markets operate only when there are property rights—when individuals control the items being traded. If one believes that the initial distribution of property rights is unfair, one can reasonably oppose the use of the market.*

Let's consider an example. Say a robber walks up to you and makes you an offer you can't refuse: "Your money or your life." You give him your money and in exchange he doesn't kill you. You're better off; he's better off; and no one else is worse off. But such an exchange is not one that, in my view, societies should condone. Put simply, the robber has no right to your life, so it's unfair for him to offer it in exchange for your money. Because the robber unfairly assumed property rights in your life, the result of the trade is unfair (although you're better off than if you hadn't made the trade).

Now let's change the example slightly. Instead of a robber, it's now an employer who makes you an offer you can't refuse: "You work for me on my terms or I'll fire you." The same unfairness argument can be made about this trade. One could argue that it's unfair because no one should have the right arbitrarily to refuse to allow a person to work unless the terms of employment are "fair."

Most Canadians don't hold that view; they believe that employment is a fair trade, within limits, as long as other jobs exist that an individual can take. But their concept of unfairness of underlying property rights determines many of their arguments in favour of government intervention, and rightfully so. Say that a firm decides that it doesn't want to hire you because you're black or a woman. Most Canadians would argue that the employer has exceeded the limitations of the "fair" employment contract at that point, because a firm shouldn't be allowed to decide whom it will hire on the basis of race or gender.

What I'm saying is that certain underlying rights—such as the right to employment—must be distributed equally for a society to be considered fair. Similarly with the right to a decent living. If the market doesn't provide that for people, then intervention is needed.

Authors: *Before we turn the pages over to Milton, let us restate Paul's four arguments in favour of government intervention.*

3 Four arguments for government intervention are:

1. Agreements to restrain trade should be restricted.
2. Informational and rationality problems necessitate government intervention.
3. When there are externalities, marginal social costs and marginal social benefits should be equalized.
4. When property rights are unfair, government should intervene to achieve fairness.

Summary: Four Arguments for Government Intervention

1. Agreements to restrain trade should themselves be restricted.
2. When there are informational and rationality problems, government should intervene.
3. When there are externalities, intervention is necessary to see that marginal social costs and marginal social benefits are equal.
4. When property rights are unfair, government should intervene to achieve fairness.

Authors: *Now go ahead, Milton.*

Four Arguments against Government Intervention

Milton: *It's always difficult to argue with Paul because he makes his arguments so clearly and convincingly. And in each of the cases he presents, I must agree that he captures a kernel of the truth. But all of the arguments suffer from a serious flaw. They assume that when the government comes in, it will actually correct a problem without introducing new problems that are even worse.*

Paul sees government as a group of individuals committed to doing good. That's not the way all governments work, as the authors point out in the opening of this chapter. The point the authors didn't make, and the point that Paul totally ignored, is that that's not the way even democratic governments operate. In my view, all government is a mechanism through which some people—people in government and people with access to government—take advantage of other people.

Once one sees government for what it truly is, then the arguments for government intervention fall apart, except for government's role in establishing a proper institutional structure within which markets can operate. But, as the authors pointed out, that general role isn't in debate.

The other roles for government are in debate. The argument against government intervention rests on the difficulty of correcting economic problems through government. Yes, all the problems Paul mentions do exist, and it would be nice if they didn't exist. But it would also be nice if diamonds grew on trees. To make the four arguments in favour of government intervention convincing, Paul would have to show that there's a better way, and that the "solution" to the problems won't make the problems worse. Paul hasn't even addressed this issue.

The reality is that government is often controlled by special interests. It's inefficient, bureaucratic, and oppressive. When you expand government, you make people worse off. So, yes, there are problems with the market, but government's attempts to correct those problems create worse problems. Laws passed in the name of the public good, in fact, generally benefit only a small group. To show you what I mean, let's consider each of the four cases that Paul presents.

1. Preventing Private Restraints on Trade Creates Even More Restraints

Milton: *There's no question that people have a desire to restrain trade, but if we look at the real world we see that the primary way they restrain trade is through governmental restrictions such as licensing requirements, anti-combines legislation, and zoning regulations. Allowing government to try to stop private individuals from restricting trade opens up a Pandora's box of new possibilities for restricting trade through government. Not only will somewhat reasonable restrictions be made, but totally unreasonable restrictions also will be made. And that Pandora's box need not be opened, because without government enforcement of restrictions, competition will soon break down any private restrictions on trade. The only long-lasting restraints are those imposed by government.*

2. Correcting Informational and Rationality Problems Creates Other Problems

Milton: *There's no doubt that informational problems like the ones Paul describes do exist. They're facts of life. But once again, using government to solve a problem creates worse problems. Say that government passes a law that all cost estimates for auto repairs must be approved as fair before the repairs can be made. Can you imagine how long you'd have to wait for the paperwork to be processed? You'd be waiting months for*

EXTERNALITIES AND PUBLIC GOODS

Externalities can be positive or negative. A positive externality is the benefit conveyed to third parties by an action in which they were not actors themselves. A negative externality is the harm inflicted on third parties by an action in which they were not actors themselves. An example of a negative externality is the negative effect of pollution on society. An example of a positive externality is the effect on society of the education of its citizens.

When actions have either positive or negative third-party effects, it's not clear that society will be better off or worse off if it follows a laissez-faire policy. Unless the government intervenes, many agreements that produce negative externalities will be allowed and many agreements that produce positive externalities won't take place. Government intervention *may* be able to make individuals take third-party benefits or costs into account.

An extreme case of a positive externality is called a public good. A *public good* is a good that an individual can consume without diminishing the amount of it that other people consume. Thus, supplying a public good conveys a positive externality not only to one or two individuals but to all individuals in the society. An example of a public good is national defence. Each person in an army who defends the nation provides defence for all in the society.

Many other activities carry with them strong negative externalities. Consider fishing Northern Cod off the coast of Newfoundland. Whenever you catch a fish, there's one fewer fish for all other people to catch. You're better off, but other people are worse off. But you're concerned only with your own welfare, so you won't take into account the harm done to other people. Activities like that which deplete or use up a commonly held resource involve significant negative externalities. If we allow everyone to carry on such activity unrestricted—if we follow a policy of laissez-faire—society as a whole will be worse off. And, this is exactly what happened in early 1995—the Northern Cod fishery was designated as commercially extinct—there aren't enough fish left to support the industry.

your car. And all that paperwork would add to your repair costs. Not only would you pay too much to have your car fixed; often you wouldn't get the car back for months.

Here's another example. Health and Welfare Canada "protects" us from unsafe drugs, but in doing so it creates enormous bureaucratic hassles for the manufacturers of all new drugs, many of which would be beneficial. For instance, it prevented a number of experimental drugs from being used on AIDS patients for years, even though their use represented many people's only chance to survive, or at least to survive longer and more comfortably. By the time Health and Welfare approved the drugs, many of the patients were dead and countless others had suffered physical agony the drugs could have lessened.

3. Correcting for Externalities Creates Other Problems

Milton: *I've heard the externality argument hundreds of times, but, I swear, every time I examine a so-called externality, I discover either that it isn't a true externality that can be corrected by government or that the way in which government will correct for the externality will cause more harm than good.*

To see this, let's first consider Paul's Exhibit 1. Is it likely that government will pass a law reducing Paul's production of steel to Q_1 and raise the price to P_1? Or is it more likely that government will simply ban production of steel at Paul's site altogether? If it bans production of a good altogether, quantity will fall to zero. The good won't be available at any price, a result that would be far worse than if the market result had been left alone. Government regulatory agencies aren't designed to do the delicate balancing of benefits and costs necessary to make the marginal changes that Paul's argument calls for. Such refinements require a scalpel, and government intervention is more like a chain saw.

The same problem of government intervention causing more harm than good exists for activities with so-called positive externalities. Government intervention simply creates a possibility for special interests to come in and channel government revenue to support their own interests. In my view, positive externalities generally are the result of a poor specification of property rights. The positive externalities argument is made by some groups attempting to use government for their own ends.

Government intervention for positive externalities inevitably means government subsidization, which must be paid for in higher taxes. These higher taxes are likely to offset the good the subsidized externalities might do; that is, higher taxes reduce private incentives to work and to undertake private economic activity. In my view and in the view of most noninterventionists generally, private activity done without government intervention involves as many, or more, positive externalities as do government-supported activities.

For example, in the early 1990s, as the threat from the former Soviet Union significantly diminished, it made sense to close a number of military bases around the country. But political pressure against doing so was intense. One argument used by supporters of keeping these bases open was that they had positive externalities: They created jobs for civilians in the area.

What's wrong with this argument is that in order to pay for these bases, government has to collect taxes, which discourages private activities. The net job creation is essentially zero. As was the case with negative externalities, even when government activities do have clear-cut positive externalities, it's not at all clear that the political process will choose the right level of the activity. Generally the political process won't produce a decision based on comparing marginal social costs with marginal social benefits. It will make the decision based on marginal political costs and marginal political benefits, which often have little or nothing to do with marginal social costs or benefits.

Finally, let's now consider the argument that Paul sneaked into his presentation in the box on externalities and public goods. That's the argument about the overuse of common resources. I suggest that overfishing is not an example of market failure. It's an example of what happens when no market exists.

Paul's argument was that species would be overfished because of individuals' failure to take into account the full social cost of catching fish. I contend that the overfishing occurred because no one owns the ocean. If someone owned the ocean, that person would take into account the fact that when someone caught a fish, the catch available to others was reduced. To prevent overfishing the owner would charge people for the right to fish and would maximize his or her wealth by seeing to it that enough fish were left in the water to reproduce for next year's fishing.

Or, alternatively, consider air pollution: If the air were owned by private individuals, those individuals would charge others for the right to pollute it and, in doing so, would decrease the amount of pollution.

Even though the air isn't privately owned, people will negotiate ways to reduce or eliminate the negative externalities of air pollution. For example, if Paul's neighbours are so worried about air pollution from the plant he proposes to build on his land, they can get together and buy his property or, at least, pay him not to build. Any other solution is simply a usurping of Paul's property rights.

4. Preventing Unfairness Creates More Unfairness

Milton: *Paul was right in saving the unfairness argument for the end because it's the argument that we market advocates find most difficult to defend against. But it, too, suffers from a serious flaw. It suggests that some standard of fairness other than the market standard exists by which to judge events.*

I contend that the market is a standard of fairness to which many people, including me, subscribe: People who are more productive and who work harder deserve more material rewards than people who don't work hard. By rewarding productivity and hard work, the market stimulates economic activity and provides benefits for everyone.

Let's consider Paul's example about the employer when he talked about "Preventing unfairness." Why is the employer the employer? Paul didn't answer that. He made it seem as if it was simply happenstance. But more often than not, the employer is the employer because he or she worked harder or was more productive than others. If society limits the gains of hard work and the freedom of people who work hard to do what they want, then society will discourage hard work. When hard work by the productive people is discouraged, society is made worse off.

That's bad, but the negative incentives created by government intervention are even worse. As soon as people see that they can get more rewards from the government than from their own hard work, productivity slows and private economic activity is discouraged. Keeping arguments about fairness out of the government decision-making process

ADDED DIMENSION

THE LIGHTHOUSE AND THE BEES

The debate about externalities, public goods, and differences between marginal social costs and benefits has long been conducted in economics. The examples that have been used are subject to much criticism.

For instance, an old textbook example of a public good that had to be supplied by government rather than privately was a lighthouse. If one person builds a lighthouse so coastal ships can avoid the rocks, the benefit will be there for others to enjoy. So, the textbook argument went, private business wouldn't provide lighthouses because lighthouses were a public good. However, upon searching the real world, people discovered that many private lighthouses existed and that firms had found ways to finance the lighthouses privately. The lighthouse example was dropped from the textbooks.

Another frequent textbook example of marginal social costs differing from marginal private costs has been the case of bees. The textbooks argued: Bees pollinate blossoms and therefore provide a positive externality. Because of this positive externality, there will be too few bees because the benefits they provide—pollination—are external to the beekeeper's decisions—to keep them for their honey.

But when researchers looked into beekeeping, they found a market in bee services. Orchard owners were renting bees from beekeepers in order to pollinate the flowers on their trees. The externality was being paid for and therefore wasn't an externality. The bee example was dropped from the textbooks.

Some opponents of government intervention to correct for externalities use these examples to argue that government shouldn't intervene on the basis of externalities, but that argument is too strong. The existence of private markets doesn't mean that the private market supplies enough of the good or service to make the marginal social cost equal the marginal social benefit. Nor does it mean that there aren't other, better examples in which there are no markets.

Two lessons should be drawn from these two examples:

1. One should always carefully consider the arguments that textbook writers make and compare those arguments to reality.
2. One should recognize that private sources of solutions to social problems may exist, and that before one advocates having government intervene to correct for an externality, one should carefully consider the private alternatives.

helps everyone, the poor as well as the rich. It creates more for everyone as the wealth spills over from the hard-working rich to the poor. The only workable standard of fairness is the market standard: Them that works gets; them that don't work go without—unless them that works want to help them that don't.

Authors: *Paul, before you respond, we'd like to summarize Milton's four arguments against government intervention.*

Summary: Four Arguments against Government Intervention

1. Preventing private restraints on trade creates even more restraints.
2. Correcting informational and rationality problems creates even more problems.
3. Correcting for externalities creates other problems.
4. Preventing unfairness creates more unfairness.

4 Four arguments against government intervention are:

1. Preventing private restraints on trade creates even more restraints.
2. Correcting informational and rationality problems creates even more problems.
3. Correcting for externalities creates other problems.
4. Preventing unfairness creates more unfairness.

Authors: *Now, Paul, you can respond, but please be brief.*

Paul's Rebuttals

Paul: *I must admit that there's a certain truth to each of Milton's counterarguments. But, in my view, government isn't nearly so controlled by special interests or so inefficient as Milton would have us believe. For every case of government ineffectiveness, I can point to a case of effective government intervention.*

As for property rights eliminating the need for government: Who is to establish those rights, if not government? Without government, productive activity would be impossible; people would spend all their time fighting over property rights. Governments use markets to avoid continually making judgements of who should get what. Once the initial property rights are established, the market decides. That method saves enormous political fighting and is good and necessary. But if the initial allocation of property rights leads to results that aren't to society's liking, then it's society's right to modify those property rights. Property rights aren't inalienable rights; they're conferred rights.

What I'm saying is that the market is not above the government. Rather the government is above the market, and a democratic government will see to it that the market's allocation of property rights is within the range of fairness that society finds acceptable. If Milton doesn't agree with society's right to change property rights, then he doesn't agree with democracy. Let me give you an example of the need for government to make decisions about fairness.

Milton says, "Private individuals should own the oceans and the air." But who decides which individuals will be the owners, and who prevents unproductive fights over the allocation of property rights? If the government didn't act to prevent private individuals from usurping common resources, the social structure would break down.

Next let me deal with the argument that government intervention is a chain saw instead of the scalpel that we need. In many cases of past regulation I think Milton is right, but he's right only because economists haven't played a significant role in helping to design the government's intervention.

All too often the type of government intervention has been administrative or regulatory. One benefit of economics is that it suggests alternatives to regulation. For example, consider pollution. If, rather than regulating the permissible amount of pollution administratively, government taxes pollution—creating activities and subsidizing the reduction of pollution—the result can be more precise and appropriate—the scalpel effect. Say that in Exhibit 2 the government determines that the additional marginal social cost of producing steel equals C_2. If government sets a firm's pollution tax on steel production at t = C_2, the firm will reduce its output to Q_1 on its own. It's a tribute to economists' influence that such taxes, called ***effluent fees,*** *are now widely used in helping deal with pollution.*

Effluent fees Charges imposed by government on pollution.

An alternative way in which the government can regulate efficiently is to foster the creation of markets. As I stated, markets don't simply come into existence; they require the definition, establishment, and enforcement of property rights.

Pollution provides an example here (again). In dealing with pollution, governments in certain areas are establishing "pollution rights." All existing firms are required to reduce their pollution by 10 percent. New firms can pollute if they pay existing firms to reduce pollution further, by an amount that will offset the new pollution introduced by the new firms. If an existing firm is willing to reduce its pollution by 20 percent, it can sell some of its entitlements to pollute to new firms and to other existing firms which, with these permits, would be allowed to reduce pollution by less than the required 10 percent. By creating these rights and establishing a market in them, government can encourage total pollution being reduced by 10 percent, while each individual firm is still free to decide how much it will reduce pollution. Firms that have a low marginal cost of reducing pollution will reduce more than 10 percent so they can sell the right to pollute to other firms whose cost of reducing pollution is higher.

Such novel plans have problems that must be worked out before they can be widely used, but they demonstrate that government regulation can be made compatible with the market.

Finally, let me comment on the "them that works gets" philosophy. It isn't so simple. There's nothing necessarily fair about the allocation of abilities. What's fair about Patrick Roy being endowed with his natural abilities and someone else being born a klutz? Should we let people starve simply because their market wage is below the subsistence wage? Society will continue to use the market only if it can adjust the distributional results of the market.

Milton's Rebuttals

Milton: *Paul concedes many of my points and differs from me primarily in judgements. But he gives few justifications for his judgements. Those justifications aren't better than the ones I initially gave, so they don't require a direct rebuttal. It's quite clear that I have a much stronger belief in the sanctity of property rights than does Paul. Because of this belief, I find it necessary to limit government by historical and constitutional constraints, such as existing property rights. I ask Paul to compare the experience*

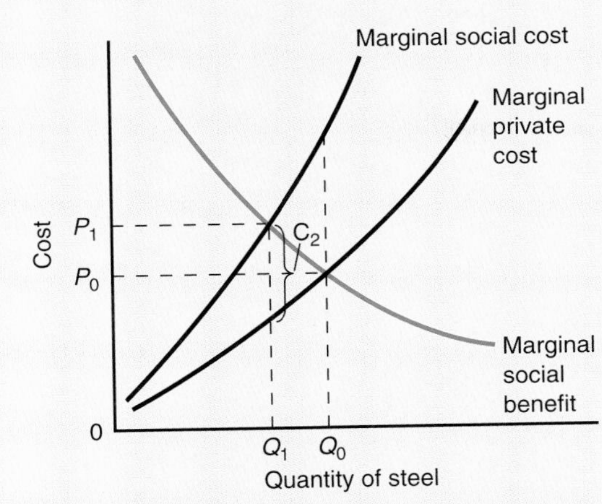

EXHIBIT 2 Regulation through Taxation

If the government sets a tax sufficient to take into account a negative externality, individuals will respond by reducing the quantity of the pollution-causing activity supplied to a level that individuals would have supplied had they included the negative externality in their decision.

of Western market economies with socialist economies if he wants an example of the power of property rights and the market.

As for interventionist economists improving the situation, I have my doubts. Often they have simply introduced new ways for government to intervene—ways that look as if they are compatible with markets, but actually require enormous government involvement.

The Difficult Decisions

At this point our debate must stop. General arguments are fine, but judging from historical experience, the debate is unending. Both sides of this debate about whether government should intervene in the market have valid points. No one general argument obviously wins out over the others. Decisions about government intervention will need to be made on a case-by-case basis, using a cost/benefit framework. In the remainder of this chapter, we look at two cases to give you an idea of the clash of these ideas in the real world.

THE DRUG LEGALIZATION DEBATE

There's no question that the use of illicit drugs costs the Canadian economy billions of dollars every year. The problem has become so serious that serious consideration is being given to the legalization of a number of illegal drugs. This legalize-but-tax alternative accepts a government role in controlling the use of drugs, but it uses market incentives to achieve a (presumably) desired end.

According to this perspective, government should legalize drug consumption but impose enormously high taxes on the sale of drugs. This possibility is sometimes called a **sin tax** approach because it discourages activities society believes are harmful (sinful) for individuals. Thus, the government is making a value judgement about what's good for individuals, but it's using market incentives rather than regulation to achieve its end. How that end could be achieved is shown in Exhibit 3.

Sin tax Tax designed to discourage activities society believes are harmful to individuals.

5 Sin taxes are designed to discourage activities society believes are harmful to individuals. Milton Friedman would likely oppose sin taxes because they involve the government trying to direct individuals' behaviour.

When legalized, drugs have a price of P_e and a quantity of Q_e. A law forbidding the sale of drugs should, in principle, reduce the supply to zero. In reality, the law would only decrease the supply somewhat, depending on the degree of enforcement of the law and people's adherence to it. The price and quantity in the market would be a black market price and quantity—the price and quantity of illegal trades.

Assuming that the law prohibiting drug trafficking decreases supply from S_0 to S_1, the equilibrium black market price of drugs is P_b and the black market quantity of drugs sold is Q_b. Notice the large difference between the free market cost of producing Q_b, which is C_b, and the black market price, P_b. The difference (the shaded rectangle) is a cost that reflects the aversion to breaking the law, either because it represents a chance of being caught and punished or because it represents the cost to individuals who find it morally wrong to violate the law (in a few minutes you'll be

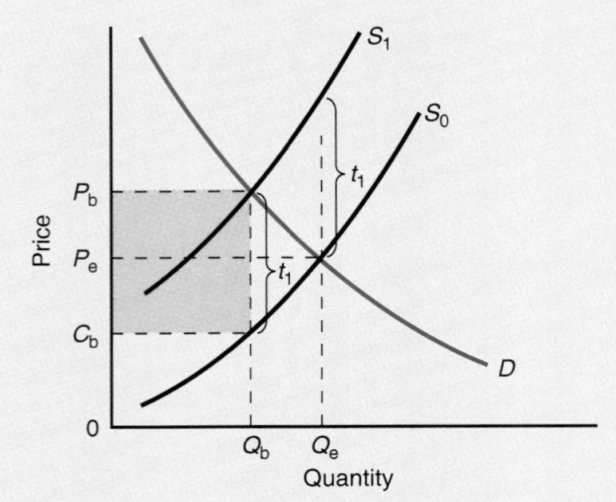

EXHIBIT 3 The Sin Tax Alternative

If drug consumption is legalized, the government can discourage drug use by imposing high taxes on the sale of drugs. If the use of the drugs is legal and no intervention takes place, along supply S_0 the price is P_e and the quantity consumed is Q_e. By instituting a high tax rate of t_1, the government can cause the supply curve to shift up from S_0 to S_1, raising the price from P_e to P_b and decreasing the quantity consumed from Q_e to Q_b. The government will receive the shaded area in taxes.

asked to explain why the government actually lowered a sin tax—you'll need to think about this morality issue).

Those suppliers who aren't caught make enormous profits. From discussions we've had with individuals exposed to the drug trade, we understand that the pay for low-level suppliers is \$50 to \$100 an hour, and for high-level suppliers it's in the \$1,000 to \$10,000 an hour range. The profit to suppliers (the shaded area in Exhibit 3) is large, as you can see. How large depends on the elasticity of the supply and demand curves, how vigorously the law is enforced, and how strongly people feel about breaking the law. The cost of producing the drugs compared to the selling price is likely to be minimal. Most of a black market drug's price is a payment for the seller's risk of getting caught.

Now let's say that instead of prohibiting drug trafficking, the government institutes an extremely high tax of t_1 on drug sales. That tax shifts the after-tax supply curve from S_0 to S_1, just as the law did, so that the price that the consumer pays to receive quantity Q_b is still P_b. Drug users are now presented with a choice: to buy illegally from a black market dealer and risk arrest, or to buy legally from a government-authorized seller at the same price but with no risk of arrest. Faced with that option, most buyers would buy from government-authorized sellers. In response, dealers would be forced to lower prices and some would be squeezed out of the market. As that happened, the government would get more of the revenue that had been going to the dealers.

The extra revenue could be substantial—perhaps as much as \$50 or \$60 billion if most black market sales at lower prices could be prevented. The government could greatly reduce black market sales if it used, say, one-fifth of the tax proceeds to increase the enforcement effort. Illegal dealers would be squeezed on both sides. Their costs would rise and their revenues would fall since they'd have to charge 10 or 20 percent less than the legal price to get people to buy their illegal drugs rather than the legal drugs. The remaining tax revenue could be used for drug treatment programs and for educating people about the evils of drugs. How much revenue the government would receive and how effective the tax would be in stopping drug use depends on the elasticities of supply and demand. A good exercise for you is to explain, assuming it could choose, whether the government should prefer elastic or inelastic supply and demand curves.

Many more arguments could be made for and against all three of these positions regarding government intervention in the drug trade. But the discussion should be enough to start you thinking about the myriad options available for dealing with society's problems and about how economics provides a way to consider the costs and benefits of the various options. Another good exercise is for you to explain why the government *reduced* taxes on cigarettes in 1993. Was it trying to encourage cigarette consumption, or was there another reason?

THE LICENSURE DEBATE

All government intervention is not the same. The government can respond to any specific problem or situation in any number of ways, some of which are preferable to others. As a result of political pressure, the important policy debates often concern not *whether* government should intervene, but *how*.

Let's consider the licensing of doctors—and consider an alternative.[1]

Licensing Doctors

In the early 1800s, medical licenses were not required by law, so anyone who wanted to could set up shop as a physician. The most popular type of medical treatment at the time was heroic therapy, which consisted primarily of bloodletting, blistering, and the administration of massive doses of mineral poisons, such as mercury.[2] The practitioners of two alternative types of medicine—homeopathy (which focused on natural healing) and eclecticism (which combined a variety of approaches)—together laid the foundation of modern medicine. These practitioners challenged the status quo by arguing that heroic therapy was not helping people. They pressured government to pass licensure laws requiring that all doctors earn a license to practise medicine by receiving training in homeopathy and eclecticism. Ever since, it has been illegal to practise medicine without a license.

6A Licensing tends to prevent incompetents from practicing, provide information to consumers, and professionalize an activity.

To get that license, one must go through an undergraduate program, four years of medical school, and a residency in a hospital for anywhere from one to seven years, as well as pass a series of Medical Board examinations.

Licensing of doctors is justified by the informational and rationality problems discussed before. Since individuals often don't have an accurate way of deciding whether a doctor is good, government intervention is necessary. The informational problem is solved because licensing requires that all doctors have at least a minimum competency. People have the *information* that a doctor must be competent because they see the license framed and hanging on the doctor's office wall.

Sometimes even when people have the information available, they don't use it *rationally*. Without licensing, businesses would be established to sell a whole set of schemes, such as using laetrile to fight cancer or using vitamin C to fight everything. According to scientific research, laetrile does not cure cancer and vitamin C does not cure everything.

A small number of economists, of whom Milton Friedman is the best known, have proposed that licensure laws be eliminated, leaving the medical field unlicensed. While such a proposal is supported by only a few economists, it's instructive to consider their proposal: Let anyone practise medicine who wishes to.

6B Licensing tends to restrict entry, restrict consumer choice, and cost money.

They argue that licensure was instituted as much, or more, to restrict supply as it was to help the consumer. Specifically, critics of medical licensure raise these questions:

> Why, if licensed medical training is so great, do we even need formal restrictions to keep other types of medicine from being practised?
>
> Whom do these restrictions benefit: the general public or the doctors who practise mainstream medicine?
>
> What have the long-run effects of licensure been?

Even the strongest critics of licensure agree that, in the case of doctors, the informational argument for government intervention is strong. But the question is whether

[1]The arguments presented here about licensing doctors also apply to dentists, lawyers, professors, and other professional groups.

[2]Bloodletting involved extracting blood from the body, on the theory that the person's problem stemmed from "too much blood." Blistering involved causing blisters to form on the body, on the theory that when they burst, they would expel the poisonous matter that was making the person ill.

licensure is the right form of government intervention. Why doesn't the government simply provide the public with information about which treatments work and which don't? That would give the freest rein to **consumer sovereignty** (the right of the individual to make choices about what is consumed and produced). As for the rationality argument, critics of licensure simply reject it out of hand. They ask: Who is the government to decide for people what is, or isn't, good for them? If people have the necessary information but still choose to treat cancer with laetrile or treat influenza with massive doses of vitamin C, why should the government tell them they can't?

Consumer sovereignty The right of the individual to make choices about what is consumed and produced.

If the informational alternative is preferable to licensure, why didn't the government choose it? Friedman argues that government didn't follow that path because the licensing was done as much for the doctors as for the general public. Licensure has led to a monopoly position for doctors. They can restrict supply and increase price and thereby significantly increase their incomes.

Let's now take a closer look at the informational alternative.

The Informational Alternative to Licensure

The informational alternative is to allow anyone to practise medicine, but to have the government certify doctors' backgrounds and qualifications. The government would require that doctors' backgrounds be made public knowledge. Each doctor would have to post the following information prominently in his or her office:

1. Grades in university.
2. Grades in medical school.
3. Success rate for various procedures.
4. References.
5. Medical philosophy.

According to supporters of the informational alternative, these data would allow individuals to make informed decisions about their medical care. Like all informed decisions, they would be complicated. For instance, doctors who take only patients with minor problems can show high "success rates," while doctors who are actually more skilled but who take on problem patients may have to provide more extensive information so people can see why their success rates shouldn't be compared to those of the doctors who take just easy patients. But despite the problems, supporters of the informational alternative argue that it's better than the current situation.

Current licensure laws don't provide any of this information to the public. All a patient knows is that a doctor has managed to get through medical school and has passed the Medical Board exams (which are, after all, only sets of multiple-choice questions). The doctor may have done all this 30 years ago, possibly by the skin of his or her teeth, but, once licensed, a doctor is a doctor for life. (A well-known doctor joke is the following: What do you call the person with the lowest passing grade-point average in medical school? Answer: Doctor.) Thus, the informational alternative would provide much more useful data to the public than the current licensing procedure.

Let's now consider two examples.

Two Examples of How the Informational Alternative Would Work

Say you're wondering whether that new mole on your arm is cancerous. What do you do? Under our current system, you ask your private physician, or you go to your local hospital and ask. The physician, most likely, won't know. He or she had two or three lectures on skin cancer in medical school and may have seen some in practice, but probably isn't a specialist in cancer. So all you get is a referral to a specialist (cost: $35 to Medicare).

Why not go to the specialist in the first place? By agreement among doctors, specialists usually will see only those patients who have been referred to them by a general physician. Now let's say that you go to the specialist, who looks at the mole and recognizes immediately that it's just a mole (cost: $50 to Medicare). But she orders a biopsy, just to be sure (cost: $20 to Medicare). She's right and you're relieved, but Medicare is also $105 poorer (and whose tax dollars pay for Medicare?). To find out from the specialist whether the mole was cancerous cost $105 and about four hours of your time. While Medicare picks up the tab, the time cost involved discourages many people (how long did you have to wait the last time you visited your physician—or even worse—the hospital?) They'll just hope the mole isn't cancerous.

Consider this hypothetical informational alternative: You go to a person who hasn't been to medical school, but who's been through a special one-year training program in diagnosing malignant carcinomas (skin cancer). The success rate of detection by such persons is 99.8 percent; the fee to Medicare is $10 if no biopsy is needed, $30 if one is. The process is quick, easy, and inexpensive.

As a second example, consider surgery. This should be the strongest case for licensure. Would you want an untrained butcher to operate on you? Of course not. But opponents of licensure point out that it's not at all clear how effectively licensure prevents butchery. Ask a doctor, "Would you send your child to any board-certified surgeon picked at random?" The honest answer you'd get is, "No way. Some of them are butchers." How do they know that? Being around hospitals, they have access to information about various surgeons' success and failure rates; they've seen them operate and know whether or not they have manual dexterity.

Advocates of the informational alternative suggest that you ask yourself, "What skill would you want in a surgeon?" A likely answer would be "Manual dexterity. Her fingers should be magic fingers." Does the existing system of licensure ensure that everyone who becomes a surgeon has magic fingers? No. To become licensed as a surgeon requires a gruelling residency after four years of medical school, but manual dexterity, as such, is never explicitly tested or checked!

The informational alternative wouldn't necessarily eliminate the surgical residency. If the public believed that a residency was necessary to create skilled surgeons, many potential surgeons would choose that route. But there would be other ways to become a surgeon. For example, in high school, tests could be given for manual dexterity. Individuals with superb hand/eye coordination could go to a one-year technical college to train to be "heart technicians," who would work as part of a team doing heart surgery.

Clearly open-heart surgery is the extreme case, and most people will not be convinced that it can be performed by unlicensed medical personnel. But what about minor surgery? According to informational alternative advocates, many operations could be conducted more cheaply and better (since people with better manual dexterity would be doing the work) if restrictive licensing were ended. Or, if you don't accept the argument for human medical treatments, how about for veterinarians? For cosmetologists? For plumbers? Might the informational alternatives work in these professions?

Some Words of Caution about the Informational Alternative

If you were convinced that the informational alternative was preferable to medical licensure, beware. The preceding discussion of licensure and the informational alternative presented only the arguments in favour of that alternative. It highlights the benefits of the informational alternative and the problems with the licensure alternative.

We presented the alternatives in a one-sided way to stimulate your thinking, not to convince you that doctors are monopolists concerned only with their own incomes and that eliminating the medical monopoly will solve our country's health care woes. Reality is far more complicated than that. A complete presentation would have discussed problems of the informational alternative and how, if chosen, the alternative could be implemented. In the real world, systems for qualifying professionals have serious problems; arguments can be made against the informational and certification alternatives that would convince you that neither is the answer.

Ultimately, one needs an intimate knowledge of the actual practice and institutions to judge whether reforms would really make things better or worse. Therein lies the problem of reform. Just about the only individuals who have detailed knowledge are those who have a vested interest in the current system. So the information you're likely to get about potential reforms may well be biased toward only those reforms that will help the vested interest.

CONCLUSION

7 Should the government intervene in the market? It depends.

As textbook writers, we wish we could say that some conclusions can be drawn about whether the government should, or should not, enter into the economy. We certainly have views about particular instances (in case you haven't guessed, we're highly opinionated individuals), but to lay out arguments and information that would convince a reasonable person to agree with us would take an entire book for each area in which government might intervene.

What we can do in this textbook is to stimulate your interest in discovering for yourself the information and the subtleties of the debates for and against government intervention. Just about every time you read, hear, or are asked the question "Should the government intervene in a market?" the answer is "It depends." If your first impulse is to give any answer other than that one, you may have trouble maintaining the appropriate objectivity when you start considering the costs and benefits of government intervention.

CHAPTER SUMMARY

- A laissez-faire policy is not anarchy.
- Possible reasons for government intervention include preventing private restraints on trade, informational and rationality problems, externalities, and unfairness.
- An externality is the result of a market transaction that is not taken into account by the transactors.
- Advocates of laissez-faire argue that government intervention usually makes the situation worse, not better.
- Making something illegal creates the possibility of a black market with large returns for breaking the law.
- Taxing an illegal activity is an alternative way of discouraging it.
- Licensure laws are often presented as helping the public, but in fact are often designed to help a particular group.
- In answer to a question "Should the government intervene?" an objective initial response is almost always "It depends."

KEY TERMS

consumer sovereignty *(358)*
effluent fees *(354)*
externalities *(348)*
government *(346)*
laissez-faire *(346)*
sin tax *(355)*

QUESTIONS FOR THOUGHT AND REVIEW

The number after each question represents the estimated degree of critical thinking required. (1 = almost none; 10 = deep thought.)

1. State four reasons for a potentially beneficial role of government intervention. *(1)*
2. Would an advocate of laissez-faire support or oppose anti-combines laws? Why or why not? *(9)*
3. Should Health and Welfare Canada's role in restricting which drugs may be marketed be eliminated? Why or why not? *(8)*
4. Pollution is often considered an externality. Should the government pass laws that prevent pollution? Why or why not? *(8)*
5. What would be the sin tax method of controlling pollution? *(4)*
6. Most redistribution in Canada is from one middle-class group to another middle-class group. What does that suggest about the laissez-faire/government intervention fight? *(5)*
7. Why would Milton Friedman likely oppose the legalize-and-heavily-tax solution to the addictive drug problem? *(5)*
8. Why would British Columbia consider legalizing heroin, as it did in early 1995? *(5)*
9. Financial analysts are currently unlicensed. Should they be licensed? Why or why not? *(6)*
10. An advanced degree is required in order to teach at most colleges. In what sense is this a form of restricting entry through licensure? *(5)*

PROBLEMS AND EXERCISES

1. The marginal cost, marginal social cost, and demand for a firm are given in the accompanying diagram. The social cost is higher than the private cost due to pollution emitted by the plant.
   a. What is the efficient level of output?
   b. Given the information in the accompanying diagram, if the government wanted to set a fee to force the firm to decrease emissions, what fee would you recommend?

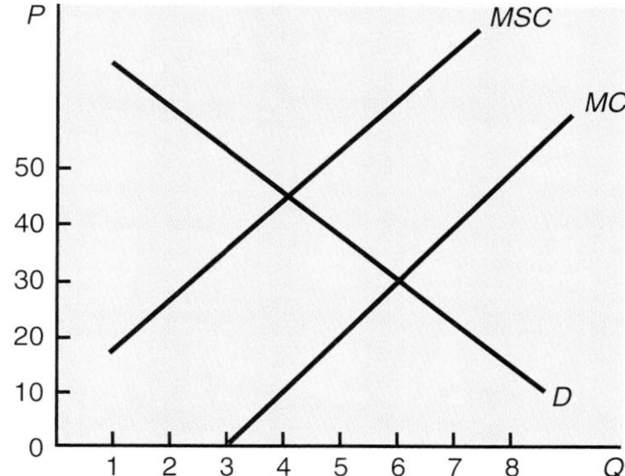

2. Congratulations! You've been made finance minister of Happyland. The prime minister is unhappy that so many of her subjects are taking illegal drugs. You recommend legalizing such drugs and then imposing a tax on them.
   a. Demonstrate graphically the supply/demand equilibrium for the use of illegal drugs before your program is instituted.
   b. What should the minimum amount of tax be if the prime minister wants to keep drug use no higher than its previous level?
   c. Show graphically the government's revenue.
   d. Your drug program failed miserably for political reasons. The prime minister fires you but secretly comes to you for advice. She has heard that a cartel or combine is taking over the drug trade and wonders what she should do about it. What advice do you give her?
3. Demonstrate graphically the effects of price controls when:
   a. There is a competitive market.
   b. There is a monopoly.
   c. Relate the results of *a* and *b* to the price controls in the health care debate presented in the chapter.
4. Economics professors Thomas Hopkins and Arthur Gosnell of the Rochester Institute of Technology have estimated that in the year 2000, regulations will cost the U.S. economy $662 billion, and that in 1992, regulations cost each family $5,700 per year.
   a. Do their findings mean that the U.S. has too many regulations?
   b. How would an economist decide which regulations to keep and which to do away with?
5. In the 1990s a debate about dairy products has concerned the labelling of milk produced from cows who have been injected with the hormone BST that significantly increases their milk production. Since this is a synthetically produced copy of a milk hormone that government regulatory bodies have determined is indistinguishable from the hormone produced naturally by the cow and has also determined that milk from cows treated with BST is indistinguishable from milk that comes from cows that have not been treated with BST, some people have argued that no labelling requirement is necessary. Others argue that the consumer has a right to know.
   a. Where do you think most dairy farmers stand on this labelling issue?
   b. If consumers have a right to know, should labels inform them of other drugs, such as antibiotics, normally given to cows?
   c. Do you think dairy farmers who support BST labelling also support the broader labelling law that would be needed if other drugs were included? Why?
6. The milk industry has a number of interesting aspects. Provide economic explanations for the following:
   a. Fluid milk is 87 percent water. It can be dried and reconstituted so that it is almost indistinguishable from fresh milk. What is a likely reason that such reconstituted milk is not produced?
   b. Canada has provincial milk-marketing regulations whose goals are to make each of the provinces self-sufficient in milk. What is a likely reason for this?
   c. A politician has been quoted as saying, "I am absolutely convinced . . . that simply bringing down dairy price supports is not a way to cut production." Is it likely that he is correct? What is a probable reason for his statement?
7. Subtle changes in the tax laws often mean enormous amounts of money to individuals and groups. Consider the case of whiskey, as did economists Jack High and Clayton Coppin. Whiskey is distilled grain. The distilling process produces poisonous impurities, called fusel oil, that must be removed before the whiskey is drinkable. One way to remove these impurities is by aging the whiskey in wooden barrels. Whiskey produced in this manner is "straight whiskey." The second method is distillation—removing the fusel oil through additional distilling. The latter method removes more impurities and is cheaper, but it results in a whiskey with little taste. However, taste can be added back through flavourings or blending with aged whiskey. Up until 1868 distilled or blended whiskey predominated, but in that year a law was passed that allowed straight-whiskey producers who stored their whiskey in government warehouses to defer their taxes on it until it was fully aged.
   a. What advantage would this law have for straight-whiskey producers?
   b. After the tax was paid the whiskey received a tax stamp, certifying that its producers had paid the tax and that their straight whiskey had been stored in a "bonded government warehouse." If you were a straight-whiskey producer, how might you try to use that tax stamp to your advantage in advertising?
   c. How might competing producers of distilled whiskey certify the quality of their product?

CHAPTER

18

Politics, Economics, and Agricultural Markets

The bourgoisie cannot exist without constantly revolutionizing the instruments of production, and thereby the relations of production, and with them the whole relations of society.

~Karl Marx and Friedrich Engels

After reading this chapter, you should be able to:

1. Explain the good/bad paradox in farming.
2. Give a brief summary of the history of Canadian farm policy.
3. State the general rule of political economy in a democracy.
4. Explain, using supply and demand curves, the distributional consequences of four alternative methods of price support.
5. Argue both sides of the question of agricultural price supports.

Agricultural markets provide good examples of the interaction of the invisible hand (the market) and the invisible foot (politics). Considering the economics of agricultural markets shows us how powerful a tool supply and demand analysis is in helping us understand not only the workings of perfectly competitive markets but also the effects of government intervention in a market. So in this chapter we consider agricultural markets and the effect of government policies on them. But bear in mind that, while the focus is on agriculture, the lessons of the analysis are applicable to a wide variety of markets in which the invisible hand and foot interact. As you read the chapter, applying the analysis to other markets will be a useful exercise.

THE NATURE OF AGRICULTURAL MARKETS

In many ways, agricultural markets fit the classic picture of perfect competition. First, there are many independent sellers who are generally *price takers*. Second, there are many buyers. Third, the products are interchangeable: Farm A's wheat can readily be substituted for farm B's wheat. And fourth, prices can, and do, vary considerably. On the basis of these inherent characteristics, it is reasonable to talk about agricultural markets as competitive markets.

In other ways, however, agricultural markets are far from perfectly competitive. The competitiveness of many agricultural markets is influenced by government programs. In fact, neither Canada nor any other country allows the market, unhindered, to control agricultural prices and output. For example, the federal and provincial governments set a minimum price for milk; buy up large quantities of wheat and stockpile it (through a federal crown corporation); and control the supply of eggs, turkeys, chickens, . . .

We could have made the list of government programs much longer, because the government has a program for just about every major agricultural market. The point is clear, however: The competitive market in agriculture is not a story of the invisible hand alone. It's the story of a constant struggle between the invisible hand and the invisible foot. Whenever the invisible hand pushes prices down, farmers use their political clout (the invisible foot) to kick them back up.

The Good/Bad Paradox in Agriculture

Good/bad paradox The phenomenon of doing poorly because you're doing well.

Agriculture is characterized by what might be called a **good/bad paradox** (the phenomenon of doing poorly because you're doing well). This good/bad paradox shows up in a variety of ways. Looking at the long run, we see that the enormous increase in agricultural productivity over the past few centuries has reduced agriculture's importance in Canadian society and has forced many farmers off the farm. Looking at the short run, we see that when harvests are good, farmers often fare badly financially; when harvests are poor, farmers often do well financially. Let's consider these two cases in some detail.

The Long-Run Decline of Farming Most countries, Canada included, began their existence as predominantly agricultural societies. When Canada was founded about 130 years ago, much of the labour force was engaged in farming, but today less than 3.5 percent of the Canadian labour force works in agriculture. That's part of a downward trend that began in the 1930s when over 30 percent of Canadians worked on the farm.

The decline in the number of farmers isn't the result of the failure of Canadian agriculture. Rather, it's the result of its tremendous success—the enormous increase in its productivity. Counting workers connected to agriculture who weren't actually working on farms, it used to take the majority of the population to provide food for Canada. Today it takes only a small proportion to produce more food than the Canadian population can consume.

1 The good/bad paradox is the phenomenon of doing poorly because you're doing well.

Exhibit 1 shows how success can lead to problems. The long-run price elasticity of demand for wheat is inelastic (i.e., the percent change in quantity is small relative to the percent change in price), as it is for most agricultural products, so the exhibit shows the equilibrium in the inelastic portion of the demand curve.

In this example, initially farmers are selling quantity Q_0 for price P_0. Their total income is P_0Q_0, shown by rectangles A and B. Now say that increases in productivity shift the supply curve out from S_0 to S_1. Output increases from Q_0 to Q_1 and price falls

ADDED DIMENSION

THE COST OF A BOX OF WHEATIES

When people think of agricultural products, they often think of the products they buy, like Wheaties. Doing so gives them the wrong impression of the cost of agricultural products. To see why, let's consider a box of Wheaties which costs you, say, $3.75.

If you look at the ingredients, you'll see that you're buying wheat, sugar, salt, malt syrup, and corn syrup. So you're buying agricultural products, right? Well, a little bit. Actually, the total cost of those agricultural ingredients is probably somewhere around 35¢, less than one-tenth of the cost of the box of Wheaties. What are you spending the other nine-tenths on? Well, there's packaging, advertising, transporting the boxes, processing the ingredients, stocking the grocery store shelves, and profits. These are important components of Wheaties, but they aren't agricultural components.

The point of this example is simple. Much of our food expenditure isn't for agricultural goods; it's for the services that transform the agricultural goods into the processed foods, convince us we want to eat those foods, and get those foods to us.

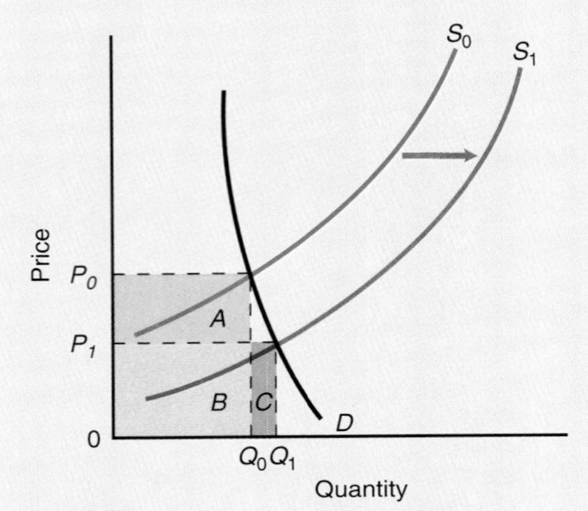

EXHIBIT 1 The Good/Bad Paradox

The good/bad paradox is demonstrated in this graph. At price P_0 the quantity of wheat produced is Q_0. Total income is P_0Q_0. But if the supply of wheat increases from S_0 to S_1 due to increased productivity, the price of wheat will fall from P_0 to P_1 and quantity demanded will increase from Q_0 to Q_1. The increase in farmers' income (area *C*) is small. The decrease in farmers' income (area *A*) is large. Overall, the increased productivity has led to a decrease in farmers' incomes.

to P_1. Income falls to P_1Q_1, shown by the *B* and *C* rectangles. Farmers have gained the *C* rectangle but lost the *A* rectangle. The net effect is the difference in size between the two rectangles. So in this example the net effect is negative.

In short, productivity has increased but income has fallen, and many farmers have stopped farming altogether. They've done well by producing a lot, but the result for them is bad. This good/bad paradox will occur whenever the supply curve shifts outward in the inelastic range of the demand curve.

Due to competition among farmers, most benefits of productivity increases in agriculture have gone to consumers, in the form of lower prices. As an example, consider chicken. In the early 1930s, some politicians running for reelection promised prosperity to the country by saying there would be "two chickens in every pot." That promise meant a lot because, in today's money, chicken would have cost $20 a kilogram. In the mid-1990s, the price of chicken had fallen to under $5 a kilogram, only about one-quarter of its price in 1930.

The Short-Run Cyclical Problem Facing Farmers The long-run good/bad paradox for farmers is mirrored by a short-run good/bad paradox: Good harvests often mean bad times and a fall in income; poor harvests often mean a rise in income.

A fact of life that farmers must deal with is that agricultural production tends to be highly unstable because it depends on weather and luck. Crops can be affected by too little rain, too much rain, insects, frost, heat, wind, hail—none of which can be easily controlled. Say you're an apple grower and you're having a beautiful spring—until the week that your trees are blossoming, when it rains continually. Bees don't fly when it rains, so they don't pollinate your trees. No pollination, no apple crop. There goes your apple crop for this year. Or, think of what happened in New Brunswick in 1994. The Saint John River rose above normal flood levels and left many farmers' fields under water during what should have been prime planting season. The result: strawberries were in limited supply that summer, and—you guessed it—at much higher prices than the year before.

The short-run demand for most agricultural goods is even more inelastic than the long-run demand. Because short-run demand is so inelastic, short-run changes in supply can have a significant effect on price. The result is that good harvests for farmers in general can lower prices significantly, while poor harvests can raise prices significantly. When the short-run price effect overwhelms the short-run quantity effect (as it does when demand is inelastic), farmers face the short-run good/bad paradox.

The Difficulty of Coordinating Farm Production This good/bad paradox caused by inelastic demand isn't lost upon farmers. They, quite naturally, aren't wild about passing on the gains to consumers instead of keeping the gains themselves. However, because agriculture is competitive, it is not in any one farmer's interest to decrease his or her supply in order to avoid encountering the paradox. Competitive farmers take the market price as given. That's the definition of a competitive industry. While it is in the industry's interest to have a "bad year" (to reduce total supply), it is in each individual farmer's interest to have a good year (to increase output) even if the combination of *all* farmers having a good year would cause all farmers to have a bad year.

It is, however, in farmers' joint interest to figure out ways to have continually "bad" years—which are, of course, actually "good" years for them. In other words, it's in their interest to figure out ways to limit the production of all farmers.

In a competitive industry, limiting production is easier said than done. It is difficult for farmers to limit production privately, among themselves, because although they make up only a small percentage of the total Canadian population, there are still a lot of them—391,000 were counted in the 1991 Census. That's too many to coordinate easily.

A Way around the Good/Bad Paradox The difficulty of organizing privately to limit supply can be avoided by organizing through government. The Canadian political structure provides an alternative way for farmers (and other suppliers) to coordinate their actions and limit supply. Suppliers can organize and get government to establish programs to limit production or hold price high, thereby avoiding the good/bad paradox. And that's what farmers have done, and that's why so many government agricultural programs exist today. Before we consider how these government farm programs work, let's briefly review their history.

HISTORY OF CANADIAN FARM PROGRAMS

2 Two reasons a persistent agricultural slump started in 1920 were (1) post-World War I demand for agricultural products declined, and (2) farm costs increased when Canada placed tariffs on imported manufactured goods.

We'll begin the story in the early 1900s when, because of strong growth in Canadian income, there was an increased demand for Canadian farm products, which led to high and growing income for farmers. The eruption of World War I in 1914 increased demand, but the depression of 1920 ended that trend. In 1921 the Canadian economy improved, but agriculture did not; it remained in a severe slump, marked by high production, low prices, and low farm income.

The reasons for this continued severe slump were various. Two important reasons were the recovery of agricultural production in Europe after the war ended late in 1918, and the high tariffs the Canadian government placed on imported manufactured goods during the 1920s.

During the war (1914–1918), the number of Canadian farms increased significantly to meet the combined demand from European countries (whose production had fallen significantly as they devoted their resources to war) and from Canada itself (which was experiencing wartime economic boom). After the war, production remained high in Canada, but demand fell as European agricultural production increased.

The impact of the low prices Canadian farmers received in the 1920s was intensified by high tariffs on imported manufactured goods. These tariffs squeezed the farmers in two ways. First, they increased the prices of goods farmers bought; and second, they further reduced demand for Canadian farm products. Unable to afford the high Canadian tariffs on their exports, the European countries, already financially weakened by the war, couldn't afford to import Canadian agricultural goods. The result of these developments was the good/bad paradox with a vengeance: low prices and high output with a tremendous fall in farm income.

The Beginnings of Government Agricultural Programs

The good/bad paradox is not a textbook concept. It has significant real-world effects. What it meant in the 1920s and 1930s was that a large number of Canadian farmers were going broke. They worked hard and got little or nothing in return. This was the time period captured in W. O. Mitchell's novel, *Who Has Seen the Wind.*

By 1929 the Canadian agricultural sector was extremely weak, but it was to become even weaker. The Great Depression that started in 1929 further devastated agricultural markets. These historical events led many to believe that competition didn't work and that the economic system used by Canada had to be changed. It was a bit like a title fight when one fighter is so bloodied and beaten that the referee steps in and stops the fight. That's what the government did; it said competition wasn't working the way society wanted it to work, and it stepped in to regulate that competition. The Great Depression marked the beginning of many of the Canadian agricultural programs that are still around today.

Agrifirms Large firms that own huge farms and operate them like big corporations.

What would have happened without these programs is unclear. Farmers might have eventually been dominated by a few large **agrifirms** (firms that own huge farms and operate them like big corporations) which could have limited production and smoothed out price fluctuations. But as we said, achieving a private organization that limits production in agricultural markets is extraordinarily difficult. Thus, such a private "solution" to the good/bad paradox never occurred. Instead, farmers used their political clout to induce the Canadian government to step in.

In 1934, the government created the Natural Products Marketing Act which created a Federal Marketing Board. The Board could control the sales of natural products. Provincial marketing boards sprang up across the country, and, after a legal challenge declared the 1934 federal Act unconstitutional, the provinces were acknowledged to have control over the sale of many products through their network of marketing boards.

Canadian Wheat Board A federal agency having control over how Canadian wheat is marketed and the price at which it is sold.

The **Canadian Wheat Board** was established in 1935. It had and continues to have control over how Western wheat is marketed and the price at which it is sold. The Wheat Board essentially offers farmers a price floor—a minimum price—when they deliver their wheat to grain elevators. The Wheat Board sets that price at a level it expects to be high enough to cover costs. When the Wheat Board sells the grain at world prices, it forwards the farmer another payment if the final sales price (less transportation and other costs) is higher than the initial price. This policy places a lower limit on the revenues the farmers will receive.

Agricultural Stabilization Board A federal agency regulating the prices of a number of commodities.

Canadian Dairy Commission A federal agency that coordinates provincial milk marketing boards.

There are a number of federal and provincial bodies charged with setting price and quantity restrictions across the country. The **Agricultural Stabilization Board** is a federal agency charged with supporting the prices of a number of commodities (cattle, hogs, sheep, and industrial milk, just to name a few) at not less than 90 percent of their average price over the previous five years. The **Canadian Dairy Commission,** a federal agency, coordinates provincial milk marketing boards to ensure that farmers receive a fair return while consumers enjoy an adequate supply. The boards do this by supporting the market price of processed products through the buying and selling of dairy products. They also make cash payments to producers under a quota system.

There are a host of other marketing boards and agencies involved in agriculture. Farmers have access to provincial crop insurance programs that protect against losses due to bad weather, and there are income support programs that help farmers over periods of depressed commodity prices. In some provinces there are loans and grants

ADDED DIMENSION

THE CARTEL PROBLEM

When facing an inelastic demand, it's in the interest of producers as a whole to limit production, but it's in any one producer's individual interest to produce as much as it profitably can. This difference between what's in the interest of an individual producer and what's in the interest of the group of producers is called the *cartel problem.* Agriculture is simply one example of the cartel problem; there are many other examples, such as oil production and manufacturing.

Producers have several methods to deal with the cartel problem. These methods differ among industries. For example, in Canada, *combines,* or *trusts,* (other names for cartels) were formed in manufacturing in which each firm was allocated market share. Production was held down by agreement. These combines were hard to enforce. Eventually, to eliminate the enforcement problem, many of the firms merged, although the amount of merger activity was limited by the Canadian anti-combines laws.

Even if a group of suppliers gains a domestic cartel, it can still face competition from abroad which can undermine the domestic cartel. To be effective, a cartel often must be an international cartel. Luckily for consumers, international cartel agreements are even more difficult to enforce than domestic cartel agreements. One reason many economists support free trade is the competitive pressure it creates for domestic producers. It places a limit on domestic cartels.

Profits aren't necessarily a good measure of a cartel's effectiveness. Often its costs will rise as workers and other factors share in the gains. That's what happened in manufacturing industries. The firms formed combines, which led to the formation of unions and the institution of government regulations, which pushed up costs. Thus, even though we don't see manufacturing firms earning enormous profits, that doesn't necessarily mean that they haven't, to a degree, limited production to raise price.

to help farmers become more efficient and expand production. All of these programs are aimed at sheltering farmers from adverse fluctuations in their incomes.

Stabilization and Support for Agricultural Prices

Let's assume that you've been hired as an economist for the Wheat Board. Your assignment is to determine a price at which the government should buy and sell wheat so as to stabilize the market by minimizing future fluctuations in its price at the lowest net cost to the government.

The jagged line in Exhibit 2 is a hypothetical line showing what the price of wheat would have been from 1900 to 1995 had there been no stabilization program. It illustrates the price pattern of most agricultural goods. Two aspects of this exhibit are easily recognizable. First, the long-run trend in prices is downward. Second, there are significant short-run fluctuations around that trend.

What price would you choose? Since your object is to stabilize price at the lowest cost to the government, you should choose a price on the P_0 line, which reflects the downward trend of prices. Setting the price at that trend price, you'd expect to buy wheat whenever the price falls below the trend line, stopping the price from falling further and pushing the price up toward the trend line. If the price of wheat rose above the trend line, you'd sell the wheat you had bought. A perfect stabilization program would eliminate all price fluctuations, other than the general downward trend of prices.

If you've set the price on the trend line P_0, it's reasonable to expect that the surpluses will roughly equal the shortages. If the government chooses a stabilization price above the trend line, on average, government will accumulate surpluses; if it chooses a price below the trend line, on average, it will have shortages and will have to buy wheat from other countries to meet the demand.

So if the government's goal is to minimize fluctuations in price at the lowest possible cost, it should choose a continually decreasing price that builds in the expectations of (1) increases in productivity and (2) a continually falling long-run price. That's what a **price stabilization program** is: A program designed to eliminate short-run fluctuations in prices but to allow prices to follow their long-term trend line.

Price stabilization program
Program designed to eliminate short-run fluctuations in prices but allow prices to follow their long-term trend line.

EXHIBIT 2 Hypothetical Decreasing Price of Wheat

If there had been no government intervention, the price of wheat would have fluctuated around a downward trend as in this diagram.

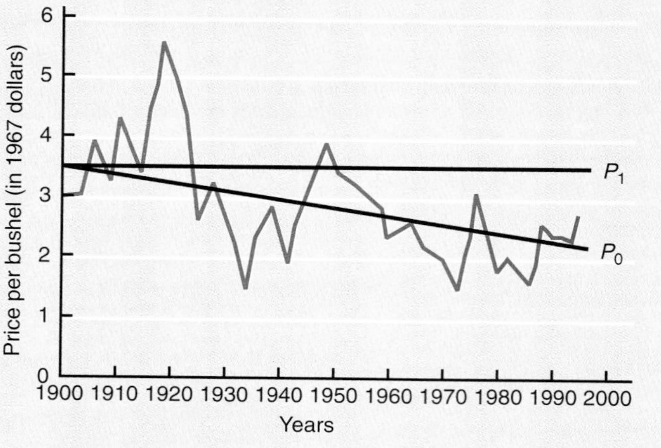

Price support program Program that maintains prices at a level higher than the trend of prices.

Farmers aren't against such price stabilization programs. However, they're generally more interested in another type of program: a **price support program.** A price support program is one that maintains prices at a level higher than the trend of prices. If price support is your goal, you won't choose a price on trend line P_0; you'll choose a price above it on a price line such as P_1. In a price support system, surpluses and shortages don't net out. Instead, when the price trend is downward, the program generates continual surpluses which the government must figure out how to manage.

Government programs have been both stabilization and support programs. That is, they've been designed not only to minimize fluctuations in prices, but also to increase income for farmers. (To stabilize is to smooth out short-run fluctuations, but not to affect the long-run trend. To support is to try to affect the long-run trend.) Farmers have come to rely on these programs to help them avoid the problems caused by the good/bad paradox.

Parity price Price that maintains the ratio of prices received and paid by farmers at the same ratio as in a base year.

The Choice of a Parity Price Some economists argue that the Wheat Board should establish a price support system that incorporates the idea of a *parity price* that farmers should receive. A **parity price** of, say, wheat, is a price of wheat that keeps farmers as well off relatively as they were in a specified base year (say, for example, the average of prices in the years 1980–1984). If farmers received the parity price for wheat, the ratio of the prices received by farmers for that wheat and prices paid by farmers would always be the same as it was in the base year. For example, say the base year price of wheat was $3 a bushel and the price paid by farmers for a composite of manufactured goods was $4. If the price of manufactured goods rises to $6 (a rise of 50 percent), the parity price of wheat also rises by 50 percent—to $4.50 in this hypothetical example.

Parity could be justified by relatively simple arguments. Farmers could argue that if they could exchange a bushel of wheat for a shirt in 1982, they should also be able to exchange a bushel of wheat for a shirt in 1995. If price parity is maintained, the relative prices of agricultural goods (and hence farmers' relative income) cannot fall. If price parity is maintained, the trend line of agricultural prices will be flat, not downward sloping.

The argument that farmers deserve price parity sounds logical on the surface, but it's flawed for two reasons. It doesn't allow for normal fluctuations in price, and it doesn't explain why the base should be the 1980–1984 period. Why not use 1995 as the base year?

To understand the base period, remember that we chose 1980–1984 to make a hypothetical case. In the real world, the government's aim would be to increase farmers' income—to support as well as stabilize prices. Therefore, officials would analyze wheat prices to come up with a period of several consecutive years when relative agricultural prices were at their peacetime high. They'd choose peacetime because wartime skews prices in ways that may be unique, and they'd choose a period rather than a single year because they wouldn't want to be seen as purposely selecting just one very high year. The base year would not be 1995 because, first of all, as we explained, the base period has several years and doesn't rely on only a single year. Second, 1995 figures won't be available until some time in 1996, and even then one won't get a clear idea of whether it's part of a multiyear period in which prices were high every year.

How high the support price might be held (which parity ratio has been guaranteed) would depend on the political power of farmers. To increase their political power they have organized a **farm lobby** (an organization of farmers whose purpose is to further political goals that will benefit farmers). Although the farm lobby might not be politically strong enough to achieve full parity, it might be able to hold the price farmers get above what the average competitive market price otherwise would be.

Farm lobby Organization formed to further political goals that benefit farmers.

How do we know that this has been the case? We know because surpluses have consistently exceeded shortages. If the government maintained prices at the average competitive price, the surpluses would be sold in time of shortage. Expressing the support price in terms of a high parity price serves a political purpose. The price support program could always be presented to the public as a limited program, going only part way to parity.

Politics and Parity If farmers are helped by farm programs, who is hurt? The answer is taxpayers and consumers. One would expect that these broad groups would strongly oppose farm programs because farm programs cost them in two ways: (1) higher taxes that government requires in order to buy up surplus farm output, and (2) higher prices for food. It's not easy for a politician to tell her nonfarm constituents, "I'm supporting legislation that means higher prices and higher taxes for you." Nevertheless, the farm lobby has been quite successful in seeing that these programs are retained.

3 The general rule of political economy states that small groups that are significantly helped by a government policy will lobby more effectively than large groups that are hurt by that same policy.

Economists who specialize in the relationship between economics and politics (known as *public choice economists*) have suggested that the reasons for farm groups' success involve the nature of the benefits and costs. The groups that are hurt by agricultural subsidies are large, but the negative effect on each individual in that group is relatively small. Large groups that experience small costs per individual don't provide a strong political opposition to a small group that experiences large gains. This seems to reflect a **general rule of political economy** in a democracy:

General rule of political economy Small groups that are significantly affected by a government policy will lobby more effectively than large groups that are equally affected by that same policy.

> When small groups are helped by a government action and large groups are hurt by that same action, the small group tends to lobby far more effectively than the large group. Thus, policies tend to reflect the small group's interest, not the interest of the large group.

This bias in favour of farm programs is strengthened by the historical representation of farmers in parliament, provincial legislatures, and legislative assemblies. Right from its beginnings the Canadian political system has reflected the importance of agriculture. Farmers' strong political representation establishes a core of lawmakers who favour price supports and price stabilization. That core, combined with the lack of political organization of large groups (consumers and taxpayers), has made it possible for the farm lobby to put together enough votes to maintain programs of farm price support and farm price stabilization. When political pressure does become intense, a bit of obfuscation can be used to get a bill passed.[1] For example, what if, instead of a price support system, one introduced a loan program? Who could oppose making loans to hard-pressed farmers?

James Buchanan won the Nobel prize in 1986 for work in public choice theory. He played a major role in establishing the importance of the general rule of political economy. © *The Nobel Foundation.*

The 1970s were good times for Canadian farmers. With land prices rising significantly and food prices high, many farmers expanded, financing that expansion by borrowing, using their land as collateral. The good times ended in the late 1970s and

[1] Obfuscation is a wonderful word meaning "to make obscure, or to confuse." It comes to us from the Latin word for "to darken."

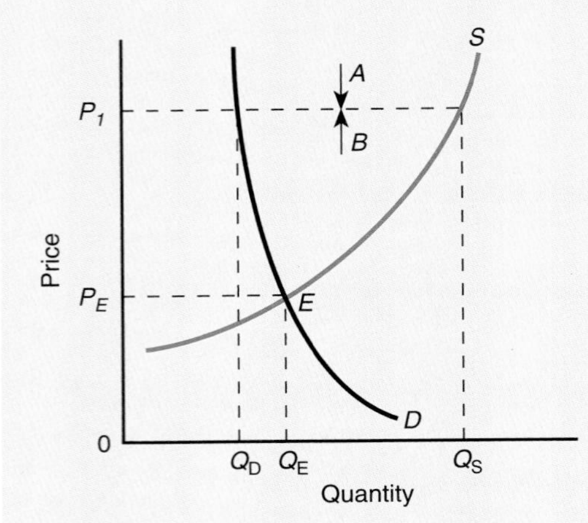

EXHIBIT 3 A Price Support System

In a price support system, the government maintains a higher-than-equilibrium price. At support price, P_1, the quantity of product demanded is only Q_D, while the quantity supplied is Q_S. This causes downward pressures on the price, P_1, which must be offset by various government measures.

early 1980s as interest rates rose substantially while land and food prices fell. Once again there was a strong push on government to help the farmer. And once again the government came through, although the huge federal budget deficit kept it from being quite as generous as in the past. In the early 1990s, farm prices had recovered from the mid-1980s slump, and the cost of the government farm programs was reduced.

The combination of acreage reduction and price support/price stabilization systems has continued through today, although the level of the programs depends on what political pressures are being applied at a particular time.

HOW A PRICE SUPPORT SYSTEM WORKS IN THEORY

Now that we've briefly reviewed the history of the Canadian government support system for agricultural prices, let's consider more carefully the theory underlying some alternative farm price support options. In doing so, we'll try to understand which options, given the political realities, would have the best chance of being implemented, and why.

Four Price Support Options

In a price support system, the government maintains a higher-than-equilibrium price, as diagrammed in Exhibit 3. At support price P_1, the quantity people want to supply is Q_S, but the quantity demanded at that price is Q_D.

At price P_1 there's excess supply, which exerts a downward pressure on price (arrow *A*). To maintain price at P_1, some other force (arrow *B*) must be exerted; otherwise the invisible hand will force the price down.

4 Four methods of price support are:
1. Regulatory methods.
2. Economic incentives to reduce supply.
3. Subsidizing the sale of the good.
4. Buying up and storing, giving away, or destroying the good.
The distributional effects are shown in Exhibit 4.

The government has various options to offset that downward pressure on price:

1. Using legal and regulatory force to prevent anyone from selling or buying at a lower price.
2. Providing economic incentives to reduce the supply enough to eliminate the downward pressure on price.
3. Subsidizing the sale of the good to consumers so that while suppliers get a high price, demanders have to pay only a low price.
4. Buying up and storing, giving away, or destroying enough of the good so that the total demand (including government's demand) increases enough to eliminate downward pressure on price.

Each of these methods distributes the costs and benefits in a slightly different way. Let's consider each method in detail.

Supporting the Price by Regulatory Measures Suppose the government simply passes a law saying that, from now on, the price of wheat will be at least $5 per bushel. No one may sell wheat at a lower price. If the competitive equilibrium price is higher than $5, the law has no effect. When the competitive equilibrium is below the price floor (say the

EXHIBIT 4 Alternative Methods of Government Price Supports

Alternative methods have different distributional consequences. The consequences of regulatory measures are shown in (**a**); of providing economic incentives to reduce supply in (**b**); of subsidizing the sale in (**c**); and of buying up and storing, giving away, or destroying the good in (**d**).

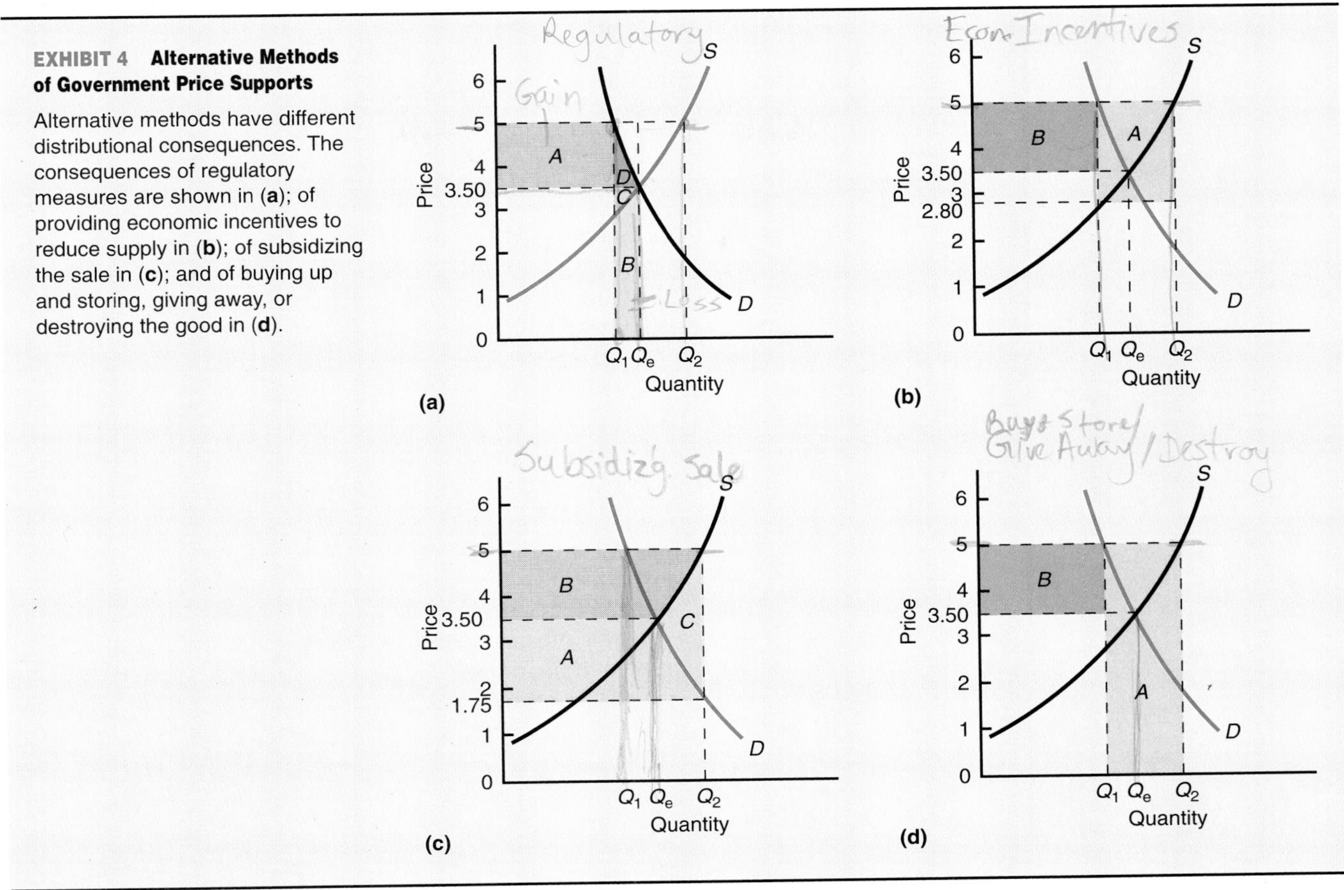

competitive equilibrium is \$3.50 per bushel), the law limits suppliers from selling their wheat at that lower price.

The price floor helps some suppliers and hurts others. Those suppliers who are lucky enough to sell their wheat benefit. Those suppliers who aren't lucky and can't find buyers for their wheat are hurt. How many suppliers will be helped and how many will be hurt depends on the elasticities of supply and demand. When supply and demand are inelastic, a large change in price brings about a small change in quantity supplied, so the hurt group is relatively small. When the supply and demand are elastic, the hurt group is larger.

In Exhibit 4 (a), suppliers would like to sell quantity Q_2 but, by law, they can supply only Q_1. They end up with a surplus of wheat, $Q_2 - Q_1$. Demanders, who must pay the higher price, \$5, and receive only Q_1 rather than Q_e, are hurt.

The law may or may not specify who will, and who will not, be allowed to sell, but it must establish some noneconomic method of rationing the limited demand among the suppliers. If it doesn't, buyers are likely, for example, to buy from farmers who are their friends. If individual farmers have a surplus, they'll probably try to dispose of that surplus by selling it on the black market at a price below the legal price. To maintain the support price, the government will have to arrest farmers who sell below the legal price. If the number of producers is large, such a regulatory approach is likely to break down quickly, since individual incentives to sell illegally are great and the costs of enforcing the law are accordingly high.

In understanding who benefits and who's hurt by price floors, it's important to distinguish two groups of farmers: the farmers who had been producing before the law went into effect, and the farmers who entered the market afterward. In Exhibit 4 (a), the first group supplies Q_e; the second group, which would want to enter the market when the price went up, would supply $Q_2 - Q_e$. Why must the second group be clearly identified? Because one relatively easily enforceable way to limit the quantity supplied is to forbid any new farmers to enter the market. Only people who were producing at the beginning of the support program will be allowed to produce, and they will be allowed to produce only as much as they did before the program went into effect. Restricting production will reduce the quantity supplied to Q_e, leaving only $Q_e - Q_1$ to be rationed among suppliers.

Grandfather in To pass a law affecting a specific group but providing that those in the group before the law was passed are not subject to the law.

This method of restriction, which is said to **grandfather in** existing suppliers, is one of the easiest to enforce and thus one of the most widely used.

When it comes to grandfathering groups *out* of production, foreign producers are perhaps the politically easiest targets. To keep the domestic price of a good up, foreign imports must be limited as well as domestic production. Canadian taxpayers might put up with subsidizing Canadian farmers, but they're likely to balk at subsidizing foreign farmers. So most farm subsidy programs are supplemented with tariffs and quotas on foreign imports of the same commodity.

Notice that with the equilibrium in the inelastic portion of the demand curve, even though the average farmer is constrained as to how much can be sold, he or she is made better off by that constraint because the total revenue going to all farmers is higher than it would be if supply weren't constrained. The farmer's total revenue from this market increases by rectangle *A* in Exhibit 4 (a) and decreases by the rectangle composed of the combined areas *B* and *C*. Of course, making the farmer better off is not cost-free. Consumers are made worse off because they must pay more for a smaller supply of wheat. There's no direct cost to taxpayers other than the cost of enforcing and administering the regulations.

Notice in the diagram the little triangle made up of areas *C* and *D*, which shows an amount of income that society loses but farmers don't get. It's simply wasted. That little triangle is a net loss to society from the restriction. It's called an **excess burden,** and it results whenever the market is prevented from operating freely. (Excess burden is also called *deadweight loss*).

Excess burden Loss to society caused by a policy introducing a wedge between marginal private and marginal social costs and benefits.

Providing Economic Incentives to Reduce Supply A second way in which government can keep a price high is to provide farmers with economic incentives to reduce supply.

Looking at Exhibit 4 (b), you see that at the support price, $5 per bushel, the quantity of wheat supplied is Q_2 and quantity demanded is Q_1. To avoid a surplus, the government must somehow find a way to shift the quantity supplied back from Q_2 to Q_1. For example, it could pay farmers not to grow wheat. How much would such an economic incentive cost? Given the way the curves are drawn, to reduce the quantity supplied to Q_1, the government would have to pay farmers $2.20 ($5.00 − $2.80) for each bushel of wheat they didn't grow. This payment of $2.20 would induce suppliers producing $Q_2 - Q_1$ not to produce, reducing the quantity supplied to Q_1. This amount is shown by the *A* rectangle.

There is, however, a problem in identifying those individuals who would truly supply wheat at $5 a bushel. Knowing that the government is paying people not to grow wheat, people who otherwise had no interest in growing wheat will pretend that at $5 they would supply the wheat, simply to get the subsidy. To avoid this problem, often this incentive approach is combined with our first option, regulatory restrictions. Farmers who are already producing wheat at Q_e are grandfathered in; only they are given economic incentives not to produce. All others are forbidden to produce.

When economic incentives are supplied, the existing farmers do very well for themselves. Their income goes up for two reasons. They get the *A* rectangle from the government in the form of payments not to grow wheat, and they get the *B* rectangle from consumers in the form of higher prices for the wheat they do grow. Farmers are also free to use their land for other purposes, so their income rises by the amount they can earn from using the land taken out of wheat production for something other than growing wheat. Consumers are still being hurt as before: They are paying a higher price and getting less. In addition, they're being hurt in their role as taxpayers because the lightly shaded area (rectangle *A*) represents the taxes they must pay to finance the government's economic incentive program. Thus, this option is much more costly to taxpayers than the regulatory option.

Subsidizing the Sale of the Good A third option is for the government to subsidize the sale of the good in order to hold down the price consumers pay but keep the amount suppliers receive high. Exhibit 4 (c) shows how this works. Suppliers supply quantity Q_2 and are paid \$5 per bushel. The government then turns around and sells that quantity at whatever price it can get—in this case, \$1.75. No direct transfer takes place from the consumer to the supplier. Both are made better off. Demanders get more goods at a lower price. They are benefitted by area *A*. Suppliers get a higher price and can supply all they want. They are benefitted by area *B*. What's the catch? The catch, of course, is that taxpayers foot the entire bill, paying the difference between the \$5 and the \$1.75 (\$3.25) for each bushel sold. The cost to taxpayers is represented by areas *A, B,* and *C*. This option costs taxpayers the most of any of the four options.

Buying Up and Storing, Giving Away, or Destroying the Good The final option is for the government to buy up all the supply that demanders don't buy at the support price. This option is shown in Exhibit 4 (d). Consumers buy Q_1 at price \$5; the government buys $Q_2 - Q_1$ at price \$5, paying the *A* rectangle. In this case consumers transfer the *B* rectangle to suppliers when they pay \$5 rather than \$3.50, the competitive equilibrium price. The government (i.e., the taxpayers) pays farmers rectangle *A*. The situation is very similar to our second option, in which the government provides suppliers with economic incentives not to produce. However, it's more expensive since the government must pay \$5 per bushel rather than paying farmers \$2.20 per bushel. In return for this higher payment, the government is getting something in return: $Q_2 - Q_1$ of wheat.

Of course, if the government buys the surplus wheat, it takes on the problem of what to do with this surplus. Say the government decides to give it to the poor. Since the poor were already buying food, in response to a free food program they will replace some of their purchases with the free food. This replacement brings about a drop in demand—which means that the government must buy even more surplus. Instead of giving it away, though, the government can burn the surplus or store it indefinitely in warehouses and grain elevators. Burning up the surplus or storing it, at least, doesn't increase the amount government must buy.

Why, you ask, doesn't the government give the surplus to foreign countries as a type of humanitarian aid? The reason is that just as giving the surplus to our own poor creates problems in Canada, giving the surplus to the foreign poor creates problems in the countries involved. To the degree that the foreign poor have any income, they're likely to spend most of it on food. Free food would supplant some of their demand, thus lowering the price for those who previously sold food to them. Giving anything away destroys somebody's market, and when markets are destroyed someone gets upset. So when Canada has tried to give away its surplus food, other foreign countries have put enormous pressure on Canada not to "spoil the world market."

Politics, Economics, and Price Supports

The four price support options we've just described can, of course, be used in various combinations. It's a useful exercise at this point to think through which of the options farmers, taxpayers, and consumers would likely favour and to relate the history of the farm programs to these options.

Which Group Prefers Which Option? The first option, regulation, costs the government the least, but it benefits farmers the least. Since existing farmers are likely to be the group directly pushing for price supports, government is least likely to choose this approach. If it is chosen, most of the reduction in quantity supplied will probably be required to come from people who might enter farming at some time in the future, not from existing farmers.

The second option, economic incentives, costs the government more than the first option but less than the third and fourth options. Farmers are benefitted by economic incentive programs in two ways. They get paid not to grow a certain crop, and they can sometimes get additional income from using the land for other purposes. When farmers aren't allowed to use their land for other purposes, they usually oppose this option, preferring the third or fourth option.

The third option, subsidies on sales to keep prices down, benefits both consumers (who get low prices) and farmers (who get high prices). Taxpayers are harmed the most by this option. They must finance the subsidy payments for all subsidized farm products.

The last option, buying up and storing or destroying the goods, costs taxpayers more than the first two options but less than the third, since consumers pay part of the cost. However, it leaves the government with a surplus to deal with. If there's a group who can take that surplus without significantly reducing their current demand, then that group is likely to support this option.

The third option, to subsidize the sale of the good so the farmer gets a high price and the consumer pays a low price, hasn't been used because it would be the most costly to taxpayers. Rather than costing $10 billion or $20 billion a year, farm programs involving direct subsidies would likely cost $60 billion to $100 billion a year. In contrast, economic incentive and government purchase programs hide the true costs of price supports better. However, direct subsidies are used in a number of developing countries where governments are under strong and conflicting political pressures from both consumers and farmers. Often the subsidies are financed by budget deficits, not taxes, so the taxpayers aren't directly confronted with the bill. (But since there's no such thing as a free lunch, they'll face the bill later when they must pay the interest on the debt.)

Economics, Politics, and Real-World Policies

The actual political debate is, of course, much more complicated than presented here. For example, other pressure groups are involved. Recently, farm groups and environmental groups have combined forces and have become more effective in shaping and supporting farm policy. Thus, in the 1990s, restrictions on supply in farming are likely to operate in ways that environmentalists would favour, such as regulating the types of fertilizer and chemicals farmers can use.

Moreover, the three interest groups discussed here—farmers, taxpayers, and consumers—aren't entirely distinct one from another. Their memberships overlap. All taxpayers are also consumers; farmers are both taxpayers and consumers; and so on. Thus, much of the political debate is simply about from whose pocket the government is going to get money to help farmers. Shall it be the consumer's pocket (through higher prices)? Or the taxpayer's (through higher taxes)? That said, the political reality is that consumer and taxpayer interests and the lobbying groups that represent them generally examine only part of the picture—the part that directly affects them. Accordingly, politicians often act as if these groups had separate memberships. Politicians weigh the options by attempting to balance their view of the general good with the power and preferences of the special interest groups that they represent or that contribute to their election campaigns.

International Considerations

The final real-world complication that must be taken into account is the international dimension. If you think government is significantly involved in Canadian agriculture, you should see its role in other countries such as the members of the European Union and Japan. When French farmers were told that government price supports were becoming just too expensive, they converged en masse in Paris and the city ground to a halt. Farmers dumped crops and fish in the street and in front of government buildings. They made their point, and the government backed off (for the time being).

Our agricultural policy is in part determined by trade negotiations with our trading partners. For example, the Canadian government could subsidize Canadian agriculture to keep Canadian agricultural products competitive with the heavily subsidized EU production. A reduction in EU subsidies could bring about a reduction in our subsidies. That's not likely given the demonstrations in Paris.

At the other extreme, the United States continually charges Canada with unfair trade practices. The U.S. government believes Canadian farmers are unfairly advan-

ADDED DIMENSION

THE WHEAT DISPUTE

U.S. TURNS UP THE HEAT ON CANADIAN WHEAT DISPUTE

Espy Says Argentina Also Worried about Lost Market Share

Reuters, Staff and Bloomberg

WASHINGTON—U.S. Agricultural Secretary Mike Espy turned up the heat on the simmering Canada–U.S. wheat trade dispute yesterday by saying Argentina shares U.S. concerns about lost market share because of sales of subsidized Canadian wheat into Brazil.

Mr. Espy, in Buenos Aires on the first leg of a three-nation trip, said his meetings with Argentine government officials had focused on reciprocal trade issues, but specifically wheat trade.

He said both countries were "disappointed with the respective loss of market share into the Brazilian wheat market because of, we both feel, the predatory pricing practices by the Canadian Wheat Board."

An Agriculture Canada official confirmed that Argentina has complained repeatedly in recent months about Canadian wheat exports to Brazil.

But he said the suggestion that Canada is squeezing Argentina out of a traditional export market such as Brazil by undercutting their price is without merit.

The milling wheat Brazil buys from Canada is mostly a higher-grade wheat that is pricier than most Argentine wheat, he noted. Argentina benefits from a preferential tariff in Brazil (2 percent versus 10 percent for Canada), the official said.

Canadian wheat exports to Brazil are on the rise. Canada sold 1.3 million tonnes of wheat to Brazil through January, seven months into the current crop year, according to Agriculture Canada. Canada sold 1.1 million tonnes the previous year and 1.7 million in 1991–92.

The official said Canada has been selling wheat to Brazil since the 1970s.

Mr. Espy used a press briefing to rail against Canadian wheat pricing practices. He said he hopes to broaden the front against Canada by enlisting Argentina and other wheat-exporting nations in the campaign.

"We are trying to take this fight beyond the bilateral perspective and internationalize it," Mr. Espy said later in a telephone conference call to the United States.

The secretary sought to portray the conflict as a dispute over open markets, not a parochial squabble between the United States and Canada over farm prices. "This is not a wheat fight. This is a free-trade fight."

The United States filed an anti-dumping suit against Canada in mid-April under Article 28 of the General Agreement on Tariffs and Trade, citing the surge in imports of Canadian durum wheat and an adverse impact on domestic producers.

Source: *The Globe and Mail,* May 17, 1994.

taged through Canadian subsidies. Several years ago U.S. officials wouldn't allow Canadian potatoes to cross into the United States because of concerns over a virus that left potato plants unaffected, but killed many other plant species. Extensive testing revealed that many Canadian potatoes were free of the virus. The U.S. potato lobby succeeded in curbing Canadian imports. Prince Edward Island potato farmers filed lawsuits claiming they lost revenues as a result of, among other things, inadequate government testing for the virus.

A **trade dispute** occurs when two or more countries disagree with each other over the terms of trade each country has set and how those terms are interpreted, administered, and enforced. Some international rule-making bodies exist to try to settle trade disputes.

Trade dispute Disagreement by two or more nations over international trade.

Recently, the United States claimed that the Canadian Wheat Board practises predatory pricing. As the accompanying box makes clear, the United States is not alone in its objections to the activities of the Wheat Board. Also note in the box that an international rule-making body is involved: GATT (General Agreement on Tariffs and Trade). We'll discuss this body and its successor in a moment.

Trade agreements often play an important role in agricultural markets. The Canada–U.S. Free Trade Agreement reduced many agricultural tariffs between the U.S. and Canada—the aim was to eliminate them gradually over a 10-year period. Since Canada exports about half of total Canadian agricultural production, trade disputes like this have made it harder for Canadian producers to receive what they believe to be fair prices.

The North American Free Trade Agreement won't do much to U.S.–Canada trade, but it should open up Mexican markets to Canadian products that faced high tariffs. That's good news for Canada, but we shouldn't be overly optimistic, since Canadian trade with Mexico is relatively small.

General Agreement on Tariffs and Trade (GATT) International agreement not to impose trade restrictions except under certain limited conditions. Replaced by the World Trade Organization (WTO) in 1995.

The **General Agreement on Tariffs and Trade (GATT)** was negotiated in the mid-1940s and originally 23 countries signed the Agreement. By the time GATT was replaced by the World Trade Organization at the end of 1994, there were 117 countries, including Canada, operating under that Agreement. GATT was the foundation of international trade arrangements. It granted tariff concessions and set the rules and regulations for international trade. Periodically it conducted meetings—called "rounds"—of its members, and a "round" could go on for years. The last round, the Uruguay Round (so-called because it was launched in Uruguay), began in 1986 and didn't conclude until the end of 1994.

World Trade Organization (WTO) World body charged with reducing impediments to trade; it replaced GATT in 1995.

GATT set the groundwork for trade liberalization. It was replaced at the beginning of 1995 by the **World Trade Organization (WTO).** Its mission is, like GATT's, to reduce tariffs and other trade barriers among countries. Many of the details of its operation have not yet been worked out, but, broadly speaking, trade disputes brought to it will be resolved by a panel of trade experts appointed by the WTO. The decisions of the panel will be binding on the disputants unless overturned by a consensus of the WTO membership. (This is different from GATT's dispute-resolution process, in which the country against whom a decision was rendered could simply ignore the decision.) A country that loses in a dispute will have two options: it can change its laws, or it can accept the WTO sanctions, which will probably be imposed in the form of tariffs.

AN ASSESSMENT OF FARM PRICE SUPPORT PROGRAMS

5 Price supports cause inefficiency and loss compared to a competitive solution. However, it is likely that, in the absence of price supports, private cartels would have been the outcome, and the price supports are the least inefficient practical solution.

This chapter's overview of government price support programs and their effects on farmers, consumers, and taxpayers should have given you a sense that, for society as a whole, the competitive solution would be a much better option than any of the other four approaches that we've discussed. Society would probably be better off, on average, if all the government farm programs were eliminated and replaced with a free market in agricultural goods. There would likely be much larger fluctuations in agricultural prices than there currently are, but the average price paid by consumers and the cost to taxpayers would both be lower.

But given the realities of the agricultural markets, it's unlikely that the competitive solution is a practical one. The inelastic demand for, and the fluctuating supply of, most agricultural goods create enormous pressure for cartelization of the various agricultural markets. In the absence of government programs, it's likely that the pressure would rise for the formation of private cartels—organizations of suppliers whose purpose is to limit supply—to stabilize and support agricultural prices. Had the government support programs not been established, agricultural production in Canada might today be controlled by four or five major firms that could limit supply even more than now. Agricultural prices might be higher and agricultural production lower than they currently are.

Had such private cartelization occurred, these firms would have initially made large profits, as did many of the first large manufacturing companies. The response to such profits would also likely have been similar. Agricultural workers would have organized and demanded safer working conditions and limited hours. They would have established pension systems similar to those that workers in manufacturing industries obtained. That would have significantly increased the costs of agricultural goods. The result might have been lower production and higher prices than we currently have.

To see the differences in the nature of production under our current system of private production and government support programs and under a system of private cartelization of agriculture, let's consider the question of industrial safety. To put the matter bluntly, one reason why Canadian farms are so productive is that farmers work extremely hard and skimp a lot on safety measures. Competition drives farmers to be productive, but it also kills and maims them. The accidental death rate for farmers is high—almost twice the death rate in mining (often considered the most dangerous occupation) and five times the national average. In a three-week period in a single year, the following accidents happened:

- A man was strangled when his clothes got caught in a swather.
- A man was buried and suffocated by corn sliding into the centre of the steel bin where he was working.
- A woman was seriously injured when her clothing was caught in the machinery of a harvesting combine.
- A man was crushed by cattle in his farmyard.
- A child suffocated in a silo.

If those accidents had happened in any other industry, there would be demands for government intervention and new safety regulations. But not in farming. It wasn't Big Business that was responsible; it was individual farmers making their own decisions. Under a cartelized system, Big Business would be held responsible, and there would be a clamour for government-imposed regulations. Such requirements would significantly increase costs and decrease productivity.

Arguments like the one we are making are always tenuous because no one can say for sure what the farm industry would have been like if government programs had never existed. For example, it's possible that, even if there had been large-scale cartelization in agriculture, international competition would have forced that domestic cartel to be competitive.

Because it's unclear what the correct hypothetical comparison is, one must be extremely careful in arguing that our present system is preferable to some hypothetical alternative, just as one must be careful in arguing that perfect competition would be preferable to the present situation.

Many economists speak rather harshly about our current government agricultural programs, comparing their waste and inefficiency with the operation of a perfectly competitive market. That comparison is problematic. An alternative to current Canadian farm programs might have been, not perfect competition, but the cartelization of the entire farming industry, resulting in higher prices, lower production, and less efficiency than the existing level.

Thus, while ideally perfect competition might be best for our society, policymakers must recognize the reality that competition isn't always the relevant alternative, given the nature of politics and the market. Relevant policy choices must be made between the two most likely alternatives, not between a tidy ideal and a messy reality. Which is the better situation? As usual, there's no easy answer.

CONCLUSION

This chapter has focused on agricultural markets, but it should be clear that the discussion is about much more than just agriculture; it's about the interrelationship between economics and politics. If individuals are self-interested maximizers, it's reasonable to assume that they're maximizers in all aspects of their lives. What they can't achieve in the economic sphere, they might be able to achieve in the political sphere.

To understand the economic policies that exist, one must consider how people act in both spheres. Consideration of the economics underlying government policies often leads to useful insights. For example, a military draft can be seen as a mechanism for focusing the costs of defence away from the taxpayer and onto a specific group of individuals—young people. The government's support for the arts can be seen as a transfer from general taxpayers to a specific group of individuals who like the arts. Government support for education can be seen as a transfer from general taxpayers to a specific group of individuals: students and instructors. These groups maintain strong lobbies to achieve their political ends, and the interaction of the various lobbying groups typically strongly influences what policies government will follow.

Economics doesn't tell you whether government intervention or any particular policy is good or bad. That, you must decide for yourself. But what economics can do is pose the policy question in terms of gains and losses for particular groups. Posing the question in that framework often cuts through to the real reasons behind various groups' support for this or that policy. Farmers aren't going to tell you that they support agricultural programs because those programs transfer money from taxpayers and consumers to farmers. Similarly, academics generally aren't going to tell you that the reason they favour government support for education is that those policies transfer money to them.

The economic framework directs you to look beyond the reasons people say they support policies; it directs you to look for the self-interest. The supply/demand framework provides a neat graphical way to picture the relative gains and losses resulting from various policies, which is why the supply/demand framework is such a powerful tool, even when few industries are actually perfectly competitive.

But as usual there's an *on the other hand.* Just because some groups may support policies for self-serving reasons, it is not necessarily the case that the policies are bad, or shouldn't be adopted. Reality is complicated with many more grey answers than black-and-white ones.

CHAPTER SUMMARY

- Because most agricultural markets have an inelastic demand, they produce a good/bad paradox for farmers.
- The history of Canadian farm programs is one of government intervention to keep prices higher than they otherwise might have been.
- Canadian agriculture is enormously productive and technically efficient.
- A general rule of political economy in a democracy is that policies tend to reflect small groups' interests, not the interests of large groups.
- Farm price support options are regulations, economic incentives, subsidies, and buying up and storing, giving away, or destroying.
- In judging a policy, the appropriate comparison is often the counterfactual. What would have happened if that policy had not been introduced?
- Reality is complicated, with many more grey answers than black-and-white ones.

KEY TERMS

Agricultural Stabilization Board *(366)*
agrifirms *(366)*
Canadian Dairy Commission *(366)*
Canadian Wheat Board *(366)*
excess burden *(372)*
farm lobby *(369)*
General Agreement on Tariffs and Trade (GATT) *(375)*
general rule of political economy *(369)*
good/bad paradox *(363)*
grandfather in *(372)*
parity price *(368)*
price stabilization program *(367)*
price support program *(368)*
trade dispute *(375)*
World Trade Organization (WTO) *(376)*

QUESTIONS FOR THOUGHT AND REVIEW

The number after each question represents the estimated degree of critical thinking required. (1 = almost none; 10 = deep thought.)

1. If the demand for farm products were elastic rather than inelastic, would the good/bad paradox still exist? Why or why not? *(5)*
2. Demonstrate, using supply and demand curves, the distributional consequences of a price support system achieved through acreage restriction. *(4)*
3. Which would a taxpayers' group prefer: price support achieved through buying up the surplus, or through providing economic incentives for not producing? Why? *(5)*
4. Say a city is establishing rent controls requiring rents to be set below market rents. What alternative methods could it use to ration apartments? *(8)*
5. What's the most-costly method of price support to the taxpayer? Demonstrate graphically. *(4)*
6. What is the least-costly method of price support to the taxpayer? Demonstrate graphically. *(4)*
7. Why do tariffs and quotas generally accompany price support systems? *(5)*
8. How does the elasticity of supply affect the cost of price supports in each of the four options listed and discussed in the chapter? *(6)*
9. Does the comparatively high accidental death rate for farmers say anything about the efficiency of Canadian regulation? If so, what? *(7)*
10. All government intervention in markets makes society worse off. True or false? Evaluate. *(8)*

PROBLEMS AND EXERCISES

1. Show graphically how the effects of an increase in supply will differ according to the elasticities of supply and demand.
   a. Specifically, demonstrate the following combinations:
      (1) An inelastic supply and an elastic demand.
      (2) An elastic supply and an inelastic demand.
      (3) An elastic supply and an elastic demand.
      (4) An inelastic supply and an inelastic demand.
   b. Demonstrate the effect of a government guarantee of the price in each of the four cases.
   c. If you were a farmer, which of the four combinations would you prefer?
2. Congratulations! You've been appointed finance minister of Farmingland. The prime minister wants to protect her political popularity by increasing farmers' incomes. She's considering two alternatives: (a) to bolster agricultural prices by adding government demand to private demand; and (b) to give farmers financial incentives to restrict supply and thereby increase price. She wants to use the measure that's least costly to the government. The conditions of supply and demand are illustrated in the accompanying diagram. (S_1 is what the restricted supply curve would look like. P_s is the price that the prime minister wants to establish.) Which measure would you advise?

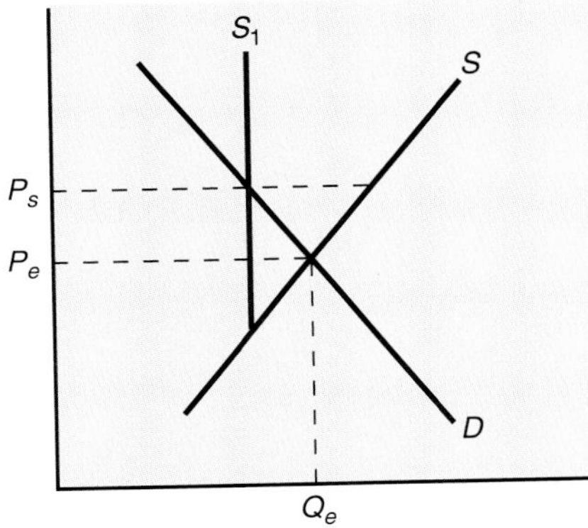

3. Suppose the government makes it against the law to grow soybeans unless the grower has been granted a government quota. It also essentially forbids soybean imports and sets a minimum price of soybeans at about 50 percent higher than the price of soybeans on the world market. This program costs the government $4 million a year in administrative costs.
   a. Are there likely any other costs associated with the program?
   b. Demonstrate graphically how to come up with about $250 million of additional costs.
   c. When "soybean land"—land with soybean quotas—is sold, what is the likely price of that land compared to equivalent land without a soybean quota?
   d. Say that, in accord with the World Trade Organization, the country agrees to allow open imports of soybeans and guarantees that all sellers receive the current high price. What will happen to the governmental costs of the program?
   e. Say the government limits the guaranteed high price to domestic producers. What will it have to do to make that guarantee succeed?
4. Say that a law, if passed, will reduce Mr. A's wealth by $100,000 and increase Mr. B's wealth by $100,000.
   a. How much would Mr. A be willing to spend to stop passage of the law?
   b. How much would Mr. B be willing to spend to ensure passage of the law?
   c. What implications for social policy do your answers to *a* and *b* have?
5. In 1998 the government of Landland will set a fee for ranchers who graze their animals on public land equal to $1.86 per animal unit per month—the amount of forage needed to feed one cow and its calf, or five sheep, for a month. The market rate for grazing on private land is expected to be $9 per animal unit month.
   a. Why do you think there is a difference?
   b. What are the advantages of setting the lower fee?
   c. Would you expect excess demand for government grazing land? Why? Demonstrate graphically.

CHAPTER

19

Microeconomics, Social Policy, and Economic Reasoning

If an economist becomes certain of the solution of any problem, he can be equally certain that his solution is wrong.

~H. A. Innis

After reading this chapter, you should be able to:

1. List three reasons why economists sometimes differ in their views on social policy.
2. Explain why liberal and conservative economists often agree in their views on social policy.
3. Explain the typical economist's view of many regulations.
4. Define cost/benefit analysis.
5. State why economists disagree about whether the minimum wage should be raised.
6. Explain why teaching a parrot the phrase *supply and demand* will not make it an economist.

One of the important jobs that economists do is to give advice to politicians and other policymakers on a variety of questions relating to social policy: How should unemployment be dealt with? How can society distribute income fairly? Should the government redistribute income? Would a program of equal pay for jobs of comparable worth (a pay equity program) make economic sense? Should the minimum wage be increased?

Economists differ substantially in their views on these and other social policy questions. As one pundit remarked, "If you laid all economists end to end, they still wouldn't reach a conclusion." Such comments have a superficial truth to them, but they also are misleading. Economists agree on many issues, and the reasons they disagree often have little to do with economics.

Understanding what economists agree and disagree about, and why, is an important part of understanding economics. Thus, this chapter considers some areas of agreement and disagreement among economists. This analysis will give you a good sense of economic reasoning as it's used in formulating social policy.

ECONOMISTS' DIFFERING VIEWS ABOUT SOCIAL POLICY

1 Economists' views on social policy differ widely because (1) their objective economic analyses are coloured by their subjective value judgements; (2) their interpretations of economic issues and of how political social institutions work vary widely; and (3) their proposals are often based on various models that focus on different aspects of problems.

Economists have many different views on social policy because:

1. Economists' suggestions for social policy are determined by their subjective value judgements (normative views) as well as by their objective economic analyses.
2. Policy proposals must be based on imprecise empirical evidence, so there's considerable room for differences of interpretation not only about economic issues, but also about how political and social institutions work. Economic policy is an art, not a science.
3. Policy proposals are based on various models which focus on different aspects of a problem.

The first and third reasons directly concern the role of ideology in economics, a controversial subject among economists. However, all economists agree that any policy proposal must embody both economic analysis *and* value judgements because the goals of policy reflect value judgements. When an economist makes a policy proposal, it's of this type: "If A, B, and C are your goals, then you should undertake policies D, E, and F to achieve those goals most efficiently." In making these policy suggestions, the economist's role is much the same as an engineer's: he or she is simply telling someone else how to achieve desired ends most efficiently. Ideally the economist is, as objectively as possible, telling someone how to achieve his or her goals (which need not be the economist's goals).

How Economists' Value Judgements Creep into Policy Proposals

Even though responsible economists attempt to be as objective as possible, value judgements still creep into their analyses in three ways: interpretation of policymakers' values, interpretation of empirical evidence, and choice of economic models.

Interpretation of Policymakers' Values In practice, social goals are seldom so neat that they can be specified A, B, and C; they're vaguely understood and vaguely expressed. An economist will be told, for instance, "We want to make the poor better off" or "We want to see that middle-income people get better housing." It isn't clear what *poor, better off,* and *better housing* mean. Nor is it clear how interpersonal judgements should be made when a policy will benefit some individuals at the expense of others, as real-world policies inevitably do.

Faced with this problem, some academic economists have argued that economists should recommend only policies that benefit some people and hurt no one. Such policies are called **Pareto optimal policies** in honour of the famous Italian economist, Wilfredo Pareto, who first suggested that kind of criterion for judging social change.[1]

Pareto optimal policies Policies that benefit some people and hurt no one.

[1] Pareto, in his famous book, *Mind and Society,* suggested this criterion as an analytic approach for theory, not as a criterion for real-world policy. He recognized the importance of the art of economics and that real-world policy has to be judged by much broader criteria than his Pareto optimality.

It's hard to object to the notion of Pareto optimal policies because, by definition, they improve life for some people while hurting no one.

We'd give you an example of a real-world Pareto optimal policy if we could, but, unfortunately, we don't know of any. Every policy inevitably has some side effect of hurting, or at least seeming to hurt, somebody. In the real world, Pareto optimal policies don't exist. Any economist who has advised governments on real-world problems knows that all real-world policies make some people better off and some people worse off.

But that doesn't mean that economists have no policy role. In their policy proposals, economists try to spell out what a policy's income-distributive effects will be, whether a policy will help a majority of people, who those people are, and whether the policy is consistent with the policymakers' value judgements. Doing so isn't easy because the policymakers' value judgements are often vague and must be interpreted by the economist. In that interpretation, the economist's value judgement often slips in.

Interpretation of Empirical Evidence Value judgements further creep into economic policy proposals through economists' interpretations of empirical evidence, which is almost always imprecise. For example, say an economist is assessing the elasticity of a product's demand. She can't run an experiment to isolate prices and quantities demanded; instead she must look at events in which hundreds of other things changed, and do her best to identify what caused what. In selecting and interpreting empirical evidence, a person's values will likely show through, try as one might to be objective. People tend to focus on evidence that supports their position. Economists are trained to be as objective as they can be, but pure objectivity is impossible.

Let's consider an example. In the 1980s, some economists proposed that a large tax be imposed on sales of disposable diapers, citing studies that suggested disposable diapers made up between 15 and 30 percent of the garbage in a landfill. Others objected, citing studies that showed disposable diapers made up only 1 or 2 percent of the refuse going into landfills. Such differences in empirical estimates are the norm, not the exception. Inevitably, if precise estimates are wanted, more studies are necessary. (In this case, the further studies showed that the lower estimates were correct.) But policy debates don't wait for further studies. Economists' value judgements influence which incomplete study they choose to believe is more accurate.

Choice of Economic Models Similarly with the choice of models. A model, because it focuses on certain aspects of economic reality and not on others, necessarily reflects certain value judgements, so economists' choice of models must also reflect certain value judgements. Albert Einstein once said that theories should be as simple as possible, but not more so. To that we should add the maxim: Scientists should be as objective and as value-free as possible, but not more so.

This book presents the mainstream neoclassical model of the economy. That model directs us to certain conclusions. Two other general models that some economists follow are a Marxian (radical) model and a public choice (conservative) model. Those other models, by emphasizing different aspects of economic interrelationships, would sometimes direct us to other conclusions.

Let's consider an example. Mainstream neoclassical analysis directs us to look at how the invisible hand achieves harmony and equilibrium through the market. Thus, when neo-Classical economists look at labour markets, they generally see supply and demand forces leading to equilibrium. When Marxist economists look at labour markets, their model focuses on the tensions among the social classes, and they generally see exploitation of workers by capitalists. When public choice economists look at labour markets, they see individuals using government to protect their monopolies. Their model focuses on political restrictions that provide rents to various groups. Each model captures different aspects of reality. That's why it's important to be as familiar with as many different models as possible.

Why Economists Advise Policymakers Who Share Their Value Judgements

Usually economists provide advice for policymakers whose values agree with their own. Economists with liberal values usually provide policy recommendations for liberal policymakers; economists with conservative values usually provide policy recommendations for conservative policymakers. Why? Because of the inevitable influence of economists' value judgements on their policy prescriptions. When economists have the same values as policymakers, they can have a better feel for a policy's harmony with the policymakers' worldview.

Let us give you a personal example. One of us has generally consulted for liberal policymakers even though the policies he's advocated are often classified as conservative. Why? Because his basic values are consistent with most liberals' values: he doesn't like people to go hungry, and he believes that we, as a society, should do what we can to help the poor. Paradoxically, much of his policy advice focuses on how existing government policies to help the poor don't achieve their desired ends, and how stronger reliance on market forces would be more effective in achieving those ends. In fact, both of us share these values, and we've found that we simply can't offer advice to politicians who, deep down, don't share our value judgements about what a just society is.

John Maynard Keynes once said that economists should be seen in the same light as dentists—as competent technicians. He was wrong, and his own experience is a contradiction of that view. In dealing with real-world economic policy, Keynes was no mere technician. He had a definite worldview, which he shared with many of the policymakers he advised. An economist who is to play a role in policy formation must be willing to combine value judgements and technical knowledge.

AGREEMENT AMONG ECONOMISTS ABOUT SOCIAL POLICY

Despite their widely varying values, both liberal and conservative economists agree more often on policy prescriptions than most laypeople think they do. They're economists, after all, and their models focus on certain issues—specifically on incentives and individual choice. All economists believe economic incentives are important, and most economists tend to give significant weight to individuals' ability to choose reasonably. This leads economists, both liberal and conservative, to look at a problem differently than other people do.

2 Liberal and conservative economists agree on many policy prescriptions because they use the same models, which focus on incentives and individual choice.

Many people think economists of all persuasions look at the world cold-heartedly. That opinion, in our view, of course, isn't accurate, but it's understandable how people could reach it. Economists are taught to look at things in an "objective" way that takes into account a policy's long-run incentive effects as well as the short-run effects. Many of their policy proposals are based upon these long-run incentive effects, which in the short run make the policy look cold-hearted. Economists argue that they aren't being cold-hearted at all, that they're simply being reasonable, and that following their advice will lead to less suffering and more people being helped than following others' advice. They ask, "How can advice that will lead to less suffering be cold-hearted?" This is not to say that all economists' advice will lead to significant long-run benefits and less long-run suffering. Some of it may be simply misguided. You must decide your position on that, but you should decide it knowing economists' defence of their policy suggestions.

Some economists argue that comparing marginal cost and marginal benefit (making efficient decisions) will lead to the most equitable and fairest systems—interpreted as most people would interpret *equitable* and *fairest.* Economists have had problems in getting their ideas fairly expressed in public because their arguments are often long-run arguments, while the press and policymakers usually focus on short-run effects. The problem economists face is similar to the one parents face when they tell their children that they can't eat candy or must do their homework before they can play. Explaining how "being mean" is actually "being nice" to a six-year-old isn't easy.

A former colleague, the late Abba Lerner, was well known for his strong liberal leanings. The government of Israel called on him for advice on what to do about unemployment. He went to Israel, studied the problem, and presented his advice: "Cut union wages." The government official responded, "But that's the same advice the conservative economist gave us." Lerner answered, "It's good advice, too." The Israeli Labour government then went and did the opposite; it raised wages, thus holding onto its union support in the short run.

Another example comes from a friend who is a World Bank economist. She was lamenting that she had to advise a hospital in a developing country to turn down the offer of a free dialysis machine because the marginal cost of the filters it would have to buy to use the machine significantly exceeded the costs of other life-saving machines. Economic reasoning involves making such hard decisions.

EXAMPLES OF ECONOMISTS' POLICY ADVICE

The best way to see the consistency and the differences in economists' policy advice is to consider some examples. Some of the following examples bring out certain common characteristics of most economists' policy advice, while others show the differences among economists in values and in empirical interpretations. Let's start with a general consideration of economists' views on regulation.

Economists' Cost/Benefit Approach to Government Regulation

3 Economists believe many regulations are formulated for political expediency and do not reflect cost/benefit considerations.

Say that there has been a plane crash in which 200 people died. Newspaper headlines trumpet the disaster while news magazines are filled with stories about how the accident might have been caused, citing speculation about poor maintenance and lack of government regulation. The publicity spreads the sense that "something must be done" to prevent such tragedies. Politicians quickly pick up on this, feeling that the public wants action. They introduce a bill outlawing faulty maintenance, denounce poor regulatory procedures, and demand an investigation of sleepy air controllers. In short, they strike out against likely causes of the accident and suggest improved regulations to help prevent any more such crashes.

Economists differ in their views on government regulation of airlines and other businesses, but economists of all ideological persuasions find themselves opposing some of the supposedly problem-solving regulations proposed by politicians. Considering why economists react this way gives you insight into their similarity.

"Count-from-1-to-10" Philosophy One reason economists unite in their opposition to many proposed government regulations is that they believe decisions should be made rationally on the basis of costs and benefits, not on the basis of political expediency.

Their position simply reflects their trained reasonableness. Reasonable people should look at the costs and the benefits of various possible courses of action, and make decisions based on those costs and benefits. After an emotional event like a plane crash, it's difficult to make rational decisions based on costs and benefits. Economists argue that laws enacted quickly in reaction to an emotional event generally will be ill thought out and will reflect the information provided by special interest groups (information that has not necessarily been processed and analyzed by independent observers). Psychologists advise patients not to make major decisions during a time of crisis; economists advise policymakers not to do so either. This advice reflects what we'll call the count-from-1-to-10 philosophy.

In advising policymakers to stop and count to 10 before recommending new regulations, economists point out that lawmakers have an incentive to act fast—to make it look as if they're doing something when the issue is hot and they're likely to get good press. But by the same reasoning, economists have an incentive to act slowly—to advise studying the issue (by hiring economists to do so) and coming to a "rational" conclusion. Whether economists are offering self-serving advice or good advice is for you to decide.

The Assignment of a Cost and a Benefit to Everything A second reason economists often find themselves united with one another but at odds with the general public is that their **cost/benefit approach** to problems—assigning costs and benefits, and making one's decision on the basis of those costs and benefits—requires them to determine a quantitative cost and benefit for everything, including life. What's the value of a human life? All of us would like to answer, "*Infinite.* Each human life is beyond

Cost/benefit approach Approach in which one assigns a cost and benefit to alternatives, and draws a conclusion on the basis of those costs and benefits.

EXHIBIT 1 The Value of a Human Life

Value of Life	Basis for Calculation (1994 Canadian dollars)
Desire for prompt coronary care	$110,000
Automobile air bag purchases	598,000
Smoke detector purchases	619,000
EPA requirement for sulfur scrubbers	830,000
Seat belt usage	898,000
Wage premiums for dangerous police work	1,410,000
Regulation of radium content in water	4,149,000
Wage premiums for dangerous factory jobs	5,311,000
Rules for workplace safety	5,809,000
Premium tire usage	5,975,000
Desire for safer airline travel	19,583,000

Source: Adapted from Stan V. Smith, adjunct professor, DePaul College of Law, and president, Corporate Financial Group, Chicago, Illinois. Used by permission.

price." But if that's true, then in a cost/benefit framework, everything of value should be spent on preventing death. People should take no chances. They should drive at 50 kilometres per hour with airbags, triple-cushioned bumpers, double roll bars—you get the picture.

4 Cost/benefit analysis is analysis in which one assigns a cost and benefit to alternatives, and draws a conclusion on the basis of those costs and benefits.

It would be possible for manufacturers to make a car in which no one would die as the result of an accident. The fact is that people don't want such cars. Many people don't buy or don't use those auto safety accessories that are already available, and many drivers ignore the present speed limit. Instead, many people want cars with style and speed.

Far from regarding human life as priceless, people make decisions every day that reflect the valuations they place on their own lives. Exhibit 1 presents one economist's estimates of some of these quantitative decisions. These values are calculated by looking at people's revealed preferences (the choices they make when they must pay the costs). To find them, economists calculate how much people will pay to reduce the possibility of their death by a certain amount. If that's what people will pay to avoid death, the cost to them of death can be calculated by multiplying the inverse of the reduced probability by the amount they pay.

For example, say someone will buy a car whose airbags add up to $500 to the vehicle's cost, but won't buy a car whose airbags add more than $500 to its cost. Also say that an airbag will reduce the chance of dying in an automobile accident by 1/720. That means that to increase the likelihood of surviving an auto accident by 1/720, the buyer will pay $500. That also means that the buyer is implicitly valuing his or her life at roughly $360,000 (720 × $500 = $360,000).

Alternatively, say that people will pay an extra $36 for a set of premium tires that reduces the risk of death by 1/100,000. As opposed to having a 3/100,000 chance per year of dying in a skid on the highway, people with premium tires all round have a 2/100,000 chance of dying (3/100,000 − 2/100,000 = 1/100,000). Multiplying 100,000 (the inverse of the reduction in probability) by $36, the extra cost of the set of premium tires, you find that people who buy these tires are implicitly valuing their lives at $3,600,000.[2]

No one can say whether people know what they're doing in making these valuations, although the inconsistencies in the valuations people place on their lives suggest that to some degree they don't, or that other considerations are entering into their decisions. But even given the inconsistencies, it's clear that people are placing a finite value on life. Most people are aware that in order to "live" they must take chances on

[2] For simplicity of exposition, we're not considering other benefits of these decisions such as lowering the chance of injury.

The Economist is a British economics magazine that closely follows economic developments in the world.

losing their lives. Economists argue that individuals' revealed choices are the best estimate that society can have of the value of life, and that in making policy society shouldn't pretend that life is beyond value.

Placing a value on human life allows economists to evaluate the cost of a crash. Say each life is worth \$2 million. If 200 people die in that plane accident and a \$200 million plane is destroyed, the cost of the crash is \$600 million.

Right after the accident, or even long after the accident, tell a mother and father you're valuing the life of their dead daughter at \$2 million and the plane at \$200 million, and you'll see why economists have problems with getting their views across. Even if people can agree rationally that a value must be placed on life—that they implicitly give their own lives a value—it's not something they want to deal with emotionally, especially after an accident. Using a cost/benefit approach, an economist must be willing to say, if that's the way the analysis turns out, "It's reasonable that my son died in this accident because the cost of preventing the accident by imposing stricter government regulations would have been greater than the benefit of preventing it."

Economists take the emotional heat for making such valuations. Their cost/benefit approach requires them to do so.

Comparing Costs and Benefits of Different Dimensions After the marginal cost and marginal benefit data have been gathered and processed, one is ready to make an informed decision. Will the cost of a new regulation outweigh the benefit, or vice versa? Here again economists find themselves in a difficult position in evaluating a regulation about airplane safety. Many of the costs of regulation are small but occur in large numbers. Every time you lament some "bureaucratic craziness" (such as a required weekly staff meeting or a form to be signed assuring something has been done), you're experiencing a cost. But when those costs are compared to the benefits of avoiding a major accident, the dimensions of comparison are often wrong.

For example, say it were discovered that a loose bolt was the probable cause of the plane crash. A regulation requiring airline mechanics to check whether that bolt is tightened and, to ensure that they do so, requiring them to fill out a form each time the check is made, might cost \$1. How can one compare \$1 to the \$600 million cost of the crash? Such a regulation obviously makes sense from the perspective of gaining a \$600 million benefit from \$1 of cost.

But wait. Each plane might have 4,000 similar bolts, each of which is equally likely to cause an accident if it isn't tightened. If it makes sense to check that one bolt, it makes sense to check all 4,000. And the bolts must be checked on each of the 4,000 flights per day. All of this increases the cost of tightening bolts to \$16 million per day. But the comparison shouldn't be between \$16 million and \$600 million. The comparison should be between the marginal cost (\$16 million) and the marginal benefit, which depends upon how much tightening bolts will contribute to preventing an accident.

Let's say that the decreased probability of having an accident because of having checked that bolt daily is .001. This means that the check will prevent one out of a thousand accidents that otherwise would have happened. The marginal benefit of checking a particular bolt isn't \$600 million (which it would be if you knew a bolt was going to be loose), but is:

$$.001 \times \$600 \text{ million} = \$600{,}000$$

That \$600,000 is the marginal benefit that must be compared to the marginal cost of \$16,000,000.

Given these numbers, we leave it to you to decide: Does this hypothetical regulation make sense?

Putting Cost/Benefit Analysis in Perspective The numbers in our plane crash example are hypothetical. The numbers used in real-world decision making are not hypothetical,

ADDED DIMENSION

HEARTBREAK COST/TRAFFIC BENEFIT

It's not only the general public that disdains economists' analyses. Sometimes economists disdain them themselves. In 1989, Herbert Stein (a well-known economist who has been, among other things, an economic advisor to a president of the United States) wrote a little piece for *The New York Times* that touched on the empirical problems of implementing cost/benefit analysis.

Stein alluded to a tendency of economists that makes ordinary people think that computer ink and not real blood runs in economists' veins; that where people anatomically locate their hearts, economists have a tidy box of microchips, electronic circuits, a few beeps, and an occasional flashing light. He invented a "newspaper article" announcing that a group of economists had studied the costs and benefits of traffic lights. The group concluded that the cost of installing, operating, and maintaining traffic lights, together with the costs incurred by motorists who lost time, wasted gas, and imposed wear and tear on their engines by stopping at red lights, were worth it in terms of lives saved in car accidents that didn't happen—but only just barely worth it. If the lights cost as little as 3 percent more or if lives were worth as little as 3 percent less, it would be cheaper to compensate accident victims and their families than to spend all that money on traffic lights.

Then, pointing out the human weakness for people to choose data to fit their value judgements, he invented another group of economists. The second group, he said, was very upset that any economic study would come to the conclusion that a social expense was worth the money it cost. In fact, the group was so upset that it was sure the first group must have made a mistake in analyzing its data, so the second group was going to conduct the study over again, convinced that this time it would come out the way their model said it should: Don't install traffic lights because they cost too much compared to the return on mere human life, health, and happiness.

Stein's playful story captures two aspects of economists that we've emphasized in this chapter:

1. Economists' tendency to view everything in a cost/benefit framework.
2. Economists'—and everyone else's—tendency to use empirical evidence selectively (that is, to use it to support positions they favour).

but they are often ambiguous. Measuring costs, benefits, and probabilities is difficult, and economists often disagree on specific costs and benefits.

Cost/benefit analyses are often used to justify what one wants to do. For example, in the 1950s, 1960s, and 1980s power companies always seemed to come up with conclusions that their projects—dams, canals, and the like—made sense from a cost/benefit analysis point of view. In the 1990s, there has been a reassessment of many of these projects, and in that reassessment many of the projects no longer make so much sense—the earlier analyses had not taken into account larger environmental costs.

Take, for example, a cost-benefit study one of us did on alleviating damages due to excessive flooding. A small community had been subjected to excessive flood damage for several years (as a result of the construction of a dam for a power utility, some residents argued). Possible remedies included flood-proofing the affected houses and building retaining walls, as well as several other options, including moving the entire community (which turned out to be one of the least-expensive solutions). The original cost-benefit project on the construction of the dam didn't take the potential for flood damages into account—it should have.

Costs have many dimensions, some more quantifiable than others. Cost/benefit analysis is often biased toward quantifiable costs and away from nonquantifiable costs, or it involves enormous ambiguity as nonquantifiable costs are quantified. An example? A large forestry firm wanted to know if it should build a logging road—at a cost of hundreds of thousands of dollars—so they could obtain access to a large stand of timber that was ready to be harvested. Their cost-benefit calculations assumed the damage to the environment from building the road and using the road would be negligible. Sixteen months after the road was built, a fuel truck on its way to resupply the harvesting operation spilled its entire load into the local stream, killing the fish and

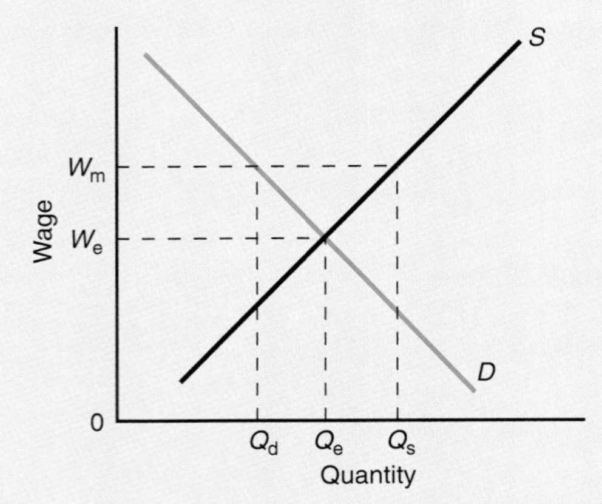

EXHIBIT 2 The Effect of a Minimum Wage

A minimum wage creates a gap between the quantity of labour supplied and the quantity of labour demanded, and hence creates unemployment. It helps those who manage to keep their jobs, increasing their wage from the equilibrium wage, W_e, to the minimum wage, W_m. But it hurts those who find that they can't get a job at the minimum wage, or keep a job they already had if the wage goes up (because the employer will just get along without that employee rather than pay more). This is shown by the distance $Q_s - Q_d$.

contaminating the area. The clean-up costs significantly exceeded the profits from the harvest.

The previous example highlights the subjectivity and ambiguity of costs, and this is one reason why economists differ in their views of regulation. In considering any particular regulation, some economists will favour it and some will oppose it. But their reasoning process—comparing marginal costs and marginal benefits—is the same; they differ only on the estimates they calculate.

Economists' Debate on Increasing the Minimum Wage

As a second case study, we'll consider economists' views of the minimum wage. The basic argument in favour of the minimum wage is that it raises poor people's income. The basic economic argument against the minimum wage is that it prevents market forces from working and creates unemployment. How it does so is captured in Exhibit 2. In it you can see how the minimum wage, W_m, set above the equilibrium wage, W_e, increases the gap between the quantity of labour supplied and the quantity demanded, and thereby creates unemployment equal to $Q_s - Q_d$. The simple argument against the minimum wage is that it creates this unemployment which hurts poor people.

5 Economists disagree about minimum wage policy because of differences in empirical estimates of direct and of side effects.

How does one compare the costs and benefits here? First, we must determine how many, and by how much, poor people will be helped or hurt. This depends on the elasticities of supply and demand. For example, say the supply and demand curves are highly inelastic. In that case, not many people will lose their jobs because of the minimum wage. However, if the supply and demand curves are highly elastic, a large number of people will lose their jobs when a minimum-wage law is introduced.

But estimating elasticities isn't sufficient to make a decision on whether a minimum wage is desirable. Another issue that must always be considered is the *general equilibrium* issue. Supply and demand are **partial equilibrium** concepts. They assume "all other things remain equal." But all other things don't remain equal. A minimum wage will cause firms to demand labour-saving machines. This will affect the demand for machines, and the demand for machines will affect the demand for labour. To consider the things that don't remain equal is to consider the general equilibrium issue. **General equilibrium analysis** is the analysis of the simultaneous interaction of all markets. To say that something is a general equilibrium issue is to say that looking at a supply/demand model isn't sufficient. Such general equilibrium considerations make policy debates much more complicated.

Partial equilibrium analysis Analysis of a part of a whole; it initially assumes all other things remain equal.

General equilibrium analysis The analysis of the simultaneous interaction of all markets.

ECONOMISTS, POLICYMAKERS, AND POLICY

Economics teaches people to be reasonable—sickeningly reasonable, some people would say. We hope that this chapter has given you some sense of what we mean by that. Economists' cost/benefit approach to problems (which pictures a world of individuals whose self-interested actions are limited only by competition) makes them look for the self-interest behind individuals' actions, and for how competition can direct that self-interest into the public interest.

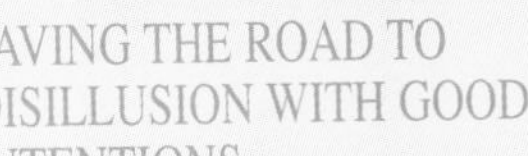

PAVING THE ROAD TO DISILLUSION WITH GOOD INTENTIONS

Suppose that you are an influential member of the government and that you and a group of your powerful colleagues are worried about how expensive housing has become. Millions of low-income people are living in run-down houses or apartments or doubling up with friends and relatives. Some even sleep in their cars or spend their lives wandering the streets without any regular place to live at all.

You're in a position to write a law and get it passed. You do pass legislation, a "Low-Income Housing Act." You state your purpose: "It is the policy of the Government of Canada to assist the Provinces and their subdivisions to remedy the unsafe and unsanitary housing conditions and the acute shortage of decent, safe, and sanitary dwellings for families of low income."

You believe that when this program gets going, old housing will be rehabilitated, new housing will be built, and these units will be made available to low-income families at rents they can afford.

You institute the program and it's initially a success: All available units are rented to low-income families at rents they can afford. But its success creates an incentive problem. Once in such a unit, a family does its best to remain there. That's not what you intended; you intended that as families benefited from this assistance, they would gradually improve their circumstances and income, and move on to homes of their own or the better apartments available on the open market. This would make room for other low-income families to move in and begin their own climb up the economic ladder.

But what's the incentive for a family fortunate enough to obtain one of these units? The incentive is to remain a low-income family in order to continue to qualify for the "decent, safe, and sanitary dwelling" where it lives. Given this incentive, there's little turnover in these units. When occupants die, relatives and even friends struggle to remain in the units under a provision that permits "remaining occupants" to continue to live there.

Another incentive problem is that landlords have no incentive to keep rents below the rent that similar units outside the program command, because as long as the rent doesn't exceed fair market rents in the area, the occupants need pay, say, only 30 percent of their monthly income in rent. Rent increases don't matter to the occupants. They continue to pay only 30 percent of their income, with the government paying the difference.

How can we be so sure about the problems of such a law? Because federal and provincial laws like this exist in Canada, and there are continual debates over the pros and cons of low-income and social housing—particularly around election time.

In an economist's framework:

- Well-intentioned policies often are prevented by individuals' self-seeking activities.
- Policies that relieve immediate suffering often have long-run consequences that create more suffering.
- Politicians have more of an incentive to act fast—to look as if they're doing something—than to take enough time to get something done well that makes sense from a cost/benefit point of view.

Policy for the Real World

We've argued that it's important for economic considerations to be taken into account in decision making, and that people are, over the long haul, rational. But in proposing policies that will work, economists must also keep in mind that, in the short run, people are often governed by emotion, swayed by mass psychology, and irrational. Politicians and other policymakers know that; the laws and regulations they propose reflect such calculations. Politicians often tell academic economists, "Yes, your arguments are reasonable, but politically I must reflect my constituents' positions. I'd be eaten alive if I followed your advice."

Politicians don't get elected and reelected by constantly saying that all choices have costs and benefits. And so, while policymakers listen to the academic economists they ask for advice, and in private frequently agree with those advisors, in practice they often choose to ignore economists' policy recommendations.

The way economic reasoning influences policy can be subtle. Sometimes one sees an elaborate charade acted out: A politician puts forward legislation that from a cost/benefit viewpoint doesn't make sense but that makes her look good. She hopes the legislation won't pass, but she also hopes that presenting the legislation will allow enough time to pass so that emotions can cool and more reasonable legislation can be put forward. Other times, compromise legislation is proposed that incorporates as much cost/benefit policy as possible, but also appeals to voters' emotional sense. So economists and economic reasoning do influence policy.

Still, all too often (in our view), economists' advice is dumped as irrelevant, and special-interest groups' policies are adopted instead. Social policy made in the real world reflects a balancing of cost/benefit analysis and special-interest desires. Walking on that political tightrope is an art in which academic economists, in their role as economists, have little training.

When they propose policies, academic economists don't have to deal with such concerns. From their ivory towers they put ideas into the real world, and they help students better understand the reasoning behind those ideas. Often the ideas don't have a snowball's chance in hell of being implemented, but the ideas do make people think and influence *the way* they think. That's the payoff many economists are looking for. You'll understand policy proposals better if you bear in mind that the goal behind them isn't always to get them implemented.

Parrots and Economic Reasoning

6 Applying economics is much more than muttering "supply and demand." Economics involves the thoughtful use of economic insights and empirical evidence.

As you can see, applying economics is much more than muttering "supply and demand" to explain every situation. Thomas Carlyle, who, as we saw in an earlier introductory quotation, argued that all you have to do is teach a parrot the words *supply and demand,* was wrong. Economics involves the thoughtful use of economic insights and empirical evidence. If this book is giving you a sense of the nature of that thoughtful application along with the core of economic reasoning, then it's succeeding in its purpose.

CHAPTER SUMMARY

- Economists differ because of different underlying value judgements, because empirical evidence is subject to different interpretations, and because their underlying models differ.
- Value judgements inevitably work their way into policy advice, but good economists try to be objective.
- Economists tend to agree on certain issues because their training is similar.
- The economic approach to analyzing issues is a cost/benefit approach.
- Economists generally have reservations about regulations.
- Economics involves the thoughtful use of economic insights and empirical evidence.

KEY TERMS

cost/benefit approach *(384)*
general equilibrium analysis *(388)*
Pareto optimal policies *(381)*
partial equilibrium *(388)*

QUESTIONS FOR THOUGHT AND REVIEW

The number after each question represents the estimated degree of critical thinking required. (1 = almost none; 10 = deep thought.)

1. Could anyone object to a Pareto optimal policy? Why? *(8)*
2. Would it be wrong for economists to propose only Pareto optimal policies? *(9)*
3. Would all economists oppose price controls? Why or why not? *(7)*
4. Should body organs be allowed to be bought or sold? Why or why not? *(8)*
5. In cost/benefit terms, explain your decision to take an economics course. *(6)*
6. How much do you value your life in dollar terms? Are

your decisions consistent in that valuation? *(9)*

7. If someone offered you $1,000,000 for one of your kidneys, would you sell it? Why or why not? *(7)*
8. Should the minimum wage be eliminated? Why? *(8)*
9. Why might an economist propose a policy that has little chance of adoption? *(4)*
10. Why is economics more than just muttering "supply and demand"? *(4)*

PROBLEMS AND EXERCISES

1. Demonstrate graphically, and explain why, both perfect competition and a perfectly discriminating monopoly lead to a Pareto optimal outcome.
2. Say that the cost of a car crash is $8,000. Assume further that installing a safety device in a car at a cost of $12 will reduce the probability of an accident by .05 percent. The plant makes 1,000 cars each day.
   a. If the preceding are the only relevant costs, would you favour or oppose the installation of the safety device?
   b. What other costs might be relevant?
3. The technology is now developing so that road use can be priced by computer. A computer in the surface of the road picks up a signal from your car and automatically charges you for the use of the road.
   a. How could this technological change contribute to ending bottlenecks and rush-hour congestion?
   b. What are some of the problems that might develop with such a system?
   c. How would your transportation habits likely change if you had to pay to drive on roads?
4. In the early 1990s, the 14- to 17-year-old population fell because of low birth rates in the mid-1970s. Simultaneously the echo from the past was the baby boom, and late-aging baby boomers who decided to have kids combined to increase the number of babies and hence to increase the number of parents needing baby sitters. What effect will these two events likely have on:
   a. The number of times parents go out without their children?
   b. The price of baby sitters?
   c. The average age of baby sitters?
5. As organ transplants become more successful, scientists are working on ways to transplant animal organs to humans. Pigs are the odds-on favourites as "donors" since their organs are about the same size as human organs.
   a. What would the development of such organ farms likely do to the price of pigs?
   b. If you were an economic advisor to the government, would you say that such a development would be Pareto optimal (for humans)?
   c. Currently, there is a black market in human organs. What would this development likely do to that market?
6. According to government statistics, the cost of averting a premature death differs among various regulations. Car seat belt standards cost $100,000 per premature death avoided while hazardous waste land disposal bans cost $4.2 trillion per premature death avoided.
   a. If you were choosing between these two regulations, which would you choose? Why?
   b. If these figures are correct, should neither, one, the other, or both of these regulations be implemented?
7. A 29-year-old politician proposed that the county government sell the organs of dead welfare recipients to help pay off the welfare recipients' welfare costs and burial expenses.
   a. What was the likely effect of that proposal?
   b. Why was that the effect?
8. Technology is being developed such that individuals can choose the sex of their offspring. Assume that technology has now been perfected and that 70 percent of the individuals choose male offspring.
   a. What effect will that have on social institutions such as families?
   b. What effect will it have on dowries—payments made by the bride's family to the groom—which are still used in a number of developing countries?
   c. Why might an economist suggest that if 70 percent male were the expectation, families would be wise to have daughters rather than sons?

CHAPTER

20

Economics and the Environment

The attempt to turn a complex problem of the head into a simple moral question for the heart to answer is of course a necessary part of all political discussion.

~Frank Colby

After reading this chapter, you should be able to:

1. List four ways in which an economist's approach to environmental problems differs from a noneconomist's approach.
2. Say why correlation does not necessarily imply causation.
3. Explain why economists often oppose direct regulation.
4. Justify the notion of an optimal level of pollution.
5. Discuss economists' concerns about voluntary programs.
6. Explain why economists believe that long-term solutions to problems involve making people pay a price that reflects the cost of an externality.
7. Apply economists' reasoning to an environmental issue that has not been discussed in this chapter.

Important areas of application of economic reasoning are the environment and resources. In the debate, economists who study and are concerned about these issues often have different views than do other individuals who are concerned about these areas but who aren't trained in economics. Some of the differences include:

1. Economists' understanding and statement of the environmental problem are likely to differ from those of conservationists without economic training.
2. Economists often oppose explicit regulation and prohibitions of certain actions (such as the use of styrofoam), preferring alternative incentive-based programs to achieve the same end.
3. Economists are often dubious about voluntary solutions.
4. Economists' methods of paying for environmental programs are likely to differ from lay conservationists' methods.

1 Four ways in which economists' approach to environmental problems differs from noneconomists' approach include: 1. their understanding of the problem; 2. their opposition to explicit regulation; 3. their dubiousness about voluntary solutions; and 4. their methods for paying.

In this chapter we consider an example of each of these differences to give you some insight into how economists think and how understanding economic principles affects one's understanding of environmental problems. Then we consider a case study of a mandatory recycling program, the economic analysis of that program, and, finally, alternatives to it.

ECONOMISTS' INTERPRETATION OF THE PROBLEM

One important difference between economists and laypeople is a result not so much of economists' economic training as of their statistical training. Having worked with statistics, economists know the difficulty of reaching definite conclusions about what's happening or will happen on the basis of what has happened in the past.

The Empirical Debate about Global Warming

Let's consider this difference in relation to the **global warming theory** (the theory that the earth is now going through a period of warming due to the rise in carbon dioxide gases caused by the burning of fossil fuels). The problem of global warming and the policies we should use to deal with it have been much in the news in the 1990s. Before one can discuss what policies to use to deal with global warming, one must answer the question: Is the global warming theory correct? It's not all that easy a question to answer.

Global warming theory The theory that the earth is now going through a period of warming due to the rise of carbon dioxide gases caused by the burning of fossil fuels.

Is the Global Warming Theory Correct? The temperature measurements in the Northern Hemisphere have been on an upward trend over the last 100 years, as we see in Exhibit 1 (a). There's no debate about that. There's also no debate about the recent increase in carbon dioxide gas in the atmosphere. But to a statistician, and hence to an economist who's trained as a statistician, those facts don't necessarily mean that the global warming theory is correct.

Correlation Does Not Imply Causation Early on in any statistics course, all economists, like all scientists, learn that **correlation** (the joint movement of data points) does not imply **causation** (that the change in one of those data points caused the other data point to change). If the global warming theory is correct, a number of conditions are necessary. These include: (1) future temperatures must not be expected to fall unless carbon dioxide in the atmosphere falls, and (2) temperatures must be expected to continue to rise as long as carbon dioxide in the atmosphere continues to rise.

2 Correlation does not imply causation.

Correlation Term in statistics meaning the joint movement of data points.

Causation Term in statistics meaning that a change in one data point causes a change in another data point.

For example, if in the 1990s temperatures fall even as carbon dioxide in the atmosphere increases, the global warming theory will be shown incorrect. But even if temperatures continue to rise, the theory *won't be proven* correct (a theory can never be proven correct); it can only be corroborated. (**Corroboration** means that the data are more consistent with this theory than with any other theory, so it makes sense to use the theory.) We generally treat a corroborated theory as correct even though we're not sure it's correct.

Corroboration Term meaning that the data are more consistent with a particular theory than with any other theory, so it makes sense to use that particular theory.

Deciding whether the global warming theory is corroborated is a difficult statistical question with no definitive answer. It requires interpretation and integration of data from many sources. Statisticians are still debating this issue. The current state of the

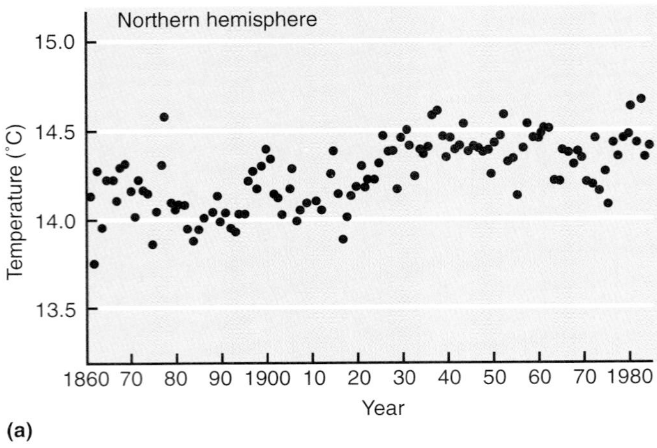

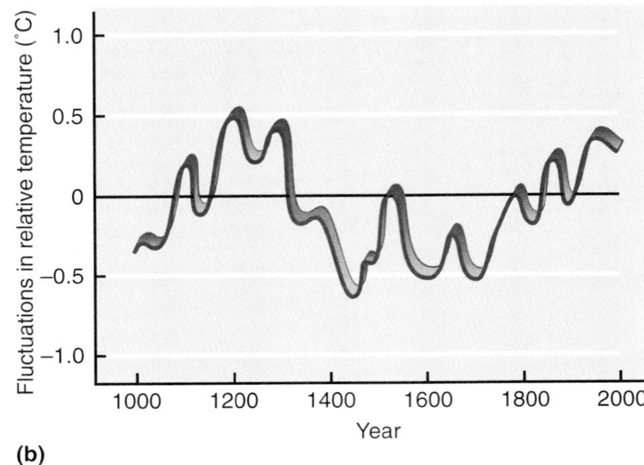

EXHIBIT 1 (a and b) Global Warming Statistics

When we look at recent data, (**a**), the global warming theory seems reasonable. But when we look at long-run data, (**b**), we see enormous fluctuations in temperature long before the appearance of the causes identified by the global warming theory.
Source: Adapted by permission from *The Changing Atmosphere* by John Firor © Yale University Press, New Haven, CT, 1990.

Nicholas Georgescu-Roegen was one of the earliest environmental economists. © *David Crenshaw.*

debate is that interpretation of the data depends on one's prior belief.[1] If one believes that it's reasonable to assume that a qualitative change in the model has taken place, then the data are consistent with the global warming theory. Statisticians who believe that the burning of fossil fuel since the 1860s is likely to have produced a qualitative change in the nature of our weather system would take this view. If, however, one presently believes:

1. That no qualitative change in the system generating these data has taken place;
2. That the general temperature pattern is subject to significant long-run cyclical fluctuations; and
3. That potential measurement problems exist—specifically, (1) that the instruments measuring temperature aren't completely representative of global conditions but are instead representative of conditions close to inhabited areas, and (2) that the precision of the instruments in early years had problems,

then the data are inconclusive. A few statisticians believe this and the debate between the two groups of statisticians remains unresolved.

The Ambiguity of Formal Statistical Results Like statisticians, economists who focus on this area differ in their assessments of what can be drawn from the data, but they're all far more careful about drawing inferences from the data than are the typical laypersons. Each year of new data provides more information. However, as you can see in Exhibit 1 (b) (which shows estimated fluctuations in temperatures over hundreds of years), temperatures have fluctuated even before any carbon fuels were burned. We have no satisfactory explanation why. Given our lack of knowledge of the reasons for these earlier fluctuations, even another hundred years of data will be unlikely to produce conclusive evidence. Still, by the turn of the century it's possible that the group believing the global warming theory is corroborated or the group believing the data are inconclusive will have strengthened its case significantly.

[1] In high-level statistical theory there's a debate between Bayesian statisticians (who believe that all statistics must be interpreted through a person's prior beliefs) and Classical statisticians (who believe that purely objective statistical estimates, not based in any way on prior beliefs, can be made). Most statisticians accept that in areas where there's a lot of ambiguity (such as in global warming) and where precise data are so limited, it's impossible to be totally objective. This doesn't mean that the scientists are doing bad science; it only means that data limitations require interpretive assumptions that cannot be fully objective. The fact that data are limited doesn't mean the policy question shouldn't be addressed. Often policy problems must be addressed long before adequate data are available.

In an article discussing global warming, the magazine *The Economist* summarizes the data's ambiguity. It concludes that it's very possible that future effects on climate "will be unlike any seen before." The writers continue:

> This is not good news for computer modellers. Climate models are derived from weather forecasting programs that are designed to provide tomorrow's weather when told about today's. As such, they may have many assumptions built into them that have nothing to do with the underlying mechanisms governing the weather and climate. They can be inspired fudges. (*The Economist,* April 7, 1990, p. 100.)

This ambiguity of formal statistical results isn't an exception; it's the rule in economics and business. But in the real world, decisions must be made before statistically conclusive evidence is in. That's where the art of economics comes into play. One must use one's judgement, accepting that it might be wrong. Based on such judgement, not formal statistical proof, many economists believe that global warming is taking place.

Statistical Inference and Policy Let's say that the global warming theory is correct. The next question is what to do about it. Here again, the economist's statistical training enters in. Economists recognize that averages aren't enough. Even if the average temperature has risen, the problem presented by that rise depends on how average temperature has risen. Advocates of the global warming theory's correctness claim that, based on a computer projection, a two- or three-degree increase in temperature will cause enormous problems for agriculture and create desert areas in much of the world. But that conclusion depends on when during the year, and where on the earth, the temperature rises.

Some economists point out that the data collected to date have suggested the rise in the average is occurring by winters becoming milder and summer temperatures remaining almost unchanged. Moreover, the warming is greater in polar regions than it is near the equator. Since such an asymmetrical change in temperature wouldn't create deserts, but would extend the growing season in a number of areas (reducing the cost of growing agricultural goods), it's not at all clear that such global warming will have dire negative effects on the world economy. In fact, a few economists even suggest that in certain circumstances such a global warming may benefit society. They would advocate doing nothing.

Other economists, such as William Nordhaus (a professor at Yale University who did a study of policy to deal with global warming), advocate a tax on the use of carbon fuels. We'll discuss economists' policy proposals shortly.

We emphasize these interpretative statistical problems here because, before discussing policy, we must recognize how important data interpretation is. Much real-world applied economics is slogging through data, bringing one's statistical training to bear on that data so that one can understand what the problem is. If you don't understand statistical inference, you are likely to go off to solve the wrong problem.

How Limited Are Our Natural Resources?

Before moving on, let's consider another debate in which many economists have questioned the conventional wisdom based on their empirical and statistical training. That debate concerns the extent to which the world's resources are limited.

Proven Reserves

The layperson's conventional wisdom is that the world is running out of resources. After all, resources are fixed and, once used up, they're gone. To support this view, statistics are often cited that we have only, say, 20 years of copper left, 30 years of fossil fuel, and so on. Economists have two problems with these statistics. The first is that the available statistics don't tell us how large existing reserves of any resource are. The statistics we have concern **proven reserves** (reserves that have been discovered and are recoverable), assuming current technology and prices. The calculation of proven reserves changes over time as more resources are discovered. As reserves run low, new exploration may well find more reserves.

Proven reserves Resource reserves that have been discovered, documented to date, and are recoverable with current technology.

ADDED DIMENSION

A STORY OF TWO BETS

The prophets of doom have been around for a long time; economists generally believe they are overstating their case, not taking into account that there is a built-in market reaction to scarcity—a rise in price of the scarce good—that eliminates the scarcity. The rise in price eliminates scarcity in two ways: (1) it decreases the quantity demanded by causing demanders to substitute, and (2) it increases the quantity supplied, through such actions as investment in new technologies that replace the resource with another resource. Most economists believe that the prophets of doom significantly underestimate both these effects. One economist who has been especially outspoken on this issue is Julian Simon, author of *People: The Ultimate Resource.*

Bet 1

In 1980, Simon challenged Paul Ehrlich, an outspoken leader of the prophets of doom (and author of *The Population Bomb*), to put his money where his mouth was. He told Ehrlich to choose any five resources that he believed would become scarce. Simon was willing to put up $1,000 to back his belief that these five resources of Ehrlich's choosing would become *less scarce* in 10 years, on average—as measured by their total price in 1980 and their total price 10 years later. Put another way, he bet their prices would rise less than the inflation. So Simon wasn't even relying on the demand response to scarcity; he was relying only on the supply response—new technological developments, the breakdown of cartels, and new discoveries.

At the time, Simon's bet seemed to be a foolhardy one. Ehrlich accepted the bet, which was to cover the period October 1980 through October 1990. If, at the end of the period, the total value for specific amounts of each resource had risen above $1,000, Simon would pay Ehrlich the difference between the $1,000 and the higher value. But if the total value had fallen below $1,000, Ehrlich would pay Simon the difference between the total value and $1,000.

Ten years pass. Guess who wins? You're right: Simon. (Otherwise we wouldn't be telling this story.) The prices of the resources had fallen (some had fallen in nominal terms!). Paul Ehrlich writes a check to Simon for $576.07 and sends it to him with no note or anything. *The New York Times* hears about the bet and, in a magazine story (Sunday *New York Times Magazine,* December 2, 1990), recounts the bet, and it becomes famous—an example of the prophets of doom being mistaken again.

Bet 2

Two years pass. An economist we know is at a conference having dinner with Julian Simon. He congratulates Simon on his bet with Ehrlich and tells him that he's generally in agreement with his attack on the prophets of doom, but he argues that Simon pushes it a bit too far. Simon says that he was not strong enough in his attack on the prophets of doom; he believes not only that resources are becoming less scarce, but that the welfare of society is continually improving, not getting worse. In fact, he says he is so sure that the future is improving that he will offer our friend a bet similar to the one he offered Ehrlich. He tells our friend: "Choose any measure of human material welfare, over any time period, in any area or community. I bet $1,000 that measure will improve."

As an example, consider the case of copper. In 1950, proven reserves were said to be enough for 27.9 production years. Thus, in 1950 one might have predicted that copper reserves would run out by 1980. That didn't happen. In 1980, proven reserves of copper were said to be enough for 38 production years, an increase of about 10 production years. Using these data, some cynical economists facetiously argue that if the trend continues, eventually the world will be swamped with copper. That obviously won't happen, but it's not clear from the statistics we have now that we should be concerned about running out of copper in the near, or even distant, future.

The Invisible Hand at Work A second problem economists have with these long-run projections about running out of resources is that the use of any resource depends upon its price. As the price rises, people use less of the resource (the law of demand)

Even though our friend agrees with much of Simon's argument, he finds Simon's statement too strong, and suggests Simon modify it slightly. Simon stands firm. So our friend asks his wife, a doctor, to come up with a statistic that would qualify as a "measure of human material welfare" that is highly likely—in fact, is almost guaranteed—to get worse (our friend hates to lose bets). They decide on the following measure: The number of full-blown AIDS cases in the United States as measured by Center for Disease Control (CDC) statistics in a one-year period, April 1992–April 1993. Our friend bets that the statistic will increase as compared to the April 1991–April 1992 period.

Simon, having stated his position so strongly, feels he must accept the bet. (Actually, he told our friend later, he believes that the bet is a bad one for him—that the relevant measure of human welfare is life expectancy rather than a particular disease, and that a one-year period is too short for meaningful tests.) A bet is made and a contract hastily drawn up. If our friend wins, Simon will donate a specified amount of money to a charity our friend designates; if Simon wins, our friend will donate the equivalent amount of money to a charity Simon designates.

Our friend, of course, thinks he has a winning bet: the number of new AIDS cases is a flow from a stock of HIV-infected people. That stock has been on an upward trend for at least 10 years and the flow from it is statistically almost guaranteed to rise in the short run.

However, about 4 o'clock the next morning he wakes up—somehow, in his sleep, he has remembered that AIDS cases had recently been redefined to include a set of women's diseases that hadn't previously been included. Depending on the decisions made by government statisticians, that redefinition could cause a one-time blip in the number of full-blown AIDS cases in the base period April 1991–April 1992. With that one-time blip, it is possible that our friend could lose the bet, since a number of AIDS cases that were actually contracted over the past 10 years could be added in the base period, artificially inflating it. With the blip, even though the number of full-blown AIDS cases has, in one sense, continually increased, the statistic measuring that increase—the number of defined AIDS cases as specified by the bet—may not have increased.

As of mid-1995 the CDC numbers were still unavailable.

Lessons

Two lessons can be learned from the two bets.

1. First, don't underestimate technological change and the positive progression of history. Simon's general position is a strong one. The world will adapt to new circumstances, and most people significantly underestimate its adaptability. People have a tendency to make unfair comparisons of past and present.
2. Second, there is no sure thing. Statistics are subject to significant deviation from what one thinks they are. Our friend thought he had a sure thing, but he may have lost on a definitional point. To understand statistics, you must understand how they are defined and compiled.

Why are these lessons important for economics? Because they play important roles in policy decisions; they urge caution in making "common sense" arguments, and in treating statistical facts as truth.

and spend much more time, energy, and money on finding alternatives. Rising price brings about technical change. If people expect resources to be in short supply in the future, the price of those resources will go up now, causing people to conserve. That's the market's way of conserving resources.

The fact that the price of a particular resource isn't going up now suggests that maybe the problem isn't viewed as that great by the people who produce, buy, and sell the resource. Economists point out that this group of people has the most information about future supplies and demand. Hence economists believe the current price tends to be a good signal about future shortages. If the current price isn't high or rising, then there are probably strong empirical data to support the view that we are not going to run out of that resource in the foreseeable future. If the price is high and rising, then one would expect that people will be undertaking more and more conservation mea-

ADDED DIMENSION

PRICING NATURAL RESOURCES

Let's consider how natural resources should be priced in a perfectly competitive market. Suppose you have $1,000 sitting in your wallet, and you have the choice of investing in a bond or buying a kilogram of a new (fictional) mineral—let's call it Wombatium. The bond pays you interest, at, say, 10 percent a year. To make you indifferent between the bond and the kilo of Wombatium, what has to happen to the price of that kilo of Wombatium over the year? If you said it has to rise by 10 percent, you've got it. (If you weren't sure about what had to happen, you need to think about what you'd have at the end of one year.)

Hotelling's Rule In a perfectly competitive market, every year natural resource prices should rise by the rate of interest.

That's the insight behind Harold **Hotelling's rule** on pricing natural resources: In a perfectly competitive market, every year natural resource prices should rise by the rate of interest.

In reality, we know there are several factors affecting the price of a natural resource: new discoveries; innovations that affect availability, such as new methods of extraction; and government policies that set price floors or price ceilings. Hotelling's rule gives us a good starting point, but it doesn't always explain what we see in the market. For example, price controls aren't a feature of a perfectly competitive market. Let's look at a real-world example.

In the early 1970s, the Organization of Petroleum Exporting Countries (OPEC) raised the world price of oil by forming a cartel that limited supply. This quadrupled oil prices and certainly wasn't tied to interest rates. It raised the costs of production substantially. Firms passed higher costs on to consumers, whose incomes were not rising at the same rate as the cost of living, and many industrialized nations fell into deep recession, with rising rates of unemployment and continually rising prices (in the macroeconomics course we give this set of conditions a special name—*stagflation).*

The federal government of the day decided that Canada had sufficient resources to allow us to set oil prices below the world price of oil—they believed that with such low oil prices our costs of production would be lower than they would otherwise be (so central Canadian manufacturing wouldn't suffer), and we wouldn't have problems as a result of OPEC's market power. The federal government established the **National Energy Program,** which put controls on oil prices, so that by 1981 Canadian prices were only half of the world price. With a change in government in 1984, the National Energy Program was abolished, and Canadian oil prices quickly became consistent with world prices.

National Energy Program A federal program that put controls on oil prices in the late 1970s and early 1980s. It was abandoned in 1984.

The National Energy Program has been sharply criticized because it led to a misallocation of resources—the invisible hand had been badly bruised by the invisible foot. In addition, the political decision to put the welfare of central Canada above that of the oil-producing provinces was unpopular on a Canada-wide basis because the oil-producing provinces were forced to accept a low domestic price when they could have been selling at a much higher world price. The residual fallout still colours federal-provincial relations.

All of this goes to show that Hotelling's rule is fine in a vacuum, but in the real world it faces several challenges both on economic and political fronts.

---

sures without any regulatory policies to induce them to do so. The invisible hand does the work. The higher price gives them an incentive to choose to conserve. But the real price of most minerals hasn't risen. In fact, real prices of most minerals have fallen over time.

Many empirical studies suggest relative scarcity declining over time. How can scarcity decline? Remember back in the first chapter when we first discussed resources and scarcity. Available resources depend upon technology—and if technology increases faster than resources are used, relative scarcity declines.

Once again, our purpose in discussing the issue of limited resources is not to argue which view is right, but simply to point out how careful one must be in interpreting empirical evidence before discussing policy proposals.

ALTERNATIVE POLICY APPROACHES

But let's now suppose that we have come to the conclusion that there's a problem—say that we've concluded that people are using too much oil. Having come to that conclusion, let's now specifically consider the differing policies to which an economist and a layperson might naturally gravitate.

One difference is that a layperson is likely to favour a program of **direct regulation,** in which the amount of oil people are allowed to use is directly limited by the government. Economists are likely to oppose that solution because it does not achieve the desired end as **efficiently** (at the lowest cost possible in total resources without consideration as to who pays those costs) and fairly as possible. As we discussed in the last chapter, for an economist, coming to the conclusion that too much oil is being consumed would imply that for some reason the consumption of oil involves a negative **externality** (the result of a decision that is not taken into account by the decision maker).

As an alternative to direct regulation, economists will likely favour some type of a **market incentive program** (a program that makes the price reflect the negative externality).

The reason for this difference between the layperson's view and the economist's view of policy is the same reason that we discussed in the last chapter: Regulation does not get people to equate the marginal costs of reducing oil consumption with the marginal benefits.

Let's consider an example. Say we have two individuals, Mrs. Thrifty using 10 litres of gasoline (which is made from oil) a day and Mr. Big using 20 litres of gasoline a day. Say we have decided that we want to reduce these two individuals' total daily gas consumption by 10 percent, or 3 litres. The regulatory solution might require everyone to reduce consumption by some amount. Likely direct regulatory reduction strategies would be to require an equal quantity reduction (each consumer reducing consumption by 1.5 litres) or to require an equal percentage reduction (each consumer reducing consumption by 10 percent).

Economists' problem with this direct regulatory solution is that it doesn't take into account the costs to individuals of reducing consumption. Say, for example, that Mrs. Thrifty could easily (i.e., almost costlessly) reduce consumption by three litres while Mr. Big would find it very costly to reduce consumption by even .5 litres. In that case, either regulatory solution would be **inefficient** (more costly than necessary). It would be less costly to have Mrs. Thrifty undertake the entire reduction. Economists would prefer a policy that would automatically make the person who has the lower cost of reduction choose (as opposed to being *required*) to undertake the largest reduction. In this case the policy should get Mrs. Thrifty to *choose* to undertake the whole reduction.

Two types of policies would get Mrs. Thrifty to undertake at least the largest share of the reduction, and economists generally favour these alternative policies if they are administratively feasible. One is to create a tax incentive to achieve the desired reduction; the other is to create a type of property right embodied in a permit or certificate and to allow individuals to trade these property rights freely. Let's consider each separately.

Tax Incentives to Conserve Let's say that the government imposes a 50¢ per litre tax on gasoline consumption. This would be an example of a **tax incentive program** (a program using a tax to create incentives for individuals to structure their activities in a way that is consistent with the desired ends). Since Mrs. Thrifty can almost costlessly reduce her gasoline consumption, she will likely respond to the tax by reducing gasoline consumption by, say, 2.75 litres. She pays only $3.63 in tax but undertakes most of the conservation. Since Mr. Big finds it very costly to reduce his consumption of gasoline, he will likely respond by reducing gasoline consumption by very little—say by .25 litres. He pays $9.88 in tax but does little of the conservation.

In this example, the tax has achieved the desired end in a more efficient manner than the regulatory solution would—the person for whom the reduction is least costly cuts consumption the most. Why? Because the incentive to reduce is embodied in the price, and individuals are forced to choose how much to change their consumption. The solution also has a significant element of fairness about it. The person who conserves the most pays the least tax.

Economists and Direct Regulation

3 Economists are likely to oppose direct regulation because it does not achieve the desired end as efficiently and as fairly as possible.

Direct regulation Program in which the amount of a resource people are allowed to use is directly limited by the government.

Efficiently Achieving a desired goal at the lowest possible cost in total resources, without consideration as to who pays those costs.

Externalities Results of a decision that are not taken into account by the decision maker.

Market incentive program Program that makes the price of a resource reflect a negative externality.

Inefficient More costly than necessary.

Tax incentive program Any program in which a tax is used to create incentives for individuals to structure their activities in a way that is consistent with particular desired ends.

Marketable certificate program A program that formalizes rights by issuing certificates and allowing trading of those rights.

Marketable Certificates and Conservation A second method of incorporating the incentive into the individual's decision is a **marketable certificate program** (a program requiring everyone to get certification that they have reduced total consumption—not necessarily their own individual consumption—by a specified amount, say 1.5 litres). Such a program would be close to the regulatory solution but it involves a major difference. If individuals choose to reduce consumption by more than the required amount, they will be given a marketable certificate which they can sell to someone who has chosen to reduce consumption by less than that amount. By buying that certificate, the person who has not personally reduced consumption by the 1.5 litres will have met the program's requirements. Let's see how the program would work with Mr. Big and Mrs. Thrifty.

In our example, Mr. Big finds it very costly to reduce consumption while Mrs. Thrifty finds it easy. So we can expect that Mr. Big won't reduce consumption much and will instead buy certificates from Mrs. Thrifty, who will choose to undertake significant reduction in her consumption in order to generate the certificates, assuming she can sell them to Mr. Big for a high enough price to make that reduction worth her while. So, as was the case in the tax incentive program, Mrs. Thrifty undertakes most of the conservation, but she reaps a financial benefit for doing so.

Obviously there are enormous questions about administrative feasibility of these types of proposals, but what's important to understand here is not the specifics of the proposals, but instead, the way in which the economists' policies are *more efficient* than the regulatory policy. As we stated before, *more efficient* means *less costly* in terms of resources, with no consideration given to the question of who is bearing those costs. Incorporating the incentive into a price and then letting individuals choose how to respond to that incentive lets those who find it least costly undertake most of the adjustment.

More and more, governments are exploring economists' policies for solving problems. Sin taxes (discussed in an earlier chapter) are an example of the tax incentive approach. Marketable pollution rights discussed in the accompanying box are an example of the marketable certificate approach. You can probably see more examples discussed in the news.

Optimal policy Policy whose marginal cost equals its marginal benefit.

The Optimal Amount of Pollution An **optimal policy** is one in which the marginal cost of undertaking the policy equals the marginal benefit of that policy. If a policy isn't optimal (that is, the marginal cost exceeds the marginal benefit or the marginal benefit exceeds the marginal cost), resources are being wasted because the savings from a reduction of expenditures on a program will be worth more than the gains that would be lost from reducing the program, or the benefit from spending more on a program will be worth more than the cost of expanding the program.

Let's consider an example of this latter case. Say the marginal benefit of a program significantly exceeds its marginal cost. That would seem good. But that would mean that we could expand the program by decreasing some other program or activity whose marginal benefit doesn't exceed its marginal cost, with a net gain in benefits to society. To spend too little on a beneficial program is as suboptimal as spending too much on a nonbeneficial program.

4 If a policy isn't optimal, resources are being wasted because the savings from reduction of expenditures on a program will be worth more than the gains that will be lost from reducing the program.

This concept of optimality carries over to economists' view of most problems. For example, some environmentalists would like to completely rid the economy of pollution. Most economists believe that doing so is costly and that since it's costly, one would want to take into account those costs. That means that society should reduce pollution only to the point where the marginal cost of reducing pollution equals the marginal benefit. That amount of pollution at which the marginal benefit of reducing pollution equals the marginal cost is called the **optimal level of pollution.** To reduce pollution below that level would make society as a whole worse off.

Optimal level of pollution Amount of pollution at which the marginal benefit of reducing pollution equals the marginal cost.

Economists Are Dubious about Voluntary Solutions

A second point upon which economists often differ from laypeople is in their view of the effectiveness of voluntary solutions. Say that one has decided that energy reduc-

ADDED DIMENSION

MARKETABLE PERMITS FOR POLLUTION

Marketable permits are being used more and more to deal with environmental issues. In many areas of North America, air quality permits are required of firms before they may begin production. The only way a new firm may start production is if it buys permits from existing firms, which are allowed to sell permits only if they decrease air pollution by the amount of the permit.

Another example of the use of marketable permits is a program instituted in California to deal with a drought. The only way a construction firm is allowed to build a new house is if it reduces existing water usage by a specific amount. To do this, the firm goes around to existing home owners, offering to put in water-saving devices for free. In some areas, more than 60 percent of the existing homes have accepted these water-saving devices, which were paid for by the construction firms and hence, indirectly, by the new home buyers.

tion is a desired goal. Often the first policy presented to achieve the desired end is the voluntary one: ask everyone to save energy, leaving individuals free to choose whether to save or not. Since it involves free choice, economists don't oppose this solution, but they often do question whether it will work in a large group.

To see why, let's consider Mr. Big and Mrs. Thrifty again. Say the government simply asks them to reduce their consumption voluntarily. Let's say that Mrs. Thrifty has a social conscience and undertakes most of the reduction while Mr. Big has no social conscience and does not reduce consumption significantly. Then it seems that this is a reasonably efficient solution. But what if the costs were reversed and Mr. Big had the low cost of reduction and Mrs. Thrifty had the high cost? Then the voluntary solution would not be so efficient.

5 Economists believe that a small number of free riders will undermine the social consciousness of many in the society and that eventually a voluntary policy will fail.

The potential lack of efficiency is not the main reason economists generally are dubious about voluntary solutions. After all, when people do something voluntarily, they are choosing to do it, and, assuming they are rational, it must make them better off or they wouldn't choose to do it. So one could argue that even in the case where Mrs. Thrifty has a high cost of reduction *and* voluntarily undertakes most of the reduction, she also has a high benefit from reducing her consumption, so the person who is undertaking the reduction is getting the benefit.

Within the economists' model of rational decision makers, the preceding reasoning is correct, but most economists are quite willing to admit that this model of rational decision makers is insufficient to capture people's complex motives and psychology. Most economists fully recognize that people have a social conscience in varying degrees and do things for the good of society as well as for their own good. However, economists point out that a person's social conscience and willingness to do things for the good of society generally depend on that person's belief that others will also be helping.

Free rider Person who participates in something for free because others have paid for it.

If a socially conscious person comes to believe a large number of other people won't contribute, he or she will often lose that social conscience: Why should I do what's good for society if others won't? This is an example of the **free rider problem** (individuals' unwillingness to share in the cost of a public good) which economists believe will often limit, and eventually undermine, social actions based on voluntary contributions. The free rider problem and its likely effect on social consciousness are the most important reasons why economists are sceptical of voluntary solutions. They believe a small number of free riders will undermine the social consciousness of many in the society and that eventually the voluntary policy will fail.

There are exceptions. During times of war and of extreme crisis, voluntary programs are often successful. For example, upon the advice of economists, during World War II the war effort was in part financed through successful voluntary programs. But for other social problems that are long run and that involve individuals accepting significant changes in their actions, generally the results of voluntary programs haven't been positive. Economists don't oppose such voluntary programs; they simply don't have much faith in them.

How to Pay for Conservation

A third way in which economists' approach to environmental policy differs from environmentalists' approach is in how to pay for any environmental program. Most environmentalists see taxes only as a way to collect the money to pay for an environmental program. Economists see taxes and other policies to affect prices as a central part of the program. In fact, for an economist the incentive embodied in the price is the single most important part of a policy.

Let's consider what this difference means. Say that the problem is too much pollution. Immediately, an economist's training directs him or her to look at the price of polluting and how that price can be raised. If there is too much use of carbon fuel, an economist immediately looks at the price of carbon fuel and how it can be raised.

Moreover, as we discussed, the economist, in deciding whether there's a problem, looks at the price and tries to reason out whether there's an externality that makes the price too low. In many cases the externality is easy to find. For example, when people pollute they don't pay for the cost of that pollution, so there is an argument that pollution is an externality and the price of polluting is too low. If there is no such externality argument, then an economist will likely conclude that there is no problem.

6 If a program requires people to pay a price that reflects the cost of an externality, it will be in their interest to change their behaviour until marginal social benefits equal marginal social costs.

In most environmental issues, it is relatively easy to conclude that there is a negative externality. Thus, economists often agree with environmentalists: There is a social environmental problem that the current market structure doesn't solve. But the answer to that problem for an economist is seldom direct regulation nor is it voluntary conservation paid for by some type of tax. Rather the economist's answer is *to find a program that makes the price people pay reflect the cost of the externality.*

A CASE STUDY: A MANDATORY RECYCLING PROGRAM

Many examples presented in this book concern the federal government and national problems. While many of the environmental issues are national and even international—such as ozone depletion and global warming—others are local.

In the remainder of this chapter we consider a local case—one you might read about in a small-town paper. That case is a mandatory recycling program instituted by a small town. We'll consider the chosen policies and some alternative policies an economically trained environmentalist might have suggested.

The case begins with trash. It seems that the people of this province were generating more trash than the existing landfills could handle. This wasn't the result of a sudden decrease in the amount of land. Rather, as people became more environmentally conscious, their concerns about the potential polluting effects of landfills increased and landfills became much more regulated. In fact, they became unacceptable to most neighbourhoods. **NIMBY** (**N**ot **I**n **M**y **B**ack **Y**ard) became the political "in" word.

NIMBY A short way to express "Not In My Back Yard" when a community objects to a proposed development in its neighbourhood.

It was decided that something must be done to reduce the amount of trash, and many communities instituted recycling programs. This is the story of the path one community followed.

The first problem they had was setting up the administrative apparatus to plan and organize the recycling program. What area would it cover? The decision: A recycling coordinator was appointed, and a regional solid waste management area was established for the community and the surrounding villages. Within that regional area, the largest town was selected for an initial recycling program.

The largest town, which we'll call Big Town (population 8,293), then appointed its own part-time recycling coordinator, a recent graduate of a local college who had majored in political science and was a strong environmentalist. Working with town planners, Big Town's recycling coordinator designed the program. Her first decision was that the plan would be mandatory. It was felt that a voluntary program wouldn't achieve anywhere near the amount of desired recycling. Big Town then enacted an ordinance making the recycling of certain items mandatory for all residents.

The second decision she had to make was what would be recycled. What was there a market for? Likely candidates included certain plastics, newspapers and magazines, glass, metal containers, and corrugated boxes. Unfortunately, upon checking the second-hand market she found that the price that could be obtained for selling most of these recycled items was very low, and that no regional market existed at all for magazines and corrugated boxes. Moreover, recycling firms would take the items only if they were "uncontaminated," which meant that not only would paper have to be separated from plastic but that various types of plastic and various types of paper would have to be subdivided. For example, one could not simply recycle "paper." One would have to separate at least four different types: newspaper, glossy magazines and catalogues, coloured stationery, and white stationery. For another example, only a few of the many kinds of plastic would be acceptable to recycling firms, and it would be costly to determine which types were recyclable and which were not. All this sorting would add enormously to the cost of recycling. In short, the cost of sorting trash would be so high that it would far exceed the payment the town would receive from recycling firms.

This led to a third decision: that householders would have to separate their trash themselves. This, in turn, meant that ordinary garbage trucks could not pick up the trash because the separated trash would have to be placed in individual compartments in the truck, and ordinary trucks aren't built that way. Therefore special new trucks had to be bought at a cost of about $80,000 per truck. Because no trash collection firm was willing to buy such trucks, Big Town had to find some way to pay for the trucks if there was to be any recycling.

The job of collecting recycled trash was put out to bid. Only one local trash collector was willing to take on the job. Not surprisingly, that company won the bid.

The final agreement was that this company would collect the separated trash once every two weeks and would be paid a $4 monthly pickup fee by every household, regardless of whether the household generated any recyclable trash. Big Town would borrow the money to buy the truck for the collector, and the collector would pay the town for its use (in instalments).

This $4 per month recycling fee was in addition to the fees that people were already paying private companies to pick up their trash. So at the initiation of the recycling program, people were faced with two trash fees: one for the regular trash and one for the separated trash.

Since there were about 2,600 households, this fee meant that the firm received about $10,400 per month (about $125,000 per year). From that it had to repay Big Town for the truck, pay for the labour to pick up the recycled items, and get rid of the recyclable items. (The administrative cost of the program, including the Big Town coordinator's salary, also had to be paid for. This cost was incorporated in the property tax rate payable to the town.)

The remaining problem was compliance—how to enforce the requirement that people recycle. This was done by providing a fine of up to $1,000 for each failure to recycle. Thus, households that put recyclable material in the regular trash instead of the separated trash risked a heavy fine. The final design of the program was as follows:

1. Every residential building had to separate its trash according to rules published by the Big Town coordinator.
2. Each household was provided with a blue plastic box into which it would sort its recyclable trash. The householder then had to carry the recyclable trash to curbside before 6 a.m. on pickup day. Pickup was once every two weeks, with the exact day depending on the neighbourhood.
3. The recycling trash collector inspected each bin and left behind any items that didn't fit the rules. For example, only plastic bottles whose bottoms bore a raised symbol including the number 2 were acceptable. If items were rejected, the collector left a notice stating the reason.
4. The recycling collector kept records of people who were not putting out the blue bins so that the town could make investigations and impose any fines that appeared justified.
5. Householders had to pay a flat $4 a month to the recycling trash collector, whether they had many, few, or no recyclable items. They could obtain any number of additional blue bins they needed, the only limitation being that

ADDED DIMENSION

THE GYP CHIPPER: THE DECISION TO RECYCLE

The *Eight-Penny News,* a newspaper for light contractors, ran an article about the Gyp Chipper—a 500-pound, 4′ × 4′ machine that "eats wallboard at the rate of 10,000 pounds an hour and costs $8,000." Wallboard (also called *plasterboard*) is the covering on most walls in houses, and when any remodelling is done the old wallboard needs to be discarded. How much is discarded? Approximately 3 million tonnes a year.

The article was written for contractors. It addressed the issue of whether it would be worthwhile to buy the machine and whether recycling wallboard would be in the interest of the construction tradespeople, called *drywallers,* who worked with wallboard. The bottom line of the article was that at "$60 [a tonne] tippage fee (the landfill cost), it probably wasn't in their interest to recycle, but at $100 or $200 [a tonne] it would be relatively easy to convince drywallers that recycling beats throwing away whole truckloads of wallboard."

they had to pay $5 for each additional one. (The first bin was free of charge because funds to pay for these had been provided by a local civic organization.)

6. It was up to the recycling collector to dispose of what was collected. If it could sell the items, it could keep the money.

The initiation of the program brought significant complaints from various groups. One group was composed of competing trash collectors whose customers were generating less trash and were therefore opting to save money by requesting fewer collections. These competing collectors were also losing business to the collector who won the bid to pick up the separated trash. The winning collector had offered a discount to the customers who also hired this company to pick up their regular trash, giving people an incentive to switch to this company.

Another group complaining about the program were residents of households who generated almost no recyclable trash yet had to pay for its collection. There were documented instances of elderly women who put out nothing but one tin can in two weeks. A third group who complained were apartment house landlords who were responsible for paying the monthly fee and/or fines but who could not force their tenants into individual compliance. A final group who complained were civil libertarians who claimed that it was illegal to search people's regular trash to be sure no recyclable items were being put into it.

Despite the complaints, the program was considered successful by most citizens. Compliance was high (about 95 percent of households), and total trash going into the landfill was reduced by one-fifth—2,000 tonnes out of a total annual trash generation of about 10,000 tonnes. In the view of the environmentally conscious organizers of the program, at least the people of Big Town were doing something to deal with the environmental problem, and that made the program successful.

An Economist's Cost/Benefit View of the Program

This view of the program's success wouldn't be shared by all. Specifically, many economists, even ones who strongly support environmental issues, would have a number of problems with it.

The first problem concerns whether a recycling program made sense at the time it was instituted. Recycled items sold for anywhere from $10 to $70 a tonne delivered to the recycling plant. Unfortunately, there were no such plants nearby. Essentially, the delivery costs, even after the items were separated, roughly equalled the value of the recycled material! This rough equality of costs presents a major problem to an economist. The first question any economist asks about a program is whether program costs exceed the benefits. Since here the delivered value of the recycled material is essentially zero, there's a significant concern about the benefit of recycling.

Deciding costs and benefits necessarily involves judgement. For example, in the publicity literature the recycling program distributed, the organizers stated that program costs were covered by the saved tipping fees (fees charged by the landfill). But for individuals, this was questionable, since the recycling program cost them $48 per year per household in direct payments but, for most people, did not reduce their trash costs significantly. Moreover, some administrative costs were part of the general town budget and not separable, so one couldn't attribute the proper amount to the recycling program. What makes it hard to come to any definite conclusion about these direct costs is that trash removal fees were rising anyhow, and the appropriate comparison is how much they would have been otherwise. So even for "direct costs" there is ambiguity.

But there is even more ambiguity in costs since for economists the comparison of direct costs and benefits is not sufficient. Because of the way the program was set up, many program costs were passed on to individuals who have to separate their trash and spend time determining what goes where. Although these costs involve no direct payment, they are included in **opportunity costs** (the costs of forgone resources). These opportunity costs of the time it takes to separate the trash do not show up when officials calculate the cost of the program, but they are still costs.

Opportunity cost The benefit forgone, or the cost, of the best alternative to the activity you've chosen. In economic reasoning, the cost is less than the benefit of what you've chosen.

If we assume that it takes an hour per week for a household to separate its trash, then each household spends a total of 52 hours a year separating trash. How should that time be valued? The time should be valued at its opportunity cost, but that opportunity cost isn't directly measurable. Some people dislike separating trash, so they would place a high opportunity cost on their time. Others might enjoy it (they are contributing to recycling); for them, the opportunity cost is zero. In fact, for them, taking part in the program can be seen as a benefit.

How does it all net out? It would take an enormous study to figure that out, and even that study probably would not come to a conclusive result. But let us say for the sake of argument that the study concluded that the appropriate value was \$2 per hour. Using this number, we arrive at a cost of \$104 per year (52 × \$2 = \$104). Thus, the yearly cost of the recycling program would be \$152 (\$48 to the collector and \$104 in householder's time) per household. The administrative costs in the first year were approximately \$20,000. There are about 2,600 households in the town, so, given these assumptions, the yearly cost of mandatory recycling is (\$152 × 2,600) + \$20,000 = \$395,200 + \$20,000 =\$415,200.

For this yearly expense, approximately 2,000 tonnes of trash is processed through the recycling program each year. Since the landfill cost of 2,000 tonnes of trash is approximately \$118,880 (\$59.44 per tonne for the town in our case study), this suggests that, if that landfill cost is the appropriate cost, the costs of this program significantly exceed the benefits. Of course, assuming the landfill cost is the appropriate cost is a big *if.* Supporters of the program see landfills as much more expensive than the actual costs, which, if true, would increase the benefits of recycling significantly.

There are also other possible benefits. For example, one could argue that separating trash is creating an environmentally aware community and is building environmentally sound habits into the population. Therefore, the argument would run, the program has significant positive external effects which should be considered.

As you can see, cost/benefit studies aren't conclusive, especially when done in a way as cursory as this one. But even a much more thorough study still wouldn't be definitive; it would reflect the assumptions put in.

Despite the ambiguity, as cost/benefit studies go, this one isn't highly favourable to the program unless one is willing to make some strong assumptions about the program's external benefits and about the value of people's time. But if these external benefits exist—if the social and landfill costs significantly exceed the actual costs paid—then for an economist the natural solution is not mandatory recycling, but is, instead, figuring out a way to get the private costs of the landfill to equal their social costs.

How would an economist handle the problem? That's unclear, but what is clear is that an economist would look much more carefully into costs and would try to build price incentives into the program. For example, if the landfill costs are only \$59.44 per tonne, then the entire program is called into question; but if the landfill costs were \$250 per tonne, the program would make sense since the savings on 2,000 tonnes would then be \$500,000, not \$118,880.

ADDED DIMENSION

NIMBY AND THE SUPPLY OF AND DEMAND FOR LANDFILLS

If the price is perfectly flexible, shortages can't exist. For an economist, the term *shortage* conveys a situation in which the price cannot rise to a level to equate the quantity supplied and the quantity demanded. Below, we consider how a shortage of landfills can occur.

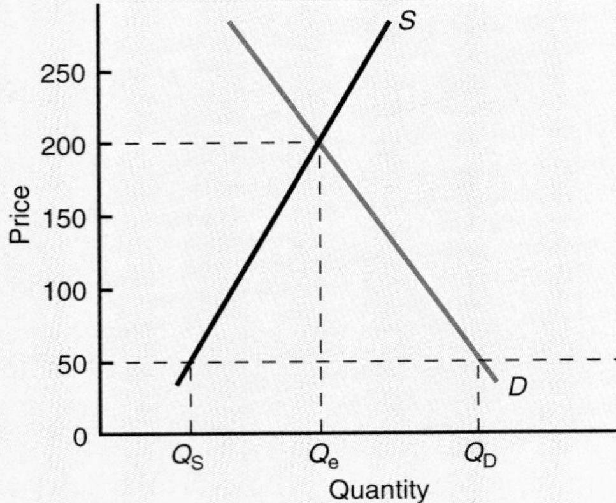

As we've drawn it, you can see that at $50 per tonne of trash dumped, the quantity of landfills demanded significantly exceeds the quantity of landfills supplied, but at $200 per tonne of trash dumped (with a large portion of that going to the town that allows the landfill), the supply and demand are equal. Why? Because the higher cost of getting rid of trash reduces the amount of trash and hence lowers the need for landfills and gets many more areas to be willing to accept landfills. Thus, supply and demand analysis suggests that NIMBY is not a necessary state of the world; it is simply a state that is characterized by too low a price of landfills and waste disposal.

In the 1980s there were dire predictions of a severe shortage of landfills. Despite that, in the 1990s, the issue, ironically, has been a shortage of waste. Many landfill owners have been trying to increase the amount of waste coming into their landfills, often by offering cut-rate prices for dumping. The reasons for this turnaround are complicated. One reason is that some of the landfills expect to be shut down and want to make money while they still can. Another reason is that some are imposing external costs on their neighbours without being concerned about these costs. A third is the success of recycling operations, and a fourth is that there never was a severe shortage. But whatever the reasons, even at existing waste-disposal prices, the predicted severe shortage of landfills that played a significant role in beginning the recycling movement has not materialized.

To decide whether there are significant external effects, an economist would ask whether landfill costs are for some reason not being determined by market pressures, or whether landfills create an externality that is not being taken into account in the price of the landfill. If either of those is the case, an economist would look for a program that would incorporate the externality into the price.

Perhaps a preferable program would be to push landfill prices up to a price that included the externality. Big Town's recycling program does not incorporate the price of the externality into the price the consumer pays. The Big Town program is financed with a flat $4 fee per month for every household. That flat fee is paid regardless of how much or how little recycling the household does. Thus, the fee provides no price incentive for recycling or for refraining from using the resources in the first place.

Now it's quite clear that one of the main pressures for recycling has been the decrease in the number of areas willing to accept landfills. But in that search for landfills, no one explored the possibility of allowing the price of landfills to rise by almost 300 percent and seeing how many areas might be willing to accept environmentally sound landfills at that much higher price.

It's likely that if areas were to receive large payments to accept a landfill voluntarily, as opposed to the landfill site being administratively chosen, many more areas would be willing to accept landfills. True, the cost of landfills would be higher, but that higher cost would create stronger incentives to recycle. Individuals would choose

Until recently landfills were the primary means of waste disposal in Canada and the United States. *© Jim Sculley/The Image Works.*

to recycle, not be forced to recycle by the threat of a fine. Thus, economists would look much more carefully at a policy that would raise the landfill cost to a level where the NIMBY pressure would be much weaker than it currently is.

Right now, most communities with landfills get nothing or only a minimal fee when other communities dispose of their trash in the landfill. Suppose a community with no landfill were to be charged \$250 per tonne of landfill accepted, with \$200 of that fee going to the community that is willing to have a landfill within its borders. At \$250 per tonne of landfill accepted, communities that were willing to have a landfill facility could fund their services—such as schools, police, fire, streets, and street lights—even as they lowered or even eliminated their property taxes. Since a \$250 landfill fee was necessary for the benefits of the mandatory recycling program to exceed the costs, if the market-determined landfill prices did not rise to that level, then an economist would seriously consider whether a mandatory recycling program made economic sense at this time.

The Economist's Perspective on Environmental Problems

A second way in which an economist environmentalist's solution would likely differ from a noneconomist environmentalist's solution is that the economist would look at the problem from a broader perspective. He or she would likely say that environmentally sound recycling is only part of the issue; the real issue is the total amount of trash generated.

For example, say that total trash were reduced by 20 percent through lower consumption of items that create trash rather than through recycling. Wouldn't that achieve the same end? Using such reasoning, an economist is likely to argue that the problem shouldn't be seen as a problem of recycling, but as a problem of trash generation. Why is trash generation the problem? Because when individuals buy goods, they do not pay the cost of disposing of those goods.

To see why this is the approach to which economists are directed, think back to our discussion of how economists view problems. They look for a reason why individual decisions might involve an externality (a result of a decision that's not taken into account by the decision maker). If there's an externality of too much trash, it is that people are not taking into account the cost of getting rid of products when they make decisions about buying the products. Thus, the externality view focuses the analysis on trash generation and not on recycling because recycling is only one of many methods to reduce the amount of trash.

What's the economist's answer to this problem? Since trash generation involves an externality, the answer is that the externality's cost must be integrated into the good's initial price. Doing so will give people incentive to create less trash by seeing to it that the price of those goods that create trash includes the cost of getting rid of that trash. Thus, rather than support a mandatory recycling program, an economist would be more likely to support (1) a "trash tax" in which the price of items sold must include the cost of disposing of the items, or (2) a "disposal requirement" on goods.

Let's consider how these economists' policies might work in regard to newspapers (a significant component of trash). We first look at the trash tax.

A Trash Tax A trash tax of, say, 10¢ per kilogram of newspaper would increase the price of newspapers significantly, causing people to demand fewer newspapers and/or publishers to print fewer pages in their newspapers. Here the reduction in trash wouldn't take place through recycling; it would take place through a reduction in newspapers demanded and/or newspaper pages supplied. This approach has an added benefit. The tax money that is generated could then be used to fund environmental programs that create environmental consciousness.

A Disposal Requirement Alternatively, the government could simply pass a law requiring publishers to cut the volume of newspapers they generate by 10 percent. In other words, newspaper publishers would be responsible for ensuring that, in total, 10 percent of their papers are either recycled or eliminated. The program would allow some newspapers to exceed a 10 percent reduction. Such newspaper firms would be given disposal certificates for the tonnage they saved in excess of 10 percent. These certificates would be marketable, which means that the firms could sell the certificates to other firms who reduced their trash generation by less than 10 percent.

Under this program, firms would have two ways to meet the law's requirements. They could either directly meet the requirement by reducing the trash they generate by 10 percent, or they could indirectly meet the requirement by buying the necessary disposal certificates from other firms that had reduced their trash generation by more than 10 percent.

This program would give newspapers a strong incentive to see that their newspapers are recycled directly. It might cause newspaper carriers to collect old newspapers when they delivered new ones. This program would also stimulate the development of a computer newspaper that would involve no paper whatsoever. People would simply wake up in the morning and flip on their computer screen or TV to get the latest headlines and the accompanying stories.

An Update on the Program and a Final Word

Three years after its implementation, Big Town's program was considered a success; Big Town's coordinator was promoted to supervise the entire multi-town region, and mandatory recycling was adopted in the entire region. In the meantime, the prices of recyclables fell even lower than they were when the Big Town program started, and there were reports of recycling centres sending their recycled material to landfills as stockpiles of those materials became larger and larger.

The region built a new recycling and trash transfer station, paid for by the taxpayers through the issuance of long-term bonds, the cost of which was incorporated into trash collection fees. It also began selling its trash for $47 a tonne to a distant incinerator that was actively seeking trash. Trash collection fees in the Big Town region went up more than 30 percent. While this was happening, the supposed landfill crisis in the province abated, and in the mid-1990s many landfills were competing to get trash.

Within the environment of the 1990s, it was unclear what role recycling was playing. Advocates who recognized and understood the cost/benefit analysis of recycling argued that, despite its poor current cost/benefit showing, recycling was changing people's habits, making them environmentally aware, and creating economies of scale that would eventually mean that recycling would make economic sense. Economic cynics argued that it was simply a program to make environmental yuppies feel good—to give them the sense that they were doing something about the environment—without significantly changing their lifestyles, and without having a significant impact on the environment.

Obviously there's much more to be discussed about economists' approach to recycling and various alternative programs, but this brief discussion should give you a sense of economists' approach and convince you that *to be an economist does not mean that one cannot be an environmentalist.* But it should also give you a sense that an environmentalist economist's approach to an environmental problem could differ significantly from the approach of an environmentalist untrained in economics.

CONCLUSION

Environmental issues are enormously complicated and require intense study before one can come up with a viable way of dealing with the problems. There are major difficulties with the economists' solutions presented here. We did not discuss those difficulties because (1) it would have made the chapter too long, and (2) it would have taken some of the sharp edge off the arguments—and we wanted the arguments to cut deeply and make you think.

The point of this chapter is not to convince you to believe one thing or another about environmental policy—the issues are too complicated for that. The point is simply to make sure you recognize how complicated they are. In elementary school and high school (judging from what our children learn), environmental issues are often presented as black and white—as positions taken by (1) the mean nasty businesspeople, or (2) the good friendly environmentalists. That characterization is far too simplistic. It does not consider the trade-offs that inevitably exist, and the difficulty of making judgements on limited data and imperfect statistics.

Economists are often seen by many laypeople as opposed to environmentalism. That isn't the case. There's no fundamental difference between environmentalists and economists in terms of beliefs or concerns about the environment. What difference there is involves initial approach. An environmental economist's initial thoughts are likely to focus on market incentives, while an environmentalist untrained in economics is likely to distrust the market's effectiveness and therefore favour regulatory approaches.

7 Economists' reasoning involves a general approach to all problems in which a cost/benefit analysis is taken and the program with the least cost is chosen.

To emphasize how economic training can affect one's view of environmental problems, this chapter's approach has been to contrast the two views, showing the advantages of the economists' approach and the disadvantages of the regulatory approaches. But the decision to write the chapter this way creates a problem in making some people believe that the economic answer is obviously the correct answer. It isn't.

The economists' approach, like the regulatory environmentalists' approach, has disadvantages. For example, if landfill prices rose significantly, people would likely burn their own trash or dump it illegally. Similarly, a trash tax would involve significant administrative problems. So you should not come away from this chapter believing that economics has all the answers, or even that economic approaches are preferable to regulatory approaches (although we believe that the economic approach is preferable). Instead we'd like you to come away from this chapter believing that economic approaches to environmental issues are worth considering, and that it is important to keep an open mind in approaching environmental problems.

CHAPTER SUMMARY

- There is no contradiction in being both an economist and an environmentalist, but an economist environmentalist's approach to solving environmental problems often differs from a lay environmentalist's approach.
- Economists often question "statistical proof" that laypeople accept without question.
- Economists generally prefer incentive-based programs over direct regulatory programs because incentive-based programs are more efficient.
- An optimal policy is one in which the marginal cost of undertaking the policy equals its marginal benefit.
- Economists are often dubious about voluntary solutions.
- NIMBY suggests that some prices are not free to fluctuate.
- All policies have problems and advantages. It is important to consider both before deciding on a policy.

KEY TERMS

causation (393)
correlation (393)
corroboration (393)
direct regulation (399)
efficiently (399)
externality (399)
free rider problem (401)
global warming theory (393)
Hotelling's rule (398)
inefficient (399)
market incentive program (399)
marketable certificate program (400)
National Energy Program (398)
NIMBY (402)
opportunity costs (405)
optimal level of pollution (400)
optimal policy (400)
proven reserves (395)
tax incentive program (399)

QUESTIONS FOR THOUGHT AND REVIEW

The number after each question represents the estimated degree of critical thinking required. (1 = almost none; 10 = deep thought.)

1. Many environmentalists agree that the data supporting the global warming theory are questionable but argue that, if the theory is correct, unless we start doing something about global warming now, it will be too late to do anything about it. Would you expect an economist to accept this argument? Why or why not? *(7)*
2. A friend tells you that by historical standards the price of gold is low, so now is a great time to buy gold. Would you agree? Why or why not? *(5)*
3. Explain why a market incentive program is more efficient than a direct regulatory program. *(6)*
4. It is sometimes said that there is a trade-off between fairness and efficiency. Explain one way in which that is true and one way in which it is not true. *(8)*
5. How would an economist likely respond to the statement "There is no such thing as acceptable pollution"? *(5)*
6. State two reasons why an economist generally opposes a solution based upon voluntary action that is not in people's self-interest. *(4)*
7. Say that the government placed a high tax on the use of oil. Would that significantly reduce the amount of pollution coming from the use of oil? Why or why not? *(4)*
8. Say that the government placed a high tax on the use of oil. Would that significantly reduce the total amount of pollution in the environment? *(8)*
9. If the price of landfills rose significantly, what problems do you see arising in the disposal of trash? *(7)*
10. How does your community deal with trash? What would an economist think of that method? *(9)*

PROBLEMS AND EXERCISES

1. There's a gas shortage in Gasland. You're presented with two proposals that will achieve the same level of reduction in the use of gas. Proposal A would force everybody to reduce their gas consumption by 5 percent. Proposal B would impose a 50¢ tax on the consumption of a litre of gas, which would also achieve a 5 percent reduction. Demand curves for two groups are shown below.

P
D (Group 1)
D (Group 2)
Q

   a. Show the effect of both proposals on each group.

   b. Which group would support a regulatory policy? Which would support a tax policy?

2. The marginal cost, marginal social cost, and demand for fish are represented by the curves below. Suppose that there are no restrictions on fishing.

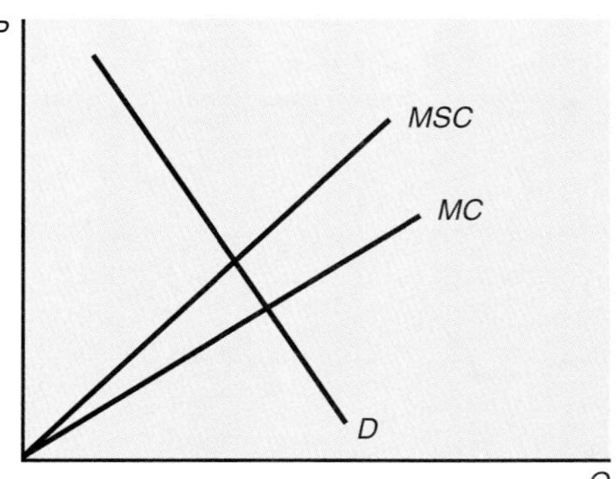

a. Assuming perfect competition, what is the catch going to be, and at what price will it be sold?

b. What are the socially efficient price and output?

c. Some sports fishers propose a ban on commercial fishing. As the community's economic advisor, you're asked to comment on it at a public forum. What do you say?

3. You are in Fredericton, watching the Fredericton Stomp—a dance homeowners do in their trash cans.

   a. What can you say about trash fees in Fredericton? Be as specific as possible.

   b. What change in fee structure might eliminate the Fredericton Stomp?

4. In *At the Hand of Man,* Raymond Bonner argues that Africa should promote hunting, charging high fees for permits to kill animals (for example, $7,500 for a permit to shoot an elephant).

   a. What are some arguments in favour of this proposal?

   b. What are some arguments against?

5. California has passed an air quality law, which requires that by 1998, 2 percent of all the cars sold in the state emit zero pollution, and that by 2003, 10 percent of all cars sold in the state meet this standard.

   a. What is the likely impact of this law in California?

   b. Can you think of any way in which this law might actually increase pollution in California rather than decrease it?

   c. How might an economist suggest modifying this law to better achieve economic efficiency?

CHAPTER

21

Growth and the Microeconomics of Developing Countries

It is always depressing to go back to Adam Smith, especially on economic development, as one realizes how little we have learned in nearly 200 years.

~Kenneth Boulding

After reading this chapter, you should be able to:

1. State some comparative statistics on rich and poor countries.
2. Define the dual economy and explain its relevance for developing countries.
3. List six problems facing developing countries.
4. Explain how the market can function in inappropriate ways when there is no well-developed public morality.
5. Explain why it is so difficult for developing countries to generate investment.
6. Summarize four debates about strategies for growth.
7. Defend the position that economic development is a complicated problem.

There are approximately 5 billion people in the world. Of these, 3.8 billion (about 75 percent) live in developing, rather than developed, countries. Per capita income in developing countries is around $700 Canadian per year; in Canada it is over $20,000.

These averages understate the differences between the poorest country and the richest. Consider the African country of Chad—definitely one of the world's poorest. Its per capita income is about $260 per year—about 1/100 of the per capita income in Canada. Moreover, income in Chad goes primarily to the rich, so Chad's poor have per capita income of significantly less than $260.

1 Seventy-five percent of the world's population lives in developing countries, with average per capita income of around $700 per year.

DEVELOPMENT: PRELIMINARY CONSIDERATIONS

Before we consider the obstacles to economic development, let's consider how a person lives on that $260 per year, as many people in the world do. To begin with, that person can't:

Go out for Big Macs.

Use Joy perfume (or any type of perfume).

Wear designer clothes.

And that person must:

Eat grain—usually rice or corn—for all meals, every day.

Mix fat from meat—not meat itself—with the grain on special occasions (maybe).

Live in one room with 9 or 10 other people.

Work hard from childhood to old age (if there is an old age). Those too old to work in the fields stay at home and care for those too young to work in the fields. (But children go out to work in the fields when they're about six years old.)

Go hungry, because no matter how many family members can work in the fields, probably the work and soil don't yield enough to provide the workers with an adequate number of calories per day.

In a poor person's household it's likely that a couple of the older children may have gone into the city to find work that pays money wages. If they were lucky and found jobs, they can send money home each month. That money may be the only cash income their family back in the fields has. The family uses the money to buy a few tools and cooking utensils.

This view of the difficult life in a developing country shows a woman washing clothes and children playing in Rio de Janeiro, Brazil. *© McGlynn/The Image Works.*

ADDED DIMENSION

WHAT TO CALL DEVELOPING COUNTRIES

In this chapter, following common usage, we call low-income countries *developing countries*. They have not always been called *developing*. In the 1950s they were called backward, but it was eventually realized that backward implied significant negative value judgements. Then these countries were called *underdeveloped,* but it was eventually realized that underdeveloped also implied significant negative value judgements. More recently they have been called *developing,* but eventually everyone will realize that *developing* implies significant negative value judgements. After all, in what sense are these countries "developing" any more than is Canada? All countries are evolving or developing countries. Many so-called developing countries have highly refined cultures which they don't want to lose; they may want to develop economically, but not at the cost of cultural change.

What should one call these countries? That remains to be seen, but whatever one calls them, bear in mind that language can conceal value judgements.

The preceding is, of course, only one among billions of different stories. Even Canadians and Europeans who are classified as poor find it hard to contemplate what life is really like in a truly poor country.

Don't Judge Society by Its Income Alone

Poor people in developing countries survive and often find pleasure in their hard lives. There are few suicides in the poorest countries. For example, in Canada the suicide rate is about 13 per 100,000 people. The U.S. suicide rate is approximately the same. In Costa Rica it's 4.9 per 100,000; in Mexico it's 1.4 per 100,000; and in Peru it's .5 per 100,000. Who has time for suicide? You're too busy surviving. There's little ambiguity and few questions about the meaning of life. Living! That's what life's all about. There's no "Mom, what am I going to do today?" You know what you're going to do: survive if you can. And survival is satisfying.

Often these economically poor societies have elaborate cultural rituals and networks of intense personal relationships that provide individuals with a deep sense of fulfilment and satisfaction.

Are people in these societies as happy as Canadians are? If your immediate answer is no, be careful to understand the difficulty of making such a judgement. The answer isn't clear-cut. For us to say, "My God! What a failure their system is!" is wrong. It's an inappropriate value judgement about the relative worth of cultures. All too often Canadians have gone into another country to try to make people better off, but have ended up making them worse off.

An economy is part and parcel of a culture. You can't judge just an economy; you must judge the entire culture. Some developing countries have cultures that, in many people's view, are preferable to ours. If one increases a country's income but takes away its culture in doing so, one may well have made its people worse off.

That said, we're ready to consider whether people in developing countries would be better off if they had more income. Most people in developing countries would definitely answer yes!

Even culturally sensitive people agree that economic growth within the context of a developing country's culture would be a good thing, if only because those countries exist simultaneously with market economies. Given market societies' expansionary tendencies, without economic growth, cultures in economically poor countries would simply be overrun and destroyed by the cultures of market societies. Their land would be taken, their agricultural patterns would be changed, their traditional means of subsistence would be destroyed, and their cultures would be obliterated. So generally the choice isn't between development and preservation of the existing culture (and its accompanying ancient ways to which the poor have adjusted). Rather, the choice is between development (with its attendant wrenching cultural transitions) and continuing poverty (with exploitation by developed countries and its attendant wrenching cultural transitions).

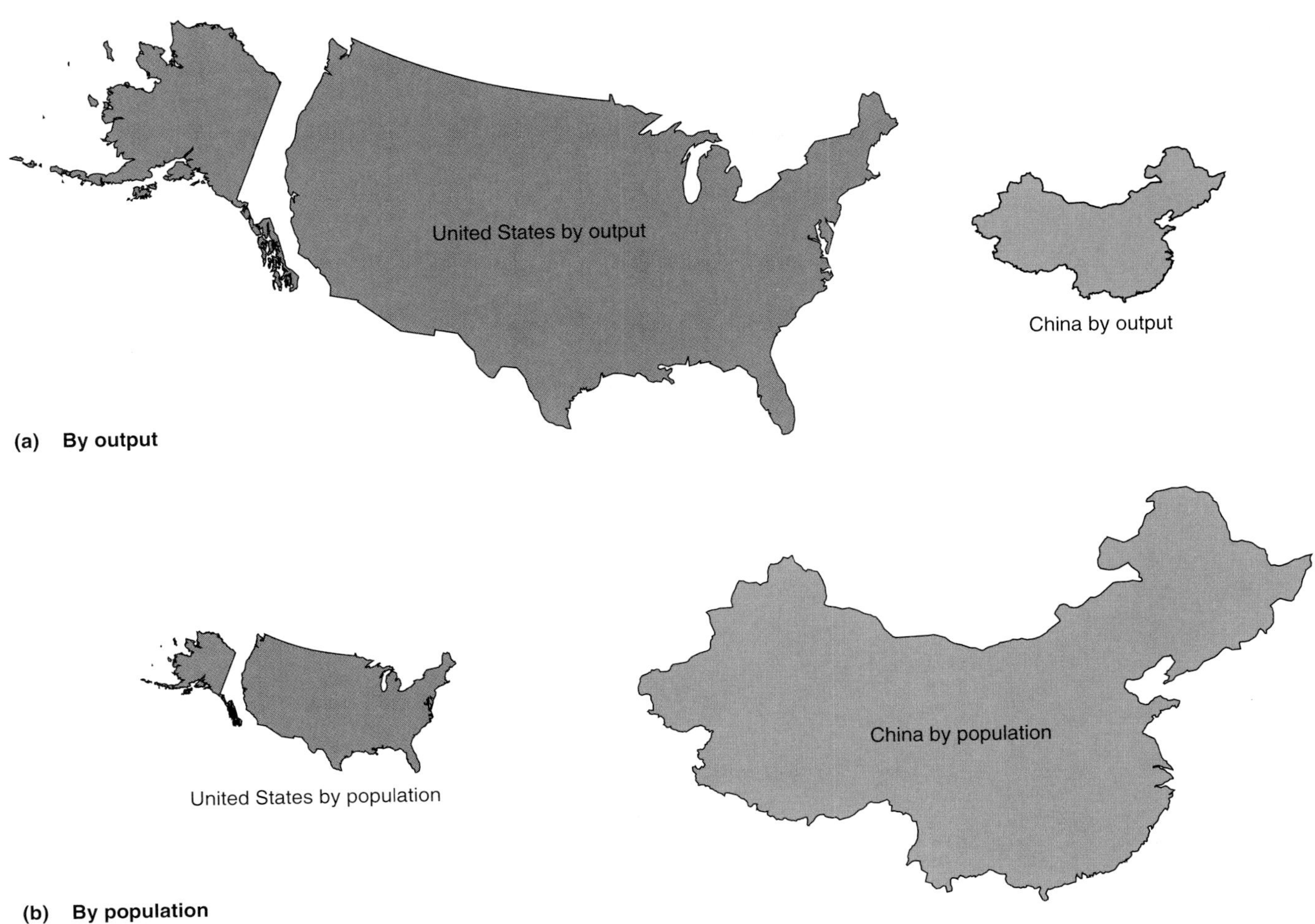

EXHIBIT 1 Comparing the United States and China by Output and Population

The areas of China and the United States are approximately equal. If, however, we were to scale their sizes in accordance with their relative outputs, as in (**a**), the United States would be shown double in size and China would be shown reduced to one fourth of its size. If we scaled their sizes in accordance with population, as in (**b**), it is China that would increase its size, more than doubling, while the size of the United States would be cut in half.

Some Comparative Statistics on Rich and Poor Nations

Exhibit 1 gives you a sense of the uneven distribution of production among one rich country and one poor country.

The low average income in poor countries has its effects on people's lives. Life expectancy is about 50 years in most very economically poor countries (compared to about 77 years in Canada and 76 in the United States). In economically poor countries most people drink contaminated water, consume about half the number of calories the World Health Organization has determined is minimal for good health, and do physical labour (often of the kind done by machine in developed countries). Exhibit 2 compares some developing countries, middle-income countries, and developed countries.

As with all statistics, care must be taken in interpreting the figures in Exhibit 2. For example, the income comparisons were all made on the basis of current exchange rates. But relative prices between rich and poor countries often differ substantially; the cost of goods relative to total income tends to be much lower for people in developing countries than for those in developed countries.

To allow for these differences, some economists have looked at the domestic purchasing power of money in various countries and have adjusted the comparisons accordingly. Rather than working with exchange rates, they compare what a specified

EXHIBIT 2 Statistics on Developing, Middle-Income, and Developed Countries

Country	Life Expectancy	Physicians per 100,000	Infant Mortality per 1,000	Percent Labour Force in Agriculture	Percent Labour Force in Industry	Illiteracy Rate	Number of Radio Receivers in Use per 1,000	Per Capita GDP (U.S. $)
Developing								
Bangladesh	53	8	108	75%	6%	65%	43	$201
Ethiopia	47	3	122	80	8	76	189	129
Haiti	57	14	86	70	8	47	47	399
Middle-Income								
Brazil	66	118	57	31	27	18	386	2,668
Iran	67	40	40	36	38	46	231	10,769
South Korea	71	83	21	36	27	4	1,001	6,483
Thailand	69	21	26	71	10	7	191	1,685
Developed								
Canada	77	224	7	5	29	3	1,029	21,623
Japan	79	33	5	11	34	1	907	26,983
Sweden	78	253	6	6	33	1	877	27,796
United States	76	250	8	4	31	1	2,118	22,219

Source: *UN Handbook of International Trade and Development Statistics,* 1993.

Purchasing power parity Method of comparing income by looking at the domestic purchasing power of money in different countries.

market basket of consumer goods will cost in various countries and use these results to compare currencies' values. This is called the **purchasing power parity** method of comparing income of countries. Making these adjustments, the World Bank found that income differences among countries are cut by half. In other words, when one uses the World Bank's purchasing power parity method of comparison, it's as if the people in developing countries had twice as much income as they had when the exchange rate method was used.

A similar adjustment can be made with the life expectancy rates. A major reason for the lower life expectancies in developing countries is their high infant mortality rates. Once children survive infancy, however, their life expectancies are much closer to those of children in developed countries. Say a country's overall life expectancy is 50 years and that 15 percent of all infants die within their first year. As a person grows older, at each birthday the person's life expectancy is higher. So if a child lives to the age of 3 years, then at that point the child has an actual life expectancy of close to 60 years, rather than 50 years.

Developing Countries Focus on Growth

Before the Industrial Revolution, when Western countries had low incomes compared to today's income in developing countries, Western economists focused on one question: What makes a society grow? By growth they meant growth of material production. It isn't surprising that the focus of the economics of developing countries is material growth: how to achieve and maintain growth in per capita income.

2 The "dual economy" refers to the tendency of developing countries to have two somewhat unrelated economies—one an internationally based economy, the other a traditional, often nonmarket, economy.

The Dual Economy The fact that the average income in a country is very low does not mean that a certain group of people in a developing country may not have incomes and lifestyles equal to, or preferable to, lifestyles in developed countries. In fact, a certain group of people in virtually every country do have such lifestyles. The income level of this group of people gives them access to Western goods, which they buy on their trips to developed countries. Given the low level of wages in their own countries, their income levels provides them with servants and "lifestyle employees" who care for their physical needs. Maids, cooks, and "housepeople" have disappeared almost entirely from Western countries, except for those employed by the very rich, but there are significant numbers of such employees in many developing countries, and even upper-middle-class families may have one or more household servants.

This bifurcation of the economy is often called the **dual economy,** one economy being an internationally based economy in which wage rates and lifestyles are the same as in developed countries, and the other economy being the traditional, often nonmarket economy. Many of the people who participate in the internationally based economic sector are what might be called "internationally mobile." They can move to some Western country if they choose. Many would not work in their own country unless its pay matched what they could earn in a developed country, and they judge themselves relative to Western standards, not the standards of the majority of citizens in their own country. It is their high income that pulls up the average income of many developing countries.

Dual economy Tendency of developing countries to have two somewhat unrelated economies—one an internationally based economy, the other a traditional, often nonmarket, economy.

The traditional economy, on the other hand, is only tangentially related to the economies in developed countries and to the international economy. It is largely domestic, and often people in it are doing today what their ancestors did hundreds of years ago. Pay in the traditional economy is generally very low; this part of the economy pulls the average income down.

The Growth Record The long-term record for most countries in achieving growth isn't good. Only a small number of countries have moved out of the "developing country" ranks. One group that has moved out is the oil-producing countries. Another group of countries, called the **Asian tigers** (for example, Taiwan, South Korea, Singapore, and Hong Kong[1]) have achieved substantial economic growth and are no longer considered developing countries by some economists. They've become middle-income countries.

Asian tigers Group of Asian countries that have achieved economic growth well above the level of other developing countries.

The Asian tigers are an exception. Considered as a group, developing countries haven't done well compared to developed countries. While from 1950 until 1990 developing countries' average overall growth rates were slightly higher than growth rates of industrial market countries, their per capita growth rates were much lower. But to catch up with developed countries, the developing countries would have to grow at a much faster rate than the developed countries.

For example, if developing countries grew 4 percent a year and developed countries grew 3 percent, after 24 years the developing countries' income would have increased 156 percent while developed countries' income would have increased 103 percent. As opposed to having 1/18 of a developed country's per capita income, a developing country, after 24 years of growth, would have improved to the point of having 1/14 of a developed country's per capita income. But even that small gain isn't occurring for many developing countries, especially those in Africa.

Geographic Grouping of Developing Countries In the 1990s, economists are moving away from grouping all developing countries together, and are separating out four geographic groupings—Asian, African, Latin American, and Middle Eastern. Because of cultural similarities, the problems of countries in each of these groupings often parallel those of others in that grouping.

As you can see in Exhibit 3, the growth rates of these groupings have diverged from one another. The Asian countries have emerged as the winners in the growth sweepstakes. As mentioned earlier, a number of the Asian countries have moved into the category of "middle-income countries." Latin American and Middle Eastern developing countries have had moderate growth—often coming in spurts—and in the first half of the 1990s, Latin American countries were in another growth spurt.

Finally come the African, especially the sub-Saharan African, countries whose growth rates have been extremely low and sometimes negative. These African growth

One of the best sources of information about development issues is the *World Development Report*, published by the World Bank.

[1] Hong Kong isn't an independent country. Since the 19th century it has been administered by Great Britain, but in 1997 it's scheduled to be returned to China, which originally owned it. However at present, economically, it behaves very much like an independent country.

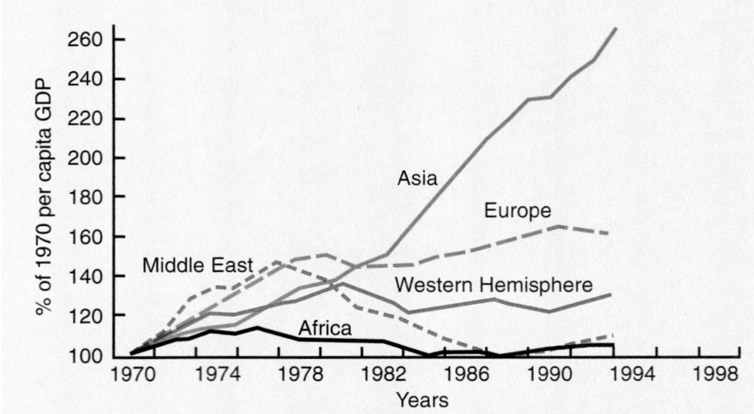

EXHIBIT 3 Growth Rates—Groupings of Countries

Since the late 1970s, African and Middle Eastern economic growth has essentially come to a halt. Only the Asian tigers have grown faster than Europe or the Western Hemisphere.

Source: *World Economic Outlook* (Washington, D.C. : IMF).

rates are more than just statistics. They represent suffering and pain. When you hear of a famine or of starvation killing thousands of people, those events will generally be taking place in an African country.

OBSTACLES TO ECONOMIC DEVELOPMENT

What stops countries from developing economically? Economists have discovered no magic potion that will make a country develop. We can't say, "Here are steps 1, 2, 3, 4. If you follow them you'll grow, but if you don't follow them you won't grow."

What makes it so hard for developing countries to devise a successful development program is that social, political, and economic problems blend into one another and cannot be considered separately. The institutional structure that we take for granted in Canada often doesn't exist in those countries. For example, economists' analysis of production assumes that a stable government exists that can enforce contracts and supply basic services. In most developing countries, that assumption can't be made. Governments are often anything but stable; overnight, a coup d'état can bring a new government into power, with a whole new system of rules under which businesses have to operate. Imagine trying to figure out a reasonable study strategy if every week you had a new teacher who emphasized different things and gave totally different types of tests from last week's teacher. Firms in developing countries face similar problems.

While economists can't say, "Here's what you have to do in order to grow," we have been able to identify some general obstacles that all developing countries seem to face. Such problems that fall within microeconomics include:

3 Six microeconomic problems facing developing countries are:
1. Political instability.
2. Corruption.
3. Lack of appropriate institutions.
4. Lack of investment.
5. Inappropriate education.
6. Overpopulation.

1. Political instability.
2. Corruption.
3. Lack of appropriate institutions.
4. Lack of investment.
5. Inappropriate education.
6. Overpopulation.

We consider each in turn.

Political Instability

A student's parents once asked one of us why their son was doing poorly in economics. The answer was that he could not read and he could hardly write. Until he could master those basics, there was no use talking about how he could better learn economics.

Roughly the same reasoning can be applied to the problem of political instability in developing countries. Unless a country achieves political stability (acceptance within a country of a stable system of government), it's not going to develop economically, no matter what it does.

All successful development strategies require the existence of a stable government. A mercantilist or a socialist development strategy requires an elaborate government presence. A market-based strategy requires a much smaller government role, but even with markets, a stable environment is needed for a market to function and for contracts to be made with confidence.

Many developing countries don't have that stability. Politically they haven't established a tradition of orderly governmental transition. Coups d'état or armed insurrections always remain possible.

One example is Rwanda, a small African country. In April of 1994, its president was killed and the entire country was engulfed in civil war. Another example of political instability in developing countries is to be found in Somalia. There, a civil war among competing groups led to famine and enormous hardship, which provoked the sympathy of the world. But attempts by the U.N. and the United States to establish a stable government by sending troops there caused as many, or more, problems than they resolved, and in 1994 the United States withdrew its troops.

The problem of political instability exists in most developing countries, but it is strongest in Africa, which, in large part, accounts for Africa's low rate of economic growth relative to that of the other geographic areas.

Even countries whose governments aren't regularly toppled face threats of overthrow, and those threats are sufficient to prevent individual economic activity. To function, an economy needs some rules—any rules—that will last.

The lack of stability is often exacerbated by social and cultural differences among groups within a country. Political boundaries often reflect arbitrary decisions made by former colonial rulers, not the traditional cultural and tribal boundaries that form the real-life divisions. The result is lack of consensus among the population as a whole as well as intertribal suspicion and even warfare.

For example, Nigeria is a federation established under British colonial rule. It comprises three ethnic regions: the northern, Hausa Fulan, region; the western, Yoruba, region; and the eastern, Ibo, region. These three regions are culturally distinct and so are in continual political and military conflict. Nigeria has experienced an endless cycle of military coups, attempts at civilian rule, and threats of secession by the numerically smaller eastern region. Had each region been allowed to remain separate, economic development might have been possible; but because the British lumped the regions together and called them a country, economic development is next to impossible.

The Influence of Political Instability on Development Do these political considerations affect economic questions? You bet. As we will discuss shortly, any development plan requires financial investment from somewhere—either external or internal. Political instability closes off both sources of investment funds.

Any serious potential investor takes political instability into account. Foreign companies considering investment in a developing country hire political specialists who analyze the degree of risk involved. Where the risk is too great, foreign companies simply don't invest.

Political instability also limits internal investment. Income distribution in many developing countries is highly skewed. There are a few very rich people and an enormous number of very poor people, while the middle class is often small.

Whatever one's view of the fairness of such income inequality, it has a potential advantage for society. Members of the wealthy elite in developing countries have income to spare, and their savings are a potential source of investment funds. But when there is political instability, that potential isn't realized. Fearing that their wealth may be taken from them, the rich often channel their investment out of their own country so that, should they need to flee a revolution, they'll still be able to live comfortably. Well-off people in developing countries provide major inflows of investment into Canada and other Western countries.

Ferdinand Marcos, former president of the Philippines, was reported to have $10 billion worth of assets scattered around the developed countries of the world. Had he invested those billions in the Philippines, he most likely would have lost all that money when he was deposed in 1986. Marcos, having placed his wealth abroad—often hiding its ownership—didn't lose it, or at least he didn't lose all of it, after being deposed. So the Philippines lost twice from Marcos's actions. First, he took money that didn't belong to him; and second, he deprived the Philippines of much-needed investment capital.

Political Instability and Unequal Distribution of Income The highly skewed distribution of income in most developing countries contributes in another way to political instability. It means that the poor majority has little vested interest in maintaining the current system. A coup? Why not? What have they got to lose? The economic prospects for many people in developing countries are so bleak that they are quite willing to join or at least support a guerilla insurgency that promises to set up a new, better system. The resulting instability makes development almost impossible.

Corruption

4 When rights to conduct business are controlled and allocated by the government, economic development can be hindered.

Bribery, graft, and corruption are ways of life in most developed countries. In Egypt it's called *baksheesh* (meaning "gift of money"); in Mexico it's called *la mordida* ("the bite"). If you want to park in a parking spot in Mexico City, you'd better pay the policeman, or your car will get a ticket. If you want to take a photograph of the monument to Rameses II in Cairo, you'd better slip the traffic officer a few loonies, or else you may get run over.

Without a well-developed institutional setting and a public morality that condemns corruption, market forces function in a variety of areas that people in developed countries would consider inappropriate. In any country the government has the right to allow imports, to allow development, to determine where you can park your car, to say whether you can take photographs of public buildings, to decide who wins a lawsuit, and so forth. In developing countries, however, those rights can be, and often are, sold. The litigant who pays the judge the most wins. How about the right to import? Want to import a new machine? That will be 20 percent of the cost, please.

Such graft and corruption quickly become institutionalized, so that all parties involved feel that they have little choice but to take part. Government officials say that graft and bribery are built into their pay structure, so unless they take bribes, they won't have enough income to live on. Businesspeople say that if they want to stay in business they have to pay bribes. Similarly, workers must bribe business in order to get a job, and labour leaders must be bribed not to cause trouble for business.

We're not claiming that such payments are wrong. Societies decide what is right and wrong; economists don't. The term *bribery* in English has a pejorative connotation. In many other languages the terms people use for this type of activity don't have such negative connotations.

But we *are* claiming that such payments—with the implied threat that failure to pay will have adverse consequences—make it more difficult for a society's economy to grow. Knowing that those payments must be made prevents many people from undertaking actions that might lead to growth. For example, a friend of ours wanted to build a group of apartments in the Bahamas, but when he discovered the payoffs he'd have to make to various people, he abandoned the whole idea.

Limiting an activity makes the right to undertake that limited activity valuable to the person doing the limiting. When bribery is an acceptable practice, it creates strong incentives to limit an ever-increasing number of activities—including many activities that could make a country grow.

Lack of Appropriate Institutions

Almost all economists agree that, to develop, a country should establish markets. Markets require the establishment of property rights—and establishing them is a difficult political process. That is the problem of a number of African countries: how to establish property rights with an undeveloped political process.

Creating markets is not enough. The markets must be meshed with the cultural and social fabric of the society. Thus, questions of economic development inevitably

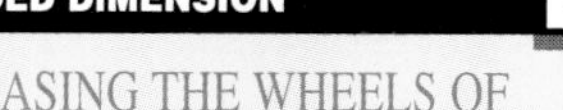

GREASING THE WHEELS OF CANADIAN COMMERCE

You might think that bribery is frowned on in Canadian business, but recent evidence suggests it pervades all sectors of the economy. A 1994 fraud survey found that kickbacks, secret commissions, and bribes made up between 4 and 13 percent of all reported frauds. That included giving gifts (lovingly referred to as *inducements*) like:

- Box tickets to games at Toronto's SkyDome.
- Two weeks in a Florida condo, with a car.
- Home renovations.
- Hockey equipment for your kids at cost.
- Airlines releasing cash to your travel agent upon receipt of your order.
- Envelopes from your wholesaler, stuffed with cash ranging from $50 to figures in the thousands, depending on your order.

Several elaborate schemes have been uncovered by the R.C.M.P., but it's hard to find corruption without a *whistle-blower.* It's not likely someone receiving kickbacks is going to have an attack of conscience, so we'll concede it's difficult to get caught with your hand in the cookie jar. That doesn't make it right. And, like telling lies, it usually catches up with you in the end.

Source: "When Gifts Become Graft: Greasing the Hand that Feeds You," *The Financial Post,* January 14, 1995, pp. 12–13.

involve much more than supply and demand. They involve broader questions about the cultural and social institutions in a society.

Let us give an example of cultural characteristics not conducive to development. Anyone who has travelled in developing countries knows that many of these countries operate on what they call "____ time," where the "____" is the name of the particular country one is in. What is meant by "____ time" is that in that country, things get done when they get done, and it is socially inappropriate to push for things to get done at specific times. Deadlines are demeaning (many students operate on "____ time").

As a self-actualizing mentality, "____ time" may be high-level mental development, but in an interdependent economic setting, "____ time" doesn't fit. Economic development requires qualities such as extreme punctuality and a strong sense of individual responsibility. People who believe their being two minutes late will make the world come to an end fit far better with a high-production country than do people who are more laid back. The need to take such cultural issues into account explains why development economics tends to be far less theoretical and far more country- and region-specific than other branches of economics.

As mentioned above, the Asian tigers have been the most successful of the developing countries. Their strategy has been a neomercantilist strategy in which the governments have played a major role in directing the economies toward establishing an export-led growth. Interest rates and currency values have been kept purposely low to encourage exports and promote growth. Governments have built the needed transportation and energy facilities, and domestic firms' home markets have been protected through a variety of nontariff and tariff barriers to imports.

There is much debate about whether the cause of the Asian tigers' success is due to their neomercantilist strategy, or has occurred despite their government-oriented strategy. Many economists believe that their cultural characteristics—hard-working, high-saving, and orientation toward trading and markets—would have led to higher growth if their governments had intervened less.

Even if the government-oriented strategy was in part responsible for their success, it is not at all clear that such a strategy can be successfully transferred to other situations since, by developing-country standards, the Asian governments are relatively stable and incorrupt.

Lack of Investment

Even if a country can overcome the political, social, and institutional constraints on development, there are also economic constraints. If a country is to grow it must somehow invest, and funds for investment must come from savings. These savings can be either brought in from abroad (as private investment or foreign government aid) or generated internally (as domestic savings). Each source of investment capital has its problems.

5 With per capita incomes of as low as $300 per year, poor people in developing countries don't have a lot left over to put into savings.

Investment Funded by Domestic Savings In order to save, a person must first have enough to live on. With per capita incomes of $300 per year, poor people in developing countries don't have a whole lot left over to put into savings. Instead you rely on your kids, if they live, to take care of you in your old age. As for the rich, the threat of political instability often makes them put their money into savings abroad, as we discussed before. For the developing country, it's as if the rich didn't save. In fact, it's even worse because when they save abroad, the rich don't even spend the money at home as do poor people, so the rich don't generate even as much as the first-round income multiplier effects in their home country.

That leaves the middle class (small as it is) as the one hope these countries have for domestic savings. For them, the problem is: Where can they put their savings? Often these countries have an underdeveloped financial sector; there's no neighbourhood bank, no venture capital fund, no government-secured savings vehicle. The only savings vehicle available may be the government savings bond. But savings bonds finance the government deficit, which supports the government bureaucracy, which is limiting activities that could lead to growth. Few middle-class people invest in those government bonds. After all, what will a government bond be worth after the next revolution? Nothing!

Some governments have taxed individuals (a type of forced savings) and channelled that money back into investment. But again, politics and corruption are likely to interfere. Instead of going into legitimate productive investment, the savings—in the form of "consulting fees," outright payoffs, or "sweetheart contracts"—go to friends of those in power. Before you get up on your high horse and say, "How do the people allow that to happen?" think of Canada, where it's much easier to prevent such activities but where scandals in government spending are still uncovered with depressing regularity.

Investment Funded from Abroad The other way to generate funds for investment is from external savings, either foreign aid or foreign investment.

Foreign aid Funds that developed countries loan or give to developing countries.

Foreign Aid The easiest way to finance development is with **foreign aid** (funds that developed countries loan or give to developing countries). The problem is that foreign aid generally comes with strings attached; funds are earmarked for specific purposes. For example, most foreign aid is military aid; helping a country prepare to fight a war isn't a good way to help it develop.

As you can see in Exhibit 4, in 1992 Canada gave about $2.5 billion U.S. dollars—about $86 per Canadian citizen—in foreign aid. For the 4.2 billion people in developing countries, total foreign aid from all countries comes to about $15 per person. That isn't going to finance a lot of economic development, especially when much of the money is earmarked for military purposes.

Infrastructure investment Investment in the underlying structure of the economy, such as transportation or power facilities.

Foreign Investment If a global or multinational company believes that a country has a motivated, cheap workforce, a stable government supportive of business, and sufficient **infrastructure investment**—investment in the underlying structure of the economy, such as transportation or power facilities—it has a strong incentive to invest in the country. That's a lot of ifs, and generally the poorest countries don't measure up. What they have to offer instead are raw materials that the global corporation can develop.

Countries at the upper end of the group of developing countries (such as Mexico and Brazil) may meet all these requirements, but large amounts of foreign investment often result in political problems as citizens of these countries complain about imperialist exploitation, outside control, and significant outflows of profits. Developing

EXHIBIT 4 Foreign Aid Given by Major Countries, 1992

Country	Development Aid 1992 (millions of U.S. dollars)	Percent of GDP
United States	$11,709	0.20%
France	8,270	0.63
United Kingdom	3,217	0.31
Japan	11,151	0.30
Germany	7,572	0.39
Italy	4,122	0.30
Austria	556	0.30
Sweden	2,460	1.03
Canada	2,515	0.46

Source: *OECD DAC Chairman's Report,* The World Bank.

countries have tried to meet such complaints by insisting that foreign investment come in the form of joint development projects under local control, but that cuts down the amount that foreign firms are willing to invest.

When the infrastructure doesn't exist, as is the case in the poorest developing countries, few firms will invest in that country, no matter how cheap the labour or how stable the government. Firms require infrastructure investment such as transportation facilities, energy availability, and housing and amenities for their employees before they will consider investing in a country. And they don't want to pay to establish this infrastructure themselves.

Competition for Investment among Developing Countries The world is made up of 15 to 20 highly industrial countries and about 170 other countries at various stages of development. Global companies have a choice of where to locate, and often developing countries compete to get the development located in their country. In their efforts to get the development, they may offer tax rebates, free land, guarantees of labour peace, or loose regulatory environments within which firms can operate.

This competition can be keen, and can result in many of the benefits of development being transferred from the developing country to the global company and ultimately to the Western consumer, since competition from other firms will force the global company to pass on the benefits in the form of lower price.

An example of the results of such competition can be seen in the production of chemicals. Say a company is planning to build a new plant to produce chemicals. Where does it locate? Considering the wide-ranging environmental restrictions in Canada, the United States, and Western Europe, a chemical company will likely look toward a developing country that will give it loose regulation. If one country will not come through, the chemical firm will point out that it can locate elsewhere. Concern about Mexico's relatively loose environmental regulatory environment was one of the sticking points of approval of NAFTA.

Focal Points and Takeoff The scope of competition among developing countries can be overstated. Most companies do not consider all developing countries as potential production and investment sites. To decide to produce in a developing country requires a knowledge of that country—its legal structure, its political structure, and its infrastructure. Gaining this information involves a substantial initial investment, so most companies tend to focus on a few developing countries about which they have specific knowledge, or which they know other companies have chosen as development sites. (If company X chose it, it must meet the appropriate criteria.)

Because of this informational requirement, developing countries that have been successful in attracting investment often get further investment. Eventually they reach a stage called **economic takeoff**—a stage when the development process becomes self-sustaining. Other developing countries fall by the wayside. This means that economic development is not evenly spread over developing countries, but, rather, is concentrated in a few.

Economic takeoff The stage of self-sustaining economic development.

Inappropriate Education

The right education is a necessary component of any successful development strategy. The wrong education is an enormous burden. Developing countries tend to have too much of the wrong education and too little of the right education.

Often educational systems in developing countries resemble Western educational systems. The reason is partly the colonial heritage of developing countries and partly what might be described as an emulation factor. The West defines what an educated person is, and developing countries want their citizens to be seen as educated. An educated person should be able to discuss the ideas of Jacque Godbout, the poetry of Lord Byron, the intricacies of chaos theory, the latest developments in fusion technology, the nuances of the modern Keynesian/Classical debate, and the dissociative properties of Andy Warhol's paintings. So saith Western scholars; so be it.

But, put bluntly, that type of education is almost irrelevant to economic growth and may be a serious detriment to growth. Basic skills—reading, writing, and arithmetic, taught widely—are likely to be more conducive to growth than is high-level education. When education doesn't match the needs of the society, the degrees—the credentials—become more important than the knowledge learned. The best jobs go to those with the highest degrees, not because the individuals holding the degrees are better able to do the job, but simply because they hold the credentials. Such credentialing education serves to preserve the monopoly position of those who manage to get the degree. It has acquired the name **credentialism.**

Credentialism Situation where individuals who hold the highest educational degrees get the best jobs simply because they have the credentials.

If access to education is competitive, credentialism has its advantages. Even irrelevant education, as long as it is difficult, serves a "screening" or "selection" role. Those individuals, who work hardest at getting into, and in, education advance and get the good jobs. Since selecting hard-working individuals is difficult, even irrelevant education serves this selection role.

But developing countries' current educational practices may be worse than irrelevant. Their educational systems often reflect Western culture, not their own cultures. The best students qualify for scholarships abroad, and their education in a different tradition makes it difficult for them to return home.

In our studies, we've come to know a large number of the best and the brightest students from developing countries. They're superb students and they do well in school. But as they near graduation, most of them face an enormously difficult choice. They can return to their home country—to material shortages, to enormous challenges for which they have little training, and to an illiterate society whose traditional values are sometimes hostile to the values these new graduates have learned. Or they can stay in the West, find jobs relevant to their training, enjoy an abundance of material goods, and associate with people to whom they've now learned to relate. Which would you choose?

Brain drain The outflow of the best and brightest students from developing countries to developed countries.

The choice many of them make results in a **brain drain** (the outflow of the best and brightest students from developing countries to developed countries). Many of these good students don't return to the developing country. Those that do go home take jobs as government officials, expecting high salaries and material comforts far beyond what their society can afford. Instead of becoming the dynamic entrepreneurs of growth, they become impediments to growth.

There are, of course, many counterexamples to the arguments presented here. Many developing countries try to design their education system to fit their culture. And many of the dynamic, selfless leaders who make it possible for the country to develop do return home. As with most issues, there are both positive and negative attributes to the way something is done. We emphasize the problems with educational systems in developing economies because the positive attributes of education are generally accepted. Without education, development is impossible. The question is simply how that education should be structured.

Overpopulation

Two ways a country can increase per capita income are:

1. Decrease the number of people in the country (without decreasing the total income in the country).
2. Increase income (without increasing the population).

In each case the qualifier is important, for income and population are related in complicated ways: People earn income; without people there would be no income. But often the more people there are, the less income per person there is, because the resources of the country become strained.

A country's population can never be higher than the natural resources that it either has, or can import, can support. But that doesn't mean that overpopulation can't be an obstacle to development. Nature has its own ways of reducing populations that are too large: Starvation and disease are the direct opposite to development. That control system works in nature, and it would work with human societies. The problem is that we don't like it.

Arthur Lewis won the Nobel prize in 1979 for work on economic development. *© The Nobel Foundation.*

Thomas Carlyle gave economics its nickname, *the dismal science,* commenting on the writings of Thomas Malthus, who, in the early 1800s, said that society's prospects are dismal because population tends to outrun the means of subsistence. (Population grows geometrically—that is, at an increasing rate; the means of subsistence grow arithmetically—that is, at a constant rate.) The view was cemented into economic thinking in the law of diminishing marginal productivity: As more and more people are added to a fixed amount of land, the output per worker gets smaller and smaller.

Through technological progress, most Western economies have avoided the fate predicted by Malthus because growth in output has exceeded growth in population. In contrast, many developing economies have not avoided the Malthusian fate because diminishing marginal productivity has exceeded technological change, and limited economic growth isn't enough to offset the increase in population. The result is a constant or falling output per person.

That doesn't mean that developing countries haven't grown economically. They have. But population growth makes per capita output growth small or negative.

Population grows for a number of reasons, including:

1. As public health measures are improved, infant mortality rates and death rates for the population as a whole both decline. (Fewer people die each year.)
2. As people earn more income, they believe they can afford to have more kids.
3. In rural areas, children are useful in working the fields.

What to do? Should the government reduce the population growth rate? If it should, how can it do so? Various measures have been tried: advertising campaigns, free condoms, forced sterilization, and economic incentives. For example, in China the government has tried imposing severe economic penalties on couples who have more than one child, while providing material incentives such as a free television set to couples who agree not to have more than one child.

China's vigorous population control campaign has had a number of effects. First, it created so much anger at the government that in rural areas the campaign was dropped. Second, it led to the killing of many female babies because, if couples were to have only one baby, strong cultural and economic pressures existed to ensure that the baby was a male. Third, it led to an enormous loss of privacy. Dates of women's menstrual periods were posted in factories and officials would remind them at appropriate times that they should take precautions against getting pregnant. Only a very strong government could impose such a plan.

Even successful population control programs have their problems. In Singapore a population control campaign was so successful among educated women that the government became concerned that its "population quality" was suffering. It began a selective campaign to encourage college-educated women to have children. They issued "love tips" to men (since some college-educated women complained that their male companions were nerds and had no idea how to be romantic) and offered special monetary bonuses to college-educated women who gave birth to children. As you might imagine, the campaign provoked a backlash, and it was eventually dropped by the government.

Individuals differ substantially in their assessment of the morality of these programs, but even if one believes that population control is an appropriate government concern, it does not seem that such programs will be successful, by themselves, in limiting population growth.

It is true that birth control programs have enabled developing countries to slow their population growth, but so far their overall effect hasn't been what planners had hoped. Summarizing past attempts, Ashish Bose (head of the Population Research Center of Delhi University in India) stated, "Looking back, high tech, money, and the bureaucracy—all these have failed."

Some people, like social scientist Julian Simon, believe that all such attempts to control population are misplaced. People are the ultimate resource, he argues, and it is inconceivable that a society can have too many people. People will design technologies that will allow ever-increasing numbers to exist in a society.

STRATEGIES FOR GROWTH: AN ONGOING DEBATE

While developing countries' problems seem overwhelming, development economists have nonetheless offered a variety of strategies for growth. These strategies have been much debated, and a brief discussion of four areas of debate is appropriate at this point. All four presume that development money is available; the debate involves how best to spend it.

Balanced versus Unbalanced Growth

6 Four debates about strategies for growth are:
1. Balanced vs. unbalanced growth.
2. Agriculture vs. industry.
3. Infrastructure vs. directly productive investment.
4. Export-led growth vs. import substitution.

In deciding how to spend your development money, do you follow an **unbalanced growth plan,** focusing on one sector of the economy and hoping that that will generate development in other sectors? Or do you adopt a **balanced growth plan,** spreading the money around and trying to spur development in all sectors simultaneously? With a balanced growth plan, you risk spreading the money so thin that nothing substantial can be accomplished. With an unbalanced growth plan, you risk creating an oasis of development that the economy cannot sustain for long. The debate has sometimes been likened to a debate about how you should pull yourself up by your own bootstraps. Should you pull one side first? Or should you pull both sides together? And how can you pull yourself up at all if you are standing on the very surface you're trying to lift?

Agriculture versus Industry

Unbalanced growth plan Plan that focuses on one sector of the economy in the hope that that will generate development in other sectors.

Balanced growth plan Plan that spreads money around in trying to spur development in all sectors simultaneously.

Most developing countries' economies depend on agriculture. Developed countries' economies depend on industry. If you have some development money, do you spend it on agriculture, where most of your production takes place, or do you spend it on developing an industrial base for growth?

The argument for spending the money on industry is that such expenditures will allow you to decrease imports and will encourage further industrial growth so you can become like the developed countries. Advocates of this position contend that agriculture is a dead-end path.

The argument for spending the money on agriculture instead of industry is that agriculture is already built into the culture of that society, so gains in a congenial area (agriculture) are much more likely to occur than are gains in an unfamiliar area (industry).

Dueling Duals Debate whether a country should focus development on agriculture or on industry.

Since agriculture is generally associated with the traditionally based economy and industry is often associated with the internationally based economy, this agriculture/industry debate might be called "**the Dueling Duals.**" Should one build up the small existing industrialized economy, widening the income and cultural gap between the two economies? Or should one narrow that gap by trying to pull up the traditional economy? Notice that since the degree of inequality is tied to the strategy a country chooses, it is not clear that the country will make the choice that offers the highest prospect for growth.

Infrastructure versus Directly Productive Investment

As we stated before, most developing countries do not have the infrastructure necessary for most kinds of production. Should you invest your development money in the infrastructure, which is indirectly productive, or in directly productive activities like building a mill or providing a fertilizer subsidy? Infrastructure investment shows no immediate monetary return. If it is to show a return, it must increase private investment which in turn generates a short-run monetary return; if private investment isn't forthcoming, the money spent on infrastructure is wasted. Thus, there is a strong incentive to use the money in directly productive investment. But directly productive investment often cannot compete internationally unless the infrastructure is in place.

Export-Led Growth versus Import Substitution

Another of the choices developing countries face is whether to focus on *export-led growth*—trying to develop industries that will compete on the world market and that are not necessarily tied to the domestic economy—or to focus on *import substitution*—trying to develop industries that will produce for the domestic economy, replacing imports. Such an import-substitution strategy is often initiated with government-imposed tariffs on imports to provide some initial protection for an industry. It is, however, often difficult for government ever to eliminate that initial tariff protection both because (1) with the protection there is little pressure on the industry to hold costs down and become internationally competitive, and (2) the size of the market often limits the use of large-scale efficient technology.

MISSION IMPOSSIBLE

7 Economic development is a complicated problem because it is entwined with cultural and social issues.

At this point in our courses, we inevitably throw up our hands and admit that we don't know what makes it possible for a country to develop. Nor, judging from what we have read, do the development experts. The good ones (that is, the ones we agree with) admit that they don't know; others (that is, the ones we don't agree with) simply don't know that they don't know.

Our gut feeling is that there are no definitive general answers that apply to all developing countries. The appropriate answer varies with each country and each situation. Each proposed solution to the development problem has a right time and a right place. Only by having a complete sense of a country, its history, and its cultural, social, and political norms can one decide whether it's the right time and place for this or that policy.

CHAPTER SUMMARY

- One must be careful in judging economies.
- The analysis of developing countries is, more and more, being divided into four geographic groupings: Asian, African, Latin American, and Middle Eastern.
- The dual structure of developing countries' economies creates political and economic tension.
- Six obstacles to economic development are political instability, corruption, lack of appropriate institutions, lack of investment, inappropriate education, and overpopulation.
- Without an appropriate infrastructure, governments can sell rights to all kinds of things and thereby limit development.
- Generating sufficient investment is a difficult problem for developing countries.
- Four debates about strategies for growth include the balanced/unbalanced growth debate, the agriculture/industry debate, the infrastructure/directly productive investment debate, and the export-led growth/import substitution debate.
- Optimal strategies for growth are country-specific.

KEY TERMS

Asian tigers *(417)*
balanced growth plan *(426)*
brain drain *(424)*
credentialism *(424)*
dual economy *(417)*
the Dueling Duals *(426)*
economic takeoff *(423)*
foreign aid *(422)*
infrastructure investment *(422)*
purchasing power parity *(416)*
unbalanced growth plan *(426)*

QUESTIONS FOR THOUGHT AND REVIEW

The number after each question represents the estimated degree of critical thinking required. (1 = almost none; 10 = deep thought.)

1. If you suddenly found yourself living as a poor person in a developing country, what are some things that you now do that you would no longer be able to do? What new things would you have to do? *(2)*
2. What is wrong with saying that people in developing countries are worse off than people in Canada? *(3)*
3. Does the fact that suicide rates are lower in developing countries than in Canada and the United States imply that North Americans would be better off living in a developing country? Why? *(5)*
4. Why are investment and savings so low in developing countries? *(5)*
5. If developing countries are so unstable and offer such a risky environment for investment, why do foreigners invest any money in them at all? *(5)*
6. If you were a foreign investor thinking of making an investment in a developing country, what are some things that you would be concerned about? *(4)*
7. Should developing countries send their students abroad for an education? *(5)*
8. How does corruption limit investment and economic growth? *(6)*
9. Should a country control the size and makeup of its population? Why? *(7)*
10. List four alternative strategies for growth and give an advantage and disadvantage of each strategy. *(0)*

PROBLEMS AND EXERCISES

1. Interview a foreign student in your class or school. Ask about each of the six obstacles to economic development and how her country is trying to overcome them.
2. Spend one day living like someone in a developing country. Eat almost nothing and work lifting stones for 10 hours. Then, that same evening, study this chapter and contemplate the bootstrap strategy of development.
3. In 1991 Germany passed a law requiring businesses to take back and recycle all forms of packaging. A large group of businesses formed a company to collect and recycle these packages. Its costs are 4.5 cents per pound for glass, 9.5 cents per pound for paper, and 74 cents per pound for plastic. This accounts for a recycling cost of about $100 per tonne for glass and $2,000 per tonne for plastic, and the average recycling cost is $500 per tonne. A developing country has offered to create a giant landfill and accept Germany's waste at a cost of $400 per tonne, which includes $50 per tonne sorting and transport costs and a $350-per-tonne fee to be paid to the developing country.
   a. Should Germany accept this proposal?
   b. Will the proposal benefit the developing country?
   c. What alternative or modification to the proposal might you suggest?
4. Say that you have been hired to design an education system for a developing country.
   a. What skills would you want it to emphasize?
   b. How might it differ from an ideal educational system here in Canada?
   c. How much of the Canadian education system involves credentialism, and how much the learning of relevant skills?
5. Asian countries have grown faster than countries in other geographic areas. These countries have followed a neomercantilist approach in which the government takes a lead role in the development process.
   a. Would you suggest other countries do the same? Why or why not?
   b. What factors might have made the Asian countries successful other than this role of government?
   c. Of the six obstacles to growth, which would you say is the most important for developing countries to focus on overcoming? Why?

CHAPTER

22

Socialist Economies in Transition

God made the world in seven days; but he didn't have an installed computer base.

~Bill Gates

After reading this chapter, you should be able to:

1. Summarize the historical roots of socialism.
2. Summarize how a centrally planned economy works.
3. Explain why most Soviet-style socialist economies suffered consistent shortages of most goods.
4. State five major problems of a centrally planned economy.
5. Summarize some transition problems former Soviet-style socialist countries are experiencing.
6. List four cautionary lessons for transitional economies in their decision to adopt Western institutions.

Most of this book has considered the operations and institutions of capitalist economies, and has discussed how economic forces work within market situations. However, as emphasized throughout this book, economic forces are at work in *all* situations. A market is simply an institution in which economic forces are allowed to predominate over political and social forces.

Soviet-style socialist economies Centrally planned economies in which the state owns most of the means of production.

In this final chapter we switch gears and look at what happens when markets aren't used. We do that by considering the operation of economic forces in **Soviet-style socialist economies**—centrally planned economies in which the state owns most of the means of production—and consider some of the explanations for why these countries have moved toward an economic organization using the market rather than planning. We'll consider how central planning has worked in practice—and how that practice differed from theory. Finally, we'll consider the ongoing transition of Soviet-style socialist economies and the problems these economies face.

THE HISTORICAL ROOTS OF SOCIALISM

The theory of modern socialist economies originated when a group of writers in the 1800s reacted to the excesses of unregulated capitalism. Looking at what the Industrial Revolution had wrought—the 10-hour work day, child labour, poor working conditions, a highly unequal distribution of income, unemployment, and starvation—they argued that there must be a better way than capitalism to organize economic society.

1 The theory of modern socialist economies originated in the early 1800s when a group of writers reacted to the excesses of unregulated capitalism.

The doctrine of socialism itself began in the early 19th century with the work of individuals such as Louis Blanc, a French historian and government official. Blanc focused on the belief that everyone who was willing and able to work should have a job. Over time, the emphasis in socialism changed from creating an economy in which everyone had a job to creating an economy that redistributed income from the rich to the poor, and then to creating an economy in which the government controlled production.

In the 1990s, with the downfall of Soviet-style socialist economies, the emphasis in socialist thinking was again changing. China attempted to merge markets into its socialist system, and the former Soviet bloc countries attempted to build new institutions in their formerly socialist economies. In the midst of these changes, socialists kept their belief in the existence of a better way, but they agree with mainstream economists that the Soviet-style socialist approach, with its combination of totalitarian political control and state-controlled economic planning, is not the way to go.

HOW A CENTRALLY PLANNED ECONOMY WORKS

2 In a centrally planned economy, central planners decide the general direction the economy will take. They make the what, how, and for whom decisions.

In a **centrally planned economy,** central planners decide the general direction the economy will take. They make the *what, how,* and *for whom* decisions. Should the economy focus on producing consumer goods? Machinery? Agriculture? Military hardware? The government's central planners decide.

In communist-dominated socialist economies like the former Soviet Union and China, or in pre-1990 Eastern Europe, the power behind the central planners was the Communist party. The Communist party nominated candidates for office. The public then ratified the choices by voting in elections in which the Communist party candidates were the only candidates. Thus, these systems were political systems as well as economic systems in which the Communist party was like an autocracy, being a government composed of a small group of people with nearly unlimited power, not of a popularly elected set of officials.

Planning in a Centrally Planned Economy and in a Market Economy

A centrally planned economy like that in the former Soviet Union differs from a market economy like that of Canada. That difference is not, however, that in one there is planning and in the other there is not. The difference lies in who does the planning, how many planners there are, and what motives guide planners' decisions.

A centrally planned economy has one central agency for economic planning, while a market economy has many planners. Since the idea of planning in a market economy may be a bit unusual to you, let's consider for a moment who does the planning in Canada.

ADDED DIMENSION

THE SEARCH FOR UTOPIA

If only the world were wonderful, or at least better than it is. How many times have you thought that? Probably many, and you're not alone. Sir Thomas More in 1515 wrote a book about such a wonderful society, which he called *Utopia.* Ever since, dream worlds have gone by the name Utopia.

In the 18th and early 19th centuries there were many dreamers of Utopia. Democracy had been ushered in and new, better forms of government were taking hold. Why not a better economy too? Not an economy in which people starved; not an economy in which people were held under the "gun" of competition—but a society of cooperation, of concern for others, and of love.

If it sounds wonderful to you, it also sounded wonderful to numerous individuals in the early 1800s, including Robert Owen, owner of a large, successful cotton mill in Manchester, England. Owen believed sufficiently in his ideas to put his money where his mouth was. To demonstrate the superiority of his utopian ideas, he bought a mill in New Lanark, near Manchester, and instead of paying low wages and tolerating unsanitary conditions, he took a strong interest in the workers' welfare. He provided decent housing, education, and low-cost goods for his workers at the company store. The mill was a success.

Owen then expanded his mission, recommending that entire towns adopt a "cooperative," not a "competitive," structure. He suggested villages of "unity and cooperation" of about 1,200 inhabitants, with each village offering a public kitchen and dining room. Parents would care for their children until the age of three, after which children would be raised by the community so that they would be imbued with the appropriate cooperative social attitude. He believed that once society saw how wonderful these communities were, all societies would voluntarily adopt the structure and soon the whole world would embrace his ideas.

To implement his plans he moved to the United States and set up a model project—New Harmony, Indiana—in 1825. Life in New Harmony was anything but harmonious. In three years Owen was broke and the project was dead—killed by internal fights and arguments. Other similar communities suffered the same fate. The experiment in voluntary socialism was a failure.

For the percentage of Canadian output controlled by the various branches of government (the public sector), the government is the planner, and its decisions are periodically ratified by the public through regularly scheduled elections. In the rest of the economy (the private sector) the planners are business executives, and their decisions are guided by the profit motive, which in turn reflects consumer sovereignty.

The multitude of planners in a market economy like Canada's makes it difficult to say exactly who decides *what, how,* and *for whom* to produce. So normally economists say, "The market decides," but it's important to remember that planning does take place in a market economy. Exhibit 1 summarizes the differences in planning in market and centrally planned economies.

Planning in Practice Planning in practice starts with a group of planners deciding what will be produced. For example, the planners in a centrally planned economy might issue a general directive like the following: "Over the next five years the focus of the economy will be on producing more machinery. Production in machinery will increase 8 percent per year. We will increase agricultural goods by 4 percent per year and consumer goods by 5 percent." This plan, of course, will be made more specific—what kinds of machinery will be produced and what crops will be focused on in each of those five years.

Even when these decisions have been made, many more specifics need to be added before the plans will be meaningful enough to be carried out. For example, managers and workers need to know not only how many tractors to produce, but also their specifications: What horsepower? What size tires? What kind of steel? What inputs will be available? To give you a sense of how extensive planning was in a centrally planned economy, consider that in 1987 the former Soviet planners set quotas and prices for more than 200,000 commodities and controlled the operation of more than 37,000 enterprises. Making such decisions requires a large planning agency.

EXHIBIT 1 Planning in a Centrally Planned and in a Market Economy

All economies require planning. The difference between a market economy and a centrally planned economy is in who does the planning and what the planners' motivations are.

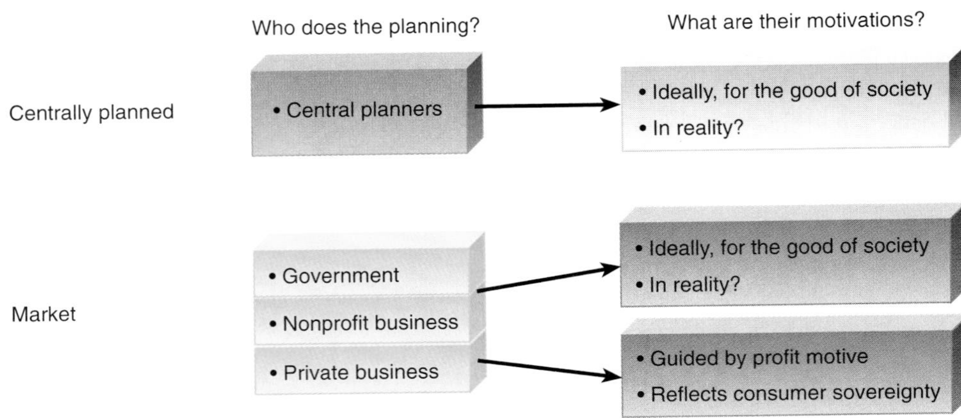

In the former Soviet planning system, an individual official in the planning agency was assigned a certain group of factories or production units, usually all in the same region of the country. This individual knew the capabilities of the factories in the region and, on the basis of that knowledge, he or she set production quotas for each factory.

For example, say the government's five-year plan emphasized plenty of bread to go around. To fulfil this plan, bread output would have to be increased by 40 percent over five years. The planners would translate that goal into an increase in the output of bread of, say, 7 percent per year, which, compounded over five years, would achieve more than the 40 percent desired growth. The planners translated these targeted increases into specific production quotas for regions containing groups of firms—8 percent for one region, 3 percent for another, and so on.

These plans would have to be translated into directives for the managers of individual factories. Thus, a bakery manager was given a set of directives specifying what he or she would be required to produce over the next year and what inputs would be available in order to meet the goal. The directive would have read as follows: "Next year you will produce 4,000,000 loaves of white bread, 2,000,000 loaves of rye bread, 1,000,000 loaves of whole-wheat bread, and 1,000,000 loaves of pumpernickel. To do so, you will be allocated 400 workers, 1 plant, and 4,000,000 pounds of grain."

This one-year directive was subdivided into monthly, weekly, and even daily input and output levels. Managers' performances were judged according to how close they came to meeting their assigned goals. Under actual conditions the plans would have been much more detailed than the hypothetical directive we've constructed, but the example gives you the general idea.

Counterplanning The preceding description may make it seem as if, in a central planning system, the various planning agencies would continually be telling the agencies below them what to do. That was true, but the information flowed both ways. Long before a final directive was issued, the higher-level planners conferred extensively with lower-level planners. They would go over what was feasible. After talking with the lower-level planning group, the higher-level planning group would usually show the lower-level group a draft plan.

Each lower-level group had a chance to point out that it wasn't allocated the inputs necessary to achieve the output quota, or that the output quota was unrealistic. They could suggest modifications to the plan. This process of modifying the plan from below was known as **counterplanning.** Counterplanning let individuals at lower levels of the hierarchy influence decisions of those at higher levels and thereby affect the decisions made by the highest level of central planners.

Counterplanning Process that lets individuals low in the hierarchy influence the planning decisions of those higher in the hierarchy.

Coordinating the Plans: Material Balances Directing and issuing detailed plans for an entire economy was a complicated procedure. The planners had to ensure that the output of firms whose products were used in the production of other products matched the inputs that the planners had assigned to the manufacturers of those other products. This coordination of directives was achieved through a system called *material balances*.

Using the **material balance** approach, essentially the planning board added up what was coming in, subtracted what was going out, and kept adjusting incoming and outgoing quantities of materials until they were equal—until the materials balanced. Hence the name *material balance*. The process wasn't easy. It was like trying to put a Rubik Cube back in the pattern it had when it came out of the box. One kept trying various combinations of inputs and outputs until one got everything to fit.

Material balance Process by which central planners adjust incoming and outgoing quantities of materials until supply equals demand (at least on paper).

To aid in this complex process of making inputs and outputs balance, economists designed and perfected some mathematical tools. These tools were important not only to planned economies; they are still important tools to Western business firms. The tools include linear programming, designed by Leonid Kantorovich (a Soviet economist), and input–output analysis, designed by Wassily Leontief (a Russian-born American economist who was interested in analyzing centrally planned economies). The two men won Nobel prizes for their work, Kantorovich in 1975 and Leontief in 1973. The material balance approach, assisted by tools such as input–output analysis and linear programming, was the most widely used system for coordinating centrally planned economic systems, and a variant is still being used in China.

Deciding What to Produce

Now that you've been introduced to the technical planning apparatus, let's consider planners' motivation in deciding what and how much of something to produce next year. There are no simple answers to these questions. The planners in a centrally planned economy could, if they desired, decide how much would be wanted by consumers next year in about the same way a firm in Canada decides. Alternatively, they could look at what was produced one year, estimate how much demand for the product would increase the next year, and base their production decisions on that estimate. Or they could base their decision on other criteria.

But whatever criteria they choose, there's a big difference in the motivation behind planning in a socialist economy and in a capitalist economy. In a capitalist economy a firm makes its profits by producing *what* and *how much* is wanted by consumers. To stay in business, firms must take the consumers' desires into account. Central planners in a socialist economy don't have to take consumers' desires into account. Central planners might realize that Twinkies will be wanted by consumers, but the planners might believe that Twinkies aren't good for people, so their decision might be to produce whole-wheat bread instead.

Central planners could follow any set of principles they wanted to in determining what output levels to assign the producers of various goods. Exhibit 2 presents a production possibility curve showing the range of choices that societies could make between investment goods and consumer goods. In the 1970s and 1980s, Soviet planners chose a point like *A*, focusing on investment goods (heavy equipment, large machines, space exploration, and military goods such as tanks and planes), having decided that these goods were what their society needed. Consumer goods (cars, household appliances, clothing) were given short shrift. Most market economies, in which the profit motive directs firms to produce what they think people want, choose a point like *B*, which includes more consumer goods.

The reason socialist planners chose a point like *A* was that higher production of investment goods was supposed to lead to faster growth, which would make up for the lower level of output (relative to Western developed countries) at which the former Soviet Union and other socialist countries started out. It's as if your economics instructor told you to work harder at the beginning of the term because it will pay off at the end. This strategy can be successful, but socialist economies, for reasons that we'll discuss later, didn't grow faster than Canada and other market economies. They grew more slowly. The payoff for choosing investment goods over consumer goods didn't come, and that missing payoff was a significant factor in the demise of centrally planned economies.

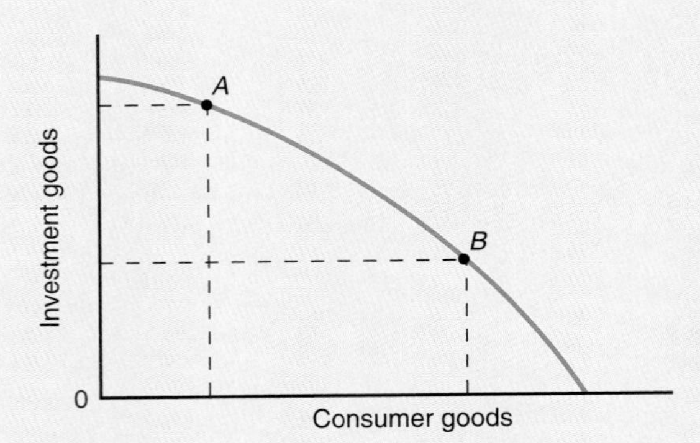

EXHIBIT 2 Choice between Investment Goods and Consumer Goods

One of the reasons socialist economies had shortages of consumer goods is that the planners made a conscious decision to emphasize investment goods, choosing a position like *A* over *B*.

Pricing in a Centrally Planned Economy

Central planners had not only to decide what goods to produce; they also had to decide what prices to charge for those goods. In a market economy, most prices are set by suppliers at a level that covers costs of production and provides them with a profit margin that they feel is appropriate. If suppliers set their prices too high, consumers will buy from other suppliers; if suppliers set their prices too low, they won't cover their costs and they'll lose money.

In a market economy, suppliers are free to adjust their prices to make the quantity demanded equal the quantity supplied. If demand is lower than expected, firms will lower their prices to stimulate an increase in the quantity demanded. If demand is high, prices will tend to rise, encouraging consumers to economize on the good, and producers to increase their production. That's what's meant by **market-determined prices.**

Market-determined prices Prices are determined by supply and demand, with suppliers free to adjust their prices to make the quantity demanded equal the quantity supplied.

In a centrally planned economy, prices are determined by the central planners, not by the market. The prices that central planners set influence the quantity demanded of various goods. When planners set a low price, the quantity demanded will be high; when they set a high price, the quantity demanded will be low. That's the same as in a capitalist economy.

What are different are the criteria that central planners use to set prices. To some degree, they set prices to cover costs (not including profits, since socialist producers aren't supposed to earn profits), but they can also set prices at the level they believe is fair or at the level they believe is the social worth of a product—in short, at whatever level they want.

Leonid Kantorovich won the Nobel prize in 1975 for work on linear programming and economic planning. © *The Nobel Foundation.*

How did central planners actually decide where to set prices? The general approach to pricing taken by socialist countries was to price necessities (like basic foods) low and luxuries (like washing machines and cars) high, independent of costs. For example, in the late 1980s Soviet rents were set at the equivalent of $95 a month for a one-bedroom apartment in Moscow. Compare this to the usual $1,000 monthly rent for a one-bedroom apartment in Toronto at that time. Medical care was free. Bread and potatoes were priced far below what it cost to produce them.

Exhibit 3 shows prices of selected goods in East and West Germany in 1988, before the two nations were reunited. After unification, East Germany's prices were changed to reflect those of West Germany.

The ability to set prices at whatever level they wanted didn't free central planners from economic forces. The laws of supply and demand still operated. There were surpluses of goods whose prices were set too high relative to the quantity supplied and shortages of goods whose prices were set too low relative to the quantity supplied.

3 Most Soviet-style socialist countries suffered from consistent shortages of goods because the planners chose too-low prices relative to demand.

Most Soviet-style socialist economies suffered from consistent shortages of most goods. Getting an apartment required a wait of five years or even longer. Getting a car required a still longer wait. This suggests that the prices the planners chose (even the relatively high prices) were too low relative to demand. This was one of people's big complaints with the centrally planned economies—a consistent shortage of goods.

EXHIBIT 3 Prices (in U.S. dollars) in East and West Germany before Unification

Item	Germany (D-mark)	Germany (OstMark)
Coffee (1 pound)	$ 3.39	$ 13.33
Colour TV set	600.00	2,000.00
Electricity (1 kwh)	.17	.03
Monthly rent	200.00	30.00
Potatoes (10 pounds)	1.80	.30
Refrigerator	250.00	570.00
Rye bread (1 kg)	.75	.10
Washing machine	400.00	1,000.00

Sources: Based on information collected by Deutsche Bank, World Bank, and estimates by authors.

When there are shortages of goods, an alternative rationing system must be established to determine who gets what. In Soviet-style socialist countries, that rationing system generally involved being a member of the Communist party or being in the in-group. Officials received "gifts," were put at the top of waiting lists, and were notified by distributors when scarce goods came in so that they could shop ahead of other people. In Romania, for example, before the revolution that broke out at the end of 1989, the communist leadership could get pretty much whatever consumer goods it wanted. That inequality contradicted the goals of communism, and the people's resentment of it was one cause of the uprisings against communism and Soviet-style socialism in the late 1980s and early 1990s. We'll cover this issue in more depth when we discuss reforms.

THE PROBLEMS OF CENTRAL PLANNING

Economists have identified five problems that tend to undermine central planning:

1. Nonmarket pricing and perverse incentives.
2. Inability to adjust prices quickly.
3. Lack of accurate information about demand.
4. Ambiguous production directives.
5. Inability to adjust plans quickly to changing situations.

Let's look at each of these problems in turn.

Nonmarket Pricing and Perverse Incentives

In a market economy, prices reflect costs—a central lesson of the economic analysis of production. The advantage of having prices reflect costs was a central lesson of microeconomic theory. Prices that reflect costs make people's decisions about what to consume and what to produce reflect opportunity cost. The result is efficient use of resources.

Central planners can override the market and choose prices that don't reflect costs. However, as discussed in Chapter 6 on consumer choice, when prices don't reflect costs, consumers have an incentive to use goods in a manner that reflects the cost to them and not the costs to the society. Economists call an incentive to use goods in a manner that doesn't reflect the cost to society a **perverse incentive.**

Perverse incentive Incentive to use goods in a manner that does not reflect that use's cost to society.

4 Five problems that tend to undermine central planning are:
1. Nonmarket pricing and perverse incentives.
2. Inability to adjust prices quickly.
3. Lack of accurate information about demand.
4. Ambiguous production directives.
5. Inability to adjust plans quickly to changing situations.

Let's say that the economic planners decide that everyone in the society deserves inexpensive bread, so they lower the price of bread from 50¢ to 5¢ for a 16-ounce loaf. Say that last year, at 50¢ a loaf, people consumed 1 million loaves, so planners figure this year, at 5¢ a loaf, 2 million loaves will be consumed. After all, how much bread can people eat? In principle, that's plenty of bread, but most likely the outcome will be a shortage of bread to eat. Why? Because at 5¢ a loaf, self-interested people will discover lots of other things one can do with bread besides eat it themselves. For example, after the fall in price, a pig farmer might buy four loaves of bread a week for his family and 7,000 loaves a week for his pigs. At 5¢ a loaf, it pays him to feed bread, rather than oats or corn, even though the equivalent amount of oats or corn would be

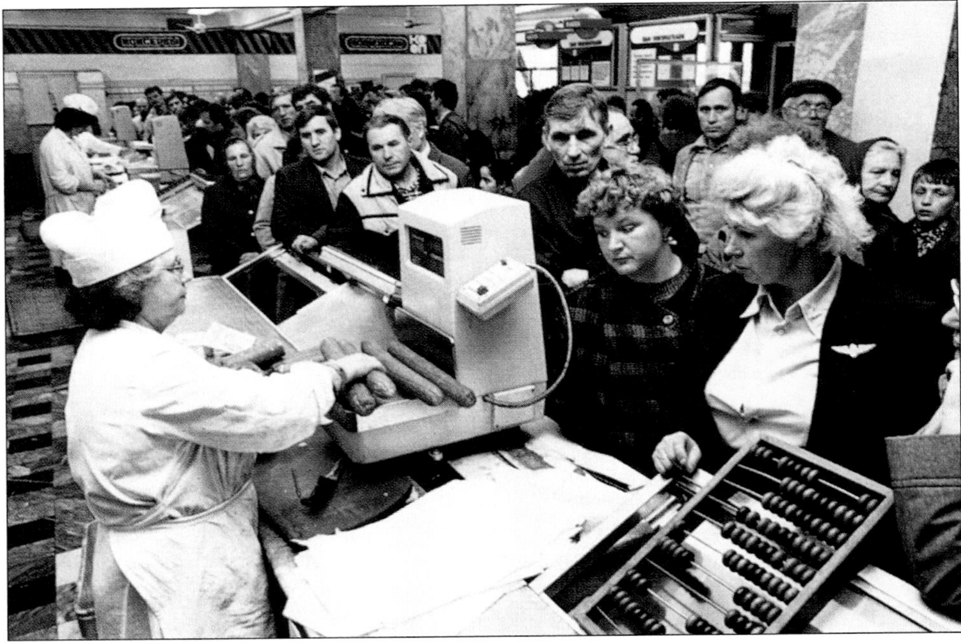

This Russian photo exemplifies the shortages and queues for food that have characterized socialist economies. *Reuters/Bettmann.*

better for the pigs and less costly to society. Pig farming will increase enormously. If the cost to society of producing a loaf of bread is 40¢ and the cost of producing oats or corn of equal feed value is 20¢, the 5¢ price of bread not only creates a shortage of bread for people to eat, but also subsidizes pig farmers. Moreover, society will be losing 35¢ (the 40¢ it costs minus the 5¢ it gets for the bread) for each loaf of bread fed to pigs while gaining only 20¢ of value in additional output of pigs. The net loss to society will be 15¢ per loaf (the opportunity cost of the oats or corn).

If central planners have a high degree of control over which, and how, inputs are used, they can stop such "inappropriate" uses of bread simply by forbidding them. But unless people are not self-interested, policing and enforcing those additional rules require an enormous amount of central control, which requires a large, costly bureaucracy and causes other problems.

Central planners must direct individuals to do what is consistent with their plan, and must enforce their directives. The market, in contrast, uses economic incentives to guide people to do what is in society's interest.

Inability to Adjust Prices Quickly

Centrally planned pricing decisions are also not consistent with quick adjustment of prices. The reason is that the information about what is selling fast and what isn't doesn't get back to the central planners rapidly enough. Why? Sales information is often delayed by the need to flow through three or four levels of bureaucracy: A salesperson must tell his boss, who must tell the regional director, who must tell the central planning assistant director—all by memo, and memos simply don't travel very fast. It's a law of nature that administrative decisions aren't made quickly. Large firms in Canada have the same problems; they tend to adjust their prices more slowly than do small firms.

The result of central planning's inability to adjust prices quickly is a surplus of some items whose price is too high and a shortage of other goods whose price is too low. Shortages and surpluses were especially apparent in specialized consumer goods such as fashionable clothing (for example, stone-washed jeans), household appliances, and novelty items. In Canada, you can walk into stores and get almost anything you want, whenever you want. As long as some person can predict a demand and make a profit filling that demand, the demand will be filled. In the centrally planned former Soviet Union, "frivolous needs" received a low priority, resulting in chronic shortages of all types of consumer goods.

China is currently changing its planning focus toward more consumer goods while simultaneously allowing more market production of consumer goods. Economic theory predicts that the market will do much better than the planners. The reason is that predicting demand for consumer items is always difficult, and central planning makes it even more difficult. In a market economy, surpluses are dealt with by running sales: "CLEARANCE SALE! TAKE 60% TO 70% OFF ALL RED-TAGGED ITEMS!" At some price, suppliers in a market economy will find demanders for those purple trousers or those dresses with last year's length.

Socialist retail firms will have trouble running sales because the need to get approval prevents them from changing prices quickly enough. So the planners' retail stores may find themselves with empty racks for jeans but overflowing racks of purple trousers.

Lack of Accurate Information about Demand

The problems caused by the planners' inability to adjust prices are amplified by their lack of information about what products are desired. In a centrally planned economy, producers have little incentive to tell the planners that their plans will create a surplus or a shortage; nor do they have an incentive to see that their goods sell. When producers are judged by their ability to meet their production quotas, not by whether their goods sell, they don't provide planners with information about what sells. Instead they provide information that will encourage planners to set production targets that are easy to meet.

The result of such misleading feedback has been the production of lots of undesirable and unwanted goods and severe shortages of desired goods. In most centrally planned economies, consumers walked around with lots of cash and shopping bags. When they saw something they needed or liked in a store, they got in line to buy large quantities for themselves and their friends—which worsened the shortage for other consumers.

Ambiguous Production Directives

Another problem that centrally planned economies had is that production directives were inevitably ambiguous. To be unambiguous, a directive must give all relevant specifications of a product. One can't simply say, "Produce 4 million tonnes of screws." One must specify size, quality, type of material to be used, and number of threads. One perhaps apocryphal story concerns a directive for chandeliers that specified only the overall weight. To meet the directive, the plant simply built one gigantic chandelier made of lead, for which no truck large enough to move it could be found. The plant met its quota, but did not produce anything useful or desirable.

This problem is a general one of administrative control and isn't confined to centrally planned economies. At General Motors, for example, until recently managers were often given quantitative goals that left out certain qualitative specifications. In the 1970s the basic goals were to produce lots of cars quickly and cheaply. The result: low-quality cars and the decline of the auto industry.

Inability to Adjust Plans Quickly

Another problem for centrally planned economies is that they do not adjust plans very well. In any economy, things never develop in quite the way they're expected to. Inevitably there are emergencies, breakdowns, and changes in priorities that require changes in the plan.

In market economies, decisions about adjusting plans are made by individuals and firms, using the information available to them. Firms react to market incentives. If there's a significant shortage of a good, its price rises and, as it does, some individual or firm has a monetary incentive to provide it. If an automobile manufacturer in a market economy finds that its steel supplies aren't being delivered on schedule, it calls other suppliers to round up an alternative supply. The market provides both the information needed to adjust the plan and *incentives* to do so.

In a centrally planned economy, all information about the need to adjust plans must go through a central office. Say an auto plant in a centrally planned economy found that steel supplies were falling short. The managers would have to call the next level of the central planning office, which in turn would have to call the next level, which would have to call the steel producers and try to find out what was going wrong. Once a decision to adjust the plans was made, the same bureaucratic procedure was followed in reverse. The producer called the subplanner, the subplanner called the planner, and so on. By the time the information led to a change in direction, most likely everyone had said, "To hell with it." Your own experiences in dealing with some large Canadian firm or bureaucratic institution may have been merely frustrating, but centrally planned economies would have driven you crazy.

In principle, planners could have built into their plans a method of adjustment—their plans could have been contingent plans. But, in practice, merely specifying the dimensions of the product made the plans so complicated that formulating contingent plans was out of the question. There were hundreds of possible contingencies, and specifying plans for them was impossible. In short, information about what adjustment to make wasn't efficiently transmitted among producers and planners in a centrally planned economy. This was the lesson of microeconomic theory: *Market prices transmit information efficiently.*

Even if such information were efficiently transmitted in a centrally planned economy, the incentive to proceed with the adjustments still would not exist. It isn't easy to adjust production plans in any economy. In a market economy, competition—the threat of losing business—keeps suppliers on their toes; they have to adjust to the changing whims of consumers because if they don't, they won't make a profit. In a centrally planned economy, the profit motive doesn't exist, so it couldn't serve as an incentive to adjust plans.

Let's consider a car production manager in a centrally planned economy who discovers that delivery of steel supplies is falling behind. The question he asks is "Can I cover my backside?" The answer: "Yes, I can blame the steel company for not meeting its plan." Since the manager can't be blamed—or fired—for the steel shortages, he or she has little *incentive* to find an alternative source of steel.

The problem becomes even more difficult with consumer goods. Meeting consumer demands is tough work. Being nice to the fickle, frivolous consumer takes effort—and unless one is profiting significantly from making that effort, being nice isn't worth it. It's not from benevolence that Kmart meets your whims; it's from Kmart's self-interest. And in centrally planned economies, meeting consumer whims isn't directly in producers' self-interest.

Again, China is currently heeding the lessons from the former Soviet Union. It is directing its retail employees to be friendly and to meet customers' whims. Chinese planners are now trying to produce what they believe the people want. Economic theory predicts that they will have trouble doing so, and will be outcompeted by firms operating in the market—if they continue to allow such firms to exist.

Central Planning, Bureaucracy, and Markets

It's important to go over these problems with central planning, not only because they provide an understanding of why socialist countries are moving away from central planning and from socialism itself, but also because you'll see many examples of such problems in Canada.

Many larger Canadian firms face the same inefficient transmission of information and lack of incentives to adjust plans that centrally planned economies do. In fact, the difference between them, as far as these problems of unresponsiveness are concerned, is just a matter of size. The Soviet or Chinese planner would deal with a supermega company consisting of the entire economy, while Canadian managers face only the particular company they work for. Like their socialist counterparts, Canadian executives are removed from the flow of information needed for them to know what consumers want. They too often lack the incentives to meet consumer demands. The managers are often more interested in office politics and internal management promotion criteria than they are in meeting consumer demands. The reason is that in large firms the profit motive exists for the *firm* but isn't directly translated to the individual employee.

Because of this similarity, much of the training and many of the tools used in Soviet-style socialist planning are identical to those taught in business schools and

ADDED DIMENSION 

THE NEED FOR PLANNING

Planned economies are often presented as the antithesis of market economies. However, while considering planned economies, remember that market economies have within them large organizations that run by plans—not by market. For example, in the United States General Motors had sales in 1993 of about $138 billion, sales larger than the GDP of all but five or six countries of the world. GM is a planned economy unto itself.

Markets could exist to coordinate activities within these firms, but they don't. Imagine, for a moment, that Canada didn't have any anti-combines laws and that one of the conglomerate companies, call it Super Pac Company, began buying more and more firms until eventually it owned all the firms in Canada. While its theoretical goals might be different, Super Pac Company would want to earn profit for its owners rather than provide a good life for its workers. Its organizational problems would be exactly the same as the problems facing a socialist planner.

Thus, the economics of socialist countries is, in a sense, managerial economics. The problems managers of large Canadian firms and central planners face are similar: how to coordinate and motivate individuals without the use of the market.

used in management. That training and the tools focus on how incentives within the system can be structured so that the system better achieves the desired goals.

Even with training, large businesses in Canada aren't especially responsive to consumers. That's why small firms and businesses are constantly springing up to fill in the gaps left by the large firms. These small firms keep the large firms alert to consumer demands. If the large firms don't meet those demands, they'll lose their market to small firms and go out of business.

Why do bureaucracies exist if they have such problems? The reason is simple: Markets have their problems too. Market economies have firms (which are essentially bureaucratic command and control organizations) because setting up markets and negotiating prices for every transaction would simply be too time consuming. Imagine the complexities if each day firms had to negotiate pay with workers, or students had to negotiate with every teacher how much they would pay for each lecture. Instead, institutions and contracts develop that remove some of those decisions from the market. For example, you pay tuition for a semester, not an amount per teacher and lecture; classes are then allocated by nonmarket mechanisms. Institutions, bureaucracies, and administrative controls exist because "the market" isn't the answer to every problem.

The difficulty, of course, is to find the middle ground between market control and coordination, and administrative control and coordination. Pinpointing that middle ground is a judgement call. Most economists are willing to make that judgement call against central planning in a large country, but similarly most economists believe that some large institutions and government coordination are necessary. The debate is about the appropriate mix.

Central Planning Is Inconsistent with Democracy

Economic efficiency is not an end in itself. It has a meaning only in relation to its contribution to the goals of society. If economic efficiency violates other goals of society, then one might say, "To hell with economic efficiency." We point this out because a second argument some economists use against central planning is that it's inconsistent with democratic institutions (to which they have an ideological commitment) and that it violates the rights of individuals. If one agrees with this argument, one would oppose central planning even if it were efficient.[1]

The ideological argument against central planning is that it gives too much economic power to the central planners and thus is inconsistent with true democracy. Holders of this view argue that unless various groups in society share economic power, government will become oppressive, trample on individual rights, and destroy

[1] We should point out that the argument also works in reverse: If one believes that capitalism and a market system violate individuals' rights, then one could oppose the market even though it is more efficient.

democracy. To give as much economic power to a small group of individuals as central planning gives can only lead to corruption. As 19th-century historian Lord Acton said, "Power corrupts, and absolute power corrupts absolutely."

Proponents of this view argue that this is what happened in many socialist countries. When it was first established, the Communist party in most socialist countries may have had society's goals in mind, but by the 1980s those in power had pursued their own welfare, not society's. Thus, the parties had failed, even on the terms that they set out for themselves.

One example of this failure was the almost total lack of concern for the environment in these countries. Water, land, and air were far more polluted than in Canada. Environmental concerns involve externalities that the market alone cannot effectively handle. So one would have expected that socialist governments would be able to internalize the externalities and deal more effectively with environmental problems than has Canada. Yet, by all accounts, they did not.

Another example concerns the distribution of income. One of the Communist party's goals was the equal distribution of income among the people, but, as Abram Bergson (an economist at Harvard University) has pointed out, the actual distribution of income was no more equal in the former Soviet Union and most other Soviet-style socialist countries than it was in Canada.

So not only did their economies provide fewer goods than are provided in market economies, those fewer goods were not more equally divided. As we discussed, many goods in those countries were rationed, but somehow Communist party members were able to get these scarce, rationed goods that nonmembers could not. Many high-level communist leaders lived in palatial homes while ordinary citizens were crammed into tiny apartments. There were even tales of government leaders having billions of dollars stashed away in foreign bank accounts.

In the early 1990s, the perception that Communist party members were being treated "more fairly" than others played a major role in the overthrow of communist-dominated socialist governments. Once those governments were out of power, it quickly became apparent how badly the communist parties had failed. In free elections, large majorities in most of the formerly Soviet-style socialist countries voted to eliminate Soviet-style socialism entirely, and the countries adopted market economies.

SOCIALIST ECONOMIES IN TRANSITION

In the 1990s, political and economic changes in Eastern Europe, the Soviet Union, and China have come so fast and so erratically that it's impossible to provide an up-to-date survey in a textbook. It is possible, however, to provide a brief background of the changes and some of the problems these countries will be experiencing.

General Transition Problems

The choices these countries face aren't pleasant. They're much larger choices than the choice of an economic system. They're choices that have political and social elements as well. For example, the republics of the former Soviet Union and Eastern European countries are combinations of distinct nationalities with their own customs and allegiances. Many of these groups want political independence. The fights about the economic system will be interrelated with these political fights. As we discussed in the previous chapter on developing countries, such political and social upheavals make it impossible for any economic system to operate effectively. So one complex problem they face is political and social instability. Markets aren't going to solve this problem.

5 The problems faced by transitional economies include the lack of political will to decide on an institutional structure, determining initial property rights, and developing a legal and physical infrastructure within which the economy can function.

A second problem they face is lack of a consensus as to which direction to follow. Some groups favour maintaining a centrally planned system. Others favour moving totally to a market economy. Still others favour what they call *a third way,* an as-yet-undefined economic system that would supposedly provide the best of both worlds. The uncertainty accompanying these potential alternative directions will make it almost impossible for any economic system to operate. Central planning doesn't work because managers at the firm level no longer see their personal and professional futures tied to fulfilment of the centrally directed plan. But neither does the market, since a well-functioning market requires the existence of a legal structure that can see

ADDED DIMENSION

STUDENTS IN BULGARIA

To give you a sense of the specific situation in these countries, we ask you to consider the plight of students in Bulgaria in 1991, when one of us was there. Before the overthrow of the socialist economy, they received free tuition and a stipend, and the universities were well funded. In the transition, education received short shrift. Stipends were eliminated, and parents' incomes had fallen by 50 percent. Faculty pay had fallen by more than that—by 75 to 80 percent—when the faculty was paid at all, which didn't happen always, because the tax system didn't allow effective collection of taxes. Schools in 1992 were starting to charge tuition, but given the economic situation, what they could charge was limited.

Fixed physical facilities were substantial, but with no operating money, they were run down; light bulbs were missing; chalk was almost nowhere to be found; and anything that broke stayed broken. Similar situations existed in all societal common areas.

Despite the physical and financial problems, the students kept coming to school and kept learning. Some professors, working with students, organized "new schools" that met in people's apartments, or wherever, to learn and study. And the students did learn—in many ways their technical training in mathematics and foreign languages exceeded the training of Canadian students whose education was far more costly and well supported.

The ability of individuals to cope, even in a period of institutional transition, is phenomenal, and often underestimated. The Bulgarian students' experience in the early 1990s is an example of that ability to cope.

that contracts are carried out, a well-defined structure of private property, and a populace with entrepreneurial skills. And who knows what the third way requires.

Specific Transition Problems

Most of these countries decided to move to a market economy. Let's consider a couple of the specific problems one of these countries, Bulgaria, faced in implementing these decisions.

Deciding on Ownership The former Bulgarian government had taken land away from landowners in the 1940s and had created collective farms. Collective farm members had lived on these farms for almost 50 years. The problem faced by the current government was how to allocate ownership of that land—should it go to the former owners, or to the current collective farm members?

The political compromise they reached was to give the land back to the former owners—or, in most cases, the heirs of the former owners—but only if these people agreed to live on the land for at least five years. Here's the problem that created: In order to establish their ownership rights, individuals who had never worked on a farm in their life were suddenly placed on a farm without equipment. It isn't difficult to guess what happened to agricultural production.

Deciding the ownership of many buildings other than agricultural structures presented the same kind of problem, and, with the changes in the legal system that were happening simultaneously, there was no way to resolve the disputes definitively. In the meantime, the buildings sat there, deteriorating. No one was willing to fix them up because no one knew who would own them.

Where property ownership wasn't in dispute, the government tried auctioning off the properties, but here, too, they faced a catch-22. Few people had any money or access to credit. Actually, it was believed some of the former communists had a great deal of money. In the first auction the government held, one of these former communists won the auction and bought a property at a price far higher than the government had expected. But when the newspapers got hold of the story, the popular uproar was so great that the government had to investigate and tried to arrest the former communist for having so much money. Needless to say, if any former communist did have money hidden in foreign bank accounts, this example discouraged him or her from using it to develop businesses in Bulgaria.

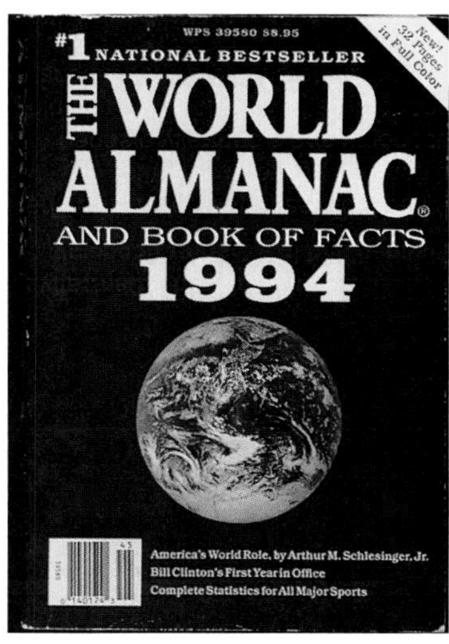

Almanacs are excellent sources of recent economic statistics.

Developing Competitive Businesses Now let us move to the problems faced by Bulgarian businesses. Sixty percent of their trade had been with Comecon countries (former socialist Soviet-bloc countries), and that trade had broken down almost completely. Serbia, on Bulgaria's western border, was effectively closed because of the war going on there. Previously, Bulgaria had been a transshipment port for Iran and Libya, but now international pressure had closed off those markets.

In the previous system, the Soviet Union had maintained a low price for the oil and raw materials it sold to Bulgaria. Consequently Bulgaria's production facilities had been designed for very low-priced oil, which made those facilities highly energy-intensive. When the price of oil rose to $20 a barrel after the former Soviet government fell, most Bulgarian production facilities were too costly to operate, no matter what the labour costs might have been. Shortages of oil meant that electricity had to be rationed. This rationing was accomplished by having the power on for four hours, off for four hours, with alternating parts of the country being affected (that is, off for four hours in one province while it was on for those same four hours in another province). The oil shortages also meant that the dangerous Chernobyl-type nuclear reactor near Sofia, the capital of the country, had to be kept operating or else electricity would have had to be rationed much more severely.

The rest of the infrastructure was similarly situated. The telephone system worked only part of the time. Bulgaria's firms had no marketing or sales departments, and no way of establishing an international marketing structure since the relative value of their currency was so low. They also faced a perception-of-quality problem: If a good came from a former socialist country, it had to be low quality; if the former socialist country tried to compete on price, the low price convinced foreigners that their perception of the quality was accurate.

We could go on, but what we have already written gives you a good sense of the dimensions of the economic problems Bulgaria, and the other transitional economies, faced.

Cautionary Lessons for Transitional Economies from Principles of Economics

What lessons do the principles of economics have for these countries? The answer is: Not a specific lesson, but an important general lesson.

The general lesson is that market institutions that encourage individual entrepreneurship—such as private property and moderately regulated markets—have done well for Western economies, and that, therefore, transitional countries should consider developing some variation of these institutions. In choosing these institutions, these countries should recognize that a market operates given an institutional and legal structure, and an entrepreneurial mindset of the population. If these countries want to develop market economies, getting an acceptable institutional structure is the first priority.

6 Four cautionary lessons for transitional economies are: (1) the Nirvana caution, (2) the QWERTY caution, (3) the tombstone caution, and (4) the transplant caution.

Economics does not say that these transitional societies should adopt Western institutions. Institutions evolve, and develop to fit the situations and problems of the time. Western institutions have worked for the West, and thus they should be seriously considered. In that consideration, transitional economies should, however, remember the following:

Nirvana caution Taking care not to assume that a country that looks extremely fortunate does not have any problems of its own.

QWERTY caution Remembering that some economies have developed for reasons that were not necessarily the most efficient or most desirable.

1. The **Nirvana caution:** When you're in a situation like the one the transitional economies are in, the Western economies look like heaven, but it is important to remember that Western economies have their own problems. If they import Western institutions, they may well import these problems as well.
2. The **QWERTY caution:** The institutions that developed in Western economies, such as the QWERTY keyboard used with typewriters and computers, developed for a variety of reasons, not necessarily because they were the most efficient or most desirable. Western institutions may exist not because they are efficient, but because their inefficiency served some group's interest.
3. The **tombstone caution:** While it seems true that economies that have markets are more efficient than centrally planned economies, that doesn't

ADDED DIMENSION 

ECONOMISTS' ADVICE IN THE TRANSITION: TANSTAAFL

Like many other Western economists, one of the authors of this book made the trip over to the formerly socialist countries. He spent two months in Bulgaria trying to understand what was going on and discussing the country's economic problems with the people there. He had an office in the former Karl Marx University (now the National Institute of International Economics), right next to the office of the university's chief administrator.

He taught classes about Western banking systems, markets, and international financial systems. Bulgarian newspaper, radio, and television reporters came to him asking what the answers were. He went over the problems and took positions on many of the controversial issues facing the Bulgarian government. But in giving advice, he made clear to the questioners that it was contingent advice—that his knowledge of their institutions and social structure wasn't deep enough to come to conclusions. He emphasized that his training allowed him to help them understand what markets could and could not do, but it did not allow him to tell them, "This is what you should do." That, they had to decide for themselves.

But wherever he went, he told the story of King Tanstaafl. He became known as the Tanstaafl professor. If the Bulgarians learn that lesson, they will do OK, because that is the most important lesson the West has for them.

necessarily mean that markets caused the higher efficiency. An efficient market can exist only in a stable legal and political setting. The existence of markets may be a tombstone over those disputes about the distribution of property rights. Settling the disputes, not the creation of markets, may be the more important issue.

Tombstone caution Remembering that markets may not be the cause of high efficiency but instead may be merely covering over disputes about the distribution of property rights.

4. The **transplant caution:** When an organ is transplanted from one body to another, it is often rejected by the body to which it has been transplanted. Similarly, rejection can occur with transplanted institutions that don't fit the cultural or social aspects of the economy to which they are transplanted.

Transplant caution Remembering that when an institution is transplanted from one economy to another, the institution can be rejected if it doesn't fit the cultural or social aspects of the economy to which it is transplanted.

The above four cautions are simply that—cautionary addenda to the general lesson that, in the competition of economic systems, Western market systems of the welfare capitalist variety have outcompeted centrally planned economic systems.

WHAT IS THE FUTURE?

As you can see, the issues facing transitional economies are challenging, to say the least. But the countries had no choice; they had to face those issues, and in the mid-1990s some of the countries seemed to be turning the corner and their economies seemed to be improving.

Still, uncertainty associated with the transition makes most economists pessimistic about the short-term prospects for the group of economies that were formerly centrally planned, regardless of which direction these economies follow. Whatever path they follow, the transition to a noncentrally planned economy is a rocky one.

We could list many more problems and decisions that these transitional economies are facing, but this brief discussion should give you a sense of the enormity of the transition problem. There are potential answers for each difficulty, but for each answer there are additional problems.

That does not mean that there are not better, or worse, answers. It is possible to take specific positions on a variety of issues, but you must carefully qualify your positions with a caveat: To understand real-world policies, one must understand economic theory, but one must also understand the culture and the institutions of the country one is advising. Without the background in either the culture or the institutions of a country, one should stick to using both the power and the limitations of economic theory, and encouraging policymakers to understand both the strengths and the weaknesses of the market. Only they can, and only they should, make the decisions that will determine their future.

CHAPTER SUMMARY

- Socialism developed as a reaction to the excesses of unregulated capitalism.
- In a centrally planned economy, central planners make the *what, how,* and *for whom* decisions.
- Centrally planned economies have been plagued by shortages of consumer goods. These shortages have been partly due to conscious decisions since central planners have generally chosen investment over consumption goods.
- Five problems of centrally planned economies are:
  1. Nonmarket pricing and perverse incentives.
  2. Inability to adjust prices quickly.
  3. Lack of information about demand.
  4. Ambiguous directives.
  5. Inability to adjust plans quickly to changing situations.
- Transforming Soviet-style socialist economies is a difficult process. Whether the transformation will succeed is an open question.
- Two specific transition problems that the formerly socialist countries have in switching to a market economy are (1) deciding on ownership, and (2) developing competitive businesses.
- The general lesson from principles of economics for the formerly socialist countries is that market institutions that encourage individual entrepreneurship have done well for Western economies, and that, therefore, the formerly socialist countries should consider some variation of these institutions. In that consideration, four cautions are: the Nirvana caution, the QWERTY caution, the tombstone caution, and the transplant caution.

KEY TERMS

centrally planned economy *(430)*
counterplanning *(432)*
market-determined prices *(434)*
material balance *(433)*
Nirvana caution *(442)*
perverse incentive *(435)*
QWERTY caution *(442)*
Soviet-style socialist economies *(430)*
tombstone caution *(443)*
transplant caution *(443)*

QUESTIONS FOR THOUGHT AND REVIEW

The number after each question represents the estimated degree of critical thinking required. (1 = almost none; 10 = deep thought.)

1. Contrast the ways a capitalist country and a Soviet-style socialist country would respond to an increase in demand for shoes. *(5)*
2. Socialist countries are fairer than capitalist countries because they price luxuries high and necessities low. True or false? Why? *(7)*
3. Perverse incentives are not only a problem of socialist economies; they are a problem of all bureaucracies organized around administrative control. Give an example of a perverse incentive you see in Canada. *(6)*
4. How would you redesign the bureaucratic structure that caused that perverse incentive? *(8)*
5. What problems would your redesign cause? *(8)*
6. If your redesigned structure would improve the efficiency of the bureaucratic structure, why hasn't the bureaucratic structure been redesigned? *(8)*
7. Market socialism is doomed to failure because prices provide information as well as coordinate action. True or false? Why? *(8)*
8. Why do many people feel that central planning is inconsistent with democracy? *(5)*
9. Explain why markets cannot resolve the ownership problem. *(7)*
10. List, and explain the relevance of, four cautions you might advise transition governments to be aware of as they attempt to develop market economies. *(6)*

PROBLEMS AND EXERCISES

1. In a centrally planned economy the government fixes the apartment rents at $50 per month, even though the equilibrium price is $100 per month.
   a. Show the likely result with supply and demand curves.
   b. Say the central planners recognize the problem and decide to eliminate the shortage by charging the equilibrium price. Show the likely result.
   c. If they do charge the equilibrium price, will the economic system be equivalent to a market system? Why or why not?
2. Research the recent economic reforms in China, Bulgaria, and Latvia.
   a. Which country has the highest growth rate?
   b. What are the reasons for this?
   c. Would a different reform path have changed the results? Why?
3. One of the specific problems Soviet-style socialist economies had was keeping up with capitalist countries technologically.
   a. Can you think of any reason inherent in a centrally planned economy that would make innovation difficult?
   b. Can you think of any reason inherent in a capitalist country that would foster innovation?
   c. Joseph Schumpeter, a famous Harvard economist of the 1930s, predicted that as firms in capitalist societies grew in size they would innovate less. Can you suggest what his argument might have been?
   d. Schumpeter's prediction did not come true. Modern capitalist economies have had enormous innovations. Can you provide explanations why?
4. Nobel Prize winner Robert Coase has argued that firms exist in those areas where command and control are more efficient than markets. Thus, a firm replaces the market with a managerial command system.
   a. If one accepts that argument, is it legitimate to argue that the Western institutions that have developed are the most efficient? Why or why not?
   b. Can one argue that such Western institutions are the most efficient institutions for the countries in which they developed, but not necessarily for other countries?
   c. A radical economist, Steve Marglin, has argued that firms develop command and control systems to protect the monopoly position of managers, not necessarily to be most efficient. How do Marglin's and Coase's views mix?

Glossary

A

abuse of a dominant position The new concept of monopolistic or abusive behaviours, it defines a number of anticompetitive acts.

accounting profit Definition of profit used by accountants that states profit is total revenue minus explicit measurable costs.

acquisition A company buys another company; the buyer has direct control of the resulting venture, but does not necessarily exercise that direct control.

Advance Ruling Certificates Issued by the Director of Investigations, these tell the parties proposing to merge that on the basis of available information, the merger will not be challenged.

Agricultural Stabilization Board A federal agency regulating the prices of a number of commodities.

agrifirms Large firms that own huge farms and operate them like big corporations.

annuity rule Present value of any annuity is the annual income it yields divided by the interest rate.

anti-combines legislation/policy Government's policy toward the competitive process.

anti-competitive behaviour Forms the basis of intervention and can be either monopolistic or abusive behaviour, merger, or restrictive policies.

arc elasticity The average elasticity of a range of points on a demand curve.

art of economics The relating of positive economics to normative economics—the application of the knowledge learned in positive economics to the achievement of the goals determined in normative economics.

Asian tigers Group of Asian countries that have achieved economic growth well above the level of other developing countries.

average fixed cost Fixed cost divided by quantity produced.

average product Total output divided by the quantity of the input.

average total cost Total cost divided by the quantity produced. Often called *average cost.*

average variable cost Variable cost divided by quantity produced.

B

balance of trade The difference between the value of goods a nation exports and the value of goods it imports.

balance of trade deficit When a nation imports more than it exports.

balance of trade surplus When a nation exports more than it imports.

balanced growth plan Plan that spreads money around in trying to spur development in all sectors simultaneously.

barrier to entry A social, political, or economic impediment that prevents firms from entering a market.

bid-rigging Potential suppliers co-ordinate their bids to ensure an equitable distribution of successful bids.

bounded rationality Rationality based on rules of thumb rather than using the rational choice model.

brain drain The outflow of the best and brightest students from developing countries to developed countries.

break-even level of income The level of employment income at which government subsidy is completely lost.

business The private producing unit in our society.

C

Canada Assistance Plan A federal program providing assistance to the provinces for welfare programs.

Canadian Dairy Commission A federal agency that coordinates provincial milk marketing boards.

Canada Pension Plan (CPP) Funded by employee and employer contributions, it provides monthly benefits to retired contributors, as well as disability and survivor's benefits.

Canadian Wheat Board A federal agency having control over how Canadian wheat is marketed and the price at which it is sold.

capital intensive Methods of production that use proportionately more capital than any other factor inputs.

capitalism An economic system based upon private property and the market. It gives private property rights to individuals and relies on market forces to coordinate economic activity.

capitalists Businesspeople who have acquired large amounts of money and use it to invest in businesses.

cartel A combination of firms that acts like a single firm.

cartel model of oligopoly Model that assumes that oligopolies act as if they were a single monopoly.

cash flow accounting system An accounting system entering expenses and revenues only when cash is received or paid out.

causation Term in statistics meaning that a change in one data point causes a change in another data point.

closed shop A firm in which the union controls hiring.

combine A combination of firms that act as it were a single firm.

comparable worth laws Laws in which government groups will determine "fair" wages for specific jobs.

comparative advantage The ability to produce a good at a lower opportunity cost (forgone production of another good) than another country can.

competition Ability of individuals to freely enter into business activities.

Competition Act 1986 legislation setting Canadian anti-combines policy.

competition policy The government's policy toward the competitive process.

Competition Tribunal The body charged with adjucating Canada's competition policy.

competitiveness A country's ability to produce goods and services more cheaply than other countries.

complements Goods used in conjunction with other goods.

concentration ratio The percentage of industry output of a specific number of the largest firms.

conglomerate A large corporation whose activities span various unrelated industries.

conglomerate merger Combination of unrelated businesses.

constant returns to scale When output rises by the same proportionate change in inputs. For example, when a firm uses twice as much labour and capital and obtains twice as much output.

consumer sovereignty The right of the individual to make choices about what is consumed and produced.

consumer surplus The additional amount that consumers would be willing to pay for a product above what they actually pay.

contestable market model A model that bases pricing and output decisions on entry and exit conditions, not on market structure.

corporate takeover A firm or a group of individuals issues an offer to buy up the stock of a company to gain control and to install its own managers.

corporation Business that is treated like a person, legally owned by its stockholders. Its stockholders are not personally liable for the actions of the corporate "person."

correlation Term in statistics meaning the joint movement of data points.

corroboration Term meaning that the data are more consistent with a particular theory than with any other theory, so it makes sense to use that particular theory.

cost minimization condition The ratio of marginal product to the price of an input is equal to all inputs ($MP_c/P_c = MP_x/P_x$).

cost shifting Adding the costs for one group to the prices paid by another group.

counterplanning Process that lets individuals low in the hierarchy influence the planning decisions of those higher in the hierarchy.

credentialism Situation where individuals who hold the highest educational degrees get the best jobs simply because they have the credentials.

Crown corporation Businesses whose major shareholder is the federal, provincial, or municipal government; usually natural monopolies in which economies of scale create a barrier to entry.

cultural norms Standards people use when they determine whether a particular activity or behaviour is acceptable.

D

deacquisition One company's sale of parts of another company it has bought.

debt Accumulated deficits minus accumulated surpluses.

deceptive marketing Marketing strategies that make consumers think that they are getting something they are not.

decreasing returns to scale When output rises by proportionately less than the change in input usage; for example, when a firm uses three times as much capital and labour and only doubles its output.

demand Schedule of quantities of a good that will be bought per unit of time at various prices.

demand curve Curve that tells how much of a good will be bought at various prices.

demerit goods or activities Things government believes are bad for you, although you may like them.

derived demand The demand for factors of production by firms; the nature of this derived demand depends upon the demand for the firms' products.

derived demand curve for labour The curve describing the demand for labour by firms; it depends on the marginal revenue product of labour—how much additional money the firm will make from hiring additional workers.

diminishing marginal utility At some point, as individuals increase their consumption of a good, consuming another unit of the product will simply not yield as much additional pleasure as did consuming the preceding unit.

direct regulation Program in which the amount of a resource people are allowed to use is directly limited by the government.

discrimination Differential treatment of individuals because of physical or social characteristics.

diseconomies of scale An increase in per-unit cost as a result of an increase in output.

dual economy Tendency of developing countries to have two somewhat unrelated economies—one an internationally based economy, the other a traditional, often nonmarket, economy.

Dueling Duals Debate whether a country should focus development on agriculture or on industry.

duopoly An oligopoly with only two firms.

E

economic decision rule If benefits exceed costs, do it. If costs exceed benefits, don't do it.

economic forces The forces of scarcity (when there isn't enough to go around, goods must be rationed).

economic institution Physical or mental structures that significantly influence economic decisions.

economic policy An action (or inaction) taken, usually by government, to influence economic events.

economic profit Definition of profit used by economists that states profit is total implicit and explicit revenues minus total implicit and explicit costs.

economic reasoning Making decisions on the basis of costs and benefits.

economic system The set of economic institutions that determine a country's important economic decisions.

economic takeoff A stage in the development process when that process becomes self-sustaining.

economic theory Generalizations about the working of an abstract economy.

economically efficient Using the method of production that produces a given level of output at the lowest possible cost.

economics The study of how human beings coordinate their wants.

economies of scale A decrease in per-unit cost as a result of an increase in output.

economies of scope The costs of producing products are interdependent, so that producing one good lowers the cost of producing another.

economy The institutional structure through which individuals in a society coordinate their diverse wants or desires.

efficiency Achieving a goal as cheaply as possible.

efficiency wages An above-average wage paid to a worker for bringing forth better effort.

efficiently Achieving a desired goal at the lowest possible cost in total resources, without consideration as to who pays those costs.

effluent fees Charges imposed by government on pollution.

eight-firm concentration ratio The percentage of industry output of the largest eight firms.

elastic Percent change in quantity is greater than percent change in price. $E_d > 1$.

entrepreneur Individual who sees an opportunity to sell an item at a price higher than the average cost of producing it.

entrepreneurship Labour services that involve high degrees of organizational skills, concern, and creativity.

envelope relationship The relationship explaining that, at the planned output level, short-run average total cost equals long-run average total cost, but at all other levels of output, short-run average total cost is higher than long-run average total cost.

equal pay for work of equal value Providing the same compensation for different jobs that require approximately the same level of training and skill.

equilibrium A concept in which the dynamic forces cancel each other out.

equilibrium price The price toward the invisible hand (economic forces) drives the market.

European Union (EU) An economic and political union of European countries that allow free trade among countries.

excess burden Loss to society caused by a policy introducing a wedge between marginal private and marginal social costs and benefits.

excess demand Quantity demanded is greater than quantity supplied.

excess supply Quantity supplied is greater than quantity demanded.

exclusive dealing A manufacturer supplies its goods on the condition that the retailer cannot carry a competitor's product.

experimental economics A branch of economics that gains insights into economic issues by conducting controlled experiments.

exports Goods produced in the home country but sold to foreign countries.

externalities Results of a decision that are not taken into account by the decision maker.

F

factors of production Resources, or inputs, necessary to produce goods.

farm lobby Organization formed to further political goals that benefit farmers.

feudalism Political system divided into small communities in which a few powerful people protect those who are loyal to them.

firm Economic institution that transforms factors of production into consumer goods.

first dynamic law of supply and demand When quantity demanded is greater than quantity supplied, prices tend to rise; when quantity supplied is greater than quantity demanded, prices tend to fall.

fixed costs Costs that are spent and cannot be changed in the period of time under consideration.

focal point equilibrium Equilibrium in which goods are consumed, not because the goods are objectively preferred to all other goods, but simply because through luck or advertising they have become focal points to which people have gravitated.

focal point phenomenon Phenomenon where a country focuses on another country as a site for business primarily because it knows the conditions in that country, while ignoring other countries that may be just as good but about which it has little knowledge.

foreign aid Funds that developed countries loan or give to developing countries.

four-firm concentration ratio The percentage of industry output of the largest four firms.

free rider Person who participates in something for free because others have paid for it.

free rider problem The unwillingness of individuals to share in the cost of a public good.

Free Trade Agreement (FTA) Trade deal signed by Canada and the United States aimed at reducing barriers to trade. It took effect on January 1, 1989.

free trade association Group of countries that allows free trade among its members and puts up common barriers against all other countries' goods.

friendly takeover When one corporation is willing to be acquired by another.

G

game theory The application of economic principles to interdependent situations.

General Agreement on Tariffs and Trade (GATT) International agreement not to impose trade restrictions except under certain limited conditions. Replaced by the World Trade Organization (WTO) in 1995.

general equilibrium analysis The analysis of the simultaneous interaction of all markets.

general purpose transfers Payments from the federal government to the provincial and local governments meant to reduce disparities between "have" and "have-not" provinces.

general rule of political economy Small groups that are significantly affected by a government policy will lobby more effectively than large groups that are equally affected by that same policy.

global corporations Corporations with substantial operations on both the production and sales sides in more than one country. Another name for multinational corporation.

globalization The cross-border spread of goods and services, factors of production, firms, and markets.

global warming theory The theory that the earth is now going through a period of warming due to the rise of carbon dioxide gases caused by the burning of fossil fuels.

good/bad paradox The phenomenon of doing poorly because you're doing well.

government The combination of federal, provincial, and local agencies whose officials are elected by the people or appointed by elected officials.

government budget deficit Situation when government expenditures exceed government revenues.

government budget surplus Situation when government revenues exceed expenditures.

Group of Five Group that meets to promote negotiations and coordinate economic relations among countries. The Five are Japan, Germany, Britain, France, and the United States.

Group of Seven Group that meets to promote negotiations and coordinate economic relations among countries. The Seven are Japan, Germany, Britain, France, Canada, Italy, and the United States.

guaranteed annual income The level of income the government would provide under a negative income tax program.

Guaranteed Income Supplement A payment to the recipients of Old Age Security benefits based on need.

H

historical costs Cost in terms of money actually spent.

homogeneous product A product such that each firm's output is indistinguishable from any other firm's output.

horizontal merger A merger of companies in the same industry.

hostile takeover A merger in which one company buys another that does not want to be bought.

Hotelling's Rule In a perfectly competitive market, every year natural resource prices should rise by the rate of interest.

households Groups of individuals living together and making joint decisions.

I

ideology Values that are held so deeply that they are not questioned.

impacted information Information that does not convey the whole story—more likely to support one point of view.

implicit collusion Multiple firms making the same pricing decisions even though they have not consulted with one another.

import control law A law preventing people from importing.

imports Goods produced in foreign countries but sold in the home country.

incentive effect How much a person will change his or her hours worked in response to a change in the wage rate.

incentive-compatible contract An agreement in which the incentives and goals of both parties match as closely as possible.

income Payments received plus or minus changes in value of one's assets in a specified time period.

increasing returns to scale When a firms' output rises by proportionately more than the change in its inputs; for example, if a firm uses twice as much capital and labour and obtains three times as much output.

indicative planning A macroeconomic policy in which the government sets up an overall plan for various industries and selectively directs credit to certain industries.

individual self-selection bias The skewing of risk and rates that would occur if individuals who are most likely to need insurance are left to buy it individually.

indivisible setup cost The cost of an indivisible input for which a certain minimum amount of production must be undertaken before the input becomes economically feasible to use.

Industrial Revolution Period (1750–1900) during which technology and machines rapidly modernized industrial production.

inefficiency Getting less output from inputs which, if devoted to some other activity, would produce more output.

inefficient More costly than necessary.

inelastic Percent change in quantity is less than percent change in price. $E_d < 1$.

infant industry argument With initial protection, an industry will be able to become competitive.

inferior goods Goods whose consumption decreases when income increases.

infrastructure investment Investment in the underlying structure of the economy, such as transportation or power facilities.

in-kind transfer Transfers of goods rather than money.

input What you put in to achieve output.

interest The income paid to savers—individuals who produce now but do not consume now.

interest groups Individuals and others who band together to encourage and protect governments spending in certain areas of the economy.

intermediate products Products of one firm used in some other firm's production of another firm's product.

internal rate of return The rate of return on an investment project.

International Monetary Fund (IMF) A multinational, international financial institution concerned primarily with monetary issues.

invisible foot Political and legal forces that play a role in deciding whether to let market forces operate.

invisible hand Economic forces, that is, the price mechanism; the rise and fall of prices that guides our actions in a market.

invisible handshake Social and historical forces that play a role in deciding whether to let market forces operate.

invisible hand theory The insight that a market economy will allocate resources efficiently.

J

just-noticeable difference A threshold below which our senses don't recognize that something has changed.

L

labour market Factor market in which individuals supply labour services for wages to firms that demand labour services.

labour productivity Average output per worker.

laissez faire Economic policy of leaving coordination of individuals' wants to be controlled by the market.

law of demand More of a good will be demanded the lower its price, other things constant. Also can be stated as: Less of a good will be demanded the higher its price, other things constant.

law of diminishing marginal productivity As more and more of a variable input is added to an existing fixed input, after some point the additional output one gets from the additional input will fall.

law of supply More of a good will be supplied the higher its price, other things constant. Also can be stated as: Less of a good will be supplied the lower its price, other things constant.

lazy monopolist Firm that does not push for efficiency, but merely enjoys the position it is already in.

learning by doing Becoming more proficient at doing something by actually doing it; in the process, learning what works and what doesn't.

limited liability The liability of a stockholder (owner) in a corporation; it is limited to the amount the stockholder has invested in the company.

loanable funds theory of interest A theory that suggests the interest rate is determined by the demand and supply of funds available for investment.

long-run decision A decision in which the firm can choose among all possible production techniques.

Lorenz curve A geometric representation of the size distribution of income among families in a given country at a given time.

low income cut-off The income level at which families spend at least 20 percent more than the average family on the necessities of life. Used by Statistics Canada to define low-income families.

low-income measure (LIM) A level of income used to measure poverty in Canada—based on 50 percent of adjusted medium family income.

M

macroeconomic externality Externality that affects the levels of unemployment, inflation, or growth in the economy as a whole.

macroeconomics The study of inflation, unemployment, business cycles, and growth primarily from the whole to the parts, focusing on aggregate relationships and supplementing its analysis with microeconomic insights.

marginal benefit Additional benefit above what you've already derived.

marginal cost The change in cost associated with a change in quantity.

marginal factor cost The additional cost to a firm of hiring another worker.

marginal physical product (MPP) Additional units of output that hiring an additional worker will bring about.

marginal product Additional output forthcoming from an additional input, other inputs constant.

marginal productivity theory Factors of production are paid their marginal revenue product.

marginal revenue The change in revenue associated with a change in quantity.

marginal revenue curve Graphical measure of the change in revenue that occurs in response to a change in price.

marginal revenue product The additional revenue a firm receives when it hires an additional worker.

marginal tax rate The tax you pay on an additional dollar.

marginal utility The satisfaction one gets from the consumption of an incremental or additional product above and beyond what one has consumed up to that point.

market demand curve The horizontal sum of all individual demand curves.

market force Economic force to which society has given relatively free rein so that it has been able to work through the market.

market incentive program Program that makes the price of a resource reflect a negative externality.

market niche An area in which competition is not working.

market structure The physical characteristics of the market within which firms interact.

market supply curve Horizontal sum of all the firms' marginal cost curves, taking account of any changes in input prices that might occur.

market-determined prices Prices are determined by supply and demand, with suppliers free to adjust their prices to make the quantity demanded equal the quantity supplied.

marketable certificate program A program that formalizes rights by issuing certificates and allowing trading of those rights.

material balance Process by which central planners adjust incoming and outgoing quantities of materials until supply equals demand (at least on paper).

mercantilism Economic system in which government doles out the rights to undertake economic activities.

merchandise trade balance The difference between the goods a nation exports and the goods a nation imports.

merger The act of combining two firms.

merit goods or activities Things government believes are good for you, although you may not think so.

microeconomics The study of individual choice, and how that choice is influenced by economic forces.

minimum efficient level of production The amount of the production run that spreads out setup costs sufficiently for a firm to undertake production profitably.

minimum efficient scale The plant size which minimizes both short-run and long-run average total cost.

misleading advertising Statements that another firm's product or service is inferior or that one's own product or services has some unique advantage that, in fact, it does not have.

MITI Japanese agency, the Ministry of International Trade and Industry, that guides the Japanese economy.

model Framework for looking at the world.

monitoring costs Costs incurred by the organizer of production in seeing to it that employees do what they are supposed to do.

monitoring problem Problem that employees' incentives differ from the owner's incentives and that monitoring the employees is expensive.

monopolistic competition A market structure in which many firms sell different products.

monopoly A market structure in which one firm makes up the entire market.

monopoly power Ability to prevent others from entering a business field, which enables a firm to raise its price.

monopolistic behaviour When a firm acts as though it were the only producer of a good or service.

monopsony A market in which only a single firm hires labour.

most-favoured nation Country that will pay as low a tariff on its exports as will any other country.

movement along a demand curve Method of representing a change in the quantity demanded. Graphically, a change in quantity demanded will cause a movement along the demand curve.

movement along the supply curve Method of representing a change in the quantity supplied. Graphically, a change in quantity demanded will cause a movement along the supply curve.

MR = MC Marginal revenue curve equals marginal cost; the condition under which a monopolist is maximizing profit.

multinational corporation Firm with production facilities and a marketing force in two or more countries.

N

National Energy Program A federal program that put controls on oil prices in the late 1970s and early 1980s. It was abandoned in 1984.

National Policy An 1879 policy that defined supportive roles for domestic Canadian companies within which they competed.

natural monopolies Monopolies that exist because economies of scale create a barrier to entry.

neomercantilism An economic system in which the government explicitly guides the economy.

Negative Income Tax (NIT) A program in which the government would subsidize households as long as their incomes fell below a certain threshold level.

Nimby A short way to express "Not In My Back Yard" when a community objects to a proposed development in its neighborhood.

Nirvana caution Taking care not to assume that a country that looks extremely fortunate does not have any problems of its own.

Nirvana criticism Comparing reality to a situation that cannot occur (*i.e.*, to Nirvana).

nonprofit business Business that does not try to make a profit. It tries only to make enough money to cover its expenses with its revenues.

nontariff barriers Indirect regulatory restrictions on exports and imports.

normal goods Goods whose consumption increases with an increase in income.

normal profits Payments to entrepreneurs as the return on their risk taking.

normative criticism The desirability of a Pareto optimal position depends on the desirability of the starting position.

normative economics The study of what the goals of the economy should be.

North American Free Trade Agreement (NAFTA) Trade deal signed by Canada, Mexico, and the United States aimed at reducing barriers to North American trade; went into effect January 1, 1994.

O

objective Term applied to "analysis," meaning that the analysis keeps your subjective views—your value judgments—separate.

Old Age Security Benefits paid to every resident of Canada at age 65.

oligopoly A market structure with a few independent firms.

opportunity cost The benefit forgone, or the cost, of the best alternative to the activity you've chosen. In economic reasoning, the cost is less than the benefit of what you've chosen.

optimal level of pollution Amount of pollution at which the marginal benefit of reducing pollution equals the marginal cost.

optimal policy Policy whose marginal cost equals its marginal benefit.

other things constant An assumption that places a limitation on the implications that can be drawn from any supply/demand analysis. The elements of the particular analysis are considered under the assumption that all other elements that could affect the analysis remain constant (whether they actually remain constant or not).

output The result of an activity.

P

Pareto optimal criterion Criterion that no person can be made better off without another being made worse off.

Pareto optimal policies Policies that benefit some people and hurt no one.

parity price Price that maintains the ratio of prices received and paid by farmers at the same ratio as in a base year.

parity ratio Prices received by farmers divided by prices paid by farmers.

partial equilibrium analysis Analysis of a part of a whole; it initially assumes all other things remain equal.

partnership Business with two or more owners.

patent A legal protection of a technical innovation that gives the person holding the patent a monopoly on using that innovation.

pay-equity laws Regulations that attempt to provide similar compensation for comparable jobs.

payoff matrix A box that contains the outcomes of a strategic game under various circumstances.

perfectly competitive Market in which economic forces operate unimpeded.

perfectly elastic Horizontal demand curve. E_d = infinity.

perfectly inelastic Vertical demand curve. $E_d = 0$.

perverse incentive Incentive to use goods in a manner that does not reflect that use's cost to society.

planning Deciding, before the production takes place, what will be produced, how to produce it, and for whom to pro-duce it.

positive economics The study of what is, and how the economy works.

predator A firm that attempts to drive out its competitors.

predatory pricing Charging low prices with the aim of driving out the competition.

prenotification When a firm must advise the Director of Investigation of its intentions before their plans take place.

present value Method of translating a flow of future income or savings into its current worth.

price ceiling A government-imposed limit on how high a price can be charged.

price discriminate To charge different prices to different individuals.

price elasticity of demand A measure of the percent change in quantity of goods demanded divided by the percent change in the price of that good.

price elasticity of supply The percent change in quantity supplied divided by the percent change in price.

price-fixing Combining with other firms to set a uniform price.

price floor A government-imposed limit on how low a price may be.

price level A composite price of all goods.

price stabilization program Program designed to eliminate short-run fluctuations in prices but allow prices to follow their long-term trend line.

price support program Program that maintains prices at a level higher than the trend of prices.

price taker Firm or individual who takes the market price as given.

principle of increasing marginal opportunity cost In order to get more of something, one must give up ever-increasing quantities of something else.

principle of rational choice Spend your money on those goods that give you the most marginal utility per dollar.

prisoner's dilemma A well-known game that nicely demonstrates the difficulty of cooperative behaviour in certain circumstances.

private good A good that, when consumed by one individual, cannot be consumed by other individuals.

private property rights Control of an asset or a right given to an individual or a firm.

privatization Finding private buyers for publicly-owned government businesses.

producer surplus The difference between the price at which producers would have been willing to supply a good and the price they actually receive.

production function Equation that describes the relationships between inputs and outputs, telling the maximum amount of output that can be derived from a given number of inputs.

production possibility curve A curve measuring the maximum combination of outputs that can be obtained from a given number of inputs.

production possibility table Table that lists a choice's opportunity costs.

production table Table showing the output that will result from various combinations of factors of production or inputs.

productive efficiency Getting as much output for as few inputs as possible.

profit A return on entrepreneurial activity and risk taking.

profit-maximizing condition Marginal cost equals marginal revenue (price). $MR = P = MC$.

progressive tax Average tax rate increases with income.

prohibition orders These tell a firm that it must stop engaging in an offensive practice or risk a penalty if it does not stop.

proletariat The working class.

property rights The rights to use specified property as one sees fit.

proportional tax Average tax rate is constant with income.

protectionist policies Policy that favours domestic products over foreign-produced products.

protective tariffs Taxes on imports of goods similar to domestic goods aimed at sheltering domestic producers from foreign competition.

proven reserves Resource reserves that have been discovered, documented to date, and are recoverable with current technology.

public assistance Sometimes called *welfare*, these are means-tested social programs targeted to the poor and providing financial, nutritional, medical, and housing assistance.

public choice economists Economists who integrate an economic analysis of politics with their analysis of the economy.

public goods Goods whose consumption by one individual does not prevent their consumption by other individuals.

Q

quantity demanded A specific amount that will be demanded per unit of time at a specific price. Refers to a point on a demand curve.

quantity supplied A specific quantity of a good offered for sale at a specific price. Refers to a point on a supply curve.

quási rent Any payment to a resource above the amount that the resource would receive in its next-best use (also called *producer surplus*).

quotas Limitations on how much of a good can be shipped into a country.

QWERTY caution Remembering that some economies have developed for reasons that were not necessarily the most efficient or most desirable.

R

rationing Structural mechanism for determining who gets what.

real-world competition A fight between the forces of monopolization and the forces of competition.

régime change A change in the entire atmosphere within which the government and the company interrelate.

regressive tax Average tax rate decreases with income.

relative price The price of a good relative to the price level.

rent An income received by a specialized factor of production.

rent seeking Attempting to influence the structure of economic institutions in order to create rents for oneself.

rent-seeking loss from monopoly Waste caused by people spending money trying to get government to give them a monopoly.

resale price maintenance When a manufacturer dictates the retail price of its goods to a retailer.

restrictive business practices Practices that prevent or make it difficult for other businesses to enter the same kinds of fields.

reverse engineering Firm buying up other firms' products, disassembling them, figuring out what's special about them, and then copying them within the limits of the law.

rule of 72 72 divided by the interest rate is the number of years in which a certain amount of money will double in value.

S

second dynamic law of supply and demand In a market, the larger the difference between quantity supplied and quantity demanded, the greater the pressure on prices to rise (if there is excess demand) or fall (if there is excess supply).

second-best criticism If the economy is not currently at the competitive equilibrium, it is not at all clear that particular moves toward a competitive equilibrium will be in society's interest.

services balance The difference between the services a nation exports and the services a nation imports.

shell corporation A structure that exists primarily to buy up other firms funding social spending on health care, welfare, and post-secondary education.

shift factors of demand Something, other than the good's price, that affects how much of the good is demanded.

shift in demand If how much of a good is demanded is affected by a shift factor, there is said to be a shift in demand. Graphically, a shift in demand will cause the entire demand curve to shift.

shift in supply If how much of a good is supplied is affected by a shift factor, there is said to be a shift in supply. Graphically, a shift in supply will cause the entire supply curve to shift.

short-run decision Firm is constrained in regard to what production decisions it can make.

shutdown point Point at which the firm will gain more by shutting down than it will by staying in business.

sin tax Tax designed to discourage activities society believes are harmful to individuals.

size distribution of income The relative division or allocation of total income among income groups.

socialism Economic system that tries to organize society in such a way that all people contribute what they can and get what they need, adjusting their own wants in accordance with what's available.

socioeconomic distribution of income The relative division or allocation of total income among relevant socioeconomic groups.

sole proprietorship Business with only one owner.

Soviet-style socialism Economic system that uses central planning and government ownership of the means of production to answer the questions: what, how, and for whom.

Soviet-style socialist economies Centrally planned economies in which the state owns most of the means of production.

special purpose transfers Payments from the federal government to provincial and local governments for funding social spending on health care, welfare, and post-secondary education.

stage of production Any of the various levels, such as manufacturing, wholesale, or retail, on which businesses are organized.

state socialism Economic system in which government sees to it that people work for the common good until they can be relied upon to do that on their own.

stock A partial ownership right to a company.

strategic bargaining Demanding a larger share of the gains of trade than you can reasonably expect.

strategic decision making Taking explicit account of a rival's expected response to a decision you are making.

strategic pricing Firms set their price based upon the expected reactions of other firms.

subjective Term applied to "analysis," meaning that the analysis reflects the analyst's views of how things should be.

substitutes Goods that can be used in place of one another.

supply A schedule of quantities of goods that will be offered to the market at various prices.

T

takeover Purchase of a firm by another firm that then takes direct control over its operations.

tariff A tax governments place on internationally traded goods—generally imports. Tariffs are also called *customs duties.*

tax incentive program Any program in which a tax is used to create incentives for individuals to structure their activities in a way that is consistent with particular desired ends.

team spirit The feelings of friendship and being part of a team that bring out people's best effort.

technical efficiency A situation in which as few inputs as possible are used to produce a given output.

technological change An increase in the range of production techniques that provides new ways of producing goods.

third dynamic law of supply and demand When quantity supplied equals quantity demanded, prices have no tendency to change.

tied-selling Access to one product is conditional on the purchase of another product.

tombstone caution Remembering that markets may not be the cause of high efficiency but instead may be merely covering over disputes about the distribution of property rights.

total cost Sum of the fixed and variable costs.

total revenue The amount a firm receives for selling its products; obtained by multiplying price by the quantity supplied.

total utility The satisfaction one gets from one's entire consumption of a product.

trade deficit The result of a country's imports exceeding its exports.

trade dispute Disagreement by two or more nations over international trade.

trade surplus The result of a country's exports exceeding its imports.

transplant caution Remembering that when an institution is transplanted from one economy to another, the institution can be rejected if it doesn't fit the cultural or social aspects of the economy to which it is transplanted.

U

unbalanced growth plans Plan that focuses on one sector of the economy in the hope that that will generate development in other sectors.

unemployment insurance Short-term financial assistance, regardless of need, to eligible individuals who are temporarily out of work.

union shop A firm in which all workers must join the union.

unitary elasticity Percent change in quantity equals percent change in price. $E_d = 1$.

utility A measure of the pleasure or satisfaction one gets from consuming a good or service.

V

value added The contribution that each stage of production makes to the final value of a good.

value of marginal product Marginal physical product times the price for which the firm can sell that product.

variable costs The costs of variable inputs; they change as output changes.

vertical merger Combination of two companies, one of which supplied inputs to the other's production.

W

wealth The value of assets an individual owns.

welfare capitalism Economic system in which the market operates but government regulates markets significantly.

welfare loss triangle Geometric representation of the welfare cost in terms of the resource misallocation caused by monopoly.

World Trade Organization (WTO) World body charged with reducing impediments to trade; it replaced GATT in 1995.

X

X-inefficiency Operating less efficiently than technically possible.

Z

zero profit condition In the long run, zero profits exist.

zoning laws Limits on the use of one's property.

Index